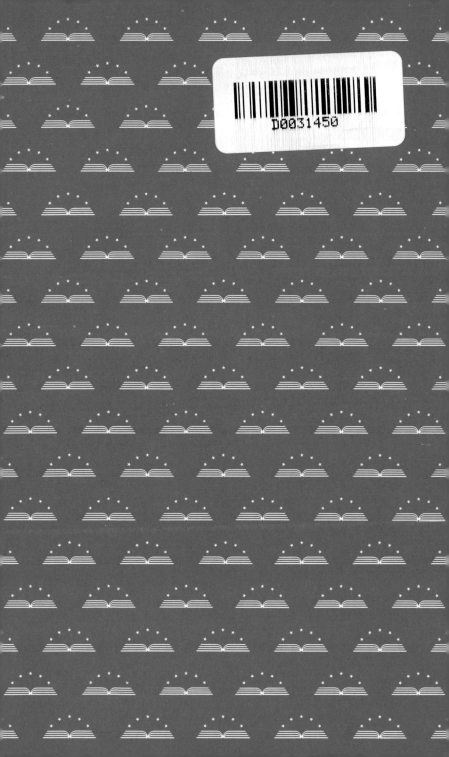

REPORTING VIETNAM

PART ONE

REPORTING VIETNAM

PART ONE

AMERICAN JOURNALISM 1959–1969

THE LIBRARY OF AMERICA

The paper used in this publication meets the
minimum requirements of the American National Standard for
Information Sciences—Permanence of Paper for Printed
Library Materials, ANSI z39.48—1984.

Distributed to the trade in the United States
by Penguin Putnam Inc.
and in Canada by Penguin Books Canada Ltd.

Library of Congress Catalog Number: 98–12267
For cataloging information, see end of Index.
ISBN 1–883011–58–2

First Printing
The Library of America—104

Manufactured in the United States of America

Contents

TIME Death at Intermission Time
First U.S. Advisers Killed in South Vietnam: July 1959 . . 1

STANLEY KARNOW Diem Defeats His Own Best Troops
Challenges to Diem: January 1961 3

MALCOLM W. BROWNE Paddy War
Guerrilla War in the Mekong Delta: December 1961 . . . 18

HOMER BIGART A "Very Real War" in Vietnam—
and the Deep U.S. Commitment
Increasing American Involvement: February 1962 26

MALCOLM W. BROWNE "The Enemy Had Left
a Display for Us"
Massacre in the Ca Mau Peninsula: February 1962. . . . 33

BERNARD B. FALL Master of the Red Jab
Interview with Ho Chi Minh: July 1962 47

HOMER BIGART Vietnam Victory Remote Despite
U.S. Aid to Diem
A Skeptical Assessment: July 1962 58

NEIL SHEEHAN Vietnamese Ignored U.S. Battle Order
Battle of Ap Bac: January 1963 68

DAVID HALBERSTAM "An Endless, Relentless War"
*Helicopter Assault in the Ca Mau Peninsula:
April 1963* 71

MALCOLM W. BROWNE "He Was Sitting in the Center
of a Column of Flame"
Suicide in Saigon: June 1963 79

MARGUERITE HIGGINS The Diem Government,
Pro and Con
Politics in Saigon: August 1963 86

JOSEPH ALSOP In the Gia Long Palace
Nhu and Diem: September 1963 91

STANLEY KARNOW The Fall of the House of Ngo Dinh
Overthrow of Diem: November 1963 94

DAVID HALBERSTAM   "They Can Win a War If Someone
  Shows Them How"
  Profile of John Paul Vann: 1962–1964   108

U.S. NEWS & WORLD REPORT   "We Are Losing, Morale
  Is Bad . . . If They'd Give Us Good Planes . . ."
  A Pilot's Letters Home: November 1963–March 1964 . . .   124

BEVERLY DEEPE   Christmas Eve Bomb in Saigon
  "The pink cloud became black": December 1963   134

RUSSELL BAKER   Befuddled in Asia
  Confusion Over Policy: March 1965   138

JOHN FLYNN   Marines Get Flowers for a Tough Mission
  First Combat Troops Land: March 1965   140

ROGER RAPOPORT   Protest, Learning, Heckling
  Spark Viet Rally
  First Campus "Teach-In": March 1965   142

MEG GREENFIELD   After the Washington Teach-in
  Controversy Over the War Intensifies: May 1965   145

DON MOSER   Eight Dedicated Men Marked for Death
  Struggle for Loc Dien: Summer 1965   153

BERNARD B. FALL   Vietnam Blitz: A Report on the
  Impersonal War
  American Buildup: September 1965   175

WILLIAM TUOHY   A Big "Dirty Little War"
  Terror and Counter-terror: Autumn 1965   187

TOM WOLFE   from *The Electric Kool-Aid Acid Test*
  Ken Kesey Addresses an Anti-War Rally: October 1965 . .   198

SPECIALIST 4/C JACK P. SMITH   Death in the
  Ia Drang Valley
  "Men All Around Me Were Screaming": November 1965 . .   208

SUSAN SHEEHAN   A Viet Cong
  A Defector Tells His Story: 1965   223

MCCANDLISH PHILLIPS   Two Hilltops in a Marine's Life
  Letters Home: April 1965–February 1966   236

HENRY F. GRAFF   Teach-In on Vietnam By . . . The
  President, the Secretary of State, the Secretary of
  Defense and the Under Secretary of State
  The Administration Defends Its Policies: February 1966 . .   242

AFRO-AMERICAN No Room in the Cemetery
A Soldier's Burial: May 1966. 259

WARD S. JUST Reconnaissance
Combat in the Central Highlands: June 1966 262

FRANK HARVEY "Only You Can Prevent Forests"
Spraying Defoliants: July 1966 281

MARTHA GELLHORN "Suffer the Little Children . . ."
Civilian Casualties in South Vietnam:
August–September 1966. 287

NEIL SHEEHAN Not a Dove, But No Longer a Hawk
Veteran Reporter Reassesses the War: October 1966 298

FRANCES FITZGERALD "The Long Fear"
Politics in the Mekong Delta: 1966 316

HARRISON E. SALISBURY U.S. Raids Better 2 Towns;
Supply Route Is Little Hurt
The Bombing of North Vietnam: December 1966. 325

BERNARD B. FALL "Unrepentant, Unyielding": An
Interview with Viet Cong Prisoners
U.S. Offensive in the Iron Triangle: January 1967 331

JONATHAN RANDAL U.S. Marines Seize 3d Hill in
Vietnam After 12-Day Push
Khe Sanh Hill Fights: May 1967. 344

WARD S. JUST Saigon and Other Syndromes
A Reporter Looks Back: December 1965–May 1967 348

DON MOSER The Vietcong Cadre of Terror
War in Saigon: June 1965–July 1967 371

JONATHAN SCHELL from *The Military Half: An Account*
of the Destruction in Quang Ngai and Quang Tin
Southern I Corps: August 1967 386

RICHARD HARWOOD The War Just Doesn't Add Up
Conflicting Views: September 1967 484

MICHAEL J. ARLEN A Day in the Life
A TV Crew at Con Thien: September 1967 490

NORMAN MAILER from *The Armies of the Night*
The March on the Pentagon: October 1967 506

PETER ARNETT Hill 875
Battle of Dak To: November 1967. 522

TOM WOLFE   The Truest Sport:
   Jousting with Sam and Charlie
   Air War Over North Vietnam: December 1967   525

CHARLES MOHR   U.S. Aide in Embassy Villa
   Kills Guerrilla with Pistol
   The Tet Offensive: January 1968.   557

DON OBERDORFER   from *Tet!*
   The Viet Cong in Hue: January–February 1968   560

LEE LESCAZE   A Third of Mytho Destroyed in
   Delta Fighting
   The Tet Offensive: February 1968   572

JOHN T. WHEELER   Life in the V Ring
   Khe Sanh Under Siege: February 1968.   576

WALTER CRONKITE   "We Are Mired in Stalemate . . ."
   Aftermath of Tet: February 1968   581

DON OBERDORFER   "An Ending of His Own"
   Lyndon Johnson Changes Course: March 1968   583

MARY MCCARTHY   Hanoi—March 1968
   An American in North Vietnam: March–April 1968 . . .   598

THOMAS A. JOHNSON   The U.S. Negro in Vietnam
   Black Servicemen and the War: 1968   615

NORMAN MAILER   from *The Siege of Chicago*
   The Democratic Convention: August 1968.   628

STEVE LERNER   A Visit to Chicago:
   Blood, Sweat, & Tears
   The Democratic Convention: August 1968.   643

JOE MCGINNISS   from *The Selling of the President 1968*
   The Nixon Campaign and Vietnam: September 1968 . . .   653

KEVIN BUCKLEY   A Small Contribution
   Firefight Near Loc Ninh: October 1968   664

ZALIN GRANT   "We Lived for a Time Like Dogs"
   American POWs in a Jungle Camp:
   July 1968–January 1969   667

JEFFREY BLANKFORT   Our Town: The War
   Comes Home to Beallsville, Ohio
   A Small Town Mourns Its Dead: Spring 1969   688

DAVID HOFFMAN Hamburger Hill: The Army's Rationale
Battle in the A Shau Valley: May 1969 698

WALLACE TERRY Black Power in Viet Nam
Racial Tensions in the Military: September 1969. 704

DANIEL LANG Casualties of War
An Atrocity and Its Aftermath:
November 1966–October 1969 709

Maps 771
Chronology, 1940–1995 775
Biographical Notes. 804
Note on the Texts 817
Notes 822
Glossary 836
Index 841

Death at Intermission Time

IT WAS a quiet evening in the sleepy little town of Bien Hoa 20 miles north of Saigon, base camp for the South Vietnamese crack 7th Infantry Division and its eight-man U.S. Military Assistance Advisory Group. The presence of the Americans symbolized one of the main reasons why South Viet Nam, five years ago a new nation with little life expectancy, is still independent and free and getting stronger all the time—to the growing chagrin of Communists in neighboring North Viet Nam. Since the beginning of 1959, Communist infiltrators have stepped up their campaign of terrorism, assassinating an average of one South Vietnamese a day, frequently hammering lonely victims to death and then hanging their battered bodies in trees under a red flag. But not since 1957 had the Communists dared attack any Americans.

In the residential compound where the eight Americans lived in Bien Hoa, Master Sergeant Chester Ovnand finished a letter to his wife in Copperas Cove, Texas and dropped it in the mess-hall mailbox. Major Dale Buis of Imperial Beach, Calif. had arrived in Bien Hoa only two days before and was showing his new friends pictures of his three young sons. Two of the officers drifted off to play tennis; the other six men decided to watch a Jeanne Crain movie, *The Tattered Dress*, on their home projector in the grey stucco mess hall. While they were absorbed in the first reel, six Communist terrorists (who obviously had cased the place well) crept out of the darkness and surrounded the mess hall. Two positioned a French MAT submachine gun in the rear window, two pushed gun muzzles through the pantry screen, the other two went to the front of the building to cover the Vietnamese guard. When Sergeant Ovnand snapped on the lights to change the first reel, the Communists opened fire.

In the first murderous hail of bullets, Ovnand and Major Buis fell and died within minutes. Captain Howard Boston of Blairsburg, Iowa was seriously wounded, and two Vietnamese guards were killed. Trapped in a crossfire, all six might have died had not Major Jack Hellet of Baton Rouge leaped across the room to turn out the lights—and had not one of the terrorists who tried to throw a homemade bomb into the room miscalculated and blown himself up instead. Within minutes Vietnamese troops arrived, but the rest of the assassins had already fled.

Time, July 20, 1959

Diem Defeats His Own Best Troops

by Stanley Karnow

SAIGON

AT THREE one humid morning last November, three battalions of paratroopers surrounded the handsome Saigon palace of South Vietnam's President Ngo Dinh Diem. Within thirty-six hours, their attempted revolt had been crushed. The rebel chiefs fled to sanctuary in Cambodia, and the rebel troops themselves, forced to surrender, tactfully reaffirmed their allegiance to the régime. Bullet holes in buildings were quickly plastered in. The dead were discreetly buried. President Diem, who has survived several serious scrapes in his six years of power, emerged from the fortified cellar of his palace with another narrow triumph to his credit. "The government continues to serve the nation," he intoned confidently, and his spokesmen dismissed the abortive *coup d'état* as merely "an incident."

So it was—just an incident. But it was the most dramatic symptom to date of a deeper disturbance that has plagued South Vietnam for a year or more. Beneath the appearance of calm and stability, and despite all the government's assurances of security, President Diem's régime may well be approaching collapse, and with such a collapse, the country could fall to the Communists. "The situation is desperate," an official told me a few weeks ago.

Bands of Communist guerrillas, directed from Hanoi in North Vietnam, roam almost every rural region, blowing up bridges, blocking roads, terrorizing farmers, and attacking army posts. This menace has been compounded by the demoralization of the peasants, the army, and what the French-oriented Vietnamese call *"les intellectuels."* Most serious of all, perhaps, is President Diem's own attitude. He seems to have survived the revolt with his ego unscathed and his faith in his own infallibility renewed.

3

Diem is a complex personality. From his mixed Catholic and Confucian background evolved a combination of monk and mandarin, a kind of ascetic authoritarian. He is a deceptively dainty-looking man; in fact, he is tough and obstinate. To a significant degree, his stubborn self-righteousness saved a régime that most "experts" considered lost back in 1955, after the Geneva Agreement had divided South Vietnam at the seventeenth parallel. Amply bolstered by American sympathy and material aid—which has totaled more than a billion dollars in the past five years—he successfully fought off the insurgent sects, consolidated a government, welcomed and resettled almost a million refugees from the Communist North. He initiated a land-reform program and embarked upon such ambitious projects as building roads and railways, extending agricultural credit, and establishing light industries.

In all his energetic enterprises, the fixation in Diem's mind has been survival. But in his concentration on survival, Diem seems to have paralyzed rather than inspired those around him. He demands absolute loyalty and has developed an inability or unwillingness to trust others. Instead, fearful of betrayal, impatient with any initiative by underlings, he has gathered all power to himself, and working as much as fifteen hours a day, he plunges into the most minute details of administration, personally signing passport applications, reserving for himself the right to approve a student's scholarship to the United States. He has even been known to decide on the distance between roadside trees.

This sort of one-man rule is not uncommon in underdeveloped countries that lack trained personnel. But it discourages the development of a responsible civil service, and it can inspire minor officials to all sorts of red tape and pettifoggery. Without any balanced administrative structure, officials turn to the most convenient source of power. Here, Diem's family —he does trust them—display their peculiar talents. They have succeeded in building a partly public, partly clandestine structure inside and outside the government. On this, Diem's power rests.

One of the President's brothers, the mysterious Ngo Dinh Can, lives in Hué, and from there controls central Vietnam. He exercises much of his authority through the National Revolutionary Movement, the pro-government political party. Another brother, Ngo Dinh Nhu, whom Diem trusts implicitly and relies upon constantly, is probably the most powerful single individual in the country after Diem himself. Educated in Paris and the leading native civil servant under French rule, Nhu is a handsome, articulate, passionate, voluble intellectual. Speaking elegant French in a voice that sometimes whines with emotion, he will declaim at length on one of his favorite subjects, the "problems of the underdeveloped country." This includes an exposition of the theory that "freedom must not prevent the march of progress."

There is considerable validity to Nhu's notion. But his ideas in action are somewhat more questionable. He has certainly helped to curtail freedom, but it is not so sure that he has done much to promote progress. He directs an avowedly clandestine movement called the Can Lao Nhan Vi—the "Revolutionary Labor Party"—which, he concedes frankly, is organized along the lines of a Communist apparatus. Its seventy thousand secret members have been infiltrated into factories, villages, government offices, army units, schools, and newspapers, where they spend part of their time collecting information about their compatriots. Nhu's pretty wife—commonly called Madame Nhu, though the family surname is Ngo—commands the ladies' auxiliary.

Although there is not a single shred of evidence against them, Nhu and his wife are believed to be at the heart of most major corruption in the country. Through his Can Lao, Nhu is said to control the wood and charcoal trade, and there are tales of his investments in Brazil, France, and Switzerland. When the Nhus are confronted with stories of their supposed venality, they simply issue denials. "It's the diplomats," Madame Nhu told me huffily during a recent chat. "They have nothing better to do than gossip. I just ignore them." Her husband tends to protest more vigorously. "Foreign powers are against us," he insists. "Everyone picks on poor little Ngo Dinh Diem and his brothers. Why? Maybe it's because we are Catholic. I don't know. But these rumors of our corruption, our stealing—all lies. Nobody has any proof."

One way or the other, however, everyone believes that the Nhus are corrupt (everyone, that is, but Diem himself, who will not even listen to charges against his family). The real or imaginary, or total or partial, misconduct of Diem's family is serious because it coincides with a period of tension generated by increased Communist terrorism. And as Communist terrorism became more acute, the growing uneasiness and insecurity sparked more vocal dissatisfaction which, not long ago, began to spread beyond the family to criticism of Diem himself.

The current Communist offensive against South Vietnam began to build up as early as September, 1959. Communist guerrillas opened their operations with teams of fifty or more, soon increasing to company strength of a hundred—their largest groups since they fought the French. They had French, British, and American weapons hidden since wartime days; newer arms—some of Czech or Chinese origin—and fresh recruits were brought in from the north.

The first big push came last January. One night, attacking in company force, the Communists raided a regimental headquarters at Tay Ninh, northwest of Saigon, and killed thirty-four Vietnamese soldiers sleeping off their Chinese-style New Year's celebration. Soon they were fanning out through the southern delta, hitting army posts, ambushing troops, terrorizing local village chiefs. It is no longer safe to travel without escort in many parts of the country, and the important commercial highway between Saigon and Phnompenh is often closed. The Communists are, at present, killing about eight hundred people per month—rural officials, troops, police, and ordinary peasants. In recent weeks they have reportedly destroyed some fifty bridges in the delta area and they have killed an American military adviser—mainly as a demonstration of their strength.

Communists guerrillas are believed to number about six thousand at the moment. Reliable intelligence sources describe them as highly mobile and extremely well acquainted with the local countryside, and there is no place in the southern delta they cannot effectively control. But they apparently do not always consider it advantageous to be aggressive. Well aware of Mao Tse-tung's art of partisan warfare, they seem to recognize that a hostile population would be to their detriment. Thus they scout villages carefully. When they take one, they hold it long enough to deliver political lectures and distribute pamphlets, then leave behind them the threat of execution if they do not get co-operation. By "co-operation" they mean information and food, perhaps recruits, maybe medical care.

The South Vietnam Army of 150,000 men, supported by American aid and trained by American advisers, seemed to lack sufficient instruction for the kind of conflict they had to fight. As in Laos and Thailand, they had been taught conventional, western methods of warfare, and they were outfitted with tanks, armored cars, and artillery.

Not until last spring—after some squabbling among various American services—was an anti-guerrilla school created in South Vietnam. But most of the army has not begun to unlearn its earlier instruction, and in many areas troops will not move at anything less than battalion or regiment strength, accompanied by elaborate armor. A more hopeful program in South Vietnam was the recent creation of a corps of thirty thousand civil guards, armed with shotguns and radios to get help when Communist partisans are sighted. They have not been operating long enough to have proved their value.

If they are to be successful, however, Diem will have to alter part of his political and administrative structure, which has seriously hindered the fight against the Communists. In each of the thirty-eight provinces, for example, the civil guard is under the orders of a semi-autonomous province chief, who is directly responsible to the president alone but usually clears his moves with brothers Nhu or Can. Often the province chiefs exercise their peculiar right to deny their neighbors "hot pursuit" of guerrillas more than five kilometers into their territory. Similar rules and regulations hamstring the army. Units may only move within their own military districts, and lateral communications between districts are poor or nonexistent.

Still another stumbling block to effective military activity has been Diem's typical propensity to ignore his senior officers. Like a model-railroad enthusiast dispatching toy trains hither and yon, he occasionally picks up a telephone in his palace and capriciously orders a battalion to pack up and move five hundred miles, without informing anyone else of the directive and leaving all his subordinates wondering which troops are where.

In any conflict against guerrillas, however, the key to success or failure lies in the rural population, and in many regions of South Vietnam the peasants' attitude to the Diem régime seems to range between plain and "hostile" neutrality.

To some extent, the army has been at fault. It has tended—as the French did so often in Indo-China—to evacuate villages at night, thereby leaving peasants to the mercy of terrorists. Like most Oriental armies it has done its share of brutalizing peasants—raping, pillaging, torturing. And often it is caught in clever Communist traps. In the Mekong River delta a couple of months ago, for instance, a Communist band captured a junk-load of rice. They carried it to a nearby settlement and distributed it free to the people, thus winning a vote of gratitude. But to consolidate this tactic, disguised Communist agents went to army officers in the vicinity and told them where the captured cargo could be uncovered. Government troops were promptly dispatched to raid the village and confiscate the stolen rice, and the final score in this ruse was one more psychological victory for the Reds, one more psychological loss for the Diem régime.

Aggravating this sort of fumbling, some of Diem's dramatic security decisions have fallen short. Late in 1959, for example, he devised a scheme to pull the peasants together in large agglomerations, officially to be called "prosperity centers" and commonly known as *agrovilles*. The laudable aim of these projects was to establish protected villages and, incidentally, to set up marketing cooperatives. Last spring, traveling with military escort, I drove down to an *agroville* at Vi Thanh, in the heart of the dangerous delta region. At first glance, it seemed magnificent compared to the scrubby farms I had seen along the way. Flanking a canal for about four miles, it had ample bamboo-and-thatch houses, each with a large garden. There were ferries to take farmers to their fields, and in the town itself there was a power plant, a school, a dispensary, and a common market; and there were plans to stock the local canals with fish to give peasants another source of income between rice harvests.

But probing a bit more deeply into the story of Vi Thanh,

I discovered some fatal flaws that, in practice, had made the entire scheme a detriment to South Vietnam's security—and perhaps explain why the government has abruptly dropped the whole *agroville* idea.

For one thing, the project ran directly counter to traditional social patterns in the region. Peasants in the delta area, unlike those in the north, have always lived on their land and not in villages. The swift and ruthless manner in which the *agrovilles* were created not only disrupted ancient customs, it also alienated more peasants than it could ever have protected. The ingenuous provincial official who was responsible for Vi Thanh was delighted to describe what he considered his achievement. In fifty days, beginning in December, 1959, with the help of the army he rounded up twenty thousand peasants—although they were in the midst of their rice harvest—and put them to work immediately. They were paid nothing, and many of them had to walk ten or twelve miles to and from the construction job every day. And when the *agroville* was finished, there was room in it for only 6,200 people, leaving some fourteen thousand others without their rice crop, without any payment for their work, and without any opportunity to enjoy the fruits of their labor.

On balance, there is no doubt that Diem has done a great deal for the South Vietnamese peasant. The accomplishments—credit, new seeds, irrigation projects, tax exemptions, land distribution, and the like—cannot be overlooked. But the individualistic, self-conscious farmer, like farmers everywhere in the world, has an inherent inclination to discount his blessings; and in critical times, such as the present, failings tend to gain greater currency than achievements.

In a different but no less serious way, the dissatisfaction of the peasants has been matched by the increasing disenchantment of Saigon's educated elite with Diem and his government.

From various conversations during the past year, I can only venture some opinions of the influences at work among the Saigon "intellectuals." Events in Korea last spring, which culminated in the overthrow of Syngman Rhee, had a profound and pervasive effect throughout Asia. In South Vietnam—as in Formosa—younger people were inspired with the fuzzy idea that they, like the Koreans, might be able to "do something," without ever specifying clearly what they wanted to do. Many, for example, would have liked to "do something" about government bureaucracy, and in many private talks, almost every Vietnamese I saw—including some public officials—vehemently wanted to "do something" about Diem's family and its influence. Several of these youths, lacking the right political connections for advancement, felt frustrated by the difficulties they encountered in trying to serve their country.

In all the recent Saigon grumbling, however, there has been surprisingly little demand for "democracy." The general displeasure, as I heard it, was with what the wits dubbed "Diemocracy"—the government's make-believe guarantees of civil liberties and fair elections. With much fanfare, extensive plans were worked out for National Assembly elections in August, 1959, and opponents of the government's National Revolutionary Movement were invited to run. But hardly had the campaign begun than opposition politicians encountered a variety of obstacles, such as having the wrong stamp or signature on their documents or displaying "illegal" placards. Those who managed to hurdle these barriers found themselves facing another block on election day. Contingents of troops were moved into Saigon, where the opposition was strongest; the troops were all under orders to vote for the government candidates.

Even so, a Harvard-educated opponent of the régime, Dr. Phan Quang Dan, somehow succeeded in winning a parliament seat. He was never able to assume it, however. With almost infantile pique, the government arrested him for such infractions as opening his campaign "too early," using "unauthorized posters," and making "false promises"; and despite appeals by three western ambassadors to Diem, Dr. Dan's election was annulled.

Although nobody was prepared to fight strongly for Dr. Dan, the government's action against him made Diem appear petty and peevish, and it diminished his prestige considerably. Last April, a group of eighteen former officials—among them several ex-ministers, the president of the Red Cross and, in spite of family ties, Madame Nhu's uncle—sent Diem a petition requesting that he "liberalize his régime, expand democracy, grant minimum civil rights," and reform the administration, the army, and the economy. Neither this modest appeal nor its signers could have been considered a menace to the régime.

Upon receipt of their petition, however, President Diem's first reaction was to have them arrested and sent to "political re-education camps," where an estimated 25,000 citizens are currently being shown the paths of righteousness. After some reflection, Diem decided to ignore them. But, coincidentally, about thirty obscure doctors, students, and journalists were picked up on suspicion of "Communist affiliations." To my knowledge, none of them—nor any other suspects—has ever been brought to trial. Frequent police roundups of this kind serve as a warning.

The rumbling of disgruntlement throughout last spring and summer did not delude Diem and his government, and much of it sounded ominously like another South Korean episode in the making. Diem was extremely sensitive to this possibility, and a good deal of his irritation was directed toward the United States, which had taken a hand in removing Syngman Rhee and was, through its diplomats in Saigon, constantly trying to press upon him the urgent need for reforms.

But heads of state, however much aid they receive, are still aware of their sovereignty; indeed, the more impoverished and indebted they are, the more sensitive and stubborn they may be in resisting the advice or pressure of an American representative. Efforts with Diem elicited only an impatient rejection of "interference" in his domestic affairs. Obliquely, one of Diem's close aides described to me how the United States had "dislocated" South Korean society.

South Vietnam and South Korea are, it seems, parallels that do not meet. Korea had an organized opposition party, a body of fairly sophisticated students, and a group of independent army officers. In Vietnam, there has not been—and may still not be—any visible alternative to Diem except the Communists. As recently as a month or two ago, his most vociferous critics could not conceive of South Vietnam without him. "We cannot abandon him," one of them said, "but he must bring in reforms." There are several reasons to believe that the paratroopers who rebelled last year shared this feeling about Diem. They were frustrated and overworked. They were irritated by political meddling in their operations, and they blamed the government for failing to generate popular support in the countryside. Despite a later government propaganda campaign to vilify them—as "egomaniacs," "Communist and colonial agents," and the like—there is scarcely any doubt that the rebels were sincere.

Over and over again during their rebellion, the paratroop officers repeated the same theme: the régime needs overhauling so its fight against the Communists can be more effective. "If we allowed things to continue," a rebel captain explained, "it's obvious that this country would be Communist in a year."

The insurgent leaders were, first and foremost, soldiers. One of them, Lieutenant Colonel Vuong Van Dong, was a native of the north who had served with the French against Vietminh. His partner in the uprising was Colonel Nguyen Chanh Thi, commander of the country's three thousand paratroopers—a veteran who had helped save Diem's life in 1955, when the régime was attacked by the piratical Binh Xuyen and other sects. Since then, Colonel Thi had been so intimate with the Ngo family that Diem often referred to him as "my son." Neither these nor any of the other military men involved appear to have had political ambitions or much political acumen. They failed to follow the most elementary procedures of a *coup d'état*, such as seizing the radio station, blocking the roads into the city, or cutting communications. At the height of the fracas, for example, it was still possible to pick up a telephone and ring the palace switchboard. This evidence points to utter naïveté. It also points to a motive behind the façade of callowness. No experienced military men would have held back their troops for thirty-six hours from attacking the palace of the president they intended to overthrow—unless, of course, they did not intend to overthrow the president.

That, in my opinion, was the reason for their restraint. They were primarily attempting to pressure Diem into reform. In their only effort to see him, they went to the chief of the American military mission, and after outlining their grievances, asked for an escort to the president. Most Americans in Saigon were sympathetic to the rebels. But neither the

general nor Ambassador Elbridge Durbrow could risk involvement in the revolt. They refused to arrange a meeting, and at
no time during the episode did Diem and the insurgents confront each other. Although they skirmished with the palace
guards, the rebels never made a frontal attack on the palace.
Indeed, their conduct throughout—as a paratroop colonel described it at the time—was "gentlemanly."

President Diem, on the other hand, was playing to win. At
the first rebel outbreak, he and his brother Nhu descended to
the palace cellar, which had recently been equipped against
the possibility of a siege. There, sitting at a table—now en-
shrined as *"la table de la victoire"*—Diem began sending radio
messages to army units in the nearby countryside. This very
practice of personally moving around troops, which so exas-
perated professional soldiers, became an essential element in
his success. He managed to contact commanders in the south
and north, and ordered them into Saigon to rescue him. They
were slow in coming. To stall, Diem agreed to a whole list of
reforms—civil liberties, free elections, a liberal economic program, a more effective offensive against the Communists, and
other changes. He also promised to dismiss the government
and form a new coalition cabinet, with himself as president.
A tape recording of these decisions had barely been broadcast
when his saviors arrived and, after some fierce fighting, sent
the rebels scattering.

Without much hesitation, Diem publicly reneged on his
promises. They were made, he explained, at a time when the
situation seemed lost and it was imperative "to preserve the
integrity of our military potentialities." He forgave the rank-
and-file paratroopers, claiming that they had assembled at his
palace under the illusion that they were protecting him. And
he reaffirmed that "republican and personalist principles"
would continue as the basis of his régime. In short, there
would be no change.

Saigon seemed calm and peaceful again. But scores were
quietly and severely settled in the days that followed. A kind
of committee of public safety, sanctioned by the government,
announced "a systematic purge in state and civic organizations
until the last suspected element is wiped out." As advertised,
it systematically aided the secret police in making arrests,

cluttered the city with vengeful posters, and failed only "to stop the indignant masses" from smashing up five newspaper offices that were guilty of printing news of the revolt.

In that sort of atmosphere it is usually difficult to assess public opinion. But in Saigon that week I discovered, on the contrary, a greater willingness in people to talk than I had ever before encountered. They had, it seems on looking back, a desire to unburden themselves engendered by a mixture of confused feelings: desperation at the rebel failure, encouragement from the attempt, and, I found everywhere, the certainty that sooner or later there would be another revolt—a successful one. "The army has lost its virginity," as a knowledgeable Vietnamese put it. "Next time it will be easier."

South Vietnam will be fortunate, however, if the "next time" there is fighting in Saigon, the anti-government forces are not Communists. For the revolt and its aftermath is bound to prove a boon to the guerrillas. It introduced an element of distrust between Diem and his army that should inevitably make their relations more brittle than ever. Beyond that, the insurrection took a moral and physical toll on the most effective army unit in the country. The paratroopers were the spearhead against the Communist partisans. From their bases around Saigon, they could be mobilized and put into action anywhere within eighteen hours. Although no casualty figures have been released, it is calculated that as many as four hundred of them may have been killed during the revolt. Some of their best officers fled with the rebel colonels; and nobody knows how many individual soldiers, beaten and ashamed, deserted to the jungles. A high-ranking apolitical military man commented sadly: "The Communists would have given three divisions to wipe out the paratroopers. We have done it for them."

If the insurrection hurt the army, it also shattered Diem's prestige. The aloof mandarin had never been loved, but he had at least enjoyed a healthy measure of respect. Diem lost ground by allowing the situation to degenerate to a point at which revolt was conceivable, especially by troops who had often served as his most trusted bodyguard. Moreover, he lost face badly by disavowing the promises of reform he had broadcast during the uprising. "We didn't want the rebels to harm him," a schoolteacher said bitterly, "but now we're sorry they didn't."

The ugly mood of the country does not seem to have affected Diem. Just after the revolt, palace officials reported that they had rarely seen him in such good humor, and a western ambassador who paid a courtesy call described him as "bouncy." His self-confidence is paralleled by his brother Nhu's somewhat alarming analysis of the "real causes" behind the country's unsettled state. In a long conversation I had with him a few weeks ago, Nhu emphasized that the principal culprits in the revolt were the "western embassies" in Saigon, and individual Americans in particular. They supposedly provoked the paratroopers to rebellion by disseminating rumors of corruption and nepotism. "Not only that," he said, "but American military advisers were helping the paratroopers during the revolt. And they volunteered—they were not invited."

To this suggestion of "colonialist" inspiration—a charge diffused widely by the government press—Nhu added another disturbing notion. He readily admitted that the country's fight against the Communists was not going well. But, he pointed out, the army rather than the government was at fault. "The army is doing its job badly," he said. "They don't know enough about psychological warfare. It's entirely wrong to suppose that the population is displeased with the government. It's the army they dislike." And hinting at possible purges to come, he added: "Every military chief must take stock of his conscience."

Nhu's analysis of events, which naturally absolves Diem of any fault, thus puts the blame squarely on the two main props of the régime—the United States and the South Vietnamese Army. This thesis—to which Diem himself certainly subscribes—is likely to create trouble in the future. Anxiety and suspicion that the United States is "interfering," as it did in South Korea, is apt to stiffen Diem against further efforts to make him liberalize. A very blunt version of this fear was expressed in a recent *Times of Vietnam* editorial, which commented: "The threat to our independence does not come from our Communist enemies alone, but also from a number of foreign people who claim to be our friends." At the same time, Nhu's criticism of the army and the possibility of purges—even if partly justified—can be hazardous for a coun-try heavily infiltrated by Communist guerillas. Military mo-rale, as the insurrection testified, has reached a low point. Should Diem inaugurate "loyalty tests" for his troops or pun-ish them for his own failings, he may find nothing between himself and Ho Chi Minh's terrorists.

Some of the president's aides, conscious of the unstable situation—and also concerned with the régime's reputation abroad—persuaded Diem to let them announce a forth-coming "reshuffle of the cabinet and a general revamping of our entire establishment." This program of "reform," which has yet to be revealed in detail, does not, however, answer the basic question of whether Diem himself can be reformed. In Saigon, as in Djakarta and Rabat and Léopoldville, the Estab-lishment is never as important as the man who manages it. Liberal constitutions, parliaments and law courts are a glut in underdeveloped countries where governments resemble noth-ing so much as the personality of the man at the top.

The characteristics that made Diem a success in 1955 and 1956—obstinacy, single-mindedness, and guile—are his most obvious weaknesses today. If he is unable to change, there is not much hope that he, or perhaps even the country, can last. In recent months, several reputable firms have declined to un-derwrite any business in South Vietnam. "No premium, no matter how high, is worth the risk," explains one American insurance executive.

The precariousness of the Diem regime, the current fight-ing in Laos, and Prince Norodom Sihanouk's unpredictable neutralism in Cambodia have combined to bring Indo-China to its dreariest days since Dienbienphu. A durable anti-Com-munism can, in time, emerge from economic and social development. The problem in a vulnerable country like South Vietnam is to survive and progress simultaneously, as Malaya did throughout the years of its emergency. This is, of course, easier to suggest than to accomplish. But neither survival nor progress is likely to evolve out of puerile slogans, secret police, and massive regiments maneuvering like ancient Asian armies of elephants. Among other things, it requires the rational use of force accompanied by long-term economic planning and efforts to arouse popular enthusiasm. It also needs an intangible: style of leadership. If Diem cannot, in some radical switch, provide these elements, he is liable to fall. The Communists are ready to fill the vacuum.

The Reporter, January 19, 1961

Paddy War

by Malcolm W. Browne

A DRENCHING, predawn dew had settled over the sloping steel deck of the landing craft, and I slipped several times climbing aboard in the inky darkness.

Soldiers cursed sleepily as they heaved heavy mortar base plates and machine guns from the pier onto their field packs on the deck.

The night was still and moonless, and the air would have been warm except for that unpleasant dew, sometimes laced with raindrops. The French used to call it "spitting rain."

This was December, 1961, and I was going out for my first look at an operation against the Viet Cong. There were no American field advisors in those days (and no helicopters and almost no communications), and I tried to stay close to soldiers or officers who could speak French. Most of them could.

The place was a town called Ben Tre in the heart of the flat, fertile Mekong River Delta, about fifty miles south of Saigon. Ben Tre, the capital of Kien Hoa Province, still takes pride in the fact that it has produced some of Viet Nam's top Communists. Ung Van Khiem, former Foreign Minister of the Hanoi government, came from here. Kien Hoa is also famous for its pretty girls.

It was about 4 A.M., and I was dead tired. I had been up late with the province chief, Colonel Pham Ngoc Thao, a cat-like man with short-cropped hair and a disconcerting walleye.

Thao had been an intelligence officer in the Viet Minh during the Indochina War, and had gone over to Diem after independence in 1954.

The night before, Thao had invited me to the opening of a theater he had had built in Ben Tre, and the curious town residents had turned out in their holiday best. The bill of fare was a traditional Vietnamese drama and some comedians, jugglers and singers. It lacked the glamour of a Broadway opening night, but it was about the fanciest thing Ben Tre had ever seen.

Two masked actors in ornate classical costume were intoning verses about a murder they were planning and the audience was murmuring expectantly when Thao leaned toward me.

"My troops are going out in the morning. We have intelligence that a battalion of Viet Cong is moving through one of my districts. I'm not going, but would you be interested?"

Just then, the action on stage reached a high point. Several actors in stilted, oriental poses were supposed to portray violence, their brilliantly colored robes swishing. Applause rushed through the theater, and children put down their pop bottles to chatter. Thao, obviously pleased, warmly joined the applause.

He always liked the theater. A year or so later, when Diem sent him on a special mission to the States, he made a special point of visiting Hollywood, where he was photographed with actress Sandra Dee. The picture was sent back to Viet Nam by news agencies, but Diem's censors prohibited its publication, presumably because they felt it would be detrimental to fighting spirit.

The 300 or so troops on the pier that morning were an odd-looking bunch, a mixture of civil guards and self-defense corpsmen. Some were in neat fatigue uniforms with helmets, others in the loose, black garb of the Vietnamese peasant, topped with old French bush hats. There were no troops from the regular army on this operation. The commander was a crusty, French-trained captain with several rows of combat ribbons on his faded olive drab uniform.

The diesel engines of the three landing craft carrying our makeshift task force belched oily smoke and we were moving, the black silhouettes of palm trees sliding past along the edges of the narrow canal. Here and there a dot of light glimmered through the trees from some concealed cluster of huts.

For a few minutes, the commander studied a map with a neat plastic overlay, making marks with red and black grease pencils, under the light of a pocket flashlight.

One of the few things Western military men have taught

Vietnamese officers to do really well is mark up maps. The Vietnamese officer studies his sector map like a chessboard. Even if he has only a squad or two of men under his command, he uses all the ornate symbols of the field commander in marking his deployment on maps. This love of maps has often infuriated American advisors, who feel more time should be spent acting and less on planning.

After a while the light flicked out. A few of the troops were smoking silently, but most had arranged their field packs as pillows and had gone to sleep amid the clutter of weapons. We were not scheduled to reach our objective until several hours after sunrise.

I finally dropped off to sleep, and must have been asleep about an hour when a grinding lurch and the sound of splintering wood roused me.

It was still pitch dark, but people were screaming, and on the deck of the landing craft, troops were rushing around. In the darkness, we had somehow collided with and sunk a large, crowded sampan. Twenty or thirty sleeping occupants had been thrown into the canal, with all their worldly possessions. A few of them apparently were hurt.

The two other landing craft were chugging on down the canal, but we had stopped. Troops holding ropes were helping swing the people in the water over to the shore. When everyone had reached safety, we started up again, people still yelling at us in the distance. We must have destituted several large families at a blow, but there was no thought of getting their names so that they could be compensated by the government. I couldn't help feeling that their feelings for the government must be less than cordial.

The sky began to turn gray, and at last we left the maze of narrow canals and turned into a branch of the great Mekong itself.

The sun rose hot and red, its reflection glaring from the sluggish expanse of muddy water. We were moving slowly ("We don't want to make too much engine noise or the Viet Cong will hear us coming," the commander told me), and the dense wall of palm trees on both banks scarcely seemed to move at all.

It was nearly 9 A.M. when our little flotilla abruptly turned at right angles to the left, each vessel gunning its engines. We had reached the objective and were charging in for the beach. As we neared the shore we could see that the beach actually was a mud flat leading back about fifty yards to the palm trees, and it would be arduous hiking getting ashore.

The other two landing craft were going ashore about one mile farther up the river. The idea of this exercise, it was explained to me, was to seize two sets of hamlets running back from the river front, trapping the reported Viet Cong battalion in the wide expanse of rice fields in between.

We slammed into the mud, and the prow of our clumsy ship clanked down to form a ramp. We leapt into waist-deep water and mud and began the charge toward higher ground.

If the Viet Cong had even one machine gun somewhere in the tree line, they certainly could have killed most of us with no danger of encountering serious fire from us. Each step in that smelly ooze was agonizingly slow, and at times both feet would get mired. Little soldiers carrying heavy mortars and machine guns sank nearly to their necks. It happened that no one was shooting at us that day.

The first squads clambered up to high ground and began firing. Two light machine guns began thumping tracers across the open rice field, and mortars began lobbing shells at random. Individual soldiers with Tommy guns (I was surprised how many of our group were equipped with submachine guns) were emptying their magazines into a string of huts or into the field. Off a mile or so to our right, noises told us that our companion party was similarly employed. It really sounded like a war.

I was standing on a high path running parallel to the river near a machine-gun position, looking out over the field where our Viet Cong battalion was supposed to be trapped. The green rice was nearly waist high, and there might easily be a battalion concealed in this field for all anyone knew.

Suddenly, a man leapt up about fifty yards away and began to run. This was it!

Every machine gun, Tommy gun, rifle and pistol in our sector poured fire at that man, and I was amazed at how long he continued to run. But finally he went down, silently, without a scream.

Our little army continued to pour intense fire into the field and several huts until it occurred to someone that no one was shooting back, and it might be safe to move forward a little.

Some of the troops began to move into the huts, shooting as they went.

Near me was a cluster of five Dan Ve (local Self-Defense Corpsmen) dressed in ragged black uniforms with American pistol belts and rusty French rifles. The group was detailed to go into the field to look for the man we had seen go down, and I went with them.

We found him on his back in the mud, four bullet holes stitched across the top of his naked chest. He was wearing only black shorts. He was alive and conscious, moving his legs and arms, his head lolling back and forth. There was blood on his lips.

The Dan Ve squad, all young peasant boys, looked down at the man and laughed, perhaps in embarrassment. Laughter in Viet Nam does not always signify amusement.

Perhaps as an act of mercy, perhaps as sheer cruelty, one of the men picked up a heavy stake lying in the mud and rammed one end of it into the ground next to the wounded man's throat. Then he forced the stake down over the throat, trying to throttle the man. The man continued to move. Someone stamped on the free end of the stake to break the wounded man's neck, but the stake broke instead. Then another man tried stamping on the man's throat, but somehow the spark of life still was too strong. Finally, the whole group laughed, and walked back to the path.

The firing had stopped altogether, and several old peasant men were talking to the officers of our party. Two of the old men had a pole and a large fish net.

The peasants—I think they were hamlet elders—walked out to the wounded man, rolled him into the fish net, and with the net slung between them on the pole, carried him back to the path. As they laid him out on the ground, two women, both dressed in baggy black trousers and blouses, ran up from one of the huts. One of them put a hand to her mouth as she saw the wounded man, whom she recognized as her husband.

She dashed back to her hut and returned in a moment carrying a bucket, which she filled with black water from the rice field. Sitting down with her husband's head cradled in her lap, she poured paddy water over his wounds to clean off the clotting blood. Occasionally she would stroke his forehead, muttering something.

He died about ten minutes later. The woman remained seated, one hand over her husband's eyes. Slowly, she looked around at the troops, and then she spotted me. Her eyes fixed on me in an expression that still haunts me sometimes. She was not weeping, and her face showed neither grief nor fury; it was unfathomably blank.

I moved away some distance to where the operation commander was jabbering into a field telephone. When his conversation ended, I handed him a 500-piastre note (worth about $5.00), asking him to give it to the widow as some small compensation.

"Monsieur Browne, please do not be sentimental. That man undoubtedly was a Viet Cong agent, since these hamlets have been Viet Cong strongholds for years. This is war. However, I will give her the money, if you like."

I don't know what happened to that money, and I didn't go near the place where the woman was sitting, but I walked into the hut I had seen her leave.

It was typical of thousands of Mekong Delta huts I have seen. The framework was bamboo, and the sides and roof were made of dried, interlaced palm fronds with a layer of rice straw thatch on top. The floor was hardened earth. A large, highly polished wooden table stood near the door. Peasants eat their meals on these tables, sleep on them and work on them. There were four austerely simple chairs. In a corner were several knee-high earthen crocks filled with drinking water. Just inside the door was the family altar, extending all the way to the ceiling. Pinned to it were yellowed photographs and some fancy Chinese calligraphy. On a little shelf a sand pot containing incense sticks smoldered fragrant fumes.

To the right, from behind a woven bamboo curtain, two children were peering with wide eyes. The eyes were the only expressive elements in their blank, silent little faces. Incongruously, one of them was standing next to a gaily painted yellow rocking horse, one rocker of which was freshly splintered by a bullet hole.

I walked out of the hut and down the path. By now, troops were strung all along the path between the two hamlets about a mile apart, and were stringing telephone wire and performing other military chores.

Snaking through the palm trees, a water-filled ditch about twenty feet across obstructed my progress. But a few yards away, a soldier had commandeered a small sampan from an old woman and was ferrying troops back and forth. I went across with him. As I continued down the path, scores of mud walls about five feet high obstructed progress. All were obviously freshly built, and most had gun slots. It was strange that no one had decided to defend these good emplacements against us.

I came to a small hut straddling the path, consisting only of upright bamboo spars and a roof. The little building was festooned with painted banners, the largest of which read *"Da Dao My-Diem"* ("Down with U.S.-Diem"). A group of young women were dismantling the hut as soldiers trained rifles at them. I was told that this was a Viet Cong "information center."

Finally, the troops began moving out from the tree line into the field itself, converging from three sides: the two hamlets and the path itself. The battle would come now, if ever.

We moved single file along the tops of the dykes that divided the field into an immense checkerboard. The thought struck me that if there were guerrillas hiding in the tall rice we would make fine targets as we moved along, but no one seemed worried.

Progress was slow. The mud dykes were slippery as grease, and every time a soldier toppled into the muddy paddy, the whole column halted as he was pulled out. I was reminded somehow of the White Knight in Lewis Carroll's *Through the Looking Glass.* Superficially, we combed the field from one end to the other, our various forces finally meeting in the middle.

A little L19 spotter plane droned overhead, radioing what was no doubt useful information to the ground commander.

It would be difficult to search that field more completely than we did, and we found not the slightest trace of a human being. Of course, the rice could easily have concealed a thousand or even ten thousand guerrillas, without our knowing.

Viet Cong guerrillas have developed the art of camouflage to an incredible degree. In rice fields, they often remain completely submerged under the muddy water for hours, breathing through straws.

But by now the sun stood like a blast furnace in the sky, and the troops were tired. A few had tied to their packs live ducks and chickens they had pilfered from the hamlets, and were looking around for level ground on which to prepare lunch.

"It looks as though the Viet Cong got away again," the commander told me. "It's time to go. It's not a good idea to be moving around out here when the sun starts going down."

By noon, 300 mud-drenched, tired troops were boarding the landing craft, and silence had settled over the hamlets again. We had suffered one wounded—a Civil Guard who had stepped on a spike trap, which had pierced his foot.

The three landing craft churned their way out into deep water, and the tension disappeared. Soldiers lighted cigarettes, talked and laughed, and spread their sopping clothing on the deck to dry.

All of them had a warm feeling of accomplishment, of having done a hard day's work under the cruel sun. The irregularity in the palm-lined shore that marked our hamlet receded into the distance.

And I couldn't help thinking of the old travelogues that end, "And so we leave the picturesque Mekong River Delta, palm trees glimmering under a tropic sun, and happy natives on the shore bidding us 'aloha.' "

from *The New Face of War*, 1965

A *"Very Real War"* in Vietnam—
and the Deep U.S. Commitment

by Homer Bigart

SAIGON, Feb. 24—The United States is involved in a war in Vietnam. American troops will stay until victory.

That is what Attorney General Robert Kennedy said here last week. He called it "war . . . in a very real sense of the word." He said that President Kennedy had pledged that the United States would stand by South Vietnam's President Ngo Dinh Diem "until we win."

At the moment the war isn't going badly for "our" side. There is a lull in Viet Cong activities, and the South Vietnamese forces are both expanding and shaping up better as a fighting force. But all that is needed to precipitate a major war is for the Chinese Communists and Communist North Vietnam to react to a build-up of American forces.

American support to Vietnam has always been based on the fear that Communist control of this country would jeopardize all Southeast Asia. And it continues despite the fact that Diem's American critics—especially liberals repelled by the dictatorial aspects of his regime—have been predicting his imminent downfall.

Diem remains firmly in charge and Washington's support for his regime today seems more passionate and inflexible than ever.

Actually the United States has been deeply involved in the fate of Vietnam since 1949 when the decision was made to subsidize the continuation of French rule against the Communist Viet Minh rebellion. The first United States Military Assistance Advisory Group (M.A.A.G.) arrived in 1951 to supervise the distribution of supplies. Thereafter the United States played an increasingly important role. To use a favorite

26

Washington term, aid was "escalated" until today $2 billion has been sunk into Vietnam with no end to the outlay in sight.

This may sound more reckless than the best brinkmanship of John Foster Dulles' days, and perhaps it is. But the United States is on this particular faraway brink because the Kennedy Administration seems convinced that the Communists won't rise to the challenge of the American presence and assistance.

The battle in Vietnam currently involves some 300,000 armed South Vietnamese and 3,000 American servicemen on one side, against 18,000 to 25,000 Viet Cong Communist regulars operating as guerrillas.

The battle that is being fought is complex—in the nature of the fighting, in the internal political background and in its international implications.

The United States does not have any combat infantry troops in Vietnam as of now, but we are getting ready for that possibility. Marine Corps officers have completed ground reconnaissance in the central Vietnam highlands, a potential theater of large-scale action between American troops and Communist forces coming down from the north.

American combat troops are not likely to be thrown into Vietnam unless Communist North Vietnam moves across the seventeenth parallel or pushes large forces down through Laos into South Vietnam.

In that case the United States would have to move in fast. Forty miles below the frontier with North Vietnam and parallel to it is Highway 9. This road has high strategic importance. Not only is it one of the few adequate roads open across the mountains to the Laotian border but it extends across Laos to Savannakhet on the Mekong River frontier with Thailand. If Highway 9 could be held from the Mekong to the sea by American, Vietnamese, Laotian and Thai forces, South Vietnam might be saved.

The situation right now is far more stable than it was last September, when the Communists were attacking in battalion strength and were even able to seize and hold a provincial capital, Phuoc Vinh, for a few hours. The September action seemed a prelude to an all-out Communist drive to overturn the Diem Government. It precipitated the present flood of American military advisors and service troops.

Today American warships are helping the embryonic Vietnamese Navy to guard the sea frontier against infiltration from
North Vietnam and U.S. Navy servicemen presently will arrive
to help clean out guerrillas from the maze of tidal waterways
in the Mekong River delta. The U.S. Army helicopter crews
have come under fire taking Vietnamese combat troops into
guerrilla zones or carrying pigs and other livestock to hungry
outposts surrounded by hostile country. U.S. Air Force pilots
have flown with Vietnamese pilots on bombing missions
against reported enemy concentrations and against two frontier forts recently evacuated by the Vietnamese Army.

So far our contribution in blood has been small. One American sergeant has been killed by enemy action and another is
missing and presumed captured. Inevitably our casualties will
grow.

It has not been easy to change from conventional warfare,
in which the Vietnamese were trained so many years by
M.A.A.G., to unconventional counter-guerrilla warfare. Under French influence, the Vietnamese had developed two ten-
dencies difficult to erase: first, the habit of staying inside forts
designed for the troops' protection rather than for the security
of the populace; second, the habit of good living—a leisurely
lunch followed by a siesta.

But counter-guerilla warfare demands hard living. Troops
must live in the jungle just as the guerrillas do and eschew the
comforts of barracks life.

There are some minor difficulties: most Vietnamese recruits
are from the densely populated lowlands—rice paddy boys
who have a fear of the jungles, not merely fear of snakes and
tigers but fear of getting lost. They move fearfully, with the
instinct of a herd, tending to bunch up and thus present fat
targets for a Viet Cong ambush.

The Viet Cong guerrillas also were former rice paddy boys,
but they became inured to hardship by on-the-job training in
the jungle. Further, the Vietnamese are somewhat smaller
than Americans, so they get weary toting eleven-pound M1
rifles and pine for the lighter French weapons they were formerly equipped with.

At a higher level, United States advisors, besides trying to
eliminate political manipulation of troops, are attempting to

dissuade the Vietnamese from launching large-scale operations based on sketchy intelligence. They see no justification for such operations until a more adequate intelligence system is developed and greater tactical mobility achieved.

Intelligence will improve only when the Government is able to break the grip of fear with which the Viet Cong muzzles the rural population. Greater mobility is being provided by American helicopter companies, but this is a costly and dangerous way to move troops.

The man who is at the center of the Vietnamese effort and who is also a center of controversy—President Diem—is something of an enigma. He is a mandarin (an aristocrat) and a devout Catholic. So there are two strikes against him at the start, for mandarins were regarded by the masses as greedy and corrupt, and Catholics as an unpopular minority.

Diem, however, has proved incorruptible. Rumors of personal enrichment of members of his family have never been proved. And Diem has been careful not to arouse Buddhist hostility. He is a man of great personal courage, but he is suspicious and mistrustful. The creation of a central intelligence agency here was delayed for months until Diem found a director he could trust.

Diem, a 66-year-old bachelor, often has been accused of withdrawing inside his narrow family clique and divorcing himself from reality. Critics say he distrusts everyone except the family and takes advice only from his brothers, particularly Ngo Dinh Nhu, his political advisor. His brother Nhu and his attractive, influential wife, are leaders, according to critics, of a palace camarilla which tries to isolate the President from the people.

As commander-in-chief of the armed forces, Diem keeps close tabs on military operations. His personal representative on the General Staff is Brig. Gen. Nguyen Khanh who has appalled Americans by taking general reserve troops on quick one-shot operations without coordinating with the area commander. Khanh is young, vigorous and driving but, according to his critics, lacking balance and experience.

Lieut. Gen. Le Ven Ty is Chief of the General Staff but he is in his sixties and lacks vigor. Consequently much of the military direction comes from the President through Khanh.

It is well to remember that Diem has been right and the United States wrong on some crucial issues. In 1955, for example, Diem wanted to crush the powerful Binh Xuyen gangster sect that controlled both the police and the gambling dens and brothels and made a mockery of government authority. President Eisenhower's special ambassador, Gen. Lawton Collins, opposed Diem's plan fearing civil war. Diem coolly proceeded to assert his power and used loyal troops to crush the Binh Xuyen in sharp fighting in Saigon's streets.

More recently the United States resisted Diem's urgent requests for aid in the creation of the civil guard and self-defense corps. The United States insisted that a 190,000-man regular army was all Diem needed for national defense. Diem went ahead and organized the two forces, arming them with antiquated French rifles. Finally, after alarm bells were ringing to the widespread revival of Communist guerrilla activity and vast sections of the countryside were lost to the Viet Cong, the Americans conceded Diem's point. Last year the United States started training and equipping the civil guard.

It is now generally agreed that the civil guard and the self-defense corps are absolutely vital. For until these reserve forces are ready to take over the defense of villages, railroads, harbors, airports, provincial capitals and so on, the army will be so tied down to static defense duties that it will not have the manpower to chase guerrillas.

Last week, in another apparent concession to Diem's wisdom, the United States agreed that any relaxation of tight political controls would be dangerous now. In a speech cleared with the State Department, Ambassador Frederick E. Nolting Jr. urged Diem's critics to cease carping and try to improve the government from within.

Just how serious the criticism is is not clear and there seems to be no agreement among observers whether the President's popularity is rising or falling. One former Diem adviser said he was shocked by the loss of support among the people in the past two years. He blamed this on the fact that Government seemed to grope from crisis to crisis without a clear policy: "It's just anti-Communist and not pro anything."

But another qualified observer, perhaps less biased, cautioned against underrating Diem. Increased guerrilla activity had not been matched, he said, by a corresponding rise in popular discontent and this failure to respond must have depressed the Communists.

Most villages, he added, were like a leaf in the wind: "When the Viet Cong enters, the population turns pro-Communist; when the Government troops arrive, sentiment shifts to the Government." But generally the village people would settle for the Government side, he said, not because they admired the Government but because they wanted peace.

Consequently the Government has a great advantage. He estimated that of the 30 per cent tending to the Viet Cong, only a third were hard-core, another third would adhere to the Communists under adversity, while the remaining third would break off under pressure.

Freedom from dictatorship and freedom from foreign domination are major propaganda lines for the Viet Cong. Americans in uniform have now been seen by the peasants in virtually all sections of the country. This has given the Communists a chance to raise the bogey of foreign military domination.

The lack of trained troops to keep the Viet Cong under relentless pressure probably will continue to handicap the military command throughout 1962, because at least a year must elapse before the self-defense units will be really capable of defending their villages.

Whether because the Army is beginning to take the initiative and is penetrating secret areas of Viet Cong concentrations or because the Viet Cong has abated its activities in order to recruit and train, the fact remains that security seems better in most parts of Vietnam.

In peaceful, booming Saigon there is much speculation on how the Viet Cong will react to an American build-up. Senior American officers have been studying an enemy guide book to guerrilla warfare searching avidly for clues, as though this modest work were the Viet Cong's "Mein Kampf."

There will never be enough troops to seal off the frontiers. There aren't even enough troops to ring Viet Cong enclaves near Saigon. Not before summer, when the civil guard and self-defense units are slated to take over the burden of defending their villages will enough troops be freed for a counter-guerrilla offensive. Then, instead of a conventional setpiece offensive of limited duration, a counter-guerrilla drive will seek to keep Viet Cong units on the run at all times, tire them out by constant pressure and force them into less hospitable country where food supplies are scarce.

The offensive cannot succeed unless the Government is able to mobilize positive popular support. This will be difficult, for the Government is just beginning to develop grass roots political cadres.

Meanwhile something more than narrowly anti-Communist goals must be offered Saigon intellectuals, who are now scorned by both Diem and the Americans. This group may be permanently alienated unless there is promise of democratic reforms. Without pressure from Washington, there is not likely to be any relaxation of Diem's personal dictatorship. The struggle will go on at least ten years, in the opinion of some observers, and severely test American patience.

The United States seems inextricably committed to a long, inconclusive war. The Communists can prolong it for years. Even without large-scale intervention from the north, which would lead to "another Korea," what may be achieved at best is only restoration of a tolerable security similar to that achieved in Malaya after years of fighting. But it is too late to disengage; our prestige has been committed. Washington says we will stay until the finish.

The New York Times, February 25, 1962

"The Enemy Had Left a Display for Us"

by Malcolm W. Browne

AT THE SOUTHERNMOST part of Viet Nam is a large tongue of land called the Ca Mau Peninsula, which juts down from Indochina, dividing the South China Sea from the Gulf of Siam. Ca Mau, the capital of this region, is the southernmost town in Viet Nam of any substance. There is more land below Ca Mau, much of which is trackless mangrove swamp and practically all of which belongs to the Viet Cong, except for a few pinpoints on the map like Dam Doi (pronounced in Vietnamese as "dom yoy").

To the west of Dam Doi is a forest about forty miles long, running along the coast of the Gulf of Siam. This forest is the base of the Viet Cong's notorious U Minh Battalion, one of the most feared units in the nation. To the east and south of Dam Doi are other important Viet Cong base areas, most of which are openly administered by the Viet Cong as "liberated zones."

There is no road connecting Dam Doi with the provincial capital of Ca Mau—only a footpath and a network of canals.

It was a scorching hot February morning when I first arrived in Ca Mau in a light plane that slid into the landing strip right in the center of town. A little river, thick with sampans, houseboats and fishing nets curves through the center of town, and the part of the city inside the curve is a thriving market place. Cool, maritime winds blow over Ca Mau in the monsoon season, but in February there is no relief from the merciless heat. No one works any harder than necessary.

Ca Mau is the capital of An Xuyen Province, one of forty-five provinces making up South Viet Nam. Each province is divided into districts, and each district is divided at progressively lower levels into cantons, villages (which are not actual towns but geographical subdivisions), and, finally, hamlets.

Dam Doi, despite its tiny population, is the capital of Dam Doi District.

I mention these trivial, administrative matters only because they have a bearing on the horror of life in places like Dam Doi. Each time an urgent plea for help passes from one level to a higher one, it must be processed through the red tape mill at each level. Really important things often have to go all the way to Saigon (which does not work nights or on weekends).

Let me set the stage a little more. At the time I arrived in Ca Mau, it happened that two battalions of Vietnamese marines, that is to say about nine hundred officers and men, were temporarily assigned to the province, to guard work crews repairing a road in the northwest part of the province. It takes that many troops to prevent a road crew from being wiped out by the guerrillas.

Of course, as soon as the road crew and the marines leave, the road is invariably ripped up and planted with mines and bamboo groves, but the exercise is presumably good training for all concerned.

An Xuyen Province is too poor and too low on the priority list to rate any regularly assigned government troops. But besides its regular army, South Viet Nam has two paramilitary forces, which do more fighting and take more casualties than the regular army. These are called the Bao An (Civil Guard) and the Dan Ve, translated either as People's Militia or Self-Defense Corps.

The Civil Guard is supposedly a provincial force. This means that if a man joins the Civil Guard, he is not as well paid as a regular soldier, but he is reasonably assured that he will always be stationed in his home province. At a lower level, membership in the Self-Defense Corps means even lower wages and fewer benefits, but it theoretically means that a man never need serve outside his home district. Often he actually lives at home, or in a compound right next to it. This system of military organization is exactly duplicated by the Viet Cong, incidentally.

In rural administrative centers, civilian government officials also are trained to fight in case of emergency. Under the defunct Diem regime, they dressed in blue uniforms and were called the Republican Youth Corps. The old name and the blue uniforms have been dropped, and they now are called the Combatant Youth.

So An Xuyen had a share of Civil Guards (dressed in uniforms almost identical to the regular army), Militiamen (dressed in black uniforms), and Youth Corpsmen.

The city of Ca Mau had (and still has) a few 105-millimeter howitzers that are fired nearly every night, supposedly to destroy Viet Cong as they attack outlying hamlets. But these howitzers rarely hit anything except an occasional hut, and their range is not great enough to do anything for places like Dam Doi.

In addition to these forces, a Roman Catholic priest of Chinese origin, the Reverend Nguyen Lac Hoa, has for years maintained his own private army of irregulars at a hamlet called Binh Hung south of Ca Mau. Father Hoa, a refugee from China and a former colonel in the Nationalist Chinese Army, settled his little band of Chinese refugees in about the most desolate and unpleasant bit of land anywhere in South Viet Nam. Almost completely cut off from the rest of the world and surrounded by large and extremely hostile Viet Cong units, Binh Hung nevertheless survived and grew.

Some Vietnamese from the province went to live in muddy Binh Hung, and Father Hoa recruited and trained his own irregular defense force, which he named the "Sea Swallows." More than one thousand men strong, this little fighting unit began to establish a reputation for disciplined and courageous fighting, and its reputation as a thorn in the very intestines of the Viet Cong began to spread.

The American Central Intelligence Agency took a keen interest in Binh Hung, and through its Combined Studies Group in Saigon and the U.S. Army Special Forces, regular airdrops of supplies began to pour into Binh Hung.

Binh Hung actually got some of these supplies before they were issued to anyone else—even the U.S. armed forces. Supplies included the new ultralight AR-15 Armalite automatic rifle—a weapon weighing only about seven pounds, capable of throwing out super-high-velocity slugs faster than a conventional machine gun. Binh Hung also was the first to get the new unsinkable Fiberglas assault boats equipped with outboard motors. U.S. planes flew down to Binh Hung at night whenever the Viet Cong mounted a large attack, dropping flares to help the defenders. An aging Chinese wearing a priest's robes and a steel helmet and pistol belt is a strange study in contrasts, but the combination worked. Since those early days, Father Hoa has given up his military command and the Sea Swallows have been incorporated into the regular national armed forces, but Binh Hung is still fighting.

At any rate, the Sea Swallows in 1962 were a valuable addition to the normal forces of An Xuyen Province. Father Hoa felt secure enough that he would even loan neighboring district chiefs a platoon or two of Sea Swallows, at times when they felt extra shotguns were needed.

In February, 1962, a thirty-one-year-old Vietnamese army captain named Tran Van Kha was the chief of Dam Doi District. They say he had a wife in Saigon with whom he didn't get along, and this was one of the reasons he welcomed his assignment to Dam Doi. He had been there about three months.

Kha was an ambitious young officer, spoiling for a fight with the guerrillas who ruled the murky jungle. He was also worried about Dam Doi's defenses.

Counting all his Civil Guards and Militiamen, he had only about a score of able-bodied men to hold the hamlet itself. Every night the guerrillas did a little sniping and probing, and you never know what may come next. So Kha sent word to Father Hoa that he would appreciate some extra men. Father Hoa obligingly sent a platoon of Sea Swallows over to Dam Doi, giving Kha a complement of sixty-four men, counting himself. That was how things stood when I arrived in Ca Mau.

It was long before dawn on a Saturday morning when Kha decided to lead his men out for a foray against the enemy. Two things probably led him to do it. One was his boredom with always sitting behind the barricades of Dam Doi, the initiative always on the side of the unseen but lethal enemy outside. The other was Kha's mistress, a girl of about twenty, in her seventh month of pregnancy. Through "contacts" of her own, the girl had told Kha, she had learned that a squad of Viet Cong propagandists was operating in a cluster of huts about three miles south of Dam Doi, and could easily be caught red-handed by such strong forces as Kha commanded. It has never been established whether or not Kha's mistress actually was a Viet Cong agent. But there is no question that this bit of intelligence she gave him led directly to his death.

By Saturday evening, Kha and his men had still not returned. A village official—a man too old to fight—was worried. He managed to raise Ca Mau by radio.

"The chief and his men have not returned after all this time. The sun is setting, and there are signs the Viet Cong may be planning an attack. Please send help. Please, please, send help," the old man said.

A radio operator in Ca Mau dutifully took down the message, and carried it to the duty officer. The duty officer asked for confirmation of the time Kha had left. Confirmation came back. The duty officer was stuck with a hot potato, and he knew it. But he manfully swung into action to pass the word to higher command.

I was having a flyspecked dinner with a major named Hoang at the time. Two listless sentries with the dark, round faces of Cambodians stood at the gate outside. A few schoolgirls in their ankle length *ao-dais*—graceful, high-necked dresses slit to the waist, and worn over loose, white silk trousers—still stood chatting in the dusk, twirling their conical hats, fluffing their long black hair, and giggling. A steady stream of bicycles hurried people home to their dinners. Somewhere in the distance, a street vendor was yelling for customers for *pho*, a savory noodle soup favored by South Vietnamese.

The house was not the best in town, but neither was it the worst. It was a simple, stucco house fit for a deputy province chief, which was the office Hoang held.

On the front porch, a squad of tough Civil Guards, their skin tanned almost black and all carrying Tommy guns, was settling down for the night, stringing mosquito nets from the railing. But apart from these cutthroats, the scene was one of complete peace.

The dinner was tough chicken chopped in small pieces without regard to the pattern of bones, cold rice, some watery soup and an aging, flyspecked salad. But the major had some good Algerian wine, and we shared it.

There were no cigars or cognac, but there was more wine

after dinner. Hoang spoke fluent French, and felt disposed to talk.

"You know, the province chief, Colonel Ut, and I were in the same class together at the military academy," he began.

"As a matter of fact, I usually got higher marks than he did. Fate plays peculiar tricks. Here am I in this miserable job in this wretched house, away from my wife and children, and there is he, in that palace of a house, a full colonel, and enjoying a full and happy life. Tonight he is holding a dinner party for some people down from the Interior Ministry. You can be sure it will be a good party! Why don't you go over?"

I said I was tired.

"Well, then. Have some more wine. Perhaps later I can escort you for some sight-seeing around Ca Mau? There's not much to see, but you shall see Ca Mau by night—the pearl of Viet Nam's buttocks."

But Major Hoang did not have an opportunity to show me around Ca Mau. (He was right. There is not much to see at night, although market stalls lighted by little acetylene lamps and fragrant with the smell of tasty soups are attractive places. Most Vietnamese provincial towns are on or near waterways, and it is always pleasant to stroll around them in the evening.)

Major Hoang was interrupted when a jeep roared through the gate, throwing gravel as it braked. The sleepy sentries snapped to attention, and the duty officer strode up to the stone bench in front of the house door where Hoang and I were sitting. He glanced at me suspiciously, saluted Hoang, and handed him a note.

Hoang frowned as he read, and then excused himself without explanation. He was locked in his combination office and bedroom the rest of the evening, and I didn't see him again until morning.

I learned the next day that Hoang had not been able to reach Province Chief Ut during the night, either because Ut was unavailable or Hoang was unwilling to break up Ut's party with bad news. In any case, Ut didn't hear about Dam Doi until more than twenty-four hours had passed since its district chief had set forth into the jungle.

It was a pleasant Sunday morning in Ca Mau. Children were strolling and laughing in the streets, and the sun was not high enough yet to make things oppressively hot. But an odd, mixed convoy of army trucks, ornately painted but rickety civilian buses, and a handful of prewar automobiles, was rolling into town—loaded to the roofs with marines in battle gear. I asked one of the marine officers what was going on, and he said he had no idea.

"We were out guarding that cotton-pickin' road project," he said, "and nothing's happened all week long. Now, all of a sudden, along comes this convoy of buses and trucks, and we're ordered back to Ca Mau. You never know what to expect in this country."

"Where'd you learn English like that?" I asked.

"Quantico," the officer snapped back. "A marine's not a leatherneck if he hasn't been there, regardless of his nationality."

I went to the province chief's house to find out what was going on.

Ut, looking dapper in camouflaged fatigue uniform with razor-sharp creases, did live in a fine house. A long driveway led to the magnificent portico of the big, yellow stucco house. The wide doorway entered on a very large reception room with black and yellow tiled floor, comfortable and fairly modern furniture, an electric overhead fan and a tray of beer and cold soda ready for all comers. On the far wall, a portrait fully eight feet high of President Diem dominated the room, flanked by yellow and red national flags and bunting.

"There may have been some trouble down in Dam Doi, a town about thirty miles southeast of here," Ut said. "We've—well, it seems we've lost contact with the district chief there. We're going to have to have a look, so I pulled back those marines for a look at the area. They'll be leaving in a few hours. Want to go along?"

I did. I loaded my few belongings into my field pack and rejoined the marines, who were resting under the trees of one of the streets.

About 11 A.M., we marched through the streets to the river front, where Colonel Ut had assembled the most incredible armada of boats I had ever seen.

The backbone of our river task force was made up of three or four salvaged and reconditioned French gunboats called

FOMs. The FOM is a steel boat about forty feet long. Its armored sides are pierced at regular intervals with gun ports. On the top is perched a slab-sided little machine-gun turret. The ship is painted black, and is altogether one of the most ugly vessels I have ever seen.

Tied up alongside the FOMs were about twenty commercial river boats about the same length. But they were made of wood with high, curving bowsprits. They were painted yellow with red trim, and each had painted eyes just at the bow, staring forward, to bring good luck to river navigators. The squat diesel engines inside their cabins were already belching smoke. Each of the boats in our fleet carried a large national flag—yellow, with three horizontal red stripes—at the stern. It looked like the beginning of some odd regatta.

The marines bundled their packs, rifles, machine guns and mortars aboard the boats, and we chugged off down the river, in single file, fifty yards or so apart. The market place, jetties and riverside huts slipped away and were replaced by a dense, green wall of palms and bamboo on both sides of the narrow river.

We all knew that the Viet Cong had sunk many a boat— even armored boats—along here, using homemade rocket launchers mounted in trees along the banks. But the marines accepted this knowledge philosophically. Rather than crouch tensely behind their rifle sights, most of them went to sleep.

The convoy threaded its way through progressively more narrow tributaries and canals, passing an occasional outpost, the defenders of which just stared listlessly at us.

It was about 2 P.M. when the convoy reached a fork in the stream along which it had been traveling. The banks at this point were so close together the long palm fronds spreading from opposite banks almost touched overhead. The fork was sharp, and the banks on each side of it were steep. They were also studded with dagger-sharp bamboo foot spikes hardened by fire.

The fork formed the apex of a little, triangular outpost defended by a dozen Civil Guards, who had used their pitiful means for fortifying the place the best they could. A big national flag was perched bravely in the middle of the jungle enclave.

"From here on we have to walk," the English-speaking marine officer grumbled to me. By now, the bows of all our ships were jammed into the muddy bank, and the marines filed ashore, many of them muttering *"troi oi"*—a mild oath ("my God") that Vietnamese troops invariably use when strenuous physical exertion appears imminent.

We moved away from the outpost along a path hemmed in by jungle and still as death in the shimmering heat. The whole column was moving single file and fairly rapidly, with no flank scouts or any other precautions against ambush. The idea now was to get to the relative safety of Dam Doi before sunset. The night belongs to the enemy, Quantico training notwithstanding.

The path ran more or less parallel to a small canal occasionally visible off to our left. Smaller canals and ditches cut across the path every few hundred yards. Some were spanned by single logs. Poles jammed into the mud bottoms of the ditches afforded hand holds on which to balance across, but the logs were slippery, and falls were frequent. Progress was painfully slow.

Every once in a while we passed a lone hut, generally neat, with a large pile of threshed rice in front of the door, a few flowers, and a water buffalo or two tethered in an adjacent shed. But no sign of human life.

It is not healthy to be in an isolated hut when either the Viet Cong or government forces come through, and it's generally safer to go off into the jungle and hide for a few hours.

There was not a trace of the enemy, either. No barricades or foot traps across the path at all, for a change.

I should note at this point that I am writing about an incident in 1962. It is more than two years later at this writing, and one aspect of operations of this kind has changed. The Viet Cong is strong enough now that it almost invariably ambushes a relief column, and does so with such strength of numbers and firepower that these ambushes are nothing short of slaughter.

The shadows grew longer, and the faint stirring of air in the treetops that comes with dusk began. Sunrises and sunsets are short in the tropics, and night quickly follows dusk. By seven every night of the year in South Viet Nam it is dark.

All at once, we began moving past huts in groups, and the path widened. Before us was a fairly wide, wooden footbridge. Beyond the bridge was Dam Doi, and we could see even at this distance that a national flag was flying.

Dam Doi, which is on the right side of the canal we had been paralleling, is bisected by a smaller canal that runs at right angles to the main one. The side of the town we were entering included a fairly large, circular market place flanked by a few fairly large, wooden buildings. Streets, actually paths of well-trampled mud, radiated from this to form the residential district of town. On the other side of the bisecting canal, crossed by another fairly good footbridge, was the military part of the town, including the district headquarters compound.

There were several hundred people milling around the market place, where acetylene lamps were already beginning to cast their harsh, white light. The people had clearly heard our approach, and had turned out for a look at their visitors. But they stared incuriously, with no noticeable expression. Most were women and children. None waved or called out. Their welcome didn't seem actively hostile, but they certainly didn't greet us like liberators, either.

The long column moved silently through the heart of downtown Dam Doi, weapons clanking, then over the footbridge, a dozen at a time. Here the main "street" ran right next to the main parallel canal. And facing the canal was the compound where we would spend the night.

District headquarters was a building with, inevitably, yellow stucco walls, black and yellow tiled floors, a small yard in front facing the canal, a flagpole in the center of the yard, and a wooden watchtower about thirty feet high in the back. A smaller building facing the courtyard, a kind of shed, was festooned with gaudy paper stars and bunting left over from an observance of *Tet*, the lunar New Year that had passed a few weeks earlier. *Tet* is by far the most important holiday in Viet Nam, and even the Viet Cong quits fighting during the four-day holiday.

But the holiday decorations looked wrong. Inside the shed, men were hammering planks together into what were obviously coffins, and the smell of death was heavy all around. A handful of women wearing white bands of mourning around their heads were wailing in front of the main building; all of them had babies in their arms.

The smell of death was coming from the canal, where an FOM gunboat was tied up. In a small sampan the FOM had towed in were two bodies, in a ghastly state of mutilation and decomposition. They were so bad that the FOM crew had not been willing to take them aboard the big boat itself, but insisted on towing them back. Two families in Dam Doi had recognized what remained of the faces as their own. These two had gone out with Captain Kha that black Saturday morning forty hours ago.

Inside the barbed wire of the headquarters compound, marines everywhere were setting up their mosquito nets and boiling rice in the pots they always carry with them. Captain Kha's dry-eyed mistress was pouring tea for the officers inside the headquarters building.

If I said that Dam Doi was completely isolated from Saigon, this was not quite accurate. Saigon's government radio station has repeater stations all around the country, so that it is possible to receive the station any place. Very few peasants own radios of their own, but every hamlet of any consequence has a radio (from the U.S. Aid Mission) hooked up to a large loudspeaker which blares away all day long. Dam Doi's loudspeaker was mounted in the watchtower. I remember that it was playing an old recording of "In the Blue of Evening" that evening. The mourners went right on wailing.

Kha's mistress gave orders for dinner to be served to all the officers (and to me), and had cots set up indoors for all of them. This was a bit of unexpected luxury, but the word had already got around that this girl might have had something to do with Kha's disappearance. Every man slept with his service automatic in reach, and took turns posting guard.

There was no idea of going out to look for Kha and his men at night, who, by this time, had been missing about forty hours. For one thing, the night is risky even for large units, and for another, Dam Doi itself had to be protected.

Kha's girl friend showed us pictures of her man, and her eyes finally began to show signs of misery. He was young and strong and ambitious, she said, and had been terribly anxious to be able to report a victory. If only he had not been so headstrong. One of the pictures showed Kha talking into a microphone in front of the big picture of Diem over the front door of the headquarters building. It was probably a rally of some kind given for some visitors from Saigon.

All through the sweltering night, the geckos (lizard-like creatures that eat bugs) trumpeted their love songs, but otherwise the night was still. Apparently the Viet Cong had no appetite for a fight with a force of marines this large.

By sunrise we had all gulped down some cold rice and were ready to move again. The direction was the same, farther down the parallel canal. It would only be a matter of three miles or so before we would reach the place where Kha had gone.

Crowds of women chattering excitedly and looking worried now crowded the compound courtyard. They were waiting for word about their husbands, sons and fathers who had gone with Kha. Outside the barbed wire, children trudged along with the marines for a few hundred yards before turning back.

The jungle was very thick again, and the path narrower than ever. We slogged along about two miles, and then sent out some scouts to the right.

The scouts moved a few hundred yards through the trees, their rifles and Tommy guns at the ready. Then they stopped. They had smelled something that could only mean we were headed in the right direction.

The whole column turned right to follow the scouts. We were soon on another path, very muddy, and heavily tracked and rutted. The smell of rotting human beings was almost overpowering, as we moved along, and a few marines tied pocket handkerchiefs over their noses. This does no good whatever, by the way.

The jungle thinned out a little, and we came to some huts— the hamlet. All of them were deserted completely; there weren't even any chickens or buffalo. Behind the huts was a water hole about thirty feet in diameter with mud sides that sloped down to the filthy water. Neatly ranged around these sides, like spokes in a wheel, were thirty bloated corpses, all in the uniform of government troops. The hot sun had hastened the decomposition of two days, and intestines had forced their way out of gaping belly wounds, making yellowish piles atop each body. Tracks showed that the bodies all had been towed to the place by ropes tied to buffalo.

From a small, bamboo flagpole a few feet away fluttered a large Viet Cong flag—red on top, blue on the bottom, with a large yellow star in the middle. The enemy had left a display for us.

Someone found a rope, and all of us got out of the way while the flagpole was pulled down. The precaution proved to have been wise. The flagpole disappeared in a geyser of mud, and grenade fragments snapped through the trees. Booby trap.

The Viet Cong no doubt held a fine victory celebration before we arrived, with drill formation, salute to the colors, photographs of the war booty, and all the rest. But now they were gone.

Under trees and in clumps of weeds we found more bodies. Among them was the body of Kha. But we could not find Kha's head, which apparently had been hacked off with a machete. Perhaps the Viet Cong stuck it on the end of a pole and took it parading around some other hamlets, as they sometimes do.

Beheading is a terrible thing to do to a man in Viet Nam. Most people believe that the loss of the head damns the spirit to an eternity of restless wandering. It is the worst way to die.

We found a little store in the hamlet, boarded up with folding, louvred wooden doors. The marines ripped the doors off, and found a large stock of joss sticks—the long, tan sticks that burn like incense, and are said to please the spirit world. The whole stock, several thousand sticks, was stuffed into jars and lighted. The burning joss didn't improve the odor of things much, but perhaps it made things better for the spirits that had left the carnage at the water hole.

We ripped the door sections from their hinges to make litters, and began the revolting job of picking up the bodies. A half-dozen marines were retching as they worked. A large sampan had pulled up to the hamlet along a creek, and the bodies were heaved aboard like sides of beef. I noticed that some of them wore the shoulder insignia of Father Hoa's Sea Swallows.

The sampan, water almost up to its gunwales, moved off, and we started probing the jungle around the hamlet in a futile quest for the enemy. Someone spotted a lone figure in black, running through the trees a few hundred feet away. The marine snapped up his BAR and emptied a whole magazine at the figure, but I don't think he hit him.

Nothing much happened from then on, and eventually we marched back to Dam Doi. The corpse boat had preceded us there, and the bodies were now all laid out on the ground in front of the administration building, wrapped in the mats that are used in Viet Nam both as mattresses and shrouds. Scores of women, all in the white dress of mourning, were wailing and prostrating themselves before the bodies of their dead men. The coffin factory was going full tilt, with old men and boys filling the little building with lumber and hammering away. Some coffins were finished and mounted on sawhorses, a candle or two on their lids.

The sun was setting again and Pat Boone was singing something or other from the tower loudspeaker. I asked an officer if he couldn't turn the damned thing off.

"Sure, but it's better not to. Our people here don't care. And for the Viet Cong out there, it's a sign we're still alive and still able to resist. With that thing playing and the flag flying, we still have something."

from *The New Face of War*, 1965

Master of the Red Jab

by Bernard B. Fall

"IT TOOK us eight years of bitter fighting to defeat you French in Indochina . . ." said the slightly built, grandfatherly man with the wispy goatee. "Now the South Vietnamese regime of Ngo Dinh Diem is well armed and helped by ten thousand Americans. The Americans are much stronger than the French, though they know us less well. It may perhaps take ten years to do it, but our heroic compatriots in the South will defeat them in the end."

After a pause he continued, speaking slowly in flawless French and looking thoughtfully out the high French window onto the manicured formal garden of his palace in Hanoi.

"I think the Americans greatly underestimate the determination of the Vietnamese people. The Vietnamese people always have shown great determination when they were faced with a foreign invader."

The speaker, looking very spry in a tropical uniform, was Ho Chi Minh, the 72-year-old president of Communist North Vietnam, who directs the guerrillas that the United States is fighting in South Vietnam. Every time an American dies somewhere in the swamps of the Mekong Delta it will be because North Vietnam hungers to extend its rule into South Vietnam, into Laos and Cambodia, into all of the fertile crescent that was once French Indochina.

No American has been to this enemy land since the last U.S. consulate was closed down in 1955 after a yearlong blockade. And the only sign of America that I saw in the whole country was, oddly enough, a copy of Doctor Spock. It remains a mystery why the suspicious North Vietnamese should have admitted me, a Frenchman now teaching at Howard University in Washington, D.C., and why they should have allowed me to spend two weeks there, touring more than 500 miles

47

around the country, including some areas that no outsider has seen in more than a decade. Conceivably it was my criticisms in previous books on Vietnam which prompted the Communists to try to convince me of their claimed achievements.

Flying northward in a Boeing Stratoliner of World War II vintage—operated by the Canadian-Polish-Indian International Control Commission that is supposed to supervise the 1954 truce—I thought for a while that the land looked much as it had when I had known it in the days of French rule. In the Red River Delta I could see dark green patches where tree-lined villages nestle between the rice fields of lush light green. But something had changed even here. Some fields no longer are small, handkerchieflike squares but are far larger than before, with no dikes to interrupt their expanse. They belong to the new collective farms. Communism already has left its mark on the landscape. And as we came in for a landing I noticed the brutal reds of new tile roofs and the glaring whites of factory walls where there once had been nothing but farmland or French forts. Here the industrialization drive of Communism had left its imprint.

Hanoi looked about as it must have looked the day after the French pulled out—no cars in the streets, the city in a state of "brown-out," a few passersby walking in an eerie atmosphere of silence, as if every noise were filtered through cotton stoppers in one's ears. In the once-fashionable "French" section of town, the stuccoed villas were in disrepair, the shops boarded up, the broad avenues empty. Not a street seemed to have been paved, nor a house repainted since the French evacuated the city.

The car assigned to me, a rickety Soviet Pobieda (Victory), took me to the hotel I had known as the Metropole. Now it was the Hotel Thong-Nhat (Unity). By coincidence I was assigned to a dining table I had occupied nine years ago, No. 2, and the waiter brought me an example of what a North Vietnamese chef thought French cooking should taste like. It was edible, but I kept thinking of French officers I had known here, one shot down over Langson, another blown up by land mines, and others long dead in the battle against Ho Chi Minh's guerrillas—the battle that Ho had won.

The only people now eating in the 75-table dining room

were a Chinese technician, silently manipulating chopsticks, and a Laotian couple. The husband, a colonel, had attended the U.S. Command and General Staff College at Fort Leavenworth, Kansas; he had also fought with the neutralist forces against the Western-backed government during the Laotian civil war. As we ate, the public-address system—perhaps in my honor—switched from a propaganda speech to a scratched record of Glenn Miller's "In the Mood."

This is official Hanoi. There is another Hanoi, full of the bustle of any Asian city, with children swarming around, street merchants peddling duck eggs, and lines forming in front of movie houses. I saw one food queue too—people lined up to buy the Vietnamese equivalent of Popsicles. Here one can see that the average citizen of Hanoi is neither well fed nor starving (in the immediate postwar period of 1945–46, nearly one million did starve to death). The basic food staples, rice and fats and sometimes meat, are rationed but at bearable levels. Adult rice rations vary between 28 and 40 pounds a month. Clothing is rationed, too, at three yards per person per year, and it lacks the gay colors that brighten many Asian street scenes. There are only two basic colors of clothes: black cotton trousers and white cotton shirts. Recently a new color has been added to the output—faded blue. As for more luxurious goods, the shopwindows of Hanoi hold out little more than a promise. They contain such items as Czech tape recorders and Russian cameras—at prices of $600 and more. Even a pair of poorly made shoes costs $8.50, two weeks' pay for an average worker, and Chinese T-shirts cost $1.25.

I was not restricted in moving around Hanoi. I was escorted on official visits by a member of the Foreign Office, but otherwise I was left on my own to go to the local markets or the movies or to visit the few Western missions still sticking it out under virtual quarantine. And although my Vietnamese is awful I found many people in markets and stores who were willing and able to talk French.

The reasons for Hanoi's general shabbiness became more clear when I got outside the city. The cement that does not go into Hanoi pavements apparently goes into five-story apartment buildings and huge factories in places where I had seen only open rice fields nine years ago. There are an electrochemical complex at Viet-Tri, a fertilizer plant at Lam-Thao, a ceramics factory at Hai-Duong, a blast furnace at Thai-Nguyen and a tungsten mine and ore refinery at Pia-Ouac which also produce uranium for Communist China's future atomic bombs. The whole Communist bloc has pitched in with close to $1,000,000,000 in aid to make the industrialization of North Vietnam a Communist success in an area where America is deeply involved. In contrast to China, the industrialization of North Vietnam is relatively easy, for it is a nation a little smaller than Missouri with a population of 17 million. A few modern machine-tool plants, for example, can change it from a machine-importing to a machine-exporting country. Its turret lathes already have made an impressive debut at the New Delhi Industrial Fair. North Vietnam is not becoming a Japan, but it is acquiring an industrial backbone stronger than that of any non-Communist country on the Southeast Asian mainland. This country is functioning, and developing at a very rapid rate.

The people working in these factories are an extraordinary collection. At the Hanoi machine-tool plant, which produces turret lathes, carpenters' planes, irrigation pumps and drills, I was surprised to meet a foreman who addressed me in purest French factory slang.

"You're damn right I talk like a Frenchman," he said. "Worked for sixteen years at the Renault plant outside Paris."

Nearby I saw an old Tonkinese woman wearing brown peasant garb, her teeth lacquered black in the traditional fashion, standing at a turret lathe with a caliper in her hand. And next to her, as at most machines, was a younger woman. "There are two workers at each machine," I was told, "because the first teaches the second. This way we won't have any trouble when we build the next machine-tool factory."

Glaring errors are still made. A senior official at the all-powerful State Planning Board, which directs the whole North Vietnamese economic machinery, filled me with complaints—including complaints about Red Chinese aid. In the case of the 400-acre Thai-Nguyen steel complex the Chinese had delivered turbines which were so huge that they could not be fitted on any available trains or trucks. Several months went by until the Red River rose high enough for the turbines to be brought upstream on barges. In many plants young engineers freshly graduated from Chinese, Russian, or East German training schools—or, as of this year, from Hanoi's own school of engineering—must step directly into top engineering jobs involving responsibility of thousands of workers.

"It often looks as if a midshipman had been given the command of a cruiser as his first post," said one of the few Western economists in Hanoi. "And it often works out the same way."

The huge Hon-Gay mining complex, which the French ran with 140 technicians and engineers, continued operating for almost seven years under the direction of two Communist cadres. Neither director had an engineering degree. People's Army colonels were in fact the directors of many of the plants I visited. That kind of militarization of industry makes for great labor discipline, but discipline alone cannot replace technical knowledge. This explains the stretch-out of the targets set for the 1958–61 economic plan and the constant lowering of targets set for 1965.

"When we first drew up our plans we just didn't know enough about statistics," said Vo Quang Anh, a leading member of the State Planning Board. "Even for the five-year plan now under way we are still sending our target figures to the individual ministries for evaluation and finding that they are set too high. And now that we know that our population increases by a fantastic half million a year . . ."

That population increase is an obstacle to all economic growth, as it is in all underdeveloped nations, and it means that even a constant increase in food supplies will not end the people's hunger. Yet partition cut off North Vietnam from its normal supplies in the South, which used to provide 225,000 tons of rice a year. Today as I saw in trips around the countryside, every available inch is under cultivation. In areas where rice won't grow, the peasants have planted corn and yams. In the long run, however, North Vietnam's hope of success depends on its being able to export industrial goods to such agricultural nations as Burma, Cambodia and Thailand.

The struggle for economic development requires an almost military discipline, and Ho Chi Minh has succeeded in imposing it on the whole country. At the basic level, six-year-old Young Pioneers are taught to "help" their parents

"correct their backwardness in economic thinking." Many a
small-time black marketeer or would-be political opponent is
turned in by his own family or his neighbor's children. On
the next level is the Street Committee, theoretically a non-
political organization of "mutual help." In actual fact the
Street Committee is an unofficial police force which plays on
a man's desire to keep the Joneses down with him if he cannot
keep up with them. To buy a suitcase, for example, you need
an authorization signed by your Street Committee. In other
words, you must explain to your neighbors why you might be
planning a trip and how you can afford it.

The Street Committee not only keeps a check on every one
of the inhabitants within its area but it also sees to it that
everyone turns out every day for early-morning gymnastics
classes directed by a voice from a loudspeaker. These loud-
speakers are everywhere, as are huge posters exhorting people
to further achievements on the "production front"; to greater
solidarity with the "heroic struggle" of the Cubans, Congo-
lese, Angolans; to continuing hatred of the United States. In
fact, Hate America Month was officially proclaimed during my
stay in Hanoi. All of this establishes an atmosphere like that
of George Orwell's *1984*—a feeling that Big Brother is everywhere and knows everything.

Aside from the Street Committees for every home, there is
the production cell for farms and factories. The production
cell sees to it not only that work quotas are met but also that
its members are properly indoctrinated. Returning to my hotel
at midnight I could often see the night shift at a printing shop,
which formerly housed the French newspaper *L'Entente*,
sitting together around a dim light bulb while a production-
cell member read aloud from the speeches of Comrade
Ko-Rut-Sop (Khrushchev).

Above all these low-level organizations there is the party
itself, an elite of faithful believers. North Vietnam's Communist *Dang Lao-Dong* (Labor Party) is 800,000 strong, and
its membership has gradually shifted from the unsophisticated
peasantry to the students and factory workers who constitute
the political backbone of the regime. Its leadership, forged
over thirty years of bitter struggle against overwhelming odds,
is tough and resourceful.

And finally, beyond the party, there is the fearsome Vietnam People's Army. The French—who have good reasons to know it well—estimate it to be one of the best combat-infantry forces in the world today. It is at the same time a thoroughly political army. Its creator and commander-in-chief, Gen. Vo Nguyen Giap, declared in his book, *People's War, People's Army*: "The People's Army is the instrument of the (Communist) Party and the revolutionary state, for the accomplishment, in armed form, of the tasks of the revolution."

From a 24-man platoon in 1944, the army has grown into a force of 400,000 men, lavishly armed with Soviet automatic weapons. Yet in spite of this modern armament the army has lost none of its incredible agility in cross-country maneuvering. Whatever training I could see in North Vietnam—none of it was shown to me deliberately—seemed to confirm that the North Vietnamese were as ready as ever to fight in the swamps and jungles of their country. I saw infantrymen dog-trotting along the roads with full field kits in the blazing tropical sun. I saw officers instructing militiamen—there are an estimated 2,000,000 of them—in how to attack concrete bunkers. They were not training to fight against an imaginary enemy but against South Vietnamese—and Americans.

As to the loyalty of those troops there is little doubt. The People's Army is better housed and fed than most civilians, and its discharged veterans have high preference for good jobs in the administration and industry. This loyalty was tested on the one occasion when a large group of Vietnamese attempted a rebellion. In November, 1956, at just the time when the Hungarians rose in revolt, 6,000 farmers in Ho Chi Minh's own native province rebelled against the collectivization of their land. Soldiers of the 325th Division unhesitatingly shot down their compatriots and restored order.

In the face of such an awesome control apparatus, reaching from the family to the armed forces, the individual discontented North Vietnamese has almost no chance of rebellion. And any guerrilla movement sponsored by South Vietnam would have little chance of surviving in Ho Chi Minh's land.

All this, and more, was in my mind as I faced Ho Chi Minh, the grandfatherly man who still holds Vietnam's fate in his hands, and his prime minister, Pham Van Dong, 56, who looks

exactly like the aristocrat he was by birth. Both men had led
Vietnam's Communist movement since its inception. Ho Chi
Minh, though all too little known in the outside world, is the
last of the Old Bolsheviks still in power. He was a senior Comintern agent at a time when Khrushchev was still on a farm in
the Ukraine. Unlike many other Communist leaders, Ho has
traveled widely. He has been to the United States (he wrote
a pamphlet on the shocking conditions in Harlem in 1918).
He even served as a pastry-cook's apprentice under the great
Escoffier at the Carlton in London. As a member of the
French Socialist Party, he was one of the founders of the
French Communist Party in 1920. As a Comintern agent,
living in Thailand in the disguise of a Buddhist monk, he organized violent dock strikes in Singapore, later turned up in
Berlin during the last days of the Weimar Republic, finally
began organizing the Vietnamese underground in 1941—with
the help of the American O.S.S.

Ho himself is reluctant to speak of his own past. "You
know, I am an old man, and an old man likes to hold on to
his little mysteries," he said to me. When I objected to this
he said with a humorous twinkle in his eye, "Wait until I'm
dead. Then you can write about me all you want." Nevertheless, before I left Hanoi I received at my hotel an unsigned
five-page typescript which contained some hitherto unknown
details about Ho's life, obviously delivered on the old man's
instructions.

Ho has, too, a kind of human vanity and gallantry that one
scarcely expects in an old revolutionary. I had brought him a
book of mine which contained a portrait of him by my wife.
"Where? Where?" he cried. "Let me see it. Providing that
she's got my goatee right . . . providing the goatee looks all
right." After thumbing through the pages and inspecting the
portrait he was pleased. "Yes, that is very good. That looks
very much like me." He looked around him for a moment,
then took a small bouquet of flowers from a vase on the table
and handed it to me. "Tell her for me that the drawing is very
good and give her the bouquet and kiss her on both cheeks
for me."

Most of my political questions, however, were answered by
Premier Pham Van Dong. He sounded almost contemptuous

of South Vietnam's President Ngo Dinh Diem, whose regime the United States is trying to uphold. "Monsieur Diem's position is quite difficult," said Dong. "He is unpopular, and the more unpopular he is the more American aid he will require to stay in power. And the more American aid he receives, the more he will look like a puppet of the Americans and the less likely he is to win popular support for his side."

"That sounds pretty much like a vicious circle," I said.

The premier's eyes showed a humorous gleam as he said that it was more than "vicious." "It is really more like a descending spiral."

There is, I fear, some justification for the Communist leader's optimism. The French lost Indochina to Ho's guerrilla armies because they had no political program that could win the support of the peasantry. In South Vietnam today, Diem's regime remains a family autocracy in Saigon, with few reforms in sight, and there is no indication that it has attracted any real support from the majority of the people. Without that support, American helicopters and modern weapons cannot do very much. And although American officials speak of fighting for years against Ho's guerrillas, I doubt that most Americans realize what such a protracted war really means.

Despite huge sums in American aid, guerrilla depredations have changed South Vietnam from an area which once exported as much as 1,000,000 tons of rice to one which has had to import 100,000 tons in 1961–62. Its exports covered only 27 percent of its imports in 1961, and that figure fell to 18 percent by mid-1962. South Vietnam is becoming, in the words of one American economist, a "nation of mendicants." For Americans, this war means not only an economic drain but a political drain. "Americans do not like long, inconclusive wars—and this is going to be a long, inconclusive war," remarked Premier Pham Van Dong. "Thus we are sure to win in the end."

Could we negotiate a settlement? Ho Chi Minh told me he was ready to negotiate with "any" South Vietnamese regime that was "willing to sit down with us at the same table and talk." Premier Pham Van Dong spoke in more detail. "We are willing to give all the guarantees necessary for the South to get fair treatment. . . . We do not envisage an immediate reunification and are willing to accept the verdict of the South Vietnamese people with regard to the institutions and policies of their part of the country." What this means, in effect, is a neutralized South Vietnam, deprived of large-scale American support and vulnerable to Communist subversion. The South Vietnamese and Americans naturally oppose this. One of Diem's chief officials even stated publicly that the American willingness to neutralize Laos meant that "the American government . . . has fallen entirely within the scope of Communist strategy."

But part of the Western reluctance to negotiate is based on a feeling that the West is on the defensive in South Vietnam, that it would be bargaining from a position of weakness. This is true if we continue limiting ourselves to anti-guerrilla warfare in the South. One of the most ominous things about North Vietnam, as I look back on it, is the air of massive tranquillity—no guards in watchtowers, no airplane patrols. The Hanoi traffic police don't even carry pistols. But the U.S. doesn't necessarily have to let the North Vietnamese remain so placidly confident.

It is one of the paradoxes of the Vietnamese war that the huge American military commitment to South Vietnam is not well suited for waging a guerrilla war but provides a strong political bargaining position. For it enables us at least to threaten direct retaliation against North Vietnam itself. While Ho's guerrillas in South Vietnam can elude American air power, his factories in North Vietnam are extremely vulnerable to it.

The North Vietnamese are very conscious of this. When I spoke to Premier Pham Van Dong I reminded him of the risk of American retaliation against North Vietnamese territory. I reminded him that he had been to North Korea and said, "You saw what American bombers can do." The premier showed he was aware of the danger. "We fully realize that the American imperialists wish to provoke a situation in the course of which they could use the heroic struggle of the South Vietnamese people as a pretext for the destruction of our economic and cultural achievements. We shall offer them no pretext which could give rise to an American military intervention against North Vietnam."

The North Vietnamese genuinely fear American retaliation. They fear it not only because it would wreck their country but because it would raise the specter of Communist Chinese intervention and occupation. Until now, North Vietnam's rulers have followed Russian rather than Chinese leadership, and they are aware of China's ambitions for expansion. If we took into account these North Vietnamese fears of outside intervention, I believe we could press more effectively for some kind of truce settlement on terms that would definitely not be a "surrender." We could demand the immediate end of guerrilla fighting in the South and a far more effective international inspection system to police the truce. We may not achieve such a settlement, but I feel very strongly that we have no reason to fear it. And we must clearly realize that the alternative means the bloodshed and misery of a long and probably inconclusive guerrilla war—a war which Ho Chi Minh is well prepared to fight.

The Saturday Evening Post, November 24, 1962

Vietnam Victory Remote Despite U.S. Aid to Diem

by Homer Bigart

THE UNITED STATES, by massive and unqualified support of the regime of President Ngo Dinh Diem, has helped arrest the spread of Communist insurgency in South Vietnam. But victory is remote. The issue remains in doubt because the Vietnamese President seems incapable of winning the loyalty of his people.

From the strictly military point of view, the situation has improved. "We are now doing a little better than holding our own," was the cautious assessment made a few weeks ago by Maj. Gen. Charles J. Timmes, chief of the United States Army element of the Military Assistance and Advisory Group.

However, no decisive turn in the military struggle is expected this year. The combat effectiveness of the South Vietnamese has been temporarily weakened by robbing rifle companies of good officers and noncoms to provide cadres for two new divisions now being created.

These new divisions will increase the strength of the regular forces to more than 205,000 by the end of this year. In addition, the Civil Guard will be expanded to 72,000 and the Self-Defense Corps to 80,000.

Assuming that the Vietcong (Vietnamese Communist) guerrillas do not receive substantial outside aid, there would seem to be valid reason for optimism. For in 1963 the Republic of South Vietnam will put well-equipped forces totaling more than 350,000 men against 25,000 guerrillas who have no artillery, no anti-aircraft guns, no air power, no trucks, no jeeps, no prime movers, and only basic infantry weapons.

Also by 1963 the Vietnamese armed forces should be adequately staffed with officers and noncoms and be somewhat better trained for fighting in jungles and swamps.

They will have more helicopters, armored personnel carriers and other gadgets to enhance mobility, more sentry dogs to sniff out guerrillas, more plastic boats for the delta region, more American advisers with fresh, new tactical doctrines.

Yet visions of ultimate victory are obscured by the image of a secretive, suspicious, dictatorial regime. American officers are frustrated and irritated by the constant whimsical meddling of the President and his brother, Ngo Dinh Nhu, in the military chain of command.

The President assumes direction of military operations. All major troop movements, all officer promotions, must have his approval. Acting on vague rumors of a coup, Ngo Dinh Nhu last February summoned elements of the Seventh Division to the outskirts of Saigon without notifying the Third Corps commander.

Failure to coordinate with area commanders has also marked the Presidential palace's use of general reserve troops. These have been dispatched on futile one-shot operations based on faulty intelligence and conducted with slipshod planning.

In situations demanding fast action or improvisation, the palace's tight control of the army has killed initiative. In June, guerrillas wiped out a convoy forty miles north of Saigon, killing two American officers. The only soldiers available for pursuit belonged to the general reserve.

Hours elapsed before Presidential consent could be obtained for the employment of these troops, and it was early evening when United States Marine helicopters put them down on the guerrillas' trail. The guerrillas got away easily despite their heavy booty in guns and ammunition.

This episode was a bitter revelation for Americans. The ambush took place on the outskirts of Bentre, a garrison town, and on a heavily traveled highway. Yet the guerrillas moved into position in daylight, prepared the ambuscade in full view of the road and waited three hours for the convoy to appear. They must have been observed by scores of peasants. Yet no one informed the garrison in Bentre.

Could this have happened if peasants felt any real identification with the regime?

A family living at the scene said it was threatened with death if it informed. But the Vietcong probably would never have undertaken this action without full confidence that the peasants were with them, or at least indifferent.

There is no accurate gauge of sentiment in Vietnam. The press is rigidly controlled and there is no freedom of assembly. Even the election scheduled for this year was canceled when the rubber-stamp National Assembly altered the Constitution to give itself another year of tenure.

In some areas the signs of disaffection are clear enough. Observers of sweeps by the Vietnamese army through the Mekong delta provinces are often struck by the phenomenon of deserted villages. As troops approach, all flee, except a few old men and children. No one offers information; no one hurries to put out flags. Most of the rural area is controlled by Vietcong, whose agents will move back as soon as the troops have departed.

President Ngo Dinh Diem is well aware of the importance of securing the countryside. His brother has the vision of concentrating peasants into "strategic hamlets" ringed with mud walls, moats and barbed wire. The object is to isolate peasants from the Communists. Brother Ngo Dinh Nhu urged the creation of 8,000 hamlets by the end of this year.

But the American aid mission has advised the regime to come up with a less-expensive plan. While appalled by the dreary regimentation of life in these fortified villages, most Americans are convinced that the strategic hamlet is part of the answer to the pacification problem. They hope to persuade the President that forced labor on hamlet defenses is not the way to win the affection of the peasants.

Besides urging the Government to pay for this labor—workers are not even fed but must provide their own food—the American mission is trying to channel aid directly to the villages in support of counter-insurgency.

In April, the Americans proposed that a trust fund equivalent to $110,000,000 be set aside from counterpart funds—local currency equivalent to American aid funds—for direct application to the provinces, districts and villages. They wanted to knife through the bureaucratic fog to insure that emergency relief, food, blankets, medicine or perhaps defense materials, such as barbed wire and cement, would reach the new villages in the critical first weeks.

This "impact aid," designed to show peasants that the Saigon regime really cared, would, of course, be handled at the scene by local Vietnamese officials; Americans would not be hanging around looking for gratitude, and peasants presumably would guess that the manna came from the Presidential Palace.

There was urgency for action, for thousands of "montagnards," the primitive tribesmen of the central plateau, were streaming into the garrison towns. Some were fed up with Vietcong demands for food and services; others were lured by reports of medical attention and other amenities offered by the United States Special Forces. The Americans saw an opportune moment to win over tribesmen who had been ignored for years by the regime.

But the plan was coldly rejected by President Ngo Dinh Diem. He did not like the "political implications," an aide explained. The President evidently scented an American plot to undermine his control over local officials.

Similarly, the President has scuttled other American proposals that might have softened his image.

One of the major recommendations of the mission here last fall of Gen. Maxwell Taylor, President Kennedy's military adviser, was that the regime liberalize itself by permitting the National Assembly to be somewhat less of a rubber stamp. It was thought that the President had agreed to permit the election of one or two independents in Saigon and that eventually political parties free of government control might be permitted to organize.

But the election has been put off for a year and meanwhile the President and his family are in no mood to relax their grip on the administration. Besides the President and brother Ngo Dinh Nhu, who has the title of "political adviser," there is Mme. Ngo Dinh Nhu, palace hostess and an influential member of the Assembly, whose "Family Bill," promulgated in 1959, prohibits divorce except under very unusual circumstances.

There are two other brothers, Ngo Dinh Can, who, like the President, is a bachelor, very strait-laced and aloof, and who

runs the northern provinces from Hue, and Msgr. Ngo Dinh
Thuc, Roman Catholic Archbishop of Hue.

All the Ngo family are Catholics. The population of South
Vietnam is predominantly Buddhist.

At the time of the Taylor mission, American officials talked
openly of "pressuring" the Saigon regime for administrative
reforms that would oblige it to relinquish some power. This
plan was hotly resented by Ngo Dinh Nhu. According to
United States Embassy officials, he incited the controlled
Saigon press to print bitterly anti-American tirades. The
campaign was hushed after a protest by the United States
Embassy.

But Washington decided it was risky to prod President Ngo
Dinh Diem publicly. Efforts to obtain major political and social reforms were quietly dropped after a few major concessions had been obtained: higher pay, fringe benefits and merit
promotions for the armed forces; creation of a National Economic Council, quite impotent, but useful as a forum; the
establishment of provincial advisory councils and village councils and, at the top, the equivalent of a National Security
Council.

These improvements failed to touch the main problem. The
Vietnamese President, according to former intimates, has become more aloof, trusting only his family, refusing to delegate
authority. American officials find that even routine matters af-
fecting the aid program must now be referred to Ngo Dinh
Diem.

"It's virtually impossible to get anything done without the
Ambassador running to the palace like an errand boy," one
official said.

Meanwhile, a complete reassessment of the aid program is
desperately needed, American officials say. Economic aid must
be more closely related to the counter-insurgency effort, they
explain, and the Saigon regime must pump an increased flow
of piasters into the countryside to pay local costs of the strategic hamlet program.

The Government, alarmed by slumping revenues, has requested a $25,000,000 United States grant, against which it
would print more piasters. But Washington is now firmly opposed to cash grants. The United States has rejected an appeal

by Vietnam for blanket waivers of the obligation in the aid program to buy American goods. Saigon had hoped for permission to spend American aid money on cheaper products from Japan. The regime particularly wanted across-the-board waivers for industrial machinery and chemical fertilizers.

This tightening of aid policies by Washington should give Ambassador Frederick E. Nolting Jr. a little leverage in his bargaining with the Presidential Palace. The Ambassador has not enjoyed much leverage.

In the last fifteen months, a parade of VIP's, starting with Vice President Lyndon Johnson and ending with the recent visit by Secretary of Defense Robert McNamara, regaled President Ngo Dinh Diem with promises of "all the help you need." Hearing his leadership lauded as an "irreplaceable asset," the President presumably assumed he could reject any proposals he disliked and still get all the money and military equipment he wanted from his friends in Washington.

Now Ambassador Nolting may be able to force action on a number of issues the Americans regard as crucial. These include a determination, long overdue, of priorities for programs such as strategic hamlets and population identification —the photographing and fingerprinting of every Vietnamese who can be caught. Perhaps the Ambassador can also revive the plan, rejected by Ngo Dinh Diem, for a rapid, uninterrupted flow of piasters to the provinces.

Finally the Americans want the President to promulgate as soon as possible a general amnesty offer. They believe the Government's psychological warfare campaign will be more effective once guerrillas learn they stand a chance of pardon if they defect to the Government forces.

Americans hope that the amnesty offer will be launched with fullest publicity, including a radio broadcast by President Ngo Dinh Diem stating the Government's policy on how the Vietcong are going to be treated, re-educated and integrated.

Apart from the purely propaganda advantage, the national amnesty would inject a note of humanity in a struggle that has shocked American military observers with it senseless brutality. American advisers have seen Vietcong prisoners summarily shot. They have encountered the charred bodies of women and children in villages destroyed by napalm bombs.

This month a Defense Department spokesman in Washington said casualties were running at the rate of five Communists to every three for the South Vietnam Government forces. But casualty figures in South Vietnam are highly suspect, for they are often based on the estimates of air observers.

Moreover, one rarely sees a uniformed Vietcong guerrilla; generally the Communist rebels are indistinguishable from peasants. Thus, many of the "enemy" dead reported by the South Vietnam Government were ordinary peasants shot down because they had fled from villages as the troops entered. Some may have been Vietcong sympathizers, but others were running away because they did not want to be rounded up for military conscription or forced labor.

The presence of American observers has had an inhibiting effect on indiscriminate shooting. United States helicopters are now being used to evacuate prisoners to interrogation centers in the rear, where prisoners are at least safe from the threat of summary execution. Later, at prison camps called "re-education centers," the prisoners are indoctrinated in "the rights and responsibilities of citizens," lectured on Vietcong crimes and told of the achievements of the Government.

Inadequate screening and identification has sometimes resulted in the unfortunate mixing of hard-core Vietcong and non-political prisoners. But the process is now being improved under the direction of Frank Walton, former deputy chief of the Los Angeles Police Department, now head of the Public Safety division of the United States aid mission.

Mr. Walton is sending Vietnamese to the United States to study prison administration. As for conditions at the forty-three "re-education centers," Walton says: "I've seen considerably worse prisons in the Southern United States." Some of the centers were well run, others overcrowded, he said. There was no follow-up rehabilitation, hence no insurance that the former Vietcong would not defect again after their release.

In the fighting areas, American advisers fresh from training camps in the United States are astonished to find that, despite all the talk back home about unconventional warfare, the tactics here remain quite orthodox.

Government forces attempt large-scale operations that seldom flush more than a handful of Vietcong. Americans have been preaching the necessity of sustained operations. But Vietnamese commanders persist in one-shot maneuvers.

"A one-shot deal is like pushing quicksilver," one adviser commented. "Communists disperse only to fill up the vacuum as soon as the troops leave."

Helicopters have made an important contribution to the tactical mobility of Government forces. They have enabled Government units to strike at former "safe havens" of the Vietcong deep in jungles and swamps, then return quickly to their posts to be available for other missions.

"Helicopters permit us to do in one day or two days what used to take two weeks," observed Col. Frank B. Clay, until recently American adviser to the Vietnamese Seventh Division.

Armored amphibious troop carriers were introduced in June. They were supposed to solve the problem of pursuit over rice paddies and swamps. It was soon evident that these vehicles cannot be used without careful reconnaissance of the terrain. They are easily balked by steep-banked canals and rivers. On one operation a whole company of vehicles was mired for hours.

Gadgets will not win this war, and neither will war dogs. Unfounded enthusiasm for sentry dogs prompted a world-wide recruitment of German shepherds. The United States advisory group wanted 1,000 dogs, but procurement was impossible. Only about 200 are currently in South Vietnam or in the pipeline. Most of the dogs that reached South Vietnam are sick. Of the five dogs assigned to the Seventh Division, four were sick and so was their trainer.

It was reported that they needed three months to adjust to the tropics. Meanwhile, someone discovered that each dog required $1.20 worth of frozen horse meat a day; a Vietnamese soldier gets by on 19 cents worth of rice.

South Vietnam is a proving ground for other interesting theories. On the central plateau, for example, David Nuttle, a civilian attached to the United States Special Forces, is experimenting with a poisonous shrub called kpung. Its leaves have nettles that cause excruciating pain that lasts a week. Mr. Nuttle proposes a double border of kpung around strategic hamlets to keep the Vietcong out.

On the political front Americans are less inventive. Washington insists there is no alternative to President Ngo Dinh Diem. United States official policy is tied to the status quo. This policy is doomed in the long run, some feel, because the Vietnamese President cannot give his country the inspired leadership needed to defeat the Vietcong.

In the last seven years, the United States has spent well over $2,000,000,000 to prevent a Communist take-over in South Vietnam. Holding the line in Southeast Asia was a major premise of the strategy for containing communism formulated by John Foster Dulles, President Eisenhower's Secretary of State, who felt the whole of Southeast Asia would go down the drain unless South Vietnam were saved.

The United States has been deeply involved in South Vietnam ever since 1954 when, after the defeat of the French in the Indochina War, Vietnam was partitioned. The Communists took over North Vietnam. With American support, Ngo Dinh Diem, a strongly anti-Communist aristocrat, rose to power in the South.

Few Americans in Saigon during the first chaotic years of President Ngo Dinh Diem's leadership had much confidence in his ability to survive. In 1955, President Eisenhower's special representative in South Vietnam, Gen. J. Lawton Collins, recommended that the United States withhold support from the aloof and obstinate Vietnamese leader.

But General Collins' recommendation was countered by reports sent to Allen W. Dulles, then director of the Central Intelligence Agency, by Col. (now Brig. Gen.) Edward G. Lansdale, the chief United States intelligence agent in Saigon. Colonel Lansdale saw no alternative to Ngo Dinh Diem. Allen Dulles persuaded his brother, the Secretary of State, that Colonel Lansdale was right and General Collins was wrong.

Those who recall conditions in Saigon at the time may now agree that Colonel Lansdale was right. Ngo Dinh Diem's rivals were either notoriously corrupt, or tagged as collaborators in the former French colonial regime, or lacking in popular appeal. Ngo Dinh Diem had some following among the Catholic refugees from North Vietnam, and these were at least reliably anti-Communist.

The little President has shown a remarkable talent for surviving coups and assassination attempts. He got rid of

Emperor Bao Dai, established control over the army, won a small war against gangster elements of the Saigon police, eliminated the private armies of two powerful religious sects, the Cao Dai and Hoa Hao, and resettled a million refugees from the north.

In the relatively quiet years between 1955 and 1958, when the Communist insurrection supported by North Vietnam began, South Vietnam made some modest economic progress. Saigon looked relatively prosperous. But United States economic aid was slow to reach the villages. And Ngo Dinh Diem did little to generate enthusiasm for his regime.

By last year the Communists controlled most of the countryside. The Vietnamese President was forced to ask for greatly increased military aid. President Kennedy responded by rushing thousands of United States military personnel to South Vietnam to serve as advisers and instructors. A United States Military Assistance Command was established under Gen. Paul Donal Harkins.

Should the situation disintegrate further, Washington may face the alternative of ditching Ngo Dinh Diem for a military junta or sending combat troops to bolster the regime.

No one who has seen conditions of combat in South Vietnam would expect conventionally trained United States forces to fight any better against Communist guerrillas than did the French in their seven years of costly and futile warfare. For, despite all the talk here of training men for jungle fighting, of creating counter-guerrillas who can exist in forests and swamps and hunt down the Vietcong, Americans may simply lack the endurance—and the motivation—to meet the unbelievably tough demands of jungle fighting.

The New York Times, July 25, 1962

Vietnamese Ignored U.S. Battle Order

by Neil Sheehan

SAIGON, Jan. 6 (UPI) Angry United States military advisers charged today that Vietnamese infantrymen refused direct orders to advance during Wednesday's battle at Ap Bac and that an American Army captain was killed while out front pleading with them to attack.

The Vietnamese commander of an armored unit also refused for more than an hour to go to the rescue of 11 American crewmen of downed helicopters and an infantry company pinned down by Communist small arms fire, they said.

"It was a miserable damn performance" was the way one American military man summed up the humiliating and costly defeat suffered by the South Vietnamese army at the hands of outnumbered Communist guerrillas in the fight for the jungle hamlet 30 miles south of Saigon.

It was perhaps the strongest criticism by an American military adviser, but others in the battle said it was not an unfair one.

They spoke of the marked "lack of aggressiveness" of Vietnamese commanders, their refusal to heed recommendations of their American advisers, refusal to carry out orders from their superiors and a breakdown in the chain of command of the 7th Vietnamese Division.

As a result, the American sources said, the government troops suffered a needlessly high casualty toll, 65 dead and at least 100 wounded, the second highest since the war against the Communist Viet Cong began.

U.S. casualties were the highest of any single battle in Viet-Nam. Three Americans, including Capt. Kenneth N. Good of Hawaii, a West Point graduate, were killed. Ten other Americans were wounded. Of 14 U.S. helicopters involved, 11 were hit by Communist ground fire and five crashed.

American advisers who took part in the battle on the edge of the Plain of Reeds recounted sorry tales of the debacle:

Government forces out numbered the Communists by 10 to 1 and were supported by planes, artillery and armor.

Yet an infantry battalion located less than a mile from Ap Bac flatly refused to advance on the hamlet even though Vietnamese and American officers at division headquarters ordered and pleaded for hours. About 200 guerrillas held Ap Bac.

The battalion commander had been killed and the other officers refused to assume command.

Capt. Good was killed while out in front trying to get the Vietnamese to attack.

A Vietnamese captain commanding an armored-personnel carrier company refused for 70 minutes to cross a canal to rescue downed U.S. helicopter crewmen and a company of Vietnamese infantry pinned down by small arms fire.

The captain kept complaining about "heavy enemy fire," even though U.S. advisers urged him to advance because the small arms fire could not penetrate the armored vehicles. He finally gave in to radioed orders and pleading from U.S. and Vietnamese officers and rescued most of the Vietnamese and American wounded.

Then the captain attacked twice but retreated after Communist fire kept picking off exposed machine gunners on the armored cars. U.S. advisers said the captain should have "buttoned up" the armored vehicles and run over the Viet Cong forward positions as he had been trained to do.

Most of the Communists were able to withdraw from the hamlet during the night because a paratroop battalion was dropped on the west side of the hamlet instead of the east, leaving an escape route into the jungles.

An American general narrowly escaped being killed when Vietnamese artillery accidentally shelled their own troops after the fight was over.

The advisers said American patience came to an end Friday when a civil guards company failed to move into a blocking position as ordered, leaving a U.S. Army major alone in a paddy field to face guerrilla stragglers.

Lt. Col. John Paul Vann, senior U.S. adviser with the 7th Vietnamese Division, quickly rounded up 60 American advisers, cooks and communications men from his headquarters and sent them to the aid of the major.

The Americans were under strict orders not to fire unless fired upon. They rescued the major and captured 17 guerrillas without suffering any casualties and then returned to their regular duties.

One U.S. adviser said bitterly, "These people (the Vietnamese) won't listen—they make the same mistakes over and over again in the same way."

The Washington Post, January 7, 1963

"An Endless, Relentless War"

by David Halberstam

THE FIRST TIME you met a member of the Vietcong there was a sharp sense of disappointment. He was not, it turned out, very different; he was simply another Vietnamese. When you saw him he was usually either kneeling and firing at you, or he had just been captured—or, more often than not, he was dead: the bodies were always lined up, their feet in an orderly row. The guerrilla wore little, perhaps a simple peasant pajama suit, perhaps only shorts. He was slim and wiry, and his face would remind you of your interpreter or of that taxi driver who drove you to My Tho. Only the haircut was different, very thin along the sides, and very long on top and in front. It was a bad haircut, and like the frailness of the uniform and the thin wallet with perhaps only a few pictures of some peasant woman, it made the enemy human. But one's sympathy did not last long; this was the same face that had been seen by the outnumbered defenders of some small outpost before it was overrun.

There were not many operations in which the Vietcong were caught; few prisoners were taken in this war. One of the few exceptions to this that I ever observed took place in April 1963, when I accompanied the new armed-helicopter units in the upper Camau peninsula on what were known as Eagle flights. An Eagle flight was risky business; it meant that a small number of elite troops circled above the paddies in the choppers, looking for likely targets. When an objective was sighted the helicopters dropped out of the sky, virtually on top of a hamlet, and the troops made a quick search, probing and scouting. If the enemy was there, other regular units, waiting in the rear with other helicopters, would be thrown in quickly. But dropping swiftly out of the sky and exploring the unknown with a handful of troops was sometimes terrifying; the helicopters have the visibility of a press box, but you were watching a war instead of a football game. When you plunged earthward, little men sometimes rushed to different positions, kneeled and started firing at the press box while your own tracers sought them out.

On that day in April the 21st Recon Company, a particularly good outfit composed largely of troops who had fought with the Vietminh during the Indochina war, was with us. We were scouting a Vietcong battalion, moving along a line of villages which we thought the battalion had been using as its main line of communication in that region. But this was the upper Camau, almost completely enemy territory, where one could find a Vietcong squad in virtually every village.

It is perhaps deceptive to use a word like "battalion" here; when such a unit attacked a given point it might number three hundred men, but immediately afterward it would break up into small groups slipping into neighboring villages and awaiting the signal for the next operation. A single large force would make too good a target for the Government; besides, by splitting up, more men could indoctrinate more peasants, and no single village would have to take on the task of feeding three hundred extra mouths.

At about eight-thirty in the morning we saw some movement in a village below, followed by a few light crackles around us. It was ground fire; the bait had been taken. We came in low over the village and saw some men scurrying to positions. Three of the helicopters, including our own, dropped their troop load while the others circled and strafed some of the positions. We were making our advance on the treeline under fire when we saw a man in a black suit desperately running across the open field. It was the dry season and the fields were covered with sun-caked mud. Suddenly a helicopter descended almost on top of the man; he stopped and held up his hands. The Vietnamese commander ran over to him. There was no weapon on this Vietcong; neither was there any of the bowing or scraping that local guerrillas posing as farmers sometimes employed.

The captured man was angry and defiant, and at first a little scared as well—until he saw me and spat at me. The commander slapped his face very hard and said something in Vietnamese. Later I was told that the captain had said to the prisoner, "The Americans are very kind. They do not kill, and they are always telling us not to kill you, but I am not so kind and I will kill you. You will see." The interpreter thought this was very funny. "You know, the enemy takes these young boys and they tell them how fierce you Americans are, and so they are all convinced that the Americans will eat their hearts for breakfast as soon as they are captured. The captain is right; you have no real taste for war." The Vietnamese commander interrogated the captured guerrilla and told us that he was well indoctrinated. "They are taught well to hate," he said a little apologetically.

It is true that the Vietcong were better at hating than our Vietnamese, though at times Government troops could be very cruel. Once, south of Bac Lieu, Vietnamese Marines had fought a particularly bitter battle but had captured a number of Vietcong prisoners. According to a Vietnamese friend of mine who was there, the enemy were very cocky and started shouting anti-American slogans and Vietnamese curses at their captors. The Marines, who had lost an officer that day and were in no mood to be called lackeys of the Americans, simply lined up the seventeen guerrillas and shot them down in cold blood. "They had to believe their own propaganda," my friend said.

The captain said that the guerrilla was probably from an elite battalion operating in the area. "I think maybe he was a squad leader." Then the officer turned and spoke briefly and intensely to the guerrilla. He was telling the prisoner that they would kill him unless he talked—and perhaps they would kill him by throwing him out of the helicopter. "The captain is very smart," said the interpreter. "It will be the guerrilla's first helicopter ride and he will be very scared." They tied up the guerrilla and placed him in the helicopter (later we were to find out that he had indeed been frightened but did not crack), and the captain and I walked back across the open field to the village. We could hear a good deal of firing, and as always I hunched over as much as I could, but the Vietnamese officer strolled casually. He carried a small swagger stick, and he looked as if he were a large landowner inspecting his plantation. I was impressed.

By the time we reached the village the troops had rounded up two more guerrillas. They did not even pretend to be farmers; they had not surrendered until they began to take fire not only from the ground, but from some of the nine other helicopters in the area. The captain was convinced that there were other Vietcong somewhere in the village, that there had been at least five or six of the enemy stationed there. But he also suspected that the others had excellent hiding places and that we would not find them. "They are probably dug in under this village somewhere," he said. He checked his watch. Time was important because the helicopters had been aloft for a long while. He told his men that they had five more minutes to search the village, then turned to the prisoners and started to talk to them. One, about nineteen years old, gave him a look of defiance and turned away, but the other, who might have been twenty-five, gave the captain a curious look. "Maybe," the captain said later, "he is a little more tired of the war and the propaganda. We shall see. The other will not talk." He was right; the next morning the elder one confessed that they were members of a battalion which had hit two outposts in the Camau the week before and had come here to rest. This guerrilla was tired; he had been fighting too long—for seven years—and he wanted to leave the Army.

At the appointed minute the troops were back. They had found an American carbine, and the captain was surprised because it was more than he had expected. The weapon had been found in a false thatch in a roof. The captain was pleased. "Good troops," he told me. "When they search they want to find something, and when they fight they want to kill."

Then the helicopters returned and we all jumped in and prepared for the next assault.

The next two villages produced only some crude grenades made by an old farmer. "The local guerrilla," said the Vietnamese captain. These were the lowest of the three types of Vietcong: they farmed in the day and fought at night, and they had the worst weapons. When I first came to Vietnam their arms were all homemade; by the time I left they were using French equipment and even some American M-1's. But even in April 1963, in a village where there were no other weapons, a homemade grenade or a rusty rifle had great power.

The local guerrillas were a vital part of the Vietcong apparatus. They gave the village a sense of Communist continuity, they could provide intelligence on Government activities and serve as a local security force for a traveling commissar, or they could guide the professional Vietcong troops. This last was particularly important to the success and mobility of the guerrillas; everywhere they went they had trained, local guides to steer them through seemingly impenetrable areas. Because of these local men the enemy's troops could often move twenty-five miles in five hours—which meant that a raiding force attacking at night was almost impossible to find by daylight. These local guerrillas were also part of the propaganda network, for in a village they might be the only ones with a radio. (Sometimes it was only the shell of a radio, but the local man would pretend he could hear news and would give out information of Vietcong victories.)

We flew back to the base to refuel, and then returned to the area. Shortly before noon we hit pay dirt. Out of one village came a flock of Vietcong, running across the paddies, and there was intense fire from the treeline. While five of our ships emptied their troops, the rest of the choppers strafed the area. Soon the guerrillas broke from their positions and ran for a nearby canal, where they might find hiding places. We came hurtling down on them at a hundred miles an hour, just a few feet off the ground. We were still drawing fire, but it was more sporadic now.

We bore down on one fleeing Vietcong. The paddy's surface was rough and his run was staggered, like that of a good but drunken broken-field runner against imaginary tacklers. We came closer and closer; inside the helicopter I could almost hear him gasping for breath, and as we bore down I could see the heaving of his body. It was like watching a film of one of your own nightmares, but in this case we were the pursuers rather than the pursued. The copilot fired his machine guns but missed, and the man kept going. Then there was a flash of orange and a blast of heat inside the ship, and the helicopter heaved from the recoil of its rockets. When they exploded the man fell. He lay still as we went over him, but when we turned he scrambled to his feet, still making for the canal, now only about fifty yards away. While we circled and swept toward him again he was straining for the bank, like a runner nearing the finish line. We had one last shot at him. Our copilot fired one last burst of the machine gun as the guerrilla made a desperate surge. The bullets cut him down as he reached the canal, and his body skidded on the hard bank as he collapsed.

We turned and circled again. All over the paddies helicopters were rounding up Vietcong soldiers. We landed near the village which other members of the Recon company were searching. The troops were gentler with the population than most ARVN soldiers I had seen; in front of one hut a medic was giving aid to a wounded guerrilla.

"I have never taken this many prisoners before," the Vietnamese captain said. There were sixteen of them. He turned to one of his men. "Show the American the poor little farmer," he said. They brought in a wiry young man. "This one says he is a farmer," the officer said. He pushed the young man in front of me and flipped the prisoner's palms over. "He has very soft hands for a farmer," the captain said. "He has the hands of a bar girl in Saigon. He is not a very good soldier yet. In a few months, though, he might have been very good."

The prisoner was beginning to tremble. The conversation in a foreign language obviously frightened him, and I was sure that this was why the captain was using English. I asked the captain what kind of enemy we had surprised. "Territorial," he said. This was the middle rank of Vietcong guerrillas; we called them provincial guerrillas. They operated in groups of up to one hundred and were often attached to the hard-core units to beef up their strength for a major attack; they would also hit smaller outposts.

"The leadership was not very good," the captain said. "If it had been a hard-core unit, there would have been more fighting and more dying. I think we surprised them."

Before we took off again, I walked over to the canal. The little soldier's body had actually crossed the finish line; his shoulder was over the bank, his blood was still running into the canal and there was a look of agony on his face.

The helicopter pilots and the Vietnamese captain decided that they had enough fuel for one more strike. The pilots were in very good humor, pleased with the day's bag. As we skimmed over the countryside once more, they boasted of how they had made the Air Force look sick again. There was a running battle between the helicopter pilots, who were Army officers, and the Air Force over the respective merits of the helicopter and the fighter plane. In particular, the feeling was very strong between Major Ivan Slavich, commander of the armed helicopter company, and Major Bill Burgin, who was the Air Force liaison man in the Twenty-first Division. Burgin called himself "the only law south of the Mekong River," and was distinguished by his violent hatred of both the Vietcong and helicopter pilots.

"Hey," said Slavich now, "go back to Bac Lieu and ask your friend Burgin if he's got a T-28 that can land in a paddy, capture some Communists and then take off again."

We hit one more village and encountered no resistance. But as I was walking toward the treeline I suddenly heard shouts and cries all around me. I was terrified, for I was unarmed and about fifty yards from the nearest soldier. Suddenly from deep bomb shelters all around me more than twenty women and children came up; they were wailing and pointing at me. Clearly, they were scared. Judging from its defensive preparations, this was a Vietcong village, and for years these people had heard propaganda about vicious Americans like me. As far as I was concerned they were dangerous too, and we stood looking at each other in mutual fear.

I yelled out to Major James Butler, asking him what to do. Butler suggested that I try to give a good impression of Americans. "Protect our image," he said. Later he congratulated me on being the first *New York Times* correspondent ever to capture a bunch of Vietcong women. I gladly turned them over to the Vietnamese captain.

The troops were remarkably restrained in what was obviously a Vietcong village. At times the quick change in Vietnamese behavior was amazing. One moment they could be absolutely ruthless; the next, they might be talking to a prisoner as if he were an old friend. The enemy was different, however; I was told by those who had been captured by them during the Indochina war that they were not so tolerant. This was hardly surprising; much emphasis was placed in their indoctrination on teaching them to hate. They were the have-nots fighting the haves, and even after capture their feelings rarely changed.

We flew back to Bac Lieu. It had been a good day. There had been few Government losses, and there was a chance that from all those prisoners we might learn something important. Everyone was tired and relaxed and happy. If nothing else, the day seemed to prove the value of the Eagle flights. Only Mert Perry of *Time*, who had also come along to observe the new strategy, seemed a bit depressed. It had been a good day, he agreed, and in one way the Government had done very well. But after all, he pointed out, it was a pretty limited business, and in the long run it might backfire. There was no follow-up; no one would be in those villages tonight working with the people. These peasants had seen helicopters and they knew that Americans flew the helicopters; they had seen killing and they had seen their men disappear. The conclusions that the villagers would draw were obvious—particularly if the Viet-cong were there to help them. Every man taken today, Mert said, probably had a brother or a son or a brother-in-law who would take his place after today.

We listened to Perry in silence, for we knew that he was right. The Government had scored a quick victory, but in Vietnam, victories were not always what they seemed. It was an endless, relentless war to which ordinary military rules did not apply. We went to bed that night a little less confident, knowing that although for the moment the enemy was paying a higher price, he was still out there somewhere in the darkness, living closer to the peasants and ready to seize the initiative once more.

from *The Making of a Quagmire*, 1965

"He Was Sitting in the Center of a Column of Flame"

by Malcolm W. Browne

THE LONG, brown joss sticks that burn at Buddhist holy places and homes throughout South Viet Nam generate a pleasing fragrance said to find favor with ghosts. But the smell of joss sticks is one that I shall never be able to dissociate from the ghastly smell of burning human flesh.

The two odors mingled June 11, 1963, at the intersection of two busy Saigon streets, to create a political explosion, the effects of which are still felt in Washington and elsewhere. I was there, and it happened like this:

On Monday, June 10, I got a telephone call at my office from a young Buddhist monk named Thich Duc Nghiep whom I had known some time. Duc Nghiep became well known to Western newsmen later as official press spokesman for the Buddhist rebels, by virtue of his fairly fluent English. At this writing, he is in the United States studying for a master's degree in comparative religion.

"We shall hold a meeting tomorrow morning at eight A.M.," Duc Nghiep said. "I would advise you to come. Something very important may happen."

For nearly a month, top Buddhist monks had been holding marching street demonstrations and hunger strikes in Saigon, all aimed at wringing concessions from the authoritarian Ngo Dinh Diem regime. Demands included one for government permission to fly the five-colored Buddhist flag in public. The Buddhists also wanted an end of alleged government favoritism to Catholics, an end to arbitrary police arrests, and "social justice for the nation."

The whole thing had been touched off on Tuesday, May 8, 1963, when Buddhists observing the birthday of Buddha were forbidden to fly their flag in the streets. A pagoda protest

meeting organized by the powerful young monk Thich Tri
Quang had been tape recorded, and the Buddhists demanded
permission to broadcast their recording on the local government radio station. Permission was denied, and several thousand Buddhist marchers led by monks headed from Hue's Tu
Dam Pagoda for the radio station in the center of town.

As the marchers approached the radio station and surged
around its entrance, the local military commander, a major
named Dang Sy, had a bad case of jitters. He ordered troops
and armored cars to move in.

Several grenades, apparently thrown by trigger-happy soldiers, exploded in the midst of the crowd. A few of the marchers (including children) were crushed under the tracks of the
armored vehicles. Eight persons were killed on the spot, and,
of the scores wounded, several died later.

The people who died in the Hue incident became the first
of the Buddhist martyrs in what was to become a fierce struggle to destroy Ngo Dinh Diem and his family.

The Diem government, rather than back down, applied increasingly harsh measures against the Hue Buddhists, and the
pleasant little city on the banks of the Perfume River became
an armed camp. In another incident later in the summer,
marchers with arms folded were blocked at a street barricade,
and staged a sit-in on the pavement. Troops dispersed them
by hurling glass containers of acid, which splashed over demonstrators and sent more than seventy of them to the hospital.

The masses of the nation were stirring, and the showdown
was nearing.

In Saigon, demonstrations by monks during the first month
after the Hue incident were orderly and staged with military
precision. Monks would converge at key parks around the city
in taxicabs and bicycle taxis with such perfect timing that for-
mations of three or four hundred saffron-robed Buddhists appeared to materialize from thin air, under the noses of security
police.

Street marches, especially on Tuesdays, became so frequent
they appeared to be losing their impact. Tuesday was the day
of choice, because the ascension of the spirits of the dead from
the Hue incident was said to be marked by seven-day intervals,
and the victims had died on a Tuesday.

Some time in late May, one of the English-speaking monks at the cluster of concrete buildings known as An Quang Pagoda had given a visitor a piece of blood-chilling intelligence. He said that two monks were planning to commit suicide publicly in support of Buddhist demands—one by disembowelment and the other by burning. The Buddhist high command (consisting of about ten top monks, including Tri Quang) had not yet authorized the suicides but was considering them, the informant said. Nothing further was said about this plan, and many people wrote it off as an idle threat, on grounds that the nonviolent Buddhist faith would never condone suicide.

But something special was in the air the morning of June 11.

I arrived about a quarter to eight at the small pagoda off Phan Dinh Phung Street where I had been advised to go. The concrete pagoda building was set in about thirty yards from the street with a muddy alleyway as an entrance. In the rear was a small courtyard, jammed with yellow-robed monks and gray-robed nuns. Loudspeakers nailed to trees and corners of the pagoda building were blaring in rapid Vietnamese.

More monks and nuns, all of them standing, were jammed in the main pagoda room, where another loudspeaker was howling.

I was shown to an alcove in which a large, gilded Buddha statue stood, and asked to sit down at a low table. Six or eight women wearing the white dress of mourning were busy preparing tea. One of them brought me a steaming glass cup of tea, and tried to smile politely, although tears were coursing down her face.

My monk informant, Thich Duc Nghiep, spotted me and came over. He whispered in my ear, "I advise you to stay until the very end of this, because I think something very important will happen."

At exactly eight o'clock, the jabber of Vietnamese from the loudspeakers stopped and the chanting of prayer began. One monk led the chanting with a microphone and another one next to him kept time, beating rhythmically on a gourd.

"Na Mo A Di Da Phat," the ancient prayer begins, each word equally accented on the same monotonous note.

It is the most hypnotic kind of chant I have ever heard, and on that hot June morning, clouds of incense in the air, I found even myself affected. All the monks and nuns joined that chant, quietly at first, then with rising, hammering volume, as the verses were repeated over and over, the tempo speeding up slightly.

Eyes all around me were fixed straight ahead, almost glazed in the absorption of fervor. But at exactly 9 A.M. it stopped.

Monks and nuns, who apparently had drilled their procedure many times, lined up in the alleyway, moving out into the street in two ranks. Some unfurled banners in Vietnamese and English calling on the government to answer the Buddhist demands. In a minute or two, the procession of 350 or so monks and nuns was formed and moving. At its head was an innovation in the street marches—a gray sedan with four or five monks riding inside. It seemed strange to me at the time that monks were now riding instead of walking.

Police ahead of the procession cleared the streets as usual, keeping clear of the marchers, and not interfering, except to shunt traffic and crowds away from the line of march. Preceding the Buddhist car by about a half-block, a white police jeep kept pace. At that time, the main crackdown on Buddhists by government officials was in Central Viet Nam, not the Saigon area.

People leaned from shopwindows along Phan Dinh Phung, and children stared at the passing procession.

The marchers reached the intersection of Le Van Duyet Street, one of the most important boulevards in Saigon, always jammed with heavy traffic. On one corner of the intersection stood the massive, gray Cambodian consulate building, with its stone lion statue. On two other corners were apartment buildings, and on the fourth corner, an Esso service station. At precisely the center of the intersection, the Buddhist car stopped, apparently stalled. The police jeep was already halfway down the next block.

The marchers began to move past the car, and then abruptly turned left into Le Van Duyet, quickly forming a circle about thirty feet in diameter, of which the car formed a link. It was now nearly 9:20 A.M.

The monks in the car had gotten out, and one of them had

opened its hood. From inside, he pulled a five-gallon gasoline can made of translucent plastic, filled to the brim with pink gasoline. Three other monks were walking from the car side by side to the center of the circle. One of them placed a small brown cushion on the pavement, and the monk in the center sat down on it, crossing his legs in the traditional position of Buddhist meditation known as the "lotus posture." This monk was the Venerable Thich Quang Duc, destined to be known throughout the world as the primary saint of modern Vietnamese Buddhism.

The three monks exchanged a few quiet words. The two who had flanked Quang Duc brought the gasoline container quickly to the center of the circle, and poured most of it over the bowed head and shoulders of the seated monk.

The monks stepped back, leaving the gasoline can next to the seated man. From about twenty feet away, I could see Quang Duc move his hands slightly in his lap striking a match. In a flash, he was sitting in the center of a column of flame, which engulfed his entire body. A wail of horror rose from the monks and nuns, many of whom prostrated themselves in the direction of the flames.

From time to time, a light breeze pulled the flames away from Quang Duc's face. His eyes were closed, but his features were twisted in apparent pain. He remained upright, his hands folded in his lap, for nearly ten minutes as the flesh burned from his head and body. The reek of gasoline smoke and burning flesh hung over the intersection like a pall.

Finally, Quang Duc fell backward, his blackened legs kicking convulsively for a minute or so. Then he was still, and the flames gradually subsided.

While the monk burned, other monks stood in positions at all four entrances to the intersection, holding banners reading: A Buddhist Priest Burns for Buddhist Demands.

City police at first watched in stunned horror, and then began running around aimlessly outside the circle of Buddhists. One of them radioed headquarters, and three or four fire trucks arrived with a platoon of helmeted riot police carrying fixed bayonets. The riot police charged down the street in a wave, but stopped short in confusion a few yards from the circle. As the fire trucks moved down the street, several monks leaped in front of their wheels, and other monks chocked themselves behind the rear wheels, making movement impossible without crushing someone.

All the while, leading monks with portable electric loudspeakers harangued onlookers, both in Vietnamese and English, with a highly emotional explanation as to why the suicide had taken place.

A black delivery truck with large Buddhist flags painted on its sides arrived, and monks unloaded a wooden coffin. The flames by now were completely out, and monks tried to transfer the charred body to the coffin. But its splayed arms and legs were rigid, and could not be forced into the box.

Seven monks shed their saffron robes (wearing brown robes underneath) and made a kind of sling to carry the body. The circle broke and formed into a procession once again, the body at its head. Marching a few blocks more, the group arrived at Xa Loi Pagoda, the main Buddhist pagoda in South Viet Nam, where a bell was tolling mournfully from the concrete tower. It was 10 A.M. sharp, and the demonstration was finished.

Quang Duc was the first of the Buddhist monks to die by fiery suicide the summer of 1963. He also was the only one to die with such elaborate public trappings. The other suicides all were sprung by surprise without processions. In Saigon, one young monk arrived in a taxi at Saigon's central market place, walked to the center of the traffic circle, and set himself afire. Three American newsmen attempting to photograph the incident were badly beaten by police. Another young monk, his clothing apparently impregnated with gasoline in advance, died on a street corner facing Saigon Cathedral one bright Sunday morning, as Catholic worshipers were arriving for mass. A policeman tried to beat out the flames, but without success.

Two monks in Hue burned themselves to death inside their barricaded pagoda, with no outsiders as witnesses. Another monk burned to death in front of a soldier's memorial, completely alone, in the coastal town of Phan Thiet. And a thirty-three-year-old nun died in flames near her pagoda outside another coastal town, the seaside resort of Nha Trang. In all, seven died, all with the blessings of the Buddhist high command.

Thich Quang Duc's body was taken for cremation at the Buddhist cemetery just outside Saigon, and monks in charge of burning the body claimed that Quang Duc's heart would not burn. A singed piece of meat purporting to be the heart was preserved in a glass chalice, becoming an object of worship.

Quang Duc's ashes were distributed to pagodas throughout the country. The yellow robes in which his body had been carried were cut into tiny swatches and distributed to Buddhist followers everywhere. Pinned to shirts and dresses, these bits of cloth were thought to have miraculous healing properties, and also were symbols of the Buddhist uprising against the government. At one point, police tried to crack down on wearers of the yellow cloth, but there were too many of them.

Tidings of miracles spread throughout the land. In the evening sky over Saigon, thousands said they could see the weeping face of the Buddha in the clouds. Traffic was jammed everywhere as crowds of people stood gazing into the sky.

Tens of thousands of followers poured through Xa Loi Pagoda each day to worship before the heart in the glass chalice.

from *The New Face of War*, 1965

The Diem Government, Pro and Con

by Marguerite Higgins

WASHINGTON.
"A SUCCESSFUL coup d'etat against Diem would probably set the war back 12 months."

The speaker was a top American diplomat on the scene in Saigon. His estimate was echoed by the British advisory mission and by most experienced foreign observers with whom this reporter spoke not only in Saigon, but also at military headquarters in the field.

And fears of a setback in the war, which after many painful false starts is finally going better, explains why the United States has so long endured President Ngo Dinh Diem, for all his authoritarian ways, his stubbornness, and his failure to make his position clear to the world.

United States policy has now wavered to the point where the government this week decided to issue what amounted to an open invitation to the Vietnamese military to take over the government in Saigon—if they could.

The change of policy has stirred an internal row in the U.S. government, and the outcome is in doubt.

The proponents of getting rid of Diem argue that his political repression has reached the point where the United States must disassociate itself from the image he has created.

The opposite view is that the Vietnamese army has quite enough on its hands fighting the Communist Viet Cong guerrillas, that one war at a time is enough. Finally, this group argues that the greatest threat to the soldier's morale is not Diem's authoritarian approach but the confusion and dismay created by Washington's unsubtle attempts to pit the army against his regime and the hints that U.S. aid may be curtailed.

In light of this clash of views inside the Kennedy administration on what to do next, anything can happen. Only two things are clear:

(1) The State Department's apparent attempt to set the Vietnamese army at the throat of the Diem regime in the middle of a war will be the subject of bitter controversy both inside this government and around the world for an unpredictable period of time.

(2) New U.S. Ambassador Henry Cabot Lodge has been put in a terribly difficult diplomatic position.

And Mr. Lodge, it can be stated on good authority, has protested at least some of the State Department's publicity tactics in the sharpest terms.

The most controversial train of events began last Sunday —before Mr. Lodge had even had a chance to present his credentials to Diem. (He did so at 11:30 a.m. Saigon time, Monday.)

Sunday night, the Voice of America broadcast a news roundup which among other things said that the U.S. might make sharp cuts in its aid program to South Viet Nam unless Diem punished the special Vietnamese troops allegedly responsible for attacks on the pagodas and arrest of the Buddhists. The Voice broadcast also for the first time stated the American government's view that the army was innocent of responsibility for the pagoda raids.

The Voice based its broadcast on a news agency story from Washington. Roger Hilsman, Assistant Secretary of State for Far Eastern Affairs, told a Voice employee that the story was good guidance and that the Voice could go ahead with the information.

And as Hilsman and the department anticipated, the part of the Voice broadcast referring to the U.S. absolution of the Vietnamese military was instantly interpreted in Saigon as a sign that Washington was encouraging the military—with its cleaned-up image—to take charge.

As to aid, it is certain, as the State Department says, that "no decision" on future cuts has been taken. It is equally certain that Diem has been warned that such cuts are likely if he is not responsive to American wishes.

The Vietnamese military are in an agonizing dilemma. As a European diplomat in Saigon put it in a message to this correspondent: "The morale of the army at the fighting level has been astonishingly immune to outside pressure up to and through the imposition of martial law. But now the high officers are bewildered. You Americans have lectured them ad infinitum about civilian rule. You Americans have lectured them ad infinitum about getting on with the war. And they want to get on with the war. These Vietnamese officers are truly dedicated.

"But now the U.S. government comes out with what amounts to a suggestion that the Vietnamese military try and take charge of the country as well as the war. The military know that the jeeps they ride in, the planes they fly, the very bullets in their guns come from the United States. What are they to do? Forget about civilian rule, and go the way of the Korean juntas? Are they to risk chaos by trying to throw out Diem by force? So long as this uncertainty about American policy exists, Washington will be responsible for sowing more and more disunity and doubt in a country that desperately needs unity and resolve. . . ."

So far the Vietnamese army has on the surface rallied to Diem to the extent of accepting full responsibility for martial law and events in the pagodas. It is possible that the Vietnamese generals were forced by the Diem family to accept this public responsibility. But one thing is certain. President Diem and his family are not about to go quietly. Diem's head is not for the taking. He is bound to fight back.

Washington's current reappraisal of policies toward South Viet Nam is in part motivated by the anxiety to avoid the danger that Diem's anti-Buddhist image might rub off on America and endanger relations with Buddhist nations. The irony here is that Washington is perfectly well aware that Diem himself is not guilty of persecution of any religion, but rather pulled in the reins harshly on the leaders of the Buddhist Association because they were waging an increasingly loud and effective political campaign against his regime.

Opposition to the Diem regime includes the outs who want in, the citified intellectuals in the bureaucracy, the universities, the military, and—equally important—Confucianists, Caodaists, Taoists, ancestor worshippers, Hoa Hao and Catholics as well as Buddhists.

President Diem does not tolerate real political opposition in the sense of forces that stand a chance of ushering his family-dominated regime out of power. South Viet Nam has the trappings of a democracy, an "elected" national assembly, a presidential race. The elections are to some degree fair. But the catch is that hardly anybody is ruled eligible for election unless he is acceptable to President Diem and family. Diem is by Western standards a dictator who holds the reins loosely when things are going well and can tighten them up cruelly when he feels threatened.

Today's secret political opposition to the Diems still appears splintered. It has no known national following.

Still the rumors this summer of possible coup d'etats have been more persistent than Saigon mosquitos. There is not one of the 20 generals in South Viet Nam's army who has not been reported to be a potential strongman about to oust President Diem and his family.

Why are so many Vietnamese intellectuals disenchanted? One reason is that President Diem, although himself an intellectual, has nonetheless displayed an attitude of disinterest toward the literati—an attitude that has given them a sense of being left out.

The only real common denominator between the splinter opposition groups is a steady soaring hatred for the fiery Madame Ngo Dinh Nhu, the President's sister-in-law, whose talk of "barbecued monks" revolted the world. In a personal interview, the beautiful Madame Nhu struck this reporter as a woman of bad judgment in the sense of insensitivity to the rest of the world—and enormous courage. And this quality of courage just makes matters worse so far as Madame Nhu's impact is concerned. If she had a bit less courage, she might speak her mind less openly—and less insistently.

A close second in unpopularity is her husband, Ngo Dinh Nhu, who is feared because of the power he wields as close adviser to the President. Counselor Nhu is also disliked in large part because it is widely assumed that Madame Nhu is merely stating what her husband really thinks.

There have been some suggestions in American circles that relations with South Viet Nam would improve posthaste if Diem would only fire Nhu and silence Madame Nhu. In this reporter's judgment, it is unrealistic to seek to split off Counselor Nhu˙from the president. President Diem gave this reporter the impression of trusting and needing his brother, indeed of being extremely proud of him for the strategic hamlet program in which Counselor Nhu has been a driving force.

Opponents of Diem usually claim that his war and national reconstruction efforts would be carried on under any successor, but more democratically. In intellectual circles, there is the conviction that more civil liberties would and could be offered if Diem were toppled.

The tragic irony of South Viet Nam today is that its worldwide image is being tarnished at a period when the war is going better than ever. Its little people are more secure from Viet Cong attack and better fed than at any time since the Communists unleashed their cruel military assault in 1961.

Is the United States going to jeopardize these real accomplishments in exchange for a coup d'etat and military dictatorship that may or may not supply the "image" that Washington desires? Is it already perhaps too late to put a halt to a train of unpredictable and chaotic events? These are the issues that are being battled out behind the scenes in Washington and Saigon as our top policy leaders try to decide where we go from here in Viet Nam.

New York *Herald Tribune*, September 1, 1963

In the Gia Long Palace

by Joseph Alsop

SAIGON—In the Gia Long Palace, President Ngo Dinh Diem's brother, the all-powerful state councillor, Ngo Dinh Nhu, inhabits a long, high room full of books and mementoes, with a view over the gardens.

It used to be an interesting, and even on occasion an encouraging, place to spend an hour or two in talk. Whatever his other failings, Ngo Dinh Nhu is an exceedingly intelligent man with an original turn of mind. Here, for instance, this reporter first heard about the strategic hamlet program, which gives the best hope of winning the civil war against the Communists. In large measure, the idea was Nhu's.

But go today to this nerve center of President Diem's government, and you will come away with a very different impression. Something of the atmosphere was suggested by the last report in this space, describing the French intrigue to defeat American policy in Viet-Nam, quite largely in Ngo Dinh Nhu's own words. Yet even this strange story, with all its mephitic overtones, does not convey the full ripe flavor.

Like a good many other clever men, Nhu has never been without vanity. It goes beyond normal vanity, however, when a man at one moment speaks of himself as the "unique spine" of the anti-Communist struggle in Viet-Nam; at the next moment remarks that he is "the only serious modern theorist of guerrilla war," and then adds:

"Even if you Americans pull out, I will still win the war here at the head of the great guerrilla movement which I have prepared."

It goes beyond normal vanity, too, when a man proclaims that "no one in this country has any ideas except me—my brother only knows how to say 'no' and no one else knows anything at all." Yet this is how Ngo Dinh Nhu now talks.

Nor is that all. He bitterly declares that he is "the lightning rod for my brother's mistakes; all are his, yet are blamed on me." He warns that if he bows to "American pressures" and retires from the scene even for a few months, "the whole strategic hamlet program will collapse, for I alone am the inspiration of the young fighters who defend the hamlets." Or he casually reveals that he has kept from his brother, the President, such a major matter as a French-sponsored overture from the North Vietnamese Communists, because he does not think that Diem would handle the problem wisely enough.

Hearing all this, you say to yourself that this man, all but openly announces that he is the real master of the Vietnamese government; yet he has somehow lost touch with the real world outside the Gia Long Palace. Yet you suspend judgment until you make the second customary call, in the more pompous rooms of the Gia Long Palace's upper floors, where President Diem receives his visitors.

Here, too, it used to be pleasant to go. Ngo Dinh Diem, it must be remembered, is a man of admirable determination and courage, who saved his people almost single-handedly from the grim Communist takeover that everyone regarded as quite inevitable back in 1954. To be sure, he has always had a way of complaining about his American allies. But in the earlier days, when the U.S. presence here was inadequate and all too often woolly minded, the complaints were frequently justified.

Now, however, what you hear is something else again. One instant, the Buddhist crisis is attributed to a well-laid plot of the Communists. And almost in the next breath, the whole ugly business is laid to "the machinations" of the U.S. Information Service.

At one moment, the course of the war is being quite rationally and sensibly discussed. But at the next moment, the danger that the vaporings of Madame Ngo Dinh Nhu and such like goings-on will turn Congress sharply against the Vietnamese aid program is being furiously dismissed as "a mere straw, whereas the beam that weighs heavy on us is the plotting of the USIS."

Here, in sum, is another man who has lost his ability to see events or problems in their true proportions, no doubt because his natural tendency to be suspicious has been daily played upon by his brother. And right here, rather than in the "plots of the CIA," is the explanation of the widespread expectation of a coup d'etat that now prevails in Saigon.

There are countless Vietnamese who are still determined not to be the victims of a Communist takeover whether by courtesy of the French, or with the help of the growing faction of American appeasers, or in any other way. Yet a success in the struggle against the Communists can hardly be expected if the real world of the leaders of that struggle has tragically contracted to the narrow limits of the palace walls. So there are likely to be changes here.

New York Herald Tribune, September 20, 1963

The Fall of the House of Ngo Dinh

by Stanley Karnow

AT THE French mission church of St. Francis Xavier in Cholon, Saigon's shabby Chinatown, the early-morning Mass had celebrated All Souls' Day, the day of the dead. A few minutes after the congregation had gone, two men in dark-gray suits walked quickly through the shaded courtyard and entered the church. South Vietnam's President Ngo Dinh Diem and his brother Nhu, both haggard after a sleepless night, were fugitives in the capital they once commanded. In the remote church they prayed and took Communion, and it was their ultimate sacrament. Within less than an hour their bloody, crumpled corpses lay ignominiously on the deck of an armored car rumbling through the Saigon streets.

Thus ended the fragile reign of the Ngo Dinh family—a stubborn, self-righteous oligarchy that, in its eight years of rule over South Vietnam, had degenerated from clumsy paternalism into almost insane tyranny. When, after careful plotting, a host of Vietnamese officers rose against it, Diem's rotted regime fell apart with surprising ease.

Not long after the smoke of rebellion had cleared away, the chief of South Vietnam's new military junta invited me into his spacious, map-lined office. Gen. Duong Van Minh, known among Americans in Saigon as Big Minh, is a heavy, fierce-looking soldier whose single tooth is a proud badge of the Japanese torture he suffered during World War II. He is a deceptively gentle man, and when he spoke of the *coup d'état* that lifted him into office, there was a discernible tone of apology in his voice.

"We sincerely wanted to work with Diem," he said. "But the guerrilla war we are waging must be fought with the hearts of the people. Diem had lost the people. Army discipline was disintegrating, morale was low. If we had been winning the war, we wouldn't have staged the *coup d'état*. We overthrew Diem in order to restore unity to the country and give a new spirit to the army—so we can beat the Communists."

Whatever future problems the new junta faces—and they will be considerable—their *coup d'état* was the only alternative to the Diem regime. For Diem's government had, in effect, ceased to function long before it completely collapsed.

An austere, inflexible autocrat, Diem could not cope with the double threat of a Communist guerrilla enemy and a growing internal opposition. Like the flawed hero of a Shakespearean tragedy, he succumbed to his own worst instincts. He withdrew from reality and, more and more, abdicated power to his neurotic, conspiratorial brother Nhu and his beautiful, arrogant sister-in-law, Madame Nhu. In the process, he gradually alienated his country's army, its intelligentsia and a significant mass of its common people.

At the same time, he estranged himself from his main foreign supporters. Mindful of its own image, Diem's own Roman Catholic Church strove to disassociate itself from a regime described by a high Vatican official as "medieval and reactionary." More important, in giving free rein to his brother's repressive policies, Diem provoked the hostility of the United States, which had dedicated men and money to help save his nation. "We wanted a change in the way this country was being run," says a top U.S. diplomat in Saigon. "If those in power couldn't change their ways, then we favored changing those in power. Don't misunderstand me. We didn't plot Diem's downfall. But we certainly created the climate and state of mind that inspired his opponents to overthrow him."

Diem had been living on borrowed time since November, 1960, when his crack paratrooper battalions surrounded his palace and then naïvely let themselves be double-crossed by his promise to reform. Again, in February, 1962, two fighter pilots attacked his palace and reduced it to rubble. The assaults against him reinforced Diem's distrust of all but his family and a handful of flunkies.

Nowhere did Diem's paranoid suspicions have a more debilitating effect than in his armed forces, where officers were judged more by their fidelity than their ability. Even imaginary misgivings about a man were enough to tarnish his career. A general who helped to save Diem in the 1960 revolt, for example, was thereafter suspect because he had too easily passed through the rebel lines. Constantly worried that his leading generals might overthrow him, Diem deprived them of troops. Experienced men like General Minh, the country's highest ranking field officer, were made presidential aides or given innocuous staff positions.

In recent months, military men were also disenchanted by widespread reports that Diem and Nhu were putting out serious feelers for a deal with Communist North Vietnam. Several times Nhu or his representatives indirectly contacted delegates from Hanoi to discuss prospects for a reunified, neutral Vietnam. Despite his professions of anti-Communism, Diem himself was thinking along similar lines: "Why do the Communists attack us so ferociously? After all, our two systems are not so much different. We're both for the welfare of the people."

Nothing so profoundly undermined Vietnamese military morale, however, as Diem's repressive measures against the Buddhists, by far the largest religious group in the country. Throughout the summer, as the Buddhist crisis developed into a broad political protest against Diem's regime, some strategically placed officers finally started to organize a revolt. There were some odd and unlikely figures among them. The military security chief Col. Do Mau, for example, was so distrusted by Diem for alleged pro-Buddhist sympathies that he felt forced to join the conspiracy. Brilliant Lt. Col. Pham Ngoc Thao, an ex-member of the Communist Vietminh and later one of Diem's close confidants, reluctantly went into opposition, convinced that only the regime's downfall could save the country.

These conspirators worked cautiously. Sometimes they met in their homes; often they talked out in the countryside; and occasionally their conversations took place in noisy Saigon nightclubs. By early autumn they controlled a powerful force of about 2,500 paratroopers, marines, infantry and armor.

While these junior officers were planning rebellion, however, a more prestigious group of Vietnamese generals, headed by Big Minh, was also considering ways of overthrowing the government. While both factions maneuvered for position, the generals sent agents out into the provinces to line up units they might use. Last August, at the height of the Buddhist crisis, they suggested to Diem and Nhu that martial law be declared and soldiers be moved into Saigon. Secretly they planned to order these legions to rebel.

Constantly suspicious, Ngo Dinh Nhu shrewdly thwarted this plan. He accepted the generals' counsel to declare martial law. But instead of letting them call in provincial troops, he turned the military control of Saigon over to a more trusted general, the yeasty little Ton That Dinh. It was under Dinh's tactical command that Nhu's Special Forces and secret police raided the city's Buddhist temples on August 21. And after that, Dinh considered himself a national hero. "I have defeated Henry Cabot Lodge," he proclaimed. "He came here to pull a *coup d'état,* but I, Dinh, have conquered him and saved the country."

In the week that followed the violent anti-Buddhist raids, the plotting insurgents in Vietnam were greatly heartened by strong signs of U.S. distaste for the Diem regime. President Kennedy had made it clear that he disapproved of the Ngo Dinh family. The U.S. aid to Vietnam was curtailed, and Ambassador Lodge bravely told Diem that his brother Nhu was undesirable. And the CIA chief in Saigon, John Richardson, the man in the American mission closest to brother Nhu, was summarily called home.

But none of these encouraging gestures made the mechanics of revolt any easier, and the insurgent generals began to work out another design. This time they concentrated on winning over the loyal General Dinh. A courageous but not very bright soldier, Dinh's fidelity to Diem was exceeded only by his monumental egocentricity. The generals played on this fatal weakness.

They softened Dinh up with flattery, telling him that he was a personage of historic proportions, and they even bribed an astrologer to depict an important political future for him. Finally, when Dinh was inflated with ambition, they urged that he ask President Diem to appoint him Minister of Interior.

The trick worked as they had expected. Diem flatly refused him. Dinh, suffering from a loss of face, went off to sulk in a mountain resort for a few days. His faith in Diem and Nhu was clearly shaken. But Dinh did not immediately swing into the insurgent ranks. Instead he returned to Saigon and, as he told me, "I decided to give Diem another chance."

General Dinh now claims that he remained loyal to Diem in the hope of reforming him. But many knowledgeable Vietnamese insist that Dinh really stayed with the ruling family in order to participate in a fantastic machination then being devised by Ngo Dinh Nhu. His network of agents had kept him informed of impending revolts, and Nhu worked out a plan to put an end to all conspiracies. It was to be a fake *coup d'état*, which Nhu called "Operation Bravo." "Coups are like eggs and must be smashed before they're hatched," he said.

On an appointed date in early November, according to the scheme, Nhu's faithful Special Forces commander, Col. Le Quang Tung, would stage a "revolt" in Saigon with the aid of hand-picked police elements. Diem, Nhu and selected members of the palace household would flee to a prepared refuge at Cap St. Jacques, a seaside resort east of the capital. General Dinh and loyal army troops would remain on the outskirts of the capital. Inside Saigon, mob violence would "spontaneously" erupt. Gangs would loot and pillage—particularly the homes of Americans. A number of Buddhist and student leaders would be somehow killed. During all this confusion, the "rebel" Colonel Tung would announce the formation of a "revolutionary government" composed of well-known political opponents of Diem. Madame Nhu's father, Tran Van Chuong, former Vietnamese ambassador to Washington but now an outspoken critic of Diem's regime, was to be named president of the new government—without his consent. Saigon radio would blare anti-American, proneutralist propaganda and an appeal to end the war against the Communists.

This charade was scheduled to last 24 hours. Then, from their positions around Saigon, the loyal troops would march into the city and easily crush the uprising. Diem would return triumphantly to his capital, reaffirm his legitimate right to power, and Nhu would have a field day. For the fake coup would have plainly "proved" that:

- Opponents to Diem were neutralists, anti-Americans and

pro-Communists. Therefore the U.S. should give up any hope for his downfall.

• Adversaries of the Diem regime could not control the plundering mobs, which directed their pillage against Americans. Only Diem could assure law and order.

• The army really supported the Diem government, since it declined to join the revolutionaries and crushed them instead.

In addition to all these important propaganda points, Nhu expected that his phony "revolt" would bring to the surface a vast number of his enemies, making them easy to mark and cut down in the future.

Hardly had Nhu conceived his bizarre plan, however, than details of it filtered back to the various men plotting against the regime. Some of them considered the fake revolt an opportunity; they advocated letting it start, then taking it over. Others disagreed on the grounds that such a complex operation would result in too much confusion and bloodshed. The junior conspirators decided to beat Nhu by staging a real coup beforehand. D day was fixed: Thursday, October 24.

The generals, however, contended that any move without the cooperation of General Dinh and his Saigon garrison was doomed. Unable to persuade the young soldiers to alter their plan, the generals sabotaged it. They sent a key rebel regiment off on a minor operation against the Communists, and the junior conspirators had no choice but to postpone their project. When one of the plotters went home on October 24, he found a CIA man waiting to ask him, "Why didn't it start this morning?"

By now the generals realized that they had to act fast, both to keep up with the impulsive junior officers and to circumvent Nhu's crazy Operation Bravo. They focused on finally signing up Gen. Ton That Dinh. It is obvious from subsequent events that they promised Dinh almost everything, including the cherished Ministry of Interior Diem had refused him. It is still far from clear, however, whether Dinh was wholeheartedly for the revolt or was playing along with both sides, ending up with whichever was victorious.

By October 29 Dinh was apparently in the rebel fold. The rebels then set a trap for Nhu by deliberately letting him learn of the coup. General Dinh dispatched one of his deputies to the 7th Division headquarters at the town of Mytho, about 40 miles southwest of Saigon. The deputy gathered a group of division officers and declared that a *coup d'état* was being organized in Saigon. He cited some of the men involved, pointedly revealing that General Dinh was "not yet involved." Just as Dinh and the plotters expected, there was an informer among the divisional officers at Mytho. Within hours, Diem and Nhu heard of the budding conspiracy. Next day, General Dinh was summoned to the presidential palace and advised that one of his deputies was a traitor. A magnificent actor, Dinh put on a noisy performance. Weeping and gesticulating, he vowed death to the renegade.

But it was beyond Nhu's understanding to consider anything so simple. Instead, he suggested that Dinh infiltrate the plot and turn it into a countercoup against the insurgents. Moreover, he ordered Dinh to prepare for action on November 1—All Saints' Day—when Saigon offices would be closed, streets uncrowded and the movement of troops relatively easy. With the air of a master conspirator, Nhu announced that this new plan superseded his earlier scheme. Ever consistent, Nhu dubbed his latest project "Operation Bravo II."

General Dinh's first problem was to evacuate Diem's four loyal Special Forces companies from the capital. He explained to Diem's faithful Special Forces commander, Col. Le Quang Tung, that fresh troops would have to be brought into Saigon for Operation Bravo II. "But if we move reserves into the city," Dinh went on, "the Americans will be angry. They'll complain that we're not fighting the war. So we must camouflage our plan by sending the Special Forces out to the country. That will deceive them."

Next day, with Diem's approval, the Special Forces left Saigon. A major obstacle to the *coup d'état* was thus removed. Now Dinh's job was to deploy his forces for the revolt.

With Diem and Nhu under the illusion that he was preparing for their protection, Dinh rapidly shifted troops in and out of Saigon. D day was Friday, November 1; H hour was 1:30 P.M. Throughout the preceding night and following morning the insurgent legions rushed to take up their position. Two battalions of marines accompanied by armored cars were readied to attack the capital's radio stations and police headquarters. A battalion of paratroopers, resting at a seaside resort 70 miles away, was ordered to rendezvous with tank and artillery units and race to the city for an assault on the presidential-guard barracks. Infantry was called in from the north and southwest.

As the troops converged on Saigon, only senior officers knew the purpose of their mission. "I told my company commanders what we were up to beforehand," a marine colonel said later, "but I lied to my platoon leaders. I told them that the police were plotting to overthrow Diem and we were going to save him." Said a paratrooper lieutenant, "When we started out, I guessed it was the coup but I really didn't know. We reached a command post in the suburbs, and a colonel said the presidential-guard barracks was our objective. 'Who is the enemy and who our friend?' I asked, and he said, 'Anyone who opposes us is the enemy.'"

By midmorning of November 1, the whole area around Saigon was in stealthy movement, and no single person knew precisely what was happening everywhere. At about nine A.M., for example, Diem's loyal navy commander, Capt. Ho Tan Quyen, was met by two subordinates who came to give him birthday greetings. Instead, they asked him to join the revolt, and when he refused, they drove him outside town and shot him.

American military advisers, who live with the Vietnamese army, were well aware that a revolt was in the making, and those attached to General Dinh's staff knew the exact time it would begin. They reported the information to their headquarters, but the U.S. commander, Gen. Paul Harkins, apparently did not believe the news. Ambassador Henry Cabot Lodge was probably less skeptical, however. At 10 A.M. he took visiting Adm. Harry Felt, commander in chief of the U.S. Pacific forces, to see Diem for an hour. It was an odd confrontation. Both Lodge and Diem knew that a major event was in the offing, and they discussed "rumors" of a revolt. But if Lodge expected the real thing, Diem awaited Operation Bravo II, his brother's complex countercoup.

As the insurgent units wheeled into striking position, the rebel generals were arranging another astute scheme. Friday was the day for their regular weekly luncheon to discuss assorted military problems. At a dining room in the Joint General Staff headquarters, they laid extra places at the table and invited a few special guests, such as Special Forces Commander Colonel Tung and other officers loyal to Diem.

At 1:30 P.M. the revolt began. Spearheading the attack, two marine battalions sped into the city. They quickly captured the police and radio stations, and a rebel officer immediately went on the air to broadcast that the revolt was on. Meanwhile, at their luncheon, the generals announced to the assembled officers that the coup had begun and invited them all to join. Almost everyone signed up. Diem's faithful Colonel Tung flatly refused. As he was taken out to be shot, he shouted at the generals, "Remember who gave you the stars you're wearing."

In the presidential palace Diem and Nhu at first figured that their own countercoup was unfolding. They fully believed that General Dinh was loyal to them and would, as calculated, turn on the plotters and take the situation in hand. Soon after the action started, for example, a police official telephoned Nhu and frantically cried that his headquarters was under attack. "It's all right," Nhu reassured him. "I know all about it."

As the afternoon wore on, however, Diem and his brother slowly began to sense that something was going wrong. They had received the expected telephone calls from the insurgent generals demanding their surrender, and they rejected them. But time and again they tried to reach General Dinh to ask when his counterattack would start. Each time they were disappointed. Dinh was not at his office, but at the Joint General Staff headquarters. "Dinh must have been arrested," Diem was heard to say, still unable to imagine that the general had betrayed him.

A bit past four P.M. insurgent artillery opened fire on his presidential-guard barracks, and Diem knew he was in trouble. He telephoned Ambassador Lodge to tell him that the army was rebelling. Coolly acknowledging that he had heard some shooting, Lodge expressed his concern for Diem's welfare and reminded him that the rebels had offered him a safe conduct out of the country. "I shall try to restore order," snapped Diem. Replied Lodge, "If there's anything I can do to assure your personal safety, let me know."

Recalling his siege in 1960, when he had stubbornly turned almost certain defeat into victory, Diem held fast. From a special transmitter inside his yellow stucco palace, he broadcast radio appeals to his provincial commanders for help. Not a single reply came back. Only five blocks from the palace Diem's praetorian guards were besieged, and the palace itself was surrounded by rebel troops and armor.

Diem had carefully prepared for every variety of attack. Under the palace, for example, he recently completed construction of a $200,000 air-conditioned shelter against aerial bombing. He had built three tunnels leading far from the palace, and he had several plans for retreat.

About eight P.M., with the palace surrounded, Diem and Nhu fled through a tunnel that took them to a wooded area near the Cercle Sportif, Saigon's sporting club. They carried nothing but a briefcase crammed with U.S. greenbacks. At the tunnel exit, a confederate was waiting to drive them to the home of a Chinese merchant, Ma Tuyen. The house had a direct link with the palace telephone. Neither the insurgent forces attacking it nor the troops defending it ever knew that night that they were fighting for an empty palace.

In their new hideout in the Chinese district of Cholon, Diem and Nhu still hoped that General Dinh would rescue them, and they doggedly continued to telephone him. It was past midnight when, for the first time that day, they reached him directly at the Joint General Staff headquarters. With the other insurgents beside him, Dinh was apparently anxious to dispel any doubts about his allegiance to the rebel cause. Using a choice lexicon of Vietnamese obscenities, he barked at Diem: "Dinh saved you m——rs many times, but not now, you b——s. You s——s are finished. It's all over."

Obstinately Diem still refused to surrender. Through his palace radio transmitter, he went on issuing appeals for help. He called on his hand-picked province chiefs to send him irregulars, and he begged for his brother's Republican Youth Corps to rise up. He even implored Madame Nhu's paramilitary women's committee to mobilize in his defense. None of them responded. Instead, messages of loyalty to the rebels were pouring in from all over the country.

At dawn Diem's palace defenders ran up a white flag. A

horde of troops and civilians, almost incredulous at the rebel victory, stormed the building. They found its ornate chambers a shambles, and they poked curiously through the rooms, stealing Madame Nhu's negligees and her husband's whiskey. Diem's bedroom was littered with American adventure magazines, and on Nhu's desk were copies of a book entitled *Shoot to Kill*. But nobody could find Diem and his brother.

By about 8:30 A.M. Cholon was fully awake and bustling. Diem and Nhu decided to seek sanctuary in the church of St. Francis Xavier. From there Diem telephoned the Joint General Staff headquarters. He offered to yield on condition that: (1) he be permitted to surrender honorably, (2) members of his family be allowed to leave the country, (3) he be maintained as president of the republic for a decent interval in order to retire gracefully. A rebel representative granted the first two points. As for the third, he said: "We'll discuss that later." Diem agreed and disclosed his whereabouts.

Within minutes, three armored cars were dashing across the city. At about 9:45 they pulled into the narrow, dead-end street facing the church. Personally commanding them was Gen. Mai Huu Xuan. A high police official in the French colonial administration, Xuan had been shunted into a minor job by Diem, and he detested the president. He was a poor choice for this delicate mission. But he was the only man who dared accept it. Asked to accompany Xuan, another general declined, saying, "Diem doesn't deserve two generals."

Despite the bitterness of their fight against him, the insurgents could not shake off their respect for Diem. When the armored cars arrived at the church, the rebels hesitated to arrest the president and his brother immediately. Instead, they sent in a once-loyal officer to lure them out. At the sight of the faithful subordinate, Diem and Nhu emerged. The rebel troops promptly seized them. They tied the brothers' hands behind their backs and unceremoniously pushed them into one of the armored cars.

For some inexplicable reason, General Xuan did not ride with Diem and Nhu. The vehicle that carried them was commanded by a tall, swarthy tank-corps major once connected with the Dai Viet party, a dissident movement that opposed both Diem and the Communists. According to some insiders, the major burned with desire to avenge a close friend whom Nhu had executed.

"As we rode back to the Joint General Staff headquarters," an eyewitness told me, "Diem sat silently, but Nhu and the major began to insult each other. I don't know who started it. The name-calling grew passionate. The major had hated Nhu before. Now he was charged with emotion. Suddenly he lunged at Nhu with a bayonet and stabbed him again and again, maybe fifteen or twenty times. Still in a rage, he turned to Diem, took out his revolver and shot him in the head. Then he looked back at Nhu, who was lying on the floor, twitching. He put a bullet into his head too. Neither Diem nor Nhu ever defended themselves. Their hands were tied."

When the armored car reached staff headquarters with the two bodies, the generals were aghast. They had not the slightest sympathy for Nhu. But for all their impatience with his policies, they had always been awed by Diem's courage and stature. Besides, they had promised him safety and now their own honor was betrayed. One of them wept openly, and General Dinh said later, "I couldn't sleep that night."

To cover their obvious sense of guilt, the generals first claimed that Diem and Nhu had committed suicide, a tale that was later amended to "accidental suicide." Privately they admitted that Diem and his brother had been murdered. Adding to the mystery, they refused to state publicly where the bodies were buried. They are believed to lie in a prison cemetery near Saigon airport.

In the days following the coup, a few well-organized gangs smashed up pro-Diem newspaper offices, including the American-owned *Times of Vietnam* (whose proprietor, Mrs. Ann Gregory, after long berating U.S. "plans" for Diem's downfall, fled to the American Embassy). On the whole, however, Saigon's citizens behaved with restrained pleasure. Girls shyly presented flowers and food to rebel heroes, and youth delegations visited army camps to make solemn speeches of gratitude to insurgent officers. Forgetting Madame Nhu's senseless ban on dancing, nightclubs went into paroxysms of twisting.

And political prisoners slowly emerged, some with horrendous tales of brutality. A slim, pretty girl of 21, arrested in a pro-Buddhist demonstration last September and held for more than a month, told me how policemen had attached electric wires to her wrists, earlobes and breasts, shocking her into senselessness during their interrogations. Harvard-educated Dr. Phan Quang Dan, one of Diem's most prominent political opponents, was held for two years in a 27-square-foot dungeon under Saigon's Botanical Gardens. One day in early 1961, Dan recounted, Nhu personally visited him to demand his allegiance to the regime. Dan refused. Nhu enumerated the tortures he would suffer, and they were applied. The doctor was shocked with electricity and gagged with water. Last September he was transferred to Poulo Condore, a kind of Devil's Island. "After the dungeon, it was luxury," Doctor Dan said. "I was able to see the sunlight and hear sounds other than the cries of people being tortured."

As dictatorships go, the Diem regime was far from the worst. Yet, during those days after its downfall, enough evidence of its tyranny flowed forth to disturb and embarrass many Americans. For this was the government U.S. reporters had been cautioned not to disparage. Looking back on that era, a veteran American official in Saigon could not conceal his disgust. "For the sake of so-called 'realism,' we abandoned our own principles," he said. "We expected the Vietnamese people to endure a regime that we ourselves wouldn't have tolerated for five minutes back home. Maybe morality has a certain place in foreign affairs."

The new military junta's alternative to Diem is not going to be town-hall democracy. But most certainly, the new administration in Vietnam will have to strive for efficiency and public support. These are not ambiguous clichés but immediate political necessities, for a significant mass of the Vietnamese public has undergone a profound transformation.

Apathetic and apolitical as recently as six months ago, the students of Saigon quite suddenly and spontaneously burst out as a fresh force in the country. The Buddhists themselves, for years fragmented and subdued, have grown into a strong, solid organization. Most important, Vietnam's young captains, majors and colonels—the men whose units gave the revolt its muscle—have taken measure of their strength and, almost to their own surprise, have found it impressive.

One evening not long ago I dined with a group of junior officers, and they talked openly of their problems. It was a refreshing change from the covert conversations during the days of Diem rule. "It's good to speak freely," one of them said to me as the meal ended. And smiling, he added, "Let's hope that we haven't just been attending the first meeting of the next revolt."

The Saturday Evening Post, December 21, 1963

"They Can Win a War If Someone Shows Them How"

by David Halberstam

FOR Lieutenant Colonel John Vann, the battle of Ap Bac and the subsequent Vietnamese and American reaction to it were a bitter disappointment. Many Americans considered him one of the two or three best advisers in the country. In September 1962, when General Maxwell Taylor had come to Vietnam on one of his frequent trips, he had lunched with four advisers of different rank who were generally considered outstanding; Vann had represented the division advisers.

Vann was a man of curious contrasts. Thirty-seven years old, one of the younger lieutenant colonels in the Army, he was clearly on his way to becoming a full colonel, with a very good chance of eventual promotion to general. (His recognizable superiority is the reason that some of the high people in the Pentagon wish that Vann had never happened, for his case documented and symbolized so many embarrassments that might otherwise have been swept under the rug.) He was clearly about to take off in his career—one of those men who reaches his mid-thirties and suddenly begins to pull away from his contemporaries.

Yet most Army officers of this type tend to be sophisticated and polished, usually with a West Point background, often from second- or third-generation Army families—in contrast to some of their colleagues who excel as combat officers, but who find other aspects of the Army a bit baffling. Vann, however, could hardly have been more different from the traditional gentleman-soldier. There was little polish to him: he was a poor boy from Virginia, who always reminded me of a good old Appalachian South redneck—and it was literally true that on operations his neck and arms always turned an angry red.

Vann had risen by sheer drive, vitality and curiosity. After one year of college he had enlisted at the age of eighteen, and became a B-29 navigator at the end of World War II. In 1950 and 1951 he commanded the first air-borne Ranger company to be sent to Korea, specializing in actions behind enemy lines and against North Korean guerrillas who were trying to harass UN forces behind our lines. After Korea the Army sent him to Rutgers to teach the ROTC units there; he learned as well as taught, going to night school and receiving his B.S. degree. Then he was assigned to the University of Syracuse (the Army is very good about encouraging its people to pick up extra degrees), where he got an M.A. in business administration and all the credits necessary for a Ph.D. in public administration. (He has written one thesis, which is all he lacks for the degree, but is not satisfied with it.) He also attended the Army's Command and General Staff College.

Vann is a blunt, essentially conservative, at times almost reactionary man. One of the ironies of Vietnam was that at a time when the Pentagon and other elements unhappy with our reporting were claiming privately that the foreign correspondents in the country were a bunch of liberals who opposed Diem on ideological grounds, much of our information came from men like Vann.

Vann had volunteered for duty in Vietnam. Once there, he had shaken a desk job; then, knowing that he was to replace Colonel Frank Clay in the Seventh Division, he had gone on as many helicopter missions in the Delta as possible while preparing to take over; by the time he left Vietnam he had participated in more than two hundred helicopter assault landings. As a result, he knew as much or more about his area of Vietnam than any other adviser—or indeed than any Vietnamese officer—that I ever met. He also *walked* through one operation every week, and even ordered his Air Force liaison officer, Major Herb Prevost, to walk with the field soldiers regularly. Hence, Prevost became that rarity in Vietnam: an Air Force man who knew something about the effect of his weapons and about the political complexities of the war.

Once a week Vann also visited the three regiments and seven provincial capitals within his bailiwick, driving to some, going by light plane to others. His Vietnamese counterparts,

Cao and Dam, who hated traveling by light plane and frequently became airsick, were delighted to have him take over these inspection tours. He frequently stayed in these local headquarters as a guest of the province chief; invariably the chief would send a girl up to the room—an attempt, Vann suspected, to get something on him and thus give the chief some leverage if there should ever be any conflict.

Vann endlessly interrogated the missionaries and priests in his area, and any time a reporter saw him, he was likely to be questioned closely about what he had seen in other parts of Vietnam.

Vann also tried to set an example by his personal courage, and his walking in the field on major operations had a considerable effect on the Vietnamese troops, who had never seen any of their own officers above the rank of captain in the field. But the walks had another purpose: they were a futile attempt to shame Vietnamese officers into walking in the paddies too. What Vann, and many others like him who tried similar tactics, failed to realize was the power of the mandarin legacy: the whole point of being a major or colonel was that you *didn't* have to go into the field, and therefore the distinction and class separation of such officers from their juniors was much sharper than in a Western army, and the prerogatives of a high rank were more fondly cherished.

What the Americans were attempting to do, by setting examples like this, epitomized our entire problem in Vietnam. They were trying to persuade an inflexible military ally, who had very little social or political sense about its own people, to do what the Americans knew must be done, but this would force the Vietnamese officers to give up the very things that really mattered to them and that motivated them in the first place. How could anyone make the Vietnamese officers see, almost overnight, that the purpose of promotion was not primarily to separate them from the misery whence they came, but to get them to inspire or lead others?

Vann also insisted on driving his own jeep unescorted after dark in an attempt to change the Vietnamese belief that the night belonged to the Vietcong. Moreover, he ordered all his advisers to go out on at least one night operation or patrol each week; this well-intentioned directive failed, simply because many of the advisers could not persuade any troops to go with them. Eventually, at Cao's request, the colonel rescinded the order.

If Vann had any shortcoming, it was one typical of the best of the American advisers in Vietnam: the belief that the adviser's enthusiasm, dedication and effort could, through diplomatic guidance of his Vietnamese counterpart, successfully buck the system. This naïveté was the result of favorable encounters with other systems, and an overly optimistic view that in time of war common sense will prevail and allies will be inclined to agree on basic goals. This hope was doomed in Vietnam; the system was stronger than the men bucking it, particularly in the pressure of the fighting in the Delta. Tantalizingly, there was always just enough of a glimmer of success, or a transitory victory or just plain luck, to make the advisers keep trying.

We reporters admired Vann greatly, not because he gave us scoops—there are no scoops in a rice paddy—but because he cared so desperately about Vietnam, because he knew so much about his area, and because whenever we were with him we had a sense that a very real war was being fought—and not fought on a peacetime footing with peacetime hours and peacetime arrogance toward an Asian enemy. The remarkable thing about Vann, and a few others of his caliber who were fully aware of the shortcomings of the war, was that they still believed that under certain circumstances the war could be pursued successfully. This was the best kind of optimism; it was not the automatic we-are-winning push-button chant of Saigon, but a careful analysis of all the problems on both sides, and a hope that there were still time and human resources enough to change the tide.

In part, the reporters believed this too; though we were frequently criticized for being too pessimistic, I believe that a more valid criticism would have been that we were too optimistic. This is debatable, of course, but I think that anyone watching so much bravery squandered during those months could not have helped wondering what would happen if that talent were properly employed.

In the days before Ap Bac, Vann was something of a celebrity and reporters were quickly channeled to his area by the

PIO's. Later, after the atmosphere began to sour in the Delta, visiting reporters and officials were sent to the montagnard region, inhabited by primitive mountain people, where they were often initiated into a tribe, watched a buffalo being slaughtered, drank rice wine (or pretended to drink the raw liquid), received a genuine montagnard tribal bracelet, and were told, with varying degrees of accuracy, that the war was going well in that region.

The first time I ever met Vann he shook hands, told me that I was lucky because there would be an operation the next day that I could go out on, and then said, "Well, Halberstam, the first thing you'll learn is that these people may be the world's greatest lovers, but they're not the world's greatest fighters." He paused, and then added, "But they're good people, and they can win a war if someone shows them how."

Over a period of time Vann and a few officers like him taught most of the foreign correspondents the essentials of guerrilla war: why the outposts were a detriment ("They know where we are, but we never know where they are"); the danger of using the wrong weapon ("This is a political war and it calls for discrimination in killing. The best weapon for killing would be a knife, but I'm afraid we can't do it that way. The worst is an airplane. The next worst is artillery. Barring a knife, the best is a rifle—you know who you're killing"); the dangers of the American material commitment ("By giving them too much gear—airplanes and helicopters—we may be helping them to pick up bad habits instead of teaching them to spend more time in the swamps than the enemy"); the importance of the weapons exchange ("I don't think the Vietcong have any problems of recruiting; I think for varying reasons they can get all the people they want. Their problem right now is getting weapons; that's the only thing limiting the size of their units and the nature of their attacks, so unless we stop arming them we'll be in a very serious situation").

There was nothing ideological in Vann's make-up; he was simply a man of consuming curiosity and drive. He ran all the time, and he forced the young American officers around him to run just as hard, whether it was in the field or playing volleyball at the old seminary, where the Seventh Division advisers were housed. It was hard for him to compromise; he once told me that the trouble with compromise was that often it meant taking a position between something that was right and something that was wrong, with the result that you ended up with something that was neither right nor wrong. In war, Vann said, that's not good enough. It was this sense of commitment, and this unwillingness to compromise and blend in with the system—the American system, which was fast becoming a parallel of the Vietnamese—that finally brought Vann to a showdown with his superiors.

In February 1963, in the midst of the dry season, the Seventh Division was still virtually inactive. It had refused to fight at Ap Bac, and now it was refusing countless other opportunities to engage the enemy at a time of year that favored the hunter rather than the guerrilla. Our intelligence had improved, and knowledge of the enemy's whereabouts vastly exceeded the Government's willingness to act on it. For weeks the officers in the advisory group waited and fumed about the sham operations that the division was launching. Finally, in the first week of February, Vann sent a long and detailed message to American headquarters. In it he noted that there were now ten points where the Vietcong were known to be located in company strength or more; about thirty-five areas where they were known to be located in platoon strength or more; and that despite this intelligence the Vietnamese refused to act. It was a very strong and fully documented indictment.

When it reached Saigon, the message created a major controversy. President Diem was already angry with Vann because of the press coverage of Ap Bac and had urged General Harkins to remove him. Consequently, Harkins was less than enchanted with Vann; in addition, he held Vann partly responsible for the press coverage of Ap Bac. The general felt that somehow Vann should have been able to manage the outflow of news better. He was so angered by Vann's latest message that he called a meeting and designated a staff officer to investigate the report. If there were any mistakes in it, he wanted Vann relieved.

The officer spent eight hours checking the intelligence reports at My Tho. On his return to Saigon another staff meeting was held, and the officer announced that the only thing wrong with Vann's paper was that all of it was true. Harkins still wanted to relieve Vann, claiming that his relationship with Colonel Dam must be unsatisfactory. After the meeting, however, several other generals on the staff persuaded Harkins that if Vann were relieved it might seriously damage the morale of the advisory group, and that when the reporters found out about Vann's dismissal it might create a major scandal. (As a matter of fact, Vann never told any of the reporters about this; I only learned of it weeks later from another staff officer who was still angry about the incident.)

Thus began the quiet struggle between the field advisers and Harkins. Gradually others became involved, but throughout this showdown Harkins was aided immensely by the traditional pressure an army places on its younger officers not to contradict a superior.

The task before General Paul Donal Harkins could hardly have been more difficult; he was a diplomat without leverage, a commander without true command authority. (For example, on Thanksgiving Day in 1962, after the largest helicopter operation of its kind had turned into a major flop—fifty-six aircraft had been used in an assault which resulted in the death of seventeen water buffaloes—Sheehan had written that the operation had taken place with the cooperation of MACV under the command of General Paul Harkins. Lieutenant Colonel Jim Smith, the PIO at the time, called Sheehan to complain about the use of Harkins' name. "Uncle Paul doesn't want his name used. We're only here as advisers," he said. Sheehan answered, "Tell Uncle Paul that he's in charge of the American Military Command here, that he's the man who released those helicopters, that those are American helicopters flown by American pilots and that his name goes in my stories.") Although Harkins was a general, his job was not so much to command fellow soldiers, but to get along with Diem and Nhu, extraordinarily difficult and suspicious allies with most unmilitary minds.

Harkins is a West Point man who served with distinction as a staff officer to General George Patton during World War II. He had been chosen for this post in Vietnam by General Maxwell Taylor, who had written the victory plan for Vietnam. Harkins was also known in Army circles as a good diplomat, a man who could be counted on to get along with a difficult man like Diem. His boiling point was relatively high and he was not likely to pound the table, speak indiscreetly to reporters or veer from the policy line. His appointment was, in fact, a substantive *part* of the policy; the hard line against Diem had been abandoned and the soft line, the tactic of smothering Diem with kindness and keeping our own people in line, was put into effect with Harkins' appointment.

The private instructions that Harkins received from Taylor are a matter of conjecture, but almost certainly they must have included the suggestion that Harkins turn his cheek to a great deal of Vietnamese mendacity. Thus, when Vann challenged the direction of the war in his area—the Seventh Division—he was raising doubts about the effectiveness of our whole policy and questioning the role of the man who had been specifically chosen because he would go along with the policy. If the Kennedy Administration, knowing that it was a tenuous policy at best, had selected as its instrument someone more likely to draw a line, there is a chance that the story of Vietnam might have been slightly different—but of course this is pure conjecture.

Even today when Washington admits to the great discrepancy between its prolonged optimism and the obviously serious existing situation, it talks in the most superficial terms about increases in terrorism and post-coup command changes, rather than facing squarely the substantive factors which, step by step, determined the pattern and rhythm of defeat.

Harkins had other problems. He had spent a lifetime in conventional-war situations and had no particular preparation for a complex and delicate political war, where the most important voices often spoke in the softest whispers. He was probably more willing to settle for the straight "kill" statistics characteristic of traditional military situations than for the circumstances which produced those statistics. One's impression was always that MACV's figures reflected what MACV wanted to hear. There was no differentiation, for instance, between Government forces killed on offensive operations and those killed in static, defensive points, though this would have been one of the truest indicators of how successfully the war was being conducted. An estimated 70 percent of the total casualties—and this remained a constant, according to American advisers—were inflicted at static points, thus proving that the attempt to mobilize the Government forces had failed.

Another factor was against Harkins: his age. He was born in 1904 and was in his late fifties during his years in Vietnam. The problems which existed in Vietnam in those days—the legacy of a colonial war, racial tension, poverty, anti-Western feeling—were alien to the experience of a military man whose formative years had been spent in far less complex situations than those created by nationalism emerging from vast colonial empires. (In this connection, I believe that part of the truly remarkable admiration for President Kennedy in much of the underdeveloped world came from the feeling of these peoples that because he was young, he *understood*.) In contrast, Lodge, though virtually the same age as Harkins, had been in politics all his life and immediately sensed the turbulence of the situation on his arrival.

The middle-aged Western military man, regardless of his nationality, has been trained in military orthodoxy and has little feel for a war practiced by guerrillas; in such a situation he clings to whatever traditional evaluations he can—such as statistics. In reality, however, statistics mean next to nothing in this kind of war and inevitably give an erroneous impression by favoring the side with the most equipment. (I remember a sharp argument between Sheehan and an American senior officer. The latter cited the high rate of Vietcong casualties and claimed that this proved that the war was being won. Sheehan insisted, however—and most guerrilla war authorities support him—that this was simply a sign that the war was being lost and that the Government was losing control of the war and the population. In a successful insurgency, he insisted, when you are doing well the casualties do not rise; they drop, and the war simply goes away.)

Consciously or subconsciously, the Army staff system tends to reflect the thinking of the senior officer. If the commander wants to see an aspect of a war a certain way, the staff will find facts to confirm their superior's thesis. "I am an optimist, and I am not going to allow my staff to be pessimistic," Harkins was quoted by *Time* in a cover story in May 1962. I remember with chilling clarity an interview I had with Harkins about the outpost problem in October 1963. Colonel Basil Lee Baker, at that time the chief PIO, was present, and he spent much of the interview interjecting bits of what he considered positive news about some place in the mountains where "hundreds of montagnards had come in," or about another place where there had been "lots of Vietcong killed, and even our own people think it's pretty good." I was convinced that he was talking not to me but to Harkins, and I had a terrible feeling that the scene resembled those taking place at Gia Long Palace, where Diem had surrounded himself with carefully chosen assistants and where bad news was softened, strained, diluted and rewritten.

For such reasons MACV headquarters decided not to listen to Vann's warnings in those crucial months early in 1963. Whether by then the situation was already beyond recall is difficult to tell; the impression of some Americans then was that there was still time. But Westerners have always underestimated the Vietcong, and it may be that even early in 1963 the guerrillas' capability was already far greater than was imagined and that they were simply not exploiting their full capacity.

Ignoring Vann's warnings meant two things: first, that the situation in the Delta would deteriorate even more rapidly as the Vietcong was permitted to move virtually unchallenged; second, that the split within the American ranks would grow sharper as more people realized that Vann was right. Some of these people included Ralph Harwood, head of the strategic hamlet program in the Delta; Vann's eventual successor, Colonel Larry Brady; and Lieutenant Colonel Elzie Hickerson, the military representative on a joint civilian-military investigative team in the Delta, who received sharp criticism from Major General Richard Stilwell, Harkins' young deputy chief of staff, because of Hickerson's pessimistic view of the Delta hamlet program. Finally, in September 1963, Rufus Phillips, who was in charge of the strategic hamlet program for the whole country, went to Washington to warn officials there of the critical situation in the Delta and of the rotten state of the hamlet program, thereby setting off a bitter reaction at MACV.

Throughout all this MACV insisted that the war was going well—though by mid-1963 it qualified this by stating that the war was being won more slowly in the Delta than in other parts of the country. By the fall of 1963 the line had been revised again: the war was still being won in the Delta, but—in the words of one of the PIO's—"the guerrillas had been pushed down south by successful operations in northern areas."

Shortly after Vann filed his report, pointing out the ARVN's failure to follow intelligence in the Delta, MACV and Harkins were to receive one more thoroughly documented warning. Once more it was from an impeccable source: Colonel Daniel Boone Porter, Vann's immediate superior and the corps adviser who was responsible for the entire Delta. Porter is a mild, professorial sort; there was always a briefcase under his arm, and he looks as if he was on his way to give a lecture on the use of the English language. But people who knew him said that he had been a fire-eater in the past; moreover, he was reputed to know as much about basic small-unit infantry tactics as any man in the Army. He was a dedicated, hardworking soldier, and those who knew him, Vietnamese and American alike, swore by him. Charged with the responsibility for the entire Delta, Porter had seen the vast disparity between Vietnamese potential and accomplishment; similarly, the optimism of his superiors conflicted with the danger signs he saw in the field.

In February 1963, Colonel Porter submitted his final report before going home. Friends who read advance copies warned him that it was unusually strong and suggested that perhaps he sweeten it by noting some of the progressive steps taken: the increased number of operations, better communications, better care of equipment, and so on. Porter declined; he had already noted some of the improvements in an earlier report, he was deeply concerned over current trends and he was going to write what he felt.

Before writing his report Porter consulted his two immediate subordinates: Vann in the Seventh Division and Lieutenant Colonel Fred Ladd in the Twenty-first. Though the report included ideas of both Vann and Ladd (who was as pessimistic as Vann, but whose division commander was more aggressive), it was, according to one officer who saw it, fully "Porterized" in its final form. Officers who read it considered it the most acute study of the situation ever made by an American. It analyzed the character of the enemy, the character of the Vietnamese peasants and the character of the Government officials.

According to one officer, Porter's final recommendation particularly angered Saigon. He suggested that responsible high American officers confront top Vietnamese officials and that they discuss their mutual problems. It should be done tactfully, the report said, but it must be done. "We would tell them our problems and they would tell us theirs. It was also quite detailed on the failings of some of their senior officers. I think what angered the American command was that it would be a terrible thing if the Vietnamese knew we felt like this—and of course we did feel like this, and of course they knew it," one staff officer said who read Porter's report.

Harkins was so upset by the report that he ordered all copies of it collected. At a meeting of senior advisers, according to one officer who attended, the general said that Colonel Porter's report would be "sanitized," and that if there was anything of interest in it afterward, it would be made available to them. The report was never seen again. This was highly unusual; most senior officers' reports were immediately made available in Saigon for other officers to read.

Unfortunately for us reporters, Porter was extremely close-mouthed about this whole affair; none of us learned of the incident until long after he had left Vietnam.

At about this time Harkins received still another report on the Delta, this time from a general on his staff. A friend of mine who saw it after it left MACV headquarters said that all along the margins of it were notes in Harkins' handwriting which said simply, "Vann," "Porter," "Vann again."

Meanwhile, in April 1963, an angry Vann was on his way home from Vietnam, his tour completed. Unlike most Americans who were unhappy with our role in Vietnam, he was not just a dissenter, but a dissenter armed. A business statistician by education, Vann had spent long hours documenting the failures and errors of the war in terms of meaningful statistics. He could point out that during his tour in the Delta the number of small outposts had not only not decreased, but that

despite their vulnerability and the fact that they sharply reduced mobility, there were actually more outposts than on his
arrival. He could prove that as everyone had suspected, the
province chief's political relationship with Diem had a direct
bearing on the number of troops he received. Long An, for
instance, a heavily populated province immediately south of
Saigon, in which the majority of the Vietcong incidents in
Vann's zone had taken place, had fewer troops than Kien
Phong, a thinly populated province in the Plain of Reeds,
which had less than 10 percent as many incidents. As a result,
by the end of October 1963 the Vietcong were virtually in
complete rural control of Long An.

Vann could also offer unique documentation of the charge
that Government commanders were unwilling to risk casualties with their ARVN troops; in his year as senior adviser fewer
than fifty of over fourteen hundred friendly troops killed were
of the ARVN, the best-equipped and best-armed soldiers the
Government had. This did not show, as Saigon liked to think,
that these troops were fighting well; it simply proved that they
were doing very little fighting at all. The casualties were being
suffered by the Civil Guard and the Self-Defense Corps, and
they were being inflicted in defensive positions at night.

After spending a month with his family, Vann showed up
for duty in the Pentagon in mid-May 1963. There he found
that no one seemed to be interested in Vietnam or in his
opinions on it, though he had just returned from perhaps the
most critical and certainly the most controversial area in this
country's only war. Although men of division-adviser rank
were normally de-briefed in Washington, the three ranking
Delta experts, Colonels Porter, Ladd and Vann, were not
asked to give their views. When Vann began a search for the
de-briefing officer, he was told that it was "Saigon's wish"
that he not be interrogated.

So at first the Colonel gave informal talks to a few friends,
but as word spread he slowly found himself in increasing demand among higher officers. Finally General Barksdale
Hamlett, the Deputy Chief of Staff of the Army, heard Vann's
briefing, and at the general's request the item was placed on
the agenda of the Joint Chiefs of Staff for July 8. Vann was
advised by some of the generals who had already heard him

talk that he must be more moderate, and that in particular he must be careful not to be critical of General Harkins, the personal choice of Maxwell Taylor, the Chairman of the Joint Chiefs of Staff.

By a curious coincidence the Chiefs had just heard another briefing on Vietnam by McNamara's special adviser on guerrilla warfare, Marine Major General Victor Krulak. Krulak was to play an important role in Vietnamese affairs as a special investigator, and according to him the war was going well. At this point Krulak had just returned from a brief trip to Vietnam and had written an extensive report, which was extremely sanguine about the strategic hamlet program. According to one member of Harkins' staff, the report had been prepared with the close collaboration of the MACV; in any case, Krulak was simply telling the Pentagon what it wanted to hear. Vann's feelings were well known, and when his appearance before the Joint Chiefs was scheduled, Krulak's office began to telephone Vann's superiors for a copy of his report. Vann was warned by several high officers to stall and not to let the report be seen by others until the last possible minute. His briefing was set for 2 P.M. on a Monday; at about 9:45 A.M. on the morning of the briefing he sent a copy of the report to Krulak's office.

Vann arrived very early for the briefing and waited outside the office of General Earle Wheeler, the Army Chief of Staff, in case there were any late developments or questions for him to answer. According to his wife, "He was as shined and polished as a man can get—John was really prepared that morning. There wasn't a wrinkle near him."

What follows is Vann's report of the incident, but it has since been confirmed by a member of Wheeler's staff.

At 10:45 A.M. there was a telephone call to one of Wheeler's aides in the waiting room outside the general's office. The conversation went like this:

"*Who* wants the item removed from the agenda?" asked the aide.

After a silence the aide said, "Is it the Secretary of Defense or the Chairman's office?"

There was more talk at the other end. "Is that an order or a request?" Wheeler's aide asked. Then, after listening to the reply, the aide said, "Let me get this right. The Chairman *requests* that the item be removed." He then added that he would check with General Wheeler and call back. Hanging up the phone, he turned to Vann and said, "Looks like you don't brief today, buddy."

In a few minutes the aide returned, dialed a number on the phone and said, "The Chief agrees to remove the item from the agenda."

And so the Joint Chiefs did not have to hear Vann's briefing, nor did anyone else during the brief period that he remained in the Army while waiting for his papers to be processed. On applying for retirement he was immediately placed under the strictest orders not to talk to anyone about Vietnam. After hearing the news in Saigon I cabled our Washington bureau and suggested that Rick Smith, the *Times* man covering the State Department, meet Vann and try to get the expert knowledge I knew was impossible to secure in Washington. Smith tried his damndest, and then cabled back that nothing "can persuade your friend Vann to unclam."

For whatever reasons—perhaps because he was not a general, perhaps because he lacked expert advice in how to handle and exploit a protest of this sort, perhaps because it was not an election year, or perhaps because no one was that concerned over the state of the war in Vietnam in those days— Vann's retirement caused little stir at the time. There were a few stories and interviews—one in the *Times*, an excellent story in the New York *Journal-American* and a good interview in *U.S. News and World Report*—but they were sparse, so the Pentagon was really never forced to explain why Vann had left the Army.

Colonel John Vann retired from the Army so that he could speak out on Vietnam. He took a job with an aircraft company in Denver—at a considerable increase in pay—and spent his spare time and weekends speaking publicly to all kinds of audiences about where we had gone wrong in Vietnam. Even today it is obvious that he misses the Army with all his heart. "You know you miss it, John," his wife said at the airport in Denver when I visited them in the spring of 1964. "You know you've never really been happy since you left."

Vann had done, however, what no other American official has done in defense of his convictions about our role in Vietnam: he thought that the lies and failures were serious enough for him to retire from a service that he loved. In temperament he is not the kind of man who protests or who rebels against the system—but he had become personally involved. He had tried desperately to warn his own country of what was happening in Vietnam, and he had failed. Everything that he had predicted would happen in the Delta had happened—and happened even more quickly than he had imagined.

When I left Vann in Denver last March, I remembered another airport scene—in Saigon, when Vann was going home, another frustrated and disappointed American whose tour had ended. A group of correspondents had accompanied some other officers and pilots to the airport to say goodbye to him, and in recognition of his remarkable courage and integrity, as well as for many happy hours together in the field, we reporters presented him with a silver cigarette case, signed by us and inscribed, "Good soldier, good friend." As Vann was about to board the plane, I told him that we had always been worried about writing about him and about his area of the Delta for fear of making life more difficult for him with his superiors. He looked at me with a very small, tight smile and replied, "You never hurt me any more than I wanted to be hurt."

from *The Making of a Quagmire*, 1965

"We Are Losing, Morale Is Bad . . . If They'd Give Us Good Planes . . ."

Air Force Capt. "Jerry" Shank is dead—a combat casualty of the war in Vietnam.

While he lived and fought Jerry Shank wrote to his wife and family in Indiana every chance he got—sometimes twice a day. Those letters make up a moving "battle diary" of a war in which more than 15,000 Americans are fighting and dying in combat against the Communists.

Excerpts from his letters are presented here with the permission of his widow. All references, by name, to his Air Force companions have been eliminated to spare them any possible embarrassment.

Nov. 14, 1963

. . . We're using equipment and bombs from WW2 [meaning World War II] and it's not too reliable. This is an interesting place here. Everybody works together, officers and enlisted. We're out there lifting bombs and such. Every possible time, we give the men a chance to ride. On a test hop or something like that—it gives them a little motivation. We can't take them on missions, 'cause we have to have our VNAF [Vietnamese Air Force] student pilot along. . . .

We 23 Air Force run the whole T-28 war in the Mekong Delta. This will give you some idea of Uncle Sam's part in the war. . . .

Nov. 22, 1963

Been real busy with the armament job—really makes a day go fast. Got all kinds of problems—can't get parts or books or charts describing the different bombs and systems. The Air Force hasn't used any of this equipment since Korea, and everybody seems to have lost the books. The main problem is personnel—no good officers or NCO's over here that really know their business. Most of them are out of SAC [Strategic Air Command] and have dealt only with nuclear weapons. This doesn't apply over here; what we need is someone from World War II. Some days it's like beating your head against a brick wall. . . .

Nov. 27, 1963

. . . Sunday all hell broke loose with the VC [Communist Viet Cong guerrillas]. We had a big airborne operation against them—both choppers and parachutes. I woke up at 4:30 to fly my first night attack—darker than hell. . . . By 9 o'clock in the morning we had launched 12 sorties, which is a lot for our little operation. The Viet Congs got one chopper and one B-26 that day, but we (T-28s) hurt them bad. There is far more detail to this, but I don't want to put it in a letter. . . .

I'm up to 20 missions now and am real confident in myself. I do good work, I feel like a veteran and I feel like a different man. I think I am older. . . .

I have changed my opinion about the VC. They are not ornery little fellows. They are mean, vicious, well-trained veterans. They are killers and are out to win. Although this is called a "dirty little war" and it is far from the shores of old U.S.A., it's a big, mean war. We are getting beat. We are undermanned and undergunned. The U.S. may say they are in this, but they don't know we need help over here. . . .

If the U.S. would really put combat people in here we could win and win fast. It seems to be the old story of a halfhearted effort. . . .

Dec. 4, 1963

. . . I have debated for a week and a half now over telling you of Black Sunday—Nov. 24, 1963. I'm going to tell you and, if you don't want to hear about these things again, well, say so. You do have a right to know. . . .

. . . This was not a typical day. We flew 20 sorties. But the VC hurt us bad. All in all that day, 23 airplanes were hit, one B-26 crew lost their lives, three choppers crashed. The VC won.

What they had done was pull into the little village and commit their usual atrocities, then pull out. But all they had were small arms and rifles on them. So headquarters thought they would teach this little group of VC's a lesson and sent this operation I spoke of in after them.

But the crafty little b——s withdrew from the town into foxholes and bunkers and hiding places they had been secretly building for a week. Also, they had many friends in there plus large antiaircraft guns and all sorts of machine guns. So when the first wave of troops went in, they thought it was just a routine chase of VC's. But they soon ran against the VC wall and we pilots soon discovered that they had more weapons than pistols and homemade guns. Shrewd plan—and they won.

. . . We could have won but I could write a chapter on that. I hope you were able to follow that, Connie. A lot happened that day and it happened fast and furious. It's not a good thing to tell a wife, but she has to know—no one else will say it—no one else can or will, I guess. There are no heroes over here but there are a lot of fine men—America better not let us down. We can use help. We can win, but America must come over, for the Vietnamese will never hack it alone. We've either got to get in all the way, or get out. If we get out the VC will be in Saigon the next day.

Dec. 14, 1963

. . . I do get a kick out of the Vietnamese people. They're poor, dirty and unsanitary according to our standards, but they're happy and some are hardworking. . . .

Dec. 16, 1963

. . . The VC's [Communist guerrillas] sure gave them a rough time.

The VC are kind of a Mafia. They terrorize and then they sell "insurance" so that the people will not be harmed again. They strike especially villages where Americans have been seen. They terrorize these villages and then blame it on Americans by saying, "If Americans hadn't come to your village, we would not have plundered and killed, so if you don't want it to happen again, pay us money and don't let Americans into your village."

So you see, they gain from this. First of all, they get money or food; secondly, they instill a dislike for Americans—dirty b——s! But I do like the Vietnamese I've met and talked to. They are friendly, happy, and childlike—good people. . . .

Dec. 21, 1963

. . . We got a briefing today of the total result of that operation on 24 November. I'll repeat it briefly.

The air power got credit for 150 to 200 killed. No one can be sure of the amount, for the VC carry off all their dead and wounded. They never let you know for sure how bad you hurt them. . . .

Anyway, there were approximately 700 VC's dug in with three 50-caliber antiaircraft guns and three 30-caliber antiaircraft guns, plus many hundreds other machine guns. They were waiting for us, but we hurt them even though we lost. We lost because we had them trapped and they got away.

It's so mixed up over here—there are over 3,000 Air Force in Vietnam, yet there are only 50 combat crews (B-26 and T-28). What a ridiculous ratio. Also, the Army tried to show the Air Force is no good and vice versa. Ridiculous. Down at Soc Trang, Army and Air Force will die for each other, but up with the colonels and generals it's a big fight for power. And most of these idiots don't even have any idea of what it's like out in combat. . . . They're trying now to find out why we pick up so many hits. The dumb b——s. We get hit more now because the VC have very fine weapons. There are Chinese over here now. . . .

I think the next few months will tell. Either the VC will quit or this will turn into another Korea. I hope it doesn't take the U.S. too long to realize this. . . .

Dec. 22, 1963

. . . Flew another mission today. We escorted three trains across no-man's land and then struck some VC's. Our FAC (the guy in the L-19 who tells us where to hit) received three hits, but we got them. I'm credited with destroying a 50-caliber antiaircraft gun. Bombed him out of this world. I guess I'm a true killer. I have no sympathy and I'm good. I don't try to rationalize why I do it. No excuses. It's a target and I hit it with the best of my skill. It's a duel; only (I repeat) only the best man wins. You can't afford to be second. . . .

Dec. 30, 1963

. . . Well, here goes. I got shot down yesterday. We were escorting a C-123 and I picked up three slugs in my airplane. One went into my fuel strainer and I lost all my fuel. I made it to a field called Pan Tho and landed safely. Me and the airplane are both okay, not a scratch except the three bullet holes. No sweat. . . .

Jan. 3, 1964

Down at Soc Trang, one of the airmen came up with the idea of putting chunks of charcoal in our napalm tanks. Napalm is a gasoline which is jelled into a mass about the consistency of honey. We carry two tanks of it, each weighing 500 pounds. When you drop it, it ignites and spreads fire about 200 to 300 feet. With charcoal in it, the charcoal is thrown about another 200 feet farther, like a burning baseball, and does further damage to VC houses. We've had it at Soc Trang and it works real well.

Tomorrow three birds are going out with one half of their load of straight napalm and the other half with charcoal napalm (Madame Nhu cocktails). A photo ship is going along to take pictures. If higher headquarters thinks it's all right, then they'll buy us the charcoal. So far we've been buying it ourselves or else "borrowing" it from the kitchen.

Jan. 7, 1964

. . . Morale's at a big low over here, especially among the combat crews. It's the same old stuff we got in MATS. No consideration for the crew.

Lost two guys today. One was a pretty good friend of mine. The only guess is—the airplane just came apart. B-26—third or fourth that have done that now. . . . Pretty bad day—just hard to find any good news to write. Can't even talk to anybody—nobody has anything to say. Just a blue day. . . .

. . . I don't know what the U.S. is doing. They tell you people we're just in a training situation and they try to run us as a training base. But we're at war. We are doing the flying and fighting. We are losing. Morale is very bad.

We asked if we couldn't fly an American flag over here. The answer was "No." They say the VC will get pictures of it and make bad propaganda. Let them. Let them know America is in it.

If they'd only give us good American airplanes with the U.S. insignias on them and really tackle this war, we could possibly win. If we keep up like we are going, we will definitely lose. I'm not being pessimistic. It's so obvious. How our Government can lie to its own people—it's something you wouldn't think a democratic government could do. I wish I were a prominent citizen or knew someone who could bring this before the U.S. public. However, if it were brought before the average U.S. family, I'm sure all they'd do is shake their heads and say tch-tch and tune in another channel on the TV. . . .

Jan. 9, 1964

. . . Had a good target today finally. Felt like I really dealt a blow to the VC. On my second bomb I got a secondary explosion. This means after my bomb exploded there was another explosion. It was either an ammo dump or a fuel-storage area. Made a huge burning fireball. You really can't tell when you roll in on a pass what is in the huts and trees you are aiming at. Just lucky today, but I paid them back for shooting me down. . . .

Jan. 15, 1964

. . . Another B-26 went in yesterday. Nobody made it out. A couple of guys I knew pretty well "bought the farm." . . .

One of the new guys busted up a 28 (T-28) also yesterday. He thought he had napalm on but he had bombs. So at 50 feet above the ground he dropped a bomb. It almost blew him out of the sky. But he limped back to Bien Hoa and crash landed. The airplane burned up, but he got out all right. . . .

. . . That news commentary you heard is absolutely correct—if we don't get in big, we will be pushed out. I am a little ashamed of my country. We can no longer save face over here, for we have no face to save.

We are more than ever fighting this war. The Vietnamese T-28s used to come down here to Soc Trang and fly missions. But lately, since we've been getting shot so much, they moved up north. I kid you not. First they didn't want to come to Soc Trang because their families couldn't come. Second, because they didn't get enough per diem [additional pay]. Third, because they didn't want to get shot at. There were a couple of more reasons, but I can't remember them. These are the people we're supposed to be helping. I don't understand it. . . .

Jan. 20, 1964

. . . I have never been so lonely, unhappy, disappointed, frustrated in my whole life. None of these feelings are prevalent above the other. I guess I should say loneliness overshadows the others, but that's really not true.

I am over here to do the best job possible for my country—yet my country will do nothing for me or any of my buddies or even for itself. I love America. My country is the best, but it is soft and has no guts about it at all.

I'm sure nothing will be done over here until after the elections. Why? Because votes are more important than my life or any of my buddies' lives. What gets me the most is that they won't tell you people what we do over here. I'll bet you that anyone you talk to does not know that American pilots fight this war. We—me and my buddies—do everything. The Vietnamese "students" we have on board are airmen basics. The only reason they are on board is in case we crash there is one American "adviser" and one Vietnamese "student." They're stupid, ignorant sacrificial lambs, and I have no use for them. In fact, I have been tempted to whip them within an inch of their life a few times. They're a menace to have on board. . . .

Jan. 26, 1964

. . . I've done almost nothing all week. I needed the rest very badly. I actually think I was getting battle fatigue or whatever you call it. I've got 50 missions, almost all without any kind of a break, and it was telling on my nerves and temper. I feel real good today after all that sleep. I kinda hate to go to work tomorrow, for we start two weeks of combat again. But I'm rested for it now and am ready. . . .

Jan. 31, 1964

. . . All you read in the paper is the poor leadership of the Vietnamese, but we are just as bad. Everyone over here seems to be unqualified for his job. Like me—I'm a multi pilot, but I'm flying TAC fighters. We have no fighter pilots in our out-fit. I'm not complaining, but, if the Air Force was serious, they would have sent over experienced fighter people. The same on up the line.

Feb. 2, 1964

. . . I'm getting to like Vietnam. Maybe I didn't say that right. I think it is a pretty country. These little villages in the Delta are about as picturesque as you'll find. Tall palm trees, fields of rice, and all kinds of flowers. The people seem happy enough, if it wasn't for the terror of VC raids. . . .

Feb. 6, 1964

. . . We scrambled after a fort under attack. We hit and hit good, but it got dark so we headed up here for Bien Hoa. Pretty hot target and we both were hit. Coming in here to Bien Hoa they warned us that VC were shooting at airplanes on final approach. Well, we made a tight, fast approach and held our lights (it was pitch black) until almost over the end of the runway. I forgot my landing gear and went skidding in a shower of sparks down the runway. Airplane's not hurt too bad. I'm not even scratched. My pride is terribly wounded. That was my 62nd mission. I thought I had it "wired" after that much combat experience. Then I go and goof so badly. . . .

Feb. 17, 1964

All B-26s are grounded, so we are the only strike force left.
. . . A B-26 crashed at Hurlburt last week. Another came with the wing just coming off. Finally the Air Force is worried about the airplanes—finally, after six of my friends have "au-gered in."

Feb. 21, 1964

. . . Tuesday evening —— —— got shot down. He fell in his airplane next to a Special Forces camp and got out without a scratch. The airplane burned completely up, though. [Another airman] was going in on his seventh strafing pass and never came out of it. Don't know what happened—whether he got shot or his controls shot out. That was two airplanes in two days. Kind of shook us up.

Not only that, the B-26s have been grounded since Monday because the wings came off one again at Hurlburt. So after the last crash the whole USAF fighter force is down to six airplanes. This should set an example of how much Uncle Sam cares. Six airplanes. Might as well be none.

. . . Rumor now is that B-26s will fly again only with greater restrictions. . . . I'm pretty well fed up. Poor B-26 jocks are really shook. That airplane is a killer.

Feb. 24, 1964

. . . We're down to five airplanes now, all of them at Soc Trang. We have actually got nine total, but four are out of commission because of damage. The B-26s aren't flying yet, but they've been more or less released. I don't know what U.S. is going to do, but whatever it is I'm sure it's wrong. Five airplanes can fight the war—that's just ridiculous. Tell this to my dad. Let him know, too, how much the country is letting everyone down. . . . We fight and we die but no one cares. They've lied to my country about us.

Feb. 29, 1964

. . . We've got a new general in command now and he really sounds good. Sounds like a man who is out to fight and win. He's grounded the B-26s except for a few flights. But they have to level bomb, not dive bomb—no strain for the aircraft that way. He has ordered B-57s (bombers—jets) to replace them, and has asked for immediate delivery. He has also demanded they replace the T-28s with the AD-6. The AD-6 is a much more powerful single-engine dive bomber. It was designed for this type of work and has armor plating. We are pretty excited about all the new airplanes. We can really do good work with that kind of equipment. . . .

March 13, 1964

McNamara [Secretary of Defense] was here, spent his usual line, and has gone back home to run the war with his screwed-up bunch of people. We call them "McNamara's Band." I hope and pray that somehow this man does something right pretty soon.

Just one thing right will help immensely. He did send a representative over here. All he did was make the troops sore.

One of our complaints was that we can't understand the air controller, so he suggested that we learn Vietnamese. We said we didn't have that much time, so he suggested we stay here for two years. A brilliant man. He's lucky to be alive. Some of the guys honestly had to be held back from beating this idiot up. This man McNamara and his whole idiot band will cause me not to vote for Johnson no matter how much I like his policies.

McNamara is actually second in power to Johnson. But, as a military man, he finishes a definite and decided last—all the way last. . . .

Rumors are fast and furious. Nothing yet on B-57s. Rumors that B-26s are all rigged up with extra fuel tanks for long overwater flights. B-26 should never fly again, even if rejuvenated. Also a rumor that B-26 pilots will get instruction in the A-1H—another single-engine dive bomber. All is still in the air—all rumors. . . .

March 22, 1964

. . . Been flying pretty heavy again. We've only got 20 pilots now and 11 airplanes. It keeps us pretty busy. Also got two more airplanes they're putting together in Saigon, so we'll soon be back up to 13 airplanes again. Hope these last for a while. . . .

That was Captain Shank's last letter. He was killed in combat two days later.

U.S. News & World Report, May 4, 1964

Christmas Eve Bomb In Saigon

by Beverly Deepe

SAIGON.

FOR A SECOND at sunset, at exactly 6 o'clock, Saigon stood still yesterday. Every one knew it was a black Christmas.

Four American nurses in silk cocktail dresses waited for an elevator in the lobby of the American officers billet where they were to eat Christmas Eve dinner. Suddenly they stopped, turned around and soon began treating a flow of wounded. Their brocades became bloodied; they never ate dinner.

A powerful terrorist bomb had ripped through the billet in the center of the city as the officers prepared to celebrate. At least two Americans were killed.

American officials here said 107 other military men, including 63 Americans—most of them field grade officers—were injured. The casualties were the most numerous of any single instance of terrorism here and compared with losses in major battles in South Viet Nam.

Not all the men had returned to quarters when the bomb went off at 6 p.m. (5 a.m. New York time) or the casualty toll might have been higher.

The bomb—which U.S. officials said must have contained at least 100 pounds of explosives—was the biggest and most powerful ever exploded against Americans in Saigon. Presumably it was set off by the Communist Viet Cong guerrillas, who had threatened fresh outbreaks of terrorism against Americans during the Christmas season. Security forces already were on full alert at Saigon airport where intelligence sources said three Viet Cong battalions were massed nearby for a mortar attack.

The explosion occurred in the ground floor garage of the building, catching many men dressing for a big party to be held in the popular rooftop officers club and mess.

Fire roared through the first three stories of the seven-story bachelors quarters, called the Hotel Brink, after the blast. Windows within a half-mile area were shattered, terrifying many of Saigon's Roman Catholics finishing up their Christmas shopping. Bleeding children, gashed by flying glass fragments, stood screaming on the sidewalks.

The U.S. Armed Forces Radio Station on the ground floor of the billet, which feeds programs to American servicemen throughout South Viet Nam, was shattered. But it went back on the air within an hour, broadcasting from a secret transmitter. Nine military vehicles on the ground were destroyed and 15 damaged. Sidewalks were splattered with blood, and debris, including heavy truck tires, was hurled through the air.

"I was in a printer's shop," an American sergeant related. "Just as the foreman pushed a button to signal the workers to go home we heard this crackling explosion.

"I rushed into the street and saw this mushroom cloud. It was pink." He laughed at the incongruity. "It was the same color as the sunset. Then the pink cloud became black."

In the rubble searchers found the body of a lieutenant colonel. Earlier, a U.S. civilian died in a hospital. Identification was withheld pending notification of kin. Authorities said more bodies might be in the rubble. None of the injured Americans was expected to die.

The Defense Department in Washington called the bombing "one of a series of apparently terroristic actions which have taken place over there," and said it was "extremely regrettable."

Late last night a Vietnamese plainclothesman seized a Vietnamese youth near the billet with what appeared to be a plunger for a detonator. He was taken away in a military jeep for questioning. Several other people also were picked up for interrogation by Vietnamese police.

The explosion was the bloodiest terrorist attack since Viet Cong guerrillas blasted the Bien Hoa Air Base in a mortar barrage Nov. 1. It climaxed a year of anti-American attacks—the bombing of a ball park Feb. 9, killing two and injuring 23; the bombing of a Saigon movie Feb. 16, killing three; the sinking May 1 of the U.S. Aircraft Ferry Card and the bombing of a sight-seeing crowd May 2 at the site of the sinking, injuring 8.

Military police said yesterday's explosion was so great the bomb could only have been carried into the garage in a vehicle. They speculated it was a jeep. Nothing was found of one parked jeep but the bumpers and a frame.

The blast broke windows of the United States Information Service conference room 200 feet away, where Saigon newsmen were meeting with press officers, and knocked out windows of the fashionable Caravelle Hotel across a mall and the Continental Hotel alongside.

Maj. Jack G. Pruett of Keene, N.H., deputy U.S. provost marshal, said:

"I was just driving up to the compound gate in my car when the thing went off. There was a blast and a fireball, with things flying everywhere."

Burning trucks in the garage set off a chain of explosions as their gas tanks went off. Police cars and ambulances caused a traffic jam in downtown Saigon and some of the wounded—several still dressed in shorts because they had been washing up—turned to taxicabs to get to hospitals.

Some soldiers braved the inferno of the building's parking lot and pushed cars and trucks away to forestall further explosions while others raced through the building's 100 residence rooms to check casualties, even while firemen fought the flames.

"I was pouring myself a Christmas toddy—a brandy and soda—when all of a sudden the bottom fell out of the glass," related one U.S. Navy officer. Three minutes later, he recalled, he picked himself up from the floor, climbed over the wreckage of his bed and door and staggered into the corridor.

One Army officer said he was drying himself after a shower when "all the windows came in on me."

Maximum security precautions went into effect throughout Saigon.

The Brink Hotel, named after the late Brig. Gen. F. G. Brink, who served as military adviser to the French here in 1952, is surrounded by a concrete wall, topped with 12 feet of wire netting. Atop the wire netting is barbed wire. Its gate is guarded 24 hours a day by three-man teams. Searchlights light up the area at night.

As night fell, Maj. Robert Schweitzer of Chicago sauntered across a plaza in sweaty fatigues and in combat boots. He carried his carbine in one hand; the other was bandaged.

"I came in from the street to help the wounded and got caught in the second series of explosions," he said.

Leaning on the fender of an ambulance, the major said that "all day long I helicoptered around Binh Long province. That's near the Cambodian border where the war is more honest."

He slid into the ambulance. "I was going to go to mass tonight," he said. "And I'm still going."

New York *Herald Tribune*, December 25, 1964

Befuddled in Asia

by Russell Baker

WASHINGTON, March 1—President Johnson, the papers say, has a pocket full of polls which show overwhelming public support for his policy in Vietnam. Question: Who is responding to the President's polltakers?

In the first place, it is almost impossible to find out what United States policy is in Vietnam, unless you are the kind of person who can get an all-night bull session with Dean Rusk or McGeorge Bundy.

In the second place, even if you can find out what the policy is, this is the most dangerous possible moment to be caught with an opinion about it.

"Look at it this way," urged a veteran Senator who has survived every major political engagement from Pearl Harbor through Panmunjom to the Congo. "Whatever the policy is will lead to either war or peace.

"If it leads to war, and the war goes badly, people who now approve of the policy will be tarred as warmongers. If the war goes well, people who now disapprove of the policy will be vilified as fainthearted patriots.

"On the other hand, if the policy leads to peace, it will mean negotiation with the Communists. If the settlement is popular, people who now disapprove of the policy will be denounced for stupidity. If the settlement is unpopular, people who now approve of the policy will be investigated as dupes of Communism."

The trick, the Senator pointed out, is to be right when it counts. This is the period after the dust has settled, when votes are being tallied and people found to have had the wrong opinion when the outcome was uncertain are being carted up to Capitol Hill in tumbrels.

The Senator refuses to have an opinion of his own about Vietnam even before his wife in the privacy of their breakfast nook. "One way or another," he explains, "Vietnam is bound to have an outcome. When that outcome is clear, I will not only have an opinion about what should have been done, but an opinion that will be proven right by history and public opinion."

To check on how widely this cynicism has infected the community, a private poll was taken last week in Washington's best informed drawing rooms. Here are the results:

Question: Do you approve or disapprove of the United States policy in Vietnam?

Approve: 4 per cent. Disapprove: 3 per cent. Undecided: 18 per cent. Confused: 52 per cent. Refused to talk to polltakers: 21 per cent. Threatened to strike polltaker: 2 per cent.

Those who had firm opinions were asked to explain them. Among people who approved, the most frequent explanations were: "Hate Communism." "Must stop gold drain." "Want peace." "If Tshombe falls, chaos will follow." "President Johnson reminds me of John Wayne."

Among the disapprovers, frequent responses were: "Hate Communism." "Ought to teach Sukarno a lesson."

The big confused bloc felt, on the whole, that while there probably was a United States policy on Vietnam, it would be hopeless for them to try to understand it in the limited lifetime available to them.

As one confused respondent put it, "Look, I'm only human. For the last three years, I've been laboring to get a firm understanding of policy in the Congo and I think I'm getting close. But Vietnam? A man doesn't have that many years."

Encouragingly, 60 per cent of the total sample showed no lack of courage about having an opinion. The confused simply thought it beyond their ability. As for those who approved or disapproved, it was clearly beyond their ability too.

Senators looking forward to the investigations that will eventually come are dispirited by the low number (7 per cent) of people now holding opinions. "After we nail the President, Rusk and McNamara," one of them complained, "the hunting is going to be mighty scarce."

The New York Times, March 2, 1965

Marines Get Flowers for a Tough Mission

by John Flynn

DA NANG, SOUTH VIETNAM
THE TWO battalions of Leathernecks came into Da Nang—one by cargo plane, one by sea—almost with an air of release. One battalion had been on board its ships off Vietnam for more than a month and had cruised closer and farther from shore in rhythm with subsequent crises. "You get damn tired floating around in circles," said Brig. General Frederick Karch, the unit commander.

The Marines had spent much of this sea duty boning up on Vietnam, its people and their customs. "If you come into something like this," commented General Karch, "the last thing you want to do is get somebody mad."

The orientation came in handy. As the Americans waded ashore, children broke through lines of Da Nang police to yell "O.K.!"—the only English expression they know. And just as the Marines were earnestly digging in along the beach, setting up a defense line against the kind of greeting for which their conventional training had prepared them—an attack by the Vietcong—along came some pretty Vietnamese girls with garlands of flowers. General Karch observed the amenities and dutifully pulled some of his men out of their foxholes to be decorated. Happily, the Vietcong did not choose the moment to attack.

Thus officially welcomed, the troops turned to the business of bringing tanks, bulldozers, advanced radar equipment and tons of C-rations ashore through a five-foot surf. The Vietnamese had turned over buildings near the landing strip to the Americans and these were quickly swabbed out and converted into a headquarters.

Wherever they stopped, even for a few minutes, the Marines dug in as protection against mortar fire. This is a precaution the Vietnamese troops have seldom used, which explains some of their casualties.

The V.C., as always, are never far away; the planes that brought in the battalion from Okinawa were shot at as they made their landing approach. General Karch plans an aggressive defense. His men are already clearing hills that the V.C. might try to use as vantage points. Helicopters patrol the perimeter to spot enemy activity. And Marine sentries, unlike the Vietnamese, are standing their posts, not sitting.

There have been reports that the Communists are sneaking in heavy artillery pieces to increase their shooting radius around the base. "If the clowns do that," Karch growls, "we'll just have to move out to the next ridge."

Life, March 19, 1965

Protest, Learning, Heckling Spark Viet Rally

by Roger Rapoport

"GET The Daily out of Viet Nam. Defoliate the Arb. Deflower the Thetas. Stop the senseless waste of human beings. Close the Union Pool."

The sign stood high above a midnight Diag throng at Wednesday night's teach-in. But aside from the few sarcastic onlookers most of the shivering crowd of over 2000 listened closely to Prof. Kenneth Boulding of the Economics Department saying, "The poorest peasant in Viet Nam should have as much right as the richest American. The world has become much too small and crowded for what we are doing."

The midnight rally was the highlight of the 12-hour marathon teach-in.

Nearly 3000 students came to hear one or more of the lectures or take part in the seminars held in Auditoriums A, B, C, and D of Angell Hall as well as six Mason Hall classrooms.

"We only expected 500 students," said Prof. Arnold Kaufman of the Philosophy Department, one of the 200 faculty members who planned the event.

Women were allowed all night permission to attend the teach-in and as Jared Stammel, '68, remarked, "This undoubtedly gave a big stimulus to the event."

By 7:45 p.m., 15 minutes before the teach-in began, Auditoriums A, B, C, and D of Angell Hall were packed to the walls.

Carl Oglesby of the speech department told students that revolutions in nations like Viet Nam may be "inspired by the monied few who exploit their power by universal bureaucratic corruption, governmental indifference to the condition of men, police-state suppression of honest dissent, no work, and no wages."

142

Three bomb scares forced evacuation of Angell Hall and an early start for the midnight Diag rally. Hecklers abounded in the crowd, like the one athlete who came dressed in an Alabama football shirt (No. 55). A group of 75 students marched through the crowd chanting "Better dead than Red." One sign read, "All the Way with LBJ"—underneath was a huge black bomb.

Nearby a student said "this thing isn't fair at all. They aren't presenting the other side. These people want another Munich." One of the faculty leaders quipped to a friend, "That guy is going to enlist tomorrow."

One student remarked, "Just look at who is leading this thing—the philosophy and psychology department. You don't see any political science people here—do you?"

At the back of the crowd a sophomore was parked on a Honda—his girl friend seated behind him. "I'd never really thought very much about this," he said, "but after tonight I think we should get out of Viet Nam."

A few feet away the Fishbowl was overflowing. Amidst the arguing and folksinging students, there were bulletin boards full of clippings on Viet Nam, 50 cent buttons asking to "Stop the war in Viet Nam," and a protest petition to President Lyndon B. Johnson.

In the midst of the turmoil was a boy collecting money for the United Jewish Appeal.

Many of the students wading through I. F. Stone's rebuttal to the State Department's "white paper" or talking to teachers did not appear to be activists. Many came—it seemed—for curiosity's sake.

In the early morning seminars were held. The topics were not planned. They were led by students and centered around such issues as student involvement and alternatives to student policy.

One professor noted that "We are to blame ourselves for the Viet Nam predicament, for we were silent and did not let our voices be heard."

Ironically, it was Republicans who came to the defense of President Johnson's current Viet Nam policy.

Chairman Albert Gamson of the psychology department noted that many sign carrying hecklers, "Came into our seminars and engaged in intelligent debate. This was our purpose: to promote serious examination of United States' policy."

Gamson added, "I learned something I should have known, how bright and serious our students are. The closeness between faculty and students was most moving."

Gamson said the faculty committee will send a delegation to Washington on April 8, 9, and 10 to ask legislative action on Viet Nam policy. They also plan to support a march on Washington April 17.

One of the sit-in guest lecturers, Arthur Waskow of Washington commented, "This teach-in is in the true spirit of a University where students and faculty learn from each other and not from the calendar."

During a 3 o'clock coffee break, many of the students relaxed over a game of bridge or merely informally discussed the night's events. A second set of seminars began at 4 a.m.

At Room 443 Mason Hall more than 60 students took seats, sat on the floor, or craned their necks inside the door to hear Prof. Prithjof Bergmann of the philsophy department speak.

Earlier that evening he had said, "We must allow the Vietnamese to be governed by the government they have chosen themselves—the Viet Cong."

By 6 o'clock 325 students gathered for the final sessions. One speaker said that the teach-in had illustrated a new dimension in education. He said the barriers between students and teachers had been broken, and claimed both were the better for it.

Towards the end one student rose and said, "I'm just a lowly freshman, but this teach-in shows me what a University has to be."

The Michigan Daily, March 26, 1965

After the Washington Teach-in

by Meg Greenfield

I. The Arrangers

A FEW weeks ago, Richard Mann, who teaches psychology at the University of Michigan and who is executive secretary of the Inter-University Committee for a Public Hearing on Vietnam, wrote a letter inviting Presidential Assistant McGeorge Bundy to participate in a national teach-in that the group planned to hold in Washington. Somewhat to Mann's surprise, Bundy telephoned him the next day in Ann Arbor and accepted the bid "in principle." Thereupon negotiations began between Bundy, the committee, Bundy's deputies, William J. Jorden and his assistants from the State Department's Bureau of Public Affairs, and a number of pro- and anti-administration professors, with a view to working out a suitable format for debating the government's policies and its aims in Vietnam.

In the course of three personal meetings and by way of innumerable phone calls and letters, it was agreed to by both sides that there would be no placards present in the hall that had been hired for the occasion in the Sheraton Park Hotel and also that there would be no demonstrations. The committee's negotiators assumed direct responsibility for seeing to it that no one would stamp, chant, march, or immolate himself in response to Bundy's presence. For what the committee understood to be "personal reasons" Bundy was not disposed to debate with Professor Hans Morgenthau of the University of Chicago, and he also was cool to Senator Wayne Morse. He accepted the political scientist and Asian specialist George Kahin of Cornell.

Another of Bundy's conditions was that his side be fairly represented on the panels. Thus it was that Bundy was permitted to provide a list of congenial—or relatively congenial—persons not in government from whom the committee was to choose one to speak at the morning meeting. When his first choice, the columnist Max Lerner, demurred, Bundy submitted the names of Wesley Fishel of Michigan State, John P. Roche of Brandeis, and Arthur M. Schlesinger, Jr., formerly of Harvard. Of these, the committee selected Schlesinger.

While Washington has experienced just about every other conceivable kind of protest in the past, it was clear to those in charge for the government side that the new technique required new and rather elaborate responses. Accordingly, the government's spokesmen were chosen with great care for their academic credentials. Many of them attended strategy sessions in the office of William Jorden, who among other duties runs a sort of State Department speakers' bureau. The bureau attempts to counter the charge of governmental unwillingness to discuss Vietnam by sending government representatives to campuses around the country, where they are then denounced as "truth squads" and "propagandists." Between them, the State Department and the White House are said to have requested (and been granted) more than three hundred tickets out of the several thousand available for the affair, and reporters did believe they discerned a pronounced and atypical enthusiasm for the government's position in the first four rows of the cavernous hall. The department had also rented the hotel's Franklin Room for the day, in the privacy of which a number of edgy-looking persons stood about waiting to meet any research emergencies.

The arrangers for the other side—chiefly teachers from the University of Michigan—were spread through a suite of stencil-littered rooms elsewhere in the hotel. There, by midweek before the Saturday event, a reporter could wander pretty much at will and observe them making such snap decisions as whether or not to continue a crucial telephone conversation with a television representative at the risk of failing to meet the plane of the Sovietologist Isaac Deutscher, who was flying in from London for the occasion. Unlike the government side, the teach-in leadership had taken its support where it could find it, and whether by reason of an excess of democracy or as a result of other pressures, it had done little or no co-ordinating or even previewing of its speeches. Thus, there was considerable surprise in the hall when Deutscher rose at the opening meeting and delivered a classical attack from the Left on Stalin for failure of revolutionary zeal. Press accounts of this remarkable episode tended to dwell upon Deutscher's physical appearance—his gestures, his beard, his resemblance to Lenin. And while such observations may have been superficial, it is nonetheless true that within minutes of embarking on his Trotskyite discourse, Deutscher had so utterly transformed the ballroom into some remoter hall in time and space and had worked such tricks upon the imagination that one expected him to be interrupted in mid-sentence by a bearded figure rushing onto the stage with an ax.

For all its more careful planning, the government side is said to have undergone a few surprises of its own, among them the speech of Arthur Schlesinger, who in turn seemed somewhat taken aback by the crowd's reaction to him. In establishing his independence of the administration, he dealt what many considered to be a superabundance of blows at Dean Rusk, the White Paper, the Dominican action, and the decision to become involved in Vietnam after the signing of the Geneva accords. Not that any of this seemed to make more palatable to the audience his arguments against a U.S. withdrawal from Vietnam or his declaration that the intellectuals of South Vietnam were not allied with the Vietcong and that withdrawal would mean "betraying people like ourselves" there. When Schlesinger had finished his remarks, members of the audience, bursting with impatience, lined up six deep at various microphones to present him with their many-parted questions of rebuttal. "When I hear questions like that, I begin to wonder whether Mac Bundy might not be right," he growled at one point to a full accompaniment of boos and hisses. "What kind of audience is this?" he murmured when he came down off the stage.

II. The Participants

The audience of course was preponderantly academic, both by profession and in style. Everyone on both sides seemed to have a favorite historical analogy at the ready, excessively courteous titles were dispensed ("Mr. Ho Chi Minh"); the grim and sidewise joke, particularly as it was offered up by Morgenthau ("the noble war we are fighting," the "poor victim of aggression"), rarely failed to get a laugh. And, not surprisingly, people who had traveled hundreds and even thousands of miles to register a protest were overwhelmingly inclined to the view that (1) the government was acting out of unexampled malignity and (2) it had caused us to be hated with renewed fervor around the world. Indeed, the mere expression of either of these sentiments tended to produce an outpouring of cheers and applause that went beyond agreement to something like exultation and which was reminiscent of nothing so much as the happy automatic shout with which New York's Democratic party workers in the election of 1960 used to greet Carmine De Sapio's every dark announcement that the nation's economy was on the verge of collapse.

Among the sponsors and supporters of the teach-in were veterans of the peace movement, which has primarily concerned itself with disarmament in the past decade and which has focused rather suddenly and late on the problem of Vietnam—A. J. Muste, Seymour Melman, Arthur Waskow, Kenneth Boulding, Herbert Kelman, Staughton Lynd. Some, such as the economist Paul Sweezy, who in 1949 was arguing the perniciousness and futility of the Marshall Plan at the Waldorf-Astoria world peace conference, have been making their dire predictions at these conventions for almost twenty years. Others who were present in large numbers probably weren't twenty years old—students from high schools and universities in the Washington area. The meeting was notable for the dearth of big names from the world of arts and letters and even more notable for its heavy weighting of sociologists, physical scientists, and, above all, psychologists. There were, for instance, 181 professors of psychology as compared with seventy-eight political scientists in the roster of teach-in sponsors.

Despite the emphasis that the teach-in's leaders placed on facts and expertise, it remained essentially an apolitical—or even an anti-political—affair. Speaker after speaker professed not to understand why, if the government was engaged in negotiations, it could not tell the people all about them. Much

of the argument seemed to be based on a psychiatric explanation of the behavior of Communist countries coupled with
a kind of mote-and-beam moral logic by which the United
States was disqualified from making even the simplest political
judgments. As one of the organizers of the teach-in, Professor
Anatol Rapoport, put it in the course of an interview, "Is it
up to us to say who is a Communist and who is not?" The
world whose outline had emerged by the end of the day's
discussions was one without people or politics but only the
reality of "social and economic forces." One of the heartiest
laughs the audience enjoyed, in fact, was at the expense of a
pro-administration panelist who went so far as to suggest that
revolutions were fomented by revolutionaries. Revolutions,
the counterargument ran, were fomented by "forces" which
were regularly exacerbated by us. "Terror on our side," said
Professor Stanley Millet of Briarcliff, "accounts for all that has
happened in Vietnam."

On the occasions when speakers for the government side
attempted to question the moral character of some of the protesters' positions, however, the protesters took shelter in a
sudden hardheaded practicality. To the observation of Professor Wesley Fishel of Michigan State University that he could
not see why they were so eager to hand sixteen million people
over to Communism, Kahin quickly replied that no one was
"eager" to do that, but one had to be "realistic." Professor
Mary Wright of Yale even found evidence of some sort of
superior life adjustment on the part of the government's critics, who were "more able" than the government spokesmen
"to accept the fact" of Communism's inroads. As the day
wore into night and a kind of combined exhaustion and stupefaction overtook the assemblage, the statements seemed to
become ever more extreme and improbable, ending with a
post-symposium outpouring from the floor. "We in the West
are irrelevant," one man sternly announced. And a young
woman associated with the American Friends Service Committee related the impression that she and Seymour Melman
had gained after a recent interview with Secretary of Defense
McNamara. There was "no question in our minds," she said,
"that the President is advised by men of unparalleled arrogance, stupidity, and incompetence." There was applause.

III. Teaching In

In an appeal for public support, the organizers of the national teach-in were at pains to point out that sponsorship of their effort implied "only a deep concern with the present situation in Southeast Asia and a conviction that questions related to peace and war should be open to responsible debate." The description could probably fit the position of any number of government supporters, and it surely was broad enough to include almost all the participants in the teach-in—from those at one end who seemed genuinely curious and troubled to those at the other who were raising money for medical supplies for the victims of "U.S. aggression." One of the built-in problems of the new movement, however, seems to be its indiscriminate generosity in granting critics of every persuasion of the government's activities in Vietnam a home within its ample tent. The dangers of the practice—diffusiveness, pointlessness, and the final lack of any coherent and identifiable argument—all seemed to be realized at the end of fifteen hours at the Sheraton Park. Nor did the combination of protest and analysis develop as a particularly happy one. The sleepless, marathon aspects of the meeting only served to blur any hoped-for sharpness of argument; selectivity and purpose were sacrificed to a public display of endurance. To whom were the participants addressing their arguments? The public? The administration? Each other? Was the teach-in a protest or was it, as announced, a chance for a great and informative debate? The question is nowhere resolved in the literature of the movement, and the participants spent a good amount of their time extolling the event as a major contribution to the process of debate in a free society. Still, it appeared unlikely that many of the teachers-in had come to Washington with a view to being taught anything at all. When I asked Dr. Rapoport on the eve of the meeting whether he entertained the possibility of changing—even ever so slightly—any of his opinions as a result of the pending exchange, he replied: "I do not feel the government has any case whatsoever."

Within the huge audience and even among the teach-in leadership, there was a fairly wide range of attitudes toward the function—particularly the future function—of the teach-in. And such differences of opinion and of degree of militancy as existed in the group seemed to be reflected in their different responses to the sudden cancellation of Bundy's appearance. Shortly after ten on Saturday morning, Richard Mann and Professor Ernest Nagel of Columbia had been called out of a meeting in the hotel and told that Jorden would take them to the White House, where Bromley Smith of Bundy's office wished to see them. Word of the cancellation started to spread around the hotel shortly after noon; and it soon was evident that there was anything but unanimity on the part of the leadership on what it meant and how to deal with it. Mann, who accepted the legitimacy of the explanation, attempted to soften the attacks Bundy's absence quite naturally provoked. A professor from Hofstra explained it all as evidence that Bundy had felt "personally threatened" by the criticism of his former colleagues. Arthur Waskow, in an impromptu press conference, averred that he had been told by a State Department official that Bundy's action was intended as an insult. "I suggest that individual press conferences take place somewhere else," another teach-in leader remarked when he came upon Waskow and the reporters outside the press lounge. Waskow finally drafted the telegram of challenge to Bundy that the group dispatched the next day, and it was somewhat milder in tone than a "minority report" version that was voted down in a sponsors' meeting that Sunday morning.

What by then had come to be known as "the question of Bundy" consumed almost as much time as the group's efforts to arrive at a conclusion on how to organize itself for political action in the future. But a good deal of time and argument was devoted to the latter problem. There were some who wanted to work through existing peace and political organizations. Others wanted to institutionalize the loose teach-in organization that had been set up. There were motions and motions to reconsider motions to set up a variety of guiding boards and committees. There were short tempers also. "I have never seen a more self-destructive act in my life," said Barry Commoner, a Washington University botanist, when a Michigan woman moved to reconsider some motion or other. How could Commoner say that, another man rose to ask, at a meeting on *Vietnam* policy of all places?

Little was settled as to future plans before the group dispersed and went back to their campuses. But it was clear that they had some decisions to make on how to bring their influence to bear on Washington, and that their problem was not unlike some of Washington's own—particularly the one the group had theoretically assembled to consider. "The administration won't talk to us," as one professor solemnly warned his colleagues, "unless we have some strength."

The Reporter, June 3, 1965

Eight Dedicated Men Marked for Death

by Don Moser

LOC DIEN, VIETNAM

EARLY on Monday morning, while the haze still blurs the dark bulk of Truoi Mountain off to the east, the old men walk through the village of Loc Dien. Like a line of ravens in their black formal robes, and holding their black umbrellas, they walk slowly, almost in lock step, through the pale green fields of young rice toward the house of the father of the vice chief. Behind them trudges Ngo Truy, the village policeman, looking out of place in his khakis and white sun helmet, and carrying his carbine over his shoulder. Truy is burly for a Vietnamese, but with large, dark eyes and a gentle manner that seems incongruous for a cop. He looks tired and he is, for he has been awake ever since he heard the shots at midnight. At first light he found the two bodies on a jungle path: one, the father of the vice chief; the other, a Buddhist leader. Pinned to their chests were statements accusing them of using their influence to turn the villagers against the National Liberation Front—the Vietcong. The V.C. had shot the vice chief's father through the chest, and treated the Buddhist leader with sacrilegious contempt—the whole front of his head was crushed in, and between his eyes was a bullet hole you could stick your thumb in. The head is very sacred to the Buddhists.

The delegation of old men finally reaches a clearing around the house of the father of the vice chief. It is a neat building of cement painted sky blue. Inside are a few wooden tables and benches where other old men sit, looking very formal and sage in their black robes as they sip pale tea. As Truy and the visitors enter, Chuong, the vice chief, comes out from behind a curtain at the back of the room. Chuong is not a pretty man—one of his eyes has a wandering cast—and now his face is drawn with grief, but he politely greets Truy and the others, offers them tea, and draws back the curtains.

The body of the old man, his father, lies on a wooden bed. It is wrapped in a sheet and the face is covered by a piece of paper. To the right, incense smolders; to the left, an oil lamp burns. The old men in black move forward to look.

As they do, someone from outside begins to scream. Chuong's sister, who lives in a nearby hamlet, has heard the news. Now she bursts out of the jungle, running, her mouth wide open as she shrieks, the noise rising in pitch and volume. Dashing across the clearing she stumbles, then comes on staggering, tearing off her conical hat and flinging it aside. She lurches through the door to throw herself on the body on the bed.

"*Cha oi, cha di mo? Cha di mo?*" she moans. "My father, where have you gone?" As she clutches at the body, the sheet slips aside, exposing one of the old man's hands. It is the hand of a farmer, brown, with dirt under the cracked nails, strong-looking even in death.

"Why have you left me?" the girl screams harshly. "You were innocent. Why did the Vietcong kill you?"

The country village of Loc Dien lies some 400 miles north of Saigon, near the old Imperial capital of Hue. Ten thousand people live in Loc Dien. The village consists of 13 hamlets or neighborhoods, sprawling for six kilometers along the River Truoi. Loc Dien lies in lush, tropical country, and its little hamlets are tucked away among thickets of bamboo and trees that hang with bananas, coconuts and breadfruit bigger than a man's head. Loc Dien is prosperous by Vietnamese standards, and lovely by any standard. Along with the peasant huts of lath and buffalo dung are many houses made of cement, again painted a distinctive blue; here and there throughout the village are little one-room elementary schools, and an occasional small Buddhist pagoda. Most peasants have some land of their own, and around the houses the jungle is checkered with small fields of rice, tea, corn, potatoes, and garden truck. On Loc Dien's few dusty streets, and on the jungle trails that connect the hamlets, pretty schoolgirls ride their bicycles, the long skirts of their white *ao dais* flowing gracefully behind. In the hamlet by the Bay of the Two Bridges small boys wade in the waist-deep water, beating rhythmically with bamboo poles as they drive tiny fish into the nets held by their parents. The farmers plow their fields behind hump-shouldered water buffalo, or sit for hours pedaling crude pumps which lift water from the irrigation ditches up over small dikes into the rice paddies. The wives heap their produce, in top-heavy piles that defy gravity, on the tops of rattletrap buses that run to the big markets in Hue; or they carry their goods in baskets to the market in the village, where they squat all day, amicably chatting among themselves and chewing cuds of mildly narcotic betel nut.

But Loc Dien is not so tranquil as it seems. Beneath the peaceful surface, the struggle between the government and the Vietcong goes on night and day. By day most of the village belongs to the government. But the night is a different matter. Eight times this year alone, small bands of Vietcong have come down from Truoi Mountain after dark, dragged a villager from his bed and shot him dead. Scores of other villagers have been kidnaped and taken away into the forest for political "education." The highway that bisects the village has been mined. Grenades have been thrown into the market place. Almost every day people find leaflets which the Vietcong have strewn the night before. Or they hear rumors from woodcutters who have encountered Vietcong in the jungle. Both leaflets and rumors promise future violence. Not long ago the Vietcong left a leaflet that named eight influential villagers they promised to execute—eight shown at the top of these pages. For these men, and for the villagers as a whole, fear is something one gets up with in the morning and goes to bed with at night.

The hub of the village of Loc Dien is the great steel bridge on which Highway One and the Vietnam Railway—the only lines of ground transportation between Hue, to the north, and the American military stronghold of Da Nang, to the south—cross the slow-rolling River Truoi. Just to the north of the bridge is the barbed-wire enclosure of an old French fort which now serves as the garrison for a Vietnamese army

NO. 1	NO. 2	NO. 3	NO. 4
VILLAGE CHIEF	VICE CHIEF	PROPAGANDIST	NATIONAL
DONG	CHUONG	CAO	POLICEMAN
			TRUONG

battalion. Just south of the bridge, in Loc Dien proper, is the railroad station, a small dispensary, and a cluster of metal-roofed open-front shops. Off the highway, on Loc Dien's dirt main street, is the village office. And there, on the Monday morning following the two assassinations, the chief of the village works at his battered desk. In the evening Nguyen Dong likes to go about barefoot and clad in floppy trousers and an undershirt, but now he wears sandals and a shirt neatly pressed in accordance with his high station. A limp, home-rolled cigaret dangles from his lower lip, dribbling ash on his papers as he works.

At 55, Dong is, in effect, the mayor of Loc Dien. He is a civilian. The chiefs of Vietnam's larger political units—the districts (equivalent to our counties) and provinces (equivalent to our states)—are army officers, military governors with enormous authority. Dong must answer to his district chief whose headquarters are 14 kilometers to the south, but Loc Dien itself, like all Vietnamese villages, is a little democracy. The chief, his vice chief, and the chiefs of the 13 hamlets are elected every other year by all the adults of the village. With his small staff—a policeman, a tax collector, an information officer, and a few clerks—Dong worries about everything from issuing marriage licenses to protecting his people from the V.C.

Nguyen Dong is tired. He has had a lifetime of war and public service. Between his inheritance from his father, a prosperous farmer, and the canny investment of his own salary in

| NO. 5 | NO. 6 | NO. 7 | NO. 8 |
| VILLAGE POLICEMAN TRUY | HAMLET CHIEF CACH | EX-HAMLET CHIEF HACH | EX-VILLAGE CHIEF VAN |

land, Dong has acquired two good cement-block houses, four water buffalo and six hectares (about 15 acres) of rice land. But he must find someone else to work his rice fields, since he dares not work in such an exposed situation himself. He has not slept in either of his fine houses for more than two years. Dong's name heads the Vietcong assassination list and he must sleep each night on a cot in the railway station, where all the hamlet chiefs and village officials gather. There a handful of village soldiers can guard them all. Sometimes Dong wishes he could quit his job as chief, but in the last election 90% of the villagers voted for him, and now he cannot resign. "I would lose their respect," he says simply.

Dong can hardly remember a time of serenity in Loc Dien. When he was a young man, the country was run by the French, through a puppet emperor. Late in World War II came the Japanese, harsh and unpredictable, and then Ho Chi Minh's Communist Vietminh. In 1947 the French began their attempt to push the Vietminh out of the Loc Dien area and there followed seven years of being in the middle of a guerrilla war. It was not very much different from today, with the villagers fearing and despising the French and Vietminh almost equally. Then, too, there were assassinations, night raids and reprisals. Dong's father was kidnaped by the Vietminh one night and never seen again. Six months after that, the Vietminh returned and burned Dong's house to the ground.

For a while, after the country was partitioned in 1954, the village had a taste of peace and growing prosperity. But by the late '50s, President Diem—and his detested brother and sister-in-law, the Nhus—had lost touch with the countryside. The Communists, who called themselves the National Liberation Front, became active again. The succession of coups and governmental overthrows since Diem's death have bewildered Dong and his villagers. They wonder cynically whether the Saigon government will ever be stabilized. Meanwhile, the amount of Vietcong influence in the village has grown steadily.

Dong maintains that only 5% of the villagers sympathize with the Vietcong. Only a few young men have gone off to the mountain to join them. But at night Loc Dien is so insecure that people tremble with fear every time a dog barks. Recently the Vietcong have attempted to drop mortar shells onto the Vietnamese battalion garrisoned at the old French fort—something they could do only by setting up their weapons within the borders of the village. But some of the rounds have been short and the villagers who live near the fort have had to dig fox holes and tunnels beneath their houses. On the 80-kilometer stretch between Hue and Da Nang the V.C. blow or mine the road and railway every night, so that rice and other goods imported from the south have almost doubled in price over the last few months. Now people can hardly afford to buy the food they need. The railroad-highway bridge over the River Truoi, just 50 yards from Dong's office, is a prime military target, and in the propaganda leaflets left by the V.C. they have promised to attack it. They have also promised to attack the railway station where Dong and the others sleep at night. They have promised to get an old friend of Dong's named Hach and cut him in half. And just yesterday the boy who herds Dong's water buffalo heard a rumor that the V.C. plan to throw a grenade into Dong's house to kill his wife and his children.

Dong rarely sees an American, for none is stationed in the village. But once in a while, when the battalion garrisoned across the river is home from the field, its American and Australian advisers come to Loc Dien for a glass of beer, or an American medic holds sick call for the villagers. When the Americans first came, the people feared they would be like the French. But the Americans played with the children, who soon followed them in droves, shouting "Hello, OK," and they were off-handedly friendly to everyone, not offending the villagers' pride, as did the French, by treating them like inferior beings. Now, when the V.C. leaflets say that the Americans rob the people of food and leave the hamlets with their pockets bulging with stolen bananas, Dong and the villagers laugh.

The summer heat in Loc Dien is a vicious thing. The humidity is like that in a greenhouse and the sun blasts straight down out of the sky. But despite the intense heat, Policeman Truy—whose name is fifth on the V.C. assassination list—still tramps the jungle trails, a growing splotch of sweat darkening the back of his khaki shirt as he tries to learn more about the killing of the Buddhist leader and the vice chief's father. Truy is a solid, gentle little man of 38 who is not only the village policeman but also the leader of the security platoon that guards Loc Dien against the Vietcong. His men belong to the Popular Forces—full-time soldiers who are paid very poorly by the government, and who serve in their own villages as a kind of self-defense corps.

As the morning goes on and Truy talks to the peasants, he puts together the pieces of what happened during the night. The pattern was familiar. At around 11 o'clock an unknown number of V.C. crept into the village, dressed in shorts and odds and ends of military clothing. In the space of an hour, groups of four or five of them appeared at houses, each of which belonged to a farmer of status in the village. They woke the inhabitants, tied the arms of the man of each family, tersely told wives and children to go back to their beds, and took the men out into the darkness at gunpoint. Two of the men were shot on the path outside, the others, presumably, were kidnaped.

The V.C. may, or may not, have been under the command of a V.C. leader known as Le Nang (Dung is another of his many aliases) who is reputed to be the V.C. cadre chief for Loc Dien. His job is to recruit men, to distribute propaganda and to carry out acts of sabotage and terrorism. Truy saw Le Nang just once, years ago, and knows that he is a big man, powerfully muscled, in his early 50s. But beyond that he is a shadowy, unknown figure. Truy knows about Le Nang's activities only from rumors passed among the peasants. In the past, they say, Le Nang was twice imprisoned as a V.C. suspect, but each time he managed to wriggle out and now he has government identity papers which enable him to live in a sampan and masquerade as a fisherman. He is supposed to keep weapons hidden on his boat, and to have cached many guns in a swamp nearby for a future attack on Truoi Bridge. There is a rumor, too, that he will soon attempt to recruit two more platoons for his guerrilla force from those living in the hamlets of Loc Dien, and that it may have been he who drew up the murder list of eight names.

The fact that the V.C. have promised to kill him does not bother Ngo Truy, for he has been fighting guerrillas half his life. As a partisan under the French he fought the Vietminh near Hanoi, and became a red beret—a paratrooper. He is a mild-mannered man, but he was in continual trouble with the French. Once he struck a French soldier who kept ordering him to do menial tasks. On another occasion he and a friend drove off a French soldier who was raping a village girl. In 1949 the French arrested Truy's brother as a Vietminh suspect and later executed him. His brother, Truy knows, was innocent.

There are two things in this world Truy desires and he can find no way of getting either. One is an education for his six children. But his salary from the government is only about 2,000 piasters a month—say, $20—and he cannot afford anything better than the Loc Dien's one-room elementary schools. The other thing Truy wants is a Browning Automatic Rifle. On paper, Truy has some 40 men in the village's Popular Force, but most of them are on permanent guard duty at the bridges on Highway One, and so Truy has only nine soldiers to protect the 13 hamlets. Truy can rarely count on help from the garrison across the river, for the battalion is usually on operations elsewhere in the province. Truy's own men are armed only with carbines and one Thompson submachine gun. When the V.C. do attack the railway station, Truy knows that they will come with many automatic weapons. A B.A.R. would be useful against them. That the V.C. will come when they are ready, he has no doubts.

*

On Tuesday morning, Nguyen Truong is happy. Truong, No. 4 on the assassination list, is an agent of the national police. He is stationed in Loc Dien, the village where he was born, to gather intelligence about V.C. activities and to ferret out V.C. suspects. He finds his job enormously frustrating. "How can I operate when everyone knows who I am?" he asks irritably. "And what will happen if I learn that one of my friends is a Vietcong?"

Today, though, one of the village's Popular Force members has picked up three strangers. They are children—two young girls in *ao dais* and a barefoot, ragged boy, all of perhaps 15. Though children do not need to carry identity cards—as Vietnamese adults do—when they leave their home village they are supposed to carry a paper from the chief vouching for their identity. These youngsters had nothing.

As Truong looks them over, his vulpine face is lit with pleasure. He is a small, thin man of 29. He wears his fingernails long to signify that he does no manual labor. His left arm bears a long white scar from wrist to elbow. The scar is the work of a Vietminh, who slashed him with a sharpened bamboo stake in hand-to-hand combat when Truong was a soldier with the French in 1954. Truong likes to show off the scar. He killed the Vietminh, and has never stopped hating them.

Now he begins barking questions at the children: What is your name? Where are you from? I have never heard of that place. Where is it? Why did you come to Loc Dien? Why do you say you do not know each other when all three of you were found together?

Big eyed with fright, the children mumble confused answers and dig their bare toes into the dirty cement floor of the office.

"You are lying!" Truong snaps at them. Standing before them, he waves a long bony finger beneath their noses and shouts, "You came here to try to gather information for the Vietcong!"

The children are too terrified to respond. Truong sits down and looks them over slowly, his eyes glittering. He will send them off to the district headquarters to be put in jail until their identities can be established. Perhaps they are innocent, but the V.C. have often used children as agents and Truong intends to take no chances.

Nguyen Truong would like to get the war over and done with. He wishes that the Americans would bomb Hanoi and kill Ho Chi Minh. And perhaps even take on China. "China," he likes to say, "is like a tiger lying ill in the forest. If we give her time to rest, she will become very dangerous."

Truong is also personally irritated by the war. He has been married for only a year, and he is afraid to stay at home with his wife at night. He does not even think it is safe to stay in the railway station with the other officials, and so he sleeps in the homes of friends, moving each night to a different house so the V.C. won't know where to find him.

Just across the highway from where Truong questions the children, a boy of 6 is being treated at the village dispensary. The V.C. dropped a mortar round on his house and each morning he comes to the little building to have the deep wound in his foot cleaned and dressed by Nguyen Ba, the medical officer. Now, grim-faced as the boy screams in pain, Ba hacks his way through a roll of bandage with a dull, rusted pair of scissors. They are the only scissors he possesses, and he must also use them to cut the umbilical cord when he delivers a baby. "They will hardly cut paper," he says angrily.

Nguyen Ba had only two years of medical school in Hue, but for all practical purposes he is the doctor to the people of Loc Dien. As such, though he is not on the V.C. assassination list, he can never feel entirely secure. On occasion the V.C. will direct their terror against any influential member of the community; schoolteachers and medical officers are especially vulnerable. Already one of Ba's assistants has been kidnaped and another, working in a village across the river, was assassinated.

For instruments, Ba has the scissors, an equally dull and pitted scalpel, a single pair of forceps and two syringes. He repeatedly requests new instruments from his superiors at the province capital in Hue, but nothing appears and in order to give injections he sometimes must buy new syringes out of his own meager salary. With medicines it is the same.

Ba has lived in Loc Dien for eight years. Dedicated to the

villagers, he works hard all day, and frequently gets up to handle emergencies in the small hours of the night. He knows that he can never become a real doctor, but he passionately wants to go to the big hospital in Hue for more study. "How can I do it?" he asks sadly. "There is no one to replace me."

On Friday morning, the village holds a funeral for Vo Van Diem, the man the V.C. shot through the head. Diem, a well-to-do farmer, headed the Buddhist political party in the village, and although this is a country funeral it is accomplished with all the pomp appropriate to Diem's high station. In a serpentine line that winds along the dikes by the rice paddies comes a procession of some 300 mourners: first the Buddhist youth club—the boys in gray shirts and broad-brimmed hats, then the small children carrying religious banners, a man strewing symbolic money along the coffin's path so the dead man will have wealth in the afterlife, men carrying a small shrine filled with burning incense, then the monks, stately in their orange robes, chanting mournfully and ringing small gongs, and at last the coffin, moving forward on the shoulders of the men and trailed by the wailing, sobbing sisters and aunts and nieces of the deceased, all in white robes of mourning.

The ceremony itself is a long drawn-out affair in the searing sun, with much chanting and ringing of gongs, but at last the friends of Vo Van Diem carry his coffin to the grave and begin to lower it on ropes. At this precise moment there is a loud *whump* off to the east. The children and the Buddhist youth, who have been behaving solemnly up till now, rush to the top of a nearby burial mound and stand there giggling and yelling as they watch four fighter bombers of the Vietnamese air force loose their sticks of bombs on the lower slopes of Truoi Mountain. For a minute or two the sounds are all mixed up together: the crumping of the bombs, the excited giggling of the children, the chanting of the monks, and the banshee wail of the women as the coffin of Vo Van Diem is lowered slowly into the grave.

On the afternoon of the day of the funeral, Ton That Cao holds a public meeting at a little cement-block schoolhouse about half a mile down Highway One from the Truoi Bridge. Cao is the village information officer, and it is his job to distribute government leaflets, put up patriotic posters and

banners, hold anti-Communist rallies and otherwise dissemi-
nate government information and propaganda to the people.
He is as much of a contact as the people of Loc Dien have
with the Saigon government. Today he has planned everything carefully. He has set up the battery-powered sound system on the porch of the school, and the triple-striped,
butter-yellow flags of the Republic of South Vietnam whip in
the breeze coming off Truoi Mountain. This morning Cao
had the hamlet chiefs spread word of the meeting, and now
down the road and through the rice paddies come the villagers. Most of them are from the hamlet where the two assassinations took place, and they still wear their black robes and
carry the black umbrellas they took to Diem's funeral.

A quick, intelligent man of 36, Cao has a little drygoods
shop in the market which earns him a good living. He accepted the job as Information Officer, which places him No.
3 on the V.C. murder list, not so much because he needed the
money as because his friend Chief Dong wanted him. Also,
one suspects, because he fancies himself as something of an
orator. Now, as he tells the villagers that there will be a minute
of silent meditation in honor of the two dead men, the black
umbrellas fold, the hats come off and the people stand bare-
headed and silent in the hot sun.

The meditation finished, Cao introduces his speakers: the
chief of the hamlet in which the assassination victims lived, a
representative of the old men, and finally a young boy who
represents the village youth. Each reads a short speech affirm-
ing his willingness to fight the V.C. They are inspiring and
patriotic speeches, but, of course, they should be. Cao and
the district information officer wrote them for the speakers.

When the last speaker has finished, Cao looks himself up
and down, buttons an open button on his shirt, steps to the
microphone, thrusts his fist into the air and shrieks, "Why do
the V.C. kill innocent people? Down with the Vietcong!"

"Down with the Vietcong!" the people shout back.

"Da dao Vietcong!" Cao shouts again and again, and each
time the people echo his cry. But looking down from his place
on the porch, among the shouting people here and there, Cao
sees a mouth set firm, a sneer.

*

There is one man from the hamlet where the two assassinations took place who has not bothered to attend Cao's meeting. He is Ngo Quan, a stooped little peasant of 59 with a face like a shriveled apple. While Cao and the villagers shout their slogans against the Vietcong, Quan is working in his fields a kilometer away. On the night the Buddhist leader was shot, Quan himself was dragged from his house by five Vietcong and taken off into the jungle. There the V.C. bragged to him about their recent military victories and scoffed at the Americans. Quan kept his mouth shut and listened, and in the morning the V.C. let him go, admonishing him to mind his own business, work in his paddy and forget about the government. That's all right with Quan. He never intended doing anything else.

Quan served with the French army during World War II, saw Toulouse and Marseilles and acquired a love for French carrots, but the experience did not add much to his sophistication. He cannot read or write and he does not listen to the radio. He knows the name of Ho Chi Minh and remembers Ngo Dinh Diem, but he has never heard of General Ky, the newest premier. He has never heard of Mao Tse-tung, or Lyndon Johnson. Just as he didn't care who won between the French and the Vietminh, he now does not care who wins between the government and the Vietcong. He doesn't care whether the Americans stay or leave. He needs no help from anybody. He has a little patch of land for himself, and when he needs more money he works by the day for the bigger landowners. All he wants to do is work his fields—just as the V.C. on the mountain told him.

That evening Bui Van Cach, the young chief of Su Lo Dong hamlet, loads a round into the chamber of his carbine, hooks a couple of fragmentation grenades to his belt, says goodnight to his wife and children and goes out into the jungle. Cach is No. 6 on the V.C. assassination list—for the best of reasons. He likes to fight. A handsome, dynamic fellow of 33, he was in a Vietnamese commando outfit that fought against the Vietminh, and since returning to civilian life he has lost none of his aggressiveness. Come nightfall, when the other 12 hamlet chiefs sleep in the comparatively secure railroad station, Cach and an odd little band of warriors lie in ambush for the Vietcong.

At dusk they assemble—as motley a group of irregular soldiers as can be imagined. Nine of the men are peasants, wearing shorts and sandals and conical peasant hats. And Nguyen Che, who in the daytime is custodian of the village elementary schools, has completed his nightly metamorphosis into a squad leader. Festooned with grenades and flares that he has scrounged from friends in the army, with a carbine in one hand, a swagger stick in the other and a cocked .45 in his belt, he cuts a figure that is simultaneously fearsome and absurd. But the Vietcong find nothing funny about him, and they have spread the word that for the death of Nguyen Che, or for any of the men in his squad, they will pay a bounty of 5,000 piasters.

Bui Van Cach is intensely proud of his little group. "The V.C. are afraid to come here," he says with a grin all across his round brown face. "The people in this hamlet believe this hamlet will never be attacked. The people say we are *their* men, not government men. They do not have to be afraid when dogs bark at night."

Now, in the gathering dusk, Cach and the grenade-laden Che move through the hamlet, informing trusted peasants where they will spend the night in case there is any trouble. Then, with their squad, they set out trip flares along the jungle trails to tip them off to any V.C. movements, and disappear into a patch of jungle near the hamlet border to lie in wait for whatever may come.

Later this same Friday night, as Cach and his men wait in the jungle, policeman Truy is also awake, standing beneath the banana trees near the railroad station and peering out into the darkness. Truy and his Popular Forces squad also lay ambushes for the V.C., but they have the additional responsibility of guarding the officials who sleep in the railroad station. So Truy never has enough men available to pose a serious problem for the V.C.

At midnight, after checking on his guards, Truy goes on into the railway station and stretches out on a mat on the concrete floor, his arm for a pillow. An hour and a half later he is shaken awake. One of the men from the patrol tells him excitedly that they have just spotted a strong V.C. unit moving up the highway toward the railroad station. Quickly Truy wakes the sleeping men. His nine soldiers and all the hamlet chiefs who possess weapons are posted at windows and among the trees just outside the station. He has 17 guns in all, and hopes it will be enough. The battalion from the fort across the river is away on an operation and Truy knows he can expect no help. If only he had a B.A.R., it would make a difference.

At 2 o'clock the night is shattered by the fire of automatic weapons as the V.C. attack suddenly from three sides. Bullets spit and whine off the concrete facing of the building. Truy grabs his carbine and starts firing rapidly at the points of muzzle flashes out in the darkness. Screaming, "We will cut off your heads!" the V.C. press forward three times and try to throw grenades through the windows, but each time the grenades fall short. Then Nguyen Lach, one of Truy's soldiers, falls to the ground, his skull creased by a ricochet. A few minutes later, by the light of a flare, Truy sees the Vietcong dragging a wounded comrade away and the attack ends as abruptly as it began.

Next night, the V.C. attack again. Once more they try to grenade the railway station; once more Truy and his men beat them off. But this time the attack is just a diversion. Half an hour later another band of V.C. attacks a highway bridge near the school where Cao held his meeting. But they, too, are driven off by the bridge guards.

On Monday morning, just one week after Truy found the bodies of the vice chief's father and the Buddhist leader, the hamlet chiefs and village officials hold their weekly meeting at the village office. Six of the eight men on the assassination list are there. Presiding, Chief Dong sits behind the stamp pad and bronze seal that are his badges of office. The policeman Truy is there, and Truong the agent of the national police, and Cao the information officer, and the brave young hamlet chief Cach, and even vice chief Nguyen Chuong, still in mourning with a piece of black cloth pinned to his shirt. When the Vietcong shot his father and the Buddhist leader, the act was, of course, intended as a warning to Chuong himself. As vice chief, Chuong is No. 2 on the assassination list. But since he sleeps in the railroad station and the V.C. cannot easily get to him to kill him, they killed his father instead. Unless Chuong quits his job next time the attack might be directed against a brother or an uncle. But no one in the family has asked Chuong to resign his post. It would no more occur to them to ask him to resign than it would occur to Chuong actually to do so. "I cannot refuse my duty," he says. Now Chuong hates the V.C. as never before, and at night he lies awake and thinks bitterly of vengeance.

As the village office begins to fill for the meeting, Do Cho arrives and takes his seat on one of the wooden benches set aside for the hamlet chiefs. Cho, a handsome, shock-haired man of 32, is the chief of the hamlet by the bay, the poorest of the 13 hamlets of Loc Dien. All of the people in the hamlet by the bay are fishermen who live in their sampans and own no land. Indeed, the songs the men sing as they drag in their nets often refer to the fact that the young girls all want to marry a farmer and have security, and none wishes to marry the poor fishermen.

Since the hamlet by the bay is so remote from the village center, V.C. come there frequently, even in the daytime, to take fish from the fishermen, paying them with worthless V.C. money. This year the V.C. have assassinated two men from the hamlet. The place is so insecure that teachers will not come there as they do to the other hamlets, and many of the children are illiterate.

The fishermen have almost as much trouble with the government as with the Vietcong. Elsewhere in the village, the people like the A.R.V.N. soldiers from the battalion and invite them into their houses. The men are well-disciplined, and if they steal or cause trouble, Captain Tung, the battalion commander, will put them in jail. But there are other government soldiers who patrol the bay in motor boats. When they visit Do Cho's hamlet, they beat up the teen-age boys, accusing them of being V.C., and two months ago they killed a respected fisherman merely on suspicion. The hamlet people are still bitter at his death.

Before long, all the hamlet chiefs have arrived and taken

their seats beside Do Cho on the wooden benches in the office. The room is stifling and overcrowded. A couple of years ago, a spacious new cement-block office building with several rooms was built with American aid money and cement. But the building was erected a kilometer down the highway from Truoi Bridge, and after the V.C. threw a hand grenade into it one day, everyone decided that it was too far from the village hub to be safe. Dong and the others thereupon abandoned the new building and moved back into their cramped old office near the bridge.

After Chief Dong calls the meeting to order, Truy speaks proudly of the performance of the hamlet chiefs and his soldiers when the V.C. attacked the railroad station. "The Vietcong thought we were just administrators," he says, his gold teeth gleaming. But then he tells the chiefs that they must improve the security of the village. The first project will be to cut down brush and trees around the railway station and at other key points in the village, so the V.C. will not be able to find cover for their attacks. All men in the village are expected to help, and work will begin immediately.

Then Chief Dong takes up the weekly business. From now on, he says, anyone who goes to Truoi Mountain to cut firewood will be arrested—there is too much chance of V.C. finding them there and getting information from them. And beginning this week the hamlet chiefs will collect from their people lists of friends and relatives who have gone to join the V.C., so that the District Chief will have more information about the local guerrillas. Also, the V.C. have been using young people as spies, and so from now on the young men of 16 are required to have identity cards.

Then Dong explains that he has received 13 radios from District Headquarters. The government cannot give these radios away, but the people can buy them for a very special price of 800 piasters—about $8. Those who purchase radios at this special price must tell the truth about the war to those who cannot afford radios. There are 13 radios and 13 hamlets, Dong says, but he has decided that only the secure hamlets will be allowed to buy them. Certain hamlets cannot buy radios because he fears that the people may listen to the Communist stations from Hanoi.

Dong's statement unleashes an uproar. "It is not fair!" the hamlet chiefs shout. Each hamlet must get a radio. For 15 minutes the chiefs argue violently—Do Cho, from the hamlet by the bay, most passionately of all. "Why do you do this?" he asks Dong. It is not legal. His people *must* have one of the radios.

Dong says nothing. He sits behind his stamp pad and bronze seal, sipping tea, impassive as a stone Buddha. At last he cuts off the argument sharply. "Each hamlet can have one radio," he says. "But if I learn that any person is listening to the Communist radio, I will hold his hamlet chief responsible." Dong's words carry an obvious warning. As chief, he not only has personal authority, but he has the ear of the all-powerful District Chief, and it is not wise to incur his wrath.

Immediately Do Cho is on his feet. He cannot accept responsibility for the people in his hamlet listening to the Communist radio. Under those circumstances he does not want a radio. Several other hamlet chiefs respond identically—now that they must accept the responsibility, they would rather not have the radios.

As Dong listens, his face remains expressionless. But he has won. One suspects that he never doubted for a moment that he would.

That afternoon, Policeman Truy journeys to the military hospital in Hue to see Lach, the soldier who was wounded when the V.C. attacked the railroad station. The man sprawls listlessly on a dirty sheet, his left arm and leg oddly akimbo. His wife, there to tend him, explains that the bullet which apparently only grazed his scalp has paralyzed the whole left side of his body. The doctors say he may be all right in a few months, but she does not know. Truy mumbles a few words of thanks and encouragement to the man. Then he fishes in his pocket and pulls out some crumpled piaster notes and puts them on the bed. He has collected this money from the grateful people, he explains. He picks up the money again and counts it, bill by bill. It comes to 500 piasters—about $5. He gives it to Lach's wife. Then he just stands there, his dark eyes sad. Lach is a good man and has served him well, but Truy knows nothing more to say.

*

Next morning, Tuesday, a peasant comes to the village office and tells Truy excitedly that Nguyen Da and his brother Thuan, two of the men who were kidnaped on the night of the assassinations, have just come limping out of the jungle. Truy gets his carbine and goes about a kilometer down Highway One. He meets the men just as they are crossing the road. Da hobbles painfully, supporting himself with a stick. He and his brother have been walking for two days and two nights, coming down from the vastness of Truoi Mountain, and Da's bare, brown feet are so cramped with pain that he can hardly stand. Truy accompanies the brothers home, and as their wives bring them tea and their children clamber onto their laps, they tell about their experiences.

They had been wakened by the V.C., told to get 10 days' supply of rice and hurried so much that Da had no chance to put on his sandals. Then, with their arms behind their backs, they were led into the jungle. For two days and two nights they walked, stopping to rest only for 10 minutes at a time. At last, deep in the jungle, they reached a "mind-clearing" camp—a big nylon tent where a dozen other kidnaped peasants from different villages were waiting. As the indoctrination began, the brothers were told curtly to name their crimes against the National Liberation Front. When the men failed to condemn themselves, they were harshly accused of spying and providing information to the government—in fact, Da and Thuan had never done so. "You deserve to be killed on the spot," they were told. They were paralyzed with fright. But then everything suddenly changed. "You deserve to be killed," said the V.C., "but since we are men of good will, you will simply be educated."

Now the brothers were treated with respect and courtesy by their captors. Each day a different instructor came to the camp and held class. The instructors were urbane men who wore military clothing, but they had the soft hands and the pale skin of men who do no hard work out-of-doors. None of them was from this part of the country—one sounded as if he might be from the north—but all were educated. Pleasantly, they informed the brothers that they would not be heavily guarded, but of course the Front must protect itself from government troops, and so there were many mines around the camp. It would be most unwise for the brothers to try to leave.

Never during the instruction was there any mention of Communism or collectivist ideology, but some telling blows were struck at the Americans. The Americans, one instructor sneered, change the Saigon government more often than a man changes his buffalo boy—you keep a boy to herd your buffalo for at least a year or two, but the Americans change the Saigon government every couple of months.

If the Americans are such great friends of the Vietnamese, the brothers were asked, why do their planes and helicopters destroy whole villages and kill many innocent people when there are only a couple of V.C. there?

In the end, the instructors told the brothers that they had better withdraw their support from the Americans, because soon the Americans will give up and go home—and the villagers won't be able to go with them.

After five days of class, Da and Thuan were released. "Go home now and tend to your rice paddies and do not work against the Front," the last instructor told them. "If you fail to do as we say, we will come to visit you again."

That evening, Tuesday, 10 days after the assassinations, the last two men on the murder list walk to the houses of friends to spend the night. Neither Bach Duc Hach nor Bach Thanh Van has slept at home in years. Hach, a vigorous man of 45 who can open beer bottles with his teeth, is a former chief of the strongly anti-Communist Su Lo Dong hamlet; Van, who at 53 is so crippled with rheumatism that he can barely walk, worked hard to build up the strategic hamlet program when he was Dong's predecessor as village chief. Neither man has held office in the past couple of years, but the Vietcong have long memories. If the V.C. do come, Hach at least wants to go down fighting. If only he had a gun, he would fight and die on the spot before he would let the V.C. capture him, and he tells his wife and children, "I want to die here in this hamlet so that you can bury me . . . and not be carried away by the Vietcong."

Every night the people of Loc Dien sleep uneasily as the artillery officer at District Headquarters, 14 kilometers to the south, fires air bursts from his two howitzers over Highway

One, hoping to catch some roving band of V.C. All night the shell bursts flicker like lightning off to the south. Tonight the attack does not come until 2 a.m., when the V.C. strike at a bridge near the south edge of the village.

Next day Truy hitches a ride down to the area to see what happened. The V.C. attacked in force, driving off the guards and demolishing the bridge with explosives. For good measure they kidnaped 10 peasants from the neighboring hamlet and laid three mines in the road. Early this morning a civilian truck hit one of the mines and its whole front end was blown away. The driver and his wife were killed.

Late in the day, Truy stops in at the little cafe near the village office to wash the dust from his throat with a beer—a refreshment he enjoys but can rarely afford.

Truy is tired, his sad eyes bloodshot. In the last 10 days he has had little sleep, and things have never been more dispiriting: the vice chief's father dead, the Buddhist leader dead, 15 kidnaped, two more dead from the mine, the railroad station attacked twice, a highway bridge blown, and his friend Lach in the hospital, paralyzed perhaps for life.

There must be something he can do, Truy says glumly to a friend, but he does not know what it is. Each time he develops a plan, the V.C. have a new plan. The people do not like the V.C. and more than anything else they want to be protected. But he cannot protect the village with his nine men, and except in the anti-Communist Su Lo Dong hamlet he cannot get anyone to create a militia.

He cannot dare to think of what will happen if the Americans leave. He is quiet for a moment and then he says, "The Americans do everything for Vietnam. They even die for Vietnam."

There is one thing he knows for sure. He will never leave Loc Dien. He could go to Hue to join the National Police and live securely and make much more money, but there he would be only a civil servant. Here the people respect him, not because he is a policeman but because they like him. They all say hello to him on the street, and when he lost his job for a while after the overthrow of President Diem, the people took in his family and housed them and fed them for a month.

This is his village and he will stay in it and try to protect the people from the V.C. He does not know about other villages, but in this village the people have borne war for 20 years, and 10 more years is nothing. If they have to, they can bear that too.

Truy is talking quickly now, his brown eyes flashing. The important thing is to keep the minds of the people—not to let them become defeatist in spirit. He must tell this to the leaders and to the militia and to his men. The people of the village want peace. But if the leaders fight, the people will follow. They will fight on until the Vietcong are defeated.

Outside the cafe, evening has come. The village is peaceful. The smell of incense is in the air. Small bats arc above the River Truoi, and in the houses the chichas, Vietnam's omnipresent little lizards, chirp as they stalk mosquitoes beneath the thatch. It has cooled somewhat after the blistering day, but the houses still hold the heat, and the people sit on their steps, old men sipping the raw homemade rice whisky they like to nip before bed. The children, restless in that hour before dark, run and play in the dusty streets, the boys shooting at each other with toy guns they have made out of bamboo and rubber bands. Most of the guns are remarkably detailed replicas of the much-admired Browning Automatic Rifle, complete right down to bipod and sights, and they will shoot their wooden bullets clear across the street.

Around dark, the streets begin to empty for curfew, and across from the cafe old Nguyen Dong comes to the door of the village office wearing his floppy pajama trousers and undershirt, a cigaret pasted on his lower lip. He stands there looking out. Pretty soon Truy goes over to join him and then, one by one, coming in from various parts of the village, the men turn up—the hamlet chiefs, and Chuong the vice chief, and Cao the information officer, and the others. They stand around for a while talking softly, their cigarets glowing in the twilight, and then they move out, a motley little band, walking up the darkening street to spend another night at the railroad station.

Vietnam Blitz:
A Report on the Impersonal War

by Bernard B. Fall

"Bernard Fall . . . is now convinced that American air- and fire-power will carry the field."   *Newsweek*, September 27

"They have made a desert, and have called it peace."
Tacitus, *Life of Agricola*

IT WAS during one of the quieter periods of his stormy tenure as Ambassador to Vietnam that General Maxwell D. Taylor developed the theme that there was not *one* Vietnam war, but 44: one for each of the provinces of the country. It was a good public relations line, and it lived at least through one or two stateside TV shows before dropping out of sight. The fact remains that there are many kinds of war that are being fought in Vietnam, often in one and the same place—from the Dr. Strangelove missions flown by B-52 superbombers designed to carry H-weapons, to the *punji* stakes covered with human excrement, one planted by the Viet Cong in the middle of a path in the hope that they will pierce a GI's boot and give him a festering wound.

But there are not 44 wars in Vietnam and there never were. There are vast areas where ricepaddy and swamp wars are fought; other areas where ridge-running prevails, as it did in the Appalachians during the French and Indian Wars; and, finally, there are even a few areas where one can engage in the kind of jungle-fighting familiar from Late Late Show films dealing with Guadalcanal. All this gets fairly abundantly reported in the American press, particularly when it involves US troops and thus allows the citation (with nickname, age, and hometown) of as many men as space and local interest permit. Of course, there are also the Vietnamese, on whose territory—the hard-nose term is "real estate"—the war is fought.

The Vietnamese fall into two categories; the Viet Cong (also known as VC, Victor Charlie, Charlie, or "the Congs"), and "our" Vietnamese, for whom there are no particular nicknames, except perhaps "our allies" or "the friendlies"; both terms followed by a guffaw.

As human beings, neither type of Vietnamese appears to be any longer of great importance. The VC is almost never seen close up; he leads a shadowy existence in deep forests and grottoes, displays no unit insignia even when he wears a uniform, carries no dogtags by which to identify him, manages to bury his weapon before he is found dead on the battlefield; and pushes his uncooperativeness with our side to the point where he—contrary to more normal armies, including the North Vietnamese when they were fighting the French—constantly changes unit numbers. This hopelessly fouls up Intelligence estimates, order-of-battle reports and other EEI's (estimates of enemy intentions). The "off-again-on-again" Northern 325th Division may well be an example of such totally unorthodox and highly unfair camouflage tactics. For all anyone knows, only a few small segments of that ten-battalion force may have been "in-country," as one says in Saigon. As of the time I left a few days ago, no Intelligence officer was ready to swear that the 325th as a unit had joined the battle in South Vietnam.

The VC, in contrast to the old rule that knowing your enemy is a good step forward to defeating him, have to most Americans (even those who fight them) remained faceless and often nameless. There are no "Wanted" posters in Vietnam offering rewards for the capture of a Communist leader. There are such posters, however—now in tatters but still quite prominent—offering rewards for the capture of various non-Communist losers of Saigon military coups. This impersonality (or depersonalization) of the enemy merely reflects how this war is being fought. When one expects to destroy the opposition through massive use of firepower from afar, regardless of whether it is from aircraft, artillery or naval turret guns, it becomes totally irrelevant to know who the leaders of the "Liberation Front" are, or whether a given VC unit commander is a local boy or from a North Vietnamese cadre. For all one cares, the chairman of the Liberation Front could work as a cleanup boy in a US mess hall in Bien Hoa, and nobody would recognize him.

In the same sense, the "friendlies" have become irrelevant. What happens (or who happens to be in power) in Saigon has largely become unimportant. Thanks to the sheer enormity and multifariousness of the American commitment, it is now possible to just about do anything without the approval or the cooperation of the Vietnamese. A few months ago, as long as "Arvin" (shorthand for ARVN, the Army of the Republic of Vietnam) troops were required to mount an operation, American advisers had to plead with often reluctant local commanders. Now, if need be, a whole operation can be mounted from stem to stern without involving a single Vietnamese. The Chulai operation was typical of this: It was American-planned and executed, and the plan was kept a secret from the Vietnamese to prevent the notorious "leaks" for which Saigon is famous. American power also has become great enough to stave off just about any kind of military disaster. When a helicopter-borne outfit of the 101st Airborne was erroneously put down in the midst of a VC assembly area a few days ago, the result should, under normal circumstances, have been unmitigated disaster. During the French Indochina War that happened several times to misdropped paratroop battalions, who invariably made a futile but heroic last stand and got wiped out because there were no reserves available and, above all, insufficient airborne firepower to make the area around the cut-off unit unlivable.

Today in Vietnam, there is *so much* of everything available that almost any kind of military error, no matter how stupid, can be retrieved on the rebound. In the case of the recent battle near Ankhé the misdropped unit was reinforced by other helicopter outfits and progressively surrounded by a protective wall of American firepower until the enemy, unable to maintain his position, broke off contact. At Bongson, on September 24, the VC overran a government outpost, but in the "reaction" operation they allegedly lost 600 men—500 of whom were killed by American aircraft. Against that kind of slaughter, the teachings of Mao Tse-tung, superior tactics, popular support for the VC, or, conversely, poor motivation among the Arvins and patent ineptness among many of their officers, and even the "mess in Saigon" are totally irrelevant. If tomorrow morning Mickey Mouse became prime minister of South Vietnam it would have precious little influence on the men of US Army Task Force Alfa (in fact, a full US Army Corps in everything but name) or on the fighting ability of the 3d US Marine Division.

Much has been said about the use of B-52's in a counter-insurgency operation or, as it should properly be called, a revolutionary war. Joseph Alsop, always willing to swallow uncritically every official handout on Vietnam, has again assured us in a recent column that the B-52's are necessary to destroy "deeply dug-in" VC installations, thus making a few underground bunkers covered with sandbags and bamboo look like the Siegfried Line.

His words had hardly appeared in print when the Air Force switched targets on Alsop and flew three raids into the Mekong Delta, followed by several raids along the Central Vietnam shore. The trouble with the Mekong Delta is that it is so flat, and the water table so high that one cannot dig a pit privy in the place without hitting water. It is well-nigh impossible to build underground positions in it. And, as official population density maps of Vietnam clearly show, the Delta has (with the exception of one single district out of perhaps thirty) an average population density of about 250 people per square mile, with one belt of districts across the whole Delta reaching the fantastic density of *one thousand people* per square mile! With an average bomb load of 500 tons per thirty-plane raid and a known bomb dispersion pattern of about 2,000 yards by 1,000 yards for such a raid, the effects of such a bombardment on a heavily-populated area can be readily guessed.

The point is that this consideration, too, has become irrelevant because it presupposes that hate or love for Saigon or the acquiescence of the Vietnamese population in its own fate, is important. In the view of many of the *realpolitiker* in Saigon and Washington, this is no longer true. Even the old-fashioned military view that a given target must be attained or destroyed before the operation can be called a success no longer holds. The B-52 raids (or "in-country" raids by smaller aircraft) do one thing regardless of whether they hit a VC

installation or a totally innocent and even pro-government village—they keep the Viet Cong on the move, day and night,
in constant fear of being hit. Gone are the days of large and
even comfortable jungle hospitals above ground; of the VC
rest camp with warm food, clean clothes and a good swimming hole; of the large ammunition depot and weapons repair
plant with electric generators chugging away peacefully. The
heavy bombers have changed all that. The VC is hunted down
like an animal. His wounded die unattended. A VC combat
unit returns from an operation only to find its camp area destroyed and its painfully-amassed rice and ammunition reserve
shattered.

And now there are research figures (for this is the most
operations-researched conflict in human history) to back up
the allegations of success through firepower. Before February
1965—that is, before the United States began to use jets inside
South Vietnam—only about two percent of VC deserters cited
air action as a reason for leaving their side. Since then the rate
has risen to 17 percent. Indeed, as many an informed observer
in Saigon will concede, what changed the character of the
Vietnam war was *not* the decision to bomb North Vietnam;
not the decision to use American ground troops in South Vietnam; but the decision to wage unlimited aerial warfare inside
the country at the price of literally pounding the place to bits.

There are hundreds of perfectly well-substantiated stories
to the effect that this merciless bombing hurt thousands of
innocent bystanders and that one of the reasons why few
weapons are found in many cases is that the heaps of dead in
the battle zone include many local villagers who didn't get
away in time. And every observer in Vietnam meets several
American officers who will curse loudly every time they hear
a jet overhead, because it again means an invisible objective
hit blindly—for an F-105 travels far too fast to see what he hits
and must be guided on his target by a "FAC"—a Forward
Air Controller in a spotter plane. The same goes for the incredible wastage of artillery ammunition. "In my area," said
an American provincial adviser to me, "we shot a half-million
dollars' worth of howitzer ammunition last month on un-
observed targets. Yet the whole provincial budget for in-
formation- and intelligence-gathering is $300."

In another instance known personally to me, a plantation hospital had been pilfered by the VC. When informed of that fact by a plantation official, the immediate reaction of the local command was *not* to pursue the retreating VC with troops—always a tiresome and risky affair—but to propose the laying-down of an artillery barrage on the plantation area. "I had the devil's own time dissuading them from it," said the plantation official later. "After all, we have 9,000 workers and 22,000 women and children here."

Here again, operations research comes to our rescue. Thus far, interrogations seem to show that there is no *positively* hostile association between the devastation wrought upon the countryside, and the United States or the Saigon government. In the words of one of the experts, the aerial attacks on the villages "of course cause unhappiness, no doubt on the part of the villagers, [but] do not cause them automatically to become VC's. In fact we have never met one who has become a VC as a result of this." But perhaps the answer should have read: ". . . who has been willing to admit that he has become a VC as a result of this." Be that as it may, and punchcard stacks to the contrary, a high-level mission was sent to Vietnam a few days ago to investigate the effects of that massive firepower on the Vietnamese. It will probably split along service lines.

The usual reply to all this is that the Communists, too, kill civilians. They murder local officials (over 400 since January, 1965), bombed the US Embassy, hit a Saigon restaurant with a mine which killed and maimed over 20 people, and so on. That is perfectly true. But their ability to do harm is immeasurably smaller than that of the other side, and there is no doubt in anyone's mind, and that includes the Intelligence specialists in Saigon, that the VC are deliberately keeping terrorism at a low level because of its psychologically adverse effects. If the VC set its mind to it, it could go on a rampage that would leave most Vietnamese urban centers a shambles (and it may yet do so if pushed back into the terrorism phase of guerrilla war as its field operations fail), but it has not thus far.

Another aspect of the progressive irrelevance of the human aspects of the Vietnam war is the universally callous attitude

taken by almost everybody toward the crass and constant vi-
olations of the rules of war that have been taking place. The
long-suffering (and far too long silent) International Red
Cross finally addressed an appeal in July 1965 to both sides,
exhorting them to live up to the Red Cross and Geneva agreements; and it was hardly an accident that Secretary of State
Dean Rusk chose August 12, 1965, the sixteenth anniversary of
the Geneva Convention on War Victims, to reaffirm America's
adherence to the treaty, which was fully ratified by the United
States Senate. Both North and South Vietnam also have ratified it.

As personal questions to both American and Vietnamese
unit commanders have shown (and I made a point of touching
on the subject with most of them), there is only the vaguest
idea among them as to what exactly is covered by the 1949
Convention; in the few cases where the terms "rules of war"
meant anything at all, the officer concerned very often confused the rules of land warfare of The Hague with the Geneva
Convention on Prisoners of War of 1929, the 1949 Convention, the Red Cross Convention, and the American Code of
the Fighting Man. Several officers would argue that the VC
were all "traitors" and thus could be shot out of hand, in yet
another misinterpretation of the laws covering treason. But in
that case, following the logic of the State Department's assertion that the North Vietnamese were "foreign aggressors,"
North Vietnamese regulars caught inside South Vietnam
would have to be treated as regular POW's, as were American
pilots until now if shot down over North Vietnam. Needless
to say, no such distinction was made between North Vietnamese regulars and VC regulars, nor between both of them
and the VC guerrillas: they are all being treated under the
same appalling conditions. The attitude of "this isn't *our* war;
it's a Vietnamese war" could hold as long as US combat
troops were not operating on their own and taking prisoners
all by themselves. Now, this is no longer possible and the Viet
Cong are in the position of virtually bulldozing the United
States into accepting responsibility for what happens to prisoners; they can shoot in reprisal American POW's whom they
hold whenever America's Vietnamese ally executes VC prisoners, as just happened in Danang. Two American servicemen

had to pay with their lives for that gratuitous gesture. The September 29 announcement by Hanoi that henceforth American pilots caught in the North will be treated as "war criminals" is a direct consequence of Washington's lack of foresight on the POW problem.

If total disregard of signed treaties is allowed to continue, then the Vietnam war will degenerate to an ignominious level of savagery far below that experienced in other guerrilla wars since World War II. During the French Indochina war neither the Viet Minh nor the French were exactly models of knightly behavior, but one-armed Monsieur Durand, the Swiss IRC representative in Saigon, could be seen visiting the camps where the French held their POW's. And while virtually 70 percent of all Frenchmen in Communist camps died from the brutal climate and disease alone, only a very few ever complained of deliberate inhumanity. Indeed, in such savage fighting areas as the Vietnamese Mountain Plateau, the 803d People's Army Regiment was often known to leave French wounded on a jungle trail, with their wounds attended, to be picked up by their own side; and the same happened in the no-holds-barred Battle of Dien Bien Phu.

To me, the real moral problem which arises in Vietnam is that of torture and needless brutality to combatants and civilians alike. The issue has been sidestepped in the United States; or worse, simply ignored as not being an "American" problem. When the famous newsreel was shot showing Marines burning down houses with lighters, the reaction among officialdom in Saigon was not so much one of distress that the incident had happened as one of furor at the reporters for seeing and reporting it. And then to see the Secretary of the Navy trying to explain the act by dubbing the village of Camné a "facility developed by the Viet Cong" hardly raises the moral stature of the whole operation. Yet, since then, charges of unnecessary brutality have again come out of Vietnam. On September 11, 1965, the *Saigon Daily News*, a newspaper published entirely for the English-speaking Western community of Vietnam, showed on its front page a large photograph of American servicemen standing with drawn weapons over a heap of what the caption describes as "dead VC"—all lying face down on the ground, *and with their hands tied behind their backs.* If, contrary to the caption, the dead were not Viet Cong but, instead, helpless villagers shot by the Communists, I'd be only too happy if some of my friends in Saigon corrected the record, or if the Pentagon would issue a detailed denial of the event and a believable explanation of what actually happened.

For the real problem of what such methods of warfare finally do, to the men who practice them or who tolerate them in their surroundings, will have to be faced up to by the United States, just as the problem of torture in Algeria finally had to be faced up to by the French: not just by their government but by every citizen, every educator and every clergyman all the way up to the Cardinal Primate of Gaul. Even the French Army was split down the middle on the subject, with some Intelligence officers (just as some of their American counterparts in Vietnam now) protesting against torture on the practical grounds that it drove the enemy to a "no-surrender" attitude, while an even smaller minority protested on strictly moral grounds. The best-known case was that of Brigadier General de la Bollardière, a much-decorated combat veteran, who resigned from his command in Algeria because, in his words, he was a paratrooper and not a Gestapo torturer. The uproar in France compelled the Paris government to appoint a Commission of Safeguard to investigate the situation; and books by survivors of such tortures, such as Miss Djamila Boupacha or Henri Alleg (*The Question*) became known the world over.

Before I went on a napalm-bombing mission in Vietnam aboard a US Air Force "Skyraider," I was given a full briefing on "E-and-E" (evasion and escape) procedures. I noted that among the items of the E-and-E kit there was a card with a copy of the Geneva Convention of 1929, informing the American pilot of his rights as a possible prisoner and of the obligations of the enemy toward him. It should not be impossible to provide every American serviceman in Vietnam (not just the pilots) with a handy resumé of *his* obligations under the existing laws and treaties toward the hapless civilian population as well as toward the enemy combatant. And while we're at it, a half-million copies in Vietnamese could be printed up for the Arvins to read at their leisure.

There is one central factor in the Vietnam situation which becomes apparent in the field, although it is not yet recognized on the campuses in the United States and, to a certain extent, in Hanoi and Peking: the immense influx of American manpower and firepower, and the ruthless use of the latter, have made the South Vietnam war, in the *short run, militarily* "unlosable." The italicized qualifiers are of great importance—and I am sure that, as in *Newsweek* of September 27, I will be misquoted by their omission—but the core proposition is essentially correct.

Early last spring, it was militarily almost feasible for the Viet Cong to destroy, in a series of brutal frontal attacks, one or two Arvin divisions; cause the defection of thousands of dispirited South Vietnamese troops; and present the United States with the *fait accompli* of a non-existing anti-Communist South Vietnam. Similar counterinsurgent nadirs have existed in other such wars: in Algeria and Cyprus, in Aden and Madagascar, in Palestine and Angola. The power of the insurgent is usually underestimated at the outset. Insurgency is at first left to the totally inadequate local police or security forces, and things go radically downhill until the Queen's Own Fusiliers or *les Paras* appear on the scene in great numbers and are promptly backed up by jet fighters roaring overhead.

The fact that the British were soundly beaten at Khartoum by the Sudanese Mahdi and at Mafeking by the Boers of Paul Kruger did not stop them from stumbling on to victory. In the battles of Hoa-Binh and Cao-Bang in North Vietnam, the French lost more troops than at Dien Bien Phu two years later, but fought on. What broke at Dien Bien Phu was France's will to resist—not her ability. And there, it seems, lies the greatest difference between Vietnam in 1954 and Vietnam now; and there perhaps also lies the secret of what may yet become Peking's and Hanoi's greatest policy error with regard to Southeast Asia. In all likelihood both Asian Communist countries (and, for that matter, a great many Europeans, and notably Frenchmen) simply thought of the American effort as being, of course, somewhat larger and more modern than what the French had been doing; but essentially of the same kind. Well, the truth is that the sheer magnitude of the American effort in Vietnam renders all such comparisons futile. The most striking example is of course the air war. Before Dien Bien Phu, the French Air Force had for *all* of Indochina (i.e., Cambodia, Laos, and North and South Vietnam) a total of 112 fighters and 68 bombers. On September 24, 1965, the United States flew 167 bombers against North Vietnamese targets alone, dropping 235 tons of bombs and *simultaneously* flew 317 bomber sorties "in-country," dropping 270 tons of bombs. In addition, a number of B-52's slammed a Viet Cong stronghold north of Saigon, known as the "iron triangle." In that single day, *even without the B-52 raids*, the US delivered more bomb tonnage than the French Air Force did during the whole 56 days of the Battle of Dien Bien Phu.

Confidence in total material superiority now pervades all of the governmental machinery dealing with Vietnam. The whole problem has in one sense become completely controllable; the build-up now can forego crash programs and emergency troop lifts. In Vietnam itself, leases and construction contracts are being let for a three-year period. From a situation full of uncertainties, Vietnam has become a perfectly manageable situation, whose difficulties can seemingly be quantified. It takes a known number of B-52 raids to liquidate the VC redoubt of "Zone D"; it took a known number of weedkiller flights to eliminate 3,000 acres of rubber forest near Bencat; it will take some 300,000 tons of imported rice (South Vietnam used to export 1.5 million tons, but that was long ago, in 1939) to keep the country from starving this year.

The one unknown quantity is the Communists. Now that the fortunes of war have turned against them, they may find it to their long-range tactical advantage to let the war die rather than to openly admit defeat at the conference table. Or they may, as they did in 1951 against France's Marshal de Lattre de Tassigny, lick their wounds for a season and revert to small-scale warfare; and simply stay alive in the hope that a Stalinist coup in the Soviet Union might bring about an American-Soviet confrontation which might provide them with the sophisticated weapons they now need to stay in business. Or they may simply conclude, on the basis of America's newfound willingness to intervene almost anywhere with troops, that "liberation war" was just another tactic that failed (just as "counterinsurgency" has failed on our side) and revert to the nuts and bolts of political agitation.

A few months ago, William J. Pomeroy, who had fought with the Huks against the Filipino government until he was captured, published a small book on *Guerrilla and Counter-Guerrilla Warfare: Liberation and Suppression in the Present Period*, in which he presents an interesting left-wing viewpoint on the causes of a Communist guerrilla failure. According to him, the Huks failed because "phases of legal struggle that were still possible and the creation of a broad united front of a nationalist character were neglected in favor of a rapid build-up of Huk armed forces."

The same may have happened to the Viet Cong in the face of the huge American military build-up, which has largely reduced the whole war to a slugging match between two military forces, the more so as the present Communist leadership in both Hanoi and the jungles of South Vietnam is so quagmired in the war and in its own rigid posture as to have no political leeway whatever. It is now Washington's turn to show whether it can come up with more statesmanship than Hanoi or the VC, or whether it will fall prey to the attractiveness of its own deployed firepower. In the latter case, a prostrate South Vietnam, plowed under by bombers and artillery and still in the hands of a politically irrelevant regime, may become the victim of aroused social and political forces for which no aircraft carrier and eight-jet bomber can provide a ready answer in the long run.

The New Republic, October 9, 1965

A Big "Dirty Little War"

by William Tuohy

SAIGON.

IN THE WAN, yellow light of an officers' mess near Saigon's ramshackle Tan Son Nhut airport, two tired helicopter pilots sipped beer after a punishing day flying missions over Vietcong territory. The men, both U.S. Army captains in their late 20's with wives and children back home, were asked what they would do if forced down in enemy-held areas.

"I'd be thinking in the back of my mind about my family," said the tall, crew-cut captain who flies a medical evacuation chopper. "I think the four of us in the crew—with four rifles and four pistols—could hold them off long enough for rescue. But if it came to the point where we couldn't resist any longer, I don't know what I'd do."

The second pilot, who commands an armed helicopter platoon, had no doubts about what he would do. "I've made up my mind," he said. "They won't take me alive. They are not going to parade me around or make me grovel."

Drastic as it sounds, the second captain's attitude was undoubtedly shared by many other Americans in Vietnam. U.S. soldiers and civilians captured by the Vietcong have been dragged through villages like prisoners in the Roman wars, jeered at, laughed at, spit upon, kept in solitary confinement, and executed. Sometimes their bodies have been mutilated.

Recently, when two captured U.S. soldiers were killed by the V.C. in reprisal for the Saigon Government's execution of three terrorists, a State Department spokesman called it "an act of wanton murder." But most U.S. servicemen took the news more stoically: they have long accepted the fact that mercy is not to be expected from the Vietcong.

The conflict in Vietnam is often called "a dirty little war." With U.S. combat troops and equipment pouring into the country, the war is getting much bigger. But it is no less dirty. In large part, it remains one of stealth, ambush, cut and run, treachery and bloody acts of terror inflicted on the populace by assailants they call "the men of the dark night."

To the aching frustration of U.S. commanders trained in more conventional tactics, this is a war in which countless hours are spent vainly tracking an elusive quarry through almost impenetrable jungle, muddy rice fields and blazing sand dunes. Friend is often indistinguishable from foe. Napalm and fragmentation bombs sometimes fall on defenseless peasants; artillery shells are fired at random into the paddy fields. An appalling number of victims are women, children and old men; some are participants but most are noncombatants.

"War is hell and, by God, this is one of the prime examples," says a top U.S. military commander. "There is no more ruthless s.o.b. than the Vietcong. This bastard will do anything that suits his purpose and he uses every dirty trick in the book."

To many, the dirtiest trick in the Vietcong manual is the widespread use of terror as an instrument of warfare. So far this year the Vietcong have murdered—by shooting, decapitation and disembowelment—about 400 Government officials, mostly at the hamlet and village level. Terrorists have mined and grenaded scores of buses and taxis, killing and mutilating hundreds of innocent Vietnamese.

Much of the terror is calculatedly barbaric. V.C. raiders in the Mekong delta gouged out a chunk of a village official's calf and ate it before killing him; in the mountains, pieces of skin were flayed from the thighs of women to force them to divulge their husbands' whereabouts. In northernmost Quang Tri Province, the wife of a bright young Vietnamese captain whose work had earned him a promotion to A.I.D. headquarters in Saigon returned home for a visit. She was seized by the V.C., disemboweled and her body hung on a fence post as a warning to those who become "U.S. agents." The catalogue of Vietcong atrocities is long and sickeningly repetitious.

Since there is no battlefront in Vietnam, terror is employed in the cities, too. In Saigon, the U.S. Embassy, restaurants, stadiums, police stations, and military billets have all been targets for bombs, *plastique* and mines. Grenades are tossed into the open windows of passing military vehicles. Sometimes, a bicycle laden with explosives prematurely detonates, leaving a gaping hole in the street.

The passenger terminal at the Saigon airport has been singled out for repeated attacks. The last time a bomb exploded there, Gen. William C. Westmoreland, U.S. commander in Vietnam, had just taken off in a helicopter and was less than 100 yards away when a puff of white smoke and debris burst through the roof of the terminal. Circling over the scene, Westmoreland calmly remarked to a passenger, "I thought they'd do that one of these days. It is typical of the Vietcong, striking a civilian terminal. They have no concern for human life." He paused, then added: "I'm always amazed they haven't been more strongly condemned by world opinion."

Nowadays, in Saigon, West German television crewmen pointedly display their national flag on their car, British citizens paint the Union Jack on their villa gates and French hotels and restaurants conspicuously fly the tricolor at every opportunity. The flag waving is not chauvinism, of course, but merely a way of saying: "We are not Americans. Don't waste your bombs on us."

But if the Vietcong cruelly employs terror, South Vietnamese troops have behaved brutally, too. Anyone who has spent much time with Government units in the field has seen the heads of prisoners held under water and bayonet blades pressed against their throats. Photographs of such incidents were common until the Government decided the publicity was not improving Saigon's public relations. In more extreme cases, victims have had bamboo slivers run under their fingernails or wires from a field telephone connected to arms, nipples, or testicles. Another rumored technique is known as "the long step." The idea is to take several prisoners up in a helicopter and toss one out in order to loosen the tongues of the others.

Some Vietcong suspects do not survive long enough for the third degree. Earlier this year, in an operation along the central coast, a Government detachment failed to flush V.C. troops suspected of lurking in the area. However, several villagers were rounded up and one man was brought before the company commander. The Vietnamese officer briefly questioned the suspect, then turned to his adviser, an Australian warrant officer, and said, "I think I shoot this man. Okay?"

"Go ahead," said the adviser.

The officer fired a carbine round point-blank, striking the villager below the chest. The man slumped and died. The patrol moved on. Later, a correspondent asked the adviser, who had seemed a decent enough fellow, why he had given his approval. The Australian cited the British experience in putting down the Malayan insurgency and said, "These people could have moved to a Government area. In this war they are either on our side or they are not. There is no in-between."

Few American military advisers would sanction such brutality or, for that matter, subscribe to the "with-us-or-against-us" theory. The most able U.S. advisers have learned to respect the subtleties and complexities of the war; General Westmoreland himself warns new arrivals of the "frustrations and perplexities" they can expect. No village is totally pro-Communist or totally pro-Government. Few peasants have the luxury to choose freely. But these lessons come slowly to newly arrived combat troops trained to assault more conventional objectives.

On some occasions the tactics of U.S. troops have been sadly inept for the situation. Thus, in a remote hamlet in the central highlands, a burly, red-faced captain entered with a patrol of paratroopers and ordered the villagers rounded up. "Ask these people where the Vietcong went," the captain told a nervous Vietnamese interpreter. An old man who might have been the village elder began speaking rapidly. "Sit down and shut up, loudmouth," bellowed the captain—in English.

Then the captain ordered a soldier, "Take him 100 yards down the road. Maybe if they think we're going to blow his head off, they'll talk."

The villagers did not talk; the women and children wailed and sobbed. Embarrassed, the paratroopers began loading two dozen peasants aboard a truck to take them to the district town. The soldiers were gentle as possible and courteous, but the villagers continued to cry. For all they knew they were being packed off to exile, imprisonment or execution. A lieutenant wondered about the efficacy of such tactics, but asked plaintively, "Well, if they're not V.C. sympathizers, what are they doing way out here? Why don't they live in the city?"

The paratroopers meant well and were only trying to do their job, but the gospel as taught at Fort Benning is often inappropriate in the villages of Asia.

To many Americans, the war in Vietnam seems bewilderingly savage. Yet there seems to be no other way to wage it.

Despite the U.S. attempt to make the struggle more conventional, it is still basically a guerrilla war and, by definition, dirty. It is also a civil war, inevitably unleashing violent passions. It is a war fought by Asian standards, without even lip service to the niceties of warfare prescribed by Western convention.

Further, many Vietnamese on both sides hold primitive animistic beliefs that are sometimes responsible for macabre brutality. They believe that eating the liver of a dead foe instills the victor with strength and courage. They believe that the soul does not immediately leave the body after death, and so, if the body is mutilated the soul is condemned to wander.

There is still another reason for much of the brutality. As Gen. Maxwell Taylor said while he was Ambassador in Saigon, "This whole war is a matter of intelligence." Intelligence, or more simply, information, is a vital commodity and the attempt to get it or withhold it explains much of the terror and torture inflicted by both sides.

American advisers find it hard to dissuade the Vietnamese from using force on prisoners. Says one U.S. specialist, "The Vietnamese do their questioning out of our sight because they know we feel guilty about their methods. They say, 'You people are a bunch of softies. This is a rough war and this is the way to get information—the only way.' So the Vietnamese major says to the American adviser, 'I suggest you take a walk and don't come back for half an hour. We're going to do this anyway, so it is better if you aren't here.'

"I myself don't believe in the effectiveness of torture, but it is very difficult to tell a Vietnamese paratrooper whose buddies have just been wiped out to go easy on a prisoner and make sure he gets back for questioning."

"There are better ways of getting information from prisoners than torture," says another American paramilitary expert. "Sure, you can start cutting off fingers and the guy will talk. But you never know whether the information is accurate. If I were being tortured, I'd whip out so much stuff it would take them six months to check it. But you can't walk away from it. You've got to watch them do it, run through five or six guys, even if it turns your insides. Then you ask, 'Why do you do it that way? Did you get any information you could act on? No? Then why not try it another way?' Most of these prisoners have been warned to expect brutality. But if you say, 'I'm your friend,' they don't know how to react. Their orders don't cover this, so being humane is much more effective."

This specialist is one of the handful of Americans in Vietnam practicing the arcane (some call it "black") art of revolutionary warfare. Their job is to train specially motivated political-military Vietnamese cadres and infuse them with skill, confidence, pride, national fervor. Since the cadres are taught to fight the V.C. on their own terms the training draws heavily on Communist techniques.

"They've had 25 years' experience at this," explains one black warrior. "Why not adapt it to our aims and resources?"

The ultimate ideological task of the cadres is convincing the people that the Vietcong is trying to steal the national revolution. Through lectures and indoctrination they teach that since the overthrow of Diem, it is the Communists—not the Government—who are the oppressors, who wish to tyrannize the people, exploit their land and will not leave them in peace. A vital practical job of the cadres is to lead platoons of local militia "like a soft wind into a hamlet," to patrol at night, lay ambushes, bribe, subvert, assassinate.

Like many other peoples, the Vietnamese have been slow to borrow from the casebook of Communist insurgency techniques—even though the enemy comes from the same cultural and ethnic stock. Then, too, the Vietnamese Army is largely a product of American training, and no soldier in the world has been more loath to adopt the bloody tactics of revolutionary warfare than the average senior U.S. officer. "It's a great pity we didn't begin training these motivated platoons when we moved back here in 1954," laments a top U.S. official.

The Americans who train these cadres pass unnoticed in the streets of Saigon, dressed in casual sports shirts. In the field they wear black pajamas like the men they train. They are fluent in Vietnamese and have a high regard for their adversaries. Their guidebooks are not U.S. Army field manuals, but the works of Mao Tse-tung, Vo Nguyen Giap, Che Guevara and the ancient Chinese military philosopher, Sun Tzu. Speaking the language of revolutionary warfare, they believe the war must be won by revolutionary means.

"This is not so much a dirty war as a different war," says one of these men. "It is total war involving all the people. The American Army thinks terror is unconventional. But terror is not unconventional to the Vietcong. It is part of the human hardware. Assassination would horrify General Westmoreland. Air and artillery, that's what the military understands. But assassination is what the peasant understands."

These specialists discuss the use of terror analytically, not emotionally.

"Vietcong terror is bloodthirsty but selective," an expert explains. "It is a scalpel, not a hammer. It is aimed at the leaders. In three years they drove out 50 per cent of the Vietnamese leaders from the countryside. They went after the very best and the very worst. As a result, there is a premium on mediocrity among civil servants. The purpose of most V.C. terror is to teach a lesson. They behead a village chief and kill his wife and kids. It's messy but the next chief won't bring his family to the town, and the V.C. will stress this in their propaganda.

"Usually, they have a specific reason for every act of terror. They don't kill for the sake of killing. But in the past six months, they have been making mistakes, probably by using poorly trained cadres. A green kid sits under a tree with orders to touch off a mine under a military truck. He gets impatient and blows up a bus.

"Terror is effective over the short range. But if you use too much, people begin to think: 'Eventually, it's going to be me, so I might as well help get rid of these guys.' And every time a father is beheaded, all his sons join the Army."

The experts turn the terror against the Vietcong; assassination teams are "sanitation" squads who take pride in their
work. "I'm a great believer in getting the guys responsible for
the war," says an American who has been trained to clean up.
"Go for the head, get the commander, or the deputy political
commissar for the whole battalion. The Vietcong is susceptible to this kind of attack because there is no clear chain of
command to assume authority and responsibility.

"I believe in bribing guards to assassinate their officers,
buying them off, working through their relatives, putting
prices on their heads, sowing suspicion in every way. In warfare you try for the command post. And killing their communications and liaison people is like putting out their eyes
and ears. I'd rather kill a political officer of a district than his
whole company, because as long as he's alive he can recruit
five companies.

"Too many people think our job is only to kill Cong," he
notes, "but ultimately it is to convert them."

In Dinh Tuong, a crucial province south of Saigon, a superb
black operation was carried out last summer. An informer fingered the top V.C. commissar in the province at a nighttime
meeting. A sanitation squad closed in and chewed up the hut
with automatic weapons fire. Killed with the V.C. chieftain
were a half-dozen of his aides. The Vietcong apparatus in the
province was paralyzed for weeks.

"If you can repeat this kind of thing with any regularity,
you'll shorten the insurgency by years," says a U.S. specialist.
"But few people know how to apply counter-terror properly.
It must be selective, discriminating and teach a lesson. A little
bit of terror goes a long way. One act will be understood by
95 per cent of the villagers concerned. You can't allow it to
be used to settle grudges. You can't allow it to turn into a
monster.

"In burning the village of Cam Ne the Marines made the
mistake of using mass terror instead of being selective. I've
been in hamlets where kids have thrown rocks at me and I've
been spat at but there is always someone who will make your
visit worthwhile. The Marines should have found out the five
or six homes sheltering snipers and burned them, and they
should have explained why they were doing it."

Nothing infuriates these revolutionary warfare tacticians more than indiscriminate air strikes and wild artillery fire in the countryside. "It's madness," says one. "The U.S. is always looking for the easy way, the gimmick. Tactical air strikes are fine when the V.C. are attacking a position, but you don't napalm a whole village because of a couple of snipers."

The specialists also criticize some aspects of the U.S. psychological warfare program. Says one: "Writing Churchillian messages to toss out of a plane is much less dangerous than getting out to the villages personally. It is much less effective, too, since most peasants have a low literacy rate.

"Leaflets are fine to warn them of air strikes. But peasants don't follow leaflets. They follow people. You've got to have cadres on the ground to follow up. Otherwise, all you have are a bunch of activity reports but no real results."

It is a brutal war in Vietnam, but the men fighting it try not to become brutalized.

"We all want to avoid wanton ruthlessness," says a senior U.S. military commander, "and we are trying to minimize the number of noncombatants under fire. But in 20 years there has been a hell of a lot of fighting. When you receive Vietcong fire from tunnels and bunkers, the only thing to do is go in after them. If you find old people and kids, it is grievous and regrettable. But there it is.

"Yet," this officer adds, "it is curious how our point of view has changed. Twenty years ago we were dreaming up every device possible to devastate people—maximum destruction from the air—and I don't recall a great deal of concern about where the bombs landed." He went on to point out that individual acts of terror, because they are more personal, in a sense, than the mass cruelty of World War II, tend to create the impression that the struggle in Vietnam is more brutal than it really is. "What is more brutal," he asked, "killing a village chief, disemboweling his wife and cutting up his kids—or blasting Hiroshima? Burying a man alive as a warning to other villagers—or exterminating six or seven million Jews? I don't think there is a higher order of brutality here than we've had in the past."

"You can't keep a war humane," adds another American. "It's hard to argue that we're not being brutalized, but I think we can still stand for a set of ethics: respect for the dignity of life, a sense of limits to what we can and cannot do, a complete rejection of the theory that the end justifies the means. This is the cutting edge between us and Communism.

"Even in practical terms we're better off being as humane as possible because then the enemy is less reluctant to surrender."

One of the most experienced practitioners of revolutionary warfare, whose work includes counter-terror, discussed his job with candor and thoughtfulness. "Look," he said, "there's no humane way to kill a man. Terror is terror. Murder is murder. Counter-terror is a word used by Americans because it sounds clean. The important thing is not the degree of cleanliness of the war but the degree of necessity.

"Let's not kid ourselves. The hero of 'Catch 22' was right—wars are basically insane. We are trying to kill each other. But I also believe in Mao's distinction between just wars and unjust wars. If you believe this is an unjust war, then you've got to get out, because you will get yourself zapped.

"The main thing is to see the relation between our aims and what the Vietnamese farmer wants—to protect his land, be left in peace, and get the V.C. out of his village. U.S. combat troops spend so much time on patrol and in bivouac that they have little contact with the people. They are more likely to become brutalized by the fighting, and this is a real danger.

"I don't think you can become really hardened if you share the involvement with the people.

"One night a Vietnamese officer and I were talking about personal things. We were sitting in a field. He showed me his wife's picture and then broke down and cried. She had left him because he wasn't at home enough. He said he still loved her. I think that when you share things like that with the people here you can't be brutalized. The important thing is to be involved."

The "dirty little war" in Vietnam is an untidy, unclear conflict, but it is the kind the United States may be fighting for many years to come—if not in Asia, then in Africa or in Latin America. It is a grim prospect, but one with a consolation of sorts. As Brig. Gen. Samuel B. Griffith, a perceptive student of insurgency, has written, "Guerrilla warfare is suffused with and reflects man's admirable qualities as well as his less pleasant ones. While it is not always humane, it is human, which is more than can be said for the strategy of extinction."

The New York Times Magazine, November 28, 1965

from *The Electric Kool-Aid Acid Test*

by Tom Wolfe

IT WAS against this backdrop, namely, the ultimate and the infinite, that an organization known as the Vietnam Day Committee invited Kesey to come speak at a huge antiwar rally in Berkeley, on the University of California campus. I couldn't tell you what bright fellow thought of that, inviting Kesey. Afterwards, they didn't know, either. Or at least none of them would own up, despite a lot of interrogations and recriminations and general thrashing about. "Who the hell invited this bastard!" was the exact wording. A regular little rhubarb they had for themselves. The main trouble with the Vietnam Day Committee was that they couldn't see beyond the marvelous political whoopee they had cooked up. Why should they? From where they were looking in the fall of 1965, they were about to sweep the country. Berkeley, the New Left, the Free Speech Movement, Mario Savio, the Rebel Generation, the Student Revolution, in which students were going to take over the universities, like in Latin America, and drive some fire up the clammy rectum of American life—you could read about it in all the magazines. And if you don't believe it, come here and watch us, Mr. Jones—and so forth.

They never looked beyond that, as I say, but it might have been no use, in any case. Maybe there was no way in the world anybody could have made the Vietnam Day Committee realize how their whole beano looked to Kesey and the Pranksters. *Come rally against the war in Vietnam*—from the cosmic vantage point the Pranksters had reached, there were so many reasons why this little charade was pathetic, they didn't know where to begin . . .

Nevertheless, Kesey was invited, and that was how the fun started. Marchers were pouring into Berkeley from seventy-one cities and twenty-eight states, for whatever such sums are worth—at any rate, thousands of students and professors from all over. There were to be teach-ins all day and also an all-day rally starting in the morning, with thirty or forty speakers to whip things up, and then at 7:30 in the evening, when the fever pitch was reached, they would all rise up off the Berkeley campus and march over into Oakland, fifteen or twenty thousand souls in a massive line, marching on the Oakland Army Terminal. The Oakland Army Terminal was where men and supplies were shipped out to Vietnam. Just to spice things up a bit—a large supply of gelignite had been stolen, and everybody had visions of Oakland, Berkeley, San Francisco, the whole clump, blowing up in a gelignite earthquake of cops, peaceniks, Birchers, and probably spades and innocent women and children. Nobody had any idea which side had stolen the gelignite, but that only made it better.

The gelignite scare seemed to give Kesey the inspiration for this prank. Kesey's saving grace was that he never got serious where he could say it just as well with a cosmic joke. Kesey's fantasy for the occasion was to come upon the huge anti-war rally as a freaking military invasion. It was a true inspiration, this fantasy. They were going to rig up the bus as a rolling fortress with guns sticking out and all the Pranksters would dress military. Then they would get cars and rig them up the same way, and at the head of the whole convoy, there would be—the Hell's Angels, in running formation, absolutely a-dangle with swastikas. *Swastikas.* It would freaking blow their minds, or at least give their cool a test like it never had before.

First they painted the whole bus a dull red color, the color of dried blood, in fact. Right on over the greatest riot of Day-Glo design in history went this bloody muck. But who gave a damn. *Art is not eternal.* Then they started painting military symbols on the dried blood, swastikas, American eagles, Iron Crosses, Viking crosses, Red Crosses, hammers & sickles, skulls & bones, anything as long as it looked rank. That very night, naturally, the seasonal rains started, and like the Chief said, art is not eternal. All the paint started running until it was the most dismal mess imaginable. Somehow that was appropriate. The next day, Gut and his girlfriend, Little People, showed up. Gut was in a kind of transition period, between the Angels and the Pranksters. He had his old Hell's Angels sleeveless denim jacket on, but he had taken the insignia off, the lettering and the emblem of a skull with a helmet on, but you could see where it had all been, because the denim was lighter underneath. It was what you might call a goodbye-but-not-forgotten Hell's Angels' jacket. Anyway, Gut amazed the Pranksters by painting a big beautiful American Eagle on the bus, a little primitive, but strong. The big hulking jesus angel had talent. The Pranksters were all pleased as hell. They felt they had brought it out of him, somehow. Gut got everybody revved up. They built a gun turret on the bus and rigged up two big gray cannons that you could maneuver. Norman made a machine gun out of wood and cardboard and painted it olive drab. Other people were knocking together wooden guns of various ridiculous descriptions. Faye's sewing machine was going. Pranksters, inner circle and outer circle, were driving in from all over. Lee Quarnstrom, of the outer circle, showed up with a huge supply of Army insignia, shoulder patches, arm patches, hashmarks, bars, stars, epaulets. Kesey was rigging up the bus with tapes and microphones and amplifiers and earphones and electric guitars. Hagen was rigging up his 16-millimeter camera and films. Bob Dylan and the Beatles and Joan Baez and Roland Kirk and Mississippi John Hurt were droning and clattering over the big speakers from over the way atop the dirt cliff. Then Allen Ginsberg turned up from Big Sur, with his companion Peter Orlovsky and an entourage of pale Chester A. Arthur High School hindus. Ginsberg sang mantras all night and jingled bells and finger cymbals. Cassady hooked down speed and worked himself up from a standing start, jerking, kicking, dancing—he seemed to be moving in time to the sewing machine on a long seam. Ginsberg seemed to be chanting in time to a Jainist's whisk broom. Cassady began fibrillating the vocal cords, going faster and faster until by dawn if he had gone any faster, he would have vibrated off, as old Charles Fort said, and gone instantly into the positive absolute. It was a nice weird party.

The next morning, October 16, the big day—the Pranksters blew the morning, naturally, all stroked out in various attitudes from the night before, and they were late getting off to Berkeley. Art is not eternal, friends. The plan was to meet the Hell's Angels in Palo Alto and go roaring down the freeway in formation. They put on Prankster tapes and Cassady got in the driver's seat. Everybody climbed on in their crazed military costumes, Hassler, Hagen, Babbs, Gretch, Zonker, June the Goon, Roy Seburn, Dale Kesey and all sorts of people, even the Mad Chemist—he showed up for this one—and Mary Microgram at the last minute. And then Kesey got on. Kesey was wearing a big orange coat of the sort highway workers wear so cars will see them. He had hashmarks on the sleeves and some kind of floppy epaulets flapping on the shoulders. He had a big orange Day-Glo World War I helmet on his head. It was so big and came down so far over his forehead his eyes were like two little flashlight bulbs under the lid. Kesey got up in the gun turret and they were off. Before they got to Palo Alto, in Woodside, in fact, the cops stopped them and hassled them and checked them over. The Pranksters did the usual, leaped out with cameras and shotgun mikes and tape recorders, filming and taping everything the cops said, and the cops left, but it ate up time.

"Aha," said the Mad Chemist, "the first skirmish."

"The Prankster Alert is out," said Babbs.

That was just about right. They kept getting stopped and hassled and checked over and losing time. They got to the rendezvous in Palo Alto—and no Hell's Angels. They waited and waited for the Angels, then gave up and took off down the expressway, to Berkeley.

They didn't get to the Berkeley campus until almost dusk, and their arrival didn't make any very momentous impression at first. Now, a full phalanx of Hell's Angels, looking like a cross between the Gestapo and the Tonton Macoute—that would have been a different story, no doubt. Good and noisy, too. But as it was, the bus just pulled into the parking lot by the Student Union building and the Pranksters cut up as best they could, ack-acking their wooden guns at birds and planes. The big rally had been going on all day. They were out on a big lawn, or plaza, on the campus, about fifteen thousand of them, the toggle-coat bohemians, while the P.A. loudspeakers boomed and rabbled and raked across them. There was a big platform set up for the speakers. There had been about forty of them, all roaring or fulminating or arguing cogently, which was always worse. The idea at these things is to keep building up momentum and building up momentum and tension and suspense until finally when it is time for action—in this case, the march—the signal launches them as one great welded body of believers and they are ready to march and take billy clubs upside the head and all the rest of it.

All the shock workers of the tongue were there, speakers like Paul Jacobs, and M. S. Arnoni, who wore a prison uniform to the podium because his family had been wiped out in a German concentration camp during World War II—and out before them was a great sea of students and other Youth, the toggle-coat bohemians—toggle coats, Desert Boots, civil rights, down with the war in Vietnam—" . . . could call out to you from their graves or from the fields and rivers upon which their ashes were thrown, they would implore this generation of Americans not to be silent in the face of the genocidal atrocities committed on the people of Vietnam . . ." and the words rolled in full forensic boom over the P.A. systems.

The first person in the Vietnam Day Committee circle to notice Kesey approaching the speaker's platform was Paul Krassner, the editor of *The Realist* magazine. Most of the Pranksters were still on the bus, fooling around with the guns for the befuddlement of the gawkers who happened by. Kesey, Babbs, Gretchen Fetchin and George Walker came on over the platform, Kesey in his orange Day-Glo coat and World War I helmet. Krassner ran his magazine as pretty much a one-man operation and he knew Kesey subscribed to it. So he wasn't so surprised that Kesey knew him. What got him was that Kesey just started talking to him, just like they had been having a conversation all along and something had interrupted them and now they were resuming. . . . It is a weird thing. You feel the guy's charisma, to use that one, right away, busting out even through the nutty Day-Glo, or maybe sucking one in, the way someone once wrote of Gurdjieff: "You could not help being drawn, almost physically, towards him . . . like being sucked in by a vast, spiritual vacuum cleaner." At the time, however, Krassner thought of Flash Gordon.

"Look up there," Kesey says, motioning up toward the platform.

Up there is Paul Jacobs. Jacobs tends toward the forensic,

anyway, and the microphone and loudspeakers do something to a speaker. You can hear your voice rolling and thundering, powerful as Wotan, out over that ocean of big ears and eager faces, and you are omnipotent and more forensic and orotund and thunderous minute by minute—*It is written, but I say unto you . . . the jackals of history-ree-ree-ree-ree . . .* From where they are standing, off to the side of the platform, they can hear very little of what Jacobs is actually saying, but they can hear the sound barking and roaring and reverberating and they can hear the crowd roaring back and baying on cue, and they can see Jacobs, hunched over squat and thick into the microphone, with his hands stabbing out for emphasis, and there, at sundown, silhouetted against the florid sky, is his jaw, jutting out, like a cantaloupe . . .

Kesey says to Krassner: "Don't listen to the words, just the sound, and the gestures . . . who do you see?"

And suddenly Krassner wants very badly to be right. It is the call of the old charisma. He wants to come up with the right answer.

"Mussolini . . . ?"

Kesey starts nodding, Right, right, but keeping his eye on the prognathous jaw.

By this time more of the Pranksters have come up to the platform. They have found some electrical outlets and they have run long cords up to the platform, for the guitars and basses and horns. Kesey is the next to last speaker. He is to be followed by some final Real Barnburner of a speaker and then—the final surge and the march on Oakland.

From the moment Kesey gets up there, it is a freaking jar. His jacket glows at dusk, and his helmet. Lined up behind him are more Day-Glo crazies, wearing aviator helmets and goggles and flight suits and Army tunics, Babbs, Gretch, Walker, Zonker, Mary Microgram, and little Day-Glo kids, and half of them carrying electric guitars and horns, mugging and moving around in Day-Glo streaks. The next jar is Kesey's voice, it is so non-forensic. He comes on soft, in the Oregon drawl, like he's just having a conversation with 15,000 people:

You know, you're not gonna stop this war with this rally, by marching . . . That's what they *do . . . They hold rallies and*

*they march . . . They've been having wars for ten thousand years
and you're not gonna stop it this way . . . Ten thousand years,
and this is the game they play to do it . . . holding rallies and
having marches . . . and that's the same game you're playing
. . . their game . . .*

Whereupon he reaches into his great glowing Day-Glo coat
and produces a harmonica and starts playing it right into the
microphone, *Home, home on the range,* hawonking away on
the goddamn thing—*Home . . . home . . . on the ra-a-a-a-
ange hawonkawonk . . .*

The crowd stands there in a sudden tender clump, most of
them wondering if they heard right, cocking their heads and
rolling their heads to one another. First of all, that conversa-
tional tone all of a sudden, and then random notes from the
Day-Glo crazies behind him ripped out offen the electric guitars and the general babble of the place feeding into the microphone—did anybody hear right—

—all the while Kesey is still up there hawonking away on
the freaking harmonica, *Home, home on the ra-a-a-a-a-a-
ange*—

—ahhhh, that's it—they figure it's some calculated piece of
stage business, playing *Home, home on the range*—building up
to something like Yah! We know about that *home*! We know
about that *range*! That rotten U.S. home and that rotten U.S.
range!—

—but instead it is the same down-home drawling voice—

*I was just looking at the speaker who was up here before me
. . . and I couldn't hear what he was saying . . . but I could
hear the sound of it . . . and I could hear your sound coming
back at him . . . and I could see the gestures—*

—and here Kesey starts parodying Paul Jacobs' stabbing
little hands and his hunched-over stance and his—

*—and I could see his jaw sticking out like this . . . silhou-
etted against the sky . . . and you know who I saw . . . and
who I heard? . . . Mussolini . . . I saw and I heard Mussolini
here just a few minutes ago . . . Yep . . . you're playing their
game . . .*

Then he starts hawonking away again, hawonking and hawonking *Home, home on the range* with that sad old setter
harmonica-around-the-campfire pace—and the Pranksters

back him up on their instruments, Babbs, Gretch, George, Zonker, weaving up there in a great Day-Glo freakout

—and what the hell—a few boos, but mainly confusion— what in the name of God are the ninnies—

—We've all heard all this and seen all this before, but we keep on doing it . . . I went to see the Beatles last month . . . And I heard 20,000 girls screaming together at the Beatles . . . and I couldn't hear what they were screaming, either . . . But you don't have to . . . They're screaming Me! Me! Me! Me! . . . I'm Me! . . . That's the cry of the ego, and that's the cry of this rally! . . . Me! Me! Me! Me! . . . And that's why wars get fought . . . ego . . . because enough people want to scream Pay attention to Me! . . . Yep, you're playing their game . . .

—and then more *hawonkawonkawonkawonkawonka*—

—and the crowd starts going into a slump. It's as if the rally, the whole day, has been one long careful inflation of a helium balloon, preparing to take off—and suddenly some-body has pulled the plug. It's not what *he* is saying, either. It's the sound and the freaking sight and that goddamn mournful harmonica and that stupid Chinese music by the freaks standing up behind him. It's the only thing the martial spirit can't stand—a put-on, a prank, a shuck, a goose in the anus.

—Vietnam Day Committee seethe together at the edge of the platform: "Who the hell invited this bastard!" "*You* in-vited him!" "Well, hell, we figured he's a writer, so he'll be against the war!" "Didn't you have enough speakers?" says Krassner. "You need all the big names you can get, to get the crowd out." "Well, that's what you get for being celebrity fuckers," says Krassner. If they had had one of those big hooks like they had on amateur night in the vaudeville days, they would have pulled Kesey off the podium right then. Well, then, why doesn't somebody just go up there and edge him off! He's ruining the goddamn thing. But then they see all the Day-Glo crazies, men and women and children all weaving and electrified, clawing at guitars, blowing horns, all crazed aglow at sundown . . . And the picture of the greatest anti-war rally in the history of America ending in a Day-Glo brawl to the tune of Home, home on the range . . .

—suddenly the hawonking on the freaking harmonica stops. Kesey leans into the microphone—

There's only one thing to do . . . there's only one thing's gonna do any good at all . . . And that's everybody just look at it, look at the war, and turn your backs and say . . . Fuck it . . .

—*hawonkawonkawonkawonka*—

—They hear that all right. The sound of the phrase—*Fuck it*—sounds so weird, so shocking, even here in Free Speech citadel, just coming out that way over a public loudspeaker, rolling over the heads of 15,000 souls—

—*Home, home on the range hawonkawonkawonka,* and the Pranksters beginning to build up most madly on their instruments now, behind the harmonica, sounding like an insane honky-tonk version of Juan Carrillo who devised 96 tones on the back seat of a Willys Jeep, saved pennies all through the war to buy it, you understand, zinc pennies until the blue pustules formed under his zither finger nether there, you understand . . .

— Just look at it and turn away and say . . . Fuck it
—*say . . . Fuck it . . .*
hawonkawonkawonka blam
—*Fuck it*—
Hawonkafuckit . . . friends . . .

There was no way one could prove Kesey had done it. Nevertheless, something was gone out of the anti-war rally. The Real Barnburner spoke, and the Vietnam Day Committee tried to put in one last massive infusion of the old spirit and then gave the signal and the great march on Oakland began, through the gloaming. Fifteen thousand souls . . . shoulder to shoulder like in the old strike posters. At the Oakland-Berkeley line there was an arrow-shaped phalanx of police and National Guard. The Vietnam Day Committee marched in frantic clump at the head, trying to decide whether to force the issue, have a *physical confrontation*, heads busted, bayonets—or turn back when they ordered them to. Nobody seemed to have any resolve. Somebody would say, We have no choice, we've got to turn back—and somebody else would call him a Martin Luther King. That was about the worst thing you could call anybody on the New Left at that time.

Martin Luther King turned back at the critical moment on the bridge at Selma. We can't risk submitting the crania of our devoted people to fracturization and degradation by those who do not shrink from a cowardly show of weaponry, he had said, going on like Social Science Negro in his sepulchral voice—the big solemn preachery Uncle Tom. Yah! yuh Tuskegee-headed Uncle Tom, yuh, yuh Booker T. Washington peanut-butter lecture-podium Nobel Prize medal head, yuh—*Uncle Tom*—by the time it was all over, Martin Luther King was a stupid music-hall Handkerchief Head on the New Left—and here they were, calling each other Martin Luther Kings and other incredible things—but nobody had any good smashing iron zeal to carry the day—O where is our Zea-lot, who Day-glowed and fucked up our heads—and there was nothing to do but grouse at the National Guard and turn back, which they did. What the hell has happened to us? Who did this? Why, it was the Masked Man—

So the huge march turned around and headed for Civic Center Park in Berkeley and stood around there eating hamburgers and listening to music by a jug band—a group that later became known as Country Joe and the Fish—and wondering what the hell had happened. Then somebody started throwing tear gas from a rooftop and Bob Scheer was bravely telling everybody to lie down on the grass, because tear gas rises—but the jug band just stood there, petrified, with their hands and their instruments frozen in the same position as when the gas hit. It seems the jug band was high on something or other, and when the gas hit, the combination of the gas and whatever they were already up on—it *pet*rified them and they stood there *in* stark stiff *medias res* as if they were posing for an Iwo Jima sculpture for the biggest anti-war rally in the history of the American people. The whole rally now seemed like a big half ass, with the frozen jug band the picture of how far they had gotten.

from *The Electric Kool-Aid Acid Test*, 1968

Death in the Ia Drang Valley

by Specialist 4/c Jack P. Smith

THE 1ST BATTALION had been fighting continuously for three or four days, and I had never seen such filthy troops. Some of them had blood on their faces from scratches and from other guys' wounds. Some had long rips in their clothing where shrapnel and bullets had missed them. They all had that look of shock. They said little, just looked around with darting, nervous eyes.

Whenever I heard a shell coming close, I'd duck, but they'd keep standing. After three days of constant bombardment you get so you can tell from the sound how close a shell is going to land within 50 to 75 feet. There were some wounded lying around, bandaged up with filthy shirts and bandages, smoking cigarettes or lying in a coma with plasma bottles hanging above their stretchers.

Late that morning the Cong made a charge. About 100 of them jumped up and made for our lines, and all hell broke loose. The people in that sector opened up with everything they had. Then a couple of our Skyraiders came in. One of them dropped a lot of stuff that shimmered in the sun like green confetti. It looked like a ticker-tape parade, but when the things hit the ground, the little pieces exploded. They were antipersonnel charges. Every one of the gooks was killed. Another group on the other side almost made it to the lines. There weren't enough GI's there, and they couldn't shoot them down fast enough. A plane dropped some napalm bombs just in front of the line. I couldn't see the gooks, but I could hear them scream as they burned. A hundred men dead, just like that.

My company, Charlie Company, took over its sector of the battalion perimeter and started to dig in. At three o'clock another attack came, but it never amounted to anything. I didn't get any sleep that night. There was continuous firing from one until four, and it was as bright as day with the flares lighting up the sky.

The next morning the order came for us to move out. I guess our commanders felt the battle was over. The three battalions of PAVN (People's Army of Vietnam—the North Vietnamese) were destroyed. There must have been about 1,000 rotting bodies out there, starting about 20 feet from us and surrounding the giant circle of foxholes. As we left the perimeter, we walked by them. Some of them had been lying out there for four days. There are more ants in Vietnam than in any place I have ever seen.

We were being withdrawn to Landing Zone Albany, some six miles away, where we were to be picked up by helicopter. About noon the column stopped and everybody flopped on the ground. It turned out that our reconnaissance platoon had come upon four sleeping PAVN who had claimed they were deserters. They said that there were three or four snipers in the trees up ahead—friends of theirs who did not want to surrender.

The head of the column formed by our battalion was already in the landing zone, which was actually only 30 yards to our left. But our company was still in the woods and elephant grass. I dropped my gear and my ax, which was standard equipment for supply clerks like me. We used them to cut down trees to help make landing zones for our helicopters. The day had grown very hot. I was about one quarter through a smoke when a few shots cracked at the front of the column.

I flipped my cigarette butt, lay down and grabbed my M-16. The fire in front was still growing. Then a few shots were fired right behind me. They seemed to come from the trees. There was firing all over the place now, and I was getting scared. A bullet hit the dirt a foot to my side, and some started whistling over my head.

This wasn't the three or four snipers we had been warned about. There were over 100 North Vietnamese snipers tied in the trees above us—so we learned later—way above us, in the top branches. The firing kept increasing.

Our executive officer (XO) jumped up and said, "Follow me, and let's get the hell out of here." I followed him, along with the rest of the headquarters section and the 1st Platoon. We crouched and ran to the right toward what we thought was the landing zone. But it was only a small clearing—the L.Z. was to our left. We were running deeper into the ambush.

The fire was still increasing. We were all crouched as low as possible, but still keeping up a steady trot, looking from side to side. I glanced back at Richards, one of the company's radio operators. Just as I looked back, he moaned softly and fell to the ground. I knelt down and looked at him, and he shuddered and started to gurgle deep in his stomach. His eyes and tongue popped out, and he died. He had a hole straight through his heart.

I had been screaming for a medic. I stopped. I looked up. Everyone had stopped. All of a sudden all the snipers opened up with automatic weapons. There were PAVN with machine guns hidden behind every anthill. The noise was deafening.

Then the men started dropping. It was unbelievable. I knelt there staring as at least 20 men dropped within a few seconds. I still had not recovered from the shock of seeing Richards killed, but the jolt of seeing men die so quickly brought me back to life. I hit the dirt fast. The XO was to my left, and Wallace was to my right, with Burroughs to his right. We were touching each other lying there in the tall elephant grass.

Men all around me were screaming. The fire was now a continuous roar. We were even being fired at by our own guys. No one knew where the fire was coming from, and so the men were shooting everywhere. Some were in shock and were blazing away at everything they saw or imagined they saw.

The XO let out a low moan, and his head sank. I felt a flash of panic. I had been assuming that he would get us out of this. Enlisted men may scoff at officers back in the billets, but when the fighting begins, the men automatically become very dependent upon them. Now I felt terribly alone.

The XO had been hit in the small of the back. I ripped off his shirt and there it was: a groove to the right of his spine. The bullet was still in there. He was in a great deal of pain, so a rifleman named Wilson and I removed his gear as best we could, and I bandaged his wound. It was not bleeding much on the outside, but he was very close to passing out.

Just then Wallace let out a "Huh!" A bullet had creased his upper arm and entered his side. He was bleeding in spurts. I ripped away his shirt with my knife and did him up. Then the XO screamed: A bullet had gone through his boot, taking all his toes with it. He was in agony and crying. Wallace was swearing and in shock. I was crying and holding on to the XO's hand to keep from going crazy.

The grass in front of Wallace's head began to fall as if a lawnmower were passing. It was a machine gun, and I could see the vague outline of the Cong's head behind the foot or so of elephant grass. The noise of firing from all directions was so great that I couldn't even hear a machine gun being fired three feet in front of me and one foot above my head.

As if in a dream, I picked up my rifle, put it on automatic, pushed the barrel into the Cong's face and pulled the trigger. I saw his face disappear. I guess I blew his head off, but I never saw his body and did not look for it.

Wallace screamed. I had fired the burst pretty close to his ear, but I didn't hit him. Bullets by the thousands were coming from the trees, from the L.Z., from the very ground, it seemed. There was a huge thump nearby. Burroughs rolled over and started a scream, though it sounded more like a growl. He had been lying on his side when a grenade went off about three or four feet from him. He looked as though someone had poured red paint over him from head to toe.

After that everything began getting hazy. I lay there for several minutes, and I think I was beginning to go into shock. I don't remember much.

The amazing thing about all this was that from the time Richards was killed to the time Burroughs was hit, only a minute or two had elapsed. Hundreds of men had been hit all around us, and the sound of men screaming was almost as loud as the firing.

The XO was going fast. He told me his wife's name was Carol. He told me that if he didn't make it, I was to write her and tell her that he loved her. Then he somehow managed to crawl away, saying that he was going to organize the troops. It was his positive decision to do something that reinforced my own will to go on.

Then our artillery and air strikes started to come in. They

saved our lives. Just before they started, I could hear North Vietnamese voices on our right. The PAVN battalion was moving in on us, into the woods. The Skyraiders were dropping napalm bombs a hundred feet in front of me on a PAVN machine-gun complex. I felt the hot blast and saw the elephant grass curling ahead of me. The victims were screaming—some of them were our own men who were trapped outside the wood line.

At an altitude of 200 feet it's difficult to distinguish one soldier from another. It's unfortunate and horrible, but most of the battalion's casualties in the first hour or so were from our own men, firing at everything in sight.

No matter what you did, you got hit. The snipers in the trees just waited for someone to move, then shot him. I could hear the North Vietnamese entering the woods from our right. They were creeping along, babbling and arguing among themselves, calling to each other when they found a live GI. Then they shot him.

I decided that it was time to move. I crawled off to my left a few feet, to where Sgt. Moore and Thompson were lying. Sgt. Moore had been hit in the chest three times. He was in pain and sinking fast. Thompson was hit only lightly in the leg. I asked the sergeant to hold my hand. He must have known then that he was dying, but he managed to assure me that everything would be all right.

I knew there wasn't much chance of that. This was a massacre, and I was one of a handful not yet wounded. All around me, those who were not already dead were dying or severely wounded, most of them hit several times. I must have been talking a lot, but I have no idea what I was saying. I think it was, "Oh God, Oh God, Oh God," over and over. Then I would cry. To get closer to the ground, I had dumped my gear, including the ax I had been carrying, and I had lost my rifle, but that was no problem. There were weapons of every kind lying everywhere.

Sgt. Moore asked me if I thought he would make it. I squeezed his hand and told him sure. He said that he was in a lot of pain, and every now and then he would scream. He was obviously bleeding internally quite a bit. I was sure that he would die before the night. I had seen his wife and four kids at Fort Benning. He had made it through World War II and Korea, but this little war had got him.

I found a hand grenade and put it next to me. Then I pulled out my first-aid pack and opened it. I still was not wounded, but I knew I would be soon.

At that instant I heard a babble of Vietnamese voices close by. They sounded like little children, cruel children. The sound of those voices, of the enemy that close, was the most frightening thing I have ever experienced. Combat creates a mindless fear, but this was worse, naked panic.

A small group of PAVN was rapidly approaching. There was a heavy rustling of elephant grass and a constant babbling of high-pitched voices. I told Sgt. Moore to shut up and play dead. I was thinking of using my grenade, but I was scared that it wouldn't get them all, and that they were so close that I would blow myself up too.

My mind was made up for me, because all of a sudden they were there. I stuck the grenade under my belly so that even if I was hit the grenade would not go off too easily, and if it did go off I would not feel pain. I willed myself to stop shaking, and I stopped breathing. There were about 10 or 12 of them, I figure. They took me for dead, thank God. They lay down all around me, still babbling.

One of them lay down on top of me and started to set up his machine gun. He dropped his canister next to my side. His feet were by my head, and his head was between my feet. He was about six feet tall and pretty bony. He probably couldn't feel me shaking because he was shaking so much himself. I thought I was gone. I was trying like hell to act dead, however the hell one does that.

The Cong opened up on our mortar platoon, which was set up around a big tree nearby. The platoon returned the fire, killing about half of the Cong, and miraculously not hitting me. All of a sudden a dozen loud "crumph" sounds went off all around me. Assuming that all the GI's in front of them were dead, our mortar platoon had opened up with M-79 grenade launchers. The Cong jumped up off me, moaning with fear, and the other PAVN began to move around. They apparently knew the M-79. Then a second series of explosions went off, killing all the Cong as they got up to run. One grenade landed between Thompson's head and Sgt. Moore's chest. Sgt. Moore saved my life; he took most of the shrapnel in his side. A piece got me in the head.

It felt as if a white-hot sledge hammer had hit the right side of my face. Then something hot and stinging hit my left leg. I lost consciousness for a few seconds. I came out of it feeling intense pain in my leg and a numbness in my head. I didn't dare feel my face: I thought the whole side of it had gone. Blood was pouring down my forehead and filling the hollow of my eyeglasses. It was also pouring out of my mouth. I slapped a bandage on the side of my face and tied it around my head. I was numbed, but I suddenly felt better. It had happened, and I was still alive.

I decided it was time to get out. None of my buddies appeared able to move. The Cong obviously had the mortar platoon pegged, and they would try to overrun it again. I was going to be right in their path. I crawled over Sgt. Moore, who had half his chest gone, and Thompson, who had no head left. Wilson, who had helped me with the XO, had been hit badly, but I couldn't tell where. All that moved was his eyes. He asked me for some water. I gave him one of the two canteens I had scrounged. I still had the hand grenade.

I crawled over many bodies, all still. The 1st Platoon just didn't exist anymore. One guy had his arm blown off. There was only some shredded skin and a piece of bone sticking out of his sleeve. The sight didn't bother me anymore. The artillery was still keeping up a steady barrage, as were the planes, and the noise was as loud as ever, but I didn't hear it anymore. It was a miracle I didn't get shot by the snipers in the trees while I was moving.

As I was crawling around looking for someone alive, I came across Sgt. Barker, who stuck a .45 in my face. He thought I was a Cong and almost shot me. Apparently I was now close to the mortar platoon. Many other wounded men had crawled over there, including the medic Novak, who had run out of supplies after five minutes. Barker was hit in the legs. Caine was hurt badly too. There were many others, all in bad shape. I lay there with the hand grenade under me, praying. The

Cong made several more attacks, which the mortar platoon fought off with 79's.

The Cong figured out that the mortar platoon was right by that tree, and three of their machine-gun crews crawled up and started to blaze away. It had taken them only a minute or so to find exactly where the platoon was; it took them half a minute to wipe it out. When they opened up, I heard a guy close by scream, then another, and another. Every few seconds someone would scream. Some got hit several times. In 30 seconds the platoon was virtually nonexistent. I heard Lt. Sheldon scream three times, but he lived. I think only five or six guys from the platoon were alive the next day.

It also seemed that most of them were hit in the belly. I don't know why, but when a man is hit in the belly, he screams an unearthly scream. Something you cannot imagine; you actually have to hear it. When a man is hit in the chest or the belly, he keeps on screaming, sometimes until he dies. I just lay there, numb, listening to the bullets whining over me and the 15 or 20 men close to me screaming and screaming and screaming. They didn't ever stop for breath. They kept on until they were hoarse, then they would bleed through their mouths and pass out. They would wake up and start screaming again. Then they would die.

I started crying. Sgt. Gale was lying near me. He had been hit badly in the stomach and was in great pain. He would lie very still for a while and then scream. He would scream for a doctor, then he would scream for a medic. He pleaded with anyone he saw to help him, for the love of God, to stop his pain or kill him. He would thrash around and scream some more, and then lie still for a while. He was bleeding a lot. Everyone was. No matter where you put your hand, the ground was sticky.

Sgt. Gale lay there for over six hours before he died. No one had any medical supplies, no one could move, and no one would shoot him.

Several guys shot themselves that day. Schiff, although he was not wounded, completely lost his head and killed himself with his own grenade. Two other men, both wounded, shot themselves with .45's rather than let themselves be captured alive by the gooks. No one will ever know how many chose that way out, since all the dead had been hit over and over again.

All afternoon we could hear the PAVN, a whole battalion, running through the grass and trees. Hundreds of GI's were scattered on the ground like salt. Sprinkled among them like pepper were the wounded and dead Cong. The GI's who were wounded badly were screaming for medics. The Cong soon found them and killed them.

All afternoon there was smoke, artillery, screaming, moaning, fear, bullets, blood, and little yellow men running around screeching with glee when they found one of us alive, or screaming and moaning with fear when they ran into a grenade or a bullet. I suppose that all massacres in wars are a bloody mess, but this one seemed bloodier to me because I was caught in it.

About dusk a few helicopters tried landing in the L.Z., about 40 yards over to the left, but whenever one came within 100 feet of the ground, so many machine guns would open up on him that it sounded like a training company at a machine gun range.

At dusk the North Vietnamese started to mortar us. Some of the mortars they used were ours that they had captured. Suddenly the ground behind me lifted up, and there was a tremendous noise. I knew something big had gone off right behind me. At the same time I felt something white-hot go into my right thigh. I started screaming and screaming. The pain was terrible. Then I said, "My legs. God, my legs," over and over.

Still screaming, I ripped the bandage off my face and tied it around my thigh. It didn't fit, so I held it as tight as I could with my fingers. I could feel the blood pouring out of the hole. I cried and moaned. It was hurting unbelievably. The realization came to me now, for the first time, that I was not going to live.

With hardly any light left, the Cong decided to infiltrate the woods thoroughly. They were running everywhere. There were no groupings of Americans left in the woods, just a GI here and there. The planes had left, but the artillery kept up the barrage.

Then the flares started up. As long as there was some light, the Cong wouldn't try an all-out attack. I was lying there in a stupor, thirsty. God, I was thirsty. I had been all afternoon with no water, sweating like hell.

I decided to chance a cigarette. All my original equipment and weapons were gone, but somehow my cigarettes were still with me. The ends were bloody. I tore off the ends and lit the middle part of a cigarette.

Cupping it and blowing away the smoke, I managed to escape detection. I knew I was a fool. But at this stage I didn't really give a damn. By now the small-arms fire had stopped almost entirely. The woods were left to the dead, the wounded, and the artillery barrage.

At nightfall I had crawled across to where Barker, Caine and a few others were lying. I didn't say a word. I just lay there on my back, listening to the swishing of grass, the sporadic fire and the constant artillery, which was coming pretty close. For over six hours now shells had been landing within a hundred yards of me.

I didn't move, because I couldn't. Reaching around, I found a canteen of water. The guy who had taken the last drink from it must have been hit in the face, because the water was about one third blood. I didn't mind. I passed it around.

About an hour after dark there was a heavy concentration of small-arms fire all around us. It lasted about five minutes. It was repeated at intervals all night long. Battalion Hq. was firing a protective fire, and we were right in the path of the bullets. Some of our men were getting hit by the rounds ricocheting through the woods.

I lay there shivering. At night in the highlands the temperature goes down to 50 or so. About midnight I heard the grass swishing. It was men, and a lot of them too. I took my hand grenade and straightened out the pin. I thought to myself that now at last they were going to come and kill all the wounded that were left. I was sure I was going to die, and I really did not care anymore. I did not want them to take me alive. The others around me were either unconscious or didn't care. They were just lying there. I think most of them had quietly died in the last few hours. I know one—I did not recognize him—wanted to be alone to die. When he felt himself going, he crawled over me (I don't know how), and a few minutes later I heard him gurgle, and, I guess, die.

Then suddenly I realized that the men were making little whistling noises. Maybe these weren't the Cong. A few seconds later a patrol of GI's came into view, about 15 guys in line, looking for wounded.

Everyone started pawing toward them and crying. It turned me into a babbling idiot. I grabbed one of the guys and wouldn't let go. They had four stretchers with them, and they took the four worst wounded and all the walking wounded, about 10 or so, from the company. I was desperate, and I told the leader I could walk, but when Peters helped me to my feet, I passed out cold.

When I regained consciousness, they had gone, but their medic was left behind, a few feet from me, by a tree. He hadn't seen me, and had already used his meager supply of bandages on those guys who had crawled up around the tree. His patrol said they would be back in a few hours.

I clung to the hope, but I knew damn well they weren't coming back. Novak, who was one of the walking wounded, had left me his .45. I lost one of the magazines, and the only other one had only three bullets in it. I still had the hand grenade.

I crawled up to the tree. There were about eight guys there, all badly wounded. Lt. Sheldon was there, and he had the only operational radio left in the company. I couldn't hear him, but he was talking to the company commander, who had gotten separated from us. Lt. Sheldon had been wounded in the thighbone, the kneecap and the ankle.

Some time after midnight, in my half-conscious stupor, I heard a lot of rustling on both sides of the tree. I nudged the lieutenant, and then he heard it too. Slowly, everyone who could move started to arm himself. I don't know who it was—it might even have been me—but someone made a noise with a weapon.

The swishing noise stopped immediately. Ten yards or so from us an excited babbling started. The gooks must have thought they had run into a pocket of resistance around the tree. Thank God they didn't dare rush us, because we wouldn't have lasted a second. Half of us were too weak to even cock our weapons. As a matter of fact, there were a couple who did not have fingers to cock with.

Then a clanking noise started: They were setting up a machine gun right next to us. I noticed that some artillery shells were landing close now, and every few seconds they seemed to creep closer to us, until one of the Cong screamed. Then the babbling grew louder. I heard the lieutenant on the radio; he was requesting a salvo to bracket us. A few seconds later there was a loud whistling in the air and shells were landing all around us, again and again. I heard the Cong run away. They left some of their wounded a couple of yards from us, moaning and screaming, but they died within a few minutes.

Every half hour or so the artillery would start all over again. It was a long night. Every time, the shells came so close to our position that we could hear the shrapnel striking the tree a foot or so above our heads, and could hear other pieces humming by just inches over us.

All night long the Cong had been moving around killing the wounded. Every few minutes I heard some guy start screaming, "No no no please," and then a burst of bullets. When they found a guy who was wounded, they'd make an awful racket. They'd yell for their buddies and babble awhile, then turn the poor devil over and listen to him while they stuck a barrel in his face and squeezed.

About an hour before dawn the artillery stopped, except for an occasional shell. But the small-arms firing started up again, just as heavy as it had been the previous afternoon. The GI's about a mile away were advancing and clearing the ground and trees of Cong (and a few Americans too). The snipers, all around the trees and in them, started firing back.

When a bullet is fired at you, it makes a distinctive, sharp, cracking sound. The firing by the GI's was all cracks. I could hear thuds all around me from the bullets. I thought I was all dried out from bleeding and sweating, but now I started sweating all over again. I thought, How futile it would be to die now from an American bullet. I just barely managed to keep myself from screaming out loud. I think some guy near me got hit. He let out a long sigh and gurgled.

Soon the sky began to turn red and orange. There was complete silence everywhere now. Not even the birds started their

usual singing. As the sun was coming up, everyone expected
a human-wave charge by the PAVN, and then a total massacre.
We didn't know that the few Cong left from the battle had
pulled out just before dawn, leaving only their wounded and
a few suicide squads behind.

When the light grew stronger, I could see all around me.
The scene might have been the devil's butcher shop. There
were dead men all around the tree. I found that the dead body
I had been resting my head on was that of Burgess, one of
my buddies. I could hardly recognize him. He was a professional saxophone player with only two weeks left in the Army.

Right in front of me was Sgt. Delaney with both his legs
blown off. I had been staring at him all night without knowing who he was. His eyes were open and covered with dirt.
Sgt. Gale was dead too. Most of the dead were unrecognizable
and were beginning to stink. There was blood and mess all
over the place.

Half a dozen of the wounded were alive. Lord, who was
full of shrapnel; Lt. Sheldon, with several bullet wounds;
Morris, shot in the legs and arm; Sloan, with his fingers shot
off; Olson, with his leg shot up and hands mutilated; and
some guy from another company who was holding his guts
from falling out.

Dead Cong were hanging out of the trees everywhere. The
Americans had fired bursts that had blown some snipers right
out of the trees. But these guys, they were just hanging and
dangling there in silence.

We were all sprawled out in various stages of unconscious-
ness. My wounds had started bleeding again, and the heat was
getting bad. The ants were getting to my legs.

Lt. Sheldon passed out, so I took over the radio. That
whole morning is rather blurred in my memory. I remember
talking for a long time with someone from Battalion Hq. He
kept telling me to keep calm, that they would have the medics
and helicopters in there in no time. He asked me about the
condition of the wounded. I told him that the few who were
still alive wouldn't last long. I listened for a long time on the
radio to chit-chat between MedEvac pilots, Air Force jet pilots
and Battalion Hq. Every now and then I would call up and

ask when they were going to pick us up. I'm sure I said a lot
of other things, but I don't remember much about it.

I just couldn't understand at first why the MedEvacs didn't
come in and get us. Finally I heard on the radio that they
wouldn't land because no one knew whether or not the area
was secure. Some of the wounded guys were beginning to
babble. It seemed like hours before anything happened.

Then a small Air Force spotter plane was buzzing overhead.
It dropped a couple of flares in the L.Z. nearby, marking the
spot for an airstrike. I thought, My God, the strike is going
to land on top of us. I got through to the old man—the
company commander—who was up ahead, and he said that it
wouldn't come near us and for us not to worry. But I worried,
and it landed pretty damn close.

There was silence for a while, then they started hitting the
L.Z. with artillery, a lot of it. This lasted for a half hour or
so, and then the small arms started again, whistling and buzzing through the woods. I was terrified. I thought, My Lord,
is this never going to end? If we're going to die, let's get it
over with.

Finally the firing stopped, and there was a ghastly silence.
Then the old man got on the radio again and talked to me.
He called in a helicopter and told me to guide it over our
area. I talked to the pilot, directing him, until he said he could
see me. Some of the wounded saw the chopper and started
yelling, "Medic, Medic." Others were moaning feebly and
struggling to wave at the chopper.

The old man saw the helicopter circling and said he was
coming to help us. He asked me to throw a smoke grenade,
which I pulled off Lt. Sheldon's gear. It went off, and the old
man saw it, because soon after that I heard the guys coming.
They were shooting as they walked along. I screamed into the
radio, "Don't shoot, don't shoot," but they called back and
said they were just shooting PAVN.

Then I saw them: The 1st sergeant, our captain and the two
radio operators. The captain came up to me and asked me
how I was. I said to him: "Sorry, Sir, I lost my —— ax." He
said, "Don't worry, Smitty, we'll get you another one."

The medics at the L.Z. cut off my boots and put bandages

on me. My wounds were in pretty bad shape. You know what happens when you take raw meat and throw it on the ground on a sunny day. We were out there for 24 hours, and Vietnam is nothing but one big anthill.

I was put in a MedEvac chopper and flown to Pleiku, where they changed dressings and stuck all sorts of tubes in my arms. At Pleiku I saw Gruber briefly. He was a clerk in the battalion, and my Army buddy. We talked until they put me in the plane. I learned that Stern and Deschamps, close friends, had been found dead together, shot in the backs of their heads, executed by the Cong. Gruber had identified their bodies. Everyone was crying. Like most of the men in our battalion, I had lost all my Army friends.

I heard the casualty figures a few days later. The North Vietnamese unit had been wiped out—over 500 dead. Out of some 500 men in our battalion alone, about 150 had been killed, and only 84 returned to base camp a few days later. In my company, which was right in the middle of the ambush, we had 93-percent casualties—one half dead, one half wounded. Almost all the wounded were crippled for life. The company, in fact, was very nearly annihilated.

Our unit is part of the 7th Cavalry—Custer's old unit. That day in the Ia Drang Valley, history repeated itself.

After a week in and out of field hospitals I ended up at Camp Zama in Japan. They have operated on me twice. They tell me that I'll walk again, and that my legs are going to be fine. But no one can tell me when I will stop having nightmares.

The Saturday Evening Post, January 28, 1967

A Viet Cong

by Susan Sheehan

HUYNH VAN KIM, who has also used the aliases Huynh Thanh and Huynh Long, joined the Viet Cong in January, 1958, when it was still known as the underground revolutionary movement. He was then twenty-one years old.

One night in December, 1957, a dozen Viet Cong recruiting agents appeared in his hamlet in Binh Thuan village, in the delta province of Dinh Tuong. Some of the agents, who were dressed as Viet Minh troops, were armed. They invited Kim and five or six other young men in the hamlet to accompany them to a base in the jungle a mile away. Kim was afraid and said he wouldn't go, but the agents told him they just wanted to have a friendly talk with him and he consented to follow them. Once at their base, the agents lectured the boys. The lectures pointed out some of the shortcomings of Diem's régime—his failure to hold the agreed-upon 1956 elections, to carry out land reform, or to remove corrupt officials. The young men were urged to join the revolutionary movement in order to work for Diem's overthrow. The agents said that this would result in justice for the people, a more equitable distribution of land, and reunification of the country. After a couple of hours, the agents let the boys go, warning them to say nothing about their activities. The agents returned every night. Each time they came to the hamlet they invited five or six young men to go with them. They came to Kim's home and invited him to lectures every third or fourth night. The agents kept asking him if he had made a decision to join the movement. At the end of a month of lectures, Kim agreed to join.

Kim, who is now a well-built, high-strung, chain-smoking young man of twenty-nine with watchful eyes, a forced smile, and a nervous habit of cracking his knuckles, joined the Viet Cong for several reasons. He was favorably impressed by the

VC indoctrination lectures; he didn't personally know of the injustices the agents mentioned—he thought his hamlet chief was all right, his grandfather owned several acres of land, and he had never heard a word about any elections—but he had no way of determining whether the injustices existed elsewhere, and the agents were so persuasive that he believed them. Kim was most eager for reunification. Many of his cousins, Viet Minh who had fought against the French, had gone north with their units in 1954, and he and their families missed them. If the country were whole again, they might return. The fact that two of Kim's older brothers had been killed by the Viet Minh while serving in the French Army left him with no ill feelings toward the Viet Minh. French troops had come to Binh Thuan on operations and had done a great deal of raping and stealing in the village. He thought his brothers would never have joined the French Army if they had seen French soldiers burn down their own parents' home, as Kim had. According to Kim, fear also played a part in his decision to join the Viet Cong. "I wasn't forced to join," he says, "but I felt a veiled threat, because the government seemed pretty indifferent or helpless to prevent the armed agents from coming into my village and taking people away for indoctrination." Kim also joined because he had no appealing alternative. He was the ninth of eleven children. Three of his brothers and sisters died of illness, in addition to the two brothers killed by the Viet Minh; Kim, two older sisters, one older brother, and two younger brothers survived. There was no primary school in Kim's hamlet. He started primary school in another hamlet in Binh Thuan village when he was twelve. He enjoyed school very much (mathematics was the subject he liked most, dictation the subject he liked least), but the road to school was flooded most of the time, making attendance difficult, and he gave up school after four years, and went to work in his grandfather's rice fields. He didn't care for the work. The VC also promised Kim he could stay near his village if he joined them, and he believed that if he was drafted into the government Army, he would be sent far from home. Kim had married a girl from another hamlet in Binh Thuan when he was eighteen. He had seen her at school and at the village market. Kim's father, a schoolteacher, had deserted the family when Kim was fourteen and had gone to live in another hamlet in the village with his mistress; Kim asked his mother to get the girl for him and she did. They had been happy together during the first three years of their marriage and had one son. Kim wanted to remain near his wife.

The day after Kim announced his decision, the agents took him to another nearby jungle base, which consisted of several well-concealed thatched huts on the bank of a creek. About thirty people, all of them South Vietnamese, lived there—ten armed senior agents and twenty newly recruited junior agents, who were not given arms. From the day they arrived at the base, Kim and the other new junior agents followed the same rigorous daily schedule—seven and a half hours of political studies, an hour and a half of physical exercise, and an hour of social life, which was devoted to learning revolutionary poems and songs. They were fed three skimpy meals a day, of rice and fish, or just rice and salt. At the political lectures, the senior agents dwelt on the evils of the Saigon government. The government was blamed over and over again for countless injustices, and for the partition of the country. The lectures were followed by discussions of the ideas that had just been repeated for hours. "During the first month, I only listened to the lecturers," Kim says. "I didn't take part in the discussions. Then I got more interested, and I also realized that it didn't pay to keep silent, so I decided to be more talkative and to show more enthusiasm. I got through the initial period of political studies in two months. For those who didn't seem as receptive to the ideas as I was, political studies lasted as long as five or six months." The lecturers told Kim, a nominal Buddhist, not to believe in the Buddha.

In March, 1958, Kim was given two hand grenades. He was assigned to escort senior agents on their nightly recruiting excursions to the villages in the area. He was supposed to help protect them and to master their recruiting technique. He still attended political lectures, but only for an hour or two a day. In November, 1959, as a result of having effectively escorted the senior agents and of having done well in his political training, he was made a cadre and became a senior recruiting agent. He was proud to be promoted. In early 1960, Kim was told of the imminent formation of a nationwide Liberation

Front. He was also told that the revolutionary movement would soon become more militant. He continued his nightly recruiting missions and his daily political studies and he was also given a little military training: he was taught how to fire, dismantle, and reassemble an old French bolt-action rifle. In his first two years with the VC, Kim saw his family only infrequently, at night, when he was on his way to a recruiting mission near his home. He was too busy in the daytime, studying or sleeping, and visits home were discouraged by his superiors. Although the food was bad and Kim had to ask his family for clothes and spending money (the VC weren't paid and were taught to regard the government soldiers as mercenaries) he was happy with his work.

On December 1, 1960, the sixty people at the base, some of them young men Kim had recruited, were divided into two groups. Thirty, including Kim, were assigned to the military section, thirty, to the political section. They were carefully primed by the senior agents for a night attack on Binh Thuan that was to take place in mid-December. On the appointed night, both sections went together to Kim's native village. The political section had a few weapons, but their main duty was to shout slogans and declarations, urging people to rise up against the government. The military team's duty was to kill certain pre-selected government officials and supporters in the village. The VC took the village completely by surprise. They had several guns, but they didn't fire a shot. They used scimitars to behead ten people in the seven hamlets in the village, including the chief of Kim's hamlet. Kim didn't kill his hamlet chief, but he killed five of the other victims, three men and two women. "It was the first time I'd done any killing, but it didn't upset me," he says. "Before we decided to kill those people, we discussed their misdeeds at length, and we had official documents to prove their guilt. The women were spies. I personally found out that they had hung up torches to warn government troops of our presence in the village when we came to recruit." That night, the government troops fired at the VC from a nearby outpost. They didn't hit any of them. After the attack, the VC returned to their jungle base.

Over the next year, Kim went on recruiting expeditions and also accompanied some of his comrades to villages in the area to assassinate government officials and soldiers, and to capture badly needed weapons. At that time, the VC at the base were poorly armed, but in most villages there was only one platoon of government militia, which couldn't protect an entire village. Government troops in nearby outposts became reluctant to leave their forts after they had been ambushed a few times when they had set out to rescue a hamlet. Occasionally, the VC clashed with government soldiers out on patrol. In one skirmish, two Viet Cong were killed and Kim was wounded; a rifle bullet grazed his right knee. He was able to run about half a mile, and then had to be carried the rest of the way back to the base by his comrades. It took his wound two weeks to heal. In 1961, fifteen VC were killed; their losses were more than made up for by new recruits from the terrorized villages. That year, the VC at Kim's base killed about fifteen government officials and soldiers, and captured a number of guns. At the end of 1961, Kim was made a political cadre and was assigned to work with the youth in Binh Thuan. He gave them political education (while continuing his own political studies) and incited them to destroy bridges, tear up roads, and demonstrate against the government.

In January, 1963, Kim was sent to a VC district headquarters near Binh Thuan. He stayed there a while and it was decided that he would be promoted from village guerrilla to the main force Viet Cong, on the basis of his good record. Kim was unhappy with this promotion. In the last five years, he had been able to spend very little time with his family, although he had never lived far from his hamlet. In 1962, his wife had left him and had returned to her father's home. Their son was living with Kim's mother. Kim wanted to be near his village, as he'd been promised when he joined the VC, so that he could see his child, but he was afraid to protest. He was sent to join a main force unit in Tay Ninh, another province in the delta. It took Kim nearly two months to make the trip from Binh Thuan to a jungle camp a short distance from the provincial capital of Tay Ninh, a distance of only seventy-five miles. He and his companions walked at night and had to check with local Viet Cong officials every step of the way. He reached his destination in early May, and was granted a week's rest. For the next six months, he was given his first real mil-

itary training. He was taught to handle recoilless and automatic rifles, machine and submachine guns, carbines, and
mortars. Kim was allowed to fire only one round of ammunition during his whole training period. He was told to shoot
at a mark on the side of a deserted government outpost, from
a distance of two hundred yards. He came close to the target
and was considered a good marksman. The second time he
fired was in actual combat. During his military training period,
Kim spent an hour and a half a day on political studies. "In
the late fifties, we were taught to fight against the national
government, but after 1961, the one point driven home to us
more than any other was the need to drive the American imperialists out of South Viet Nam," he says. "We were told to
attack them at every opportunity, to keep them from taking
over our country." In October, 1963, Kim was assigned to a
main force battalion stationed in Tay Ninh province. He became a mortar crewman and had his first chance to fire the
mortar on the night of November 1, 1963, when his battalion
attacked a government outpost in a nearby province. Over the
following months, Kim's battalion attacked a number of other
government outposts, most of them in Tay Ninh province,
and got into several minor and two major clashes with government troops. In February, 1964, when Kim's battalion was
attacking an outpost in Tay Ninh, ten of his comrades were
killed. Kim and four other VC were wounded. A bullet grazed
Kim's thigh, but it didn't hit a bone and he required no sur-
gery. The Viet Cong considered this a major engagement and
a victory, because they overran the outpost. In the second major clash, in July, 1964—the biggest action Kim has ever taken
part in—his battalion attacked another outpost in Tay Ninh
and ambushed a government relief column. The fighting went
on sporadically for two days and two nights. One hundred
VC were killed and fifty wounded. Fifty government troops
were killed and the battle was considered a defeat. "Practically
all of our casualties were inflicted by bombers and armored
personnel carriers," Kim says. "The airpower was so terrible
we couldn't overrun the outpost and seize any weapons. With
airpower, the VC could give the Army a much rougher time."

When they weren't fighting, Kim and the men in his battalion spent their time attending political lectures, receiving

additional military training, and collecting provisions from the villages in the area. They sometimes slept at battalion headquarters, sometimes in VC villages, and sometimes, when traveling, in the jungle in hammocks. "It was especially uncomfortable when it was raining," Kim says. "We often had to work too hard when we were badly fed. But I liked the spirit of democracy and that made up for many things. We were free to criticize any officials or commanders, no matter how important they were, and they had to admit their shortcomings and promise to do better in the future. We didn't have to fear criticizing people. We were criticized often ourselves. Criticism sessions were held once a week."

At the end of August, 1964, Kim's mother came to Tay Ninh to see him. She begged him to leave the Viet Cong. Kim's older brother and one of his younger brothers were still in Binh Thuan, working in the rice fields, but one of his younger brothers had gone to Saigon to study and had become a government policeman. Kim's mother was in tears when she told Kim she wanted her sons on one side. "I'd been having serious doubts about the VC and I wanted very much to be stationed back home again, but if my mother hadn't come to see me, I would have kept my rebellious ideas to myself," Kim says. "I felt very sorry when I saw my mother weeping. I began saying I wanted to go home, and I was severely criticized at the criticism sessions for being selfish. One day, I lost my temper. I almost shot a man who had criticized me especially sharply. As a result, I was sent to a reeducation center for recalcitrant elements, in September, 1964." At the VC reeducation center in Tay Ninh province, Kim and forty other "recalcitrant elements" spent their time listening to political lectures and doing a few other chores, such as growing vegetables and building huts. They didn't have to fight. "During the first months, I couldn't help showing my resentment," Kim says. "I realized that wasn't getting me anywhere, so after a while I began to pose as a docile element and to master the lectures. After a few months, I was asked whether I wanted to continue with the Front or rejoin my family. I knew this was a test. No one is allowed to retire from the VC until he's very old, very sick, or seriously disabled. I was afraid to arouse suspicion, so I said I wanted to

continue. They sent me out on several food-buying missions.
I didn't try to escape, because I knew I was being watched
closely. I was released from the reeducation center in July,
1965, and sent to a different regiment in Tay Ninh, to wait for
a new assignment. The regiment was based in the jungle, very
close to the Cambodian border." While waiting, Kim was sent
out on various missions. Once, he was sent to a village about
five miles from the regimental base to tell the village cadres
to take special care to prevent defections, because the government was going to drop leaflets over the village describing its
"Open Arms" program in the next few days. According to
the government, Viet Cong who surrendered would receive
amnesty under the Open Arms program. The cadres were told
to tell the VC that the program was a hoax, and that the
government would torture defectors to death. Kim's regimental headquarters had received word of the imminent leaflet drop from VC infiltrated into the Open Arms program.
Kim was often dispatched on food-buying missions. One day
in August, 1965, he and three comrades were sent to a village
a few miles from regimental headquarters to buy rice and fish.
Dried fish was not available in the large quantity they had
been ordered to get. Kim's friends returned to regimental
headquarters in the afternoon, with the provisions they had
succeeded in purchasing. Kim stayed on in the village to try
to buy more fish. He spent the night under the watchful eyes
of the local VC agents. The following day, there was a government operation in the village. The local VC cadres had to
flee, so the tight VC control system was temporarily relaxed.
Kim had been looking for an opportunity to defect from the
Viet Cong. He decided that this was an excellent moment,
because no one was watching him. He went to a farming area
at the foot of the Black Lady mountain, where peasants were
working in the rice fields under the protection of a government outpost. He stayed with the peasants until four in the
afternoon, and then boarded a civilian bus with them. The
bus took him to the provincial capital of Tay Ninh. When he
arrived there, he asked his way to a police station. At the Tay
Ninh police station, Kim told officials he had been a VC for
seven and a half years, and had decided to defect to the

government side. He asked for amnesty under the Open Arms
program.

Kim had wanted to leave the Viet Cong ever since his transfer to the main forces in early 1963. He was tired of fighting.
He had killed over fifteen people in addition to those he had
killed in his village in December, 1960. He feared that he
would be killed himself in the stepped-up fighting. He had
also become disillusioned with the VC. "I was enthusiastic
about the Viet Cong during my first years," Kim says. "I
couldn't continue school, or do anything else I wanted to do,
and I didn't like working in the rice fields. The VC seemed
to be the only good chance I had to advance. When I was
recruited, I was told that we would win in two years, and that
all the people would be happy and the country reunified. After
1962, the prospect of victory and reunification grew dimmer,
because the government was reinforced with American weapons and men. I was most enthusiastic about the Viet Cong in
1962, before my wife left me, when we were doing well and
victory seemed to be in sight. Then I began to realize we
might have to fight for years to reach the target we had
thought within our easy reach. By early 1965, I even thought
we might lose, if the Americans stuck it out in Viet Nam. We
were told the Americans wouldn't stick it out, but we had
been told in 1964 that the Americans wouldn't dare bomb
North Viet Nam, and we knew that they eventually did. We
also learned that the higher VC casualty figures were being
hidden from us. It's true that our political education was intensive, but only fresh recruits believed entirely in what they
were told. That's why most of the Front's real achievements
are made by the young. People who have been with the Front
for some time have had opportunities to test their side's assets.
They come to realize that a good deal of what the political
commissars taught was questionable. Many men who have
been with the Front for a long time become dissatisfied and
want to return to their families, but they don't act on their
dissatisfaction. They are afraid, and they realize that once
they've been in the Viet Cong, they don't have much of a
future out of it. Many VC officials are really dedicated. They
control the others, and push them to get things done. I prob-

ably would never have gotten started on the road to defection if my mother hadn't come to see me in Tay Ninh. I didn't like to see her weeping."

When he arrived at the police station in Tay Ninh and said he wanted to defect and get amnesty, Kim gave the officials there some Viet Cong papers—his purchasing orders for the dried fish—to prove his case. The officials kept him at the police station for three days and three nights. During that time, he underwent two four-hour-long sessions of questioning. He was asked about the activities and whereabouts of certain VC units, and was asked to give the names of high-ranking VC officers under whom he had served. Since many VC had aliases (Kim was called Huynh Thanh as a Viet Cong village guerrilla, Huynh Long when he was transferred to the main forces) he didn't know how helpful the names he supplied would be. After three days, he was taken to the Open Arms center in Tay Ninh, where he spent two weeks undergoing several more sessions similar to the ones at the police station. He was then taken by helicopter to a military compound at Bien Hoa, the headquarters of the third Army corps, which was in charge of Tay Ninh province, where he was interrogated for another two weeks. His questioners were very nice to him and were the first people since his defection to ask him about his personal life. They offered to help him find a job when he had gone through the Open Arms program. In September, Kim was sent to a military installation in Saigon—he had never been in the capital until then—and he spent almost a month there undergoing two long sessions of questioning every day, except Sunday. His interrogators, three Army intelligence officers, asked him to give them information about units he had been with, and about other units in the delta with which he was familiar. "I was treated badly by those officers," Kim says. "They always insisted I was telling them lies. They often beat me with a small stick, slapped my face, and insulted me. They asked me what a certain VC regiment did, and I told them it was a logistics and supply regiment. They beat me and told me they knew it was an important fighting regiment. It wasn't. The ARVN has more troops and better equipment than the VC—the VC fight in sandals, the ARVN soldiers have boots—but ARVN intelligence is very poor. The ARVN would be more effective if it had intelligence like the VC's. The Viet Cong have agents everywhere, from peasants in hamlets to high-ranking Army officers in Saigon. I've never seen evidence that the ARVN has infiltrated the VC." In October, Kim was abruptly taken to an Open Arms center in Saigon, a cluster of buildings with dormitories accommodating about a hundred defectors. Upon arrival at the center, Kim was given three hundred piasters. Each subsequent day, he has been given eighteen piasters, six for each meal. He usually skips breakfast and uses six piasters for cigarettes instead; he spent the three hundred original piasters on cigarettes, too. During his first six weeks at the Open Arms center, Kim followed a schedule similar to the one he had followed when he first joined the Viet Cong; it included six and a half hours of indoctrination a day. "I've been treated well, and I've been eating better on two meals here than I did in the Viet Cong on three," Kim says. "The living conditions are fine, but the VC political education seemed much more interesting to me. VC lecturers are very articulate. They use concrete words, which appeal to me. VC lecturers are South Vietnamese. The lecturers at the center were born in North Viet Nam and in the central part of South Viet Nam. They speak with a different accent than I do, and they expound too many abstract ideas. They confuse me. They talk about the history of Viet Nam, the fallacies of Communism, and the aggressive activities of Communism in the world. I cannot grasp what they mean, because everything is too general. At the center, we can feel very much at ease and we can afford to be absent-minded. I had to be very attentive at VC lectures and I had to repeat the ideas all the time. If I were a lecturer, I would enforce the Viet Cong's harsh policy. A teacher has to be strict to drive ideas into students' heads. I think the system at the center is much too relaxed, and it's very difficult for students to master ideas. The lecturers keep on talking about the revolutionary war council and its revolutionary policy, but they haven't told us who's in charge of the government. A few people got so bored with the aimless lectures that they just took off. The security is very loose. I could have escaped if I had wanted to."

Kim has had time to think a few things over since finishing

the six weeks indoctrination course at the Open Arms center
in Saigon. He used to believe that the United States wanted
to take over South Viet Nam to get its minerals, forests, and
rice, as he had been told by the VC. He no longer believes
this. He thinks the United States is so prosperous that the
Americans do not need anything in Viet Nam. He now believes individual people in the United States are good; he has
a few reservations about the American government, because
he thinks it is making people demonstrate against the war in
Viet Nam. "I don't think the demonstrators are sincere," Kim
says. "I think they're tools of the United States government.
The American government cooks up the demonstrations to
cover its real intentions. It is trying to mislead Hanoi into
thinking the United States will pull out of Viet Nam while it
is actually escalating the war. It's not good for a government
to do this." Kim was against all bombing when he was in the
Viet Cong, but now he says he is in favor of bombing North
Viet Nam and VC bases in the south. "But I'm against bombing South Vietnamese hamlets, even if there are VC in them,"
he says. "If you want to get the support of the general population, you have to work on the political front. You shouldn't
kill people and destroy their property. If you do that, the people will get dissatisfied with you and the Viet Cong will have
a good chance of getting the support of those who live
through the bombing." Kim used to think the VC would win
the war. He now believes the government will win, as long as
the Americans don't withdraw (and he doesn't think they will)
and as long as the Americans and the government forces are
fighting only VC and North Vietnamese troops. "I think the
government side would win, even if the Communist Chinese
sent troops," Kim says. "Numbers don't mean anything, and
the Chinese are quite backward in weaponry. But if the Soviet
Union became deeply involved, to the extent of sending
troops, the Russians would win, because they would only get
involved if they really understood the war. The Russians have
had much more experience in international wars than the
Americans. In 1945, the Russians liberated Germany and
launched the world-wide Socialism drive. They've had more
practice helping people fight for a cause. The Russians are also
much more advanced in technology than the Americans. They

were the first to send up spaceships. But they won't send troops, because the Russians and the Chinese don't get along well, and the Chinese won't let them."

When Kim leaves the Open Arms center in Saigon in a short while, he will go to Bien Hoa, where the authorities who interrogated him there have promised to help him find a job. He hopes his mother and his son will be able to join him in Bien Hoa. His wife has remarried. He does not blame her for anything, but he still loves her. He would like to remarry, but he doesn't know if he will be able to, because he expects difficult days ahead financially. Kim knows he must stay in a city. He wouldn't be safe from the VC in the countryside, or in a small district town. Kim doesn't speak English, and he doesn't think he will be able to find a decent job. "My prospects don't look too good," Kim says. "I'm grateful to the government. I've been nicely treated since I left the Viet Cong. But I would still like to go to school and I'll never be able to. The VC are right in saying that there are no real opportunities for poor people in this country. I feel a little bit sorry about having killed so many people, but my conscience is pretty much at peace, because I acted under conviction. I often wonder if I'll ever find anything to believe in again. I've spent so much of my time in the jungle that I don't think I'm good for anything now anyway. When I first left the Viet Cong, I worried what would happen to me if they won the war. I don't place as much value on my life now as I did then. I'm no longer afraid of dying. I don't think the VC infiltrators in the Open Arms program will kill me. I'm not worth it. But if they do—well, if I die today, I won't have to die tomorrow."

from *Ten Vietnamese,* 1967

Two Hilltops in a Marine's Life

by McCandlish Phillips

WHILE Richard Marks was at the Hackley School in Tarry-town he was a quietly agreeable, serious boy. Sometimes he would roam the school's wide hilltop clearing and gaze down at the silvery Hudson or climb to the highest outlook to trace the shimmering outlines of the vast city to the south.

Two hilltops became important in Ricky's life. He loved the high hill at Tarrytown, with its tall shade trees and spell-inducing vistas and the ivy that rustled against the weathered gray stones of the central building. He was one of 380 boys at the preparatory school in 1961 to 1963.

The other hill is just called Hill 69, a combat outpost in Vietnam from which, in the words of one of his letters, "they will probably try to push us off in the next few nights."

"It is now dusk and we are observing artillery fire in the area around us—it is truly beautiful in a morbid sort of way," he wrote to Peter Whiting, a mathematics instructor at Hackley.

This letter, and dozens of others received from combat zones by his mother and Mr. Whiting, tell a story of troopship impressions, excitement at travel, loneliness, yearnings, fright in battle and cherished plans for civilian tomorrows—a story known to thousands of American youths now serving in Vietnam.

The letters of Pfc. Richard E. Marks of the United States Marines—written in small-figured longhand and often run-ning to five pages—trace the expanding consciousness of a young man placed under prolonged and terrible stress.

For Ricky Marks, the transitions from boyhood, to raw Ma-rine recruit, to assault trooper "trained to kill," to the inten-sity of battle were very swift.

He was born in New York City and reared in Eastchester

and California. His father, Robert B. Marks, vice president of a music publishing firm here, died in 1963.

He entered Hackley as a freshman in 1961, but quit school after his sophomore year. After working briefly, he joined the Marines.

Snapshots sent home show Ricky as a trim, muscular young man 5 feet 10 and 150 pounds, before a low-grade fever began to gnaw him down.

Ricky became a helicopter assault machine gunner in one day (they told him he'd have to learn "the hard way.") At the age of 18 he found what it was to be "scared to death" and to feel his bones "aching all the time."

The monsoons and combat patrols of Vietnam stripped him of 30 pounds.

Last July his sergeant told him he had nine more months in Vietnam. "I'll go crazy," he wrote in a letter to his mother, Mrs. Stephen Kramer. "So far we have already had six Marines in the battalion go crazy, and one Sea Bee. This place is too much for an extended period of time."

As he saw men die, whole companies almost wiped out, Ricky, however, came deeply to believe in the military job of "restoring peace to this troubled land."

From a combat perspective in Vietnam, the letters show, the matters that began perplexing Ricky early were the student demonstrations here in support of Vietcong ambitions and—in his view—political interference with pursuit of the enemy in Vietnam.

"The only complaint I have about our work here is that we cannot do a complete job," his letter last July 30 to Mr. Whiting said. He cited "red tape" that prevented seizing strategic advantages.

"I have seen on more than one occasion when artillery targets (a large number of V.C. troops) were left unfired upon because the permission to fire had to be okayed by so many people and finally approved by the local Vietnamese officials—who in many cases have been proven to be working for the V.C."

He expressed anger when an air strike was banned against "a meeting of local V.C. leaders and some Chinese advisers . . . in a valley just outside our [area]."

"The local Vietnamese officials vetoed the mission because there were some cows in the area that might be killed. With foolish circumstances such as this, our forces in Vietnam will never be effective. We will only be effective here when the decision power is returned to the battalion and to company commanders and taken out of the hands of the politically polite, nonmilitant and usually V.C.-oriented men who now have it."

On July 7 he asked Mr. Whiting:

"How can these people [college and university demonstrators] be serious? Don't they realize we are fighting the same type of bid for world take-over here in Vietnam, as we did against Hitler in Europe, and Japan in the Pacific? . . . We can fight the war now in Vietnam, or in 10 years in Mexico or South America, and maybe even in our own United States."

This winter, Ricky began to count the days—120, 90, 75—until his time in Vietnam would be up. His letters show increasing eagerness to get back to the States and to visit the Tarrytown campus.

His mother has 77 letters and Mr. Whiting has 11. The first of the letters are filled with Ricky's impressions of his first ocean voyage.

From the Pacific, after half a day in Honolulu on April 7, 1965, he wrote his mother and his married sister, Sue, that "Waikiki Beach is all and more than it is described as—the beaches are beautiful and the water is a clear, pale blue. The surfers are at it from sunup to past sundown—the bikinis are all, and less, than described."

On April 8, while at sea, he wrote:

"Tonight I went topside at about 10 P.M., and it is beautiful out—it is a half moon, and the night is clear and warm. The moonbeams were dancing on the water, which is calm as a summer lake. . . . It makes me feel good to know from here on out there is no one to fall back on but myself—I must accept the responsibilities for all my faults now.

"One of the guys here just asked me where I was from—where is my home? The more I think of it I haven't really any home to call my own, except the Marine Corps. Being on board ship gives a person a lot of time to think about things. I've done a lot of thinking, and have a lot to do."

On April 11, still at sea, he wrote his mother:

"Last night I saw 'Charade.' Cary Grant and Audrey Hepburn—an A.O.K. flick. We will land in Okinawa on Monday morning. . . . According to rumor we are going to Vietnam."

Things moved fast then. He thought he would have a month's special combat training in Okinawa. The reality of war began to come into sharp focus. On April 24, he wrote Mr. Whiting:

"Well yesterday it all came out. Two companies of our sister battalion were almost wiped out by the Vietcong. For the first time I finally realized how serious Vietnam is. Guys I had been with the week before aboard ship were now dead. At first I was sad, then I was angry, and finally I became scared—I still am.

"We are scheduled to leave next Monday and I will be in Vietnam on Wednesday. That means contact by next Friday. That is one day I do not look forward to—I would rather face Mr. Bridges when he was furious. [A reference to the guidance director at Hackley who had remonstrated with Ricky about his grades.]

"I am attached to an M60 machine-gun team, and I know nothing about machine guns—the way my platoon commander put it: 'You'll have to learn the hard way.' At any rate, this is one time I will not fall asleep in class. I'm going to make the first helicopter assault landing, and I don't want to miss my chance to practice."

In one letter to his mother there is this request:

"Send me one bottle of Scotch packed in popcorn—not only can I eat the popcorn, but it also absorbs much of the shock to the package."

He joined the Book Find Club from Vietnam, asked his mother for the Old Testament and some plays of Shakespeare and for "Sam Durell" books because "he is a modified James Bond."

"We love to get pictures of pretty girls, as you must know," he wrote from Manhdong. "We have all been without the pleasure of female companionship for four months." Later he wrote that he was "a real monsoon veteran—it has rained for 16 days straight now."

As the young Marine went through frequent combat and saw men die, he became surer and surer of why he was there.

"I, as a member of the Fourth Marines, am not only helping to further Marine tradition, but I am also, in a small and important way, helping to write 20th century history," he wrote proudly from the front.

"Each night they probe our lines and throw hand grenades," he wrote Mr. Whiting from Chulai on July 30. "Due to the noise of the rain and the wind, it is extremely hard to hear them moving in the brush—and obviously much harder to see them. Some day soon, the V.C. will mass and overrun our outposts and then try to destroy the airfield we are guarding.

"Many lives will be lost on both sides, but the airfield will not fall. We are outnumbered here, but we are also determined."

"My bones are aching all the time, and I am always tired," he wrote on Aug. 15, 1965, after four months in Vietnam. He had lost 30 pounds.

His mother wrote to Senator Jacob K. Javits expressing worry about her son. Ricky wrote her that the letter "made me seem like the only person over here involved in the war."

"Just don't write anymore—O.K.?" he asked. "There are 45,000 other Marines over here who had stood watch, run patrols, lost weight, had fevers, and seen action, and a hell of a lot of them will never see home again."

The letters express a deep contempt for the aims and acts of the Vietcong, particularly rape, and a determination to drive them out. But in the gung-ho Marine, the letters show, the civilian remained.

To Mr. Whiting he wrote of a classmate:

"I have been corresponding with Roger B. He told me he has left the University of Pittsburgh, and is joining the Marine Corps. No, I did not suggest it. As a matter of fact, I think he is a damn fool."

The letters are of dreams, too. Several tell of his decision to get a high school diploma and then to study law in night classes after his discharge.

On Feb. 5, he wrote: "I have just returned today from a patrol that lasted seven nights and six days . . . the whole time out there I was scared to death . . . today I was overjoyed at being alive . . ."

Not long ago, Mr. Whiting wrote to tell Ricky that excerpts from his letters were to run in the Hackley alumni journal. The Marine replied that he had never been able to get any work of his into the school literary or newspapers "and now, out of a rainy Vietnamese sky, I'm in print. . . . It is hard to find words to tell you how wonderful that makes me feel."

At Danang he enjoyed an unexpected breather. "All of the helicopters have been diverted, therefore our patrol today, which would have required helicopters, has been canceled, thank God," he wrote. "I figured this patrol I would get a Purple Heart. Nothing serious—just enough to shake the insides out of me."

As the days on his calendar of combat duty in Vietnam dropped from many to few, he wrote Mr. Whiting:

"Please put me down to attend all the events of the Homecoming. From the invitations I realize that many additions have come to the school. . . . But the old traditional rivalry of Riverdale and Hackley has not changed. I suppose there are some things in the world that never change."

Ricky was invited by Mr. Whiting to address the student body on April 4. He will not be there.

Instead, a memorial service for him will be held in King Chapel at the school next Sunday afternoon.

Ricky's Marine dog tag rests now on a table in an apartment in Manhattan: "MARKS, R.E. 2030503 USMC A M JEWISH."

Last Feb. 14 he was riding in an amphibious tractor near Danang. The machine touched a mine. Light flashed up all around it and he "sustained multiple extreme burns of the entire body," as the military telegram said.

Ricky was buried on Feb. 21 at Arlington National Cemetery on a gentle slope just below the crest of a hill. He was 19 years old.

The New York Times, March 6, 1966

Teach-In on Vietnam By . . .

. . . The President, the Secretary of State, the Secretary of Defense and the Under Secretary of State

by Henry F. Graff

WASHINGTON.
HOWEVER future historians may write about Vietnam, contemporaries know that the war has entered a new phase in the past few weeks. The fulfillment of the promises made at Honolulu by President Johnson and in Asia by Vice President Humphrey and other members of the Administration depends not only on the national purse but even more heavily on military success in the field. Plans are being made in conformity with this fact. The plans, as always, reflect the temper, the mood and the assumptions of the principal policy-makers.

In the third week of February, I had the opportunity to assay these elements of decision-making in conversations with President Johnson and some of the men around him. I had talked to some of the same men last June, just before the big build-up of ground forces in Vietnam. Among those I talked to this time, in addition to the President, were Secretaries Rusk and McNamara and Under Secretary of State George W. Ball. Once again, I was looking for responses to the kinds of questions which historians know ought to be answered in the heat of crisis.

The round of conversations began early on the morning of Washington's Birthday. It was a brisk, clear day and the public buildings were almost deserted. The flags were at half-staff in mourning for Admiral of the Fleet Chester W. Nimitz. I remember thinking, as I walked toward the Department of State, that the city had an air of melancholy appropriate to the subject I had come to discuss.

I called first on George W. Ball, Under Secretary of State, a lawyer by profession, who has been in and out of Government service for 30 years. I wanted especially to talk to him because, in the aviary of Vietnam policy-making, he is sometimes labeled a "dove."

My first question was: What lay behind the peace offensive of last December and January.

It was, he said, an effort to break the deadlock with Hanoi. Several East European countries "had indicated that their efforts at seeking to end the war were foreclosed by the air offensive against the North." This, he said, had been implied by the Soviet Union, too, "but mostly by the East Europeans."

I asked Ball if the cessation of the bombing in the North had taken place with an eye to the possible favorable political effect it could have in some places here at home. Ball replied that politics can never be excluded—"nor should you or could you." But he went on to point out that the holiday season had advantages, because Christmas and the Vietnamese festival of Tet coincided. The "general stand-down over Christmas" set things in motion, he said.

We turned to the matter of the resumption of the bombing. Ball said—neither apologetically nor defiantly—that he had argued the case against resumption. Out of personal conviction and at the request of the President, he often plays the role of "devil's advocate."

As we talked, he proceeded to give me what he described as "the balance of elements" for and against the resumption. There had been, he said with impressive precision, four arguments in favor of resumption, and he ticked them off. First, it was necessary in order to maintain the morale of the South Vietnamese Government and of our own men—by denying the enemy immunity from the cost of aggression. Second, it was necessary in order to provide a partial interdiction of military goods from the North to the South—"to make the flow of supplies more costly to North Vietnam." Third, it was necessary in order ultimately to convince North Vietnam that the war is not worth the economic price. Fourth, it was necessary because, with no response to the cessation coming from Hanoi, to continue the pause "empty-handed" might have been understood mistakenly as a sign of weak intent.

Next, Ball stated the arguments he had offered against resumption. First, with the increased American presence, beginning in February, 1965, the morale of South Vietnam has no longer been at issue.

Second, although bombing to interdict supplies could make them more costly, it had not been shown that bombing could ever stop those supplies altogether—or even limit them to the point of creating hardships for the Communists in the South. Ball said the effect of bombing, especially in a police state, could be "to dig people in further." He had learned this, he said, from his experience as a director of the United States Strategic Bombing Survey at the end of the Second World War.

The third point bore on the question of China. There are, Ball said, really two wars in Vietnam, one in the North and one in the South. China could be expected to respond one way when a "war of national liberation" was at stake and another way when "the survival of a sister Communist republic was at stake." If air attacks on the North caused Hanoi to become "less free to make decisions without reference to Peking," the attacks could become an "impediment to peace."

When the points on both sides were carefully weighed, the controlling one, he thought, was the one relating to interdiction. He called that argument "very impressive." It is necessary, he said firmly, "to do everything possible to minimize our losses."

Ball concluded this part of our conversation by saying that President Johnson had designated him to write the brief opposing resumption. (I afterward was told that this document of 18 pages, and of "rare brilliance and lucidity," reached the President one midnight and that he read and pondered it immediately for three hours, calling a meeting on it later the same day. Out of the discussion of the pros and cons came the President's insistence that the bombing be strictly controlled and directly related to military targets that sustain Communist efforts in the South.)

What, I asked next, is the position of China with respect to our presence in Vietnam? Ball's answer was that of a man who has lived with the question a long time. He was sure that the Vietnam conflict increases the pressure on China because it affects the competition within the Communist world.

China, Ball went on, probably doubts that we intend ever to get out of Vietnam. They just "don't know how anxious we are to get out of there," Ball said. The Chinese, he continued, hope the United States will regard itself as "stuck in a glue pot, and will tire and quit." While waiting, the Chinese will fight to "the last Vietnamese."

At this point, I asked Ball to do some predicting: What is an informed guess as to how things will go from now on? One outcome to be looked for, he said, is a disintegration or unraveling of the Communist ground forces. Hanoi, he felt certain, will decide what to do only *after* the Vietcong fall apart. He stated his opinion that the Vietcong are now finding it harder and harder to retrain and regroup. They are losing their sanctuaries and must keep moving, a "demoralizing and debilitating experience." The Vietcong are becoming increasingly aware, he said, that they are not going to win.

In his opinion, the war will not end on a single day. It will, he said, paraphrasing T. S. Eliot, probably end "with a whimper not a bang." Peking, Ball thinks, can accept the defeat of the Vietcong—unless the war takes a course more directly involving China's vital interest. However, he added quickly, "I think you can do a great deal in the South with relative impunity."

After lunch, I went to the Pentagon to see Secretary McNamara. He motioned me in warmly and I sat down in the armchair next to his huge desk. I put to him as my first question one which has come to fascinate me: What has happened in the country that the internationalism of a few years ago seems now far less attractive to so many thoughtful Americans?

"You mean neoisolation," McNamara said. "I should by now have given more thought to this question." He proceeded to deal with it.

One explanation, he said, is that "Communism has evolved —it has changed—in the Soviet Union. It has become less violently aggressive." This development, he went on, "is a product of two things. First, the rising standard of living, and, second, the increase of personal freedom." As the Soviet Union has become "less monolithic" and as nuclear weapons have become more frightening, the West has become less united. "I think," he said, "it's the military action we are forced to take which is the reason for so much dissatisfaction among intellectuals."

Of course, McNamara said, neoisolationist ideas are being fueled by misinformed people. He reached behind him to pick up that morning's Washington Post, and read to me from Walter Lippmann's column. In it, Lippmann quoted Hanson Baldwin of The New York Times to the effect that the United States does not have the ready strength to fulfill its foreign policy commitments. McNamara said Baldwin's argument is not supported by fact, but is the "viewpoint of the lobbyists for the militarists in the country."

McNamara now went on to say how strong the United States is. Imagine, he said, we have 300,000 men in combat without having imposed economic controls and without calling up reservists. He called the accomplishment "unbelievable."

He said that General Westmoreland can plan to drop in Vietnam this month two and a half times the average monthly tonnage of explosives dropped in Korea. And he commenced to read to me from a paper in his pocket the specific figures for bombs, rockets, small-arms ammunition, grenades, and mortar and artillery shells. He took care to say that Westmoreland would not need to use all this power: "I can't imagine he's going to find targets to fire all this stuff at."

We turned now to another theoretical subject. How, I asked, do we confront the Red Chinese? Clearly, *this* question McNamara had already put his mind to. We must, he said, obtain multilateral recognition of the threat China poses to Asia and surrounding areas. "Multilateral action must be brought about by the nations threatened," he insisted.

He told of how he and Rusk had attempted within NATO to "get a dialogue started" with the European nations on the question of dealing with Chinese expansion. "It is debatable whether one nation alone can do this," he declared, explaining that he doubted that such a policy would be "politically acceptable."

He added that he thought one of the elements in neo-isolationism has been the unilateral action taken of necessity by the United States. Latterly, more allies have come in and there is a growing concert of response.

Is there a danger of a belligerent riposte by the Chinese to the steps we are taking in Vietnam, I asked. "You are always running risks when dealing with a belligerent power," he replied. He commented quickly that we ran the same risk by our actions in Korea and in behalf of Taiwan. He also added the point that Ball had made, that the Chinese response was not likely to involve war "so long as we do not appear to be striking to overthrow the regime of North Vietnam but only to support the people of South Vietnam in shaping their own destiny." He concluded, "The risk of unlimited war is not very great."

I now reminded McNamara that when we talked last June he had said that we were not moving in the direction of a "land war" in Asia. Did he still have that opinion? Yes, he said, there is no "overt land war" in process. He defined such a war as one in which substantial units of Chinese or North Vietnamese were to enter the fighting "under their own flags."

Can you tell me, Mr. Secretary, I asked bluntly, how large a commitment of men the United States is prepared to make in Vietnam? "I can't answer that," he said—and quickly amended it to: "I don't answer that." He discoursed on the enormous mobility and firepower of the American soldier. "The thing we prize most deeply," he said, "is not money but men. We have multiplied the capability of our men. It's expensive in materials but cheaper in life."

Now I asked McNamara what the word victory, as many —including Vice President Humphrey—are now using it, means. He answered that he tries to avoid such words as "victory" or "win"—which he called "color words." He prefers the phrase "favorable settlement," he said.

And how, I inquired, did he think a "favorable settlement" would be brought about? He said the North could cease

"feeding the fires of subversion and aggression in South Vietnam and the N.L.F. [the National Liberation Front] could
reduce its activity against the South and withdraw to live in
peace. The people could then shape the outcome."

Could China abide such a result, I asked. Yes, McNamara
answered. He thought China might charge the defeat of the
Vietcong to the other Communist states, which could be
blamed for not having sent in sufficient material.

As I prepared to leave, I asked McNamara if there was anything he had done in his five years as Secretary of Defense
which he wished he had done differently. I was thinking of
Vietnam but he quickly adverted to the Bay of Pigs. *That*, he
said, was "a serious error." President Kennedy had taken full
responsibility, he commented sadly, "but I was in the room."
He added: "We're not likely to make that kind of mistake
again—of being so uncertain of our estimates."

And what about the course of the decisions respecting Vietnam? There should, he said, be a critique of the whole episode, but it will be years before we reach it. The lessons, he
said, are not completely clear. But some are worth talking
about.

My next stop was Dean Rusk's office. I began by mentioning his presentation of the Administration's position before
the Senate Foreign Relations Committee the previous week.
He quickly shifted the conversation to a by product, the sug
gestion by James Reston of The New York Times that the
Secretary had enunciated a "Rusk Doctrine," committing the
nation militarily to protect some 40 countries. Rusk commented tartly: "I didn't vote for a single one of those commitments. They did"—meaning the members of the Senate.
And, he added, "when you go into an alliance you have to
mean it."

Rusk, talking of his critics, stressed that "one thing really
hasn't gotten through"—that this country means what it
says it means. He stayed on the subject: "I saw Chairman
Khrushchev threaten President Kennedy with war over Berlin.
And President Kennedy responded: 'If that's what you want,
O.K., but it'll be a very cold winter.' " The Soviets, Rusk said,
had to believe that war would be the result of their bel-

ligerence. The same thing, he went on, had occurred at the time of the Cuban missile crisis: "They had to believe our President meant what he said."

It is most important, he declared, that "when President Johnson says, 'You're not going to have Vietnam,' " he must be believed. "If ever the other side concludes that a President does not mean what he says, we're finished."

Then, in a pensive tone, he said: "Most totalitarian countries make a mistake about what a democracy will do at the end of the day." They regard us "as sloppy people with our hands in our pockets." Hitler, he said, made the same wrong judgment.

I switched the discussion to the question of what had happened to the internationalists of only a few years ago who now were saying we ought not to be so heavily committed in the world. Rusk responded by saying that liberal intellectuals had always made a distinction between Fascism on the one hand and Marxism on the other with respect to the intensity of their feeling. "They are more concerned with the Hitler kind of problem" was the way he put it.

Then he said with fervor: "A certain kind of liberalism is jaded and cynical." And he added: "Don't ask me to call a man a liberal who wants to turn over to a totalitarian regime more than 14 million South Vietnamese."

Rusk thought also that some people pinned too much hope on the idea of *détente* with the Soviet Union—"when the Soviets won't push the idea until it fits their needs." People's hopes, "which went far beyond realities," were built exclusively on the nuclear test-ban treaty. "It was a great step, but it did not signal a change of heart in the Communist world." Many came to regard Khrushchev as "an affable old grandfather." But, Rusk clinched his point, "he was 68½ when he put missiles in Cuba."

Rusk, in a matter-of-fact tone now, said that because there was so much hope for a general peace, the war in Vietnam had come as "a rude shock." Some people wanted to put the problem out of sight. Their feelings of frustration, he said, have come in part because "the problem itself arose ambiguously." The aggressors "sneaked" into the area rather than marching across the border.

Rusk turned again to the critics. Many of those who oppose Administration policies, he said, "are not disclosing their premises." At least, he commented, Senator Morse says openly: "South Vietnam is not worth the life of a single American soldier." Others, he maintained, do not state the basis of their position. Yet, he said, "the 'buts' add up to withdrawal."

We moved the conversation to the subject of China. The American people are worried, Rusk said. "They ought to be," he added, "because China is capable of grossly irrational decisions." Since 1945 there has been a possibility of a bigger war in every crisis—and he listed Greece, Berlin, Korea and Cuba. "If we leave the impression with the other side that we can't face the risks, then we'll never settle these questions."

I asked Rusk to talk to me about the peace offensive. How hopeful of good results were the participants? There were, he replied, only marginal hopes. But they were substantial enough to keep it from being "a phony propaganda play." Then he pointed out that since June, 1961, the United States has not been idle in seeking peace in Southeast Asia. In the past year alone, he remarked, more than 125 efforts were made.

In 1961, he said, President Kennedy had suggested to Khrushchev in Vienna that "we all get out of Laos." Khrushchev agreed, but he would not include Vietnam in the agreement. This, Rusk said, "could have been a contribution to peace." Hanoi, in violation of the agreement, left its forces in Laos and later infiltrated them into South Vietnam. Rusk said he thinks the Soviet Union acted in good faith, but that the split between Moscow and Peking was already having an effect on the chances for peace in that part of the world.

He talked of the bombing pause of last May. "By the third day," he said, "we had the answers." Peking said "no" on the radio and Hanoi refused to receive our message. Gromyko told him in Vienna, he said, that the pause and message were an "insult."

But, thereafter, several countries in Eastern Europe were saying the United States could not get talks started unless the bombing stopped. "We tried to find out what would happen if we did," he said. But we received no answer.

The longer bombing pause, Rusk said without anger, was "harshly and negatively" received. The other side simply said:

"Recognize the N.L.F. as the sole bargaining representative of South Vietnam, accept the Four Points, and get out." He commented that it is a mystery, though, as to why Hanoi did not make it difficult for us—by an ambiguous response of one kind or another—to resume the bombing.

The resumption of bombing was a unanimous decision of the President and his senior advisers, Rusk said. He observed: "No President has spent more time than President Johnson gnawing into difficult questions." "The impression he sometimes gives of being impetuous on major issues is false," Rusk wanted to make clear.

China, however, was the lodestone and we were drawn back to it. Rusk said he is sure that there is a "flash point" and "both sides are being very careful." "We don't want blind events to take over." At the moment, we "don't see a movement of forces suggesting a substantial deployment of men to the South," he stated solemnly as he knocked wood on the edge of his desk. "We will be watchful."

I asked Rusk, as I had asked McNamara, if there were some things in respect to Vietnam in the last five years that he wished had been done differently. Rusk answered that he thinks that after the Vienna meeting in June 1961, we should have put down "a lot of blue chips immediately" to head off "the other side" and to say, "You can't have South Vietnam." (Secretary McNamara had earlier suggested to me that he wished we had examined our objectives more profoundly and completely five years ago.)

Rusk said he believed that such action would have prevented misunderstanding with the Communist world. In this regard, he said that during 1964 the Communists had concluded that all the U.S. wanted was to save face. They misunderstood: "We were not interested in saving face but in saving Vietnam."

Now I asked Rusk how he thought the war would end. He said: "They won't come to the table so long as they think they can get South Vietnam by force. If they decide they can't win they may come to the conference table to see what they can get there." They may, he said further, "just let things peter out the way the Greek guerrillas did." This may involve, he thought, a decision on their part to stop for a while and wait for another day. (McNamara had also implied the same possibility.)

Rusk also suggested that the denouement could come suddenly. He recalled for me how cryptically and unexpectedly word reached the United States in 1949 that the Soviet Union was ready to lift the blockade of Berlin.

"The other side is hurting," Rusk observed. The signs are increasing. He listed some of them: The Vietcong and the North Vietnamese lost more men last year than the total United States loss in the Korean war; prisoners report that Ho Chi Minh's statement about being ready to fight a 10-to-20-year war has had a depressing effect on morale; the other side cannot sustain a battalion in combat more than 24 hours because of the intense firepower to which they are exposed; there is no rest for their soldiers, who are always on the move; defections are up fourfold. Rusk concluded: "On the present basis, they are not going to come out of it like they had hoped."

Of course, he said, a question is: "What are the big brothers going to do?" The evidence is that they are "more cautious in action than in words." "It's a tough game we're playing and we could be wrong," he warned. And he added quickly: "The President cannot rely on a guess on this subject." "Everybody can say, 'Sorry, boss, I was wrong,'" except him.

Those who make policy, Rusk continued, can "draw no doctrinal conclusion about what the other side will *not* do. Decisions have to be based on all contingencies and all consequences of various alternatives." "If the other side is as concerned as they ought to be in similar fashion, maybe we'll get some peace out of it at some point."

In response to a question of mine, Rusk switched back to the subject of the hearings held by the Senate Committee on Foreign Relations. He stated with some heat that Senator Fulbright declares we ought to offer "the other side" something. Yet, Rusk said, "nobody is offering us anything."

As our talk on Vietnam was drawing to a close, Rusk seemed to sum up his feelings on the critics. He said plaintively: "We're caught between the hawks and the doves."

The next morning, I had an appointment at the White

House to see the President. He greeted me in his oval office, and immediately led the way into what he had called, the last time I saw him, his "little office," a place he can retreat to just off the main room. Mr. Johnson asked me if he could get me a soft drink; he was having one. I accepted. I sat on a small sofa. The President sat in an easy chair facing me. Press Secretary Bill Moyers, who had joined us, sat across from us.

The President turned to me, his mind plainly on the American soldiers in Vietnam and began to talk.

He was proud, he said, that we had moved between 150,000 and 200,000 men into Vietnam with "the greatest efficiency in the history of the world." He spoke of the medical facilities which had been built and of the care which is waiting for our wounded when they arrive from the field. General Westmoreland, he said, has called our Army "the most mobile

---

'The Steaming Jungle'

Among the Presidential advisers to whom I talked was McGeorge Bundy, then still Special Assistant for National Security Affairs, now departed from Washington to be president of the Ford Foundation. To him, too, I put the question: What has happened to the liberals, who only recently were earnest supporters of America's involvement in the world?

Bundy seized on it. "It's the part of the world we're in," he began, "and it's the steaming jungle."

The liberals, he said, "never learned internationalism with respect to Asia." "If Kennedy were doing it [that is, waging war in Vietnam], they'd be less distressed. They are a prejudiced lot who don't distinguish between style and substance; they don't realize the President has his fist in the dike—he's not MacArthur; he's not Goldwater."

Bundy completed his point: "The aggression in Vietnam is less clear-cut than in Korea, and so it does not force a moral judgment as it did then. This helps our liberal friends cover their shame."

—H.F.G.

---

under any flag, the best-equipped and the one with the most firepower per man." He said he had asked Westmoreland if he was short of anything and he had replied that he was short of nothing that affects the effectiveness or morale of our men.

The President returned to thoughts of the casualties. "We have," he said, "the lowest ratio of dead to wounded we've ever had," and he attributed that to the mobility of our forces. He marveled at how, through the use of helicopters, it is possible to move a man from the battlefield to a hospital in 30 minutes to an hour. He had praise not only for the medical people but also for the search-and-rescue units.

Then Mr. Johnson alluded to the Vietcong losses. He said they had suffered close to 30,000 killed, wounded, missing and captured in two months. "We don't think Hanoi has yet realized how serious it is," he observed gravely. "They are looking at things through rose-colored glasses, intoxicated perhaps by the debate back here." He said it will take awhile for "their own casualties to catch up with them."

The President shared with me the weekly cable to him from Ambassador Henry Cabot Lodge in Saigon, which had just arrived. It was labeled "Secret Nodis" ("Nodis" is Government language for "not for distribution"). It summarized for the President the important events of the week. It contained the information, for instance, that in one battle Vietcong machine-gunners had been found dead manacled to their weapons. Lodge also reported that he had had lunch with some elements of the First Cavalry Division and that one soldier had told him he found it easier to understand the draft-card burners than the prominent men who seemed willing to carry on the debate at home interminably.

The cable also expressed the concern of the American community in Saigon that this is "the only war we've fought in this century where important men kept flailing policy after it has been debated and decided."

Mr. Johnson spoke sadly about some of the opposition. Senator Fulbright and the others, some of the strongest critics, he noted, had voted for the SEATO treaty—under the provisions of which the United States defends the legality of its presence in Vietnam. Mr. Johnson and John F. Kennedy had been ill at the time the treaty was before the Senate, although the President remarked that he would have voted for it. "I didn't make this contract," he said, "but I intend to keep it."

He told me how he had gone to Congress for the resolution of support in August, 1964, informing the lawmakers that "he wanted them in on the take-off as well as the landing." He explained how he had helped give President Eisenhower a similar resolution to protect Taiwan. He continued calmly: "We inherited this involvement, this commitment, and we are there. I want Congress to go with us." The Communists need to know where we stand.

I asked: Mr. President, how do you account for the opposition to the fighting—Senatorial and otherwise? He replied that there is a strong strain of "cultural alienation" in it, by which he means a feeling that the Vietnamese "are not our kind of people, that they're an ancient people unconcerned with change and reform, that they are so different from us that it would be impossible for us to help them.

"You may think this is begging your question, but I have heard this from the most pronounced critics of our policy. They write off Asia and say: 'Concentrate on Europe. Our destinies are inseparable. Our customs are common.'

"These people may be sincere, but I believe they are wrong. They ignore the fact that the desire to be independent is as color-blind as aggression. They think the hope of catching up with the times is American—or European—exclusively. What we're fighting for is not European or Asian or American—it's basic to man's nature everywhere. We want to give peaceful change a chance to work in Asia as it has in Europe." (At one point, the President said to me, in obvious sorrow, that India may lose as many people by starvation this year as the entire population of Vietnam.)

Mr. Johnson reverted to the subject of the Senate hearings. The Senators came up with "no alternative plan, no alternative program." They could have recommended that we withdraw, that we accept the enclave idea, that we bomb North Vietnam harder, or that we strike China with nuclear weapons. But their main point was, "We're going to get into a war with China." As if they were the only ones who had given any thought to the difficulties we face out there!

The President anticipated the question I had next in

mind—What are the chances that China will come in?—for he spoke it and answered it: "I don't think anybody knows. I'm no expert. Of course, if we spit in her face, that's one thing; but if we don't, most experts don't believe she will want to get involved that way. In the meantime, though, what are we supposed to do—lie paralyzed in fear? That is what they [the Communists] would like us to do."

Now the President referred to what the public-opinion polls show. A solid 10 per cent, he explained, "are hotheads—Goldwater types"; 10 per cent "are ready to run." "We can never change their minds—and it's a mistake to think we can. Every concession we have made to the critics has been met with another demand and—they will never be satisfied. I have listened to them patiently: now I have to prosecute our policies to the best of my ability, hoping they will realize what is at stake."

This led him again to pose a question and to answer it: When is it going to be over?

"When Churchill said we shall fight on the beaches, and in the streets, he did not say when it would be over. When the aggressor changes his mind, it will be over—but not before—not unless the American people succumb to the temptation to take the easy way out. I can't say when this will be over—I would have to take the Fifth Amendment if asked to answer that one precisely," he quipped.

But the President tried to answer the question for me, anyway. He said General Westmoreland is more optimistic. The North Vietnamese casualties are very heavy. The defections are doubling—"averaging 1,700 a month, with 2,000 this month." "After the Alamo, no one thought Sam Houston would wind up so quick," he said in an aside. And then he mused, "Who knows how long, how much?" The important thing is: Are we right or wrong? "I believe we are right."

I broke in to ask him to tell me about the new phase of the war. His face lit up spontaneously. The war is two-pronged, he said. He made two fists. He thrust one forward signifying the military side and then the other signifying the economic and social side. This was the side he plainly *wanted* to talk about. He said proudly: "I want to leave the footprints of America there. I want them to say, 'This is what the Americans left—schools and hospitals and dams.' " Shortly afterward, he said: "We can turn the Mekong into a Tennessee Valley."

The President talked of the income of the Vietnamese as "$65 a year," and of how they need schools, health measures and agricultural assistance. "We can teach them to read and write," he said with elation. He explained that we are trying to introduce television in Vietnam. He said the domestic help at Lodge's quarters were wide-eyed in amazement when they first saw TV, beamed from a plane. He rose out of his chair, his own eyes wide and with his arms raised to illustrate how amazed they probably had looked. Then he said softly: "I remember the first time I heard radio."

The President continued. He said he was asking Ambassador William Porter to be in the economic and social field a counterpart to General Westmoreland. The work of uplifting South Vietnam, he said, is "tough." "You build schools and hospitals and the Communists tear them down. That is just one more reason I get so frustrated when people charge that we should be more sympathetic to the Vietcong. What has happened to American liberalism that it would ignore such tactics? There are times when it seems the Vietcong have more negotiators in their behalf than our soldiers do."

As to the Vietcong in negotiations, Mr. Johnson said soberly: "We'll work out a way for them to be heard—if Hanoi will let them—or if they want to. But history makes it clear that when you bring the Communists in, they can chew you up if you are not as smart or as prepared as they are."

Mr. Johnson shifted now to his impressions of Premier Ky. Ky, the President said with delight, "sounded like Rex Tugwell."* I asked him what he meant, and he recalled that Tugwell in the early days of the New Deal had said that we must "roll up our sleeves and remake America." Ky, in the President's opinion, "is talking like Tugwell—we're hoping he can perform like Tugwell."

As for the South Vietnamese people: "They have 700,000 men fighting. We're not giving them up." He insisted: "We're fighting for a special objective. We don't want to destroy

---

*Rexford G. Tugwell, one of Franklin D. Roosevelt's Brain Trusters and later Governor of Puerto Rico, helped to frame the Agricultural Adjustment Act.

China or North Vietnam. We just want to have them leave these people alone."

To illustrate, he reminded himself of how, years ago, Huey Long had gone into Arkansas to campaign for Hattie Caraway for the Senate.* He told the story with zest and in lively detail, reminding us that the only thing Long wanted to do was "just to protect this poor little helpless woman from those powerful interests arrayed against her."

Mr. Johnson returned to the matter of our strategy. Our aim in bombing, he said, is "not to destroy or kill civilians but simply to stop Hanoi from bringing the stuff down into the South." He said he had been advised by General Eisenhower to let the Communists know there are no sanctuaries from which aggression can be directed.

And, again, Mr. Johnson repeated his main idea: "They" must stop their aggression. "If they'll go home tomorrow, we'll come home."

---

*Hattie Caraway, the first woman U.S. Senator, was appointed to her late husband's seat in 1931. She won her first full term in 1933 by defeating six male opponents in the Democratic primary, with the support of both F.D.R., then Presidential candidate, and Senator Huey Long, the Louisiana Kingfish, father of Senator Russell Long. She was defeated in the 1944 primary by Senator J. W. Fulbright.

The New York Times Magazine, March 20, 1966

No Room in the Cemetery

WETUMPKA, Ala.—PFC Jimmy Williams's uniformed body was lowered in a grave in the piney woods of South Georgia Monday while a grieving mother pondered the fates which denied him a final resting place in his hometown.

And it may be that the 4000 citizens of this little town 13 miles northeast of Montgomery are searching their collective conscience for an answer to why they could offer only a pauper's grave to their first casualty of the Viet Nam war.

"My son died fighting on the front for all of us. He didn't die a segregated death, and he'll not be buried in a segregated cemetery," Mrs. John Williams, mother of the Green Beret paratrooper, declared.

City officials had claimed there was no room for the dead soldier in the segregated city cemetery. Mayor Demp Thrash said the only plots available were for paupers in the rear of the burial grounds.

Friends and neighbors of the 19-year-old youth, who was killed in Viet Nam May 19th when grenade fragments ripped into his body, crowded funeral rites at the Newton Church of Christ in Montgomery Sunday.

The flag-draped coffin was buried with full military honors in the Andersonville (Ga.) National Cemetery, a 100 miles from Wetumpka. It was the nearest available funeral site, an Army spokesman said.

Mrs. Williams, a 38-year-old practical nurse, has filed a complaint with the Justice Department. Under the public facilities section of the Civil Rights Act, the government could take the case to court using the mother's complaint as grounds for entering the dispute.

A spokesman for the Justice Department said the department would press the case despite the mother's decision to take the son to Andersonville.

Mrs. Williams said she had reconciled herself to the distant burial.

"I don't have any animosity toward anyone. I couldn't love Christ whom I cannot see, and hate the Mayor. Whatever we sow, we shall reap. If they (the city officials) think they've done right, well, maybe they have," she said.

"I did not want my son buried in an out-of-the-way place for unknown people. My son was not a shoe shine boy like his father. He was a soldier, a paratrooper in the Green Berets.

"He was not fighting a second-class war, and did not die a second-class death," the grief-stricken mother continued.

"I wanted him to be buried near his home because I know this is what he would have wanted," she added.

Mrs. Williams says she has been unable to find work since three of her six surviving children entered previously all-white schools in Wetumpka last fall. The town's population includes some 1,500 colored persons.

Mr. Williams, 49, was a shoeshine boy for the mayor, a barber, 25 years ago. He currently works for a local glass company.

Jimmy, the oldest of the seven Williams children, joined the Army two years ago upon graduating from high school. He was sent to Viet Nam in February.

Last Tuesday his body, guarded by military men, was sent home for burial. A military survivors assistant assigned to aid the Williams family, Lt. Robert L. Kraselsky, said the only site he could acquire in the town was the paupers' section.

W. T. Goodman, the funeral director handling the arrangements, said there were no cemeteries exclusively for colored persons in the town.

"Someone, somehow always found a plot for the deceased through friends or relatives. Many were buried in countryside cemeteries in the county," he revealed.

The Rev. Fred Gray, who officiated at the funeral rites, accused city officials of being unconcerned about the death of their first casualty of the Viet Nam war. Not until the burial furor arose did the city fathers bother to express condolences to the family, he said.

Mayor Thrash said that at the present the 200-year-old cemetery has slaves on one side and colored persons on the other, and whites in the middle. "We aren't going to dig up slave graves for anybody," he said.

Thrash revealed plans for expansion of the cemetery. "If they want to move the boy back, they're welcome to it," he said.

Afro-American (Baltimore), June 4, 1966

Reconnaissance

by Ward S. Just

IN THE SUMMER of 1966 yet another monsoon offensive was predicted in Pleiku and Kontum provinces in the Central Highlands. American intelligence said the North Vietnamese were infiltrating from Laos into Pleiku and Kontum in battalion- and regimental-sized units, well fed, well trained and well and heavily armed. The theory of the enemy objective, which had been expounded in one form or another for two years, was that Giap's regulars would "cut the country in half," driving east from the Laotian border to the South China Sea. It was an implausible theory, owing as it did practically nothing to logic: the North Vietnamese did not have the men to hold a line across the waist of South Vietnam, neither did they have the weapons to ward off attacking American aircraft. Much more plausible was the theory that the North Vietnamese were invading to make the highlands so hazardous that the Americans would be forced to concentrate large numbers of troops there.

But everybody believed the scissors theory, probably because it made rich newspaper copy. An American general once admitted that what the command had in mind was that if the North Vietnamese cut the country in half they would have a marvelous propaganda victory. The reverse was also true, and therein lay the *raison d'être* for the theory. The operative line was given at a Westmoreland press briefing in 1966: "They tried to cut the country in half but we stopped them."

There were a few amateur strategists who insisted that the country was already cut in half, obviously so by the inability of an ordinary citizen to drive from Saigon to the Demilitarized Zone. But these objections were swept aside as the work of cranks. As far as the American command was concerned, the North Vietnamese went on trying to cut the country in half and the American Army went on stopping them. Thus was the territorial integrity of South Vietnam preserved.

No one knew what the strategy really was. Some of the military thinkers believed that all Ho and Giap had in mind was sending as many troops as they could afford, punishing the Americans to the limit of endurance, and assaulting air-fields and base camps until the allies quit from exhaustion. It was, as Westmoreland often said in 1967, a war of attrition; grand strategy did not as a practical matter exist. It was tactics that counted, and what was meant by tactics were the thousands of small-unit engagements from the Camau pen-insula to the DMZ. The sum of these equaled the whole, or should have.

I flew from Saigon to Pleiku and then to the Special Forces camp at Dak To early in June, 1966. I had been told in Saigon that American intelligence officers had identified new North Vietnamese units prowling the highlands. The 1st Brigade of the 101st Airborne Division was to move out into the jungles to find the enemy. It was regarded in Saigon as an important campaign: whatever the argument on whether or not the enemy objective was to cut the country in half, there was no doubt that the highlands themselves were imperiled.

It was the North Vietnamese who drew first blood: on the night of June 6, a battalion hit an American artillery base just north of Dak To and nearly overran it. Firing at point-blank range, the Americans had managed to beat back the attack. Following normal procedure, enemy troops had carried their dead from the battlefield. Only two bodies were left behind, but the artillerymen were confident many, many more had died. No one knew how many. What was surprising was the closeness of the engagement. "You could see the enemy," said one young artillery captain, in wonder. "They saw us and we saw them." It didn't happen that way very often, which lent an interesting and appealing tone to the opening engagement of the operation which would be called Hawthorne, or the campaign for the control of the Central Highlands.

The commander of the 1st Battalion, 327th Infantry of the 101st Airborne Brigade, Major David Hackworth, was stand-ing amid the ruins of the camp when I alighted from a helicopter in the company of one of the ubiquitous public

relations men of the American Army. We had been flying for
nearly an hour, trying to find the base which was neatly hidden in the crotch of two hills. It had been an unnerving ride,
since the hills were nominally, or more than nominally, enemy
territory. Hackworth briefly explained the situation, then said
with a grin that he was sending one of the reconnaissance
units ("recondo," in Airborne argot, meaning commando/
reconnaissance) deep into the mountains to find the enemy
base camp, and to try in the process to round up enemy stragglers. Hackworth was so cheerful about the prospect of heading into the mountains that I instantly asked to go along. He
said fine, then introduced me to Captain Lewis Higinbotham,
the commander of the 42-man Tiger Force, as the recondo
platoon was known. "You'll like Higinbotham," Hackworth
said. "He's a good killer."

Hackworth had words for the men of the Tiger Force, who
were now assembling their weapons and gear, and the words
went like this: "Goddamnit I want forty hard-charging fuckin'
dicks. And if anybody ain't a hard-charging fuckin' dick I want
him out."

"Fuckin'," muttered one of the men.

"Right," said Hackworth.

"Fuckin'," the trooper muttered again.

The English language, like everything else in Vietnam, became unreal after a time. Hackworth's words were—words.
He might have appealed for forty soft-bellied capons, or forty
fine, aggressive young American soldiers, or forty draft-
dodgers, or forty journalists, or forty fat congressmen from
Texas. As it was, he appealed for forty hard-charging fuckin'
dicks. It didn't matter. I unconsciously wrote the words in my
notebook.

Then Hackworth turned to me, banging the palms of his
hands together. Matters were looking up. "My God, we
chased them for five days over every flipping hill in Vietnam.
Five days! And they hit us back here. They kept one hill ahead
of us. One hill all along the way. Well, now they've had it."

The Airborne had that reputation.

A unit assembles its reputation from many sources, but
mainly from its commanders. These were the commanding
general, Brigadier General Willard Pearson, and the two bat-

talion commanders, Lt. Colonel Henry Emerson, and Major Hackworth. There were others, but these were the principal ones. They were professional soldiers, none more so than Pearson, who was the architect of the Brigade's bold and successful jungle tactics. Briefly, these were to probe as far into enemy territory as possible, make contact, then reinforce by helicopter. It required using small units as bait, which you could do only if your men were anxious to fight, and had proved it by signing on as paratroopers, for more money and prestige in the services. Pearson's reputation as a soldier was excellent, but he had strange lapses when dealing with men. Once, approaching a particularly difficult mission, he promised a company of infantry a case of beer if the mission were successful. In those circles, a case of beer was regarded as barely adequate for one man, let alone 200. Pearson, the strategist who wanted to carry the war to the enemy on the enemy's terms, was regarded with a mixture of respect and astonishment.

Not so Hackworth and Emerson. They were quite simply admired, as men and as soldiers. Personal courage is a very attractive quality in men. It is the one quality, as someone said, which guarantees all the others. Hackworth had it, and so did Emerson. They were brave men, without being excessively reckless or self-conscious about it. Hackworth was especially appealing. He seemed to be amused at the whole apparatus of the war in Vietnam; he knew that things were never what they seemed, and that you kept your sanity only by admitting a whole range of possibilities. That day, in the center of the artillery fire base, he strode around with a tiny riding crop, disheveled, unshaven and profane, and after a bit took Higinbotham aside to brief him on the mission.

Lew Higinbotham looked an unlikely killer. Slim, bony-faced, Texas-accented, he was polite and grim, and the dirt deliberately smeared over his cheeks and chin did not conceal youth. He was in his middle twenties, unmarried, a career soldier. Higinbotham had been in Vietnam more than two years, most of it spent in the Delta south of Saigon as an adviser to Vietnamese troops. This was his first mission with the Tiger Force. It was an elite unit and Higinbotham was anxious to do well; he liked the Vietnamese, but preferred to work with Americans. The forty-two men under his command were a rugged and motley lot, bringing to mind one of those posses assembled from the worst saloons on Main Street in the Grade B horse operas. Unshaven, dirty, unlettered, mean, nervous; one was in flight from his third wife, another (so the story went) from the police, a third was in Vietnam because he liked to kill Charlie Cong. Some of the others had the spirit of buccaneers, fugitives from a safe society. They liked the adventure, and the weapons. One of them regularly sent the ears of dead Viet Cong to his wife, through the army postal system. Half the platoon was Negro. One of these, informed that a journalist would be along on the patrol, became helpless with laughter. He doubled up, face shaking with mirth at the madness of it all. "Sheet," he said. "Shee-it."

While the men got their gear together, checked weapons and gathered up food and ammunition, I prowled around the edges of the artillery base. There were dark streaks of blood where men had been carried off the night before. Part of a torso lay just beyond the security perimeter. On the top of a small rise I looked north, and saw high hills without signs of life. There were no villages in this part of Kontum. There were some Montagnard tribesmen, but nothing else. In the old days of the French occupation, the hills were often used for tiger hunts. We loaded into helicopters and were off.

The land north of Dak To was rugged and uneven, high hills and thick jungle laced with trails. It was cool as we were dropped at four o'clock in the afternoon in a high stand of elephant grass. The trees had two growths of branches, one about six feet up the trunk and the other about twelve feet. They blotted out the sun. The light appeared to come through a great green-glass bottle without rays or beams. Higinbotham and I moved beneath one of the trees, and waited until the rest of the forty-two were accounted for. There was another captain there, and Higinbotham introduced him as Chris Verlumis, a 27-year-old career man from Oakland, California. Verlumis was the commander of headquarters company, to which the Tiger Force was technically attached. It was Verlumis's first week in Vietnam, and his first patrol. Higinbotham was not happy about the arrangement, because Verlumis technically outranked him—or was, in any case, in command of a larger unit. If there was trouble, and there was bound to be trouble, Higinbotham did not want to have to worry about another captain. And he didn't want to be second-guessed. Higinbotham had told all this to Hackworth. But Verlumis wanted to come, and so Verlumis came.

We moved out along a trail north and west roughly in the direction of the Laos border. Right away we fell upon a two-man position carved into a bush. It was deserted. The trail was well-traveled, and almost immediately there was another small hut ("hootch," to American soldiers in Vietnam) and then a third. Then, as we wound up the trail, there was a small base camp, perhaps large enough to accommodate a squad of a dozen men. In Vietnam action usually comes without warning. All of these installations on the trail were signs, warning signals that enemy troops were there. Higinbotham knew it and the men knew it. I knew it.

We were moving quickly, winding up the trail as the light faded and noting all the signs of enemy occupation. Then there was a burst of machine-gun fire, a shout, and all of the men flopped, and scurried off the trail into the shelter of the trees and bushes. The firing had come from the rear of the column, three fast bursts and now it was silent. Higinbotham urgently radioed his rear squad. One enemy soldier was dead, but one of our own men was hurt.

Private First Class Richard Garcia was lying off the trail, blood leaking from a wound in his chest. Three men stood over him, while the medic punctured his arm with a morphine needle. The men moved their feet and talked quietly to Garcia, although he was nearly unconscious. He had been hit by one of our own bullets; it is difficult to see in the jungle. No one knows where the enemy is, and the frightened man sprays with his weapon. He fires it in bursts, and none too accurately. One of these had caught Garcia in the lung. The medic was working frantically, muttering and cursing under his breath. Suddenly Garcia sat up, and looked straight at the medic: "I can't breathe. I am going home. I am going to be OK." Then he was dead.

Fifty yards away, the men of the rear squad were looking after the dead Vietnamese. He had been shot in the chest, but that was only the most recent wound. His head had been bandaged, and so had his leg. Higinbotham, looking at the body, decided he had been on his way back to the base camp for medical attention. He was probably one of those wounded in the attack on the artillery fire base the night before. Next to the body lay a battered, damaged AK–47 submachine gun. That was the standard weapon of the North Vietnamese Army, Soviet-designed and manufactured in China.

Higinbotham reported both deaths to battalion headquarters. "We've got a KIA, one of theirs and one of ours," Higinbotham said. The G–2 (intelligence officer) on the other end of the line warned him to be on the watch for more enemy. "Maybe a battalion more," the G–2 said.

The light was going, almost visibly as lights dim in a theater, and Higinbotham decided to stay where he was for the night. Garcia's body was taken down to the trail and three men prepared it for transport on a litter. His arms were folded on his chest, and his blouse pulled up tight over his face and head. Then the body, compact in the camouflaged uniform, hatless, was tied to the litter, and the pack was tied to the body; lying there that night Garcia looked comfortable. Higinbotham said it was possible he was killed by rifle fire from the Vietnamese, but most likely not; most likely he was killed from our own lines. It was a matter of fire discipline, Higinbotham said; there was never enough of it, and too many people were killed needlessly. But you couldn't prevent all of it. With all the lead flying around, people got hurt; it was not a factor you could control.

The men arranged themselves in a star-shaped defense, three to a group. One man in each group stayed awake at all times. There would be no talking or smoking and the radio would be off. The jungle in Kontum goes dark before seven. The wetness comes as it grows black, and except for the chattering of the small birds and animals it is silent; after a while the bird and animal sounds become part of the silence. Because of the rot which turns the plants to phosphorus, the jungle floor is brilliant with light, enough light to see your fingernail or read the dials on a wristwatch. I had a small flask of whiskey, which I passed to Higinbotham and Verlumis and the radio operator, Terry Grey. We talked quietly of one thing and another, colleges, life on the West Coast, and then tried to sleep. I recalled a line from A. J. Liebling that when he was in an uncomfortable or dangerous spot during World War II, and he was trying to sleep, he thought about women. It seemed a sensible and distracting idea, so from nine that night until seven the next morning I thought about women.

We awoke slowly and crawled quietly from beneath the bushes to stretch as daylight came. With it came the second omen. There was a shout, a rattle of gunfire, and we were all on our bellies in that awful initial confusion. Suddenly a sheepish private stood before Higinbotham. There were three armed Vietnamese, uniformed and not alert, the private said. They stumbled into camp, saw the Americans, and fled. The GI's, equally startled, had time for only a half-dozen rounds. The three enemy soldiers scampered across a small stream and disappeared into the bush. Higinbotham shook his head, and smiled. "Oh hell, they probably spent the night with us," he said. "They probably thought we were the 226th North Vietnamese Regiment, for crissakes." Higinbotham reported the incident to G–2, which received the information without comment.

A long-range reconnaissance patrol cannot operate once its presence is known to the enemy. Twice the Tigers had been forced to fire. Now three Vietnamese had seen them, and had escaped, and were certainly bound for their headquarters. None of this could have been foreseen, and there was nothing to be done about it. But it was terrible luck. Security, to the extent that there was any in the middle of a jungle in the middle of enemy territory, was compromised. It had to be considered compromised, although the mission itself was not in doubt. The mission went on. There was no place to go but forward, deeper and higher into the hills, discovering enemy base camps and rounding up stragglers. The patrol was still well within the range of the brigade's artillery, and the operations officer was keeping careful check on our precise location. Word has been fed back that the enemy was known to be operating in the area; but Higinbotham knew that.

The objective now was to find a landing zone for a helicopter to come in and "extract" Garcia. Garcia was a burden and there was no room now for burdens. "I don't like any part of it," Higinbotham said.

Kontum that day was marvelously cool, and we crossed half a dozen small streams on our way up the hill. There was no movement except for an occasional exquisitely colored butterfly. The men moved very quietly and carefully. A clearing was found, and Garcia lifted out; the helicopter crew left a dozen cases of C rations behind. The men dug into the cases labeled, in the weird army phraseology, MEAL, COMBAT, INDIVIDUAL—like that, with commas. They were looking for cigarette packages and fruit. Each meal carton contained a little package of condiments: salt, pepper, sugar, powdered cream, coffee, gum, toilet paper, matches, and a package of five cigarettes; the brands were Camels, Chesterfields, Salems, Newports, Winstons, or Pall Malls. At least two of the large cases were untouched, so a hole was dug and they were buried. We moved out again.

The trail meandered into deeper jungle, with base camp following base camp. Higinbotham decided by one in the afternoon that his band had uncovered a staging area capable of accommodating a regiment of 1,000 men. The knowledge was not comforting. The men, in soft hats, their faces smeared with mud, carefully cradling weapons, kept silently climbing, turning their eyes off the trail and into the bush.

In two years in the Delta, Higinbotham had acquired a passable knowledge of Vietnamese. When his lead squad found a small arrow-shaped sign with the words *Anh Ban Di Trung*, he knew we were on the right trail, the pigeons among the cats. The words translated, "friends go straight"; it was obviously an enemy message. And with the Vietnamese talent for confusion, at the point of the sign the trail forked, with no clear indication which trail was meant. One branch led upward, along the small stream. The other moved left, down the hill. At the fork there were two huts where the command group waited: Higinbotham sent patrols down each trail. The first, led by Sergeant Pellum Bryant, almost immediately saw three enemy soldiers in the khaki uniforms of the North Vietnamese Army. Bryant opened fire with his M–16, and began heaving grenades. Everyone in the command post was flat on his stomach, waiting. The firing went on for five minutes, then ceased and Bryant returned to Higinbotham. He had got one, but the others had fled. Now from the other trail the radio crackled that there was resistance, that one Tiger was seriously wounded and the others pinned down.

Strung out in a long, thin line, the men moved down the trail and up to the ridge line. The patrol that had been hit was on the other side of the hill, which was not sharp but rolling, covered by deep jungle and ending in a steep ravine. At the top of the hill the men shed their packs, and a six-man patrol headed downslope to learn the American casualties and assess the strength of the enemy. It was impossible to judge distances because of the thickness of the cover.

The patrol reported back that the enemy had moved out; there was no more firing. Higinbotham nodded and, leaving six men behind to guard the rear, began to move down the trail to the ravine. It was a two-foot-wide trail that wound down and into a tiny cleft between the two hills. It then curled up the next hill. Edgy, edgy enough that a man snarled if you stumbled and stepped on his heel, the platoon moved down. There was a wounded GI in the crotch of the hills. He had been shot through the neck beside a cache of enemy rockets and grenades. The grenades were in a cave, carefully covered with tarpaulin. Four men went down to get the wounded man, crawling past the body of an enemy soldier whose head had been blown off in the firing ten minutes before. The wounded man was hurting, and scared. The hill was very steep, and the four found it difficult to slide down.

"You don't feel no pain, baby," the medic said, putting a needle into the man's arm. "You gonna be all right, baby. You gonna see that girl." The talk was all nonsense, meant to distract. The medic was wrapping a bandage around his comrade's neck. Another medic put a plasma needle into his right arm. The man's shirt was soaked with blood from the wound.

"I knew it," the wounded man said. "I knew that my chip was cashed in."

"We gonna get the MedEvac," the medic said.

"Well, that pilot better be there when I get there." Then, "You think I got a Stateside wound?"

The medic was worrying about the stretcher.

"Litter?"

"Litter!"

"Bring the litter, goddamnit."

"I wonder why my stomach hurts so much."

"Don't worry. This happens to everybody."

The wounded man, Private First Class Frank Wills, was at the base of a 45-degree incline. But the litter was there now, and the four men struggled and worried him up to the trail which led down from the ridge line.

It was very quiet, and no movement from anything. There were no birds or animals or butterflies, and the men were still and silent. Wills had become half-delirious from pain and fear. He asked again why his stomach hurt so much. Then he told the medic he had one hundred dollars in his pocket. "Take it and hold it for me," he said. Wills was thinking about going back home to Miami.

But the medic wasn't listening. No one was. Higinbotham was worried about Wills and whether a landing zone could be carved out of the hillside. It couldn't, and Higinbotham knew that. He also knew that his patrol was deep inside enemy lines with no way to get out, except to walk out. The patrol had found what it had come to find; the problem was what to do with it now. Enemy troops were obviously all around, and they knew that the Americans were there. Higinbotham squatted on the trail and wondered what to do.

The trail wound down from the ridge line perhaps one hundred yards. There were foxholes and bunkers all along it. Six men were at the top, guarding the packs, six more at the base. Higinbotham, Verlumis, Wills, the radio operator, Terry Grey; and twenty-five regulars were strung out along about fifty yards of the trail. There were plenty of grenades and plenty of ammunition. But Higinbotham thought about the deployment, and shuddered. They were not enough, not nearly enough if the enemy attacked from the ridge line; and the assumption had to be that that was what they would do.

"Hey, Mr. Reporter!" It was the trooper who found my presence so mirth-provoking. He began to laugh again, and so did I. It was an absurd predicament.

"You picked a great patrol," Higinbotham said.

"Mr. Reporter, how much you get paid for this?" the trooper asked.

"Not enough," I said.

"Damn," Higinbotham said, looking again at his maps.

Higinbotham's worries were not mine. Since the death of Garcia the night before, I had tried to concentrate on journalism. I had worked at taking careful notes and photographs, and now reflected on the similarity of the soldier and the war correspondent, the basic text for which comes from Joseph Heller's novel, *Catch–22*. On the one hand, no one wants to get ambushed or to be where bullets are fired in anger. On the other, if nothing happens there is no story. If the patrol does not meet the enemy, there is nothing to write about. It becomes a pointless exercise, a long walk under a hot sun. If the patrol does meet the enemy you are likely to be killed or wounded, or at the very least scared to death. *Catch–23*.

It was a bad catch. I worked at disbelief. You switch off, and pull all the plugs, severing connections. Your movements become slow and deliberate, and your consciousness seems to move back in time. The point is to maintain control. With forty-one men in the middle of a clearing in the middle of Kontum in the middle of a war, you are standing—nowhere. For distraction, think about women or squat down and pick blades of grass, chew them and put a film in the camera. Focus the lens. Make pictures of the American infantry. Transcribe dialogue:

"Sheet, I wrote her back she do anything she want."

"Well, we over here and they're there."

"Fuck that noise."

"Yeah."

"You hear Tomkins get killed?"

"Yeah?"

"Sheet, a mine blew him up and there was nuthin' left but nuthin'."

"Sheet."

"I tell you, Man, this is some kind of war."

"Sumthin' else!"

"Crise, I was in a platoon and there's nuthin' left of that platoon now. I'm the only one left."

"Gimme some fruit."

"Trayja fruit for some butts."

"Fuck you."

"Three butts."

"Whyn't you pick up the butts back there when we got 'em?"

" 'Cause I was on point savin' your ass in case old Charlie come along."

"Gimme the fuckin' fruit."

"Three butts."

"Sheet, man, I ain't got but half a pack."

"Goddamn I got to get this weapon *fixed*."

"Hey, Mr. Reporter. What the fuck you doing here?"

At two-thirty in the afternoon the first grenade crashed down the ridge line. It went wide with a *thump*. Then *thump! Thumpthump!* Again, closer.

In the first fifteen minutes, three died and six fell wounded. The firing came from three sides, hitting the Americans at all points on the trail. The men guarding the packs at the top of the trail scattered under a hail of machine-gun fire. Only a few actually saw the enemy, who were maneuvering and firing as they maneuvered. Higinbotham at his command post half-way down the line knew the danger of the situation better than anybody else. He collected the first reports from his sergeants. The reports were only that there were a lot of enemy, and it was impossible to tell how many. Higinbotham called Hackworth at battalion headquarters and requested artillery fire and air support. It would come in the next four hours, 1,100 rounds of 105 and 90 rounds of 155 artillery. There would be air strikes, and the noise would be as if the world were coming apart.

No one knew then and no one knows now how many North Vietnamese there were. They did not have mortars, so the unit was probably company-sized or smaller. But they had grenades and small arms and automatic weapons, and good cover to shoot from. They fought from concealed positions and they had the element of surprise and knowledge of the terrain. It was, after all, their base camp.

American artillery shells fell in a wide semicircle just beyond the American positions. They were hitting at the ridge line and beyond, but the Vietnamese fire did not lessen. The planes attacked with a roar and without warning; because of the heavy cover they could not be seen. One fist-sized piece of shrapnel landed two feet from Higinbotham, but he did not cease talking into the field phone, precisely locating the positions of heaviest enemy fire. While the shells were landing, Americans were dying; a half dozen in the first half hour, another six in the five succeeding hours of combat.

In the command post, enemy rifle fire was hitting five feet high. We were all down, scanning the jungle and watching that part of the trail we could see. Behind us, down the line, men were maneuvering and shouting at each other. Higinbotham was superbly cool, talking quietly and easily into the field telephone which was the only link with safety. As long as the artillery held out the Vietnamese could not advance; that was our theory, desperately clung to. Meanwhile the rifle fire got heavier and closer. The bullets were sounding: *Pop!*

Verlumis had left the command post to crawl up the trail toward the heaviest fighting. Pellum Bryant, the senior noncommissioned officer, was below rallying the dozen or so who had fallen under his command. One of the other sergeants was dead. Bryant was the only unwounded man in his eight-man squad. Pinned down by an enfilade of fire, he had huddled in an enemy foxhole. When the fire slackened, he poked up his head and fired bursts. It was Bryant alone who was protecting the rear flank.

By four-thirty in the afternoon, after two hours of fire, the situation was almost lost. The fight had been following a rhythm, with heavy bursts of fire and then silence except for an occasional rattle of a machine gun. The Americans had been pushed back into a tiny area about the size of a basketball court, with Higinbotham and the radio as its nucleus. Bryant was now fighting just a dozen yards to the rear. Hackworth, speaking with Higinbotham, said there was a full company of infantry a mile away. He was ordering them to reinforce.

"You've got to try it," Higinbotham said over the radio. For the first time, his voice cracked and became unsure. There was a 26-year-old advertising account executive or civil servant or department store clerk, or a good old boy at the night baseball game, but not a captain of infantry in the U.S. Army. "If you don't get up here soon, we're all gonna die. If you don't get up here soon, I'm gonna melt."

There was another crackling over the telephone; Hackworth

had gone off. Then, barely audibly, but precisely, as if he were reading from a piece of paper, Higinbotham said: "Dear God, please help me save these men's lives."

It got worse after that, and for Higinbotham it was the worst time of all. It was his first patrol with the Tigers. He didn't know the men, either their names or where they came from or how long they had been in Vietnam. Now he had gotten them into this. Higinbotham sat with the radio, his back against a tree, and prayed that it wouldn't be as bad as he thought it was.

The sniper fire came closer, nipping the tops of the branches of the bushes. The artillery seemed to be hitting indiscriminately, as Higinbotham called it closer to the American lines. But there were no lines any more. There was only a group of men huddled silently on a trail that led nowhere down from a ridge line that did not even show on the map. Bryant was on his own, and so was Verlumis. Higinbotham was worried about the artillery, and the tactics were taking care of themselves.

A wounded infantryman, his voice loud as a bullhorn, was calling from the left flank. "You've got to get me out of here!" He was repeating it. The voice was strong and deep, but it cracked with agony and pain. He repeated it again and again. As he screamed and moaned I moved forward. I went forward about five feet and then stopped, still safe. The wounded man was probably twenty yards away, although the jungle was so thick it was impossible to tell. I had the idea that I might save his life.

I looked around at the others and then the wounded man screamed, and was silent. I waited for a minute and then crawled back the five feet. I had spent twenty minutes deciding whether to get the wounded, who had been screaming and pleading for help. Now I didn't have to think about it. He was dead. Verlumis had given me a .45 pistol and now I took it out of its holster for the first time. I was lying on my stomach handling the .45, having dismissed the wounded man from mind. It was easier holding a .45 pistol.

Fifteen yards in front of the command post there was a dip that plunged almost straight down into the ravine. From that direction a voice came: "Airborne!" No one answered. Hig-

inbotham and the radio operator and I looked at the spot
where the voice came from. The radioman unhitched a grenade from his ammunition belt, and cradled it like an apple.
The voice could belong to anyone, but the odds were better
than even that it belonged to a North Vietnamese. I thought
of identifying questions to ask. The only two that came to
mind was the name of the manager of the New York Yankees,
and whether or not Marilyn Monroe was dead or alive. My
mind wouldn't work. I thought of asking who wrote the Declaration of Independence, but then figured that a trooper
probably wouldn't know the answer. Then I remembered that
I didn't know the name of the Yankee manager. Stengel was
dead. Or not dead, retired someplace. These thoughts were
moving so slowly I could almost see them in my mind's eye.
I was closest to the dip and now aimed the pistol straight at
it, or just above it. The radioman had not thrown the grenade
and all of us were in a state of suspended animation. But then
a voice said, "Christ, don't shoot," and a sweat-drenched
head appeared over the lip of the ravine. The head belonged
to an American.

There were now seven in the command post, and a 360-
degree defense. We had been joined by a young rifleman. Still
inexplicably careful about journalism, I asked his name; it was
Private First Class Sam Washburn, of Indianapolis. Washburn
had dived over a bush and told Higinbotham: "I got two
Charlies and the captain got one. The captain's dead. We were
lying on the trail firing at the Charlies and I looked over and
asked him how his ammo was and he was dead." Higinbotham said nothing, did not comment on Verlumis, and continued to talk the artillery in. "I don't think there's anybody
else back there," Washburn said. "I mean, any Americans."

That meant that the command post, and the seven of us,
were the front. There was no protection up the trail. The cries
of the wounded were getting louder as the men pulled back
into a tighter circle. The command post was filling up with
wounded, those who could crawl back or who were carried
back by the medics. I would hear only secondhand the horrors
endured by the men up the trail; they had been under heavy
bombardment for more than three hours. There was no firing
from the command post because the enemy could not be seen.

But then came the grenades. They were coming closer, just off the mark. That was when the awful fear set in. It was the fear of sudden realization that the North Vietnamese were lobbing grenades and there was no way to stop them.

The faces were all drawn up tight, and there was no talking. A company of reinforcements was on its way, but had got lost. No one knew whether it would arrive in time. Hollow-eyed and distracted, the men moved slowly as in a dream; or perhaps it was me, clammed up and lying flat in that taut circle. In Vietnam if you are thirty years old you feel an old man among youngsters. I was thinking about being thirty, and holding an automatic pistol I didn't know how to fire, when Washburn leaned over and very quietly, very precisely, whispered "grenade." He probably yelled it, but I was switched off, half-deaf from the pounding of the artillery and the 500-pound bombs and it seemed to me that the warning came in a whisper. Then he gave me a push. There was a flash and a furious burst of fire; the grenade had landed a yard away.

I couldn't get my feet down. I was lying on my back, almost standing on my head, and my feet wouldn't come down. Through the numbness and the red haze, I could see Washburn firing, although his hand was blown to pieces, and the radioman using his grenade launcher. Higinbotham was firing, too; but my legs wouldn't come down. Then they were down and I yelled for a medic. "I'm hit!"

"You're OK," Higinbotham said.

"The hell I am," I said. "I'm hit."

"I mean it," he said.

"Christ almighty there's blood everywhere," I said.

"You're all right."

"Goddamnit I'm not."

There was very little pain, just shock and a terrible feeling of relief. I was out of it. The terror was in the knowledge that you might lose control. You had to keep control, and you could feel it slipping away. You were half-crazy looking at the firing. The medic had scrambled up and I called for morphine. My arms and legs were shaking uncontrollably. The medic tackled me and punched the needle into my arm and began to bandage my head and back. The morphine restored the control. My hands and legs were still shaking but I was all right. Higinbotham was grinning. The medic said to take it easy. When the shaking stopped fatigue came.

"You're all right," Higinbotham said.

"I'm not all right, goddamnit," I said.

But we were both laughing, me from shock and Higinbotham from the fact that the attack had been thrown back. The grenades fired by Terry Grey, the radioman, had done it.

"Where are the VC?" I asked.

"We stopped the bastards," Higinbotham said.

I thought that line was in the best MGM tradition, and told Higinbotham so. None of it seemed real, lying in a godforsaken jungle in the middle of a godforsaken war. There were five dead North Vietnamese on the trail a dozen yards away. That was the point of farthest enemy advance. Higinbotham told me of this, and then the firing began once more. He ducked down to work the field telephone and I crawled off beneath a tree as the rat-a-tat-tat of explosions started again. I had lost the pistol and my pack, but I had the camera and my notebook. I thought it would be all right, and anyway I was out of it. There were nineteen wounded men and a dozen dead, and I was one of the wounded. The next two hours were very slow hours. Then the company of reinforcements arrived, crashing through the jungle with banshee whoops and rifle fire.

And that black humorist.

"Where's that newspaper fella?" he asked Higinbotham.

"He got hurt," Higinbotham said.

"Hurt? Sonovabitch."

I thought it would be all right until I saw the helicopters which would take the wounded out; some, like Wills, had lain on the jungle floor for five hours. There was no landing zone, so the helicopters hovered at 100 feet and lowered a T-bar. Strobe lights illuminated the jungle as arc lights illuminate a stadium. The first helicopter took three wounded. A man was strapped onto the T–bar and slowly lifted 100 feet. You ascended alone into the eye of the light, and heard the crack and thwup of bullets, and realized that the enemy, still entrenched on the ridge line, were shooting. They were shooting at the wounded men being pulled into the helicopter. You heard the bullets as you were rising and your body went stiff and you pulled out all the plugs. You gripped the T–bar and made a number of very difficult promises if God got you safely into the helicopter. But when you got there, you said instinctively, I made it. And over and over again, Jesus Christ.

There is no real epilogue to the reconnaissance patrol of the Tiger Force. Its activities that day went unnoticed in the American press because that same afternoon, on a hill only two miles away, Captain William S. Carpenter called napalm on his position after his company had been overrun. Operation Hawthorne, which lasted the better part of a month, was said to be a success. The Americans claimed 1,200 enemy dead, to 250 of their own. In the succeeding twelve months infiltration would continue. Almost eleven months to the day after the opening round of Hawthorne, a battalion of the 173rd Airborne Brigade would get ambushed and badly mauled by a force of North Vietnamese infantry. Lew Higinbotham, who by then had been transferred from the 101st to the 173rd Airborne, was operations officer that day. "How is it?" Higinbotham asked the platoon leader. "Good clean fun," the lieutenant replied. That was at 10 A.M. At ten-twenty the radio went dead; every man in the platoon was killed, or badly wounded. The wire services said the engagement took place a few miles north of Dak To, the Special Forces camp in Kontum province.

from *To What End: Report From Vietnam*, 1968

"Only You Can Prevent Forests"

by Frank Harvey

ON ONE CORNER of the Tan Son Nhut Airfield were some very beatup-looking twin-engine airplanes, gunked up with a film of something or other, covered with big and little metal patches, and smelling like leaky kerosene drums. They were the C-123 Providers, twin-engine transports built by Fairchild-Hiller, which have been adapted to spray 2-4D to kill plants and trees, which is obvious as you look at the long spray tubes hanging under the wings. The code name for these defoliation planes is "Ranch Hand," and the pilots of these planes are said to be the most shot-at people in the war. They are known by the crude but descriptive name of "magnet-asses." Ranch Hand's motto, placed there over the Ready Room door at Tan Son Nhut is there to remind the pilots of their mission: "Only You Can Prevent Forests."

Maj. Ralph Dresser, USAF, a rugged All-American football player from Texas, was Ranch Hand's commanding officer when I visited their headquarters. He was a very formidable-looking man, the kind you could well imagine coming through the line digging with his cleats on legs like big sinewy pistons, head about three feet from the ground, about as easy to stop as a charging African buffalo. He had a powerful neck, a grim look around the mouth and eyes, and yet he had one of the most charming personalities I encountered in Vietnam. He was intuitive about divining what I wished to know about his operation and most articulate and factual about telling me. He spoke softly, almost gently, and yet I would as soon have offended Maj. Dresser as gone over and tweeked the nose of a Bengal tiger. He gave the impression that if he decided to he could simply grab your arm, tear it off and hand it back to you. He ran a taut, self-contained outfit, had, at that time, flown 278 missions personally and his plane had been hit 78 times.

The Ranch Hand shop was tucked back behind an old hangar that had once housed General Ky's Coup Squadron, and Ky's present headquarters were embedded in great coils of accordion barbed-wire and high piles of sandbags a few hundred feet from Dresser's door. There were a few people around, Dresser said, who might want to eliminate Ky from the scene and he wasn't taking any chances. I noted that there were wicked-looking guys with submachine guns sitting unobtrusively in little niches of the sandbag walls, and also around the small landing area that Ky used to come and go from his fortress in a helicopter.

Dresser showed me around the squadron rooms. It was a Spartan place. The familiar sign, FUCK COMMUNISM, which was painted horizontally in stripes of red, white and blue, was tacked to one wall. Each crew member had been permitted to design and assemble his own idea of a survival kit, and there were some exotic items hanging on the pegs in the Personal Equipment room. Two places on the human body seemed to concern the Ranch Hand troops the most: the head and the testicles. One man had designed a bizarre steel helmet with a steel visor that could be lowered over the eyes, and it looked very much like the jousting headgear used by the knights of old. Steel jock-strap covers were popular. And, of course, the paint jobs on the helmets were exotic, to put it mildly. "The boys are motivated," Dresser said. "They're all volunteers." He smiled slightly. "You wouldn't stay in this business long if you didn't dig it," he said. "It gets a bit hairy."

Ranch Hand operated on a six-day week, two-mission-per-day schedule. A mission lasted from 40 minutes to two hours—depending on the target. The seven-plane squadron had, at that time, earned 27 Purple Hearts and seldom returned from a mission without bullet holes, largely because the defoliant spray must be applied from a height of 150 feet at a speed of 130 knots. Any higher and the spray doesn't get on the foliage in sufficient strength. Any lower and the foliage is overkilled—a waste of expensive chemicals. An average 11,000-pound load costs $5,000, takes four minutes to spread and kills everything green over 300 acres.

Dresser's C-123s operated 10 to 15 knots above stalling speed (the speed at which the plane quits flying with the engines still running smoothly, because the air quits rushing tightly over the wing to give it lift—and breaks up into whorls, eddies and burbles, which give no lift). When this happens, the airplane simply dives uncontrollably into the ground. Ten knots isn't much leeway between life and death. Particularly since the planes must make steep banks, as much as 60 degrees, at 100 feet of altitude—and a banking plane needs much more lift than one flying straight and level. In pilot language, they operate "at all times on the ultimate edge of the airplane's performance envelope."

The 1,000-gallon chemical tank is carried inside the fuselage with tubing out to the spray nozzles. The spray operator sits inside an armor-plated box near the rear cargo door and monitors the pump that forces the spray out of the dispensing tubes. I sat in the box and it seemed to afford pretty fine protection, but Dresser said that was apt to be an illusion because the plane often banked so steeply that the ground gunners were shooting almost straight into the box and had, in fact, hit the occupant in this manner a few times.

The pilot triggered the actual release of the spray from up front because he has a better look at the area and a better knowledge of how to release most effectively. Normally a C-123 would spray an area 14 to 17 kilometers long by 80 meters wide. When the ground fire started to crackle (it sounds like popcorn popping, Dresser said) a crewman hurls out a smoke grenade to mark the spot and the escort planes—Skyraiders or B-57 jets that are "flying shotgun"—roar in with guns blazing and bombs tumbling to suppress the fire.

The morning I talked to Dresser, Ranch Hand lost a C-123 to ground fire up near Danang. Rescue helicopters got the crew out but several men were very seriously injured. The VC were attacking both the downed spray plane and the rescue chopper. They detest the mission, which is probably understandable. Dresser said the Mekong Delta missions were the worst. The Delta country is flat, and the Vietcong gunners can see you coming for miles. They have time to get set, draw a bead and let fly. Dresser said he came in about five feet off the deck, his props leaving a white, frothy wake on the water of the rice paddies, then popped up to 150 to spray. "Even so," he added, "we get nicely ventilated very often on those Delta runs."

The areas sprayed most often are those along highways and railroads to make it more difficult for the VC to ambush convoys. It often happened that the VC mined a road, blew up a vehicle—tank, six-by, or antitank vehicle—which blocked the road. Then the guys in the underbrush zeroed in on the men and machines in the rest of the convoy, which were bottled up by the damaged point vehicle. It did not seem to me that the Americans were using our famous Yankee ingenuity in these probing patrols over roads they thought might be mined. Dick Cloy, outside Can Tho, said he sent an M-113 armored personnel carrier over the perimeter road from his village back to town to "blow up any mines they might have buried in the night." And I saw a number of newsreels showing damaged tanks that had been put out of action on roads up north of Saigon. I recalled the old French trick they'd been using when I went through Vietnam in 1954 to protect their railroad locomotives. They'd been chugging around the country with a couple of flatcars up front, so that if the tracks were mined the flats got it and not the engine. It seemed to me that a "mine-detector" tank could have been constructed by a savvy mechanic crew. They could merely have welded a bumper to the front of the tank—say about 10 feet long—with a set of bogie wheels that would press hard on the road, and trigger the mine, before the main treads of the tank arrived.

Dresser's men sprayed the perimeters of Special Forces camps out in the jungles to give the defenders a field of fire. This was also done around the perimeters of large air bases, where thick high stands of swamp grass were often found, and where snipers hid to take potshots at planes that were landing or taking off. When I was at Binh Thuy, for example, a DC-3 cargo plane was hit by a sniper at high noon while taxiing out for a takeoff. The shot came from the tall grass. The sniper was never caught.

Rice and other crops that might provide food for the VC were sprayed and killed. It takes three to five days before the sprayed leaves start turning brown and dying. A tree then dies in five to six weeks. The defoliant kills the plants and trees by overstimulating growth. The plant "grows itself to death."

"This is a very touchy thing," Dresser told me. "A mission to kill crops is particularly serious. We have to take it right up to the American Ambassador himself for approval. It can boomerang badly if it's not handled right."

Peasants who lose their crops are supposed to be paid in full for their losses. Unfortunately, they aren't always paid in full. Greedy province chiefs and sub-chiefs sometimes pocket the money the U.S. earmarks for peasant victims of Ranch Hand.

"The VC tell the peasants that our spray is deadly poison," Dresser said. "I'm going to show you now that it isn't."

He stuck his finger under one of the spigots of a dispenser drum, then licked the oily stuff. "It tastes like kerosene with chemical overtones—not good, but hardly a deadly poison unless you drink it, which nobody is likely to do."

Dresser and I walked around one of the Ranch Hand planes. It was a sorry-looking mess, coated with spray, pockmarked with patches that covered bullet holes, squat, dirty, ugly. It did seem, however, an appropriate machine for the job it had, which was certainly ugly too. "We are the most hated outfit in Vietnam," Dresser said. "Nobody likes to see the trees and the crops killed. But we're in a war, and Ranch Hand is helping to win it. The Ranch Hand mission is effective and necessary."

Dresser is right on all counts. Ranch Hand spray missions to defoliate the main trails, river banks in the Delta and truck routes over which the North Vietnamese infiltrate and resupply the South. Defoliation has also been used with great effectiveness in the Demilitarized Zone between North and South Vietnam to uncover ammo dumps and truck parks there. There has been talk of a massive effort to spray a wide buffer strip across the DMZ—a sort of "Dresser Line" so to speak—but the argument is that the VC would skirt it, just as the Maginot Line was skirted through Holland. The Big Defoliator—tactical atomic bombs—has been suggested, and may eventually be used—but Ranch Hand won't drop them. They'll come out of jets if they come at all. A C-123 couldn't possibly escape its own blast if it tried to deliver A-bombs, unless, of course, they had delayed fuses or floated down with parachutes.

It is good to report that the defoliant used by Ranch Hand does not permanently sterilize the soil. The climate and rainfall in Vietnam is such that trees and plants grow back rapidly, so that no permanent damage will be done by this operation. Ralph Dresser, who went to college in San Antonio to learn how to grow things—not kill them—is glad. He has no quarrel with the trees. Just with the VC.

from *Air War—Vietnam*, 1967

"Suffer the Little Children . . ."

by Martha Gellhorn

WE LOVE our children. We are famous for loving our children, and many foreigners believe that we love them unwisely and too well. We plan, work and dream for our children; we are tirelessly determined to give them the best of life. "Security" is one of our favorite words; children, we agree, must have security—by which we mean devoted parents, a pleasant, settled home, health, gaiety, education; a climate of hope and peace. Perhaps we are too busy, loving our own children, to think of children 10,000 miles away, or to understand that distant, small, brown-skinned people, who do not look or live like us, love their children just as deeply, but with anguish now and heartbreak and fear.

American families know the awful emptiness left by the young man who goes off to war and does not come home; but American families have been spared knowledge of the destroyed home, with the children dead in it. War happens someplace else, far away. Farther away than ever before, in South Vietnam, a war is being waged in our name, the collective, anonymous name of the American people. And American weapons are killing and wounding uncounted Vietnamese children. Not 10 or 20 children, which would be tragedy enough, but hundreds killed and many more hundreds wounded every month. This terrible fact is officially ignored; no Government agency keeps statistics on the civilians of all ages, from babies to the very old, killed and wounded in South Vietnam. I have witnessed modern war in nine countries, but I have never seen a war like the one in South Vietnam.

My Tho is a charming small town in the Mekong Delta, the green rice bowl of South Vietnam. A wide, brown river flows past it and cools the air. Unlike Saigon, the town is quiet because it is off-limits to troops and not yet flooded with a pitiful horde of refugees. Despite three wars, one after the other, the Delta peasants have stayed in their hamlets and produced food for the nation. Governments and armies come and go, but for 2,000 years peasants of this race have been working this land. The land and their families are what they love. Bombs and machine-gun bullets are changing the ancient pattern. The Delta is considered a Viet Cong stronghold, so death rains from the sky, fast and indiscriminate. Fifteen million South Vietnamese live on the ground; no one ever suggested that there were more than 279,000 Viet Cong and North Vietnamese in all of South Vietnam.

The My Tho children's hospital is a gray cement box surrounded by high grass and weeds overgrowing the peacetime garden. Its 35 cots are generally filled by 55 little patients. One tall, sorrowing nun is the trained nurse; one Vietnamese woman doctor is the medical staff. Relatives bring their wounded children to this hospital however they can, walking for miles with the children in their arms, bumping in carts or the local buses. Organized transport for wounded civilians does not exist anywhere in South Vietnam. Once the relatives have managed to get their small war victims to the hospital, they stay to look after them. Someone must. The corridors and wards are crowded; the children are silent, as are the grown-ups. Yet shock and pain, in this still place, make a sound like screaming.

A man leaned against the wall in the corridor; his face was frozen and his eyes looked half-mad. He held, carefully, a six-month-old baby girl, his first child. At night, four bombs had been dropped without warning on his hamlet. Bomb fragments killed his young wife, sleeping next to her daughter; they tore the arm of the baby. As wounds go, in this war, it was mild—just deep cuts from shoulder to wrist, caked in blood. Yesterday he had a home, a wife, and a healthy, laughing daughter; today he had nothing left except a child dazed with pain and a tiny mutilated arm.

In the grimy wards, only plaster on child legs and arms, bandages on heads and thin bodies were fresh and clean. The children have learned not to move, because moving hurts them more, but their eyes, large and dark, follow you. We have not had to see, in our own children's eyes, this tragic resignation.

Apparently children are classified as adults nowadays if they are over 12 years old. During a short, appalled visit to the big My Tho provincial hospital, among hundreds of wounded peasants, men and women, I noted a 13-year-old girl who had lost her left foot (bomb), sharing a bed with an old woman whose knee was shattered; a 14-year-old girl with a head wound (mortar shell); a 15-year-old girl with bandages over a chest wound (machine-gun bullet). If you stop to ask questions, you discover frequently that someone nearby and loved was killed at the same time, and here is the survivor, mourning a mother or a little brother: loneliness added to pain. All these people suffer in silence. When the hurt is unbearable, they groan very softly, as if ashamed to disturb others. But their eyes talk for them. I take the anguish, grief, bewilderment in their eyes, rightly, as accusation.

The Red Cross Amputee Center in Saigon is a corrugated tin shed, crowded to capacity and as comfortable in that heavy, airless heat as an oven. Two hundred amputees, in relays, have lived here. Now 40 Vietnamese peasants, male and female, ranging in age from six to 60, sit on chromium wheelchairs or their board beds or hobble about on crutches and, though you might not guess it, they are lucky. They did not die from their wounds, they are past the phase of physical agony, and in due course they will get artificial arms or legs.

The demand for artificial arms and legs in South Vietnam may be the greatest in the world, but the supply is limited; for civilians it had run out completely when I was there. These maimed people are content to wait; Saigon is safe from bombs, and they are fed by the Red Cross. To be certain of food is wonderful good luck in a country where hunger haunts most of the people.

A girl of six had received a new arm, ending in a small steel hook to replace her hand. Bomb fragments took off the lower half of her arm and also wounded her face. She has a lovely smile, and a sweet little body and she is pitifully ugly, with that dented, twisted skin and a lopsided eye. She was too young to be distressed about her face, though she cannot have felt easy with her strange arm; she only wore it to have her picture taken.

An older girl, also a bomb victim, perhaps aged 12, had lost an eye, a leg and still had a raw wound on her shoulder. She understood what had happened to her. Since the Vietnamese are a beautiful people, it is natural that they should understand beauty. She hid her damaged face with her hand.

A cocky, merry small boy hopped around on miniature crutches, but could not move so easily when he strapped on his false, pink-tinted leg. Hopefully he will learn to walk with it, and meanwhile he is the luckiest person in that stifling shed, because the American soldiers who found him have not forgotten him. With their gifts of money he buys food from street vendors and is becoming a butterball. I remember no other plump child in South Vietnam.

A young Red Cross orderly spoke some French and served as interpreter while I asked these people how they were hurt. Six had been wounded by Viet Cong mines. One had been caught in machine-gun cross fire between Viet Cong and American soldiers, while working in the fields. One, a sad reminder of the endless misery and futility of war, had lost a leg from Japanese bombing in World War II. One, the most completely ruined of them all, with both legs cut off just below the hip, an arm gone, and two fingers lopped from the remaining hand, had been struck down by a hit-and-run U.S. military car. Thirty-one were crippled for life by bombs or artillery shells or bullets. I discussed these figures with doctors who operate on wounded civilians all day, and day after day. The percentage seems above average. "Most of the bits and pieces I take out of people," a doctor said, "are identified as American."

In part, it is almost impossible to keep up with the facts in this escalating war. In part, the facts about this war are buried under propaganda. I report statistics I have heard or read, but I regard them as indications of truth rather than absolute accuracy. So: there are 77 orphanages in South Vietnam and 80,000 registered orphans. (Another figure is 110,000.) No one can guess how many orphaned children have been adopted by relatives. They will need to build new orphanages or enlarge the old ones, because the estimated increase in orphans is 2,000 a month. This consequence of war is seldom mentioned. A child, orphaned by war, is a war victim, wounded forever.

The Group orphanage, in the miserable rickety outskirts of Saigon, is splendid by local standards. Foreign charities have helped the gentle Vietnamese nuns to construct an extra wing and to provide medical care such as intravenous feeding for shriveled babies, nearly dead from starvation. They also are war victims. "All the little ones come to us sick from hunger," a nun said, in another orphanage. "What can you expect? The people are too poor." The children sit on the floor of two big, open rooms. Here they are again, the tiny war wounded, hobbling on crutches, hiding the stump of an arm (because already they know they are odd): doubly wounded, crippled and alone. Some babble with awful merriment. Their bodies seem sound, but the shock of war was too much for their minds; they are the infant insane.

Each of the 43 provinces in South Vietnam has a free hospital for civilians, built long ago by the French when they ruled the country. The hospitals might have been adequate in peacetime; now they are all desperately overcrowded. The wounded lie on bare board beds, frequently two to a bed, on stretchers, in the corridors, anywhere. Three hundred major operations a month were the regular quota in the hospitals I saw; they were typical hospitals. Sometimes food is supplied for the patients; sometimes one meal; sometimes none. Their relatives, often by now homeless, must provide everything from the little cushion that eases pain to a change of tattered clothing. They nurse and cook and do the laundry and at night sleep on the floor beside their own wounded. The hospitals are littered with rubbish; there is no money to spend on keeping civilian hospitals clean. Yet the people who reach these dreadful places are fortunate; they did not die on the way.

In the children's ward of the Qui Nhon provincial hospital I saw for the first time what napalm does. A child of seven, the size of our four-year-olds, lay in the cot by the door. Napalm had burned his face and back and one hand. The burned skin looked like swollen, raw meat: the fingers of his hand were stretched out, burned rigid. A scrap of cheesecloth covered him, for weight is intolerable, but so is air. His grandfather, an emaciated old man half blind with cataract, was tending the child. A week ago, napalm bombs were dropped on their hamlet. The old man carried his grandson to the nearest town; from there they were flown by helicopter to the hospital. All week, the little boy cried with pain, but now he was better. He had stopped crying. He was only twisting his body, as if trying to dodge his incomprehensible torture.

Farther down the ward, another child, also seven years old, moaned like a mourning dove; he was still crying. He had been burned by napalm, too, in the same village. His mother stood over his cot, fanning the little body, in a helpless effort to cool that wet, red skin. Whatever she said, in Vietnamese, I did not understand, but her eyes and her voice revealed how gladly she would have taken for herself the child's suffering.

My interpreter questioned the old man, who said that many had been killed by the fire and many more burned, as well as their houses and orchards and livestock and the few possessions they had worked all their lives to collect. Destitute, homeless, sick with weariness and despair, he watched every move of the small, racked body of his grandson. Viet Cong guerrillas had passed through their hamlet in April the old man said, but were long since gone. Late in August, napalm bombs fell from the sky.

Napalm is jellied gasoline, contained in bombs about six feet long. The bomb, exploding on contact, hurls out gobs of this flaming stuff, and fierce fire consumes everything in its path. We alone possess and freely use this weapon in South Vietnam. Burns are deadly in relation to their depth and extent. If upwards of 30 percent of the entire thickness of the skin is burned, the victim will die within 24 to 48 hours, unless he receives skilled constant care. Tetanus and other infections are a longtime danger, until the big, open-wound surface has healed. Since transport for civilian wounded is pure chance and since the hospitals have neither staff nor facilities for special burn treatment, we can assume that the children who survive napalm and live to show the scars are those who were least burned and lucky enough to reach a hospital in time.

Children are killed or wounded by napalm because of the nature of the bombings. Close air support for infantry in combat zones is one thing. The day and night bombing of hamlets, filled with women, children and the old, is another. Bombs are mass destroyers. The military targets among the peasants—the Viet Cong—are small, fast-moving individuals. Bombs cannot identify them. Impartially, they mangle children, who are numerous, and guerrilla fighters, who are few. The use of fire and steel on South Vietnamese hamlets, because Viet Cong are reported to be in them (and often are not), can sometimes be like destroying your friend's home and family because you have heard there is a snake in the cellar.

South Vietnam is somewhat smaller than the state of Missouri. The disaster now sweeping over its people is so enormous that no single person has seen it all. But everyone in South Vietnam, native and foreign, including American soldiers, knows something of the harm done to Vietnamese peasants who never harmed us. We cannot all cross the Pacific to judge for ourselves what most affects our present and future, and America's honor in the world; but we can listen to eyewitnesses. Here is testimony from a few private citizens like you and me.

An American surgeon, who worked in the provincial hospital at Danang, a northern town now swollen with refugees and the personnel of an American port-base: "The children over there are undernourished, poorly clothed, poorly housed and being hit every day by weapons that should have been aimed at somebody else. . . . Many children died from war injuries because there was nobody around to take care of them. Many died of terrible burns. Many of shell fragments." Since the young men are all drafted in the Vietnam Army or are part of the Viet Cong, "when a village is bombed, you get an abnormal picture of civilian casualties. If you were to bomb New York, you'd hit a lot of men, women and children, but in Vietnam you hit women and children almost exclusively, and a few old men. . . . The United States is grossly careless. It bombs villages, shoots up civilians for no recognizable military objective, and it's terrible."

An American photographer flew on a night mission in a "dragon ship"—an armed DC-3 plane—when Viet Cong were attacking a fortified government post in the southern Delta. The post was right next to a hamlet; 1,000 is the usual number of peasants in a hamlet. The dragon ship's three guns poured out 18,000 bullets a minute. This photographer said: "When you shoot so many thousand rounds of ammo, you know you're gonna hit somebody with that stuff . . . you're hitting anybody when you shoot that way . . . a one-second burst puts down enough lead to cover a football field. . . . I was there in the hospital for many days and nights. . . . One night there were so many wounded I couldn't even walk across the room because they were so thick on the floor. . . . The main wounds came from bombs and bullets and indiscriminate machine-gunning."

A housewife from New Jersey, the mother of six, had adopted three Vietnamese children under the Foster Parents Plan, and visited South Vietnam to learn how Vietnamese children were living. Why? "I am a Christian. . . . These kids don't ask to come into the world—and what a world we give them. . . . Before I went to Saigon, I had heard and read that napalm melts the flesh, and I thought that's nonsense, because I can put a roast in the oven and the fat will melt but the meat stays there. Well, I went and saw these children burned by napalm, and it is absolutely true. The chemical reaction of this napalm does melt the flesh, and the flesh runs right down their faces onto their chests and it sits there and it grows there. . . . These children can't turn their heads, they were so thick with flesh. . . . And when gangrene sets in, they cut off their hands or fingers or their feet; the only thing they cannot cut off is their head. . . ."

An American physician, now serving as a health adviser to the Vietnamese Government: "The great problem in Vietnam is the shortage of doctors and the lack of minimum medical facilities. . . . We figure that there is about one Vietnamese doctor per 100,000 population, and in the Delta this figure goes up to one per 140,000. In the U.S., we think we have a doctor shortage with a ratio of one doctor to 685 persons."

The Vietnamese director of a southern provincial hospital: "We have had staffing problems because of the draft. We have a military hospital next door with 500 beds and 12 doctors. Some of them have nothing to do right now, while we in the civilian hospital need all the doctors we can get." (Compared to civilian hospitals, the military hospitals in Vietnam are havens of order and comfort. Those I saw in central Vietnam were nearly empty, wasting the invaluable time of frustrated doctors.) "We need better facilities to get people to the hospital. American wounded are treated within a matter of minutes or hours. With civilian casualties it is sometimes a matter of days—if at all. Patients come here by cart, bus, taxi, cycle, sampan, or perhaps on their relatives' backs. The longer it takes to get here, the more danger the patient will die."

There is no shortage of bureaucrats in South Vietnam, both Vietnamese and American. The U.S. Agency for International Development (A.I.D.) alone accounts for 922 of them. In the last 10 years, around a billion dollars have been allotted as direct aid to the people of South Vietnam. The results of all this bureaucracy and all this money are not impressive, though one is grateful that part of the money has bought modern surgical equipment for the civilian hospitals. But South Vietnam is gripped in a lunatic nightmare: the same official hand (white) that seeks to heal wounds inflicts more wounds. Civilian casualties far outweigh military casualties.

Foreign doctors and nurses who work as surgical teams in some provincial hospitals merit warm praise and admiration. So does anyone who serves these tormented people with compassion. Many foreign charitable organizations try to lighten misery. I mention only two because they concentrate on children. Both are volunteer organizations.

Terre des Hommes, a respected Swiss group, uses three different approaches to rescue Vietnamese children from the cruelties of this war: by sending sick and wounded children to Holland, Britain, France and Italy for long-term surgical and medical treatment; by arranging for the adoption of orphans; and by helping to support a children's hospital in Vietnam—220 beds for 660 children. This hospital might better be called an emergency medical center, since its sole purpose is to save children immediately from shock, infection and other traumas.

In England, the Oxford Committee for Famine Relief (OX-FAM) has merged all its previous first-aid efforts into one: an OXFAM representative, a trained English nurse, is in Vietnam with the sole mission of channeling money, medicine, food, clothing and eventually toys (an unknown luxury) to the thousands of children in 10 Saigon orphanages.

Everything is needed for the wounded children of Vietnam, but everything cannot possibly be provided there. I believe that the least we can do—as citizens of Western Europe have done before us—is to bring badly burned children here. These children require months, perhaps years, of superior medical and surgical care in clean hospitals.

Here in America there are hopeful signs of alliance between various groups who feel a grave responsibility for wounded Vietnamese children. The U.S. branch of Terre des Hommes and a physician's group called The Committee of Responsibility for Treatment in the U.S. of War-Burned Vietnamese Children are planning ways and means of caring for some of these hurt children in the United States. Three hundred doctors have offered their skills to repair what napalm and high explosives have ruined. American hospitals have promised free beds, American families are eager to share their homes during the children's convalescence, money has been pledged. U.S. military planes, which daily transport our young men to South Vietnam, could carry wounded Vietnamese children back to America—and a chance of recovery.

The American Government is curiously unresponsive to such proposals. A State Department spokesman explains the official U.S. position this way: "Let's say we evacuate 50 children to Europe or the United States. We do not question that they would receive a higher degree of medical care, but it would really not make that much difference. On the other hand, the money spent getting those 50 children out could be better used to help 1,500 similarly wounded children in Vietnam. It seems more practical to put our energies and wherewithal into treating them on the scene in Vietnam." The spokesman did not explain why we have not made more "energies and wherewithal" available to treat the wounded children, whether here or in Vietnam. Officially, it is said that children can best be cured in their familiar home environment. True; except when the home environment has been destroyed and there is no place or personnel to do the curing.

We cannot give back life to the dead Vietnamese children. But we cannot fail to help the wounded children as we would help our own. More and more dead and wounded children will cry out to the conscience of the world unless we heal the children who survive the wounds. Someday our children, whom we love, may blame us for dishonoring America because we did not care enough about children 10,000 miles away.

Ladies' Home Journal, January 1967

Not a Dove,
But No Longer a Hawk

by Neil Sheehan

AMERICANS, because they are Americans, arrive in Vietnam full of enthusiasm and with the best of intentions. After a prolonged period of residence, they leave with their enthusiasm a victim of the cynicism that pervades Vietnamese life and with their good intentions lost somewhere in a paddy field. I am no exception. When I first walked across the tarmac of Saigon's Tansonnhut Airport on a warm evening in April, 1962, nervous that the customs officers might not accept the journalist's visa I had hurriedly obtained from the South Vietnamese consulate in Hong Kong, I believed in what my country was doing in Vietnam. With military and economic aid and a few thousand pilots and Army advisers, the United States was attempting to help the non-Communist Vietnamese build a viable and independent nation state and defeat a Communist guerrilla insurgency that would subject them to a dour tyranny. This seemed to me a worthy cause and something that needed to be done if other Southeast Asian peoples were to be allowed some freedom of choice in determining their course in history. Although I often disagreed with the implementation of American policy during my first two years in Vietnam, I was in accord with its basic aims.

I remember distinctly the thrill of climbing aboard a U.S. Army helicopter in the cool of the morning and taking off across the rice fields with a South Vietnamese battalion for a day's jousting with the Vietcong guerrillas. There was hope then that the non-Communist Vietnamese might win their war. I was proud of the young American pilots sitting at the controls in the cockpit and I was grateful for the opportunity to witness this adventure and to report it. We are fighting now, I used to think, and some day we will triumph and this will be a better country.

There were many disappointments those first two years, but when I left Vietnam in 1964, I was still, to use the current parlance, a hawk. I returned to Saigon in 1965 for another year. Now I have left again, and much has changed. There were 17,000 American servicemen in Vietnam at the time of my first departure and there are now 317,000 and I, while not a dove, am no longer a hawk.

If I had been wiser and could have foreseen the present consequences of that earlier and relatively small-scale American intervention in the affairs of this country, I doubt that I would have been enthusiastic during those first two years. I realize now, perhaps because this past year has impressed upon me more forcefully the realities of the war and of Vietnamese society, that I was naive in believing the non-Communist Vietnamese could defeat the Communist insurgency and build a decent and progressive social structure.

At a farewell dinner before my second departure from Saigon, the conversation drifted to the endlessly discussed but never resolved problem of gaining the sympathy of the peasantry. My host was a Vietnamese general, involuntarily retired through the vagaries of Saigon politics. To amuse us, he recounted an episode that had occurred in mid-1953 while he was commander of Franco-Vietnamese troops in the province of Buichu in what is now Communist North Vietnam.

That year, the Vietminh guerrillas, as the Vietcong were formerly called, accelerated their land-reform program. Communist cadres began confiscating the rice fields of landlords and dividing them up among the peasantry. To compete with the Vietminh and to arouse some popular support for the cause of his feeble Government and for France, the pro-French Emperor, Bao Dai, issued a decree reducing land rents from the traditional 40 to 50 per cent of the rice crop to 15 per cent.

Buichu was a predominantly Roman Catholic province. The two principal landlords there were the Catholic Bishop and the father of the Interior Minister in Bao Dai's Government. My host knew he would have to gain the Bishop's cooperation if he was successfully to enforce the decree.

"Impossible," said the Bishop. "How can I feed 3,000 priests, nuns, seminarians and coolies on 15 per cent of the crop?"

"I agree, Your Excellency," said my host, "it will be difficult. But perhaps it is better to make sacrifices now while there is still time. If we don't do something to win the sympathy of the population, you may lose more than your rice. You may lose your Bishopric, your land and perhaps even your head."

"Impossible," said the Bishop. "I will write to the Interior Minister."

Three months later, for attempting to implement the decree despite the Bishop's opposition, my friend was removed on the initiative of the Interior Minister. By the following summer, the Vietminh were so strong in Buichu that the French decided to evacuate the province. The Bishop, his priests, nuns and seminarians fled to Hanoi and thence to South Vietnam when the Geneva accords shortly thereafter sealed France's defeat at Dienbienphu and divided Vietnam at the 17th Parallel.

Over the 13 years since 1953, the United States has supplanted France in Vietnam. Yet among the Vietnamese themselves, the two opposing sides have changed little,

Precolonial Vietnam was administered by mandarins drawn from the merchant and land-owning families. When France colonized the country in the 19th century, much of this native aristocracy became, in effect, colonial civil servants, intermediaries between their own people and the foreigner. During the First Indochina War these Vietnamese, with a stake in the traditional society which a French presence would preserve, cooperated with France. Now the same Vietnamese, for identical reasons, cooperate with the United States.

Air Vice Marshal Nguyen Cao Ky, the current Premier of South Vietnam, was a French pilot. On occasional visits to the countryside he appears before the peasants in a trim black flight suit with a lavender scarf around his neck and a pearl-handled pistol at his waist—a kind of Asian Captain Marvel.

The Deputy Premier, Lieut. Gen. Nguyen Huu Co, and

other generals in the Saigon military junta, were officers or sergeants in the French colonial forces. Their fondness for French cuisine, snappy uniforms and cocktail parties and receptions creates a pale but faithful reflection of the social round of colonial days. They are the Vietnamese who have inherited the worst of two cultures—the pretentiousness of the native mandarins and the rigidity of the French colonial officers and administrators. Premier Ky and the earlier successors of Bao Dai have also promulgated rent-reduction and land-reform laws at the urging of American advisers eager for social progress. All of these measures have been sabotaged because the regimes were and are composed of men who are members of, or who are allied with, mandarin families that held title to properties they have no intention of renouncing. While there are some patriotic and decent individuals among them, most of the men who rule Saigon have, like the Bourbons, learned nothing and forgotten nothing. They seek to retain what privileges they have and to regain those they have lost.

In Vietnam, only the Communists represent revolution and social change, for better or worse according to a man's politics. The Communist party is the one truly national organization that permeates both North and South Vietnam. The men who lead the party today, Ho Chi Minh and the other members of the Politburo in Hanoi, directed the struggle for independence from France and in the process captured much of the deeply felt nationalism of the Vietnamese people. Perhaps because of this, the Communists, despite their brutality and deceit, remain the only Vietnamese capable of rallying millions of their countrymen to sacrifice and hardship in the name of the nation and the only group not dependent on foreign bayonets for survival.

It is the tragedy of Vietnam that what began as a war of independence from France developed, as a result of its Communist leadership, into a civil conflict. Attempts to describe the current war as a geographically based struggle between North and South Vietnam breaks down almost immediately when it is recalled that Premier Ky and several other important members of his Government are North Vietnamese by birth, who fled south after the French defeat, while Pham Van

Dong, the Premier of North Vietnam, was born in the South. The war is, rather, a struggle between differing elements of the Vietnamese people as a whole.

The division of the country into two separate states at the 17th Parallel in 1954 was a provisional arrangement ending one scene in the drama. Vietnam's larger political realities extended then and still extend now in both directions across the demarcation line. North Vietnam controls and supports with men and matériel the Vietcong guerrillas in the South because the Vietcong leaders, although native Southerners, are members of the Vietnamese Communist party and obey orders from the Politburo in Hanoi.

In 1958 the late President Ngo Dinh Diem organized a Committee for the Liberation of North Vietnam, and since 1960 the Saigon Government, with American connivance and aid, has been smuggling saboteurs and commando teams into the North in a so-far vain effort to instigate a guerrilla movement among the Northern Catholics and mountain tribesmen. The opposing sides, in short, have never recognized the 17th Parallel as a permanent boundary and have violated the frontier whenever it suited them.

Communist leadership of the anti-colonial movement led to the involvement of Vietnam in the larger context of the cold war and brought the intervention of the United States, first to aid the French, and then to develop and support a non-Communist administration and army in the South. For its own strategic and political ends, the United States is thus protecting a non-Communist Vietnamese social structure that cannot defend itself and that perhaps does not deserve to be defended. Our responsibility for prolonging what is essentially a civil conflict may be one of the major reasons for the considerable amount of confusion, guilt and soul-searching among Americans over the Vietnam war.

I know this is true in my own case and in the case of many Americans of my acquaintance who have lived for long periods in Vietnam. We are continually chagrined to discover that idealism and dedication are largely the prerogative of the enemy. The American soldier makes the lack of aggressiveness of the Government forces the butt of unending gibes. He grows to hate "Charlie," the G.I. slang name for the Vietcong guerrilla and the North Vietnamese regular, because "Charlie" kills his friends, but he soon learns to respect Communist bravery and cunning.

An American general recently paid a strange tribute to a Vietcong guerrilla who held up an entire U.S. Army infantry company for an hour in the jungle north of Saigon. The guerrilla was the lone survivor of several Communists defending a bunker. He fired off all his own ammunition and that of his dead comrades, and hurled back at the Americans the grenades they tossed into the bunker. He was finally killed while throwing rocks in a last gesture of defiance. "If one of our men had fought like that," the general said, "he would have been awarded the Medal of Honor."

Since the beginning of last year, Hanoi has increased the size of its regular army contingent in the South to a total of about 47,000 men. In the face of sustained bombing of the road and rail system in the North and the Ho Chi Minh Trail through Laos, the Communists continue to infiltrate men at an estimated rate of 4,500 to 5,000 a month. Many of these young men are conscripts who march south because of pressure on themselves and their families. Yet, once in the South, they fight well, and desertions are few despite the hardships and the severe losses through disease and battle. The Vietcong guerrillas have also managed steadily to expand their forces through recruitment and conscription.

The Saigon regime, on the other hand, has experienced great difficulty in increasing the strength of its armed forces because of a very high desertion rate. Desertions are greatest among conscripts, an indication that the average South Vietnamese feels little or no commitment to defend his own society. About 85 per cent of Saigon's armed forces are, consequently, volunteers who take up arms for pay. This gives the Government forces a distinctly mercenary cast that affects both their attitude toward the population and, except for a few élite units, their performance in combat.

From the contrast in behavior of the two sides, I can only conclude that Vietnamese will die more willingly for a regime which, though Communist, is at least genuinely Vietnamese and offers them some hope of improving their lives, than for one which is committed to the galling status quo and is the creation of Washington. The official assertion that the Communist soldier endures the appalling conditions of his daily life and behaves so commendably in combat out of terror of his superiors becomes patently ridiculous to anyone who has witnessed a battle. Terror may drive a man to march toward the enemy's guns, but it will not make him fight valiantly. The course of the conflict has made apparent that the Communists are able to arouse and to exploit the native Vietnamese qualities of hardihood and resilience and to convince large numbers of their people that the cause of *their* Government is just.

Most non-Communist Vietnamese are incapable, because of the values of the society in which they live, of looking beyond individual and family interests. Their overwhelming concern with "me and my relatives" deprives the society of a social consciousness Americans take for granted in their own culture and fosters the corruption and nepotism that exist throughout the administration. The disease of corruption appears to be worsening in direct proportion to the burgeoning amounts of American aid flowing into the country. Stories of embezzlement are legion and repeatedly embitter Americans.

Province and district chiefs' positions are frequently sold to the highest bidders by those responsible for making the appointments. The incumbent is then expected both to recoup the cost of his job from corruption and to make payoffs to the higher officials who sold it to him. Some American officials with long experience in Vietnam estimate that about 20 per cent of United States aid supplied for counter-insurgency projects in the countryside finds its way to the Vietcong and that another 30 to 40 per cent is diverted by Government officials. Cement, roofing, steel bars and other building materials destined for schools and refugee housing mysteriously end up on the open market or in private villas and apartment buildings. "What gets down to the poor son of a bitch in the paddy field," one official said, "is a trickle." A U.S. Army Special Forces captain once told me how he had arranged for rice to be flown in American planes to a camp of several thousand refugees in a remote area who were suffering from malnutrition. The local district chief confiscated the rice and sold it to the refugees at exorbitant prices.

While Americans worry about winning the war and creating an effective Vietnamese Government that can gain the support of its people, the mandarin families that run the regime have a different set of priorities. In one important province on the central coast this spring a rare honest and effective Vietnamese official, who was a favorite of the Americans, was fired because he began to talk about corruption by the two senior military commanders in the region. He was replaced by a cousin of one of the generals.

Numerous complaints from the American Embassy led Premier Ky to warn his fellow generals at one meeting of the junta that they were embezzling too much and should exercise some restraint. Their reply was that they had to think of their families. Vows by the Premier that corrupt officials will be shot have brought periodic headlines in the Saigon newspapers and the execution of one Chinese businessman and a half-dozen common hoodlums. Ordinary Vietnamese assume that Premier Ky has found it imprudent to arrange firing squads for some of his colleagues on the junta. One general's wife is sometimes referred to as "Queen of the Payoff."

Promises of land reform are solemnly reported in the American press and are apparently taken with some seriousness in official circles in Washington. I have often wondered why, since the promises are never carried out and the speeches made today are practically identical in content and phrasing to those made four years ago by some other Government leader. To gain their own ends, Asians frequently tell Americans what they think Americans want to hear. The Vietnamese, possibly because of their greater experience with Americans, seem to have developed a particular talent for this. Last April, during one of his more candid moments, Premier Ky told a group of correspondents: "Never believe what any Vietnamese tells you, including me."

In February, amid the hoopla following the Honolulu conference that was to lead to an intensive program of social, political and economic reform, the junta organized a "Social Revolution Day" in Saigon. Two thousand civil servants, soldiers, students and religious leaders were assembled on the lawn of the former presidential palace in the center of the city. The social reformers arrived in their Mercedes-Benz sedans and, dressed in well-tailored suits or bemedaled uniforms, began to read the usual speeches. The scene had a disturbing atmosphere of *déjà vu*. Within 10 minutes, a segment of the crowd, less polite than the rest, began walking out in boredom. The police, having apparently anticipated what would happen, had locked the gates of the palace grounds. No one was allowed to leave until the speeches had ended, despite a good deal of shouting and arguing back and forth through the steel bars.

The current social system discriminates against the poor and prevents social mobility. The mandarin families resist all efforts to change it, since it works in their favor. Although the United States has spent millions of dollars building primary schools in Vietnam, for example, it has been unable to bring about any fundamental reform of the Vietnamese educational structure, which makes certain that the sons of the prosperous, and almost no one else, will achieve the secondary education necessary to social advancement—whether in the army, the civil service or the professions.

Sending a peasant boy to primary school and then making it virtually impossible for him to achieve a decent secondary-school education fosters discontent, rather than lessening it. There is considerable evidence that many young Vietnamese of peasant origin join the Vietcong because the Communists, who have been forced by the nature of their revolution to develop leadership from the countryside, offer them their best hope of avoiding a life on the rung of the ladder where they began—at the bottom.

A friend of mine once visited a hamlet with a South Vietnamese Army major who is one of the few field grade officers to defeat the system by rising from a humble beginning. The major spoke to the farmers in peasant dialect instead of in the sophisticated urban Vietnamese most Government officials use.

"You're not a major," said one farmer in astonishment.

"Yes, I am," said the major.

"No, you're not," said the farmer. "You talk like a peasant and no peasant could become a major."

A drive through Saigon demonstrates another fashion in which the social system works. Virtually all the new construction consists of luxury apartments, hotels and office buildings financed by Chinese businessmen or affluent Vietnamese with relatives or connections within the regime. The buildings are destined to be rented to Americans. Saigon's workers live, as they always have, in fetid slums on the city's outskirts.

Since 1954, the United States has poured more than $3.2-billion of economic aid into South Vietnam, but no Saigon regime has ever undertaken a low-cost housing project of any size. The Singapore Government, in contrast, is erecting thousands of low-cost housing units for its people.

While Vietnamese with influence prosper in the cities and towns, the war has created a different world in the countryside. It is a world in which the masses of the peasantry no longer live—they endure.

Each afternoon, in the air-conditioned press-briefing room in Saigon, the United States Military Command releases a communiqué reporting that 300 or more "enemy structures" have been destroyed by American fighter-bombers or by the guns of Seventh Fleet warships that day. The statistics imply sound military progress until a visit to the countryside reveals that what is meant by an "enemy structure" is usually a peasant hut in a hamlet the Communists control, or which the American and South Vietnamese authorities suspect the Communists control.

No comprehensive statistics on civilian casualties are available. The nature of the war would make the assembling of such statistics very difficult, but the military authorities have also never seriously attempted to gather them.

An indication of what civilian casualties may be, however, is given by the fact that American and other foreign medical teams working in three-quarters of the country's 43 provinces treat 2,000 civilian war-wounded each month. If one accepts the normal military ratio of one dead for two wounded, the monthly figure is 1,000 civilian dead.

The number of wounded handled by the medical teams, I

believe from my own observation, is merely a fraction of the total. The medical teams treat only those wounded who reach the hospitals in provincial capitals. There are undoubtedly many more who never get that far. These victims are helped at Government district headquarters or militia outposts, or by Vietcong field hospitals and dispensaries—or they simply survive, or die, without treatment. Most of the wounds I have seen in the provincial hospitals are the type a victim could survive for two or three days without medical attention. Wounds that require rapid treatment are not usually in evidence, presumably because the victims die before they can obtain hospitalization.

Although civilians are being killed and wounded by both sides, my own investigations have indicated that the majority of civilian casualties result from American and South Vietnamese airstrikes and artillery and naval gunfire. Last November, I found one fishing village in Quangngai province, on the central coast north of Saigon, in which at least 180 persons—and possibly 600—had been killed during the previous two months by aircraft and Seventh Fleet destroyers. The five hamlets that composed the village, once a prosperous community of 15,000 people, had been reduced to rubble.

The gun and the knife of the Vietcong assassin are, in contrast, far more selective than cannon and fragmentation bombs; the victims are usually limited to Government officials and sympathizers. It has been estimated that, over the past decade, about 20,000 persons have been assassinated by Communist terrorists. This is a gruesome total, but the annual average is a great deal lower than the probable yearly number of ordinary civilian victims of the war.

Lack of sufficient American troops to occupy and hold ground when it has been wrested from the Communists is one of the major reasons for the extent of damage to civilian life and property. Once a battle has ended, the American and South Vietnamese troops withdraw. The theoretical follow-up by South Vietnamese territorial forces, police and administrators to pacify the region does not materialize except in a very limited number of instances, and the Vietcong guerrillas and their North Vietnamese allies move in again. The Americans eventually return and the same region is thus fought over repeatedly.

It would be easy to blame the American military authorities for the destruction, but this would not be fair. The Vietcong and the North Vietnamese regulars habitually fortify hamlets with elaborate trenchwork and bunker systems. Infantry attacking in classic style across open paddy fields would suffer prohibitive casualties. Under these circumstances, military commanders can only be expected to use whatever force is at their disposal.

Gen. William C. Westmoreland, the United States military commander in Vietnam, has ordered that all possible care be taken to avoid killing and wounding the innocent and that, whenever feasible, civilians be warned to leave their hamlets prior to airstrikes and artillery bombardments. Unfortunately, General Westmoreland's order has sometimes been ignored by subordinate commanders.

Hamlets are also habitually bombed and shelled at the request of a South Vietnamese province or district chief who has been told by some paid informer that Communist troops are present there. Information from informers is notoriously unreliable, the peasants are often not responsible for the presence of the Communists and, since ground units do not exploit the bombings and shellings, these attacks seem to have negligible military value. American officials excuse the practice by claiming that the Vietnamese, as the legal authorities, have the right to destroy their own hamlets, even if Americans perform the destructive acts—a fine bit of legalism that ignores the basic moral issue. I have occasionally thought that the practice results largely from the cynicism of South Vietnamese officialdom and a superfluity of aircraft and artillery.

The extraordinary firepower of American weaponry, whose ferocity must be witnessed to be comprehended, is another contributing factor to widespread civilian suffering. On an average day, U.S. warplanes alone loose 175 to 200 tons of explosives on the South Vietnamese countryside. Then there are the thousands of artillery and naval shells and the hundreds of thousands of rounds of mortar and small-arms ammunition.

The cratered landscape seen from an airplane window is an excellent advertisement for the ingenuity of American munitions makers.

The flow of refugees from the countryside is the most eloquent evidence available of the gradual destruction of rural society under the impact of the war. The number of refugees has now passed the million mark. It takes a great deal to make a Vietnamese peasant forsake his land and the graves of his ancestors.

Most refugees I have questioned told me that the Vietcong taxed them and made them work harder than usual, but that they could live with the Communists. They left their homes, they said, because they could no longer bear American and South Vietnamese bombs and shells.

If resettled properly, the refugees could conceivably develop into an asset for the Saigon Government. Yet, true to its usual behavior, the regime neglects them and the majority are left to shift for themselves. Refugee slums have risen in the cities almost as fast as G.I. bars.

Deserted hamlets and barren rice fields, now a common sight, are other evidence of what the war is doing to rural South Vietnam. In several provinces on the northern central coast as much as one-third of the rice land has been forsaken. The American policy of killing crops in Communist-held areas by spraying them with chemical defoliants from aircraft is hastening this process. During the first six months of this year 59,000 acres were destroyed.

The corrosive effect on the country of the American presence is not confined to military operations. Economically and culturally, the advent of the Americans has introduced maladies only time can cure. One is inflation. The primitive economy, already seriously disrupted by the war, has now been swamped by the purchasing power of tens of millions of dollars being dispensed for the construction of bases, airfields and port facilities and by the free spending of the individual American soldier.

This year the United States will pump a minimum of $140-million into the Vietnamese economy to cover the locally generated costs of the construction of new bases and the maintenance of existing ones. This sum constitutes about one-seventh of the country's entire money supply. American troops are themselves currently spending another $7-million a month.

The moral degeneration caused by the G.I. culture that has mushroomed in the cities and towns is another malady. Bars and bordellos, thousands of young Vietnamese women degrading themselves as bar girls and prostitutes, gangs of hoodlums and beggars and children selling their older sisters and picking pockets have become ubiquitous features of urban life. I have sometimes thought, when a street urchin with sores covering his legs, stopped me and begged for a few cents' worth of Vietnamese piastres, that he might be better off growing up as a political commissar. He would then, at least, have some self-respect.

Rarely in any war has the name of the people been evoked more by both sides than in the Vietnam conflict. Yet the Vietnamese peasantry, who serve as cannon fodder for Communists and non-Communists, remain curiously mute—a hushed Greek chorus to their own tragedy.

The conditions of life in Vietnam will probably always make an accurate assessment of the peasants' attitudes toward the war impossible to obtain. I have received the impression, however, on visits to accessible hamlets, that many of the peasants are so weary of the fighting they would accept any settlement that brought them peace.

Last March, I spent two days in one hamlet south of the port of Danang on the central coast. A company of U.S. Marines had seized the hamlet from the Vietcong six months previously, and a Government pacification team, protected by the Marines, was working there. In three years, the hamlet had changed hands three times. There were almost no young men in the community. Roughly half of the families had sons, brothers or husbands in the Communist ranks. The remaining families were about equally divided between those with neutral attitudes and those who were Government sympathizers.

The morning after I arrived, the peasants, under the supervision of the Government pacification workers, began constructing a fence around the hamlet perimeter to keep out Vietcong infiltrators. Through an interpreter, I asked two farmers among a group of old men, women and children digging postholes if they thought the fence would be of any use.

"Maybe it will," one said, "but I don't think so. A fence won't keep out the Vietcong."

"What did the Vietcong make you do when they controlled the hamlet?" I asked.

"They made us pull down the fence we had put up before, and dig trenches and lay booby traps," the second farmer said.

"Well, if you don't think the fence will do any good," I asked, "why are you putting it up?"

"We are just plain farmers," the first peasant said, glancing apprehensively at a policeman a few feet away with a carbine slung across his arm. "We have to obey any Government here."

As he spoke, a Vietcong sniper, hidden in a patch of sugar cane beyond the paddy fields, fired two shots. The old men, women and children scurried for cover, their fear and lack of enthusiasm for fence-building evident on their faces.

During a tour of South Vietnam in 1963, Gen. Earle G. Wheeler, chairman of the Joint Chiefs of Staff, referred to the conflict as a "dirty little war." While the Vietnam conflict may be even dirtier now than it was in 1963, it can no longer be termed little.

Reliable statistics are very elusive in Vietnam, but I would estimate that at least 250,000 persons have been killed since the war began in 1957. Last year, according to official figures, 34,585 Communists were killed and the Saigon Government forces suffered 11,200 deaths. Through mid-September of this year, again according to official statistics, 37,299 Vietcong and North Vietnamese regulars have died in battle and 7,017 Government troops have been killed.

American losses remained at a relatively low level until 1965, when the Johnson Administration committed ground combat units and began to create an expeditionary corps. That year, 1,369 American servicemen died in North and South Vietnam and neighboring Laos, and 6,114 were wounded. This year, as American offensive operations have picked up stride with the strengthening of the logistical apparatus, casualties have soared to 3,524 killed and 21,107 wounded, through mid-September. American dead are now averaging nearly a hundred a week and can be expected to increase as the expeditionary corps grows and more Americans are exposed to hostile fire.

The attitudes of the leadership in Hanoi and Washington indicate that the contest is far from being resolved. The rate at which North Vietnam is infiltrating its regular troops into the South and the willingness of the United States to engage its own ground forces and to escalate the air war against the North portend several more years of serious bloodshed. The world may hope for peace, but neither side has yet hurt the other sufficiently to prevent it from continuing. Both sides are trapped in a dilemma created by their history and political and strategic considerations. Washington cannot withdraw its troops from South Vietnam, as Hanoi demands, without making certain an eventual Communist seizure of power there and negating all the efforts of the last decade to maintain a friendly Government in Saigon.

Hanoi's best chance of winning now lies in prolonging the bloodletting to the point where the American public will tire of a war for a small land whose name most Americans cannot even pronounce correctly (they tend to say "Veetnam"). If the North de-escalates the fighting it will remove the principal source of political pressure on the Johnson Administration— the number of coffins being flown home from Saigon. Without the killing, the United States might be able to occupy South Vietnam indefinitely. The fact that 60,000 U.S. troops are stationed in South Korea brings no demonstrators into the streets and arouses no anxiety among American mothers, because the shooting in Korea has stopped.

A year ago, I worried that the patience of the American people would run out, that Ho Chi Minh would have his way and that the United States would lose the Vietnam war. This fear no longer troubles me nearly as much. I have the feeling that somehow we can muddle through this grim business. We may not win in Vietnam as we won in World War II, yet we may well prevail. Given our overwhelming military superiority, it is entirely possible that Washington, over a period of years, may be able to destroy the Vietcong and North Vietnamese main-force units in the South, and to transform what is currently a militarily sound but politically weak position into one of some, if doubtful, political strength.

Rather, my quiet worry concerns what we are doing to ourselves in the course of prosecuting and possibly some day winning this war. In World War II and in Korea the aggression of one state against another was an established fact. The United States acted with clear moral justification and Americans fought as they always like to think they fight—for human freedom and dignity. In Vietnam this moral superiority has given way to the amorality of great power politics, specifically, to the problem of maintaining the United States as the paramount power in Southeast Asia. The Vietnamese people have become more pawns in the struggle. Whatever desires they might possess have become incidental. The United States can no longer make any pretense of fighting to safeguard South Vietnam's independence. The presence of 317,000 American troops in the country has made a mockery of its sovereignty and the military junta in Saigon would not last a week without American bayonets to protect it.

Precisely because the Saigon Government represents nothing beyond its administration and army, the United States has had to fall back on its own military force to maintain its position and to win the war. Washington can dispense the latest in weaponry, but the First Air Cavalry Division and the Third Marine Amphibious Force cannot inspire the loyalty of the Vietnamese peasantry, and General Motors cannot manufacture decent non-Communist Vietnamese leadership, effective government and dedication. Only Vietnamese can supply these and the non-Communist Vietnamese have proven themselves incapable of providing them.

Thus, in the final analysis, American strategy in Vietnam consists of creating a killing machine in the form of a highly equipped expeditionary corps and then turning this machine on the enemy in the hope that over the years enough killing will be done to force the enemy's collapse through exhaustion and despair. This strategy, although possibly the only feasible alternative open to a modern industrial power in such a situation, is of necessity brutal and heedless of many of its victims.

Despite these misgivings, I do not see how we can do any-thing but continue to prosecute the war. We can and should limit the violence and the suffering being inflicted on the civilians as much as possible, but for whatever reasons, suc-cessive Administrations in Washington have carried the com-mitment in Vietnam to the point where it would be very difficult to prevent any precipitate retreat from degenerating into a rout. If the United States were to disengage from Vietnam under adverse conditions, I believe that the resulting political and psychological shockwaves might undermine our entire position in Southeast Asia. We shall, I am afraid, have to put up with our Vietnamese mandarin allies. We shall not be able to reform them and it is unlikely that we shall be able to find any other Vietnamese willing to cooperate with us. We shall have to continue to rely mainly on our military power, accept the odium attached to its use and hope that someday this power will bring us to a favorable settlement.

But I simply cannot help worrying that, in the process of waging this war, we are corrupting ourselves. I wonder, when I look at the bombed-out peasant hamlets, the orphans beg-ging and stealing on the streets of Saigon and the women and children with napalm burns lying on the hospital cots, whether the United States or any nation has the right to inflict this suffering and degradation on another people for its own ends. And I hope we will not, in the name of some anti-Communist crusade, do this again.

The New York Times Magazine, October 9, 1966

"The Long Fear"

by Frances FitzGerald

THE Delta is silent below Saigon. Where the land falls away to sea level, the waters of the Mekong fan out, pulse like plasma through the dark silt and infuse it with the slow, rich life of rice, sugar cane, and bananas. The Delta nourishes the country and is silent, complete within itself. On its rivers and along the grey strips of road, cargoes of rice move east to Saigon, west to Cambodia and to the North, as they did in the days of Indochina. The old habits persist. And the Revolution goes on until, after twenty-one years, the word has lost its sense; revolution on revolution, and still no change. Following the Confucian cycles of duty to the family and to the land, which encompasses its dead and its living, the villagers look away from the outside world, which has brought them so little. Independence, Communism, and the Republic rest like empty word-shells above the cycle of the seasons and the routine of the civil war.

The war in the Delta remains in a curious stasis. To the North the big fighting units—the Americans and the North Vietnamese—polarize the country, meeting pressure with increased pressure and widening the instability to draw ever new men, new territories into the vacuum of war. Except for the backwash from this building current, the Delta maintains a balance, a harmony of opposition between the Liberation Front and the Government in Saigon. Along the roadsides, above the bridges, between a hamlet and its backdrop of jungle, the Popular Forces, the barefoot black-clad boys with old carbines, wait eternally behind mud-walled forts in a clutter of nursing women, chickens, and half-naked children who play in the dust. Outside the forts in the paddies or in their dark tunnels the Viet Cong farmer-guerrillas work for their families and wait through the same long fear of their likenesses, their brothers. Though the war ebbs and flows through them, the soldiers change it little; whether drafted by the Viet Cong or the Government, they are bound together by a network of lifelong ties. When the net breaks, there is violence.

An outpost is overrun one night, and by the next morning eight are dead, eight have fled, and eight have deserted to the Viet Cong. A Government battalion encircles a company of guerrillas—leaving a breach through which the enemy can retreat without bloodshed. But the Viet do not see it and, thinking they are surrounded, fight their way out over the battalion at the cost of many lives. When there are casualties, the injured must take revenge, as must any family in the hill towns of Sicily. Who is winning the war? An absurd question. Nothing moves, nothing happens except that, little by little, the strain tells on all of the people.

In his high-ceilinged villa General Dang Van Quang, 4th Corps Commander and supreme representative of the Government in the Delta, receives Air Vice-Marshal Ky with the easy manners of a secure man, a partner. Two weeks before his troops won a great victory—an event which, despite its apparent sanguinity, went unremarked in the American press—and the General has invited the Prime Minister, the Defense Minister, and the Chief of Staff to distribute the medals and citations. [General Quang is now in the Ky cabinet.]

On the couch before the French window General Ky sits talking with nervous, catlike gestures. Beside the slim Northerner, General Quang looks solid, self-assured as a baron whose estates have prospered in a time of trouble; his roundness of stomach, his constant joviality conceal his nimbleness of wit and limb. Laughing, he calls for the servants to bring coffee and hot towels and waves across at his wife and her retinue of women who stand at the foot of the grand staircase waiting to join the party. Outside the French window a well-tended lawn, broken by a sandbag emplacement, slopes down to the river which, with its slow traffic of sampans, curves about the small provincial capital of Can Tho. Since the French resident vacated the villa, since the civil servants, the planters and their wives left Can Tho with its generous white buildings, its open plazas and its gardens, neither the view nor indeed the town itself has changed appreciably.

The General laughs again. He is always laughing—perhaps

at nothing so much as his own good luck to command the richest region of the country and the only part of Viet Nam where foreign troops with their impersonal machines of war and their floods of new money have not yet come to disorder the old system. In his still granary the General remains untroubled by the Buddhist monks and the articulate politicians who have rent apart the army in the central provinces and Saigon. Here, where politics are less a matter of principle than a matter of day-to-day business, the war allows for a certain latitude, a moderation. Later in the morning the Prime Minister and the generals will settle down in the soft dusty heat of the plaza and patiently wait out the two hours of parading and speeches.

It will be a fine ceremony with parti-coloured bunting and high school girls all in white and the provincial gentry—the officers, a few civil servants, and the ranking wives with their spike heels and their small diamonds—applauding politely. One by one the soldiers, shy and disorganized by the heat, will come up to receive their medals; now and then an American advisor in the same green uniform and red neckerchief will step up looking like a pale, retarded child among his smaller classmates. It will be a fine ceremony with flags and patriotic music at an uncertain tempo, and after his box lunch Prime Minister Ky will reboard his airplane and fly back to Saigon, having learned nothing, having given no instructions.

The Delta remains silent. It is perhaps too complicated, too meshed within its own harmonies to respond to Hanoi or to Saigon with one or even a dozen clear answers. Since the Vietnamese settlers moved down from the crowded North into the Kingdom of the Khmers one and two centuries ago, the South—unlike the Centre and the North—has been for most of its history under direct French rule.

Building their villages on the strips of high ground along the rivers, the people, except those few who went to Saigon for a French education, sealed themselves off to work the virgin land and to multiply until their numbers reached up beyond five million, or to more than one-third of the population of the Republic of Viet Nam.

Like the colonial administration, the Government and, to a large extent, the National Liberation Front hover over the villages without touching the life of the people. Where there is authority, it is that of a local warlord, a guerrilla chieftain or a priest who has shaped a community around his person. Below the two governments with their clear opposition, their linear structure of power, the religious sects, the ethnic minorities, the competing branches of each government, the villages, and the families weave their own designs into the war.

One Catholic priest, who feeds his orphans and school children on American voluntary relief funds, protects his flock— and his temporal power—by paying tribute to the Viet Cong. The owners of a rice mill process "Viet Cong" and "Government" rice indiscriminately and pay taxes to both sides.

As army officers and guerrilla chieftains must exchange military glory for a regular supply of merchandise, so the people must sacrifice killing in the interests of survival. The war has been going on for a very long time; it has become the system. To end it might stanch the flow of blood, but it would dislocate the structure of society.

The Air America pilot swings his Beechcraft in a tight gyre over the airstrip of the province of An Giang. Cutting the last loop too short, he grazes the runway and pulls back at the control for another approach. He is taking no chances with ground fire—or perhaps he has forgotten where he is, for the provinces of the Delta look so much alike with the wheeling mirrors of water, the thatched huts, and the coconut stands in a jade sea of rice. And there are so many names—An Giang, Kien Giang, An Xuyen, Kien Hoa, Dinh Tuong. . . .

But the Hoa Hao sect controls An Giang, and there are no Viet Cong in the province—or at least none to speak of. The relationship between the two facts is not strictly causal, though *mystique* is *politique* in Viet Nam, and the fundamentalist Buddhist sect with its million adepts constitutes a political force in the Delta second only to the Viet Cong. Since the Government learned to appoint Hoa Hao officials to An Giang, it has been the only province in the country where officials and Americans travel without guns.

To drive through An Giang is, for an American, to drive out of Viet Nam into a mirage of the country at peace. Ten miles of road back into the hamlets of polished wooden houses free of the barbed-wire weed that chokes the rest of the country, ten miles of gardens with their spirit altars and earthenware jars filled with rainwater.

Then to Chau Doc and the river, the ancient road of the country, past the fishing weirs, the flat boats that move against the current under the arc of a rattan sail and further into the mirage to a place that is perhaps at the back of the mind of Viet Nam, somewhere that has been half-forgotten. The small children wade in the shallows, plunging their baskets into the mud to trap the small bottom fish.

They are there, waiting at the landing. The Central Committee of the Hoa Hao—twelve men in shiny grey business suits and pointy shoes that squeak as they walk. Courtly, they bow from the waist and feign to ignore the muddy boots and open shirts which their visitors have been so naïve as to bring into their country. "We are enchanted to welcome you."

The committeemen murmur greetings preserved over the long seasons of disuse in their prewar elegance. Preserved, perhaps, by the virtue that their private army gained by killing—and, it is darkly rumoured, eating—so many Frenchmen during the War of Liberation.

The President of the Central Committee, an old man with the gait of a judge and the wicked smile of a child, ushers the company into a garden of chipped hedges and flowering trees where under a pavilion a long table is set for tea. "Let me show you the sacred places of our cult," he offers courteously. His gold teeth glitter.

The pavilion is a sanctuary. Here the Prophet Huyn Phu So, the founder, was born and here, after his illumination, he preached in the one year that was given to him, 1939, the year of the Cat. Here is the altar with its brass vessels and the crimson cloth that signifies the Buddha.

The Hoa Hao make no idols, burn no incense, and have no priesthood, for the Prophet brought the people back to the fundamental teachings of the One Buddha. Here is a picture of the Master as a young man. (The painted face behind the glass is sallow, diffident, the face of a young man set apart from the world, as if by a persistent disease. The Prophet's mandarin robes are of real silk, stuffed above the surface of the canvas; his feet are painted.) "Listen to the chanting," the President says. "Our adepts are calling out the prayers from the prayer tower in the village. Here is a photograph of the Prophet's mother. She lives here with us in the village. She is eighty-three."

We, the American guests, sit down with the Central Committee on carved black chairs around the table, and the Committee press upon us sarsaparilla, sweet cakes, and metaphysics. Who are they, these spry old men who live out here in the back of beyond in their shiny suits, in their Mormon-like zeal, in their memories of a too recent—and for that reason somehow questionable—Prophet?

"The West has made great progress in learning about the world through science, but there are some things that you will never understand and these are the mysteries." The President's eyes sparkle at his barefaced cliché. "You see, it is quite simple. The Hoa Hao have faith, and therefore there are no Viet Cong in our province. We are the blessed of Buddha. It is quite evident that we must be blessed because no sooner is the country threatened—seven hundred million Chinese, *figurez-vous!*—than we are granted a great and powerful protector in the United States."

The old man beams. He has made for our benefit such a limpid description of that human tangle which Viet Nam has spent twenty-one years in the knotting. In a softer voice he goes on to expound one of Saigon's more intricate political squabbles with whose details he is—perhaps by occult perception—absolutely familiar.

"There is," the old man continues, "no use asking which military régime is better than the next or what good can come of the Constituent Assembly. What Viet Nam must have is a revolution. Have you seen any revolutionary leaders among our chiefs of state?" he asks archly.

"You have heard, of course, of metempsychosis. Viet Nam is passing through a period of troubles—collectively we are paying for the sins of our previous incarnations. Soon, however, the period will end. We are near to finding a coalition with a leader who will deliver us from our condition."

Who, when, how, what coalition we, the Americans, ask eagerly.

The old man twiddles his hearing aid and looks puzzled. "Ah," he says finally, "you do not quite understand. I am no prophet. I can not foretell the exact time when the Saviour will come."

Among the inhabitants of An Giang province speculation into the apocalypse is a generalized, if somewhat diversified, occupation. The United States A.I.D. (Agency for International Development) organization is a sect of two foreign service officers who have quit diplomatic life in the world's capitals (temporarily) to live in An Giang and to devote themselves to soybeans.

"Soybeans!" these adepts cry ecstatically. "This year the farmers—on their own—have planted two hundred hectares of America's finest soybeans. Next year there will be six hundred hectares, and the year after that. . . ." The vision is blinding, for An Giang is a Priority Area in President Johnson's and Premier Ky's Revolutionary Development Program.

Not only soybeans but also two crops of rice a year, a primary school in every hamlet, a pig in every pigsty, bridges, wells, and cottage industry will one day be manifest in the province.

"The key to it all is rural electrification," explains one adept confidentially. "You see, when a family has an electric circuit, the wife—the woman is always the instigator—will ask her husband for an iron. He'll buy the iron, and she'll ask him for a radio or an oven. He'll have to work harder to buy her the oven—perhaps growing soybeans or planting a second crop of rice.

"But the wife won't be satisfied. She'll want a television set because the people next door have one, a washing machine, a Waring Blendor . . . and pretty soon, look what has happened! Viet Nam is a Developed Country."

The Delta perhaps demands every reserve of mysticism from the Americans who live there. As advisors to the army and to the administration, they have as much influence over the course of events as the moon has on the earth. Progress, that linear, non-Confucian concept, turns full circle in Viet Nam from progress in not losing to progress in not winning.

If there are other signs of forward movement, they are esoteric, invisible. This autumn when the monsoon floods descended on the upper regions of the Delta, the soybeans in An Giang province did not survive the disaster.

Happily, in the province and district capitals, the American military advisors are capable of imaginative triumphs unmatched by most civilians.

"The doctor says that ninety-five per cent of all Vietnamese babies have black behinds," says the staff sergeant with conviction. "You see, look at this one. Google, oogle. Isn't that the sweetest thing?" He lifts the half-naked child high up above the mess hall table and presses it close up against his gentle horse face. The child wiggles and gurgles with pleasure.

"Yes," says the Major. "Doctors say that most Vietnamese children have such birthmarks and that they are associated with syphilis in the parent."

The Major is heavy with authority. Over the meatloaf and the ketchup he has delivered a series of pronouncements which, more than the barbed wire and the artillery cover from the province headquarters, seem to provide him with a sense of security. "The Vietnamese peasant just wants to be left alone; he doesn't know a thing about Communism. . . .

"My counterpart, the district chief, is a swell little guy. If there were only more like him the war would be won in. . . .

"They have been fighting this war for twenty years and they are tired. . . ." Each statement a sandbag, a regulation bulwark against the lush jungles of the Delta which threatens to creep over sanity.

The Major lives with a lieutenant, a staff sergeant, a corporal and a radio operator in the centre of An Xuyen, the province of mud flats at the very base of the Delta, four per cent of which is controlled by Government troops. A rich province, An Xuyen knew nothing but exploitation from the French and from the Diems; its ample forests, once strongholds of the Viet Minh, now provide rest and recreation areas for the Viet Cong.

Devil's Island—that's what they call the ugly tin and thatch-built province capital which during the monsoon season looks like the back of a rhinoceros wallowing in the Mekong mud; Cam Au is a barracks, a market place for the Chinese, and a disposal centre for civil servants who have been caught with their hands in the till.

When the Major drives to Cam Au each day along the ten miles of road pitted with Viet Cong mine holes and coloured "secure" on the map, he keeps his rifle loaded against the chance of sniper fire. The sniper may be a Viet Cong or it may be one of the Government soldiers who, for reasons of his own, is gunning for an American advisor.

"The war isn't going to be won this way," said the Major, patting his M.16, "but rather with medicine and . . . things like that." When he speaks of the army's civic action program, a new expression dawns on his honest face. Civic action, the magic formula taught in the new army manuals: Just follow the instructions, and the war becomes an exercise in social welfare.

Like the General Issue Playboy pinup and the sociological pronouncements, the handouts of rice to the priests and candy to the children are for the Major anxiety repellents. They lift the great silence of the Delta, hold it up from bursting the eardrums.

In An Xuyen, as in most of the Delta provinces, the balance of power has been established and, short of foreign occupation, there is little to be done. Meanwhile the war goes on like an endless game of chance whose rules are unknown.

Vogue, January 1967

U.S. Raids Batter 2 Towns; Supply Route Is Little Hurt

by Harrison E. Salisbury

HANOI, North Vietnam, Dec. 25—Hanoi's Christmas quiet was shattered at 2:30 P.M. today when an air alert sounded, antiaircraft guns roared and a United States plane was reported shot down.

Residents in the center of Hanoi reported that they had heard the sound of aircraft shortly after the alert sounded. Almost immediately, antiaircraft guns fired and the United States plane was reported downed. Another alert was sounded when a second plane appeared about 12 miles from the city.

Hanoi's alert was apparently the same as that touched off in Namdinh, 50 miles to the southeast, where this correspondent was inspecting earlier bomb damage. The alarm sounded at Namdinh at 2:26 P.M., when it was announced the plane had been sighted approaching from the north.

Mayor Tran Thi Doan, a petite 40-year-old woman, led a group of officials to a shelter beside the City Hall, where she continued to tell of a series of 51 raids on the city up to Friday. None of the raids, as far as she knew, had ever been announced in the West.

The Namdinh alert continued until 2:47 P.M.—which residents thought remarkably long since fast-flying planes had time to make several round trips from the vicinity of Hanoi in that period. However, this duration may have been occasioned by the reported downing of the American plane. The 2:26 alert at Namdinh was the third on Christmas Day. Namdinh officials attributed the alerts to American reconnaissance, which they believed had been continued despite the Christmas truce.

Christmas wasn't a joyous occasion for Namdinh although strings of small red pennants decorated the old gray, stucco

Catholic church and a white Star of Bethlehem had been mounted on the pinnacle of the tower. Few Americans have heard of Namdinh, although until recently it was the third largest North Vietnamese city.

Mayor Doan regards her city as essentially a cotton-and-silk textile town containing nothing of military significance. Namdinh has been systematically attacked by American planes since June 28, 1965.

The cathedral tower looks out on block after block of utter desolation; the city's population of 90,000 has been reduced to less than 20,000 because of evacuation; 13 per cent of the city's housing, including the homes of 12,464 people, have been destroyed; 89 people have been killed and 405 wounded.

No American communiqué has asserted that Namdinh contains some facility that the United States regards as a military objective. It is apparent, on personal inspection, that block after block of ordinary housing, particularly surrounding a textile plant, has been smashed to rubble by repeated attacks by Seventh Fleet planes.

The town lies only 20 miles inland, which may explain why the Seventh Fleet seems to have made it its particular target. The textile plant, whose most dangerous output from a military point of view would presumably be cloth for uniforms, has been bombed 19 times, but is still operating under great difficulty.

Other industries in Namdinh include a rice-processing plant, a silk factory, an agricultural-tool plant, a fruit-canning plant and a thread cooperative. All have been damaged in raids. The least affected operation is the rice mill, which is working at normal capacity.

Street after street in Namdinh has been abandoned and houses stand torn and gaping. One deserted street is Hang Thao or Silk Street, which was the center of the silk industry. Almost every house on the street was blasted down April 14 at about 6:30 A.M. just as the factory shifts were changing.

Forty-nine people were killed, 135 were wounded on Hang Thao and 240 houses collapsed. Eight bombs—MK-84's—accomplished this. These are huge weapons weighing about 2,000 pounds.

The residents of Namdinh have become specialists in

United States weapons. They rattle off names like MK-81, MK-83 and MK-84 and various categories of missiles, including Bullpups, as baseball fans do batting averages; most attacks have been carried out by F-105's and F-4's but B-57's, A-3's, A-4's and A-6A's have also been used.

Another target in Namdinh has been the Dao (Black) River dike. The dike has been hit six times and there have been many near-misses. Breaching of the dike would seriously affect the region's rice agriculture. However, supplemental and reinforcing dikes have been built. And with a plentiful labor force always at hand to repair gaps quickly, the danger of serious damage by air attack seems minimal.

Why have American planes devoted all this unannounced attention to Namdinh? "Americans think they can touch our hearts," Nguyen Tien Canh of Namdinh's City Council said, apparently meaning that Americans thought they could intimidate the populace by continuous attacks.

A second suggestion was that the unannounced assault on Namdinh was supposed to be an object lesson to show Hanoi what United States air power could accomplish if it were directed more powerfully to North Vietnam's capital.

Whatever the explanation, one can see that United States planes are dropping an enormous weight of explosives on purely civilian targets. Whatever else there may be or might have been in Namdinh, it is the civilians who have taken the punishment.

A brief tour of Namha Province in which Namdinh lies, shows Namdinh is far from being exceptional.

President Johnson's announced policy that American targets in North Vietnam are steel and concrete rather than human lives seems to have little connection with the reality of attacks carried out by United States planes.

A notable example is Phuly, a town about 35 miles south of Hanoi on Route 1. The town had a population of about 10,000. In attacks on Oct. 1, 2 and 9, every house and building was destroyed. Only 40 were killed and wounded because many people had left town and because an excellent manhole-shelter system was available.

The community had no industry, but lay astride a highway and a railroad line running from Hanoi, which had a couple of sidings in town. Presumably, planes were attacking the railroad. But in the process they destroyed another residential community.

Since bombing is far from an accurate process, at best, and since people in Vietnam work, live, study and amuse themselves in the same streets as those on which military targets are situated or on adjacent blocks, the outlook is for more destruction, to life, residential quarters, schools and every other variety of nonmilitary facility. The same rule applies whether the target is so-called Hanoi vicinity, a crossroads, a village or a hamlet.

Effect of Bombing on Route 1 Minimal

HANOI, North Vietnam, Dec. 26—Viewed from air reconnaissance or on photographic maps, National Route 1, the old French-built highway that runs south from Hanoi to Saigon, must look like a bombardier's dream target.

The highway and a railroad run parallel only a few feet apart, mile after mile, straight across the table-flat delta of the Red River. The highway is marked by lovely, regularly planted shade trees, and camouflage, disguise or concealment is utterly impossible.

This is no jungle country. This is no tricky mountain terrain. This is rich, flat ricelands crisscrossed by irrigation flows and paddy fields. The railroad and highway could not be a plainer target if they were picked out by continuously flashing beacon lights.

It is easy to imagine Air Force strategists inspecting a map and concurring that Hanoi's southward supply services can easily be interdicted by a few easily placed bombs.

But appearances can be remarkably deceiving, as ground-level inspection of Route 1 quickly discloses. Viewed on the ground, it is obvious that the "dream target" is in reality a snare and a delusion.

The railroad and highway have been bombed again and again and again, but it is doubtful that rail traffic has ever been held up more than a few hours, and the highway seems capable of operating almost continuously regardless of how many bombs are dropped.

The secret of the railroad is simple and it lies beyond the ability of air power to interdict.

If the track uses small, light equipment when a bomb smashes the rails or overturns a car, removal and repair problems are simple. Gangs of workmen can easily clear the line. Moreover, repair materials probably sufficient to construct two or three additional railroads are kept on hand, seldom more than a few hundred yards from any possible break.

The same thing, only more so, is true of the highway, which can be repaired and restored even more rapidly by the use of readily available manpower and repair materials similarly stockpiled in advance, apparently along the whole expanse of Route 1.

The results of American bombing of the route are readily visible—particularly in small villages and hamlets along the route. They have suffered severely, often being almost obliterated. But the effect on transportation has been minimal.

Another factor in this situation is not visible to reconnaissance planes. This is that almost everything movable in North Vietnam can be moved equally well either by train or by truck, and the truck routes are virtually noninterdictable.

There is a third major alternative—human backs, bicycles and carts. As the Korean War demonstrated, where trucks and human carrying power are available as alternatives, it is impossible to interdict supply movements.

Even in the region of the Seventeenth Parallel, which divides North and South Vietnam, where United States bombs have leveled the whole countryside, movement continues by night with little impediment.

A basic flaw in the bombing policy from a military viewpoint would seem to be its failure to take into account the nature of the country and the people to which it is being applied. If the Pennsylvania Railroad and the major highway to Washington were bombed out, the disruption of United States supplies and services would be enormous and the military consequences in wartime would be grave.

Here it is hardly felt. Traffic and supplies simply flow around and past the point of interruption and the damage to rail or highway is quickly made good. The principal sufferers are the people who have the misfortune to live along the railroad and highway and on whose homes far more bombs rain down.

Another example of the ground-level reality of United States bombing compared with the communiqué version relates to air attacks carried out Dec. 13 and 14 in Hanoi. One of the United States targets was specified by the communiqué as a "truck park at Vandien."

Vandien is in the southern part of Hanoi along Route 1. Administratively it is separate from Hanoi, but actually it is a continuous part of the urban center. United States maps show the truck park as situated just east of Route 1.

In fact, there is a large, open area with light buildings and compounds that may or may not have been a truck park, lying possibly a quarter-mile east of Route 1, which has been badly smashed by bombs.

But the bomb damage does not halt at the compound lines. It extends over an area of probably a mile or so on both sides of the highway, and among the structures destroyed in the attack was the Vietnam-Polish Friendship senior high school, lying on the west side of the highway, probably three-quarters of a mile from the presumed United States target.

It is the conviction of the North Vietnamese that the United States is deliberately directing bombs against the civilian population although ostensibly contending that "military objectives" are the target.

The New York Times, December 27, 1966

"Unrepentant, Unyielding"

An Interview with Viet Cong Prisoners

by Bernard B. Fall

LAI-KHÉ, SOUTH VIETNAM

TWO YEARS AGO, Lai-Khé was a tranquil place hardly an hour's ride from Saigon, and the home of the *Institut de Recherches du Caoutchouc du Vietnam*, a research institute jointly financed by the French rubber plantations in Vietnam. There was some rubber production as such, but the low, yellow-stuccoed laboratory building with its neat rows of glittering instruments and vats full of creamy latex, the clean native village of the rubber tappers, and the spacious villas for the French scientists and administrators, gave the whole place the air of a well-funded American agricultural college. The war changed all that, for Lai-Khé is at the edge of a forest complex situated between two rivers which eventually merge about 20 miles from Saigon, thus forming a triangle pointing at South Vietnam's capital. In a series of swift attacks on the Vietnamese Army posts at the edge of the forest in late 1964, the Viet Cong had completely dismantled the whole government civilian and military apparatus in the area and taken over the town of Ben-Suc, a pleasant little place inside a meander of the Saigon River, big enough to appear on most maps of Vietnam.

Repeated attempts by the Vietnamese to retake the area failed (the stripped hulls of three American M-113 armored personnel carriers lost to accurate Viet Cong fire still lie near the road to Ben-Suc), and even a push by the US 173rd Airborne Brigade in 1965 yielded no tangible results. Progressively, the 210 square miles of forest between Ben-Suc and Ben-Cat acquired its sinister reputation as the "Iron Triangle," said to contain not only crack VC elements, but also the

command structure of MR-4, the Liberation Front's 4th Military Region covering the Saigon area. It was from the Iron
Triangle that the repeated successful VC penetrations of Saigon's huge Tan Son Nhut airbase had come. As long as the
Iron Triangle existed, Saigon itself would be exposed to the
threat of attack. The decision was therefore made late in 1966
to destroy the Iron Triangle in the largest concentrated attack
by US Forces since the Vietnam war began. The operation,
begun on January 8, opened with the 1st Infantry in position
on the Iron Triangle's northern base, with the 25th Infantry
Division 196th Light Brigade blocking all escapes on the left
flank across the Saigon River, while the ARVN's 5th Division
and parts of the 173rd Airborne Brigade held the right flank.
Other units, including the ARVN 8th Infantry which, the year
before, had broken at Ben-Suc, further reinforced the assault
units. In all, 28 combat battalions—over 30,000 men with
their logistical support—and 35 artillery batteries (140 field
guns) had converged on the Triangle. But the key actors, on
the American side, were not the men, but the unleashed
machines.

For days before the actual attack, the windows of Saigon
had been rattling from concentrated B-52 raids on the Triangle, at least 13 of them in eight days, unloading hundreds of
tons of heavy explosives on every raid, plowing under the Viet
Cong's incredibly extensive network of underground tunnels
and depots. Thanks also to American technology, the Air
Force cartographers are capable of providing the military with
fantastically detailed photo maps *in color* within a few hours
after the strikes. On these maps, the trails of the bomb carpets
in the jungle look like the tracks of tiger claws on an animal's
skin—claw marks that are three miles long and over 100 feet
wide. Whenever the strategic bombers were not over the Triangle, artillery barrages and the hammering of the light
fighter-bombers saw to it that no Viet Cong would try to
break out from the hell that the Triangle had become.

But the newest weapon of them all and, in its own way, the
most incredibly impressive for all its civilian normality, was an
assemblage of perhaps 80 bulldozers, in many cases airlifted
into the midst of the jungle by huge "Skycrane" helicopters
or the somewhat smaller "Chinooks." Their job was simple:

eliminate the jungle once and for all. By the third day of the battle, huge yellow scars had begun to be clearly visible in the deep jungle green as the bulldozers began to plow down the jungle as if some insane developer were suddenly hell-bent on covering Vietnam with Levittowns or parking lots. Such Viet Cong hideouts or tunnels as there were, either were crushed or their exits bulldozed shut, for in many cases the adversary (as well as civilians) hiding in the tunnels disappeared in their deepest recesses rather than surrender. "Tunnel rats," American soldiers specially picked for their small size and equipped with gas projectors and what looked like flamethrowers, sometimes penetrated for hundreds of meters into the burrows, looking for what was said to be a veritable "subway" crossing the whole Triangle. It was never found and perhaps never existed.

Inexorably, the bulldozers bit into the countryside, cutting huge swaths of cleared land right across the Triangle. They were followed by flamethrower tanks and teams on foot, destroying the felled trees with fire. And not only the trees: every human inhabitation within the beaten zone, be it an isolated hut which may have been used by the Viet Cong, or a whole little hamlet inhabited for years by charcoal kilners—non-white Saigon cooks with charcoal almost exclusively—went up in flames. There was one day toward the end of the week in which the air was totally still and the sky as transparently fresh and pure as on a spring day in America. Yet as I joined a new unit within the Triangle by helicopter, the whole sky, literally in a 360° circle, was framed in by perfectly straight black columns: the earth was being scorched on the whole perimeter of the Iron Triangle. And the town of Ben-Suc was among them.

Ben-Suc had been occupied in less than two minutes by two battalions of the 28th Infantry, followed by Vietnamese troops, while overhead loudspeaker helicopters instructed the population to stay put, for "anyone seen running away will be considered a Viet Cong." The 3,500 women, children and old men (there was not one able-bodied man in the lot) stayed put as Vietnamese Navy landing craft beached in front of the village and began to take aboard the population for a 10-mile ride downstream to a temporary refugee camp at Phu-Cuong.

They went without offering resistance, believing that they would merely be taken away temporarily until the operation was over. But Operation "Cedar Falls" (the code name for the whole undertaking) was, in the words of a briefing officer, an "operation with a real difference"—there would be no coming back, because Ben-Suc would be put to the torch and then razed with bulldozers, just like the forest and part of the rubber plantation. A clamor arose as the women begged to be allowed to return long enough to dig up their meager treasures, for as in Europe during the Thirty Years War, the peasants of Vietnam have long resorted to burying their money and jewelry in earthenware jars to keep them from being pilfered by government troops or taxed away by the Viet Cong. The respite was granted and the American troops even made arrangements to evacuate the most precious movable belongings of the villagers, their buffaloes and wagons.

"Make damn sure the buffaloes stay with the refugees and don't end up in the market place," I overheard the earnest young major in charge of the evacuation say to one of his subordinates escorting the landing craft.

As the burning houses began to collapse and the bulldozers methodically bit into the remaining standing walls, a new town seemed to emerge altogether from the debris. Ben-Suc was honeycombed with tunnels, trenches and stone-lined bunkers, and every house was built atop huge rice caches carefully lined with wicker mats. There were hundreds of tons there (the total "take" in the Triangle was 3,170 tons), far in excess of what Ben-Suc could have produced, let alone saved from previous crops.

"You see," said the young major, "Ben-Suc was a major transit point of supplies both for War Zone 'C' and probably the VC's central headquarters. The stuff would come up here by motor sampan and the population then transfers it on its buffalo carts and off it goes into the deep jungle in escorted convoys."

"Look at the rice," he said, picking up a handful which he carried in the breastpocket of his combat jacket, "there are at least 20 different brands here from all over South Vietnam and probably from the US, too. I've sent a batch down to Intelligence. They'll find out where it came from."

He looked back on smoking Ben-Suc with real affection as he held its rice in his hand.

"Would you believe that we offered the women that they could take the rice with them as their own if they told us where the rice caches were? *Not one* of them spoke up. Now *that's* loyalty."

As he spoke, he opened his hand to let the golden rice grains fall on the ground, stopped in mid-gesture, and put the rice back into his pocket. I scooped up a handful from the smoldering heap to my right and put it in one of my pockets. That much of Ben-Suc would stay alive. Later, what was left of Ben-Suc would be obliterated by Air Force bombers in order to destroy whatever underground caches and depots had been missed by the bulldozers.

In the evening at the mess tent, the day's doings were toted up as officers from nearby units came in for briefing and for a hasty bite to eat. There were over 400 dead by "body count," 62 prisoners, 18 machine-guns (including three brand-new American M-60's), more than 200 individual weapons (there would be close to 400 by the end of the operation, along with 508 enemy dead and 6,000 displaced civilians), and miles and miles of destroyed tunnels.

A whole jungle hospital, with two levels below ground and one above ground, had been captured.

"You should have seen the equipment," said the G-2. "Some of the stuff was good enough to be used in our hospital. West German surgical scissors at $45 apiece by the trunkful; French antibiotics."

Now, according to an order issued by General Westmoreland, on September 20, 1966, in compliance with Article 33 of the 1949 Geneva Convention, "captured or abandoned medical supplies or facilities will not be destroyed intentionally." I was told, however, how the field hospital had been disposed of.

"Well," said an eyewitness, "we removed all the medical equipment, and then all there was left was just another empty bunker and tunnel system. So we destroyed it like everything else." The same also happened to a smaller VC aid station.

An NBC television crew with a neighboring outfit witnessed and photographed the mutilation of a dead enemy soldier, but

the NBC hierarchy in New York, mindful of the uproar created more than a year ago when an enterprising CBS cameraman filmed the burning of a village with cigarette lighters,
"killed" the sequence. Conversely, a reporter for a Texas
newspaper was wounded that day by a VC sniper while he was
flying about in a med-evac helicopter clearly marked with large
red crosses. It is this kind of mutual barbarization, the needless cruelties inflicted far beyond military necessity, which will
make the Vietnam war stand out in modern history.

"You should see 'em," said the burly prison camp commander. "Unrepentant, unyielding. The only thing they're
sorry for is that they got taken alive."

He was referring to Professor Vinh Long and Middle-
Level Teacher Tran Van Tan, captured in the Iron Triangle,
and probably the highest-ranking Liberation Front cadres thus
far to fall into American hands. Both were native Southerners,
Vinh Long being born in Danang, and Tan in the province
of the Iron Triangle. Both had gone to North Vietnam in
1954 when the country was partitioned, and both had gone
on to higher studies. Long got his AB in physics and mathematics in 1963, Tan an AB in education in 1962. Both were
"finds" in their own right, since they were involved in
running the general education department of MR 4. [*For
security reasons, we have substituted fictitious names for the
real names of the prisoners interviewed by Mr. Fall.*—THE
EDITORS]

The prisoner-of-war enclosure of the 1st Division was a
small clearing in the rubber tree forest, surrounded by con-
certina barbed wire in which two squad tents had been
erected. Within the enclosure was an even smaller enclosure,
housing three captive women, one of them a pretty 19-year-
old Eurasian girl with long red hair and freckles, but almond-
shaped eyes. "She was a cook in the outfit," explained an
escort.

Vietnam can be bitingly cold in January and we were shivering in our jungle combat uniforms, particularly after a night
spent rolled in a poncho liner. The prisoners were lying on
normal Army cots and had been issued three woolen blankets
each, and each of them seemed to have his share of C-rations.
Courteously sitting up on their cots as we approached, they

looked, wrapped in their blankets, like green-clad desert Arabs. Intelligent, ascetic faces with deep-burning eyes, showing no fear—just curiosity as to what next. I first sat down with Vinh Long, flanked by a Vietnamese sergeant acting as an interpreter and an American captain. The captain was showing signs of a very bad cold, sneezing and fumbling through his pockets for an absent handkerchief. The Vietnamese prisoner picked up the C-ration box, searched around in it and came up with the tiny roll of toilet paper it contains, which he handed to the captain.

Long said that he spoke no French, but he spoke Russian. I explained to him in Russian that I was a college professor myself, not a soldier, and that I was not interested in military information. I also apologized for my bad Vietnamese and for the fact that I'd have to use an interpreter. That's all right he said, now clearly relaxed. Who had ordered him to return South?

"The party. But I would have gone in any case because I wanted to. I was happy. I visited Hanoi before I left."

He had left the North in December 1963 for the Duong Minh Chau area—the headquarters area of the Liberation Front. Before his departure from the North, where he has been stationed with the 338th Division at Xuan-Mai (he offered no information on units except those already known from papers captured with him), he had been briefed on the war here.

"We were given an accurate picture of what was going on in the South and told that victory would be easy. Of course, with the Americans here, it's not so easy." He picked up a cigarette in the C-ration carton, offered the others around, and then looked straight at me.

"But we'll win, anyway. Every country in the world helps us. Look at the American, Morrison, who committed suicide because he disagreed with American policies."

True, I said. But how about the other 200 million Americans who don't kill themselves?

"The Liberation Front forces will win in any case, because all the Vietnamese people help us. This war can only be settled among the Vietnamese themselves. The Americans and their allies must go."

But he had seen the Americans, now. Realistically, could they be made to go?

"Lots of American soldiers do get killed in battles, look at Chulai, Pleiku, Tayninh. We can do it."

To the Viet Cong, those battles, which we either claim as having won ourselves (Chulai), or as having suffered only minor losses (Pleiku), represent major victories. I said that I feared he was confusing the Americans with the French. The French weren't one-tenth as powerful as the Americans.

"Oh, I know the French were weaker than the US is, but we'll still win because our cause is right. Do the Americans think they can stay with this kind of war for 30, 40 years? Because that is what this is going to take."

The members of the Front are known to practice self-criticism. If he were to criticize himself for his activities over the past year, would he do something differently? There was a momentary lowering of the head, and a great deal of pride in the short answer: "I wouldn't change a thing."

And what would he do after all this was over?

"When I get out of this a free man, I will again work for the Liberation Front."

There was a poem, in wartime France, about a resistance member who had given exactly that answer to a German military court:

> *Et si c'était à refaire*
> *Je referais ce chemin . . .*

Yes, but that was 23 years ago, and the Nazis were the bad guys, and here the Free World is fighting the good fight with billions of dollars' worth of firepower against bad guys like Long and the freckle-faced cook.

"I told you," said the captain. "Unrepentant. Unyielding."

Tan was less tense than Vinh Long; perhaps because we had switched from a Vietnamese interpreter to an American GI (one of the few real side-benefits of this whole mess is that the US Armed Forces are going to have more Vietnamese linguists than all the universities of the whole world taken together; and that is *not* a figure of speech). Tan, in addition to education, had minored in anatomy and physiology and had been the inspector of the VC's educational system for the military zone. Though having fought in the Viet Minh against the French since 1950, he only joined the Communist Party here in South Vietnam in 1966, and like Vinh Long, he was sure that his side was winning.

"It's only natural that we should receive help from North Vietnam. After all, we're all Vietnamese, aren't we? Just as the Saigon government gets American help, the Front gets help from the socialist countries." There was a pause, and Tan said with great emphasis: "And it will never stop. *Never*. Even if their help does not rise above the present level, we'll win."

How did he feel he was being considered in the movement, being an intellectual, I asked. Wasn't he treated with a certain amount of suspicion?

"Oh, there is a certain amount of suspicion against intellectuals, but that is understandable. After all, being intellectuals, they are divorced from the masses and the working class, in particular.

"We Southern cadres are not discriminated against by the Northerners, although it did happen that some of the 're-groupees' [Southerners who went to the North in 1954 and then were reinfiltrated. B.F.] would desert from homesickness once they came South again. It doesn't affect our status at all."

But as a man trained in dialectical materialism, how could he dismiss American power so lightly in his estimates of the outcome of the war? That, to him, was no problem at all:

"After all, the Front is fighting a just war, as a true representative of the South Vietnamese people. This being a just war, we shall win."

But other "just wars" were lost in other places . . .

"Indonesia?" he interjected helpfully.

No, I said, but Greece, Malaya and the Philippines for example. As an intellectual, he could not dismiss these defeats lightly, unless he felt that these wars weren't "just wars."

"Not at all. They were just wars, to be sure, and the people were defeated, but only temporarily. The will to fight on remained in their hearts and they surely will rise again. But here, there won't be even such a temporary setback. The party has been active in South Vietnam for 36 years and thus defeat of its organization is impossible now.

"Here, the guerrillas will become stronger and stronger with the help of the socialist countries."

Yes, but did not the Sino-Soviet split introduce a weakening factor in this aid effort? Now he was on the defensive for the first time.

"Those struggles for greater socialist unity no more affect the socialist camp's effort in Vietnam than the French-American dispute affects power relationships in the West."

Come now, I said, if you read *Pravda* and the *Peking Review* and the incredibly severe mutual accusations between Peking and Moscow, you wouldn't describe this as a "struggle for greater unity."

"Let's not get into this. We'll win in any case."

Even if South Vietnam is totally destroyed in the process by American artillery and bombers? He had seen what happened here. It's happening all over the country. There was a hurt look in his eyes as the implication sunk in: "If South Vietnam is lost, we have got nothing left to live for. We would rather be dead than live as slaves. Have *you* ever seen anybody who wants to live as a slave?"

No, I had never seen anybody who wanted to, but I'd seen plenty of cases where people *had* to because they were given no choice. And I cited, on his side of the fence, the Budapest uprisings, and on our side, the Dominican Republic operation.

"These are small things," was his reply. And what did he think of how this whole war got started, I asked.

"Ah, the Americans are sly and clever," said Tan, whereupon the Americans present broke out in uncontrolled laughter. The interpreter explained to Tan that the Americans themselves never thought of themselves as either sly or clever. He nodded pensively, as if this were an important revelation.

"You know, they never smile," said the captain to me. I told him that considering their position and what was in store for them—transfer to the far-from-tender South Vietnamese —I wouldn't smile, either.

"The Americans," Tan went on, "took over military planning for the Saigon government. Their economic experts forced the South Vietnamese to work for them and Diem persecuted everybody. He would have killed us all, and that is why we revolted."

Tan, who had been silent for a moment, looked up and asked the interpreter if he, too, could ask me a few questions since I was a professor. Of course, he could.

"Do you know whether we will be treated as prisoners according to the Geneva Convention?"

Obviously, word must have gotten around among the Viet Cong about how badly most of the prisoners are still treated on this side, all promises of improvement notwithstanding, with the Americans reluctant to intervene once the prisoners have been transferred. All that I could say lamely was that he was being treated according to the Convention right now.

"Do American families approve of their soldiers here killing innocent people?"

Most of them weren't aware of innocent people being killed here, I said. As for the soldiers themselves, they were carrying out orders just as he was.

"Yes, but I'm here as a Vietnamese, in my own country. Why are the Americans all over the place, in Greece, in Laos?"

Well, they were helping their own allies, just as he expected the socialist camp to help him. But the socialist camp's aid was "political," he retorted. To which I answered that the Chinese weapons we had captured yesterday did not look "political" to me. A quick fleeting smile conceded the point to me.

"You may be right on that, but after all, it is the Americans who are the aggressors."

Why were the North Vietnamese so difficult about negotiations? I asked. On this, he was probably to the left (or was it right?) of official Front and North Vietnamese policy. Like Ambassador Henry Cabot Lodge here, who feels that negotiations are pointless if "victory by fade-out" can be achieved—a point which he has repeatedly made ever since September 1965—Tan felt that there was little to negotiate since his side was winning and since Vietnam was "one country."

Contrary to the Front's and Hanoi's avowed programs, he felt that reunification would come rapidly if the Americans were to leave. In fact, he did not believe that a divided Vietnam would "work." I told him that, for the sake of world peace, both Germany and Korea had accepted more or less permanent division.

"That's all right for them. But we rose up and fought for our own independence. We don't want to stay divided."

Yet, when asked what he would have done differently, Tan said that he would have negotiated last year, before the massive input of American troops, and he came through with a small truth which confirmed what intelligence specialists here had been wondering about for quite a while:

"You know, this is no longer the 'Special War' General Taylor talked about, but a new type of war [here the interpreter was faced with one of those party neologisms for which there was no acceptable single word] where outside forces became primary.

"The decision that the character of the war had changed was made late last year here in the South, either by the People's Revolutionary [i.e., South Vietnamese Communist] Party, or by the Central Committee of the Liberation Front. But when I was captured I did not yet know what this decision entailed."

As far as is known, the decision entails the maintenance of large units in reserve at more or less secure bases, while small forward units inflict heavy losses on the allied forces. How well this tactic works was shown this week, when the US suffered the highest casualties of the war (1,200 in one week) all as a result of dozens of pinprick attacks.

But Tan knew that he was on the right path. As I was getting up to leave, he said earnestly: "We are not fighting here to have a cease-fire and prolonged division. It is the Americans who sent their troops here. They will have to make the decision to leave. Nobody can make it for them."

As I walked out, after he had ceremoniously shaken hands with the captain, the interpreter and me, Tan said something very rapidly.

"He's asking you to thank the American people and Lord Russell for what they are doing."

Back at Division, reports were still filtering in. Ben-Suc was now totally evacuated. A herd of 61 reluctant buffaloes which proved intractable to adult Americans—it seems to be true that buffaloes find the white man's smell offensive—had required the re-airlifting in of 10 Vietnamese buffalo-boys aged six to 10 who rounded up the two-ton beasts without much difficulty. The town was now bulldozed flat and awaited its final airstrike.

Standing in his map tent, the brigade commander was going through the details of the pull-out, for after all the blood and the firepower spent here, the Iron Triangle would not be held.

"We just haven't got the troops to stay here, and the Arvins [for ARVN, the South Vietnamese Army] simply won't."

"In other words," I said, "the VC will move right back in again."

"Sure," said the general. "But they'll find their dugouts smashed, huge open lanes in the forest, and at least we'll have helicopter LZ's [landing zones] all over the place. Next time's going to be easier to get back in."

As I walked out of the command post, a short, whitewashed obelisk caught my eye, standing at the entrance to Lai-Khé. It was a monument to the dead of the 2nd Moroccan Spahi Regiment, the 2nd Cambodian Mobile Battalion, the 3rd and 25th Algerian Rifle Battalions, and 3rd Battalion, 4th Tunisian Rifles; who had died for the Iron Triangle between 1946 and 1954.

The New Republic, February 4, 1967

U.S. Marines Seize 3d Hill
in Vietnam After 12-Day Push

by Jonathan Randal

HILL 881 NORTH, South Vietnam, May 5—Weary and grimy
United States marines today secured this last major height
commanding the isolated airstrip and valley of Khesanh.
Nearly half the American combat troops here were killed or
wounded in the 12-day campaign.

Gen. William C. Westmoreland, the American commander
in Vietnam, echoed Marine fears when he warned during an
inspection visit to Khesanh: "I don't think the battle is necessarily over. I anticipate further fighting in the general area."

The general spoke of "tremendous" casualties suffered by
the 95th and 18th Regiments of North Vietnam's 325th Division. American spokesmen said they had lost 570 confirmed
dead, with 598 more deaths listed as probable.

But General Westmoreland said nothing about casualties in
the two marine battalions here, officially given as 160 dead
and 746 wounded.

The final assault on Hill 881 North began yesterday afternoon. By nightfall, Company E of the Second Battalion,
Third Marine Regiment, held part of the crest. Once heavily
wooded, the hill was now a wasteland pounded by hundreds
of tons of bombs and thousands of artillery shells.

At dawn, Company E pushed off to take the final bit of
enemy territory. But shortly after 7 A.M. the marines ran into
sporadic fire from small arms and automatic weapons.

Rather than risk the kind of infantry assault that had cost
them dearly earlier in the fighting, the marines pulled back
again. This time they shelled and bombed the North Vietnamese position for two and a half hours.

But when the marines advanced, again they met enemy fire
from five bunkers that had somehow survived the full might

of American air power and artillery over four days. In the final fighting, three North Vietnamese soldiers were killed, seven United States marines were wounded and 17 enemy weapons were captured.

"How they got through 1,000-pound bombs is what gets me," said First Lieut. Jack Adinolfi of Greenville, N.Y.

His comment reflected the thoughts of many marines who were surprised by the aggressiveness of the enemy troops since the start of fighting for the triangle of hills dominating the approaches to the Khesanh airstrip, five miles to the southeast.

The triangle is strategically important because from here, American 175-mm. guns can fire shells 20 miles, reaching almost to the Laotian border in the west and 15 miles into North Vietnam.

This makes it dangerous for the North Vietnamese to mass a large force in the area for an all-out attack on military outposts in South Vietnam. It also inhibits the enemy's movements of supplies.

The dusty red hills—861, 881 South and 881 North—take their designations from map markings showing in meters their elevation from sea level. The plateau has been struck by more than 2,000 mortar rounds and 1,200 artillery shells since the Americans dug in here two months ago.

At no point did the enemy flee the battlefield as he has often done in Vietnam, although by the time Marine riflemen reached the summits, bombs and artillery had reduced the opposition to sporadic firing.

Hill 861 was taken a week ago. Hill 881 South was occupied Tuesday.

After the marines took 881 North, General Westmoreland said the enemy had definitely come from Laos across the mountainous border that lies seven miles northwest of the hill triangle.

To strengthen Marine fire power, 4.2-inch mortars were moved to Hill 881 South and a battery of 105-mm. howitzers advanced from the airstrip farther west in the coffee-growing valley.

Marine officers said they would start extensive patrolling in the mountains surrounding the triangle.

The cost of the campaign is illustrated by the casualties suf-

fered by Lieutenant Adinolfi's company. Since its arrival in
Vietnam two weeks ago, it has lost 89 men dead or wounded
out of 220.

Standing in the valley, where many North Vietnamese bodies
still lay unburied, the lieutenant said, "I never cease to marvel
at what marines do."

"We learned our lesson real hard and real fast," he said,
"and if any of those S.O.B.'s are crazy enough to come up
here tonight, they're going to get killed."

His company learned its lesson before dawn Wednesday
when two North Vietnamese companies dented its perimeter
along the southeastern slope of Hill 881 North. The company
lost 22 dead and 69 wounded, but ultimately held its line.

The company commander and a medical corpsman were
wounded and the air observer was killed by shrapnel from
an armed Marine helicopter that accidentally sprayed their
position.

The lieutenant assumed command. "Some of the guys had
their boots off and it was raining when they hit at 4:30 A.M.,"
he said. "It was a real nightmare."

"I was sitting in the command bunker just praying for it to
get light and for another Marine company to help re-establish
the defense perimeter," he said. The enemy had pushed within
45 yards of his command post.

The marines counted 82 enemy dead including 15 snipers
whose heavy bolt-action rifles were fitted with telescopic
sights.

During the attack the marines were momentarily thrown off
guard, the lieutenant said, by North Vietnamese dressed in
American uniforms and helmets stripped from the dead.

"They were shouting out in English things like 'Corpsman!
Corpsman!'" the lieutenant said. "One of our medical corpsmen fell for it, and was killed."

"There were marines out there in the trees," he added,
"wounded, screaming and fighting like crazy for their lives.
Our chief corpsman was in the command post. He wanted to
go out and help them, but we could not spare him. He damn
near cried himself to death."

By now, the lieutenant said, his company is accustomed to

everything the enemy can throw out. "Once you get mortared—and it usually happens here at dawn and dusk—you just get used to it."

What the men of his company found harder to accept was a message they discovered in bunkers studding the hill.

"There was one pamphlet in English," the lieutenant said, "showing a Vietnik demonstration at home, with a woman holding a sign saying: 'My son died in vain. Don't fight. Go to prison.'"

On the other side were excerpts from speeches by Senators Wayne Morse of Oregon and Ernest Gruening of Alaska and an anti-American statement by the British philosopher Bertrand Russell.

The New York Times, May 6, 1967

Saigon and Other Syndromes

by Ward S. Just

SOUTH VIETNAM was the same, winter and summer. There were monsoons during both seasons, and in January and February in Saigon you could set your watch by the onset of the three o'clock rain. There was some change of temperature in the northern provinces, but in the south it was always hot. The heat was wet and close, and made you feel as if you were wrapped in a dripping blanket. It was so much a part of living in Vietnam that it was rarely mentioned. On nights when the temperature dipped below seventy-five, the Vietnamese would pull on sweaters and complain of the cold. In the air-conditioned offices of USAID and JUSPAO Vietnamese girls would wear heavy clothing over their filmy *ao dais*. It is best to remember that everything in Saigon and in the Delta south of Saigon took place in the heat.

The city was unique, a combination of Vienna in the 1930's, London in the 1940's, and Algiers in the 1950's. The war, an East Asian theater of the absurd, gave the city its connection with the 1960's. The war seemed to rock along without plot, rhyme or reason. The tension and vitality that war brings to any city was not from Hemingway and Orwell, but from Pinter and Beckett.

The first impression was the city, and the long, low descent over the twisting tributaries of the Mekong, the canals and watery fields of the Delta shimmering off to the south, the jerry-built shacks of the refugees on the fringes of town, Tan Son Nhut Airport itself in the heat, and the fighter planes stacked on the runway along with the Boeing 707 jets of the commercial airlines.

The traveler arrived in one of the big planes, staring out the window, the engines roaring, silent inside, after a day and a night from New York or Washington. There were the dregs of a cup of coffee, or a Bloody Mary, and bad nerves from listening, since Guam, to the rock and roll of the Supremes, the trio from Detroit, piped from special transistorized tapes through a stethoscope-like apparatus that fitted into both ears like gum and blotted out everything but the roar and heave of the engines. Fingers became a fist and tapped on the blue padded armrest, until the throb of the music became one with the plane. It was the velocity of both that brought the traveler into Saigon and the war, face pressed against the cabin glass:

> Baby, baby
> Whenever you're near
> I hear a symphony
> Each time you speak to me
> Baby, baby
> Whenever you're near
> I hear a symphony
> Baby, baby
> Whenever you're near
> Baby, baby
> I hear a symphony.

Down, and a shudder as the engines were reversed. The traveler exited into bright sunlight and the odor of jet fuel, and walked one hundred yards to the low white building with the signs in the inexplicable language. There were Americans everywhere. Soldiers were sprawled sleeping in the dirty terminal, which was chaos except for a small nook on the west side where Vietnamese passengers waited patiently for their Air Vietnam flights to Quang Ngai or Pleiku or Phan Rang. There was the interminable wait while immigration officials wrestled with the blue passports bearing the unpronounceable American names, and then a five-mile drive through the clogged streets to the hotel. The streets were jammed even by Asian standards, the city hung over with a heavy blue pall from the exhausts of ancient cars and Japanese motorbikes, a Honda-heaven, as someone called it, Lambretta-land. The old Peugeots and Citroëns driven by men in white suits, the delicate ladies with parasols, were relics of another Saigon. The Vietnamese drove as though crazed, thrusting the tiny yellow-and-blue taxicabs around the three-wheeled pedicabs and embassy

Mercuries with skill and audacity. They yielded only to the brawny, menacing Americans driving U.S. Army two-ton trucks, who expected all civilian traffic to halt and make way. Finally everything ceased and the cars sat idling, clumped in fat, thick bunches at traffic lights. It was impossible to catch anyone's eye. All the eyes were turned inward, looking backward. The sense one received was of a heavy city, bloated, disheveled, peopled by ghosts. The Vietnamese at the side of the road, on bikes and walking, were tightly contained, wrapped in a cocoon of privacy.

At Le Van Duyet Street a young girl on a black Solex motorbike attempts a traverse from the center of the street. She does not look to the left or the right. She keeps her dark eyes on the handlebars and one hand on her conical hat, and moves across the traffic, which avoids her or halts abruptly. The exhaust on the pavement is thick and the girl has a sheer white scarf across her mouth. She makes no hand signal, no sign to indicate her passage. She simply turns the wheel of the black bike and moves, her *ao dai* gently fluttering in the breeze, back stiff, eyes set. She turns, and starts slowly up the street.

Squalor gives way to two-story American villas with lawns and white concrete walls and armed guards close to the center of town. At Duong Pasteur Americans in shirt sleeves appear on the street, walking with determination. MACV headquarters, a three-story French villa with a forest of antennae and sandbagged bunkers, stands around the corner from Marie Curie lycée, the most fashionable girls' prep school in Saigon. And at the center of town itself it is the Americans who are hurrying, weaving their way through the crowds. The Vietnamese wander, stopping to chat and buy a bottle of Bireley orange soda from cornerside vendors. The Americans rush, long-legged and sweating, impelled by urgent business. They tower over the Vietnamese, and sometimes in their hurry and impatience they place both hands on fragile oriental shoulders and gently ease bodies out of their way. Finally there are the beggars and the crippled, the tipsters and the bar girls, off-duty American infantrymen, Vietnamese businessmen, and young ARVN lieutenants, of Tu Do Street. Tu Do had been called the Rue Catinat under the French but President Diem decided, as part of a general campaign of de-Frenchification, that the street needed a new name. He called it Tu Do, which means freedom.

The airport route gave intimations of what the rest of the city was like, away from Tu Do and downtown and the handsome villas of Cong Ly Street. The slums grew out from the central city, away from the core. Unlike the large American metropolis, the core of Saigon was a haven for what remained of the Vietnamese middle class, those who had not rented their houses to the Americans. Saigon slums, swelled by the refugees, grew on the outskirts, vast accretions that proliferated as inevitably as coral, a hut at a time, each more squalid than the last. The slums were geographically linked by fetid canals, commercially dominated by Chinese merchants, and largely disregarded by an indifferent Saigon government. The American aid mission had other preoccupations, so Saigon grew as the war grew. There was nothing to be done about it. By mid-1967 the war had thrown up a vast urban proletariat which lived precariously on the fringes of all the large cities; in a year and a half, Saigon's population rose from two to three million (according to the most reliable estimates). The refugees, cut loose from their village moorings, from their ancestral graveyards, the *dinhs*, and the hierarchy, drifted aimlessly in a bewildering and hostile environment. Families splintered and farmers became cyclo drivers and girls left home to work in the American bars, or as waitresses or laundresses on the American bases. This was said to be an inevitable concomitant to the war, and for the moment a tolerable (and inescapable) price to pay for the fight against Communism. Strangely, the Viet Cong did little to exploit the situation. They, like the Americans and the Saigon government, concentrated on the villages. No one was very happy about the refugees, but no one saw very much that could be done about them. They were very low on all the lists of priorities, safely forgotten in the press of more urgent business. American officials liked to contend that the refugees were fleeing Communism, and therefore could be regarded as a net plus in the war effort. But no one took this argument seriously. The refugees were fleeing the war, and its bombs. A family found its way to Saigon or Nha Trang or Qui Nhon on the basis of rumor that fortunes could be made from the Americans. You would sometimes see the refugees, singly or in families, having made their way to the center of Saigon. There, on the busiest street corners in town, they would stand hesitating and uncertain near the curb, muttering to passers-by, asking for alms, extending mahogany-colored hands and grabbing at your shirt.

If the refugee came from a village in the Delta he headed for Saigon because he had been told it was the capital of his country. The city held little of the symbolic value for the Vietnamese that Rome does for the Italians or London for the British. It was the foreigners, first the French and later the Americans, who made Saigon the capital of South Vietnam. It was necessary for bureaucratic and political reasons. Educated Vietnamese, when they thought about it at all, regarded Saigon as a synthetic city dominated by foreigners and ruled by a junta of generals. They thought of Saigon as the provincial Spanish think of Madrid: a non-capital, unrepresentative, artificial. The center of Vietnamese political life was the village; everything else was bureaucracy.

Most Vietnamese loathed Saigon, or what Saigon had become, and the more thoughtful tended to regard it as the symbol of the new colonialism, with its corruption and war-dominated economy. Intellectuals often spoke of corruption as if it had been an American invention, imported to South Vietnam for the specific purpose of weakening the fiber of the people. In fact official corruption on a grand scale was always present in Vietnam, a direct descendant of the Mandarin tradition; it was only the opportunities that were now so much greater. Saigonese pointed to the bloated wages of the bar girls, the lethargy and arrogance of the civil servants, the *nouveaux riches* among the officer corps of the army, the refugees in District Nine, and saw Pompeii in its last days. They saw Vietnam collapsing under the weight of American power and influence, as any weak society is bound to do when confronted by a stronger one. To the Vietnamese it was an atmosphere of menace and when the city administration removed the tall and graceful elms from Cong Ly Street to make way for the immense American military trucks, it seemed the final bit of decay, the last links with the old days.

The remembrance of the past persisted. Very few Americans knew Saigon in conditions other than those of wartime, and tended to doubt the descriptions of deterioration under the American occupation. In some ways Saigon was no worse than Paris or Rome, or any other large city that makes a point of catering to large numbers of foreigners. The central problem, unlike Paris or Rome, was the terms of the American involvement: not quite an occupying power, but a good deal more than a mere ally, the Americans *settled* in Saigon. The ambiguity of the position—was Henry Cabot Lodge a proconsul? an adviser?—resulted in a breakdown of law where Americans were concerned. The Americans were above the law, feared and therefore largely ignored by the national police and the Saigon government, which accorded them special privileges.* One of the most trivial, but significant, examples was the license plate TN. Cars with TN plates were allowed to park in the restricted lot in front of the American post exchange in downtown Saigon, directly to the rear of the National Assembly Building. U.S. authorities were convinced that one day the Viet Cong would attempt to blow up the PX, as in 1965 they had blown up the American Embassy. The PX was the single enduring symbol of American wealth and the American way of living, a gigantic Macy's of tape recorders and cameras, pearl necklaces, bathing trunks, Scotch whiskey, Crest toothpaste, plastic ice trays, cigarettes and *Playboy*. Ordinary cars driven by Vietnamese—or cars with Vietnamese plates driven by Americans—were shooed away by rifle-carrying MP's. The TN plate also enjoyed precedence on river ferries, and excused the driver from the payment of tolls. The procedure was reminiscent of the Chicago mayor who distributed to his cronies personal cards reading: "This man is my friend." The Americans were the friends of the Saigon government, and while the TN plate may have been a small concession for the intro-

---

*As an experiment late one night, three Vietnamese-speaking American diplomats attempted to pay a parking ticket at the 1st District police headquarters. They were not permitted to pay it. The Vietnamese official on duty appeared to regard the attempt to pay as a trick, and fearing censure from higher authority if he accepted money from an American, he steadfastly refused to have anything to do with the matter. It had never been done before. The Americans reported there was a good deal of laughter in the police station.

duction of 500,000 American troops in Vietnam, it was a meaningful one to the Vietnamese. It was yet another layer of privilege.

The effect of the American presence could have been worse. As it was, most of the trouble did not come from the official community but from the drifters who collected in Vietnam to work for the American construction cartel, RMK–BRJ. The trouble was invariably liquor and sex, and sometimes illegal money-changing, but in these contests the Vietnamese always gave as good as they got. The effect was less ecological than economic. The Vietnamese were not soft, and the Vietnamese spirit bent but did not break. Henry Cabot Lodge devoted much of his second tour to minimizing the effect of his compatriots on Vietnam society, and it was an extraordinary achievement that the number of Americans living in Saigon stayed at about 17,000 while the troop commitment in the country as a whole grew from less than 200,000 to nearly 450,000 in Lodge's eighteen months as ambassador. MACV headquarters was eventually moved from the villa on Cong Ly Street to an immense low-slung building called Pentagon East, at Tan Son Nhut Airport, and with that began the slow exodus of colonels from the downtown B.O.Q.'s (Bachelor Officers' Quarters).

It was difficult to imagine Saigon as the pearl of the Orient so beloved of travel writers. The villas were large and handsome and there was a zoo, a cathedral, a river and expensive shops and decent hotels downtown. But it was not a city of rhapsody. Perhaps in comparison to Vientiane, Luang Prabang or Phnom Penh, it had a certain sleazy Gallic charm; but those were not exactly five-star standards. When Vietnamese spoke of the collapse of Saigon, what they meant was the loss of sovereignty and character, and in another sense of virginity. They spoke of the three thousand years of Vietnamese history and culture and how these were being subverted by the gauche and rude Americans. But examples of this superior culture were scarce, and even the most sympathetic observers were cautious in their estimates. The arts did not flourish in South Vietnam. Painting, for example, was either florid and photographic or pastoral and imitative of the French Impressionists. *Kim Van Kieu*, the Vietnamese equivalent of *The*

Song of Roland, was not highly regarded by scholars, except as an interesting myth charmingly rendered. There were no Huckleberry Finns, Fausts, or Classical Books of Odes in Vietnamese literature; nor a Lao-tse or Confucius for metaphysics. Her heroes were warriors like Cong Ly or tigerish female saviors like the Trung sisters. Music was derived from the Chinese; sculpture, to the extent that it existed at all, was Cham. When the Vietnamese spoke of their four thousand years of Vietnamese history and culture what they really meant was their way of life. But through all those four thousand years their way of life, more often than not, was war.

So the city yielded up its soul to the Americans as it had done to the French. Some of the old symbols remained, but they were fragments of a French civilization: the opera house, now the building of the National Assembly, white-domed and vaulted with electric fans and birds careering in and out of the wide open windows; the sporting club, *Cercle Sportif*, once stiff and formal but now reminiscent of a down-at-the-heels plantation house in the Mississippi Delta, the old retainers dismissed and the house occupied by Snopeses. There was a *club nautique* and the race track at Phu Tho. The old-timers spoke of the excellent food, classical French cuisine, at the Guillaume Tell and L'Amiral, and the special atmosphere of Cholon, the Chinese quarter of Saigon. These all remained, now with a Yankee admixture. Many of the signs were now in English, and there were MP's on Tu Do Street and colonels in the pool at the *Cercle*. The American symbols tended to be fewer and uglier: Pentagon East, the hangars and modern morgue at Tan Son Nhut, traffic lights, and concrete B.O.Q.'s in Cholon. The traffic lights were the main American achievement.

The town, punch-drunk as it filled up with people, reeled from month to month. The Continental Palace Hotel retained its Humphrey Bogart air and a guidebook described the Caravelle as the *ne plus ultra* of modern Indochina inns. The old-timers fed on memories: of tiger hunts in Kontum and bird shoots in Camau, weekends at Cap St. Jacques, leisurely drives through the mountains to Dalat, water skiing on the Mekong. In remote parts of the country, village elders still thought that Ngo Dinh Diem was president, or that the French still ruled.

Plenty of tourists came to look at the war. They were army generals and diplomats from Washington, congressmen, American mayors (Sam Yorty made so many trips to Vietnam his critics grumbled that Los Angeles was the only city in America with a foreign policy), newspapermen, novelists, social scientists, baseball players, movie stars, businessmen on the make, doctors inquiring into civilian casualties, students working in the provinces, and the foreign observers: British parliamentarians, Spanish internists, Israeli generals. The standard tour for visitors was three weeks, enough to journey to Hue and speak with militant Buddhist monks, or to the Central Highlands to watch the shooting, or to undertake an automobile drive through the Mekong Delta. Three weeks was sufficient time to learn the ambiguities. One's attitudes depended a good deal on what expectations one brought to Vietnam. It was no trick to find the facts to back up the impressions, or the preconceptions: facts were everywhere, and with suitable discrimination could be used to support almost any argument. One visitor thought the war was going well, another badly. A third thought it was unwinnable. A USAID economist insisted that the Americans were building an industrial apparatus that would make South Vietnam the Japan of the 1970's and 1980's. Another American economist looked at the war damage and declared the country was destroyed for a generation.

The war hypnotized, and those whose business it was to observe it came to regard it as a drama whose characters and plot were only dimly perceived. It was not, and never could be, a question of good guys against bad because the Vietnamese half of the equation was variable. The matter has been put with great precision by the playwright Harold Pinter, who in fact was speaking of his own plays but might well have been talking about the war, the Vietnamese, and the Americans: "The desire for verification is understandable, but cannot always be satisfied," Pinter said. "There are no hard distinctions between what is real and what is unreal, nor between what is true and what false. The thing is not necessarily either true or false. It can be both true and false . . . A character on the stage who can present no convincing argument or information as to his past experiences, his present behavior, or his aspirations, nor give a comprehensive analysis of his motives, is as legitimate and worthy of attention as one who, alarmingly, can do all these things. The more acute the experience the less articulate the expression."*

There had to be an articulate framework for the half-coherent mumblings of officials and their dramatists, and for correspondents in Vietnam this was provided in the five o'clock briefing, which was held each afternoon in an auditorium in the JUSPAO building at Le Loi and Nguyen Hue Streets in downtown Saigon. It followed by thirty minutes a curtain-raising briefing by an ARVN major on Vietnamese military activities. Correspondents showed a pass to a Marine guard at the door of JUSPAO, and negotiated a maze of corridors to arrive at an air-conditioned auditorium. The briefing began with news of civilian interest: Viet Cong terrorist attacks, a medical team newly arrived from Germany, a congressional delegation departing and holding a press conference at Tan Son Nhut. Then came the colonels. There was a ground briefer and an air briefer. The air briefer discussed air strikes in North Vietnam, their number, duration and effectiveness. Occasionally the authorities would display an Air Force or Navy colonel, just back from a bombing run over Hanoi or Haiphong, who would submit to questions.

The briefing was the official version of the day's events. It was most competently done. The ground-briefing colonel stood on a well-lit stage behind a wooden lectern and discussed the previous twenty-four hours of what he called Free World Military Activity. (The Free World, in South Vietnam, was the Americans, the Koreans and the Australians. They acted "in support" of the ARVN's who, as we shall see, belonged to another world.)

"Twelve KIA, no captured," the colonel said. "Friendly two KIA, twelve WIA. Three missions flown in support, also artillery."

"What happens now?" a correspondent asked from the rear of the auditorium. The room is not large enough to accommodate all of the correspondents, and many of them are standing at the rear scribbling notes on the printed handout.

*Quoted in the *New York Times Magazine*, October 1, 1967.

Most of the briefer's information is already in the handout. (Or, as it was, the three handouts, one each from the Army, Navy and Air Force.) Occasionally there were special handouts from a particular division or corps command. And of course there were often handouts from the Australians and the Koreans, not to mention the other countries which had commitments of one sort or another: the Philippines, New Zealand, Thailand, Spain, Germany.

"The operation is continuing."

"Continuing?"

"Continuing," the colonel said.

"For how long will it continue?"

"I can't speculate on that."

"Where is it, again?"

"Here"—consulting the map which is projected on a large screen behind the lectern—"it's about sixteen clicks (kilometers) west of Quang Ngai City."

"So that would be Task Force Oregon."

"It would, yes sir."

"And if I am not mistaken, that is the first time Task Force Oregon has moved west of Quang Ngai."

"Approximately."

"We have moved south of Quang Ngai on, let's see, two weeks ago last Monday. And we moved north after that attack on the air base. We have not moved west until today."*

"That is correct."

"Are the ARVN's in on this?"

"Yes, in a way."

"What are they doing?"

"They had that at their briefing."

There is a short pause, and then the correspondent goes on:

"I wasn't at their briefing."

---

*This sort of question became known as the "left-handed battalion commander" syndrome. It was a function of journalistic desperation to differentiate one military operation from another. An enormous effort was made to establish a "first" or "most" or "least" in the lead of a newspaper article. It was surmised that the classic lead for the non-event of a fruitless operation would be that a left-handed battalion commander, "for the first time," led it into battle.

"We cannot comment on Vietnamese operations," the colonel says, crisply. "This is the Free World Briefing. The ARVN briefing is at four-thirty. We comment on the Free World Forces and the ARVN's comment on the ARVN's."

"Well, can you do it on background?"

"We do not usually do that. Where would you be if you have everybody commenting on everybody else. This is Free World. The other is ARVN."

"Perhaps on background."

"The ARVN's set up their own briefing so they could handle it fully. This is for the Free World only." The colonel pauses, then recognizes a trim, precise officer in the rear. "Ben?"

A full colonel comes striding down the aisle. "I don't see what is so difficult about it," he says. "The ARVN's comment on the ARVN's and we comment on the Free World. That is the way it is set up now."

"Well, I thought you could do it backgroundwise."

"Well, hell, what's the difference?" This from a third correspondent in a seat at the front. "Why can't it be done on background, with no attribution?"

What is happening here is that the correspondents are searching for an opening to catch the colonels in a lie, or if not a lie at least a misconception. It is a grand game, reminiscent of arguments about angels dancing on the heads of pins. None of it is of any importance. The briefing became an exercise in methodology, a means of exposing the inherent error of body counts, weapons counts, search and destroy missions which had turned left at the wrong coordinate; a meticulous search for conceptual error.

The colonel, who understood the implications of the bored accents of the correspondent, looks distastefully at the men in the chairs in front of him. Then he goes to the map.

"On background: they are here"—pointing at the map, the stick striking a coordinate—"and here."

"North and west."

"That is correct. North and west."

"Thank you. Blocking positions?"

"Yes, they are blocking. They are blocking for the American battalions."

"This is all west of Quang Ngai?" It is a correspondent who has come in late.

"That is correct."

"Thank you. What are you calling this?"

"The ARVN's call it Operation Lam Son Two. But—this is all in the handout, you know—we call it Operation Mastiff." The colonel consults his notes and speaks softly into the microphone. "It's multi-battalion."

Then he goes on to discuss the other operations that day.

The dialogue is formal, polite in an almost Victorian way. The colonels call the correspondents "Sir." The correspondents mostly call the colonels "Colonel." No one would suspect that the colonels hate the correspondents and the correspondents distrust the colonels. It is mostly a hangover from the bad days of 1963 and 1964 when the correspondents thought everybody was lying to them. The colonels believe many of the correspondents to be leftist agitators. But they are bound together by the formality of the briefing, and manage to coexist. There are even some close friendships. But not many.

The briefing was the principal source of news giving the official version of the war. It was one version among many, all of them inaccurate in the singular, but the one from which most newspaper-reading Americans received their perception of the war. From the briefing came the war story, or the front page wire service article which began, "American pilots flew 198 missions over North Vietnam yesterday, striking rail yards, storage areas, and troop concentrations . . ." It was a bad way to learn anything about the war, either the terms on which it was being fought or the means by which it might be won. This was not because colonels were lying to journalists, but because by the time news percolated up from the battle zone it was either badly garbled or hopelessly out-of-date or both. The only consolation for the correspondents was that they knew instinctively that the versions of the war which came from Saigon were intrinsically sounder than the versions from Washington. However inaccurate and misleading the view from Saigon, the view from Washington was always more so: Washington was a mirror-image away from reality. Saigon was the source of it all. What was going on elsewhere, in

Moscow and London and the other capitals, was a reaction to what was happening in Vietnam. The Viet Cong mortared an outpost at Lai Khe, a long string from the American Embassy in Saigon to the White House in Washington jerked, and there was a reaction. McNamara came for a three-day inspection tour, and by looking at his appointments list and the cities he planned to visit, you knew what he was going to hear. Would he talk with McChristian? Vann? Ellsberg? Would he go to Dong Ha?

MACV prepared for the McNamara visits by drawing literally hundreds of colored charts, each meant to show how the war was going. The civilians, amateurs to a fault, took it more casually. One high-level briefer who declined to speak with notes was confounded by a request from SecDef (as McNamara was known) to distinguish between revolutionary development and pacification. He said that the two were about the same. They were not, Ambassador Lodge broke in. So two of the highest officials in the civilian mission fell to bickering among themselves as McNamara looked on with distaste. Of course the argument was much more significant than the military briefings with their statistical certainties and quantitative measurements of progress. The American mission could never make up its mind as to what was pacification and what was revolutionary development, and that was just the trouble. These too became matters of methodology. It was a question of which Jesuit was in charge.

You were your own Jesuit in Vietnam. From the roof of the Caravelle Hotel it was possible to watch an Air Force DC–3 drop chandelier flares on the far side of the Saigon River. Somewhere there was trouble, an outpost under attack, or two patrols that went "bump" in the night—and leaning over the entrecote grille to pour another glass of Bordeaux you would ask your dinner partner where she was going tomorrow, and what she hoped to see. The girl was blond and Radcliffe and in Vietnam on assignment for magazines. In time she would come to grasp the Vietnamese condition as well as anyone in the country, but then she was a very shy girl, uncertain why she was there. She talked about the Buddhists in the I Corps, and said she was going to Quang Nam province.

She wants to talk about Vietnam, but her dinner partners want to hear about New York and Washington and the mood in the United States. There is a long dialogue about what Vietnam is doing to America, as ice cream and coffee makes its way around the table.

There is a commotion now, and heads turn to the west where flares are just appearing. There are two, four, five flares and the diners strain to hear. They are listening for explosions. The explosions come and someone nods. Yes, they are mortaring Tan Son Nhut. A wire service man quietly leaves the table to make a telephone call.

It is early enough, barely after ten, so following a drink in the NBC suite the party moves on downstairs. The journalists check the room clerk at the desk for cables, and then begin a slow crawl down Tu Do Street. The party walks across Lam Son Square in the rain, avoiding a beggar with his hat in his hand who has stationed himself under the awning of the Continental Palace. One of the girls looks at the beggar, reaches into her purse, and gives him a twenty-piaster piece. Back again across the square, dodging traffic; but a jeep crashes through a mud puddle and everybody is splashed. They watch the disappearing red lights and mutter. Son of a bitch. The Goddamned American army think they own this town.

There are half a dozen children in the wake of the party, which is now cruising past the Air France office with its advertisements of Paris, Geneva, Rome, and the Riviera. The children are asking for money: Gimme 5 P, they say, Gimme 5 P. The new girl scrambles around in her purse for change, but the others hurry on. The children are always around the Caravelle and the entrance to the Tu Do Street bar district. None of the regulars in Saigon pay them any attention. Children on the street begging for money are a part of the town, like jeeps that go splashing through mud puddles.

In the Sporting Bar the group bunches together at one end, watched closely by an American construction worker at the other end. He is looking at the American girls, pretty and round-eyed, soft hair, white skin, alive and laughing. The lights are low, as they are in all the Tu Do Street bars, and in the background, from a Panasonic hi-fi system, was music from the Armed Forces Radio Network broadcasting station.

Some of the bars had television but this one only had radio. It was playing rock, in between pleas for the GI's to go to church. This was a variation on the theme of atheists in foxholes, a soft-selling singing commercial delivered in close harmony, Ink Spots–style:

> Don't you get a little lonely
> All by yourself
> Out on that limb
> Without Him?

The last is drawn out, Himmmmmmm. This follows a subtle if insistent message to the troops not to kill prisoners, and to support the Chieu Hoi (defector) program. Each defector, AFRTS noted, "means more support for the GVN, less firepower for the VC." There are also appeals to use the zip code when writing home. Half a dozen times throughout the day the station would honor the Unit of the Day. This always seemed to be a transportation or quartermaster command deep in the bowels of Saigon or Nha Trang. And the news: *"American paratroopers, striking deep at a Communist base area near Pleiku, are heavily engaged tonight. Early reports say that more than fifty Communists have been killed in the four-hour-long firefight. United Press International reported that a battalion of the 101st Airborne Brigade jumped off at noon . . ."*

This was background to conversation at the Sporting Bar. The place was full, the girls in residence hitching up their hip-huggers and shuffling the playing cards. They played gin rummy with the men, often stationing girl friends behind the GI so they could peek into his hand. There was no need for complicated hand signals: no GI could understand the language so the girls could cheat *en clair*. The GI's knew this but didn't mind. They flew into Saigon with three months' pay after six months in Pleiku and didn't care about being cheated; getting out of Pleiku was enough. They sat drinking beer and talking, the GI's to the GI's and the bar girls to each other. They played cards because no one understood enough of each other's language to talk.

On Tu Do Street, the bar girls were not necessarily prostitutes. Some were but many were not. Most of them had

Vietnamese boyfriends who managed to keep an eye on them, either by working in the bars themselves as busboys or by arriving at curfew time on Hondas to drive them home. Some Americans felt that the girls were the principal financiers of the Viet Cong war effort, and there was probably some truth to this. The Americans were not especially fond of Vietnamese girls: their undisguised mercenary instincts were unappealing, and their language unfathomable. But mostly they were held to be unresponsive. "I told her I would give her a thousand piasters if I could screw her," went the classic GI line, "and two thousand piasters if she would screw me back."

All very cynical. But the saddest sight I have ever seen is Tu Do Street at TET, the Vietnamese New Year, celebrated by the Americans as the time to bomb or not to bomb. Traditionally at TET Vietnamese return to the village where they were born. It is the greatest festival of the year, combining something of Christmas, Easter and Thanksgiving. It is a time of fireworks and presents, of drinking and honoring family and ancestors. The bars at TET are filled with girls who have no place to go, disowned as they are for becoming courtesans to the Americans. So they sit in their hip-huggers and miniskirts and vinyl spike-heeled shoes and drink Coke, dreaming of home. No amount of attention can bring them out of it. They are deep-sad and crying with longing.

So the crowd from the Caravelle sits in the Sporting Bar and talks about the war. One of the Americans is living with a Chinese girl. They converse in pidgin French when they converse at all, and now she is wedged silently into the group at the bar, staring into a 7-Up and holding the American's hand, as he leans across her to talk animatedly to a Vassar graduate. Beer arrives, is drunk, arrives again. The construction worker edges over and wants to talk. Ignored, he retreats for ten minutes. Then he comes back again and puts an arm around one of the American girls; he says he just wanted to do it. He means no harm.

Look, we're just trying to talk among ourselves.

Haven' seen a round-eyed woman for six months, the construction man says. He is red-faced and bleary with whiskey.

Well, find one someplace else.

Who 'n hell you guys think you are?

Look, friend, we don't want to bother . . .

Snot-noses.

OK, let's go.

And the crowd from the Caravelle, all bills paid, gets up to leave. They depart quickly, in a group, leaving the construction worker behind, angry and wanting to fight. They walk down Tu Do Street, everybody agreeing that it was a bad idea to leave the Caravelle. There are so many Americans in town it is impossible to go somewhere and have a drink without some drunk bothering your girl. Well, that ended it. The hell with Tu Do Street. It's nicer to drink at the Caravelle, anyway, and that way there are no problems. Back to the NBC suite. Edith Piaf, Charlie Byrd, and Beethoven. Room service ice. Nice.

"We all lived the same," said the middle-aged woman, talking rapidly. "Ate the same food, were hungry together, took the bombs together. In the middle of the city during the siege you could hear the shell come out of the gun, and hear it hitting, usually nearby. If you were riding on a tram when it was hit, you were hit along with the people in it. There was a common danger. There was very little liquor, and the food was terrible."

That was Martha Gellhorn on the Spanish Civil War. She had come to Vietnam to write a series of pieces for the *Guardian*. Vietnam was only the latest in a series of Gellhorn-written wars, beginning with Spain and then China, Europe in World War II, the Middle East, Greece, and now Asia. Her position on Vietnam was formed before she arrived, but the atmosphere of Saigon did nothing to undermine it. She was against the war on all counts, and would denounce it to all comers. She supported an immediate withdrawal and some kind of reparations payment. She thought American policy amounted to genocide. One of her points of reference was the Spanish war. "Nothing *but*," she said when I asked her if the correspondents covering that war regarded it as a noble one. "And we knew we were right. We knew, we just *knew*, that Spain was the place to stop fascism. This was it. There was no other place."

It seemed anachronistic in the cool world of 1967, where

reporters of my generation prided themselves on a professional detachment. The compulsion was to tell it like it was, even if what it was was your own country at war and the way it was, if told truthfully, was not "helpful" to the effort. There was no sense in Vietnam of a war which would halt the advance of Communism; it was simply "the Vietnam war" and to those who lived there it was a war largely without ideology, always excepting the majors, colonels and generals of the army, who did see it as a struggle between the free world and the non-free world. Because of the doubts over the legitimacy of the struggle, and the conditions of life in Saigon, a man felt vaguely like a voyeur. Part of the schizophrenia was the imbalance between the field, where the war was being fought, and Saigon, where it was being managed. The correspondent of the Washington *Post* was not obliged to live in a Special Forces Camp at the Cambodian border, or to eat C rations in a jungle for a fortnight. In Spain the correspondents felt closer to the war and less like spectators at least in part because of the common privations. It seemed to me an appealing thought, and I wondered if the reporting would be different if Saigon were under siege and bombs burst nightly in Lam Son Square, if food and liquor were scarce. Would the perception of the war be altered if there were no Sunday night dances at the Brinks B.O.Q. in downtown Saigon? Would the cause of the war seem nobler if the Saigon government and the Americans were under greater pressure? But how would Hemingway and Matthews and Martha Gellhorn have reacted if it had been the loyalists who bombed Guernica?

In Vietnam it became a compulsion to get out of Saigon and into the field as often as possible. The justification was that the countryside was critical to the winning of the war, and in part that was true. But the reasons really had to do with conscience, and the impulse to find reality. If Saigon was unreal, then the war must be real. The part of Vietnam that was straight and without corkscrews was the shooting war. It was the only part of it that made sense without qualifications. All of the arguments and the doubts became irrelevant when men fought to survive. When I would comment that the battlefield behavior of American troops was almost the only fact about Vietnam that I found admirable, Martha Gellhorn snorted and said it was a case of "just buddies." The idea was that men were not fighting for any reason, or any ideology, but because they were there; they fought for their friends.

That was probably true, for any difference that it made, but it surely did not detract from the extraordinary courage shown by the men who were there, fighting a war to no applause. Second only to safety, the mature infantryman values comfort, so after struggling through a Viet Cong minefield in the afternoon it was quite possible, indeed likely, that he would receive a hot meal delivered by helicopter to the bivouac that night. If the infantryman got to Saigon he could telephone home; some of them called from their base camps, reversing the charges. Every tiny MACV outpost in the most remote province had its supply of cold beer and English gin, and nightly Hollywood movies. This was taken along with the fighting in the jungles and paddies, which was as terrible as fighting is anywhere.

"In Spain, correspondents actually went hungry," Martha Gellhorn had said. People went hungry in South Vietnam, but they were not the correspondents. I suppose that it doesn't matter whether correspondents are hungry or not, or whether there are dances at the Brinks or English gin at the MACV compound in Camau. Every soldier likes hot meals in the field, and the Caravelle is superior in every way to a foxhole. And none of these things are crucial to whether or not the war in Vietnam is a just war or a winnable one. The nobility of the war is a matter for historians. It is enough for a journalist to report that the atmosphere in Saigon was destructive, and tended to infect.

This will be called, not without some justification, the hairshirt analysis of the Americans in Vietnam. It is not the whole story, but it is one part of it, and because the attitudes of Americans in Vietnam were critical to the way the war was fought, it is worth pursuing. For all the good works, the money and the hospitals, the volunteer doctors, the aid projects, the dams and the schoolrooms, the truth is that it was an unequal war, and everyone knew it. There was no Viet Cong air force, let alone Viet Cong B–52 bombers, and no artillery fire bases (although in time the North Vietnamese would cause havoc with Russian-made mortars and rockets).

I have no doubt that the Communists, if they had possessed the aircraft and bombs, would have used them far more ruthlessly than the Americans used them. As it was, they had tools that were much more effective in a people's war. The basic and most useful question is not and never has been the effect of American firepower on the Vietnamese—it is the effect on the Americans, who bear responsibility for its use. It would somehow have seemed more reasonable if there were convincing evidence that the B–52 strikes and the artillery bombardments at night were helping the war effort, rather than hurting it. But there was no such evidence. The Americans were in Vietnam with the most powerful air force and the finest army in the world, and they could not halt the aggression. Battles erupted and were won, but the war seemed no closer to ending; the battles seemed then like scenes in an endless play, leading from nowhere to anywhere. The fight was unequal.

What the hell does it take to win this thing? asked a general late one night. *What do we have to do to them?* He had watched that day as the helicopters brought back green body bags from the field. The bags were lumpy and heavy with the dead. The helicopter crewmen unloaded the bags and laid them side by side in the dust near the airstrip, then took off again for another load. Nearby there was a billet of Vietnamese soldiers. As the bodies were being laid out you could hear the laughter and sounds of roughhouse from the ARVN compound. Vietnamese were not impressed by death, ours or theirs, and their lives were not changed by it. The general, fighting back an awful rage, strode off in the direction of his helicopter.

Some of the Americans would say that the trouble lay in the instinctive knowledge that they were not fighting for the existence of America, nor for any tangible set of ideals, but for a mythical Vietnam, one which had been celebrated by Eisenhower, Kennedy, and Johnson but which did not in fact exist. This was the Vietnam of the brave, freedom-loving Vietnamese. I knew very few brave, freedom-loving Vietnamese. They had other names for it, and other concepts, but those were in a different language, literally and figuratively, which neither translated nor traveled. It was very well to speak of the loss of Southeast Asia, of a gigantic domino board whose final domino was Washington or Waikiki, but the war was in Vietnam; its justification, for those who were there, had to be in the context of Vietnam and the Vietnamese. The SEATO agreements were not persuasive arguments sitting around a tent in Kontum, and while a general could make them, and believe them, he could not get truly inspired by them. If Ngo Dinh Diem was the Winston Churchill of Southeast Asia, as then Vice President Johnson described him in 1962, who then was Ho Chi Minh? Hitler? When Diem was overthrown in 1963, he was regarded as a despot. What did that make Ho? And where then were the brave, freedom-loving Vietnamese?

The population did not engage in the struggle. The Viet Cong did not regard American weaponry as decisive. And the inequality of the struggle, 500,000 men and their machines for so little advance, only increased American frustrations. It *was* unequal, and therefore unfair. It went against the American grain. When the guerrillas bombed a billet or assassinated a district chief, the Americans called it terrorism. They had to call it terrorism because guerrilla warfare did not fit the scheme of war as they were fighting it. American aircraft were first sent out after the mortaring of the airbase at Pleiku, an attack described as terrorist in character. The efficiency of the U.S. Air Force made it inevitable that in time the air war in the North would become the principal fascination of the Vietnam conflict. It was what the Americans did best. The bombing of the North came as a direct and logical consequence of the frustrations of the ground war in the South. Now it is a war out on its own, a private war with MIG's, SAM missiles, anti-aircraft fire, Russian and Chinese ships in the Haiphong harbor, and all the rest of it. Can Hau Nghia province be pacified or the Vietnamese political process inspired as a result of a dogfight between Phantoms and MIG's over Hanoi?

But how could you change it? The war was not a tennis match, with seeds, or an auto *grand prix* with corrected times for the slower cars. You did what you had to do to win, or what you thought would bring victory closer. If it seemed that bombing a power plant in Hanoi would save the lives of American soldiers, you bombed the power plant. And if after two and a half years of bombing the war seemed no closer to solution, you did not claim that bombing was a failure. You claimed that there was not enough of it, or that it wasn't begun early enough, or that crucial targets were excused from destruction. How could millions of pounds of bombs over enemy targets conceivably be a failure? The logic was inescapable. In Vietnam a moderate was a man who thought that the only thing worse than winning the war was losing it, for what would come with defeat would be far worse than anything that would come with victory. So the war was fought, and a plausible and powerful case can be made that given the situation in 1965, all the combat troops should have been committed at once; once the interventionist course had been decided, the Americans then should have pressed ahead on a one hundred percent basis, with troop call-ups and rationing at home. But it happened piecemeal, and hindsight is an unfair tactic to use in talking about American policy in Vietnam. In prosecuting a conventional war against a skilled guerrilla army operating among, at best, an indifferent population, there was a heavy psychological price to pay. And the Americans were paying it.

A sergeant major, one of the most decorated noncommissioned officers in the army, a veteran of Europe and Korea and a line sergeant in Vietnam, talked about the Viet Cong one day at the base camp of the 1st Infantry Division. He described an action just ended, where a squad of Viet Cong had fought to the last man to hold an indefensible position. There was an escape route, but the enemy did not use it. "We had to kill every one of them," the sergeant major said. "But the thing was they stayed, even though they knew what we had. They knew we had a full company, with artillery and mortars and the rest. They fought all day, *and they knew what we had.*" It confounded the rules of military logic as the sergeant major knew them. He said that he didn't care what the colonels at MACV said about the Viet Cong. "For my money, the Viet Cong is the best fighter I have ever seen anywhere. Man for man, he is as good—maybe better—than we are." Then, with no sense of irony but only saying what was true and factual, he added, "Of course, that's because he's fighting in his own country."

from *To What End: Report From Vietnam,* 1968

Peter Arnett in 1963, with field gear. *(AP/Wide World Photos.)*

Daniel Lang, 1945. *(Courtesy Margaret Lang.)*

Stewart *(l.)* and
Joseph Alsop,
1955. *(AP/Wide
World Photos.)*

(L. to r.): David Halberstam, Malcolm W. Browne, and Neil Sheehan, 1963.
(Photo: Horst Faas.)

Ward Just *(l.)* in South Vietnam, 1966. *(Courtesy Ward Just.)*

Neil Sheehan,
Saigon, 1963.
*(UPI/Corbis-
Bettmann.)*

Harrison E. Salisbury testifying before the Senate Foreign Relations Committee about the bombing of North Vietnam, 1967. *(UPI/Corbis-Bettmann.)*

Mary McCarthy, 1964. *(AP/Wide World Photos.)*

Marguerite Higgins, 1966. *(AP/Wide World Photos.)*

Wallace Terry, Bien Hoa, South Vietnam. *(Photo: Dick Swanson, Life, courtesy Wallace Terry.)*

Bernard B. Fall. *(Courtesy Dorothy Fall.)*

Bernard B. Fall, on February 21, 1967, the day before his death. *(Photo: Sgt. Burch, USMC/Defense Dept. Photo.)*

Press briefing in Saigon. *Front row (l. to r.)*: Pham Xuan An *(Time)*, Seymour Topping. *Second row:* Neil Sheehan, Malcolm Browne. *Third row:* Father O'Connor (Catholic News Service), Keyes Beech. *(Photo: Horst Faas.)*

Neil Sheehan, Saigon, 1963. *(Photo:François Sully, courtesy Archives and Special Collections, Healey Library, University of Massachusetts at Boston.)*

John Flynn in Vietnam, 1966. *(Photo: Paul Avery.)*

Jack P. Smith, 1965. *(Courtesy Jack P. Smith.)*

Lee Lescaze. *(Courtesy Rebecca Lescaze.)*

Lee Lescaze. *(Courtesy Rebecca Lescaze.)*

Charles Mohr *(Photo: François Sully, courtesy Archives and Special Collections, Healey Library, University of Massachusetts at Boston.)*

Zalin Grant *(r.)* with General William C. Westmoreland in Danang, 1966. *(Courtesy Pythia Press.)*

John T. Wheeler *(l.)* with photographer Horst Faas, 1967. *(Courtesy Horst Faas.)*

Thomas A. Johnson (wearing glasses, with camera) and soldiers of the 173rd Airborne Brigade, 1968. *(Courtesy Thomas A. Johnson.)*

Don Oberdorfer *(r.)* with Eugene Black, head of the World Bank, in Vietnam, 1968. *(Courtesy Don Oberdorfer.)*

Stanley Karnow at Angkor Wat, Cambodia, 1967. *(Photo: Jean-François Chauval, courtesy Stanley Karnow.)*

Martha Gellhorn, 1977. *(Photo: Ian Berry/Magnum.)*

Don Moser *(r.)* with *Life* photographer John Olson at a firebase in the Central Highlands. (*Courtesy Don Moser.*)

William Tuohy, Hue, February 1968. *(Courtesy William Tuohy.)*

Steve Lerner *(upper l.)* with Allen Ginsberg, William Burroughs, and Jean Genet *(center row, l. to r.)*. Democratic National Convention, Chicago, 1968. *(Photo: Copyright © Fred W. McDarrah.)*

Norman Mailer at Republican National Convention, Miami, 1968. *(Photo: Copyright © Fred W. McDarrah.)*

Walter Cronkite with Lyndon Johnson, 1969. *(AP/Wide World Photos.)*

Beverly Deepe. *(AP/Wide World Photos.)*

Joe McGinniss, 1970.
(Photo: Tony Camerano,
AP/Wide World Photos.)

Press card issued to Jonathan Randal, 1972. *(Courtesy Jonathan Randal.)*

Jeffrey Blankfort at a Joan Baez concert, Greek Theatre, Berkeley. *(Photo: Marvin Collins, courtesy Jeffrey Blankfort.)*

Frances FitzGerald touring refugee camp near Danang, 1972. *(Photo: ©Philip Jones Griffiths/Magnum, courtesy Life.)*

Meg Greenfield in 1978, after receiving the Pulitzer Prize for Editorial Writing. *(AP/Wide World Photos.)*

Homer Bigart, 1965. *(AP/Wide World Photos.)*

The Vietcong Cadre of Terror

by Don Moser

HAVING synchronized watches and gone over the plan one last time, the three men struggled through the thick late-afternoon traffic toward the Ong Lanh marketplace—Sam and Tam on their motorbikes and Trong on his bicycle. The peasant woman was there waiting, sitting with her baskets of produce, just at the spot that Sam had shown her.

Sam sat astride his cycle for a moment, checking the scene. The two baskets of crude sugar were beside her. Good.

He got off and walked toward her. "How is your business today?" he asked.

"I have sold half my sugar," the woman replied.

"Did you get a good price?"

As they made casual conversation, Sam looked over the baskets. Each had a bit of wire protruding from the side. Sam opened one of the baskets and scooped some of the sugar from it; the woman did the same with the other. Sam had been meticulously trained, but this was the first operation he had run by himself, and he wanted everything to go smoothly. He plunged his hand into the remaining sugar and felt about. The day before, in the Secret Zone outside Saigon, he had carefully blocked the mine into position and now he found it still perfectly aligned with the crude but effective sighting wire. The second basket was all right too.

Without talking, he and the woman carried one of the baskets to Trong's bicycle and lashed it to the side, the wire pointing out. Trong and Tam meanwhile were tying the other basket to Tam's motorbike. To anyone in the busy marketplace who might be watching, they were just men buying sugar.

Sam then got on his own cycle and rode along to the little park by the waterfront. He sat down on a bench there—a small man, nondescript and inconspicuous. When the others

371

arrived they did not greet him. Tam went across the park and found a bench by himself. Trong sat on the other end of Sam's bench, but the two men did not speak.

It was a long wait. Sam did not normally smoke, but he smoked now. He read the newspaper. He watched the boats out on the Saigon River, the Americans enjoying themselves speeding up and down in motorboats and drifting by in little sailboats. He was worried about Trong. Tam was an old hand, a professional, but Trong was only 19 and he had handled nothing but a couple of grenadings, never a job like this.

Trong was nervous. "I am afraid it will go off early," he blurted finally. "While I am still on the bicycle."

Sam tried to settle him down. "Do not worry," he said. They had prepared the watches themselves, he explained. They had tested them carefully, and they were very good watches, the best kind. The boy should be patient now, and calm.

At precisely 7:45 Sam reached into his pocket and took out the wristwatch and the tiny battery pack. The watch had no second hand or hour hand, and he set the minute hand exactly 40 minutes back from the wire inserted through a hole drilled in the face. At 8:25 the hand would touch the wire and close the circuit.

He passed the watch to Trong, and the boy walked over to his bicycle. Pretending to fix something on the bike, Trong swiftly connected the watch to the mine in the basket and scooped sugar over it.

Then, instead of waiting for another 15 minutes as he was supposed to do, Trong climbed on his bicycle and took off down the street.

Sam stared. This could be disastrous. The whole operation could fail. Trong would park his bicycle at the target site far too early—and parked bicycles bearing large, suspicious-looking burdens were not ignored by the police. Five to seven minutes was the maximum time allowed according to directives, and Trong would arrive at the target more than 15 minutes early.

Sam moved quickly to his motorbike and took after the boy. Trong was pedaling fast. Sam pulled up alongside and motioned sharply with his hand for Trong to slow down. But the boy did not even acknowledge him. He just kept pedaling, his face tight with fear.

There was nothing more Sam could do. He sped on ahead to the My Canh floating restaurant, parked his motorcycle at the appointed place and sat down on a bench to watch. Trong arrived a few minutes later, parked his bicycle near the restaurant entrance—as the plan had specified—and fled. *Too early, too early.*

At 8:15, exactly on time, the experienced Tam pulled up and parked his motorcycle, positioning it carefully so that the wire on the basket was aimed directly at the restaurant where all the Americans and their Vietnamese friends were dining. Then Tam walked nonchalantly down the street, got onto Sam's motorbike and rode away. *Three minutes.*

Sam got up and strolled down the street. The police had noticed nothing. Perhaps the plan would work, after all. At precisely 8:20 Tam's motorbike disappeared in a blast of flame and smoke as the huge claymore mine drove its hundreds of steel pellets through the side of the restaurant. In two or three minutes policemen and firemen and soldiers would be milling about at the scene, right in front of the second mine on Trong's bicycle.

A taxi came down the street and Sam flagged it. "God, something exploded there!" Sam said as he got in.

The taxi was halfway down Flower Street when the second mine went off, and Nguyen Van Sam did not even hear the explosion.

In the two years from the day he blew up the My Canh floating restaurant in June 1965, killing 44 Americans and Vietnamese and wounding 80 more, until his capture last July 31—the very day that he intended to pull his biggest coup—Nguyen Van Sam commanded 28 other terrorist operations in the city of Saigon which were directly responsible for the deaths of 58 Vietnamese and Americans, and for injuries to 226 more. Sam was the leader of Special Action Unit 69, an element of one of the most lethal terrorist organizations in history: F-100.

F-100—known also as C-10, C-44 and by various other cover designations—is an organization of trained, professional terrorists. Its various cells and spin-off special action units have run every major terrorist operation in Saigon for the past two and a half years. Besides the My Canh restaurant, these include the bombings of the U.S. Embassy, the Metropole enlisted men's quarters, the Victoria officers' quarters and the National Police Headquarters. It was F-100 which rocketed the Vietnamese National Day celebration, attempted to mortar General Westmoreland's headquarters, and did mortar Independence Palace during Vice President Humphrey's recent visit. F-100 agents have also carried out assassinations, grenadings and small-scale attacks beyond count. At a conservative estimate, F-100 has killed at least 250 people and wounded 1,400 more.

While it is commonly supposed that Vietcong terrorism is haphazard, or spur of the moment, F-100's operations are planned with an almost fanatical attention to detail, painstakingly rehearsed, carried out with split-second timing, and endlessly critiqued. F-100's table of organization includes mapmakers, photographers and demolition experts. It has its own finance section, its own communications section and a specialist who converts wristwatches into mechanisms for detonating time bombs. Though some of its most active cells have lately been broken by the Vietnamese police, the parent organization itself has continued to grow in size and power. From its base deep in the Secret Zone of the jungles of Binh Duong province, and under the direction of a man known only as Brother Hoang, F-100 has the primary responsibility for terrorism not only in Saigon but in every other city and sizable town in the vicinity.

F-100 was formed early in 1965, when the three sapper platoons that had handled all Saigon terrorism were combined under a single command. Today it includes sapper units of all sizes and functions: groves, groups, cells, inter-cells, and special action units, of which Sam's Unit 69 was one. F-100's setup calls for a roster of 1,200 men although its actual strength is much less. Its arsenal includes every weapon from a heavy mortar on down, and the unit has even issued instructions explaining how its men can make flame throwers from commonplace equipment easily found in Saigon—instructions which, fortunately, have not been put into practice.

F-100's men must move constantly between Saigon and

headquarters in the Secret Zone of the jungle areas outside the city. There is no problem: excellent counterfeit I.D. cards are turned out on the V.C.'s jungle printing presses, and legitimate blank cards stolen from government offices are available on the black market at prices ranging from 5,000 to 20,000 piasters. Throughout the city the organization maintains a vast system of safehouses—secret meeting places—purchased with an apparently inexhaustible treasury. Some of these safehouses are private dwellings. Others are small business establishments such as bicycle repair shops or food stores, and no trouble is spared to make the cover perfect. One of the unit's more active operatives, a man known as Chin the Barber, was trained in all tonsorial techniques before setting up a safehouse in a barbershop.

All of F-100's agents use aliases and cover names. In Vietnam people are often known by their filial rank. The second son, for example, is known as "Brother Three" (no one gets the rank of one). This custom makes a convenient basis for F-100 cover names; agents are often known just by their filial rank numbers and initials. Nguyen Van Sam's commander, for example, is called 7-N. These numerical names are also sometimes used as sign and countersign. When two agents meet, neither being certain of the other's identity, one man will ask, "Are you Brother Four?" The other will reply, "Yes, are you Brother Six?" If the two numbers add up to 10—or whatever the correct code number for the day is—each man knows that he has made the correct contact.

To maintain security, F-100 uses a system of "compartmentalization" or "vertical organization." The unit is divided into many small cells, and each man knows only his immediate commander. He may only know his comrades in the cell by aliases and see them only during operations and planning sessions.

Messages between command levels are commonly written in invisible ink made from the Chinese herbal medicine used for treating cold sores. Dispatches into the city are often carried by non-V.C. who have no idea that the paper-wrapped parcel they are delivering actually bears invisible plans for blowing up a police station. To maintain compartmentalization, agents use letter-drops—prearranged spots where messages are dropped off by one agent and picked up by another, neither man learning the identity of the other.

Recruits for F-100 are schooled in sabotage techniques in the Secret Zone, and during classes, to keep identities secret, they are separated from each other by sheets of cloth or opaque plastic. They are led about blindfolded and allowed to bathe or relieve themselves only separately or at night. After returning to Saigon, a recruit gets further on-the-job training. His squad leader gives him a grenade, drives him about on the back of a motorbike until he finds a good target, and observes how the new man performs. The scores of apparently random grenade attacks in Saigon are nearly all training exercises of this kind.

Weapons and explosives are smuggled past police checkpoints and into the city by the "ant method." Instead of a single truck carrying 200 pounds of TNT, scores of couriers using many routes of access bring in a pound or two each. F-100 is ingenious. Grenades are hidden inside pineapples, blocks of TNT are stuffed into hollow lengths of bamboo, messages are secreted in loaves of bread and sewn into potatoes. Recently an American official in one U.S. office in Saigon—an admitted admirer of the female form—was attracted each morning by a curvy Vietnamese girl in his office. But when she went home at the end of the day, she no longer seemed so appealing. For a while the American thought he was simply tired from the day's work and therefore less appreciative. "But then I knew I wasn't getting that old," he said. When he ordered a body search pulled on the girl next morning, police found her brassiere packed with plastic explosives. A few more days and she would have had enough smuggled in to blow the building off the map.

During 1965 and 1966, two cells of F-100—B-4 under a graduate science student and demolitions expert named Tuan, and B-5 led by a mastermind named Bay Be—ran a series of spectacularly successful operations in Saigon. Working sometimes separately, more often in concert, Tuan and Bay Be and their small groups hit the U.S. Embassy, killing 22 and wounding 179, the Metropole enlisted men's billet, killing 13 and wounding 152, the Victoria officers' billet, killing eight and wounding 126. They grenaded bars and restaurants all over town, and even mounted an incredibly brazen attack on the National Police Headquarters itself. In this intricate commando-style raid, Bay Be and his men sped up to the compound gates in two cars and laid down a screen of automatic-weapons fire while another man drove a third car into the middle of the central compound and blew it up right under the noses of the cops. Then, covered by a preplanned diversionary attack on a nearby police substation, Bay Be and all of his men escaped scot-free. For the police, the attack was doubly humiliating because it is the Vietnamese police, rather than the military, who are directly responsible for fighting F-100.

Early in 1966 the national police Special Branch got its first big break with the aid of a Mata Hari–style double agent who established herself as Tuan's girl friend and confederate. The girl set up a tailor shop as a safehouse for Tuan and his men. From Tuan's point of view everything was perfect. The girl was his lover, the tailor shop was a good cover, and explosives were sent in from the Secret Zone, hidden in bolts of cloth. He did not know that the tailor shop was bugged, that his conversations were recorded, and that the woman who appeared frequently to order clothes was a Special Branch agent picking up the tapes from Tuan's girl friend.

By January 1966 Tuan had worked out a formidable plan to blow up an American billet called the Alabama. He constructed an ingenious water cart. Anyone looking in the top would see that it was filled with water and if one turned the spigot, water ran out. But underneath the shallow layer of water lay 300 pounds of TNT. Just as Tuan and his men wheeled the water cart up to the Alabama, the police closed in.

Bay Be, the B-5 commander and most active terrorist of all, was also unlucky in love. He began a dalliance with the wife of another V.C. The outraged man defected and gave police the location of Bay Be's safehouse. Bay Be was arrested a few days later. A Special Branch captain thereupon saw a way to make Bay Be's capture pay further dividends. The Vietnamese Buddhists were in the midst of their 1966 demonstrations and the captain forced Bay Be to write a letter to his commander, suggesting that F-100 exploit the political crisis with a series of grenadings and minor incidents which the government would blame on the Buddhists. Many cadres should be sent in, Bay Be wrote, to work under his direction.

The letter went back up the line, the plan was approved, and F-100 started sending agents down to the city. In one week Special Branch arrested 10 key men. Ironically, the Buddhists on their own created a great deal of trouble during this period and the F-100 commander, misinterpreting who had been responsible for what, sent a message down to Bay Be, congratulating him on his effective exploitation of the situation.

Its two top cells broken with the capture of Bay Be and Tuan, F-100 subsided briefly. Then Cell B-11 and Grove A-4 went into operation with heavy weapons, shelling Tan Son Nhut airbase and the National Day celebration in the center of Saigon. In Cholon, the Chinese quarter of the city, a Chinese sapper unit also began working, although its relationship with F-100 was and is unclear. Some police believe that the organization may be a Maoist group only casually related to the Vietcong. The bombing of the Nationalist Chinese Embassy in September of 1966, however, had all the earmarks of an F-100 operation. But in the city itself, a great deal of the terrorist work was taken over by Special Action Unit 69, under the command of Nguyen Van Sam.

Nguyen Van Sam does not fit the image of a master terrorist. He is a small man with a hedgehog shock of hair and a disarming smile. He appears to be neither an ideologue nor a pathological killer, but a craftsman who has learned well a certain line of work and takes professional pride in his competence: he would approach the problem of blowing up a building in about the same frame of mind as a plumber tackling a blocked drain. He was born in 1932 in Binh Duong province, the son of a Buddhist farmer. He never attended school, but worked as a buffalo boy until he was 16, when he was recruited by his uncle into the Vietminh. During the resistance against the French he was a liaison agent, running messages from one Vietminh unit to another. When the country was partitioned in 1954, Sam went to the North where he became a truck driver and later a driving instructor. In 1963 he was recruited into Unit B, an organization for training saboteurs and terrorists to be infiltrated into the South, and attended Unit B's highly secret special school in Ha Dong province. For six months he was trained in techniques of sabotage, assassination and terrorism. He learned how to build mines and time bombs, how best to sabotage ships, offices, trains and airplanes. He received political indoctrination and studied until his head swam. In 1964, Sam infiltrated back into the South, and headed for F-100's headquarters in the then Secret Zone in Cu Chi outside Saigon. With a fake identification card, Sam took a bus to Saigon. There, riding behind another agent on a motor scooter, Sam began learning every street and alley in the city. For the next few months he traveled back and forth between the city and the jungle. Romance can flower even among the Vietcong; in the Secret Zone, Sam fell in love with a short, rounded V.C. liaison girl and the two were married by Sam's commander.

After the success of his first independent operation at the My Canh restaurant, Sam's life fell into a weird sort of routine. When he was in Saigon, only one man—his reliable deputy Tam—knew where he lived. Sam would meet his men by prearranged appointment in a coffee shop. They would then go to one of the outdoor TV receivers scattered throughout the city and stand in back of the crowd talking softly while pretending to watch the program. Each operation was planned to the last degree. Sam and his men scouted proposed attack sites for days. They prepared meticulous maps, plans, sometimes even took photographs. The plans were then carried or forwarded back to the Secret Zone for approval by Sam's commander, 7-N. When the plan was approved Sam and his men practiced the operation on a sand table until they had every movement letter perfect. Meanwhile, the necessary weapons and explosives were smuggled into the city to him.

Over the months, Sam rolled up an impressive list of accomplishments. In February of 1966 he mined the Vietnamese General Staff Headquarters gate, killing 13 and wounding 60. In May he mined an American bus station, killing five and wounding 29. Around election time in September of 1966 he ran six operations, killing one and wounding 27, and the following month he hit the Ky Son American billet, killing three and wounding 10. He bombed a warehouse in December and for the first few months of 1967 grenaded and mined several

U.S. and Vietnamese military and police vehicles. On July 10 he mined the Capitol billet, killing four and wounding 27.

By this time, Sam had invested several hundred thousand V.C. piasters in a network of safehouses. He had a virtual motor pool of old cars, motorbikes and bicycles—he went through a lot of bikes and motorcycles because they were used to bear the mines and explosives and were commonly blown up in his attacks. He had a budget of 40,000 piasters a month for operating expenses, ran a training program for new recruits, and he had munitions cached all over the city.

In April of last year Sam moved his wife and their baby son into one of the safehouses in the city, obtaining the necessary identity documents for them all by the simple expedient of telling a district chief that he was a refugee from a V.C.-controlled area and therefore not on any census rolls. He established himself—or rather his wife—as a seller of soup, rice sticks and sweets.

But Sam was not happy. His superiors were demanding an impossible amount of work from him—10 to 20 operations a month. It took a long time to train "a good fighter." All too frequently his men were captured by police, it was getting harder and harder to find replacements and the bombing in the Secret Zones and the improved government control of the roads made it more difficult to get explosives into the city. Once Sam did get three big claymores and buried them along a canal in the city. But then a boat family came along, upended their sampan on his buried mines and started to repair it. For a month they camped on top of the precious mines while Sam fumed helplessly.

Moreover, Sam was growing tired of the war and tired of the killing. He was a fighter. He had always known that he had to go on fighting and that one day he would die. This had not bothered him before, but now he had a baby boy, and he hated the idea of dying without seeing his son grow up.

But work was work. In June, with his deputy Tam and the others, he began to plan his most ambitious operation yet: an attack on JUSPAO—the big Joint U.S. Public Affairs Office in the heart of Saigon. His plan called for using three huge DH-10 mines, each capable of blasting through eight inches of reinforced concrete from a distance of 100 feet. Two of the mines would be set to go off at 12 noon, as the Americans in the office were swarming out for lunch. The third would go off seven minutes later, just in time to catch the rescue workers and police. Sam was sure the blasts would kill at least 100 people.

But in an office at Saigon municipal police headquarters a barrel-shaped, flashing-eyed man was waiting for Sam to make a mistake. He was Pham Quant Tan, chief of Saigon's Special Branch. Captain Tan is a former intelligence and psychological warfare officer who devours books on criminology, chain-smokes king-sized cigarettes and functions best at 3 or 4 o'clock in the morning. During those small hours he prowls his city, meets with his agents and informers and tirelessly interrogates suspects. Captain Tan has the patience of a cat watching a mousehole, and he is obsessed with the idea of catching terrorists. One of his diversions is the Asian chess game known in Vietnam as Co Tuong, and he is the master of a maneuver involving the two powerful "cannon" pieces. This maneuver he calls "double morte"—double death. Captain Tan is a very tough man.

While the Vietnamese police have earned something of a reputation as people not to be taken prisoner by, torture is not the captain's line. He likes to think of himself as a psychologist, and to watch him deal with a prisoner is to see a craftsman happy in his work. He interrogates prisoners for weeks, even months. "You squeeze them like a lemon, until you have every drop of juice," he says. He keeps a suspect perpetually off-balance. When a man is brought in for interrogation Captain Tan may bark a question the moment the suspect walks in the door. Next time he may ignore the man entirely for half an hour while pretending to peruse papers on his desk. During questioning his moods shift rapidly from purple-faced rage to bland reassurance. But mostly he is paternal, concerned, an agreeable relief from the surly jailers.

"Are you getting proper food?" he enquires solicitously of a prisoner. "Perhaps you would like some breakfast." Or: "Are you in good health? Your color does not look too good." His tongue clucks sympathetically and he produces vitamin pills from his desk. "You must take these, one each day, and you will feel better."

Captain Tan's interrogations form floral patterns; his questions circle, wander apparently aimlessly until the trap is set, then suddenly drive right at the guts of things.

The captain had known about Special Action Unit 69 for some time when, acting on an informer's tip, he put out an alert for the young man named Tam. When Tam was picked up at a police checkpoint he was carrying five wristwatches prepared as time-bomb detonators. In spite of this solid evidence, Tam refused to talk during an entire night of questioning at a police precinct headquarters. Next morning, the captain took over the interrogation personally. When the terrorist was brought to his office Tam refused to speak or sit down. The captain stared at him. Then he told a subordinate that no one else was to question the man or even speak to him, and that he was to be placed in solitary confinement. "All right, you refused to speak," the captain said to Tam. "I will let you rest now till 9 o'clock. You can prepare all your lies in your mind. After 9 p.m. I will begin my investigation."

That night the captain had his men take Tam out of the cell, offer him food, coffee and cigarettes. Then they brought him to the captain's office. Again the V.C. refused to sit down. Captain Tan simply smiled and took out his military identification card. "I show you this to show you that I am not really a policeman," he said pleasantly. "Until recently I have always been a soldier, an infantry captain. So we are both soldiers, both fighters. So let us talk together as soldiers."

Then he began to ask, very conversationally, questions about Tam's personal life. He took no notes, and the questions were very innocent. Eventually Tam began to talk. After 20 minutes, Tam sat down for the first time. For two days the captain interviewed the V.C. until he felt that he had found the man's weakness. Finally he ordered Tam brought to his office again. "You are a sentimental guy," Captain Tan said brusquely. "I know what you want to do—you want to die. You don't want to denounce your friends, you want to die with honor as a man who would not talk. You want to be a martyr—you want your name to be among those of the heroes.

"But I am not so stupid as to let you die that way. I will tell you what I am going to do if you do not begin to talk.

Late tonight I am going to take you and your motor scooter and a big truck and go to the street near your house. I am going to smash the motor scooter and then drive the truck back and forth over your head a few times. Then I am going to call the newspapers. And tomorrow the newspapers will say that you got killed by a hit-and-run driver. So none of your friends will ever know that you were a martyr who refused to talk. You will just be a man who died like a dog in the streets."

Tam began to talk. He was, he admitted, the deputy leader of Special Action Unit 69. He started leading the police to hidden weapons caches. Ultimately the police were to discover 295 charges of TNT, five claymores, six pistols, one machine gun and 108 grenades. He told the captain that his leader was the man named Sam, who lived in a house on Bay Coc Street.

Captain Tan was now ready to set what he calls "the rat trap." He stationed five of his plainclothes agents around the house on Bay Coc Street and sat back to wait.

Sam, meanwhile, knew that something had gone wrong. He and Tam had planned to meet in front of a shop on Nguyen Hue Street to work on plans for the JUSPAO building attack. When Tam did not appear at the appointed time, Sam grew nervous. Tam was not the kind of agent to be late. Sam was upset anyway. His wife had had a miscarriage and was in the hospital. Everything seemed to be going wrong.

Sam waited at the rendezvous for two hours and then left, feeling deeply troubled. Tam was the only one of his men who knew where he, Sam, lived. Tam was a trusted deputy, but if he had been captured . . .

Sam slept that night at one of his safehouses. The next evening, still not having heard from Tam, he went to the house of a shopkeeper named Minh, an agent who had been keeping the mines for the attack. Minh's wife met him at the door. She did not know that her husband was a terrorist, and Sam said to her: "Is your husband here? He promised to sell me some rubber bands."

The woman was frightened. Her husband was gone, she said. Some men had come to her house, bringing the man she knew as Tam with them. Tam had led them to a place in the house where some mines were hidden. The men took the mines and her husband away with them.

Sam realized that the visitors were undoubtedly plainclothes policemen. Tam had indeed been arrested—and, furthermore, was talking. That night Sam stayed in the house of another agent named Dong, but couldn't sleep. Next morning he sent a message by courier to his commander in the Secret Zone explaining what had happened. Then he got his wife from the hospital. She must go to the Secret Zone immediately. He would follow her as soon as possible, but for now he had to stay in the city to find out how many of his men had been captured and how many of their weapons caches had been discovered. His wife, long accustomed to a life on the run, said nothing. She would simply do as he told her.

Sam returned to Dong's house. A little later there was a commotion outside. Sam looked out and saw Tam in the street with a group of plainclothesmen. Tam seemed to be pretending that he could not remember which of the houses on the street belonged to Dong. Obviously he was trying to delay the police long enough for anyone inside to escape. Sam slipped out the back door and got away with seconds to spare.

There was now clearly no safe place left in the city for Sam to hide. He took a bus out of town and stayed with his sister in Long An province for two days. To return to the city would be fatal, but Sam felt that he must make one last check on the house and weapons cache on Bay Coc Street. Perhaps Tam would not reveal that one. So on the 31st of July, the very day that he had planned to assault the JUSPAO building, Sam returned to Saigon. When he reached Bay Coc Street he looked around very carefully. Some cycle drivers, a couple of men playing elephant chess at the edge of the street, the usual gaggle of children—nothing out of the ordinary. He went on down toward the house.

At 6:45 that evening Captain Tan was enjoying the rare treat of a dinner at home with his wife when the telephone rang. It was the duty officer. The trap had sprung. When Tan reached his headquarters his men brought Sam in to him. This, the captain felt sure, was the man he had been waiting for. He ordered the blindfold removed. Sam stood there blinking in the bright light. Captain Tan watched him carefully. Suddenly Sam started screaming: "What do you bring me here for? Kill me! I want to die! I will never tell you anything!" Then he started yelling about the ultimate victory of the Liberation Front. "I want to die!" he shouted again.

Captain Tan smiled. This was the kind he liked. The silent ones, the calm ones like Tam, were difficult. But this one, this man who wanted to yell and scream his undying loyalty to the Front—this one would be easy.

Life, January 12, 1968

from *The Military Half:*
An Account of the Destruction
in Quang Ngai and Quang Tin

by Jonathan Schell

THIS BOOK is about what is happening to South Vietnam—to the people and the land—as a result of the American military presence. I shall not discuss the moral ramifications of that presence. I shall simply try to set down what I saw and heard first-hand during several weeks I spent with our armed forces in South Vietnam last summer. What I saw and heard had to do mostly with the destruction that was going on in South Vietnam, but at the same time I found that the peculiar character of this war tended to be defined for me by how the men in our armed forces reacted to the various special conditions of the war: the immense disparity in size and power between the two adversaries, the fact that Americans are fighting ten thousand miles from home, the fact that the Vietnamese are an Asian and non-industrialized people, the fact that we are bombing North Vietnam but the North Vietnamese are incapable of bombing the United States, the fact that our bombing in South Vietnam can be met only by small-arms fire, the fact that it is often impossible for our men to distinguish between the enemy and friendly or neutral civilians, the anomalousness and the corruption of the Saigon government, the secondary role played by the South Vietnamese Army we are supposedly assisting, the fact that the enemy is fighting a guerrilla war while we are fighting a mechanized war, and, finally, the overriding, fantastic fact that we are destroying, seemingly by inadvertence, the very country we are supposedly protecting. Like many Americans, I am opposed to the American policy in Vietnam. As I came to know the American men who were fighting there, I could feel only sorrow at what they were asked to do and what they did. On the other hand,

386

I could not forget that these men, for the most part, thought they were doing their duty and thought they had no choice, and I could not forget, either, that they were living under terrible stress and, like fighting men in any war, were trying to stay alive and hold on to their sanity. If our country stumbled into this war by mistake, the mistake was not theirs. If our continuing escalation of the war is wrong, the guilt is surely not theirs alone. If one disaster after another is visited upon the Vietnamese people, these disasters are the inevitable consequence of our intervention in the war, rather than of any extraordinary misconduct on the part of our troops. Thousands of Americans, of course, have lost their lives or been wounded in Vietnam, many of them in the belief that they were fighting for a just cause, and some of the men I came to know in Vietnam will lose their lives or be wounded in that same belief. Some of our men have been brutalized by the war, just as I might have been brutalized if I had been fighting beside them, and just as men on both sides of all wars have been brutalized. Yet some of them have done the job assigned to them without losing their compassion for the non-combatant Vietnamese, or even for the enemy in combat. In this article, however, I am not writing, essentially, about the men in our armed forces. I am writing about a certain, limited segment of the war—about the destruction by the American forces, as I observed it (mostly from the air), of a particular rural area of South Vietnam. All of us must share the responsibility for this war, and not only the men who bear arms. I have no wish to pass judgment on the individual Americans fighting in Vietnam. I wish merely to record what I witnessed, in the hope that it will help us all to understand better what we are doing.

IN THE SPRING of 1967, the United States Military Assistance Command in South Vietnam formed a new force, called Task Force Oregon, by assembling the 196th Light Infantry Brigade, the 3rd Brigade of the 4th Infantry Division, and the 1st Brigade of the 101st Airborne Division in Quang Ngai Province, which is the fifth province south of the Demilitarized Zone along the coast of the South China Sea. The cre-

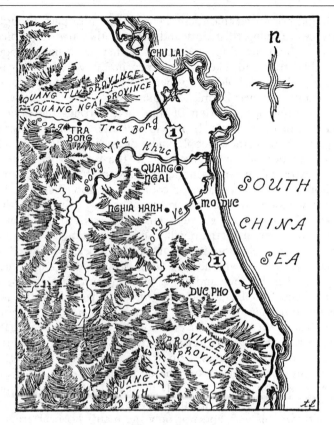

ation of Task Force Oregon, which was to operate under the
command of the 3rd Marine Amphibious Force, freed elements of the 3rd Marine Amphibious Force, which had been
conducting operations in Quang Ngai since May of 1965, to
move north to help combat increased activity along the Demilitarized Zone. The Annamese mountain range swings close
to the sea in Quang Ngai Province, and between the mountains and the sea is a strip of arable flatland eighty kilometres
long, twenty-five kilometres across at its widest point, and ten
kilometres across at its narrowest point. The Allied Forces divided this strip, which supports more than eighty per cent of
the province's population, of approximately six hundred and
fifty thousand, into four Tactical Areas of Responsibility, of

roughly equal size, and assigned one each, from north to south, to the 196th Light Brigade, to a brigade of Korean Marines that had landed in Quang Ngai in the summer of 1966, to a brigade of the Army of the Republic of Vietnam (abbreviated as ARVN and pronounced "Arvin" by the Americans), and to the 3rd Brigade of the 4th Division. The 1st Brigade of the 101st Airborne Division was reserved as a roving force that could be flown anywhere in the province by helicopter to launch surprise attacks on enemy units. The principal mission of the troops that formed Task Force Oregon was to find and kill soldiers belonging to what are called mainforce units of the Vietcong (or V.C., or National Liberation Front) and to the Army of North Vietnam who were operating in Quang Ngai Province. In order to break up any fixed patterns of operation that might help the enemy to predict their movements, elements of Task Force Oregon sometimes went outside Quang Ngai, carrying their operations into Quang Tin Province and Binh Dinh Province, which are adjacent to Quang Ngai on the north and on the south.

Task Force Oregon's area of operation was part of a mountainous coastal region of South Vietnam that stretches south from the city of Hué to Binh Dinh Province, and had traditionally been known for its natural beauty and its poor, proud, and hospitable people. Because even the narrow strip of flatland that lay between the mountains and the coast in this region was too sandy for good crops, a large proportion of the villagers long ago took up other occupations, such as fishing in the South China Sea and lumbering in the mountains. Many took up home crafts, and the area became famous for silk and for mats woven of reeds that grew on the banks of the local rivers. Predominantly a rural people, the natives of these mountainous provinces spoke with a broad, flat accent that had a simple, country ring to the ears of a Vietnamese from Saigon. They were also reputed to be shorter than most other Vietnamese, and to have plain, clear features, square jaws, and bold, frank natures. As late as 1964, most of the primary schools in the area adorned their walls with the traditional Vietnamese motto "Though your clothes may be soiled, keep your honor unspotted." Perhaps because the land was too poor to provide an adequate base for large fortunes, wealthy people in these provinces were particularly conscientious about giving their children the best education possible. Before the country was partitioned in 1954, the academic standards in most parts of what is now South Vietnam were far below the standards in the North, but students from the mountainous coastal provinces were noted for giving an excellent account of themselves at Hanoi University, which was regarded as the best in the country at that time. A large number of Vietnam's most popular writers were born in the region, including the late novelist Nhat Linh, who attacked the colonial French and corrupt Vietnamese officials in novels of social protest, and later became a hero to young people in Saigon when he led a movement of scholars and students against the regime of President Diem. The mountainous inland regions of the northern provinces were populated by primitive tribes known to the French as Montagnards, who lived by burning away patches of the forest, cultivating the cleared land until the soil was exhausted, and then moving on to another site.

Historically, the people of the region were rebellious and aggressive. It was from the provinces of Quang Ngai and Binh Dinh that the rulers of the Nguyen dynasty, in the sixteenth century, launched their long drive southward; when the French began their subjugation of Vietnam, in the late nineteenth century, it was in Quang Ngai and Binh Dinh that armed resistance to French rule was strongest; and it was in these provinces, again, that peasant rebellions first broke out, in the nineteen-thirties, against Vietnamese officials who served the French. After the Second World War, when the Vietminh, the anti-colonial predecessor of the National Liberation Front, launched the revolutionary campaign that eventually expelled the French from Vietnam, Quang Ngai became a principal center of revolutionary activity, and French troops never succeeded in entering the province in force. In 1948, for purposes of fighting the revolution, Ho Chi Minh divided the nation into military zones of four types, which he called "free zones," "guerrilla bases," "guerrilla zones," and "occupied zones," and he designated the provinces of Binh Dinh, Quang Ngai, and Quang Nam (north of Quang Tin) as free zones, meaning that those areas were to be considered already freed from the French and from the Emperor Bao Dai. The town of Duc Pho, in the southern part of Quang Ngai Province, became one of the largest rest centers in the country for Vietminh soldiers. The women of Duc Pho had always been famous for their beauty and their fiery, independent spirit, and there was a ditty that warned the "fighting man" who came to Duc Pho to be faithful to his jealous Duc Pho girl friend or risk losing his manhood at the girl friend's hands. In 1954, when many of the Vietminh soldiers and political organizers withdrew to the North, enough of them stayed behind in Quang Ngai and the provinces adjacent to it to insure that the influence of the government in Saigon would not penetrate beyond a few of the region's larger towns. By the early nineteen-sixties, a whole generation of young people in rural areas had known no government other than that of the Vietminh and the National Liberation Front. Not only had they learned to read and write in Vietminh and National Liberation Front schools but they had also learned to sing revolutionary songs, accompanying themselves on the guitar or mandolin, in the course of a drive by the Front to teach young people to play musical instruments. In early 1962, because these provinces were known to be National Liberation Front strongholds, the government in Saigon launched its Strategic Hamlet Program with particular vigor there. The program was intended to separate the people from the Front soldiers and organizers who lived among them, and as a means of accomplishing this the government ordinarily forced the people to leave their villages and to construct fortifications and new habitations at another site. Under a *corvée* system it had devised, it made each man responsible for constructing a certain yardage of wall around the strategic hamlet. If a family refused to move to a strategic hamlet, troops of the South Vietnamese Army might burn its home and its fields; by the end of 1962 parts of Quang Ngai—particularly areas near the mountains—were dotted with the ruins of burned houses. In Quang Ngai, as in other parts of the country, this program aroused hostility toward the government in Saigon, and within two years it was abandoned, to be reconstituted later as the New Life Hamlet Program. Usually, when the government succeeded in constructing a strategic hamlet, the Front quickly reëstablished—or simply maintained—contact with the villagers at their new site, and, consequently, in almost every case the strategic hamlets themselves were under the control of the Front. Supporters of the Front often wrote mottoes on the gates and walls of the strategic hamlets. One inscription, a couplet from the classical Chinese, appeared with particular frequency. It read, "How long can the Great Wall stand/ When its base is not the heart of the people?"

At the end of August, 1967, after four months of military operations, Task Force Oregon announced that it had killed, and counted the bodies of, thirty-three hundred enemy soldiers, had "detained" five thousand people, and had captured eight hundred firearms in caches or on or near the dead. It also announced that two hundred and eighty-five Americans had been killed and fourteen hundred wounded. During that August, I travelled as widely as I could in Quang Ngai Province, in order to talk with military people and civilians, and to observe what the effect of the Allied military operations had been, and I also observed several of the military operations themselves, as they were being carried out by Task Force Oregon in the northern part of Quang Ngai and just across its northern border, in Quang Tin. During my travels in Quang Ngai Province, I learned from civilian officials that since the Marines arrived, in 1965, military operations had swelled the number of people in government "refugee camps" by over a hundred thousand, bringing the official count of these people to a hundred and thirty-eight thousand around the middle of August. The American and Vietnamese officials who managed the camps estimated that about forty per cent of the province's population had passed through the camps during the preceding two years. Over the same period, the Marines, the Army, the Korean Marines, and the ARVN had destroyed approximately seventy per cent of the villages in the province—which means seventy per cent of the houses. I first became aware of this destruction when I spent several days in early August flying, as a reporter, in the back seat of one or another of several two-seat, single-propeller Cessna O-1 Forward Air Control planes (abbreviated FAC, and pronounced "Fac") that flew daily visual-reconnaissance flights over the entire heavily populated coastal strip of the province. (The

FAC planes, throughout South Vietnam, were always flown by Air Force pilots.) Some of the planes flew over single districts once a day for several weeks at a stretch, and the pilots became very closely acquainted with the terrain. Whenever it was possible, I checked my estimates of the percentage of houses destroyed against their estimates. In several districts, I was also able to check my estimates with the local ground commanders, although no figures of this kind were kept officially. From the FAC plane's prescribed flying altitude, which was fifteen hundred feet, I found it difficult to distinguish people, unless they were wearing their large brown conical straw hats, but I could easily distinguish houses and the remains of houses. The houses in Quang Ngai had been loosely grouped in groves of trees that stood out like dark-green islands in an expanse of lighter-green or yellow rice fields. From the air, the roofs of houses that were still standing appeared as dark-brown squares; the ashes of houses that had been recently burned appeared as gray squares; and the rain-washed clay foundations of houses that had been destroyed more than a month or so earlier appeared as red or yellow squares. When houses had been burned by troops on the ground, their walls—of clay-and-bamboo or stone—were usually still standing, but the walls of houses that had been bombed or bulldozed were flattened, or strewn over the rice fields. The pattern of destruction was roughly the same throughout the densely populated area of fields and villages lying between the mountains and the sea. Villages remained standing in a long belt a few kilometres wide bordering Route 1, a partly paved two-lane road running the full length of the coastal strip and approximately bisecting it. The rest—with certain exceptions, which I will mention—had been destroyed.

In Binh Son, the northernmost district of Quang Ngai Province, beyond a belt about two kilometres wide along the road, the houses that had stood on the flatland to the west of the road had been destroyed all the way down to the Song Tra Bong ("*song*" is a Vietnamese word for "river"). In the Song Tra Bong Valley, which had formerly been cultivated as far as about fifteen kilometres inland, between the mountains, the houses on the north side of the river had been destroyed as far as about ten kilometres inland. Beyond this, deep in the mountains, the town of Tra Bong, which had a population of several thousand and was also the site of a large Special Forces camp, remained standing. The Special Forces camp stood apart from the village, on a small hill. Bare of trees and grass, the camp was ringed by several rows of barbed wire, outside which were fences of sharpened bamboo poles, with rows of zigzagging trenches outside these. Inside all this was a cluster of low, heavily sandbagged huts with tin roofs. To the east of Route 1, in Binh Son District, beyond the belt of undestroyed houses along the road, seventy or eighty per cent of the houses had been destroyed all the way to the sea. South of the Song Tra Bong, in Son Tinh District, which was the Tactical Area of Responsibility of the Korean Marines, the situation was much the same. Along the south side of the Song Tra Bong, there was a Revolutionary Development project near the village of An Diem, about five kilometres west of the road, and the houses remained standing along this stretch of the river, although, as I have noted, the houses right across it on the north side, in the Tactical Area of Responsibility of the 196th Light Brigade, had been destroyed. On the coastal side of Route 1 in Son Tinh—again excepting the belt of a few kilometres along the road—from eighty to ninety per cent of the houses had been destroyed all the way to the sea. Along the Song Tra Khuc, which marks the southern border of Son Tinh District, the houses remained standing as far as ten kilometres away from the road on the mountain side, but beyond that, starting at the point where the river valley begins to wind between the mountains, they had been destroyed. Within one wide bend of the river, which described a full horseshoe, I could see networks of trenches that had been built by the National Liberation Front running down the center of many villages, and sometimes linking two or more of them. Throughout the province, I saw the black entrances to caves and networks of tunnels, which the entire population used as bomb shelters, and which the N.L.F. used as bunkers, hiding places, and escape routes, but in this bend of the river they were particularly numerous. Still deeper in the mountains, the village of Phuoc Tho remained standing, next to a Special Forces camp on a hill. All the houses of the village were crowded together in a square a hundred metres on a side, which was surrounded by a trench, and single houses out in the fields had been razed. This indicated that Phuoc Tho had been converted into a strategic hamlet. Like most of the province, the valley of the Song Tra Khuc was spotted with craters of all sizes. Craters from artillery fire, which were a yard or two wide, peppered the rice fields and the former villages, and craters from delayed-fuse bombs, which were as much as thirty feet across and seven feet deep, and many of which had filled with water, dotted the landscape with little ponds. Anti-personnel bombs, which explode on contact, had made shallow craters that spread out in rays across the fields, like giant yellow asterisks, and napalm strikes had blackened the fields in uneven splotches. What had formerly been dense woods on the mountainsides that rose up from the culti-vated valley in a series of delicate ridges were just as badly torn up.

The two districts to the south of the Song Tra Khuc— Nghia Hanh and Tu Nghia—which were the ARVN's Tactical Area of Responsibility, were the least heavily destroyed of Quang Ngai's districts. Quang Ngai City formed the center of a large undestroyed pocket that extended eastward all the way to the coast and, in places, extended westward along the south bank of the Song Tra Khuc almost all the way to the mountains. In the southern half of Nghia Hanh District, how-ever, there had been considerable destruction near the moun-tains. To the south of these two least heavily destroyed of the province's districts, and divided from them by the slow-mov-ing Song Ve, are Mo Duc and Duc Pho Districts, which were the Tactical Area of Responsibility of the 3rd Brigade of the 4th Division and were the most heavily destroyed of the prov-ince's districts. Except in four small areas, from ninety to a hundred per cent of the houses in these two districts had been destroyed, along Route 1 as well as away from it. The less heavily destroyed areas consisted of an intact stretch about four kilometres in diameter around the village of Mo Duc; a strip about seven kilometres wide extending north from the town of Duc Pho along the western side of Route 1 for about five kilometres, where about half the houses remained stand-ing; the southernmost fifteen kilometres of the coastline, where, again, about half the houses remained standing; and, finally, a region three or four kilometres long and wide around the Song Tra Kau—a small river just north of Duc Pho—and near the mountains, where about sixty per cent of the houses remained standing. As I flew over the coast of Mo Duc District, where over ninety per cent of the houses had been destroyed, I asked the pilot about the people who had lived there, and he answered, "All the personnel that were down there were pretty much V.C."

The villages had been destroyed in many ways and in a great variety of circumstances—at first by our Marines and later by our Army. In accordance with the local policy of the 3rd Marine Amphibious Force, a village could be bombed immediately and without the issuing of any warning to the villagers if American or other friendly troops or aircraft had received fire from within it. This fire might consist of a few sniper shots or of a heavy attack by the enemy. Whatever the provocation from the village, the volume of firepower brought to bear in response was so great that in almost every case the village was completely destroyed. A village could also be destroyed if intelligence reports indicated that the villagers had been supporting the Vietcong by offering them food and labor, but in such a case the official 3rd Marine Amphibious Force rules of engagement required that our Psychological Warfare Office send a plane to warn the villagers, either by dropping leaflets or by making an airborne announcement. Because it was impossible to print rapidly enough a leaflet addressed to a specific village and specifying a precise time for bombing, the Psychological Warfare people had largely abandoned leaflet drops as a method of warning, and had begun to rely almost completely on airborne announcements. There was no official ruling on when troops on the ground were permitted to burn a village, but, generally speaking, this occurred most often after fire had been received from the village, or when the province chief had given a specific order in advance for its destruction. In some cases, the villagers had been removed from an area in a big-scale operation and then the area had been systematically destroyed. By the beginning of September, there had been two large Army operations of this kind. Five thousand inhabitants of the valley of the Song Ve were made to leave their homes. In Binh Son District, along ten kilometres of coastline south of the former village of Tuyet Diem, five thousand people were "extracted." But for the most part the destruction occurred sporadically and piecemeal, without a guiding plan. Although most of the villages in the province had been destroyed, the destruction of villages in large areas was not ordinarily an objective of the military operations but was viewed as, in the words of one official, "a side effect" of hunting the enemy.

*   *   *

THE COMMONEST TACTIC of large-scale American military operations in Quang Ngai was to suddenly lift troops in on all sides of a reported enemy unit in an attempt to close a trap on it and destroy it. By the end of August, the 1st Brigade of the 101st Airborne Division had attempted three times in Quang Ngai, and also once in Quang Tin, to trap a large enemy force in this way—first in Operation Malheur I, next in Operation Malheur II, then in Operation Hood River, and, finally, in Operation Benton, this last being in Quang Tin— but in each case the trap had closed empty, and the brigade had had to measure the success of the operation by the amount of small-unit fighting it encountered, which was often considerable. In Duc Pho and Mo Duc Districts, the 3rd Brigade of the 4th Division had been fighting on a different principle. Instead of conducting large sweeps according to a detailed plan, it had been sending many company-size units into different parts of the field simultaneously and maneuvering them according to day-to-day assessments of the situation in each small area. On the briefing maps, the paths of a half-dozen units twisted, turned, and doubled back on each other. By the end of August, all the units were operating in an area where most of the villages had already been destroyed, and a great part of their effort consisted in searching for the enemy in networks of tunnels that honeycombed the area.

This area included the region in which it had been estimated that there were still some fifty-two thousand people living, and because these people used the tunnels as their dwellings, and also hid in them when air strikes, artillery fire, or ground fire alerted them to the approach of American troops, the greatest problem that the 3rd of the 4th faced in

conducting tunnel warfare was to distinguish enemy soldiers
from civilians. Furthermore, the reprisals against the villages
had impelled a number of women, old people, and children
to take up arms against our troops. Many Vietnamese of the
district threw their lives away in desperate, impossible attacks
on our troops—attacks that were apparently motivated by
pure rage. I heard one officer tell wonderingly of two old men
who had rushed a tank column carrying only rifles. "That's
when I stopped worrying about shooting the old men," he
added. A G.I. told me that he had discovered an old woman
trying—and failing—to fire a machine gun at his unit while
two small children attempted to guide the ammunition belt
into the firing chamber. In the mountain valleys, there had
been several cases of attacks with bows and arrows.

Of the civilians in general, an officer related, "We've had
tremendous difficulty in hunting them out of the tunnels. We
usually try to persuade them with loudspeaker teams to come
out, but they just won't. So sometimes we pump tear gas into
the tunnel and then blow the place up. I remember once there
were several people in the tunnel and we sent down two V.C.
defectors in front of our tunnel rat." "Tunnel rat" is a nickname given to American soldiers—usually small soldiers—who
have been chosen to enter the tunnels to search for supplies
and for the enemy. "After they had gone down about two
levels, someone in there fired on them. They came out and
we talked some more with loudspeakers, but whoever was
down there wouldn't come out. We must have blown half of
that hillside away."

After the teller of the story said this, another officer, who
had been listening, leaned over the table and said hurriedly,
"Of course, we knew that there were some hardcore V.C.
down there with those people."

The first officer continued, "Often the local V.C. will be
armed with only one hand grenade. Once, we made an announcement into a tunnel and a grenade flew out and killed
one of our soldiers. Then a kid about fourteen years old ran
out, and we shot him. The grenade was all he had. But I guess
he had completed his mission. He had killed an American."

In the *Screaming Eagle*, which relates each week's most dramatic combat stories, there appeared on August 30th an ac-

count of one of the 1st of the 101st's tunnel-warfare episodes during the period when this brigade was conducting Operation Malheur I. Under the headline "CONG YANKS CONG," it read:

In a day-long hide and seek contest, paratroopers of the 101st Airborne matched Communist resistance with American determination and won the prize—feet first. . . . Spec. 4 Donald R. Kinton, Kreole, Miss., entered the cave and the quartet began enlarging the hole in the cave floor.

Once the hole was expanded, Kinton, armed with a lighted torch, crawled into the tunnel.

He saw a VC about to pull the pin on a grenade. Kinton thrust the burning torch into his face and scrambled out of the tunnel.

The grenade was a dud.

Disgusted with the stubborn enemy, the paratroopers dropped several grenades into the tunnel opening.

When the smoke and dust cleared away, one VC crawled out of the hole and surrendered. . . .

Legari [Pfc. Vito Legari, West Islip, Long Island, New York] decided to enter the tunnel for a look around. An enemy bullet zipped by his head.

The paratroopers pulled back to map new strategy. Third Platoon joined them in suggesting tactics they hoped would force the stubborn enemy to surrender.

A Claymore [a mine that can be aimed to project steel pellets in a given direction] was set off in the tunnel opening.

The VC responded by throwing out a grenade.

Another dud.

The prisoner was sent back to the tunnel opening where he tried to talk his comrades into surrendering.

Nothing happened.

In contempt, Staff Sgt. James A. Ross, Canton, Ohio, dropped another grenade into the tunnel and brought the prisoner back again to persuade them to surrender.

One of the hesitant VC responded, bringing two weapons with him. He explained there was one Viet Cong left in the tunnel and two dead.

Apparently, the report of one remaining stubborn VC was too much for Mr. Pham Minh Cong, interpreter working with "A" Company.

In anger, Mr. Cong threw his helmet to the ground, went into the tunnel and came back dragging the last VC by his heels.

It had taken nearly all day to capture the three prisoners, but it was worth it. The platoon had captured an area VC commander, his assistant, 70 pounds of documents, more than 700 pounds of rice, a typewriter, and medical supplies.

In conversations and in the *Screaming Eagle* I found very little hatred for the enemy expressed. More often, I heard expressions of respect, especially when the enemy was compared to the Vietnamese we were supporting and working with. Nonetheless, most officers spoke of very high morale among our troops. The August 16th edition of the *Screaming Eagle* ran an article on the high morale of some veteran troops which gives a picture of an attitude that the 101st's leadership regarded as a good one for the troops to have toward their work and the war. The article reads:

Duc Pho—Three paratroopers of the 101st Airborne have the unusual distinction of serving two continuous years in the same unit under seven different commanders. Each has extended his tour of duty in Vietnam a minimum of two times.

Staff Sgt. James Howard, Detroit, Staff Sgt. Pablo Gonzales, San Antonio, and Spec. 4 Roger W. Drought, Janesville, Wis., have been with Troop A of the 2nd Sqdn. (Abn), 17th Cav. since the 101st arrived in Vietnam in July, 1965.

"We sailed over on the USNS General Leroy Eltige," said Drought. "The trip took 22 days and, as I recall, we ran out of fresh water."

The three men have been everywhere in Vietnam the 101st has been sent. They agree the stay at Tuy Hoa, one of the 25 locations occupied by the Screaming Eagles, was the best.

"Tuy Hoa was great," said Drought. "There was a nice beach, a nice town, and plenty of action in the field."

The constant moving doesn't bother them.

"It's just another day's work," said Gonzales. "I've been doing it now for 20 years."

"You get used to it," added Drought. "You even begin to look forward to the moves."

Each paratrooper has seen seven troop commanders come and go. "They've all been good commanders and we have a great unit," said Gonzales. "But then we're prejudiced, having been in it for two years."

Why do men extend tours in Vietnam? The three paratroopers each had their reasons.

"Work here is better than the spit and polish of stateside duty," said Drought. "Here you can see more results of your work."

Howard believes soldiering in Vietnam to be more realistic. "When you go on alert here," he says, "it's the real thing."

Gonzales, close to retirement, thinks Vietnam is the place for a career soldier to be. "I just felt I should finish my Army career here," he said.

The three paratroopers have seen friends leave and return.

"Right now there are guys back in the brigade who have come back," said Drought. He plans to extend again and, perhaps, again.

"I encourage a man to stay if it can benefit his career," said Howard, whose tour is up in August, but [who] is considering staying. "But then no one has ever really tried to talk me into going home," he smiled.

Most of the American soldiers I met in Vietnam supported the war effort as a whole, but I also met a number who expressed doubts. One evening in late August, at the Duc Pho base, I joined a group of four draftees who had entered a small shack to get out of a heavy rain that had continued all day and was turning the base into a sea of mud. They were engaged in a lively argument about the war. Two were deeply disturbed by the war, one was doubtful about certain aspects of it, and one supported it enthusiastically. The conversation was being carried on principally between the two men who were most deeply disturbed—Brandt and Sproul, I will call them. The man who supported the war—I will call him Dehlinger—only looked up occasionally from a pistol he was cleaning to interject a few remarks. The fourth man, whom I will call Jackson, also had comparatively little to say.

"When I got here, some of the villages were wiped out, but quite a lot were still there," said Brandt, a private from California. "Then every time I went out there were a few less, and now the whole place is wiped out as far as you can see. The G.I.s are supposed to win the people's confidence, but they weren't *taught* any of that stuff. I went through that training, and I learned how to take my weapon apart and put it back together again, and how to shoot, but no one ever told me a thing about having to *love* people who look different from us and who've got an ideological orientation that's about a hundred and eighty degrees different from us. We don't understand what they're thinking. When we got here, we landed on a different planet. In Germany and Japan, I guess there was a thread of contact, but even when a Vietnamese guy speaks perfect English *I* don't know what the hell he's talking about."

"No one has any feelings for the Vietnamese," said Sproul, a private from Texas. "They're lost. The trouble is, no one sees the Vietnamese as people. They're not people. Therefore, it doesn't matter what you do to them."

"We interrogate our prisoners in the field, and if they don't coöperate, that's it," said Brandt. "Our prisoners are usually people that we have just picked up in a hamlet that should've been cleared. But there are insufficient facilities for the people in the refugee camps, so they come back, and they're automatically considered V.C. Then we give it to 'em."

"Those V.C.s are hard to break," said Sproul. "One time, I seen a real vicious sarge tie a V.C. upside down by the feet to the runners of a chopper and drag him three thousand feet in the air, swinging out over the paddies. When he came down, hell, he was blabbering it. Another time, I seen them get a bunch of V.C.s in a chopper. They push out one first, and then tell the others that if they don't talk they go out with him. And they talk."

I asked Sproul what he was going to tell people about the war when he returned to the United States.

"Maybe when I go home I'll just crawl back inside myself, and not say a word," he answered. "Things are so violent nobody would believe it. And I don't want to die of frustration trying to convince them."

(The remark "They wouldn't believe it back home" was one that I heard almost every day in Quang Ngai, from the many who supported the war as well as from the minority who did not. While I was riding in a jeep at the Chu Lai base, the driver, who had spent time in the field, suddenly turned to me and said, "You wouldn't believe the things that go on in this war."

"What things?" I asked.

"You wouldn't believe it," he said, with finality.

"What kind of things, then?" I asked.

"You wouldn't believe it, so I'm not going to tell you," he

said, shaking his head to show his determination not to tell me. "No one's ever going to find out about some things, and after this war is over, and we've all gone home, no one is ever going to know."

I could not persuade him to elaborate.)

In response to what Sproul had said, Jackson, who was from Georgia, spoke up. "I know. I've seen all that stuff. I've seen the G.I.s out in the field get angry and beat people up—women and all—but I just turn myself off. I know it's wrong, but I just don't say anything about it."

The conversation in the shack turned to the question of whether we should be in Vietnam at all. Sproul thought we should not be. Brandt was unhappy with the war, but he was afraid that we might have to fight another war somewhere else if we didn't fight this one. Jackson thought we should drop nuclear bombs on North Vietnam, and on China, too, if necessary, rather than continue to fight what he saw as an unwinnable war in South Vietnam.

When Communist China was mentioned, Dehlinger looked up to say, "They killed a Red Chinese at Kontum."

"How do you know he was a Chinese?" Brandt asked.

"They can tell by the way they look."

"Well, how did they know he was a *Red* Chinese?"

"Any old Chinaman comes from China, doesn't he?" Dehlinger answered, and he went on to say, "I've seen about forty dinks get zapped in the field, and I can tell you that I want to get out there and pop some more dinks!" The four soldiers all laughed at this sudden resolute declaration.

A few minutes later, Brandt said, "Yesterday, I was out on a Medevac"—a Medevac is a helicopter that carries the wounded from the field to hospitals—"and three civilians had got shot up real bad. There was a little boy and two women. One of them was really messed up. She had three or four major bandages. But they were just chuckin' her onto the helicopter like cordwood. There was a strap hanging down from the ceiling of the chopper with a buckle on it, and it slapped the woman in the face as they tossed her in. Now, some G.I. could have pushed that buckle aside and *then* put her in, couldn't he? And her blanket blew off, leaving her sort of half naked. Now, you'd think that some G.I. would have put that blanket *on* again. But no. I remember once, when I was on a ski slope, I broke my leg. It was excruciating! I remember when the guy came along to take off my boot he was real careful not to cause me any more pain, and I really remember that. You really remember kindness when you're really suffering. Like if someone does something nice for you when your mother dies. That's when you really remember it. They drop those millions of leaflets, but they won't put on the blanket."

On August 19th, I flew in a "bubble," or OH-23, helicopter over the northern twenty kilometres of the coast of Duc Pho and Mo Duc Districts, and had a chance to view at first hand the areas I had seen on the Duc Pho artillery maps and had been discussing with the men of the 3rd of the 4th for the last several days. The OH-23 seats two people inside a clear-plastic bubble that affords a view in all directions except through a small steel plate underfoot and through the seat backs. The engine sits, uncovered, directly behind the bubble, and supports the long rotor blades on a metal shaft; behind the engine a thin, sticklike tail supports a small rear rotor. The machine rests on narrow metal runners. Originally, the Army had brought the OH-23 to Vietnam strictly for reconnaissance flights, but the 3rd of the 4th had converted it into a gunship by dangling an automatic weapon by a piece of wire in the open doorway on one side of the bubble. The OH-23 pilots, who were Army men, went out daily over the destroyed, but still inhabited, areas on what they called "squirrel-hunting missions," to find the enemy and either kill them with the dangling machine gun or call for artillery fire. They informed me that in the course of three months their body count had reached fifty-two, which was more than the larger Huey gunships of the 3rd of the 4th could claim for that period. "The Huey has to start its run on a target from much farther away than we do, and has to pull off sooner, and it can't fly low at all," a young pilot told me while I was talking with a group of OH-23 pilots.

I asked whether they considered everybody who remained in the destroyed areas to be one of the enemy.

"They've had a chance to get out," the pilots' commanding officer answered. "But they're not *all* V.C., I guess. Sometimes they just go back to their fields. But anyone of military age is a pretty sure bet as a V.C. It's definitely a V.C.-controlled area. We've got shot at in that area ever since we got here. A lot of times, you see a guy taking a shot at you and a woman and kid are standing right nearby. I used to hesitate to call artillery strikes on them, but I'm getting over that now."

The purpose of the flight I went on was only to convey me from the Duc Pho base to the city of Quang Ngai, but the pilot offered to take me on a detour over the areas where he and his fellow-pilots hunted the enemy. Since there was no gunner aboard, it would not be possible to fire on anyone the pilot might identify as a Vietcong soldier during our flight. We left shortly after five o'clock—about half an hour before sunset. Flying in the bubble gives one an entirely different sensation from flying in any other aircraft. In contrast to the Huey helicopter, a ten-passenger craft that takes off and lands slowly and hesitantly, like a boat leaving or approaching a pier, the bubble seems to leap effortlessly into the air, like an elevator in a modern office building. Aloft, you find that as you face forward or to either side no part of the helicopter is visible except the control panel at the front, the tiny floor, and the edge of your seat, which sticks out several inches beyond the edge of the floor. Most helicopters fly over the landscape, above the treetops and house roofs, but the bubble flies *within* the landscape—often among the trees and level with the houses, when they are not too close together. Above rice fields, it easily skims along at an altitude of six or eight feet. Flying in this tiny, agile craft, with all the machinery out of sight behind you, you feel a tremendous freedom to go wherever you please—as though you could alight on a tree branch, like a bird, or fly right in at the door of someone's house and then out through a window.

As we flew east toward the coast, I saw that the destroyed area began on the outskirts of the base. Tracks made by tanks, bulldozers, and armored personnel-carriers crisscrossed the red-earth foundations of the houses; not even the ruins were left standing. We soon passed beyond these former villages and arrived over a wide belt of rice fields lying between Route 1 and the coast. The fields were covered with craters but were still cultivated; people wearing the loose black garment of the Vietnamese peasant were bent over at work in the rows of rice. The fields were littered with scraps of paper, which covered the field divides and had sunk into the shallow water between them. The pilot explained that these were Psychological Warfare leaflets. (An average of a million leaflets were being dropped on Quang Ngai Province every day.) We crossed a tree line at the eastern edge of the rice fields and entered an area where the homes of between twenty and thirty thousand people had been loosely grouped in villages along a coastal strip that was about twenty kilometres long and four kilometres wide. The houses along this strip had been destroyed almost without exception. In the coastal area of Duc Pho District, approximately two-thirds of the houses had clay-and-bamboo walls with thatched roofs, and the rest had stone walls with red tile roofs. Where soldiers had set fire to a house on the ground, the back-yard garden and fence, the well, the hedge, the stone gateposts, and the surrounding palm glade or bamboo grove remained standing, but the house that had provided a focus for this setting, and had received the shade of the trees, was missing; only a square of ashes and debris remained on the foundation. In places where the villages had been shelled, bombed, or strafed, the destruction had not been so selective. "General-purpose" bombs had sent out hails of steel fragments and shock waves, and, near their craters, the upward force of the blasts had torn off the leafy tops of the palm trees, leaving only the trunks standing, with their shattered tips pointing at the sky. Shrapnel had cut down many trees halfway up their trunks, or lopped off their branches, or, in places, thrown whole trees fifty or a hundred yards into adjacent fields. In places where napalm had been used, the yards and fields were blackened and leafless in large splotches. Many artillery and bomb craters were partly filled with leaflets that had been carried across the fields by winds. It did not appear that the destruction had been carried out systematically. The ruins of most of the villages displayed the marks of many methods of destruction. Knowing that the artillery often simply "covered" large areas several kilometres on a side with harassment-and-interdiction fire over a period of days, I found the senseless-looking pattern of craters—dotting the open fields as well as the tree lines and the villages—more understandable. Tanks and armored personnel-carriers had cut their own roads through the landscape. Apparently, the drivers had chosen to travel through the fields rather than use the existing roads, which were likely to be mined.

The families who had returned from the camps, or had just stayed on in the area, lived underground. The dark mouths of their caves dotted the tree lines of the back yards. As we flew overhead, whole families sitting in the yards of destroyed houses tilted their heads up and froze in position to watch us out of sight. It was nearly six o'clock now, and many families were crouching around fires, cooking their dinners. Pots, bedding, and a few pieces of furniture lay out in the yards. In some places, the spindly frames of tiny huts had appeared. Everywhere there were mounds of hay about three feet high, and I later found out that these were small, wall-less individual sleeping shelters consisting of straw thatching mounted on sticks. Some people had built their straw shelters out in the center of the fields, away from trees and bunkers—perhaps because they knew that our Army, believing all bunkers and caves to have been constructed by the Vietcong as fortifications, treated them as prime military targets. Firewood, most of it beams from the destroyed houses, lay about in piles. Children played in the dust, and generally there were far more children, women, and old people in sight than men. Small boys were riding in from the fields on the backs of water buffalo. The pilot noticed artillery shells sending up puffs of whitish smoke in several spots near one edge of these fields, and took care to skirt the area by about a kilometre. The people below continued to work outside their shelters and did not show any sign of noticing the artillery shells that were exploding nearby. The pilot flew the bubble out over the rice fields, and we raced across them at a height of fifteen feet. He pointed out a few scraps of twisted metal and machinery lying in a scorched circle in one of the fields and said that his helicopter had been shot down there a month before. He and his gunner had landed without injury. Once they were on the ground, guerrillas had shot at them from a tree line, and they had fired back. Fifteen minutes later, they had been rescued by another helicopter. A minute or so after he'd pointed out the spot where he crashed, he performed one of the bubble's many aerial stunts. He raced toward the tree line and then, when it seemed that we would crash into the trees, suddenly brought the helicopter sharply upward and arrested its forward motion, so that it rolled up over the trees and house ruins and came to a stop in the air as though it had been caught head on by a blast of wind. As we floated slowly just above the half-destroyed trees, the pilot exclaimed, "Look! There's one!" In a rising tone of tense excitement, he continued, "See? See? He's hiding!" I looked down and saw a youth crouching on a path next to a line of trees. The pilot wheeled the bubble and headed it back toward the youth, who then stood up and began to chop at a log with an axe. "See? Now he's pretending to be working!" the pilot said. An instant later, he cried out, "Look! There's another. She's hiding! See how she's hiding?" I looked down and saw that as our bubble drifted in a slow arc a woman in black edged carefully around a thin tree, always keeping on the opposite side of the trunk from the bubble.

We flew inland to the other side of Route 1, where the villages had also been destroyed. Rushing low across the darkening landscape, we passed over a field of tall grass, and the pilot said, "I killed four there. They ran for a bunker, but they didn't make it." We came to a destroyed village that had stood in the shade of rows of trees. A line of smoke rose from an orange dot of flame in a thicket, and the pilot said, "There's a V.C. havin' his supper. There shouldn't be anyone down there. He shouldn't be there." We began to fly a meandering seaward course down the Song Ve, which marked the boundary between the 3rd of the 4th's Area of Responsibility and the South Vietnamese Army's Tactical Area of Responsibility. A naked boy stood washing a smaller naked boy in a broad bend of the river, which was clear, with a sandy bottom. The two froze and watched as our helicopter passed over them. The spans of two bridges lay twisted in the river. On the south bank, where the 3rd of the 4th had been operating, piles of bricks and ashes and skeletons of blackened poles stood on the foundations of houses, and the fields were brown or black, or had gone wild, but on the north bank, where the South

Vietnamese Army had been operating, the trees and fields were full and green—it might have been a different season there—and the houses remained standing, next to their vegetable gardens, yards, and palm trees. As we returned toward Route 1, we crossed over to the north bank. Smoke from supper fires rose from dark courtyards. People carrying loads on shoulder poles walked homeward down the sides of the road, and girls glided down other roads on bicycles. When the pilot set me down on a small helicopter pad within the American Advisory compound on the edge of Quang Ngai City, night had fallen. Inside the compound, all was American, and there was nothing to indicate that I had not magically been set down within the United States itself.

The buildings of the compound were of white clapboard, and neatly ordered, and the busy sound of conversation floated out of a brightly lit dining hall, where food was being served buffet style. Soldiers and civilian advisers with fresh shirts and neatly combed hair laughed and chatted as they entered an air-conditioned movie theatre. I went into the officers' bar and sat down next to a table of officers who were singing as they drank. Their voices were loud and unrestrained, and they banged their glasses on the table to keep time. The lyrics of one of the songs—a song that was apparently meant, in part, to ridicule the idea that civilians are unnecessarily killed by our air strikes, and one that I was to hear again, in many variations, during my stay in Quang Ngai—went:

> Bomb the schools and churches.
> Bomb the rice fields, too.
> Show the children in the courtyards
> What napalm can do.

*   *   *

AT THE BEGINNING of 1967, American officials in Vietnam, both military and civilian, commonly expressed the view that the "generation of refugees" was an unfortunate but unavoidable consequence of conducting effective military operations. By August, most officials were declaring that the removal of people from their original homes and villages was in itself a valuable tactic in the struggle against the National Liberation Front. Military men, in particular, were fond of quoting Mao Tse-tung's dictum that in guerrilla warfare the guerrillas are the fish and the people are the water. They argued that they could catch the fish only by drying up the water. I heard Mao Tse-tung's metaphor mentioned in this connection on at least five occasions in Quang Ngai. In an article titled "The Cause in Vietnam Is Being Won," which appeared in the issue of *The New York Times Magazine* of October 15, 1967, General Maxwell D. Taylor, former chairman of the Joint Chiefs of Staff and former United States Ambassador to South Vietnam, explains the logic of population control and, without naming the camps as such, describes the advantages to the South Vietnamese government of having from three million to four million of the country's population of roughly seventeen million in or around government-controlled camps:

As an indicator of progress in pacification, there has been an encouraging increase in Government control in rural areas in recent months. Indeed, since mid-1965, there has been an increase of some 3 million people in rural areas clearly under Government control. About 1,200,000 of this increase has occurred in the last six months. Concurrently, the Vietcong-controlled population has decreased by more than a million since 1965, the remaining Governmental gains having come from contested areas. In that year, it was estimated that 26 per cent of the total population (including the cities) was under Vietcong domination; now it is down to 14 per cent. If one includes the cities, the total population under secure Government of Vietnam control has increased from 6.6 million in mid-1965 to 10.8 million in mid-1967. . . .

Population liberated from Vietcong control is a double asset from our point of view. Not only are these people freed from the tyranny of Vietcong domination, but they are withdrawn from among the human assets so necessary to support the guerrilla movement. The Vietcong are necessarily parasitic upon the rural population from whom they drew recruits, porters, food and other forms of help. Without this rural support, the local guerrilla movement risks atrophy and progressive attrition.

I met a young American lieutenant colonel in Binh Son District who was discouraged by the current situation in the province but thought that things would improve greatly if a sweeping plan he had in mind should be put into effect. After talking for over a year with Vietnamese whose command of English was poor, the colonel had developed a very slow, careful style of enunciation and had come to employ a minimal basic vocabulary. This way of speaking had become such a habit with him that at times he used it even with Americans, especially when he was trying to elucidate difficult points. His slowness of speech was accompanied by strong emphasis on every important word and a tense, passionate gesticulation with his fists that expressed his total dedication to his work. Sometimes he would expend so much energy explaining an idea about the future of the province that he would have to slump back in his chair with a weak smile of exhaustion when he had finished.

While I was with the colonel, I heard him tell an observer from the American headquarters for Pacification in Saigon, who had come to evaluate the "potential" of the province for Revolutionary Development, which is the South Vietnamese government's response to the Vietcong's political-indoctrination program, and is usually abbreviated as revdev, or R.D., "Look, the V.C. get their people to support them. They *organize* the people. Those people are *alive*; they are highly *motivated*. But the people who are supposed to be on our side are just *blobs*." He screwed up his face in chagrin and clenched his fists in front of him. "The refugees sit around all day doing *nothing*, and *we are doing nothing about it*," he continued, coming down hard on every word. Then he outlined his plan for reconstruction. "We've got to get these people out where they can get killed," he said, then stopped himself, smiled, and added, "Don't get me wrong. I don't want them to suffer any more than they are suffering now. They've suffered too much already, but what I mean is, we've got to give them some *reason* to support the government. We have to give them some motivation to defend themselves. Now they don't have any jobs, or houses, or anything that they can get excited about, and I don't blame them for being apathetic. Look at the camps. *Anybody* would be apathetic." The first requirement for reconstruction, as he saw it, was security, and for this he envisaged a vast, superbly conducted training program for the local young men, who would learn a new self-confidence and the will to defend their villages against the National Liberation Front. Next, the villages would have to be physically rebuilt—"preferably by the villagers themselves." He said, "The Vietnamese have to do it themselves. We always try to do it for them, to give it to them. I know what a tremendous temptation it is to give candy to kids. It makes you feel good inside. You're No. 1. But for every piece of candy you give a kid, you're destroying the kid's faith in his father, who can't give him any candy. I have seen so many cases of Americans who want to play Santa Claus and feel warm all over, but this kind of thing is only corrupting, and it destroys the people's pride. If only we could learn that!" The next part of the plan involved the creation of a democratic village government, chosen by the people themselves and responsive to their aspirations. Finally, the change at the local level would be accompanied by the total abolition of corruption at the provincial level, and the beginnings of a nationwide changeover to civilian rule. In short, the colonel wanted to see a vigorous, democratic, prosperous, happy, entirely new and changed society rise from the ashes of Quang Ngai to resist the National Liberation Front because the local villagers felt a spontaneous love for their new life and a deep enthusiasm for a wholly reformed government of South Vietnam.

I pointed out to the colonel that approximately seventy per cent of the villages in the province had already been destroyed, and asked if he saw this as a serious obstacle to the realization of his plan.

"I know it," he said. "In the fifteen-kilometre stretch of coast of our area of operation there are just *two* villages still standing, and if anyone tells you there are more they are liars. One thing is that the Vietnamese can rebuild their houses very quickly, with very little trouble at all." He then patiently described to me in detail how the thatch-roofed houses that had made up about eighty per cent of the homes in the province were constructed. "The thing is, we've got to change the population patterns," he went on. "It's these widely dispersed *population patterns* that allowed the V.C. to get going in the first place. So we won't necessarily move the people back to their original villages. If we could change the population patterns, getting people consolidated into tighter areas, we could put up defenses, and the government could control them more easily. We could check them every night for I.D. cards, and in that way keep the V.C. from infiltrating."

When the colonel had concluded his remarks, the observer from Saigon said that he would like to spend a day and a night in a village of the district with his Vietnamese interpreter, to judge for himself whether conditions were ripe for a Revolutionary Development Program, and he asked the colonel to recommend a village. Clapping a hand to his forehead, the colonel laughed in dismay, and said, "You can't sleep in a village. I couldn't let you do that. We don't have any villages an *American* could spend the *night* in."

AFTER completing Operation Malheur II in the Song Ve Valley, the 1st Brigade of the 101st Airborne Division took another hop in its drive northward and launched Operation Hood River in the Song Tra Khuc Valley. The hope was to trap a large unit of the enemy by landing on the hills above the valley and sweeping down into it from all sides, but, as in the two earlier operations, the trap closed empty. Sporadic contact with the enemy was common during these sweeps, but this time it was lighter than usual. The official figure for enemy killed during the two weeks of the operation was seventy-eight, and the figure for American casualties was three killed and thirty-eight wounded. The troops, and the artillery and aircraft that supported them, did, however, destroy most of the villages in the river valley and on the coastal plain at its mouth.

In mid-August, when I first arrived at the Chu Lai base, which is situated just north of Quang Ngai Province, in the southern part of Quang Tin Province, and which was the headquarters for Task Force Oregon at that time, I was given a briefing on the composition of the enemy in Quang Ngai Province by the head Information Officer for the task force, Major Patrick H. Dionne, who is a portly man with a round face and a smile that appears, along with an outstretched hand, as soon as someone enters his office—a greeting that seems to say, "We're going to get along fine!" (Throughout my stay in Quang Ngai, I was given perfect freedom to see whatever I wanted, and was encouraged by Major Dionne and other Information Officers to fly in FAC planes and accompany operations on the ground as often as possible.)

"We're here to sell the government of South Vietnam to the people in this province," Major Dionne said. "The trouble is, they don't *want* to have the government sold to them, so what we are really doing is cramming the government down their throats. This place has been V.C. ever since the Japanese, so they've never really had any contact with the government." Picking a pink card out of a desk file for reference, he continued, "There are from seven hundred thousand to a million people in Quang Ngai. About half of these are under G.V.N. control and a quarter are V.C. supporters. We've got quite a large number of refugees in the province. They fled the V.C. or left their area because of combat, and now the G.V.N. controls them. We've got both local V.C. and N.V.A. units in the province. The 3rd N.V.A. Division is based in Duc Pho District."

I asked if these North Vietnamese Army soldiers had infiltrated into South Vietnam recently.

"Actually, these are the ones that came down in 1954 and stayed, and they organized the local people to support Hanoi," Major Dionne said. "You might say that the people are North Vietnamese–oriented—living on this side of the D.M.Z. The N.V.A. here are the old Vietminh who stayed on. They have their families down here and don't really have too much to go back to up North. Then, there's the V.C.—the local-force guy and the main-force guy. The local-force guy lives at home and is poorly armed—a squad might have two rifles and six hand grenades—but he's highly motivated, and does the political cadre work. As opposed to the N.V.A., the local V.C. is a loner—with a lot of other loners. They feel pretty sure that they are going to succeed. The main-force guy is organized in units and roves around. He's better armed."

When I spoke with American officers about the civilians who were sometimes killed in our bombings of villages judged to be hostile, they often brought up the fact that the Vietcong also mistreated and killed civilians in *their* operations.

During my month in Quang Ngai Province, two incidents of this kind figured heavily in Army press releases, in battalion newspapers, and in Psychological Warfare posters and leaflets. On August 9th, the Vietcong had attacked a village along Route 1 that was supposed to be protected by Popular Forces stationed there. The Popular Forces had fired at the Vietcong, but without venturing outside their fortified positions, and the Vietcong had destroyed a dozen houses with satchel charges and killed and wounded several villagers; they had, however, left the medical dispensary, which was financially supported by Americans, untouched. Army photographers arrived the next morning to take photographs of civilians wounded or killed in the attack. Later, these photographs were printed on propaganda posters and were also released to the press. The other incident was the discovery of two men that the Vietcong had held prisoner for several months. The August 16th edition of the *Screaming Eagle* reported the discovery as follows:

DUC PHO—"God, they were a mess," said one paratrooper. "They looked like something out of those World War II prison camps." The 101st Airborne trooper was shocked at the physical condition of two South Vietnamese soldiers liberated from a Viet Cong prison camp near here during Operation Malheur II. The prisoners were emaciated, haggard and beaten. Eyes and cheeks were sunk into their gaunt faces and their voices weak and inaudible due to lack of strength. Both suffered from malnutrition and exhaustion.

"They were in pretty bad shape," said Lt. Corky Boswell, Chico, Calif. "The VC had beaten them, used them for laborers, and fed them just enough to keep them alive. And that wasn't very much, as you can see. . . ." The two former prisoners, exhausted, and limited in their knowledge of enemy movements, were of little help. "We can't help you," said Xuan.

"We just dug tunnels. They watched us carefully all the time and never talked in front of us."

Major Dionne expressed deep disgust with the Vietcong for attacking the village on Route 1. "O.K., so maybe one of our artillery rounds goes astray and hits a friendly village every once in a while," he said. "But I don't know." Major Dionne's expression became disturbed. "With a hidden device—a V.C. mine . . . I mean, *I* get paid to wear the uniform, so if something happens to me it's not so bad. But these poor old buzzards don't get paid for that. I don't know . . ."

Every few weeks or so, the Vietcong overran another village along Route 1 that was supposed to be under the protection of the Popular Forces. In October, I asked U.S. AID officials in Washington how many village officials had been assassinated by the Vietcong in 1967 in Quang Ngai Province. When AID or any other government agency gives statistics on "village officials" killed, these may include officers of the Popular Forces and members of the Combat Youth—these are both lightly armed groups of villagers recruited to defend their own villages against the Vietcong—and Revolutionary Development workers, Civic Action cadres, interfamily chiefs, security agents, and a great variety of other types of individuals. For the period from January 1st to October 1st, AID listed a total of eighteen "village officials" as having been killed by the Vietcong in Quang Ngai. They consisted of three Revolutionary Development workers, three hamlet chiefs, two Youth Cadre members, one Civic Action cadre, four Popular Forces officers, one Combat Youth member, one chief of a rehabilitation center, one former village security agent, one village security agent, and one former interfamily chief. Usually, the Vietcong were careful to bomb only the houses of government employees, and several Americans expressed horror at the coldblooded premeditation of these assassinations. "We may have accidents," said one, "but we never set off a mine or shoot a bullet with some specific guy's name written on it in advance."

Major Dionne told me that Task Force Oregon's proudest nonmilitary achievement was the opening of Route 1 to traffic. When the task force arrived, it found that the Vietcong had blown up almost all the bridges on the road. Task Force Oregon engineers rebuilt the bridges and then opened the road to public traffic in a big ceremony, with several high-ranking officers of Task Force Oregon and the province chief present. Several times each week, American teams swept the road for Vietcong mines, finding an average of two a week. A light traffic of bicycles and motor scooters began to travel between certain towns, although other stretches were still unused.

Later on, Major Dionne told me, "When I get to wondering what this war is all about, I take a trip up to the base hospital. You know—a guy smilin' at you, saying that he's going to be up in a few weeks, when what he doesn't know is that he's lost the use of his legs and is crippled for life. And when I see what these boys are willing to sacrifice, that really makes me see what it's all about over here."

I also spoke briefly with an Intelligence captain assigned to the FAC control desk about the character of the enemy. "They have a parallel structure," he told me. "The orders originate in Hanoi and go to COSVN." He pronounced it "Cosvin" and explained that it meant the Central Office of South Vietnam.

I asked if he would tell me what he meant by a parallel structure.

"O.K., let's take a look at Communism—at North Vietnam, the U.S.S.R., and China," he said. "They all have a front organization that tells the people that the government has moral objectives that are sound. All these countries have that in common."

"What does the front organization consist of?" I asked.

"It's the fact that they have a President."

"How does this apply to the National Liberation Front?"

"I don't know precisely how the front and the real government are related, but the front is the organization that tries to tell them that Communism is a good deal."

"If there is a parallel structure, what is parallel to what?" I asked.

"The Front is one—the National Liberation Front—and the other . . . Oh, hell, I can't think of the other. Did you read Allen Dulles' book about intelligence?"

I said I hadn't.

"It's described in there. There's the apparatus that spreads Communism. But I forget what they call it here." (That night, the captain came in to tell me he had done some research and had found the name that had eluded him earlier—it was the People's Revolutionary Party.)

Conversations in Vietnam tend to become muddled because many meanings are attached to a few favorite terms, as in the above conversation, in which the Intelligence captain often failed to make it clear when we meant "front" in the sense of the National Liberation Front and when we meant it in the sense of a cover, or front, organization. Later, I was talking with the same captain about "the V.C. infrastructure," and I suddenly realized that this term, which he had used at the beginning of the conversation to mean the political or-ganization of the Vietcong at the local level, had changed as we talked to mean the wood-and-packed-mud "infrastruc-ture" of the Vietcong's tunnels and bunkers. "Parallel struc-ture" is another of the favorite terms, and it can apply to the Vietcong governmental apparatus, which "parallels" the South Vietnamese government, or to the American advisory system, which also "parallels" the South Vietnamese govern-ment, or, as in my conversation with the captain, to the "par-allel structure" of all Communist governments, including the National Liberation Front. (The word "structure" is itself a favorite in Vietnam. The military refer to all Vietnamese houses as "structures.")

AFTER completing Operation Hood River, the 1st Brigade of the 101st Airborne Division was to move north once again and launch Operation Benton, in the southern part of Quang Tin Province. I flew over the Song Tra Khuc Valley in FAC planes—assigned by the Air Force to the 1st Brigade of the 101st Airborne Division—during the last two days of Opera-tion Hood River. FAC pilots had two duties. The first was to fly over specified areas noting anything that seemed suspicious to them and choosing targets to recommend for air strikes. The targets were not further examined at first hand, and un-less they were found to be near friendly troops or in "no-strike zones" they were bombed. Some FAC pilots flew over a certain area every day for several weeks at a time, acquainting themselves with it as thoroughly as they could from the air with the aid of maps. Other pilots would be assigned to the brigade, and would fly over the brigade in all its operations, wherever it went. The FAC pilots' second duty was to guide fighter-bombers to their targets. Air Force spokesmen were always careful to stress the point that a FAC pilot could not, on his own authority, call planes to bomb a target—that the Army had to give its clearance in every case. In practice, this meant that when a FAC pilot spotted something he wished to have bombed he would radio its position to the DASC (Direct Air Support Center) office for his military corps area and enter a request for a flight of fighter-bombers. DASC would weigh the urgency of the mission against other requests made for fighter-bombers at that particular time, and decide which of the requested targets should be bombed by the limited number of planes that were aloft or "on hot pad alert," ready for immediate takeoff. The Air Force divided all air strikes into two categories, which it termed "pre-planned strikes" and "immediate strikes." A pre-planned strike was scheduled any-where from twenty-four hours to two weeks in advance of the time of the bombing, and an immediate strike was carried out within a few hours, at most, of a call from ground troops or from a FAC pilot who had spotted what he judged to be enemy activity. In conversation with a FAC pilot, I once said "planned strike" instead of "pre-planned strike," by mistake, and was swiftly corrected. When I asked what the difference between the terms "planned" and "pre-planned" was, the pilot answered, "*All* our strikes are *planned*. We *have* no *unplanned* strikes."

At the Danang airbase, I received a briefing from a major on the role of FAC pilots in I Corps. When I asked what kinds of targets were usually hit by pre-planned strikes, he answered, "In the mountains, just about anything that moves is consid-ered to be V.C. We've cleared most of the people out of there, and anything that's left has got to be V.C. No one else has got any reason to be there. We go after enemy base areas and V.C. r.-and-r. centers." The Army refers to the overnight way stations where Vietcong soldiers are believed to sleep as "r.-and-r. centers," after the Army's own practice of sending its troops for one week of "rest and relaxation" each year in a foreign capital, like Bangkok, Tokyo, or Sydney. "Most of the action is in the lowlands," the major continued. "There we hit mostly the bunkers and fortifications. The V.C. hide in there, and store their supplies in there, too. Of course, we can never hit *all* the bunkers. Also, we hit fortified villages. In some of these villages, the lines of trenches and bunkers are amazing. It looks like World War I. These fortified villages are all known to be enemy installations. I mean, they've been shooting at people and harboring the V.C. But before we hit any place we send a Psy War craft in to warn the villagers to escape. We used to drop warning leaflets, but they didn't do much good, so now we've switched over to announcing. We give the people at least a good ten or fifteen minutes to get out of there before we put in a strike. But it's the immediate strike that gives the best results. That's where you get your K.B.A.s." The initials stand for "Killed by Air." "Of course," the major added, "enemy troops in the open are the kind of target that we all like the best."

I asked him what was involved in getting clearance for an air strike.

"First, we check the area for friendly troops, and then, when the request goes in to DASC, the province chief has to give his O.K.," he said. "We *never* put in a strike without first getting permission from the province chief. He's a Viet-namese, and he knows the local conditions, so he's the man in the final analysis who knows who's friendly and who's un-friendly. And, after all, it's their country, so they ought to know what's going on." (Later, I asked Province Chief Hoang Dinh Tho, of Quang Tin Province, about the specific steps that were usually taken in securing his clearance, and learned that at the beginning of each operation in his province he designated certain regions—typically, those surrounding dis-trict capitals—as no-strike zones, and gave the ground com-manders of the operation a free hand in deciding which targets to bomb in the rest of the area of operation.)

The major explained that the Vietnam Air Force (or VNAF, pronounced "Veenaf" by the Americans) had its own organ-ization, separate from the United States Air Force but flying out of the same bases. VNAF supported ARVN with A-1 pro-peller-driven fighter-bombers—a type of plane that was last used by our Navy in the Korean war. "VNAF has its own FACS," the major told me. "They work just the way we do. One-half of the base is for VNAF and one-half for us."

I asked what VNAF FACS did, mostly.

"VNAF FACS usually cover convoys," the major replied. "They're pretty much tied up with that. But it's a very nec-essary function—to cover those convoys. VNAF uses one side of Danang. We built the facilities just the same as the Amer-ican facilities, but separate. But they don't know how to take care of something nice. You go over there now, and it's a stinking mess. You know what one of the first things they did was? They unscrewed the taps and spigots in the bathrooms and took them into town and sold them."

I asked whether American FACS guided the VNAF fighter-bombers to their targets.

"Those old A-1s that VNAF uses are a lot slower than our planes, and more accurate, so they don't use any FACS for that," the major answered.

I learned that ideas for targets of the American fighter-bombers were gathered mainly from the recommendations of ground commanders, FAC pilots, and "agent reports"—the name given to most other sources of information. Occasionally, a province chief would order a town burned or bombed. All targets were described to DASC in terms of their coördinates on a military map, and DASC would relay these coördinates to the FAC pilot who was guiding the air strike. The FAC pilot would locate the target point on a similar map that he carried with him in the plane. The maps were crosshatched by a grid. The horizontal lines, spaced two centimetres apart, were numbered from 01 to 99, and the vertical lines were similarly spaced and numbered. Each square formed by the lines represented one square kilometre on the ground. The coördinates were given in six figures divided into two groups of three—691 873, for example. The first two digits of the first group of three designated a vertical line, and the first two digits of the second group of three designated a horizontal line. The third digit of the first group indicated a distance, in hundreds of metres, east of the vertical line on the map, and the third digit of the second group indicated a distance, in hundreds of metres, north of the horizontal line. However, the hundred-metre intervals were not drawn on the map, so the pilot had to estimate for himself what one hundred, or three hundred, metres along the lines amounted to. And even if the pilot estimated accurately, the smallest area that could be designated by this system was a hundred metres square. (Everything within the hundred-metre square northeast of the coördinates 691 873 was designated by those coördinates.) On about half the missions, DASC would give the FAC pilot a description of the type of target that was to be located in the hundred-metre-square area designated by the coördinates. Some of the official descriptions, such as "bunkers," "military structures," and "enemy hamlet," referred to targets that could sometimes be spotted from the air, but other descriptions, such as "V.C. r.-and-r. area," "suspected enemy troop concentration," and "infiltration route" did not, and in these cases the pilot had to rely entirely on his coördinates. Once the pilot had found the target area on his map, he would plot its position on the ground by using as reference points prominent topographical features that showed on his map; in the mountains he would use the configurations of the ridgelines as reference points, and in the flatlands he would use rivers, roads, and villages. After finding the target on the ground, he would relay the coördinates by radio to the fighter-bombers when they came overhead. Just before the strike, he would "mark" the target by hitting it with a phosphorus rocket, which sends up a highly visible cloud of white smoke and also splashes burning phosphorus over a twenty-yard area. Then, using the smoke as a guide, the fighter-bombers would fly over the target, dropping their bombs or cans of napalm, or hitting it with rockets or strafing fire. The FAC plane meanwhile circled slowly nearby, watching the strike and telling the pilots of the fighter-bombers by radio how far from the target they were hitting. Usually, there were two or three fighter-bomber planes on a mission, and each plane flew two or three passes, depending on what armament it was carrying. When the strike was completed, the FAC pilot would fly over the area again and make a Bomb Damage Assessment Report—usually called the B.D.A. Report—to DASC and to the fighter-bomber pilots. The B.D.A. Report included the percentage of "Bombs on Target" and the percentage of "Target Destroyed." The pilot would also report any "Military Structures Destroyed." When there were friendly ground troops in the area near the target, the ground commander would radio the coördinates of their position to the FAC pilot, who would relay the information to the pilots of the fighter-bombers. The FAC pilot would make contact with the commanders of nearby artillery batteries, too, to check the trajectory of artillery shells being fired at that moment, so that he would be able to avoid them. A FAC pilot told me that one in twenty FAC pilots was killed during 1966, but he explained that he and his fellow-pilots felt less fear than many G.I.s on the ground who had a smaller chance of being hit. In the air, you didn't know when you were being shot at until a bullet came very close to the plane, or actually hit it, the pilot said, and he described a bullet passing close by as making a snapping sound, "like someone closing an ashtray in the back seat of your car." The fighter-bomber pilots made no decisions about targets themselves. A fighter-bomber pilot who was based at Danang told me, "We are going four or five hundred knots, and we can't see much ourselves. I've never seen a body or a person yet, and I've been on over a hundred missions. It's virtually impossible to see any movement on the ground. The FAC is the expert. We're only experts on delivery."

In August, there were six FAC pilots detailed to the 1st Brigade of the 101st Airborne Division. During Operations Malheur I and Malheur II, they had flown out of Duc Pho, but as the brigade moved north for Operation Hood River and Operation Benton, the FAC pilots shifted their base of operation north to Chu Lai. While the brigade was conducting an operation, the FAC pilots always kept one plane aloft over the area of operation during daylight hours. Each pilot usually flew a three-hour shift each day, though occasionally, when an emergency called for it, each would fly a six-hour shift. From August 10th to August 21st, I flew with the FAC pilots attached to the 1st of the 101st almost daily, lived with them in their quarters, and ate my meals with them on the base.

On August 10th, the next-to-last day of Operation Hood River, I flew in the early morning with a FAC pilot from Texas who had a thin face and a slight frame and was about thirty years old. I shall call him Captain Reese. The standard FAC plane was a Cessna O-1 Bird Dog. It seated two, one in front and one in back; had a single propeller; and was armed with four tubes containing phosphorus rockets, two tubes being mounted under each wing. It could fly as slowly as forty miles an hour, and could hold an extremely tight corkscrew turn when the pilot wanted to look at one small area of ground for a sustained period. Before climbing into the plane, Captain Reese picked up a flak vest, a helmet, a submachine gun, and a survival kit, the last two for use in case the plane was hit and had to make a forced landing. On the flight line, where the planes sat enclosed by steel walls to protect them from shrapnel in mortar or rocket attacks, three young mechanics lounged shirtless in the heat, waiting to refuel O-1 planes or repair their engines. Although it was against the rules, the pilots occasionally let the mechanics climb into the pilot's seat and taxi the planes across the fifty-yard stretch of asphalt between the fuel pump and the protective walls.

Just before our plane went out on the runway, one of the mechanics, who was pulling safety rods from the rocket tubes on the wings, asked Captain Reese, "You gonna get any of 'em today, Captain?"

"I dunno," answered Captain Reese.

The mechanics often asked the pilots about their missions, but they rarely got answers any more revealing than this. During most of the day, the mechanics sat on wooden boxes around a soft-drink cooler that was protected by a canvas roof, and read back issues of *Stars and Stripes*, or looked for the hundredth time through a few thumb-greased copies of *Sir!* and *Escapade* magazines. Beyond their little spot of shade stretched a landscape of hot asphalt, shimmering corrugated metal, and airplanes. Part of their job was to assemble phosphorus rockets and load them under the wings of the FAC planes. The rockets were about a yard long and came in three pieces, which the mechanics had to screw together. I once asked a mechanic who had just dumped a case of four rockets on the asphalt whether a rocket would explode if he tossed it up in the air and let it fall onto the runway. He picked up a front section, which was marked "Warhead," and, dangling it about five feet off the ground, said, "It would go off if I dropped it from here. If it gets on you, it'll burn right through you for days and it won't go out with just water. You have to put it out with a special chemical we've got over there in the shed." The mechanics did not learn about any military operation that the FAC planes supported until four or five days after it had been launched, when a copy of the Task Force Oregon mimeographed *News Sheet* might reach them, and they could read, for example, "The infantry units mounted a three-pronged attack, and in the ensuing ground action tallied 44 enemy killed, bringing the body count to 65 for the action north of Duc Pho," or "Two Chinese mines were discovered by the airborne-infantrymen as they searched for the enemy in heavy jungle west of Quang Ngai City. One detainee, suffering a bullet wound in the back, was turned over to authorities. The paratroopers captured three enemy weapons and one and one-half tons of rice." Every once in a while, one of the mechanics would get a word or two out of a FAC pilot about a current operation, and he would relay the information to the other mechanics with studied nonchalance, as though he always had an inside line on what was going on. But usually the mechanics just fuelled the planes, watched them disappear in the sky, read old magazines, and listened to the day-long thunder of bombs on the other side of the mountains.

When Captain Reese and I had strapped ourselves into our seats, a young mechanic waved us forward onto a siding of the runway. Captain Reese had to wait for an F-4 fighter-bomber to take off ahead of us. The F-4 was mottled with green and brown camouflage paint and had a heavy, sharklike body with stubby wings, downward-slanting tail fins, and a drooping black nose, which was just rising off the runway as the plane crossed our bow. For a few seconds, the deep roaring of its engine filled one's head completely, overpowering thought. In a quarter of a minute, the orange-tipped blue flames of its afterburners were vanishing in the distance as it rose at a steady steep angle.

Captain Reese taxied onto the runway, and our small plane lifted off the asphalt after running only a hundred yards or so down the runway, which was two miles long and stretched out of sight in front of us like a turnpike in a desert. As soon as the plane was off the ground, Captain Reese turned southwest and started a climb to fifteen hundred feet. According to regulations, the FAC pilots were not supposed to fly below that altitude, but almost all of them frequently broke this rule, and sometimes they went down as low as a hundred feet. ("As soon as I heard that rule, I knew that it was one of the rules made to break," a FAC pilot once said to me. "You can't even see people from one thousand feet. You can't see anything unless you go down there.") Captain Reese guided the O-1 over the brown, abandoned rice fields and blackened ruins of the villages in the western part of Son Tinh District. There was a heavy, high gray overcast.

Using a headset and a microphone wired for the back seat, I asked Captain Reese what types of target were most common and what the targets of the present mission were.

Speaking through a microphone the size of a lima bean that reached around on a small metal arm from the side of his helmet almost into his mouth, Captain Reese answered, "Oh, usually we get a V.C. base camp, burn off a village, or hit a supply depot. Today, we're going to hit a suspected enemy troop concentration at 324 733." (All figures given for coördinates in this account have been changed.)

I asked how it had been decided to bomb this target.

"I don't know. An agent reported it, or something, I guess," he said.

We crossed a small ridge of hills and came out over the Song Tra Khuc Valley. The cultivated fields were pale green, and the forests on the mountain slopes were a vivid deep green under a sky that was darkening before rain. Several miles to the west, where the valley vanished into the mountains, curved plumes of rain trailed down from the cloud cover, and to the east more plumes of rain descended into the sea. The air below the clouds seemed oddly clear, and tall, bluish mountains were visible far to the west, above the delicate ridges of nearer, smaller mountains. The line between the sea and the sky was lost in a uniform grayness, and a large blue island, clearly visible twenty or more kilometres offshore, seemed to be floating in the sky. The tops of four or five of the low mountains on the north and south sides of the valley were bald and blackened. Captain Reese explained that intensive bombing and machine-gun fire were usually directed at hilltops—often starting forest fires—in order to kill anyone there before our troops made a landing. In the valley, the cultivated fields were marked with craters of all sizes. Five or six thin, straight columns of smoke rose from the valley floor. "They're burning off some hootches. This is a solid V.C. area," Captain Reese told me. He circled lower, for a closer look. In that part of the valley, widely separated clusters of houses stood along a line of trees bordering a small stream. Troops were advancing across a rice field and entering a courtyard that was surrounded by three houses. A minute later, as they reappeared in a field on the other side of the yard, a spot of flame began to spread on the roof of one house, then on the roof of another, and soon all three roofs were collapsing in flames. Captain Reese brought the plane back to fifteen hundred feet and headed southwest again, toward his target area. Below us, the gray squares of freshly burned houses dotted the ground. Arriving over the target area, Captain Reese found that the hundred-metre square designated by the coördinates included a wooded ridge and a small ravine lying halfway up a mountain about three thousand feet high. The side of the ravine across from the ridge was lined with rows of crops stretching up the steep mountain slope.

"They want us to hit that ravine," Captain Reese said. "That's the target."

At eight-forty-five, the flight commander of three F-4 fighter-bombers radioed to say that they had arrived over the general area.

"Tell me what ordnance you've got, and all that jazz," the Captain said.

"We've got six napes, six seven-hundred-and-fifty-pounders, and six two-hundred-and-fifty pounders. Can you use it?" the flight commander answered.

"We can use all that. I'll mark the target for you," the Captain replied.

Throughout most of the strike, the pilots communicated in relaxed, genial voices and with a perfectly flat intonation, which came across the headsets with a nasal, buzzing quality, perhaps because the pilots placed their lips against the tiny microphones as they talked. Captain Reese spotted the three F-4s through the clear roof of the cockpit as they cut under the clouds above us. Wheeling his plane over the target, he went into a sharp dive, and threw a switch to fire a phosphorus rocket from a tube under his wing. The rocket did not fire. "Damn. Won't fire today," he said. He banked around again, brought the plane into another dive, and threw another switch. Once more, the rocket failed to fire. On his next pass, he dropped a smoke grenade by hand out the window, and it failed to explode. He dropped three more grenades in succeeding passes, and these, too, were duds. The fifth grenade

trailed a thin line of smoke from the plane down to the top
of the ridge, and a large puff of white smoke soon appeared
over the trees. "I want it right down in that valley. You can
come in from the east and break west," Captain Reese told
the flight commander, and then he began to fly in a tight circle
a few hundred yards from the target. As the O-1 was closing
its second full circle, he lined up the first fighter-bomber in
his front windshield, and he held it in view while it went into
a low dive over the cleft. The bombs travelled diagonally
earthward and landed on the wooded ridge. A visible shock
wave sprang outward from the point of impact, and a cloud
of brown smoke shot up several hundred feet above the
woods. The fighter-bomber pulled up at a sharp angle, presenting its belly, with the bombs grouped under its stubby
wings, to our view. "Real fine!" exclaimed the Captain.
"That's right in there! Next time, try to get it fifty metres
south, down in the valley." The next plane, diving from the
same angle, landed its bombs farther up the ridge. "That's
real fine," said the Captain. The third plane sent two silver
canisters of napalm toppling down, end over end, and they
also landed on the wooded ridge. A pillar of black smoke, with
a thick column of orange fire boiling briefly at its core, puffed
up over the trees, and red globs of burning jelly splashed outward over the jungle. The next two loads were also napalm,
and they also hit the top of the ridge. After the third napalm
strike, the flight commander asked, "Do you want it down
pretty much in the ravine?" and Captain Reese answered,
"Yes, right down there in the ravine." The next three passes
put bombs in the ravine, filling it with brown smoke. With
that, the strike was over, and the Captain flew back across the
target area. Large brown holes had been opened up in the
woods, with blasted trees lying in pieces around the edges.
Globs of napalm still burned in patches on the ground and in
tree branches. At the bottom of the ravine, two bombs had
landed directly on a tumbling stream. Above the trees, a flock
of birds flying in tight formation wheeled swiftly in circles.
One bomb had landed on the cultivated side of the ravine. "I
don't see anything," the Captain observed to me, in a tired
voice. Then, to the flight commander, he reported, "A hundred per cent of Bombs on Target. Fifty-per-cent Target

Coverage. Thank you very much, sir. I've never marked this area before, and I don't seem to mark it very well."

"Not at all," answered the flight commander. Throughout this strike, as in most of the strikes I accompanied, the FAC pilot and the flight commander addressed each other in polite, almost humble tones.

I asked the Captain who had cultivated the fields.

"That's just Montagnard farming. You'd be amazed at the places they farm," he said.

Captain Reese headed the plane back eastward over the Song Tra Khuc Valley. The line of smoking houses along the river was now a kilometre long, and led away from the river into the fields, where two flaming houses marked the troops' advance units. Since the Captain had no further need to talk with the flight commander, he listened in on fragments of conversations on the ground. Communications between ground units crackled into our ears between bursts of static.

"We've captured one Charlie, but we haven't interrogated him yet," said a voice.

"Did he have a weapon?" asked another.

"He had on the black pajamas, short type, but he didn't have a weapon," the first voice replied. "Most likely he hid it somewhere. We found him four hundred metres south of where we were last night."

To me, the Captain said, "Yesterday, five of them ran into a hole, and came out shooting, and got killed. All the villages around here have foxholes and bunkers under them. This place is almost entirely V.C.-controlled, or pro-V.C."

I asked whether the bunkers did not also serve as bomb shelters for the general populace.

"No," he said. "The V.C. build them—or force the people to build them—strictly for the V.C.'s own protection."

Below us, the lines of smoke from the burning houses had mingled to form a thin haze, which drifted eastward down the valley. DASC at Chu Lai radioed to say that the fighter-bombers assigned to the second target had been diverted to a more urgent mission and would not be coming.

"Well, we'll have to hit it tomorrow, or something," Captain Reese remarked to me.

I took advantage of the lull to ask him about the bombing

policy—that is, the policy on the bombing of villages—that he, as a FAC pilot, helped carry out.

"We've got two kinds of strikes—pre-planned and immediate," he answered. "The pre-planned strikes are when we say, 'O.K., you people have been bad now for two or three months, and we haven't been able to talk you into being good, so we're going to wipe you out. You've got twenty-four hours to get out.' Usually, we give them twenty-four hours. That's the pre-planned. Then there's the immediate strike. Now, when there's an Army unit near the village, and they get fire from the village, they say, 'O.K., you people quit shooting or we're going to hit you now—right now.' Of course, that would be in a case where almost everyone in the village is pro-V.C. Technically, the village doesn't have to be warned of a strike when we are flying in conjunction with an operation, like we are now."

While we were talking, we had reached the entrance of the valley, where the river flowed out onto the coastal plain. Here, also, smoke was rising from a roadside, and houses were aflame. The lines of smoke were spreading westward, toward the troops of the 1st Brigade of the 101st, who were moving eastward as they burned more houses. "Those guys down there burning off those hootches are Civilian Irregular Defense Forces," Captain Reese said. "They're Montagnards trained by the Special Forces."

A single main road ran the length of the valley, following the meanderings of the river. Between the villages being burned by the Civilian Irregular Defense Forces and the villages being burned by the 1st Brigade, the road was crowded with cattle and with people carrying double loads on shoulder poles. Near the road, a Special Forces camp had been dug into the bald summit of a round hill that stood alone on the valley floor, overlooking a large village where houses were jammed together inside a small fortified square. Captain Reese said he thought that the village was probably a "new-life" hamlet and would be spared destruction.

As we turned westward again, I asked him about his aerial-reconnaissance duties, and how he distinguished houses and trails used by the enemy from those used only by civilians.

"You look for changes—something that's different," he

said. "Normally, you're at fifteen hundred feet, searching for trails and tree lines, and looking for hootches. It's almost a fact that anything out in the open is friendly, so anything you see in the trees you suspect is unfriendly, because it might be V.C. We report hootches that are hidden in tree lines."

I pointed out that, except in the "new-life" hamlets, almost all the houses were built in the shade of tree lines.

"Yeah, they'll be built in the tree lines," he said. "But out in the sticks, if you spot a hootch with no fields around, it's probably V.C. Maybe a rice-storage house."

I asked who lived in the mountains.

"Just the Montagnards and a lot of Vietnamese," he said. "They've taken most of the people out of the mountains, so nobody has any business being here except the V.C. Even the Montagnards here are kind of coöperating with the V.C. We watch for trails up in the mountains, too."

I had noticed that many of the hilltops were cultivated and that most of these were laced with webs of foot trails, and I inquired about the trails.

"I'll look real close at the trails," the Captain said. "If someone walks through one, the grass gets bent."

I asked whether he could spot freshly bent grass from his airplane.

"Oh, yeah, you can tell," he said.

DASC called again, to say that a flight of two fighter-bombers had not expended all its bombs in a previous strike and had been looking for a target for the rest, so DASC had suggested Captain Reese's second target.

To get to the second target, we headed south and crossed a thousand-foot ridge into a small, high abandoned valley, where the rice fields—thickly terraced ones—had already gone wild and the house foundations were half overgrown. Four straight, mile-long avenues of craters from B-52 strikes criss-crossed the valley. The path of craters from one strike began on the ridge on the north side of the valley and marched across the fields and a stream, straight up the southern hillside, and out of sight beyond. The coördinates described a hundred-metre square in a wide stretch of woods on the southern hillside. "We're going to hit a place the troops were in a week ago," Captain Reese said. "They found some hootches and burned them off. Then, yesterday morning, a FAC pilot spotted some smoke comin' out of there. There wasn't supposed to be any smoke comin' out of there, so we're going to hit it today." Then, looking at his control panel, he exclaimed, "Hell, I forgot to pull the safety switch on the rockets! *That's* why they wouldn't fire." He went on, "You can see that they've hit this target before." He indicated scores of bomb craters and irregular splashes of brown and black from napalm strikes that scarred the woods in the target area. "It's a V.C. base area," he said. "It's got a number. All the base areas have got numbers."

The fighter-bombers for the second strike arrived over the valley and radioed that, all told, they were carrying six five-hundred-pound bombs and four tubes of rockets, with nineteen to a tube. Captain Reese brought the O-1 into a dive, and there was a sharp metallic explosion as a phosphorus rocket fired off our right wing. This was followed by the appearance of a pillar of white smoke rising from the woods. The Captain instructed the flight commander that the F-4s should land their bombs forty metres west of the smoke. Two bombs sent down in the first pass hit a hundred metres east of the smoke. The bombs sent down in the second pass landed fifty metres east, and in the third, and final, bombing pass the bombs landed within thirty metres of the white smoke. The strike continued with four volleys of rockets. Each volley spread over sixty or seventy metres of the woods, sending up puffs of brown smoke, and the rockets were all on the target or within thirty metres of it. Afterward, Captain Reese guided the O-1 into a descending tight spiral over the bomb craters to observe the damage. At the edge of one hole in the woods he saw a pile of debris that he judged to be the remains of a hut, and in his Bomb Damage Assessment Report he mentioned one "Military Structure Destroyed." At eleven o'clock, he headed our plane back to Chu Lai.

The Chu Lai base had expanded steadily since it was founded, in 1965, and by August of 1967 it was about ten miles long and five miles wide, and occupied what must be one of the world's most beautiful stretches of coastline. A wide beach of pure-white sand runs the length of the base in a gently curving crescent, and the water of the South China Sea is a bluish green, even on cloudy days. Along parts of the shore, a warm surf rolls evenly toward the beach across long sand-bars; a mountain island lies off the coast. The area occupied by the base had once been heavily populated. A three-mile-long hilly promontory forming the northern tip of the base had been the site of a dense conglomeration of fishing villages. As the base expanded, leaflets were dropped on these villages announcing that they were going to be destroyed in order to make room for the base. (In the catalogue of leaflets used by the Marines and Task Force Oregon I saw several leaflets of this kind.) The people were evacuated, the villages were bull-dozed away, and the Americans laid out their installations on the stretch of bare earth.

Upon landing, Captain Reese started back to headquarters in a jeep. The twenty-minute drive from the FAC flight line to the Task Force Oregon headquarters led through several miles of bulldozed fields of sand and dirt dotted with warehouses, munitions dumps, and repair sheds, and then ran along the beach for a mile or so. The sky was still overcast, and the beach was empty. Beer cans were strewn on the sand around simple canvas roofs on pole frames, which served as canopies for evening cook-outs. (When the sun was out, the waves were usually dotted with heads and with men riding the surf on air mattresses, and the beach was usually covered with sun-tanned soldiers in bright-colored boxer-style bathing trunks.) Beyond the beach, the road continued up a hill and out onto the rocky promontory at the northern tip of the base. At the top of the promontory, Captain Reese turned right and drove into the command complex of Task Force Oregon. In the center of a dirt parade ground that was surrounded by low, tin-roofed barracks, the American flag and the South Vietnamese flag (three horizontal red stripes on a yellow ground) flew at ex-actly the same height on two flagpoles standing side by side. Two gaily painted Buddhist shrines, each about ten feet tall and adorned with Chinese characters, also stood on the parade ground. These were the only traces of the Vietnamese villages that had once stood on the site of the base.

Captain Reese had a light lunch and then went to his quar-ters for a long nap. At just about any time of day after eleven in the morning, two or three of the six pilots could be found sprawled on their beds, asleep in the breeze of an electric fan. The pilots took turns standing by at a central control desk, which was in one of the barracks on the parade ground. It was in constant communication with DASC and with the FAC pilot who was aloft. Although the FAC pilots almost never flew after dark, one of their number helped supervise, from the central control desk, any bombings carried out at night, and coördinated night flights of AC-47s (this was the military version of the DC-3, and was nicknamed Spooky) that supported troops on the ground with heavy fire. On nights when the fighting on the ground was particularly intense, a pilot would have to stay up all night at the control desk and sleep the next day.

Except when the FAC pilots were flying missions, they lived entirely within the confines of their base. It would have been perfectly possible for any one of them to pass his entire one-year tour of duty in Vietnam without ever talking to a Vietnamese or setting foot inside a Vietnamese village or city other than Saigon. Except for their r.-and-r. trips to foreign cities, and occasional expeditions in the FAC planes to the Danang airbase to buy beer and soft drinks, on what they called "the soda-pop run," the pilots' daily lives revolved solely around their missions, their quarters, the central control desk, and the dining halls, bars, and movie theatres in the officers' clubs. The FAC pilots' quarters, which they called the Hootch, con-sisted of one of the several rows of tin-roofed barracks, which had mosquito netting serving as the upper half of the walls. The barracks was partitioned into three rooms, containing four beds each, and the beds were separated by tall metal clothes cabinets. Most of the pilots had decorated their walls with *Playboy* Playmates of the Month. On the wall next to one major's bed, Miss May of 1967, who is shown standing on a sun deck with her pink shirt open, dwarfed a dozen small snapshots of the major's wife, in one of which she was stand-ing, arms akimbo, in a bathing suit on a beach, and of his eight-year-old son, shown standing beside a lake and holding a small fish up to the camera. On the major's desk were a can of spray insecticide, a Reader's Digest volume of condensed books (featuring President Eisenhower's book "At Ease," which is subtitled "Stories I Tell to Friends"), a can of Pepsi-Cola, a softball, a dozen loose bullets, and a life-size wooden carving of a fist with the middle finger upraised. The Vietnamese do not use the gesture of raising the middle finger, and this kind of sculpture had been developed especially for American soldiers looking for souvenirs of Vietnam. Sometimes the younger pilots played darts on a board that hung on one door, and they also occasionally played Monopoly. A refrigerator was kept stocked with beer and soft drinks. Because of the heat, most of the pilots had at least two beers or soft drinks a day. Each was on his honor to put fifteen cents in a common refreshment fund in a box in the back of the refrigerator every time he took a drink, but someone who, it seemed, had not been wholly able to put his trust in an honor system had halfheartedly attempted to revise it by taping to the front of the refrigerator door a sheet of paper with everyone's name on it, on which each person was supposed to mark down the number of drinks he had taken and the number he had paid for.

Around the central control desk, and in other places where the pilots gathered, an atmosphere of perpetual low-keyed, comradely humor prevailed. There was a steady stream of light remarks. One man who was standing idly around said to another, with weary joviality, "It's a beautiful, beautiful war!" The second man said, "It's the only one we've got." A FAC pilot entered a room full of FAC pilots and said, "Here are our hard-working FAC pilots," in a tone that indicated neither that they were hard-working nor that they weren't. In this way, the FAC pilots rarely talked about the war directly, and yet never quite got away from the subject, either. The relaxed style of their humor was, I thought, caught quite precisely in their choice as their squadron's emblem of Charles Schulz's comic-strip dog Snoopy, who daydreams of fame as a First World War flying ace. On the outside of the door of the central-control-desk office, Snoopy was depicted, in a sketch, wearing goggles and a scarf that trailed out behind him as he went into a dive in a First World War Sopwith Camel biplane. Cartoon bombs exploded below him. (On a wall of the Duc Pho central-control-desk office, there was a large painting of Snoopy accompanied by a speech balloon that had him saying

"Curse you, Charlie Cong!" The Task Force Oregon *News Sheet* reproduced one episode about Snoopy in each of its issues, and the pilots of the 20th Tactical Air Support Squadron in Danang carried calling cards that depicted Snoopy in his biplane firing a machine gun. On a wall of the squadron's office was a large color poster that bore a reproduction of a painting of an American pilot walking sadly through a prisoner-of-war camp. A vow not to give the enemy any information that was not required by international law was printed below the picture. The pilots, who flew regularly over North Vietnam, had pencilled a beard and mustache on the grave, pious, spotlighted face of the captured American.)

At the Chu Lai officers' club for Task Force Oregon, drinks were twenty cents each, and the pilots usually had three or four rounds each evening before supper. One pilot observed, "At these prices, you can't afford *not* to drink." On the evening of August 10th, the FAC pilots drove to the Marine dining hall, which was a favorite of theirs among the base's many dining halls. Ham, chops, steak, and chicken were served there. They were all prepared in the dependably appetizing style of an excellent truckers' diner on a big American highway, and you could have as much as you could eat. Some Korean officers sat grouped together at several tables. Most of them were enjoying the Korean version of r. and r.—a visit to an American base like Chu Lai, where they were allowed to eat in the American mess halls, shop in the American PX, and swim on the safe stretch of beach occupied by the base. Conversation at dinner usually revolved around matters having to do with the flying life. Often, the pilots discussed the day's events, sometimes criticizing or praising the accuracy of certain missions of fighter-bombers. They stuck fairly closely to day-to-day events and to the technical problems of bombing missions, such as what altitude is best to bomb from and how to tell if a bomb is "hung" on the wing after the bomb release has been triggered. This evening, they discussed an incident in which a pilot had spotted a man on the ground, had judged him to be a Vietcong soldier when he attempted to escape observation by running into a grove of trees, and had called in planes to bomb the trees. This incident, which in itself was quite ordinary, had one unusual aspect: the

FAC pilot had been flying outside his assigned area, and the bombs had only just missed some American troops nearby.

Another pilot said that he, too, had spotted a Vietcong soldier and had later guided an air strike onto the woods the man had disappeared into.

I asked him how he had been able to tell that the man was a Vietcong soldier.

"Well, he walked real proud, with a kind of bounce in his gait, like a soldier, instead of just shuffling along, like the farmers do," the pilot answered.

During my stay with the FAC pilots, they never discussed the progress of the war as a whole, nor did they ever express any hatred for the enemy. They talked a lot about pensions and salaries, they complained about the administrative sloppiness of the promotion procedures, and they discussed the advantages of various cities for r.-and-r. tours (Thai women had good figures; Hong Kong had good cheap clothes, hi-fi equipment, and cameras). The pilots laughed when they read in the *News Sheet* that lectures on venereal diseases, and how to tell if you had any of them, were going to be given to the men just before they went on r.-and-r. tours. The armed services displayed a completely tolerant attitude toward the soldiers' patronage of brothels in Vietnam and in the Asian cities used for r.-and-r. tours. In Hong Kong, until very recently, the Army employed a prostitute of mixed Chinese and Portuguese parentage, who spoke understandable English, to brief the soldiers on how to pick up prostitutes among the city's bar girls without getting into fights or getting fleeced. The briefing was intended to minimize the ugly incidents that occur when a soldier is overcharged or misunderstands a girl's intentions. The pilots talked a great deal about the living conditions and the food on other bases. Once, at dinner, Captain Reese got into a long discussion about food with another pilot, and as he ate a plateful of ham, he gave a detailed description of a chicken dinner he had eaten at the Duc Pho base. Then, beginning on a piece of cake, he described to me the breakfast at the Marine dining hall in which he was eating at that moment. "They have terrific breakfasts here," he said. "Every day, they have eggs, bacon, pancakes with butter and

maple syrup, toast, milk, raspberry jam, grapefruit juice, coffee, and tea—the works. Real fine breakfast."

Although the pilots never spoke angrily of the Vietcong,
they often spoke disparagingly of the Army, compared to the
Air Force; they called Army men "grunts." Their feeling
about the Army seemed very much like one ball club's or
college fraternity's feeling about a rival, but occasionally they
expressed a bitterness that went beyond such friendly rivalry.
One pilot told me, "The Army guys sometimes don't care
what you have to do, so long as they get an air strike. But
I'm not going to send men on an impossible mission to get
killed like that. I'm responsible to the Air Force, too, and I've
got to think of Air Force safety. Sometimes it's kind of hard,
because you have to look a general in the eye and say, 'No,
sir, I can't do that.'" I was surprised at the intensity of the
rivalry not only between the services but between units in the
same service. The men of the 1st Brigade of the 101st Airborne,
who were extremely proud of their paratrooper training, referred contemptuously to all infantrymen as "legs." Once,
when I was driving inside the Chu Lai base on a cruelly hot
afternoon with a paratrooper of the 101st, he refused to pick
up a hitchhiking soldier, on the ground that the soldier was
a "leg," and "no leg is worth picking up." High officers of
the 101st and the 3rd of the 4th maligned each other, in my
presence, by claiming that the other brigade's body count was
falsified. "The 3rd of the 4th count the probables in their body
count," an officer of the 101st told me. "We don't deal with
probables. We only deal with confirmed kills counted by sight.
That's the only way." On another occasion, an officer of the
3rd of the 4th made the same charge about the 101st, and
added that the 101st's "weapons-kill ratio" was much worse
than the 3rd of the 4th's, the implication being that the 101st
was far less discriminating than the 3rd of the 4th when it
came to deciding whom to kill. Men of both the Army and
the Air Force made derogatory remarks about the Marines.
One soldier of the 101st told me that the Marines were "no
different from the Vietcong" in their handling of prisoners. I
asked if he meant that they beat the prisoners. "Hell, *we* work
'em over before we talk to 'em," the soldier said. "The Marines are a lot worse than that. They're just like the V.C."

After dinner that evening, the pilots had a choice of two movies, one at an outdoor theatre on the beach near the Marine dining hall and the other up at the Task Force Oregon officers' club. The officers' club stood on the crest of a five-hundred-foot hill, overlooking a brushy meadow that swept down to the sea. A number of tables with chairs were arranged in a large, three-walled room under a broad, barnlike palm-leaf roof; the front was open to the ocean. In back, there was a long bar with a television set at one end, swivelling barstools, a dart board, and bartenders who wore gaudy Hawaiian shirts. Movies were shown in front. The club commanded a view of the entire twenty-kilometre crescent of beach. Even on the hottest, stillest day, a fresh breeze blew in off the water. At night, out on the ocean, the lamps that all local fishing boats were required to keep burning after dark glowed from miles away. On most evenings, the booming of artillery and bombing sounded steadily, sometimes lighting up the night sky down the coast. During some operations, flares, which are fired by artillery or dropped from planes, and descend slowly on parachutes, seemed to be hanging over the mountains throughout the night. Two hundred yards from the club, the helicopter landing pad for the base hospital sat on a high ridge, from which there was a sharp drop to the sea. Several times each day, a helicopter would fly up the coast at full speed and settle rapidly onto the asphalt, which was in full view of the front of the officers' club and looked from there like a small black stage. Two figures would run up to the helicopter and then run back to the hospital, bearing a man on a stretcher. If the cloth over the man covered him only up to his shoulders, the man was wounded, but if the cloth covered his face the man had died. Inside the club, the hospital landing pad was visible only from a few front tables, and most of the officers did not notice when a helicopter arrived, but when the officers were standing in front of the club at their weekly outdoor barbecue, tending their steaks in the charcoal pits, the arrival of a helicopter at the hospital caused a brief slackening in the din of conversation as the officers looked up from their drinks and steaks to watch the two figures bearing a wounded or dead man into the hospital.

Once every few weeks, on nights that did not precede mil-

itary operations or important pre-planned strikes, some of the
FAC pilots, I was told, would get together to get drunk. One
evening, Captain Reese and two other pilots, whom I will call
Major Nugent and Captain Leroy, returned to the FAC pilots'
quarters from the officers' club talking in booming voices and
laughing loudly at everything any of them said. Major Nugent
had apparently half-seriously yielded to an Army officer's urging that he enter airborne training school, and Captain Reese
was snickering and teasing him about it. "Why would anyone
want to jump out of a perfectly good airplane? You must be
out of your gourd!" he exclaimed seven or eight times, provoking a more uproarious laugh with each repetition. His idea
that you should stay in an airplane until it was shot down
reflected his loyalty to the Air Force and his contempt for
paratroopers. About midnight, when Captain Leroy was on
his way to bed, he tripped over someone's box of gear and
fell on the floor. Later that night, an unidentified person threw
a glass of water on another pilot as he slept.

* * *

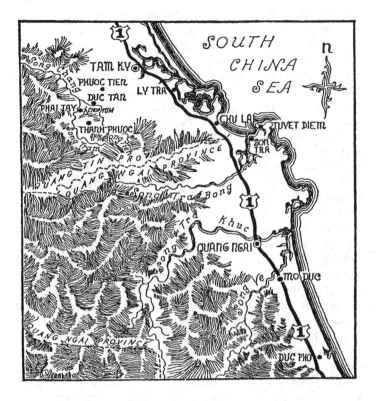

ON AUGUST 13, 1967, two days after Operation Hood River
came to an end, Task Force Oregon launched Operation Benton. In Quang Ngai Province I had seen the results of the
American bombing, shelling, and ground activity but, for the
most part, I had not seen the destruction take place. Now I
was about to observe in detail the process of destruction as it
unfolded in Operation Benton, in which Task Force Oregon
went over the northern border of Quang Ngai into Quang
Tin Province. I spent several days flying in FAC planes attached
to the 1st Brigade of the 101st Airborne. On August 12th, I
flew over the area where Operation Benton was to be carried
out. This was a three-hour reconnaissance mission, with a
pilot whom I will call Major Ingersol. Major Ingersol was a few
years older than the other pilots, and he was more reserved.

At the FAC pilots' quarters on the base at Chu Lai, he often read paperback mysteries or other novels while the rest of the pilots joked together. When he did enter into the conversation, he ordinarily spoke in serious, measured tones, which did not quite fit in with the usual light banter. Once, when the other pilots were sitting around drinking and discussing the figures of Thai bar girls, his contribution to the conversation was "I've heard that there are some exquisite restaurants in Bangkok." Another time, while chatting with a captain in the FAC central control room, he expressed a keen appreciation of the natural beauty of Quang Ngai. "It's a lovely countryside," he said. "One of my favorite activities is following waterfalls up through the valleys. It's a shame we have to destroy it."

While Major Ingersol and I were flying to the area of the new operation, he described to me his method of distinguishing Vietcong soldiers from the rest of the population. "You know that they are V.C.s if they shoot at you or if you see them carrying a weapon. Those are about the only two ways," he said. In the matter of trails through the woods, he had subtler criteria. As we passed over the flank of a tall mountain, he pointed out a trail, almost as wide as a small road, that ran up the mountainside from the valley. The trees were tall and dense, and the path was visible as an occasional gap in the jungle foliage. About halfway up the mountain, this large, clearly distinguishable trail began to get narrower. For a stretch, it apparently continued under the dense foliage, because farther up the mountain it became visible once again, but then it was lost to sight altogether. "This is the kind of thing we look for," Major Ingersol said. "See how that trail disappears up there? That indicates to us that there is probably a base camp up there. These trails that go up into the mountains and disappear are often V.C. trails. Also, we look to see if the trails have been freshly used."

I remarked that from fifteen hundred feet it must be very difficult to tell whether a trail that was mostly covered by dense jungle foliage had been used recently.

"Even then you can tell," Major Ingersol said. "You see, the V.C. use water buffalo and other large animals to carry their equipment around, and they leave marks. These trails often get hit by artillery fire at night." As we flew over a thirty-foot-wide crater that had eliminated one section of a footpath, Major Ingersol commented, "Now look down there. See how someone has built the trail *around* the crater? This is the kind of sign you look for." He said that he also looked for bunkers to recommend as bombing targets. And, as still another example of the kind of suspicious sign he looked for on his reconnaissance missions, he told me that in one small field high in the mountains there was a small herd of water buffalo that disappeared from sight every few days. "We speculate that the V.C. use those water buffalo to carry things," he said.

Major Ingersol spent most of his three hours flying over a maze of little hills and valleys, for these were to be the scene of Operation Benton. The area of operation was a rectangle of about ten by twenty kilometres lying southwest of Phuoc Tien, a town in the southern part of Quang Tin Province. The 1st Brigade of the 101st was to launch the operation the next morning in an area ten kilometres on a side, and two days later some units of the 196th were to be lifted into an area of equal size to the east. I had decided that, within the area of operation, I would concentrate my attention on a somewhat smaller area, clearly discernible both on aviation maps and on the ground, and observe it from FAC planes on as many of the first few days of Operation Benton as I could, in order to see how bombings were carried out during a large military operation. Just southwest of Phuoc Tien, which lies in a valley of rice fields surrounded by foothills, two small rivers—the Song Tien and the Song Tram—join to form a single stream, called the Song Chang. (The Vietnamese word *"song"* means "river.") Within the fork of the rivers stands a small mountain, about a thousand feet high, called Chop Vum, and around its base there were at that time a number of villages and scattered houses. To the south of Chop Vum, a narrow dirt road ran east and west through thickly settled fields. I decided to observe an area six kilometres square surrounding Chop Vum, and henceforth I will refer to this as the Chop Vum area. It was bordered, roughly, on the east by the Song Tien, on the west by the Song Tram, on the south by the road, and on the north by the Song Tien again, for this river bends sharply to the west after flowing north for about six kilometres. Between Chop Vum and these boundaries, just beyond which rose an encircling range of two- to three-thousand-foot mountains, spread a landscape of tiny forested hills, seldom more than fifty feet high, standing like chains of islands in a sea of small terraced rice fields. A few of the knolls and knobs were smooth-topped and rolling, but most of them were very steep, and rose abruptly from the rice fields, like miniature models of the mountains surrounding them. Most of the houses were not in villages but stood scattered among the fields. Wherever the land was only gently inclined, it had been terraced and planted with crops. Along the sharp ridge of one small hill, a footpath ran to a small pocket of flat land near the top. In this pocket, farmers had planted rice and built several houses that commanded a view of most of the valley and the mountains beyond. Nearly all the houses near Chop Vum had front yards where chickens and ducks could run about, vegetable gardens in back, and a ring of hedges and trees around house, yard, and garden. One species of palm tree, which had a single crown of leaves and grew to be fifty or sixty feet high, was particularly common in the gardens. Small, winding paths ran from house to house on top of the field divides and up and around the knobby hills, and every crevice or fold in the skirts of the mountains seemed to have a house tucked in it. The arrangement of the houses allowed a dense population to live separate lives with considerable privacy. In only a few places were as many as fifty or sixty houses grouped together to form villages, and even in these places the houses were not lined up side by side on streets but were separated by yards and by groves of bamboos and palms. The layout of the villages conformed to the bumps and hollows of the landscape, instead of dominating it with a symmetrical design. The village houses were linked by paths, and these paths led, ultimately, into an indistinct, curving main path that ran near all the houses. The village of Phai Tay stood at the base of Chop Vum, within the fork of the Song Tram and the Song Tien; the village of Duc Tan stood on the north bank of the Song Tien about two kilometres northeast of Phai Tay; and the village of Thanh Phuoc was sprawled along both sides of the road that formed the southern boundary of the area. In Thanh Phuoc, two stone churches stood within fifty yards of each other on opposite sides of the road. Each of them was about three stories high and seventy feet long, was faced with intricately carved stucco, and had a cross on the roof.

The afternoon I flew over this landscape with Major Ingersol, several herds of water buffalo were wallowing in the clear water of the rivers. There were people bent over at work in the water of the rice fields, and in the yards. The area had been heavily battered at some earlier date, and gray and red squares of what had once been houses dotted the landscape. Roughly one house in twenty had been destroyed. Many fields were totally taken up by craters, and the forest on the hillsides was blackened and pockmarked. On two adjacent knolls, perhaps a hundred feet high and five hundred feet wide at their bases, the woods had been almost entirely destroyed by bombs that had left overlapping craters. Each type of terrain —the mountains, the fields, and the yards of the houses— seemed to have received the same amount of bombing, as though the fighter-bomber pilots' intent had been to cover with equal quantities of explosives the areas marked out by the squares on their maps. Smaller craters, from artillery fire, spotted the fields and yards but were not large enough to show up in the thick forest. Many of the artillery craters were yellow and fresh, but all the bomb craters were partly overgrown with bushes and vines, and so must have been at least several months old.

I asked Major Ingersol when these bombings had occurred, and he answered, "Well, only the Marines were operating around here before Task Force Oregon arrived, but I don't think they got up this far. But it looks like they did. I don't know. It looks like it happened quite a long time ago, anyway."

Having surveyed the future area of operation, Major Ingersol flew south across several ridges of mountains toward the Song Tra Khuc Valley, in northern Quang Ngai Province. On the way, he indulged in his favorite pastime of viewing waterfalls. "You can see that FAC-ing *can* be pretty boring, especially on these strictly V.R. missions," he said. "V.R." stands for "visual reconnaissance." "I'll show you some of the waterfalls up here. They're just beautiful. This is some of the most beautiful mountain countryside I have ever seen." Before we came to a waterfall, he would describe it to me in detail from memory, telling me whether or not it had a pool at the bottom, whether it cascaded over a cliff or flowed down the rocks, and how many tiers it had. One of his favorite waterfalls—a long, cascading one with a large, clear pool in a rock bed at the base—had been bombed since he last saw it; he pointed out a crater on its lip.

By the time we started back to Chu Lai, it was late afternoon, and the sun was large and red beyond the dark mountain ridges. Over the plane's radio, a voice from somewhere said, "Hey, we're having a party over in D 19 tonight, with lots of free booze. Come on over."

Another voice answered, "I'll make it if I can, but I don't know if I'll be able to get over tonight. Thanks a lot."

*   *   *

On the morning of the third day of Operation Benton, I flew over the 1st of the 101st's area of operation with Major Billings, whom I had flown with during Operation Hood River. I saw that, except for two or three houses, the village of Duc Tan, which had stood below the evacuated command post, had been destroyed. Some groups of houses in Duc Tan had been completely annihilated by bombs; the only traces of their former existence were their wells or back gardens. Other houses had been burned to the ground by napalm. Most of the fields around the destroyed village had been eliminated by the deep craters of delayed-fuse bombs or else had been covered with debris. More craters were scattered across other fields in the Chop Vum area and across mountainsides, and the gray squares of freshly burned individual houses dotted most of the landscape. Major Billings told me that these houses had been burned by phosphorus rockets fired from helicopter "gunship" patrols. A few minutes later, I watched a gunship cruise low over the landscape. It wheeled suddenly and fired several phosphorus rockets into a group of three houses that stood in a clump of palms. White smoke puffed up, and the houses burst into flames. The helicopter circled and then charged the houses again, firing more rockets into the fields and gardens. Several hilltops and small mountains that had been green and wooded when I saw them three days earlier were burned black by napalm. Fresh artillery craters were spattered over the fields around the landing zones. At that point, approximately twenty per cent of the houses in the Chop Vum area had been destroyed.

Major Billings had been assigned to guide a "preplanned strike," but before he could locate the target on the ground a ground commander called for an "immediate" strike, which meant a strike carried out a few hours, at most, after it was requested, whether by a ground commander or by a FAC pilot. "We picked up some sniper fire earlier this morning from a couple of hootches down below us, at about 384 297, and we'd like you to hit it for us," the ground commander said. Major Billings flew over the hundred-metre square described by the coördinates, and found that it included the two large stone churches along the road, in the village of Thanh Phuoc. The ground commander was in charge of a hilltop landing zone that was a little over half a kilometre from the churches. When he had received the sniper fire, he had apparently scanned the horizon, noticed the two church steeples, which were the only buildings that stuck up above the lines of trees, and decided that the snipers were firing from the churches. In front of one church, a white flag flew from the top of a pole as high as the church itself.

"Let's have a look and see what's down there," said Major Billings. He took our plane on a low pass over the churches. The churches were surrounded by twenty or thirty houses. About half of these had stone walls and red tile roofs. The others had clay-and-bamboo walls and thatched roofs. One thatch-roofed building was perhaps fifty feet long and thirty feet wide, and appeared to be some sort of gathering place. Flower gardens were in bloom in front of both churches. Behind both, plots of vegetables stretched back through glades of palm trees to rice fields. After climbing to fifteen hundred feet again, Major Billings got into contact with the ground commander and said, "Two of those structures seem to be structures of worship. Do you want them taken out?"

"Roger," the ground commander replied.

"There seems to be a white flag out front there," Major Billings said.

"Yeah. Beats me what it means," the ground commander replied.

An hour later, three F-4 fighter-bombers reached the target area, and the flight commander radioed to Major Billings—who had spent the time trying to spot suspicious activities—to say that they were prepared to strike with seven-hundred-and-fifty-pound bombs, rockets, and 20 mm.-cannon strafing fire.

"We can use all that good stuff," said Major Billings.

"What kind of a target is it?" asked the flight commander.

"They're military structures. You can tell by how they look that they're military structures," Major Billings answered. Just then a fleet of ten helicopters moving in tight formation arrived at the hilltop landing zone. Major Billings went on to say that he would have to wait until the helicopters left before he gave clearance to bomb.

I asked him whether he thought it was necessary to bomb the churches.

"Well, if the V.C. don't care and just go in there and use the place to fire on our troops, then we've got to wipe it out," Major Billings said. "And the V.C.—the V.C. are *the first ones to blow up a church*. They go after the churches on purpose, because the churches won't always go along with what the V.C. are doing. *They* don't care at all about blowing up a church and killing innocent civilians."

As the helicopters rose from the hilltop, Major Billings said to the flight commander, "Believe it or not, two of those big buildings down there are churches. I'll check with the ground commander again to see if he wants them taken out."

"No kidding!" said the flight commander.

"Say, do you want those two churches hit down there?" Major Billings asked the ground commander.

"That's affirmative," the ground commander replied.

"O.K., here goes," said the Major. Then, addressing the F-4 pilots, he said, "Make your passes from south to north. I'll circle over here to the west."

The Major brought the O-1 into a dive, aiming its nose at

the village, and fired a phosphorus rocket. Its white smoke rose from a patch of trees fifty yards to the south of one church. "Do you see my smoke?" he asked the flight commander.

"Yeah, I got you," the flight commander said. "I'll make a dry run and then come in with the seven-hundred-and-fifty-pounders."

A minute later, an F-4 appeared from the south, diving low over the churches in a practice run. As it pulled out of its dive, it cut eastward and began to circle back for the next pass. A second F-4 made its dive in the same way, and released its bombs. A tall cloud of brown smoke rolled up from the vegetable garden in back of one of the churches.

"That's about a hundred metres off," Major Billings said. "See if you can move it forward."

"O.K. Sorry," the flight commander said.

The third plane also sent its bombs into the vegetable garden. The first plane, on its second pass, sent its bombs into rice fields about sixty yards to one side of the churches. Three pillars of brown smoke now rose several hundred feet in the air, dwarfing the churches and the houses. On the second plane's second pass, a bomb hit the back of one church directly—the church with the white flag on the pole in front.

"Oh, that's nice, baby, real nice," Major Billings said. "You're layin' those goodies right in there!"

When the smoke cleared, the church was gone except for its façade, which stood by itself, with its cross on top. The white flag still flew from its pole. The third plane sent its bombs into the rice fields to the side. The first plane fired rockets on its third pass, and they landed in the vegetable garden behind the destroyed church, leaving it smoking with dozens of small brown puffs. Several of the rockets from the next volley hit the other church, obliterating its back half and leaving two holes the size of doors in the roof of the front half. Four or five of the houses around the church burst into flame.

"That's real fine!" said Major Billings.

"Where do you want the twenty mike-mike?" asked the flight commander. ("Twenty mike-mike" is military slang for 20-mm.-cannon strafing fire, which fires a hundred explosive shells per second.)

"Lay it right down that line you've been hitting," Major Billings said. "Put it right down across those hootches, and we'll see if we can start a few fires." (Strafing rounds often set houses on fire, whereas bombs rarely do.)

As one of the F-4s made the first strafing run, the path of fire cut directly through the group of houses around the churches, sparkling for a fraction of a second with hundreds of brilliant flashes.

"Goody, goody! That's right down the line!" exclaimed Major Billings. "Why don't you just get those hootches by the other church, across the road, now?"

"Roger," answered the flight commander.

On the second strafing pass, the flashing path of shells cut across the group of houses on the other side of the road.

"Real fine!" Major Billings said. "Now how about getting that hootch down the road a bit?" He was referring to a tile-roofed house that stood in a field about a hundred yards to the west of one church. The path of fire from the third strafing pass—the final pass of the strike—cut directly across the house, opening several large holes in its roof.

"Right down the line!" Major Billings said. "Thanks, boys. You did a real fine job. I'm going to give you ninety-per-cent Target Coverage."

"Did I get any K.B.A.s?" the flight commander asked. (The number of killings credited to each pilot is not kept as an official statistic, but most pilots try to keep track of their K.B.A.s informally.)

Major Billings, who told me he had not seen any people in the area, either before or during the strike, answered, "I don't know—you'll have to wait until ground troops go in there sometime. But I'd say there were about four."

As the two men were talking, perhaps a dozen houses in the strafed area began to burn. First, the flames ate holes in the roofs, and then they quickly spread to the walls, turning each house into a ball of flame. Most of the houses burned to the ground within a few minutes, leaving columns of black smoke rising from the ruins.

Major Billings called Chu Lai to give his Bomb Damage Assessment Report. "There were two Permanent Military

Structures Destroyed, ten Military Structures Destroyed, and five Damaged," he said.

I asked him whether he considered the houses and the churches military structures.

"Oh, that's just what we call them," he replied.

A few minutes later, the ground commander on the hilltop got in touch with Major Billings to request another immediate strike. "There's a row of bunkers down below our hill here, along a tree line, and we've seen the V.C.s down there," the ground commander said. "We see their heads poppin' in and out. We'd like to get an air strike put in down there."

Major Billings flew over the spot the ground commander had indicated, and found a line of trees about half a kilometre from the hill. The dark openings of several bunkers showed on the near side, and a row of several houses was standing on the far side.

"I've got you," Major Billings said. "Do you want us to put 'em in along that tree line down there? There are a couple of hootches down there, too."

"Affirmative. We've been getting trouble from that whole general area down there."

"O.K.," said Major Billings wearily, pronouncing the first syllable long and high, and the second low. "We'll do that as soon as the fighters come in."

Three F-4s arrived in the area twenty minutes later, and the flight commander announced that they were carrying napalm and thousand-pound bombs, which are the largest normally used in South Vietnam.

The first bombs of the strike landed about a hundred metres off target. One bomb turned an entire rice field into a crater about thirty-five feet across and six feet deep, and splashed mud over the surrounding fields. The next two bombs annihilated two houses with direct hits. Two more bombs landed next to the tree line, breaking most of the trees in half and hurling one palm tree fifty or sixty metres into a field.

"O.K., you got that tree line real good," Major Billings said. "Now let's get some of those hootches to the south of it with the napes." He directed the pilots to a group of a dozen houses that stood about forty yards from the tree line. The first canister landed beside two houses, which were instantly engulfed in napalm. When the smoke cleared, only the broken, blackened frames of the houses remained in the intense blaze, which continued after the houses were burned to the ground, because the napalm itself had not yet finished burning.

"Beautiful!" cried Major Billings. "You guys are right on target today!"

The next canister did not land directly on any of the houses, but it landed close enough to splash napalm over four of them, and these houses immediately burned down.

With the strike completed, Major Billings told the fighter-bomber pilots, "I'm giving you a hundred-per-cent Target Coverage. Thank you very much. It's been a pleasure to work with you. See you another day."

"Thank *you*," the flight commander answered.

Major Billings' three hours of flying time were up, and he turned the plane toward Chu Lai. Fifteen minutes later, we landed.

AFTER we had taxied to a halt at the fuel pump, a young mechanic asked, "How'd it go, Major? Did you get some of 'em today?" He spoke with a nonchalance that failed to disguise his intense interest in getting an answer.

Instead of just replying "I dunno," or "Real fine," as he and the other pilots usually did, Major Billings burst out "We bombed two churches!" and gave a laugh that seemed to register his own surprise and wonderment at the act.

That afternoon, back at the FAC pilots' quarters, Major Billings, scratching his head and staring into the faces of the other pilots, exclaimed, again with a laugh, "I put in a strike on two churches!"

"No kidding," said one.

"They had a white flag in front of them. That damn white flag is still standing," the Major said.

"Yeah, I saw the white flag when I was out today," Lieutenant Moore said. "We'll have to get that white flag. It's a matter of *principle*."

The conversation turned to the subject of accidental bombings, and Major Billings, who had been a bomber pilot in both the Second World War and the Korean War, told of an ill-conceived bombing run he had once made over North Korea. "There was a big building right in the center of a town, and they told me it was a real important military headquarters," he said. "The target was so important that they sent two reconnaissance planes to guide me right to it. I laid my stuff all over it. About three days later, I found out that the place was really a school, and about a hundred children had been killed. They weren't going to tell me about the mistake, but I found out."

A man I have called Major Nugent said, "In early '65, there was a pilot who accidentally bombed an orphanage and killed a lot of kids. When he found out about it, he was so shook up that he voluntarily grounded himself for good. He said that he'd never fly again."

"That's the way you feel when something like that happens," said a man I have called Captain Reese, whom I'd also flown with during Operation Hood River.

"No—I mean, you can't let it get to you, or you couldn't go on," Major Billings objected. "It gets completely impersonal. After you've done it for a while, you forget that there are people down there."

"Yeah, everything looks so calm up where we are," Major Nugent said. "We can't even tell when we're getting shot at. We forget what's going on down on the ground. It's the guys on the ground—the ground troops—that really have it rough. They really know what's happening."

The extreme solemnity that had descended on the group seemed suddenly to generate an opposite impulse of hilarity, and small, irrepressible smiles began to appear on the pilots' faces.

Captain Reese turned to me and asked if I had ever heard the songs about the war that they occasionally sang.

I said that I had heard one such song.

"Shall we tell him?" he asked the other pilots. They all looked at each other, and before anyone could answer, Captain Reese sang rapidly:

> "Strafe the town and kill the people,
> Drop napalm in the square,
> Get out early every Sunday
> And catch them at their morning prayer."

Major Billings then recited the words of another song:

> "Throw candy to the ARVN,
> Gather them all around,
> Take your twenty mike-mike
> And mow the bastards down."

At dinner in the Marine dining hall that evening, after a few drinks, the pilots began to make jokes in which they ridiculed the idea that the bombings they guided were unnecessarily brutal by inventing remarks that might be made by men so bloodthirsty that they took delight in intentionally killing innocents. The joke-tellers appeared to bring out their remarks with considerable uneasiness and embarrassment, and some of the pilots appeared to laugh unduly long in response, as though to reassure the tellers. All the jokes seemed to deal, indirectly, with the conflicts of conscience that had arisen in the conversation at the pilots' quarters during the afternoon.

When the main course was nearly finished, Major Nugent asked Captain Reese, "Git any woman and children today?"

"Yeah, but I let a pregnant woman get away," Captain Reese answered.

Lieutenant Moore's heavy-browed, serious, wooden face began to reflect a struggle between his usual gravity and a rebellious smile. "When we kill a pregnant woman, we count it as two V.C.—one soldier and one cadet," he said.

Everyone laughed loudly.

"Bruce got a bunch of kids playing marbles," said Major Nugent.

The group laughed again.

"I got an old lady in a wheelchair," Lieutenant Moore said, and there was more laughter.

"You know, when I flew over Japan, *anything* was fair game," Major Billings said. "They really were merciless, and they shot at everything. I remember I once saw an old guy riding a bicycle down the road, and I came up behind him, putting my fire in the road. The guy's feet started going faster and faster on the pedals, and just before my fire caught up with him you would never believe how fast the old bugger's feet were flying!"

The idea that civilians were often killed in the bombings they guided rarely arose in the pilots' conversation, and now that it had come up—if only to be debunked—the pilots made their jokes in the casual, familiar tone that marked most of their conversations. Yet the laugh that followed Major Billings' story erupted with a sudden force that seemed to take the men themselves by surprise. I sensed that their laughter eased a tension that had been building up during the session of jokes—eased it, perhaps, because this usually straightforward, informal group of men had found it a strain to have a largely undiscussed subject standing between them. Lieutenant Moore was so severely racked with laughter that he could not swallow a mouthful of food, and for several seconds he was convulsed silently and had to bend his head low with his hands over his mouth. Tears came to his eyes and to Major Nugent's.

"Oh, my!" Lieutenant Moore sighed, exhausted by all the laughing. Then he said, "I didn't kill that woman in the wheelchair, but she sure bled good!"

Nobody laughed at this joke. A silence ensued. Finally, Captain Reese suggested that they find out what movies were playing on the base that night.

*   *   *

DURING my stay with the FAC pilots, they and other officers said again and again that we could win the war quickly if only we weren't under so many restraints. They spoke mainly of three kinds of restraints. First, they said that except where troops were engaged in battle, villages could not be bombed until the villagers had been warned by a leaflet drop or a loudspeaker announcement. Second, they said that when we wanted to turn an area into a "free-strike zone"—that is, an area in which we could bomb at will, and without warning—the villagers had to be evacuated. Third, they said that we could not destroy an area until we had cleared the action with the province chief. To find out about the warning system,

I spoke with the Psychological Warfare Office for Task Force Oregon; to find out about evacuation I spoke with the Civil Affairs Office for the 101st Airborne Division; and to find out about the clearance system I spoke with the province chief. Having flown over Operation Benton during its first five days, I confined my inquiries to that operation in that period. All in all, my investigation disclosed that the procedures for applying these restraints were modified or twisted or ignored to such an extent that in practice the restraints evaporated entirely, though enough motions were gone through to create the illusion of restraints in the minds of the officers.

At the Task Force Oregon Psychological Warfare Office, the lieutenant colonel in charge told me that his people had dropped 1,515,000 leaflets over the area of operation and had made one announcement, but that all these had been of a very general nature, and none had warned of impending air strikes. He showed me a copy, in the original English, of each of the leaflets that had been dropped, including a group that the men at the Psychological Warfare Office refer to as "the Chieu Hoi mix" ("Chieu Hoi" means "Open Arms"), which consists of various leaflets encouraging members of the Vietcong to defect to the side of the G.V.N.—that is, the South Vietnamese Government. Some are threatening, showing photographs of the naked corpses of Vietcong soldiers riddled with bullet holes and heaped in piles, and others are conciliatory, showing photographs of smiling defectors along with signed statements saying that life in the government camps is prosperous and happy. The Psychological Warfare planes also dropped a hundred and eighty thousand copies of Leaflet No. 47-65, which is titled "Vietcong Mines Cause Senseless Deaths" and shows a cartoon drawing of several farmers reeling from an explosion in a rice field. The caption reads, "The V.C. mine your rice fields and cause you to go hungry. You must help the ARVN and the Marines to stop the Vietcong and deny the Vietcong any of your own rice." On the back is this text: "Vietcong mines kill Vietnamese on the roads, in the villages, and in the rice fields. Help your friends and neighbors by reporting such V.C. activities." Finally, they dropped a hundred thousand copies of Leaflet No. 167-66, which shows a cartoon drawing of a boorish Communist Chinese official laughing cruelly and spilling food all over a table as he eats a lavish meal while at his feet a moronic-looking Vietnamese with a Vietcong star on his tattered conical hat crouches under the table and picks up scraps of food from the floor. The text on the back reads:

APPEAL TO THE V.C. TO REJECT THE RED CHINESE AS THEIR MASTERS

The Red Chinese Communist masters of the Vietcong have declared that the South Vietnamese people must pay more and more to support the unjust war of the Vietcong. Still the Vietcong soldiers go hungry and they are not paid. Where does the rice and money go? Think about it! Refuse to give your rice and money—don't let the Chinese Communists make fools of you.

The colonel gave me a short briefing on the activities of his office over the previous three months. "We drop leaflets based on the desire to exploit their vulnerability," he told me. "We drop more than a million a day. We use mostly Cessna O-2s for the drops, but now we are getting in C-47s, and they can drop two million leaflets in one flight." (Later, I looked at the office notebook of leaflets—well over a thousand of them, of different types. The book is divided into "Campaigns," such as "Support G.V.N.," "V.C.," "Instructions to Civilians," "Chieu Hoi," and "Health." The "Health" leaflets give tips on personal and public hygiene. For example, they advise the villagers always to boil water before drinking it, to cover their garbage, and to sleep under mosquito nets. The leaflets usually end with the assurance that the G.V.N. "cares for the people.")

The colonel went on to say, "We also have a new aircraft that carries an eighteen-hundred-watt bank of loudspeakers effective up to five thousand feet. We've got several standard tapes that we can run off here. We played the national-reconciliation tape for a couple of hours over Benton. We make our own tapes here, too, using *hoi chanh*"—returnees, that is—"the way we do with the leaflets. Sometimes we play a tape *and* drop the leaflets. The *hoi chanh* tell how well they've been treated, and that kind of thing."

I asked what the national-reconciliation tape said.

"Well, I don't have a translation of the actual words, but

the general idea is to get them to return to the government cause," the colonel said. "We get the targets for the different kinds of leaflets through intelligence and interrogation of *hoi chanh*. We try to cause disaffection between the top V.C. and the V.C. rank-and-file, and we advertise the Chieu Hoi Program. One of our big problems here is lack of support for the government, but this problem exists for the V.C., too. A lot of the people are in the V.C. because of force, and there are a lot in because it is the thing to do—because the neighbors are doing it. Last year, there were a hundred and sixteen defectors in Quang Ngai. I Corps, which includes Quang Ngai and four other northern provinces, has a high rate of defectors."

"Do you estimate the rate of defectors as the number of *hoi chanh* in the population of the province or as the number of *hoi chanh* in the estimated number of enemy troops in the area?" I asked.

"I don't know the precise details of how they measure it, but anyway it's very high here," the colonel answered, and he continued, "We've also got posters that we put up in the area. On the fourth of May, the V.C. blew up some houses at Ly Tra and Li Tinh, a few kilometres southeast of Tam Ky, in Quang Tin. So we made up some atrocity posters." The colonel got up from his desk to show me some large posters on an easel that stood at the back of his office. They featured photographs of the burned or blown-up bodies of women and children, and scenes of destroyed houses followed by scenes of Vietnamese reconstructing a village. The colonel, however, was not sure that the destruction of villages and the killing of villagers was always an unsound tactic on the part of the Vietcong, and after gazing gravely at the poster for a moment he smiled and said, "But the distribution of atrocity posters has to be limited. Sometimes they influence the people the wrong way, and help out the V.C. Sometimes it is just what the V.C. want."

The colonel then said that many ground units were aided by loudspeaker teams who broadcast ahead of the American troops, encouraging the enemy to surrender. In combat, the Psychological Warfare Officers preferred to play tapes rather than use live voices. "That way, the guy is sure to sound confident, and we avoid fluttery, scared-sounding voices," the colonel explained. "Sometimes they use the tapes to broadcast from the perimeter of the U.S. troops. Mostly, we play music and interrupt it with what we call our commercials. We use nostalgic music to make the V.C. feel lonesome and want to go back home. We know from research that flute music is nostalgic to the Vietnamese. We've got three main pieces— one with a man, one with a woman, and one with a flute. The man and the woman sing of their lovely home. The Viet-namese are very closely related to their land. There is an old Vietnamese legend about a commander who was so good on the flute that all the enemy dropped their weapons and went home when he played it. We haven't had that happen yet. But I want to emphasize that in all our leaflets and pamphlets we *tell only the truth*. This is, of course, to establish our credibility, so that the people can depend completely on the truth of what we say."

I pointed out that we had destroyed about forty per cent of the houses in the Benton area of operation during its first five days, and asked him how he viewed this.

"We do destroy villages, and we have to," he answered. "But there are rules of engagement that prevent us from just arbitrarily bombing any friendly village. Whenever there's time, we get a Psy War bird out there to warn them. That way, we keep from hurting as many civilians as we can. Also, when the V.C. set off a mine in the road, and someone in-nocent gets killed, the V.C. exploit us and say, 'See what the American artillery has done!' So we drop our standard leaflets about V.C. mines."

The colonel also told me about units called audio-visual teams, which showed movies in the camps and villages when they got a chance. "They show American films, usually— mostly Westerns," he said. "Once, they showed 'The Swinger.' That wasn't too good. That was a mistake. They won't show that one again. But we try to show pictures that portray the American way of life. We're careful to show them things they understand. For instance, if you show them a science-fiction movie, they won't know what's going on. Walt Disney pic-tures are good, because the words aren't too important. In between reels, we show cartoons and shorts that liberally assert our propaganda. A lot of these are made by the South Vietnamese Ministry of Information. One shows a North Vietnamese soldier goofing up—falling into a canal, and that kind of thing. Another shows how a *hoi chanh* decided to defect. Sometimes we get the village chief to address the people between reels. You see, they don't have any TV or movies or record-players, or anything. So when we show them something, they gobble it right up. What we are accomplishing is to leave a good taste in the mouths of the children, so that when they grow up and the V.C. try to persuade them they'll remember the nice things the Allies did for them."

As I passed out of the colonel's private office into a larger room, which was filled with the desks of other Psychological Warfare Officers, a captain was calling out to a lieutenant, "Hey, Ray, what about a nice nostalgic tape by a woman?"

"Fine!" answered the lieutenant. He was peering at the Psychological Warfare Office target map, which was enclosed in a folder decorated on the outside with two *Playboy* Playmates of the Month.

A minute later, the captain handed the lieutenant the English original of a leaflet to read.

The lieutenant objected that a curfew that was announced in the leaflet should read, "From sundown to sunrise," instead of "From 6:00 P.M. to 6:00 A.M." "The Vietnamese don't know what time it is," the lieutenant said. "They don't have any watches."

"Sure they do," the captain replied. "You look around the bases and you'll see they've all got watches."

"Yeah, on the bases," the lieutenant said. "But you go out on Route 1, where they're carrying wood and rice and stuff, and I'll give you a double mixed drink for every watch you see."

"All I know is we announced the last curfew by the hours," said the captain, and the two men moved on to another question.

A chart on the wall next to the captain's desk showed in one column the number of leaflets dropped each month so far in 1967, in a second column the number of defectors for each month, and in a third column the number of defectors for each month of 1966. The captain told me, "We keep tables on how many defectors we get every month to gauge how effective we've been, and we feel pretty good about the fact that we've had more *hoi chanh* this year than in the same months last year, because this is where we measure the results. This is where we can see we are really doing something." There was, however, no correspondence between the number of leaflets dropped during the months of Task Force Oregon's operations and the number of defectors in those months.

I visited a small tent serving as the Civil Affairs Office of the 1st Brigade of the 101st Division, to ask how many people had been evacuated from the Benton area of operation, and learned that Operation Benton was not supposed to "generate any new refugees." Apparently, word that the camps had been able to provide care—and then only minimal care—for only a fraction of the area's dispossessed people had reached Saigon, and Task Force Oregon had been requested to conduct operations in a way that would not result in a great increase in the number of people arriving at the camps. During the first week of Operation Benton, Task Force Oregon's solution to the problem was to conduct the operation as usual but omit the step of evacuating the villagers, either before or after their villages were destroyed. I learned this when, on the sixth day of the operation, I asked the major in charge of the Civil Affairs Office how many of the seventeen thousand people who lived in the area of operation had been evacuated, and he told me that fifteen people had been lifted out by helicopter and that a hundred more were waiting for transportation. I pointed out that about forty per cent of the houses in the area had already been destroyed without any warning to the villagers, and the major told me that, with the help of the Psychological Warfare Office, the Civil Affairs Office had devised a more flexible plan, which would be put into action during the second week of the operation; this was intended to offer the inhabitants of the area what the major described as a "free choice" between going to the government camps and remaining on the sites of their homes. Each American soldier would be given a handful of leaflets designed expressly for Operation Benton, and would himself pass them out to the people of the area when his commanding officer instructed him to do so. The leaflet to be employed—No. 244-133-68—was titled "Move to Ly Tra Refugee Camp," and read:

The American soldier who handed you this is here to help you free yourself from the Vietcong and the North Vietnamese invaders who bring upon you the ravages of war. He will take you and your family to Ly Tra, where the G.V.N. will protect you. There you can live a peaceful, prosperous life without fear for the lives of your beloved ones. You will go to Ly Tra by helicopter and will be able to take only the personal possessions you carry. The G.V.N. has a refugee center at Ly Tra that will give you aid until you can reëstablish yourself.

If you desire to go to Ly Tra, touch the American soldier on his shoulder. He will understand. Get your belongings together and follow the American's instructions. If you do not wish to go to Ly Tra, tear this leaflet in half. He will understand that you do not wish to go.

I asked the major in charge of the Civil Affairs Office what he thought the purpose of Operation Benton was.

"The province chief has told us this is pretty much a hundred-per-cent V.C. area," he answered. "We consider just about everything here to be a hard-core V.C., or at least some kind of supporter. Before they bomb an area, a Psy War bird always goes in ahead. This is an operation to catch the V.C., not to clear the area. You can't just go around moving everybody out all the time."

I asked if the Civil Affairs Office had any further plans for the people in the region.

"Now you're getting out of our area," he answered. "*We* don't have any plans for the immediate future. It's the responsibility of the G.V.N. and the ARVN to carry out Pacification and Revolutionary Development."

While we stood talking, a captain at a desk nearby received a phone call, and after he hung up he said to the major, "That was the colonel, and he wants those two villages burned. He said the province chief requested it."

A tall young lieutenant in fatigues and an undershirt, on the other side of the tent, interrupted the conversation to ask, "What about the people?"

"The colonel said we're not supposed to bring out any refugees," the captain replied.

"What do you mean? How can we burn a village if we're not going to bring out the people?"

"Well, those are the colonel's orders."

"Look," the lieutenant said, standing up. "We have our rules of engagement, and we can't just go around burning villages without taking care of the people. That's just ridiculous! Can you have any respect for a colonel who gives an order like that? I mean, no kidding—can you?"

"The province chief ordered us to do it," the captain said. The lieutenant sat down again.

A sergeant from the Operations Office spoke up to say, "The Vietnamese can relocate themselves. That's the way they are. Every two years or so, they'll just pick up their sticks and move on to somewhere else on their own. That's the way it was in Korea, too. The villages got wiped out there, too, and everybody just picked up their stuff and went somewhere else. Those aren't houses. They're just huts. Take, for instance, all those people who came down from North Vietnam for religious reasons. The North is Catholic and the South is Buddhist. That's one reason why they don't like each other." Actually, of course, both North Vietnam and South Vietnam are predominantly Buddhist, with a Catholic minority.

The next day, I drove to Tam Ky, the capital of Quang Tin Province, to see Lieutenant Colonel Hoang Dinh Tho, who is the Province Chief, and ask him about his role in providing clearance for Task Force Oregon's activities for the first five days of Operation Benton and in his province generally. His office was in a large two-story building in the ornate, pastel-colored colonial French style, which stood in a large courtyard at the end of a long driveway lined with trees, on the outskirts of Tam Ky. At the entrance to the driveway, two three-story modern-style stucco towers stood like giant bookends on a plain that had had its trees bulldozed away for security. There was a guardhouse beside one of the towers, and beyond them coils of barbed wire stretched out into brown fields. A Vietnamese officer there explained to me that an arch was to have stretched between the towers but that materials had run out. He said that the trees had been planted as a special project in an effort that President Diem had made to beautify the country. Flanking the office of the Province Chief were two long, low buildings occupied by officers of the ARVN and their American advisers. Just as I arrived—it was shortly after noon—a pickup truck pulled up to one of these buildings. In the back of the truck, an American soldier holding a shotgun guarded about twenty Vietnamese, whose heads were covered with muddy sandbags. In their blindness, some had clasped hands and others had their arms around each other. A Vietnamese officer shouted something to them, and they removed the bags and looked about them, blinking in the whitish noon sun. Five of them were young women, eight or nine were young or middle-aged men, three were old men, and two were young girls with still boyish figures. When they had helped each other climb shakily off the truck, they were delivered into the hands of a tall, young, collegiate-looking American soldier with a shock of straight dark hair, who appeared to be intensely irritated by something. "Get over there!" he shouted to the people, pointing with a sheaf of papers he was holding toward one end of the building. The people looked in the direction he indicated but did not move. "I said *get moving*!" the young soldier shouted, and struck an old man—who happened to be standing near him—in the face with his sheaf of papers. The old man fell back, his gaze riveted on the young American, who then turned away and stalked ahead of the group, his face red and furious. Four American officers who had been standing on a porch talking and watching the prisoners get off the truck went inside the building. The people filed around a corner of the building and were led toward a small, whitewashed, windowless structure that stood alone in a withered field. Several ARVN officers who had been lounging outside it began to pick themselves up sluggishly as the people came in sight.

I asked an American officer passing through the square who the Vietnamese prisoners were.

"Detainees," he answered. "They picked them up back in the mountains somewhere, and now they're taking them out back for interrogation." (Several times during my stay in Quang Ngai and Quang Tin, I saw groups of detainees, always with sandbags over their heads, being herded into airplanes or trucks under the guard of Americans carrying shotguns. I learned at the Task Force Oregon Information Office that

ninety-three per cent of them were eventually cleared as innocent and released.)

In due course, I was received by Colonel Tho, who is about
forty and is shorter than most of his countrymen. He has
strikingly clear and handsome features, he was immaculately
groomed, and he displayed a solid, if inelegant, command of
English, which he had acquired during two years of military
training in the United States. It had recently been reported
in the Vietnamese military press that Colonel Tho had insisted
that several air-conditioners intended for his own spacious offices be installed in an ARVN hospital instead. I mentioned this
to him when I met him, and he laughed in delight and embarrassment, brushing the matter away with a sweep of his
hand. Colonel Tho then motioned to an American officer
standing behind him, who stepped forward for a few seconds
to introduce himself, in a hushed voice, as Lieutenant Colonel
Robert O. Lynch, Senior Adviser for Quang Tin Province,
and then stepped back, solemn-faced, like a well-trained butler. Throughout the interview, Colonel Tho laughed often
and gesticulated expansively, and Colonel Lynch sat silent, apparently to avoid cramping the Province Chief's style with an
overbearing American presence.

We sat down around a small coffee table, and I asked Colonel Tho what his role had been in the planning of Operation
Benton, and whether he had restrained Task Force Oregon
from any bombings or shellings during the first five days of
the operation. I learned that his method of giving clearance
in an American military operation was not to review the targets of individual air strikes or shellings but to give the American ground commander a blanket clearance before the
operation was launched. The Chop Vum area had been covered by such a clearance, and Colonel Tho had received no
information on the results of any American air strikes, except
in terms of enemy casualties, since the beginning of Operation
Benton.

"The American Army comes to me to ask my permission
for running the operation, and I tell them the areas they can't
bomb," Colonel Tho told me. Later, I learned that he had
been called to a meeting two days before the operation and
had been asked to specify the no-strike zones. It had then

been agreed not to operate within several kilometres of the town of Phuoc Tien. "Outside of Phuoc Tien, the ground commander decides where to bomb," he went on. "Sometimes I give permission to burn a fortified village on the ground, but not so many in this operation. Just one or two. Sometimes the villages support the V.C., and they are *too strong*, so they must be destroyed."

I asked him about his plans for the civilians in the area.

"No refugees this time, unless they *ask* to come," Colonel Tho said. "We take out only villagers who are friendly to protect in the government area. For relatives of the V.C., maybe they have to suffer some."

At this point, Colonel Lynch looked up, and, after asking and receiving the Province Chief's permission to speak, he said, "Of course, when we *do* have to destroy a village, in almost every case we warn the people in advance with announcements or leaflets. We're very careful about that."

I asked Colonel Tho if there were any plans for securing the area after Operation Benton was over.

"Well, maybe, sometime, but now we don't have enough troops," Colonel Tho said. "This operation is just to get the main-force V.C. units. This war has many faces. Sometimes we find V.C., and move some people for economic war. Sometimes economic war is most important. Population control. Change the population patterns."

I observed to the Province Chief that the two churches in Thanh Phuoc had been bombed, and asked if he had heard about that.

"Oh, yes," he said. "I got the report this morning that V.C.s blow up two churches."

I said that I had seen American planes bomb the churches.

The Province Chief laughed for several seconds, and said, "Well, in the fighting you cannot always tell what is happening, and you cannot always tell the difference between just regular houses and church."

Later, I spoke with a captain in the ARVN who had been in and out of the northern provinces since the end of the Second World War, and he expressed alarm at the policies that our military had developed in I Corps over the past year or so. "The Americans are destroying everything," he said. "If they get just one shot from a village, they destroy it. We have an expression: The American S-5 builds a village and the American S-3 destroys it." S-5 is the Civil Affairs Office, and S-3 is the Operations Office. "I helped give out rice and building materials in one village, and three days later it was completely bombed. They bomb villages with the families of our troops living in them. A soldier comes back from Saigon and finds that his family has been killed. They bomb the rich and the poor. The rich man is the V.C.'s enemy. We should protect him. But now he has two enemies: the V.C., and the Americans who bomb all the houses. They even bomb the houses of the local militia. Who has made this new policy? The Americans never try to protect a village. Just one V.C.—*just one*—can enter any village with a machine gun and the people are helpless against him. What can they do? Nothing. He shoots, and then their village is bombed."

*   *   *

On August 28th, when Operation Benton came to a close, Task Force Oregon announced that the troops taking part in it had killed, and counted the bodies of, three hundred and ninety-seven of the enemy, and that forty-seven American soldiers had been killed. Into an area of ten by twenty kilometres they had dropped 282 tons of "general-purpose" bombs and 116 tons of napalm; fired 1,005 rockets (not counting rockets fired from helicopters), 132,820 rounds of 20-mm. explosive strafing shells, and 119,350 7.62-mm. rounds of machine-gun fire from Spooky flights; and fired 8,488 artillery rounds. By the end of the operation, the Civil Affairs Office had supervised the evacuation of six hundred and forty of the area's seventeen thousand people, to the vicinity of government camps.

The reports that were sent back to Saigon to form the overall statistical picture of the war could be divided into two kinds. One kind measured the achievements of the American efforts in Vietnam in terms of materials expended—whether these were bombs dropped, artillery shells fired, Psychological Warfare leaflets dropped, pounds of rice distributed, or gallons of defoliants sprayed. Like the Psychological Warfare Officer for Task Force Oregon at Chu Lai who was encouraged by the fact that his people had stepped up the rate of leaflets dropped over Quang Ngai Province to a million a day, and like the artillery officer in Duc Pho who took pride in the fact that his men had fired sixty-four thousand and forty-four shells into two districts in three and a half months, most American officers and officials found cause for optimism in the sheer scale of the outputs of our efforts. The other kind of statistical report measured American achievements in Vietnam in terms of some of the effects of all this activity. The Bomb Damage Assessment Reports filled out by the FAC pilots were a good example. The terms "Military Structure," "Suspected Enemy Troop Concentration," "Percentage of Target Destroyed," and "Percentage of Bombs on Target," which described the bombing targets and the bomb damage, were devised by higher-ups, and the FAC pilots' only track-keeping duty was to write figures into the blanks. With this system, only results of the kind we intended to bring about were reported to Saigon, and the vast "side effects," such as the destruction of villages in large areas, went unmentioned. It is perhaps not very surprising that the Bomb Damage Assessment Reports supplied no blanks for "Homes Destroyed" or "Civilians Killed."

A further problem was that the terms employed in the Bomb Damage Assessment Reports often did not correspond to what the FAC pilots saw on the ground. When a FAC pilot guided an air strike onto a target that was defined by his coördinates only as a patch of jungle a hundred metres square, and was termed a "Suspected Enemy Troop Concentration," or guided an air strike onto a village that was described as an "Enemy Sniper Position," there was no meaning in a figure for the "Percentage of Target Destroyed," and little meaning in a figure for the "Percentage of Bombs on Target." Since the pilots could never know how much of the real target—the enemy troops—had been destroyed, they fell back on simply reporting how many houses had been destroyed, or how much of the hundred-metre-square patch of jungle had been torn up, as though this had been the objective of the bombing. Also, since the enemy was fighting primarily a guerrilla war, and built virtually no "military structures," the FAC pilots came to apply this term to any building that the planes happened to bomb. (Some of the bunkers and caves used by both the N.L.F. and the civilians might accurately have been called "military structures," but the Bomb Damage Assessment Reports listed these in a separate category.) Most of the terms used in the Bomb Damage Assessment Reports seemed to have been devised for something like a bombing raid on a large, clearly visible, stationary military base, and not for the bombing of guerrilla forces in the setting of fields, villages, and jungle which the FAC pilots actually guided. Finding himself having to guide air strikes with the aid of a set of instructions that had little relevance to his actual task, each FAC pilot had to improvise his own ways of trying to tell where the enemy was operating. This was how Captain Reese came to think that he could spot, on the trails, grass that had been freshly bent by the passage of enemy troops, and that he could distinguish enemy houses from civilian houses by whether they were in the tree lines or not; how Lieutenant Moore came to think that he could tell a farmer from a soldier by the way he walked; and how Major Billings came to believe that he could tell enemy soldiers from civilians by making a low pass over the fields and seeing who ran for cover, and that he could judge whether a wisp of smoke hanging over the woods was rising from the fire of a Montagnard or from the fire of a Vietcong soldier.

WHILE some units of the 196th Light Infantry Brigade were helping the 101st Airborne in Operation Benton, other units of the 196th launched a separate, nameless operation along the northernmost five kilometres of coastline in Quang Ngai Province. Because American troops had been fired on almost every time they entered this coastal area, the 196th Light Brigade had decided that the best course of action would be to evacuate its inhabitants, who were thought to number five thousand; to destroy their villages; and to convert the area into a free-strike zone. The first stage of the operation was planned for the morning of August 21st, when elements of the 196th would make a surprise landing in amphibious tractors (usually called Amtracs) at Tuyet Diem, a fishing village on a small peninsula. During the next three hours, the population of the village, estimated at six hundred, would dismantle their houses and take the beams and roof thatching, and also all their possessions and animals, down to the beach and aboard two landing craft that were to be brought near the shore in front of the village. Then, according to the plan, the landing craft—making as many trips as necessary—would sail down the coast to a lot that had been cleared in preparation for the operation, and the villagers would set up their village in the new spot. The newly cleared lot had formerly been the site of a large village called Son Tra, which had been shelled by the Marines about two years before. At that time, its people had been evacuated to a roadside a few kilometres away, where they erected huts to live in. A week before the operation that was to destroy Tuyet Diem was launched, the Army arranged to employ the villagers of Son Tra to level the ruins of their old village in preparation for the arrival of the villagers of Tuyet Diem. The villagers of Son Tra were given hints that they were clearing their old village in preparation for their own return. By conveying these hints, the Army hoped to prevent the National Liberation Front from guessing that the site was being cleared in preparation for a new military operation. The Americans who planned the evacuation of Tuyet Diem and the other coastal villages were much gratified by the neatness and simplicity of their plan, especially when they compared it with other evacuation projects that had been carried out in the province. As they saw it, the evacuation would not create "refugees" of the kind that had proved such a burden in the government camps. One colonel said of it, "We're just going to interrupt the villagers' work for six hours. They're not going to lose their chance to work, like the other refugees we've got. They can just bring their boats down the coast and start right up again with the new village. The real beauty of this is that all we have to supply is one day's food. They're going to bring their houses right along with them, so we won't need to bring any extra supplies for houses. This isn't going to be like those operations where five thousand people come into a camp with nothing to eat and nowhere to stay. This is going to be the best Civil Affairs operation we've run yet. The refugee people have been preparing for it for a full week." Mr. Ernest Hobson was far from happy about any operation that would increase the number of displaced people in the province, but, he, too, said that the evacuation of Tuyet Diem was much the most carefully planned operation of the sort so far.

The American planners were particularly pleased with the arrival of a three-man Vietnamese Cultural Drama Team—a troupe of actors organized by the South Vietnamese government and sent on tour throughout the country—which would perform for the villagers during their first evening at the new site. The evening before the evacuation, the Cultural Drama Team performed for an audience of about a hundred G.I.s in an open movie theatre at one of the base camps of the 196th Light Brigade. Standing under floodlights on a low stage, two youths dressed in the black garments of farmers sang several rock-and-roll songs in Vietnamese, accompanying themselves on electric guitars. They then switched to Vietnamese songs for a time, and wound up with "When the Saints Go Marching In," which they sang in English, in high, reedy voices. The second half of the performance was a magic show. Whereas the singers had remained perfectly deadpan throughout their concert, the magician, who couldn't have been more than eighteen, never once relaxed a wide, tense smile as he moved through his routine, and he moved through it as though every step and every flourish of his hands had been mapped out in advance. Among other tricks, he made a glass of water disappear; folded up a dollar bill in a piece of paper, burned the paper, and pulled the bill, intact, from the ashes; made three scarves tie themselves together in midair; and produced a bouquet of paper flowers from his assistant's ear. At the beginning of the magic show, the G.I.s clapped politely, but their interest soon waned, and then, the audience having suddenly been attacked by a swarm of large, bumbling insects that resembled fat dragonflies, the magician lost its attention completely. After the show, a colonel who was involved in the planning of the evacuation made a sour face and said to a fellow-officer, "Are *they* going to play tomorrow night? I don't think *I'd* want to watch them if *I'd* just been moved out of *my* village."

The next morning, I accompanied the soldiers of the 196th Light Brigade that landed in Tuyet Diem. The troops as-

sembled at four-thirty at the top of a gently rising field in front
of the base camp, and at five o'clock the men started walking
down a dirt road to the beach in two single lines, each man
keeping ten yards between himself and the man in front of
him. A three-quarter moon faintly illuminated the road from
behind a high cover of thin, milky clouds. A deep thumping
of artillery shells landing in rapid series, which had begun at
about one o'clock, continued well into the morning at a
stepped-up pace, and to the east, over the peninsula where
the troops were to land, the sky periodically flashed a dull
yellow. The morning was warm and muggy, and the troops,
in their battle gear, began to sweat freely. The double column
descended from the high ground in front of the camp and
approached the clusters of tiny huts that the villagers of Son
Tra had built themselves. Single candles burned in several huts
as people rose for the day. A low sound of talking in the
houses ceased as our presence became known; a dog barked
and was silenced with a sharp word. A small girl stood in a
low doorway and watched the troops pass, and a woman at a
well paused with her hands on the well rope. An old man
stood naked in a small dirt yard in the dim moonlight. When
the troops had been walking for fifteen or twenty minutes, a
single line of ARVN soldiers passed wordlessly between the two
American lines, heading in the opposite direction. A rooster
crowed, although dawn had not yet broken. The column
halted.

Abruptly, someone called out, "Where the fuck are we?"
The voice was shockingly loud in the silence of the dark road.

"Ah, shit, we're lost," someone else said angrily.

An officer walked up to the head of the column, and after
a minute the column started to move again. The two lines,
observed by four silent young Vietnamese men who were
squatting in a row on a stone wall, passed through a wooden
gate onto the beach. An elderly fisherman in black stood mo-
tionless by his boat, smoking a cigarette, as the soldiers filed
past him. Apparently, the leaders had taken a wrong path, for,
after another halt, they led the column through a brambly
field to the road they had just left. Ten minutes later, the
soldiers arrived on the beach again, at a point where two Amtracs were waiting on the sand. The men had a brief rest, and

most of them got out cigarettes and began smoking. When the order came, they climbed eight-foot ladders running up the sides of the Amtracs, and sat down on their metal decks.

In one Amtrac, a platoon sergeant grumbled loudly as the men were seating themselves, "Everyone around here is a goddam Yankee. All Ah see is goddam Yankees everywhere Ah go." To a G.I. near him he said, "You're a Yankee, aren't you, soldier?"

The soldier did not answer.

"Ah ain't no Yankee, Sarge," another soldier said.

Presently, the ponderous, box-shaped Amtracs rolled off the beach into the water. The point of departure was just inside the mouth of the Song Tra Bong river, and the square-bowed Amtracs had to buck a heavy incoming tide to get out to sea. Then, after a twenty-minute voyage across calm water, we came in sight of Tuyet Diem. It was almost full daylight. From the water, only ten or twelve of the houses in the village could be seen. As the invasion force approached, a woman on a front porch who was gathering something into her arms went on with her task, and a man standing up to his knees in the water next to a fishing boat and working with its rigging kept on doing so, and glanced up only briefly, as though the arrival at Tuyet Diem of two Amtracs bearing American soldiers were an everyday occurrence. The Amtracs rolled up on the beach, and the soldiers jumped quickly to the sand, a few of them falling over backward under the weight of their ammunition belts, heavy packs, and weapons. One squad walked quickly up a rough pasture, with their M-16s in firing position at their hips. Another filed north along the beach. Rounding a rocky promontory, the men of this squad arrived at the edge of the village, which fronted on a crescent of white sand and was protected at each end by several giant gray boulders—some as large as two-story houses—extending into the sea. At the north end of the cove, a stony island no more than fifty feet across, which was topped with a stand of straggling pine trees, helped provide a lee for the beach. Out at sea, a fleet of half a dozen fishing boats under full sail was visible on the horizon. (These fishing boats drew only two feet of water, were about six feet wide and thirty feet long, had long, heavy bowsprits, and sailed under a gaff rig.) Facing the water were half a dozen stone houses of two or three rooms. Some had porches whose roofs were supported by gaily painted stone pillars. The walls of these houses were decorated with molding, and the cornices, windowsills, and door frames were painted with patterns in bright blues, reds, oranges, and greens. Palm trees and bamboos arched above the houses, casting a mottled shade.

Several families stood watching silently as the troops filed into the village. The soldiers, too, were silent. Each of the Vietnamese, male or female, wore a simple black collarless garment with three-quarter-length trousers. Each of the women and the little girls wore her hair long down her back, held in place with a silver oval clasp. Most of the villagers had bare feet, and children under three wore no pants. A few soldiers poked their heads briefly in at doorways, but most of them simply walked along the pathways between the houses, intently scanning the scene around them as they proceeded; they were on the lookout for signs of the enemy. Only the sergeant who had been complaining about Yankees on the Amtrac was more aggressive in his search. He walked directly up to a neatly-groomed, wiry middle-aged man who, with his wife and son, was standing in front of one of the most prosperous-looking houses, and, pointing inside, demanded, "What's in here?" Getting no answer, he went inside, pointed to a large ornate chest, and said, "Open this."

The Vietnamese man looked at him questioningly.

"*Dammit, Ah said open this!*" the sergeant shouted, striking the chest with his gun butt.

The man opened it, revealing a pile of folded clothes. The sergeant poked inside with the barrel of his gun and then left.

Outside again, the sergeant demanded, "Where V.C.? *Beaucoup* V.C., hunh?" ("*Beaucoup*" is a standard word in G.I. pidgin Vietnamese.) No one replied. As he passed another house, he noticed that the shutters on a side window were wired closed, and he bashed at them with his gun butt, but they did not break open, and he continued on his way without bothering to enter the house, whose front door stood ajar.

A few moments later, the sergeant pushed aside a curtain over the front entrance to a third house, and found himself facing an old man who was sitting on the floor just inside, bobbing his head and saying something that sounded like "Ow-ow-ow-ow-ow."

"Ow-ow-ow-ow-ow," mimicked the sergeant. "You're fuckin' crazy, that's what. Ow-ow-ow-ow-ow."

A central path wound back through the village, which was spread out on a hill. Directly behind one of the shore-front houses, a pile of rubble lay on a house foundation, and a palm tree about ten inches thick had been snapped in two halfway up, so that its leafy head—still green—was bowed into a neighbor's yard. "Artillery," a soldier remarked when he came upon the scene. Farther up the hill, the houses were poorer and were crowded closer together. Most had one or two rooms, were built of clay packed into woven bamboo frames, and were roofed with thatch. At the crest of the hill, the landscape opened out onto about two acres of flat rice fields. The troops who had headed up through the pasture when they debarked from the Amtracs were sitting on a steep, sandy hill that rose immediately behind the rice fields and gave them a view of the entire village. A dozen houses that were as large and well made as those on the shore surrounded the fields. Two other houses bordering the fields were in ruins. Recent artillery fire had made several big craters in a young crop of rice, and had sprayed mud over what remained of the rice shoots and onto the grassy embankments dividing the fields. The central path that led up the hill from the sea ran along its crest, parallel to the shore, for a few hundred yards, and then descended the hill to the shore farther north, at a place where treeless dunes covered with beach grass swept back from a long white beach.

Half an hour after the troops arrived, a Psychological Warfare Team consisting of an American and a Vietnamese began making announcements with a tape recorder and a loudspeaker. They announced that American troops had arrived to free the villagers from Vietcong domination, and ordered them to dismantle their houses and load the building materials, their possessions, and their animals on the landing craft (which had not yet arrived) within the next three hours. They also announced that the soldiers would help the people carry their possessions down to the boats. The commanding officer did not issue an order to this effect to his soldiers but allowed each man to decide for himself whether he would carry anything. The two landing craft arrived shortly after the announcements, one pulling up in the cove in front of the center of the village and the other at the long stretch of sand to the north. The villagers began to work as soon as they understood the nature of the situation. American troops that had entered other villages in Quang Ngai had usually found few able men, but at Tuyet Diem they found that a third of the families had men at home. Everyone, from the very old down to children of five or six, began carrying bundles to the beach. The villagers kept their stores of rice in waist-high pottery jars, and these were the most difficult objects to carry. Little girls and old women who were not accompanied by men importuned the American soldiers for help by tugging at their sleeves and attempting to pull them along to their houses. Four or five soldiers consented to help, and at once three or four little girls and a few old women gathered around them and tugged at their sleeves, trying to pull them in different directions, and smiling coaxingly or making sad faces. Neither the young men nor the young women ever smiled or asked for help. Most of the villagers set about carrying their belongings down the hill with a cold, fierce determination. Working against the three-hour deadline, they balanced huge loads at the ends of bamboo poles and made for the beach at a rapid, smooth, dancing jog. One old woman wept freely and loudly as she walked down the hill with a load. Other women wept soundlessly. One young woman's eyes streamed, even though her features were tightly composed, as she bent her energies to the work. All the children over five or six worked silently and hard, without any urging from their parents. Children of nine or ten carried two- and three-year-old brothers and sisters to the beach, leaving the heavier burdens of food, cooking utensils, and furniture to their parents. On the long open beach, the smallest children stood crying in groups of two and three next to their families' furniture and bundles of belongings. The four or five Americans who had taken up shoulder poles smiled and winked at one another with embarrassment as they passed on the path, in the manner of adults who have good-naturedly consented to take part in a children's game. To most of the soldiers, the villagers' possessions looked hardly worth carrying anywhere. Besides their jars of rice, the villagers wished to bring down large jars of *nuoc mam*—a major food staple for them, made of fermented fish, which gives off an odor that is usually disagreeable to Americans smelling it for the first time. They also carried bundles of twigs and reeds for firewood. When one American soldier was asked whether he intended to carry any of the villagers' belongings to the boats, he looked around him at the bundles on the beach and said, "What? *Me* carry *this shit?*" The villagers were wiry and strong, and even the women carried loads sufficient to tax a young G.I. (When a G.I. relieved one old woman of two bundles of firewood, he lifted them to his shoulder, and then set them down again and handed one to another soldier to carry and, looking at the frail old woman, put on an expression of amazement for the benefit of the other soldiers.) The combat soldiers in Vietnam are unusually big men, even by American standards, and at Tuyet Diem they loomed over most of the village men by more than a head. Some of the village women, apparently equating size with strength, led American soldiers to absurdly heavy loads and motioned to them to carry these to the beach. One old woman led an American at a half run to her hut, where she began desperately digging with her hands into the packed sandy earth of its floor. At length, she uncovered two huge jars of rice, each weighing about a hundred and fifty pounds. She secured one jar to each end of a shoulder pole with a wire hook and motioned impatiently to the American to take them away. Later, he and a man from the village together carried a jar at a time, with difficulty, down the path, one of them at each end of a shoulder pole.

Around eleven o'clock, the sun began to burn through the clouds, and the Americans who had been carrying belongings sat down and stopped work for the day, almost overcome by the heat. At eleven-fifteen, a sudden burst of machine-gun fire sent up a line of small geysers in the cove, about fifty feet from the shore. The commanding officer sent a patrol out along the beach, but the source of the fire was never ascertained. These were the only shots fired that day. (The Tuyet Diem operation was unusual in its lack of contact with the enemy. The military can almost never predict when the enemy will choose to resist in force, but most operations encounter sniper fire, at least, or small-unit fighting that results in both American and enemy casualties.)

The landing craft had been able to pull up to within ten yards of the shore, where the water was waist-deep. Each time a landing craft departed, many of the villagers, believing that the last boatload of belongings was leaving, waded deep into the water with bundles in their arms, and the soldiers on board shouted at them, "No more! That's all!," and attempted to prevent them from pushing their bundles onto the lip of the craft. Once, as a landing craft pulled away from the shore, a man ignored the protests of a soldier who stood at the rear of the craft, and, wading out up to his shoulders, tried repeatedly to shove a bundle of cooking utensils aboard. The soldier, becoming angry, pushed the man's bundle into the water. Some two dozen ARVN troops arrived late in the morning on one of the landing craft. They did not carry anything to the beach. One of them had brought a transistor radio, and a group of Americans persuaded him to tune it to the American armed-forces radio network. Light music, of the kind usually heard in restaurants or elevators in the United States, issued across the crowded beach. Another group of American soldiers sat on a poncho eating combat rations and drinking the milk of coconuts they had taken from nearby trees. Several soldiers had brought cameras, and they took pictures of the villagers carrying loads to the beach, and also of the landing craft jammed with firewood, furniture, bundles, jars of food, hobbled animals, and villagers. (The military in Vietnam apparently encourage the men to take snapshots of the war to send home. In the photographic department of the Danang PX, there hung a poster showing a picture of houses and palm trees silhouetted against a conflagration that filled most of the poster with red-and-orange flame and black smoke. In the foreground was a larger-than-life-size profile, in black silhouette, of the helmeted head of a G.I.; he was holding a camera to his eye and pressing the shutter. A caption at the bottom read, "SEND HOME A PHOTOGRAPHIC HISTORY OF THE WAR IN VIETNAM.")

To get their belongings from the beach to the landing craft, some villagers made use of large, shallow baskets woven of reeds and waterproofed with a coating of tar or resin. (The fishing villages along the coast in Quang Ngai use baskets of this type as small boats. It was in these simple craft that the villagers had first launched out on the water as children; in front of other coastal villages I often saw the water dotted with children in baskets, who propelled themselves about at a surprising speed with a sculling stroke of a single paddle.) During the morning, men who had been out in their fishing boats returned to Tuyet Diem, and helped carry belongings to the landing craft. By noon, it was apparent that the population of the village was not six hundred, as had been thought, but about fifteen hundred, so the deadline for the dismantling of the village was extended until late afternoon.

At Son Tra, where the villagers were being landed after their journey down the coast, a team of American soldiers had been detailed to help them carry their possessions ashore. Around the newly cleared lot that was to be the villagers' new home, a barbed-wire fence had been erected to insure that everyone checked in through a registration tent, for fingerprinting and questioning, and through a Red Cross tent, for a brief medical checkup. Perhaps because the number of people so far exceeded expectations, rendering the medical and security facilities inadequate for even the most cursory checking, someone had cut a large breach in the fence, and several hundred villagers had poured through to claim spots on the lot. On the lot, three stone buildings, including a roofless church, remained standing. Children's line drawings of helicopters, cattle, pigs, and gunboats had been scratched into the paint on the inside walls of one building. At one end of the lot was a little rocky hill that had been reduced to a blackened knob dotted with shattered stumps of trees during the Marines' bombing and shelling about two years before. Because of the delay in the schedule, American officers at Son Tra decided to postpone the destruction of the village of Tuyet Diem until the next day, and to blow up only the wells that night, to keep the Vietcong from getting water there. The officer detailed to the task said that because they were good, deep wells, with stone shafts part way down, he would need several hundred pounds of explosives to destroy them all.

An ARVN sergeant had been appointed "village chief," to control and organize the Tuyet Diem villagers at their new site. The Americans present always referred to him by his new title and spoke to him with the same humble deference that I had seen accorded to Lieutenant Colonel Tho in Quang Tin. The village chief was a tall, thin young man with a tight-lipped, impatient air, who wore a freshly pressed khaki uniform, stiff and glistening with starch, and French-style glasses with rims of clear plastic that extended only across the top of the lenses. At about two o'clock, when I arrived at the beach in front of the lot, he was in a state of fury because the gap in the barbed-wire fence had rendered the registration procedure meaningless. He paced up and down just inside the barbed-wire fence shouting through an electric bullhorn, telling the villagers they should remain on the beach, but his order came much too late; about half the new arrivals had already entered the empty lot. At one point, nine middle-aged and elderly men approached him, with their conical straw hats in their hands, and a spokesman for the group told him that the villagers were afraid the Vietcong would come to Son Tra to kill them in the night, because they had not resisted evacuation from their homes in Tuyet Diem. The newly appointed village chief interrupted the spokesman in midsentence and, shaking with anger, shouted that he would listen to no demands of any kind at that moment, because no one was supposed to have even come through to his side of the fence yet. The spokesman started to say something more, and the village chief rushed at him and, in swift succession, struck him on the face with the front and then the back of his hand and kicked him on the hip. The spokesman fell back as he was beaten, and said nothing more. Several American officers were sitting nearby in a jeep talking, and one of them—an adviser to the new village chief—remarked to me, "Looks like they're having a little row." At my request, he went over to the chief with his interpreter to ask what had happened, and after returning and explaining the situation to me he observed, "The village chief believes that you have to be tough at first to gain their respect in order to control them."

Because the villagers had had neither the time nor the manpower to dismantle their houses and load the materials on the landing craft, as the Army had originally planned, and no building supplies had been made available, the villagers slept for the next few weeks under pieces of cloth propped up on sticks, or under their tarred basket boats. During that time, they began constructing makeshift dwellings of poles that they cut for themselves in a patch of woods nearby. The first night, they camped here and there all over the lot, but the next day they learned that theirs was only the first of a number of villages to be moved into the enclosure, and they were made to squeeze into one corner at the back. That day, the village chief performed his first administrative act, which was to take everyone's identification card away, so that no one could leave the enclosure. The same day, the Army decided to evacuate another village right away, and consequently a thousand more people arrived on the lot, bringing the official estimate of its population up to twenty-five hundred. Even then, only half the lot could be used, for more villages were scheduled for evacuation in the near future. Later that week, troops of the 196th Light Brigade blew up and then burned the empty village of Tuyet Diem. The Army put off the evacuation and destruction of the other villages until after the Presidential election, on September 3rd, because the troops of the 196th were needed to provide security around the polls.

Like most of the American military in Vietnam, the Army men who evacuated the villagers from Tuyet Diem and then destroyed the village saw what they were doing as only the first stage of a long-range benevolent plan for all of South Vietnam, in which the country would be rebuilt and then would develop a free and democratic government. This first stage of the plan—the destruction of the villages—usually went very smoothly, and gave rise to considerable optimism among the Americans who carried it out, but the second stage—the stage in which the Vietnamese and their American civil-affairs advisers were to rebuild and reorganize villages like Tuyet Diem, and were to stitch the whole society back together again—turned out to be infinitely more difficult than anyone had expected, and the people who were to carry it out could not even begin to match the scale of destruction with their construction. More often than not, the reality of the villagers' new life under the South Vietnamese government turned out to be a crowded tent in a government camp or a bare lot like the one in Son Tra. Many optimistic Americans,

including reporters as well as military men and civilian officials, tended to set off the destruction caused by the military
effort against the construction resulting from the civil-affairs
effort, seeing the two results as separate but balanced "sides"
of the war; and, looking at our commitment of men and materials, they were often favorably impressed with the size of
the constructive effort, almost as though it were being carried
out in one country while the military effort was being carried
out in another. But, of course, the two programs were being
carried out in the same provinces and the same villages, and
the people who received the allotments of rice were the same
people whose villages had been destroyed by bombs. The
Vietnamese civilians felt the effects of the two programs not
as two abstract "sides" of the war but as a continuing experience in the single reality of their daily lives, and, from their
point of view, the aid given them by the Americans and the
South Vietnamese government amounted to only a tiny measure of compensation (although extravagant promises were
made in the leaflets and in other propaganda) for enormous
losses and suffering. Many Americans, both civilian and military, tended not to see beyond the particular program they
were involved in. Civil-affairs officials, forgetting that it was
American firepower that had been the original direct cause of
the destitution of the vast majority of the people in the camps,
were puzzled when these hungry, tired people showed little
gratitude for the help that the Americans and the G.V.N. were
giving them. Many of the civil-affairs officials were working
exhaustingly long hours and doing the best job they could
with their limited time and resources, and they could not see
why the people should complain and expect more than they
were getting. Many military men, for their part, were loyal
only to *their* duty—that of conducting military operations.
Having efficiently carried out the "military half," they saw it
as the responsibility of the Vietnamese government and of the
American civil-affairs advisers to carry out the "civilian half"
by taking care of the people who had been hurt or dispossessed in the "military half." (Thus, although, in the two
weeks of Operation Benton, Task Force Oregon destroyed
about sixty-five per cent of the houses of an estimated seventeen thousand people, the officer in charge of the 101st's

Civil Affairs Office had been able to answer my question about the future of the area's population by saying, "*We* don't have any plans for the immediate future. It's the responsibility of the G.V.N. and the ARVN to carry out Pacification and Revolutionary Development." He did not know that the G.V.N. had no plan for these people.) But because, along with the destruction of villages, American military operations brought death to many civilians, American civil-affairs workers, no matter how well intentioned they might be, and no matter how well supplied they might someday become, could never, from the point of view of the villagers, "balance" the sufferings caused by the military, or undo what they had done, which was often absolute and irreversible.

from *The Military Half: An Account of the Destruction in Quang Ngai and Quang Tin*, 1968

The War Just Doesn't Add Up

by Richard Harwood

THE SUMMER'S EVENTS in Vietnam have generated a major conflict between the American Government and the press. It is a conflict of judgment over the course of the war.

A substantial majority of the correspondents in Vietnam believe and are reporting that the war is going badly, that no victory is in sight, that the effort to pacify the peasantry has been unproductive.

To the Johnson Administration in general and to the President in particular, such assessments are incorrect and uninformed. As The Washington Post reported Aug. 18, "Recent newspaper reports that little progress is being made in Vietnam and that the military situation is stalemated are hotly disputed by the White House."

The reports in question have come from Peter Arnett and Horst Faas of the Associated Press, both of whom have spent more than five years in Vietnam; from R. W. Apple Jr. and Thomas Buckley of the New York Times; from Ward Just of The Washington Post; from Sol Sanders of U.S. News and World Report, and from other correspondents, both American and foreign, representing newspapers, magazines and the television networks.

"This war," Just wrote in June at the end of an 18-month tour in Vietnam, "is not being won . . . It may not be winnable."

" 'Stalemate,' " Apple wrote early this month, "is a fighting word in Washington . . . But it is the word used by almost all Americans here, except the top officials, to characterize what is happening."

The private comments of most (although not all) of the correspondents in Vietnam are even more pessimistic and more disillusioned than their stories reflect. One correspondent for a major American publication has spoken often this summer of a personal crisis of conscience: "If I had any guts, I'd quit and join the peace movement."

He is admittedly a dove. But it is not only "doves" among the correspondents who have lost faith in the ability of the Americans to salvage their $25-billion-a-year enterprise in Vietnam.

The negativism in dispatches has been so pronounced that the official spokesman for the U.S. Mission in Saigon, John McGowan, was led to remark last month: "The pessimism among the correspondents has never been deeper than now." From all accounts, however, the President is getting few, if any, pessimistic reports from his subordinates in Washington or Vietnam.

"(He) tells visitors," the papers reported last month, "that every responsible official he has sent to Vietnam reports that there is no stalemate; that the Communists are suffering heavy losses, have a shortage of medicine and food, are finding it increasingly difficult to move supplies and face morale problems."

These officials include Gen. William C. Westmoreland, Defense Secretary Robert McNamara and the chairman of the Joint Chiefs of Staff, Gen. Earle Wheeler, all of whom have emphasized "progress" in their assessments of the war this summer.

One result of this conflict is public confusion, which the opinion polls reflect. Another result is mistrust between the press and American officialdom involved in the war in Vietnam. At a social gathering in Honolulu a few weeks ago, a correspondent was introduced to an admiral, who curtly announced, "If I'd known you were a newspaperman, I wouldn't have shaken your hand."

The press corps, at times, has been no more gracious. Many of the statements issued by the American establishment in Saigon these days are challenged bluntly as propaganda or self-delusion.

This "credibility gap" is a product of many factors, not the least of which is ignorance. The state of the enemy's morale, for example, influences any assessment of the war. But neither the CIA nor the American correspondents can say with certainty whether the morale of the Vietcong and the North Vietnamese is up or down at any given time.

The Johnson Administration, on the basis of intelligence estimates, nevertheless insists that the enemy is "hurting badly." On the other hand, correspondents and American troops who observe enemy units in action are impressed by their aggressiveness, their fighting ability and the quality and quantity of their arms. North Vietnamese units in Kontum Province, for example, have not bothered in recent months to pick up American weapons left on the battlefield except as souvenirs to take home.

Another area of ignorance involves enemy troop strength and enemy casualties. American military commanders have said all summer that the enemy force numbered between 295,000 and 300,000 men and that it was growing larger each month. American civilian officials, such as pacification chief Robert Komer, have been skeptical of these estimates and have predicted that they would be corrected downward.

Last month, they were revised downward. The revision, military spokesmen said, was a result of heavy enemy casualties and not simply an arithmetical recalculation. The difficulty with that explanation, in the minds of some correspondents, is that U.S. estimates of enemy casualties often appear to be little more than wild guesses.

On June 19 and 20, for instance, elements of the U.S. Ninth Division attacked Vietcong positions at Apbac village in Long-an Province, 15 miles south of Saigon. The Americans had heavy casualties but claimed to have killed 255 of the enemy.

Two reporters, Lee Lescaze of The Washington Post and Robert Pisor of the Detroit News, interviewed all of the surviving officers and senior NCOs who took part in the fight. From their estimates, Lescaze and Pisor concluded that the number of enemy killed was between 54 and 70.

The following week, a company from the 173d Paratroop Brigade was virtually annihilated in a five-hour fight at Newdakto in Kontum Province. Gen. Westmoreland called the engagement a major victory and the brigade commander reported 475 enemy killed.

Subsequently, the U.S. command in Saigon unaccountably

reduced the enemy losses to 106. The estimate of troopers who survived the fight was 230. The number of enemy bodies found was 44.

The significance of such numbers is simply that they often spell the difference between "victory" and "defeat" in given engagements. And inevitably they provoke the question: Which numbers does the White House receive in its reports from the field?

This speculation carries over into other aspects of the American effort in Vietnam. A correspondent traveling in the Delta south of Saigon in June was informed by American officials there that only about 1.5 million of the region's 5.7 million people lived in "secure" areas controlled by the Saigon government. American officials in Saigon disagreed vehemently after the figures were published in The Washington Post. More than three million Delta people, they claimed, were "secure" and under government "control."

A few weeks later, the New York Times reported that "official United States data" showed fewer than 500,000 people under "total government control" in all of South Vietnam, excluding large cities such as Saigon. Since there is only one major city in the Delta (Cantho with a population of 200,000), the implication was that there is gross confusion among American officials over the degree of "security" in the country. Again the question presents itself: Which figures does the President read?

The White House was informed early in the summer that the troops under the command of Premier Ky in Saigon had shown dramatic improvement in their combat skills. Ky's armored squadron, as an example, killed 125 enemy troops for every ten fatalities they sustained, according to American commanders.

Assuming the correctness of the ratio, however, the performance of these squadrons—each containing 500 men—was not necessarily impressive. In all of 1966, the Eighth Armored Squadron killed one enemy soldier, the Fifth killed 12, the Tenth killed 23 and the Ninth killed 148. Total enemy dead: 184. Presumed Armored losses: 14 killed.

A single U.S. Marine battalion of about 1000 men claimed more enemy kills and lost more dead that these four armored squadrons in three days of fighting at the Demilitarized Zone in Quangtri province the first week in July.

Another problem contributing to the "credibility gap" is the different yardsticks applied by the correspondents and the American military establishment.

To the correspondents and to Marine riflemen at the DMZ, U.S. losses have been appalling and military gains nonexistent in recent months. Marine casualties along that frontier between North and South Vietnam have exceeded 10,000 since Jan. 1. Not a foot of ground has changed hands permanently.

To the generals, however, and presumably to the Pentagon and the White House, the military gains have been impressive; the Marines have prevented a full-scale invasion of the South. As for the casualties, they are not disturbing in terms of the manpower available in the United States.

A final element in the credibility debate is the judgments that both the correspondents and the American Government have made in the past. Major elements of the press expected the overthrow of President Diem in 1963 to lead to major reforms in Vietnamese society. That failed to happen. The press was generally confident in 1965 and 1966 that the American buildup in Vietnam would dramatically change the course of the war. Most correspondents have now abandoned that view.

The Government's record is equally spotty. Secretary McNamara predicted in late 1963 and again in 1964 that some American troops would soon be brought home. Instead, there has been a steady buildup in American troop strength. Secretary of State Dean Rusk said in February, 1964, that the South Vietnamese had reached a position where "they themselves can handle this problem primarily with their own effort." Instead, American troops have taken over more and more of the fighting and have become more and more involved in the civil pacification effort.

Early in July, Gen. Wheeler announced that "we have the initiative, the military initiative, and this is the basis upon which wars are won." Less than three weeks later, Gen. Westmoreland told a press conference that American troops in

South Vietnam were on the "defensive" and were fighting a "defensive" war.

Thus the President has one point of view and many of the correspondents in Vietnam have another. So the public is likely to continue to get wholly conflicting assessments of how it is going over there.

The Washington Post, September 3, 1967

A Day in the Life

by Michael J. Arlen

SAIGON

ONE Thursday morning recently, very early—about six o'clock—but with the sun already up and the air already sticky and warm, John Laurence, who is twenty-seven years old and a correspondent with C.B.S. News, pulled himself out of bed at the slick but not notably comfortable Marine-built press center at Danang, put on his green combat fatigues, filled up his two canteens with purified water in the kitchen, and, together with his cameraman, a twenty-five-year-old named Keith Kay, and his sound man, a thirty-one-year-old Vietnamese named Pham Tan Dan, headed off in the direction of Con Thien, a Marine artillery outpost three-quarters of a mile south of the Demilitarized Zone. Con Thien isn't very far from Danang—about a hundred miles—but it is hard to get to nowadays. Laurence and his crew took one of the big C-130 transports that make regular thirty-minute flights to the Marine base at Dong Ha, then boarded a truck in a convoy that leaves Dong Ha each morning on the westerly route along what's still called Route 9, toward the village of Cam Lo. There were about twelve vehicles in the convoy, mostly trucks, and mostly carrying ammunition, food, water, mail, and some Marines who had been on leave or in hospitals and were being returned to duty at the artillery batteries. Laurence rode in an open truck with a dozen Marines, his sound man, Dan, nearby, and Kay, the cameraman, perched on the cab, half-leaning against a machine gun mounted there. The young Marines read the comics from last Sunday's paper and talked easily among themselves. One asked Laurence what he was doing there, and he said he was going out to do a show about Con Thien.

"When's it going to be on?" the Marine asked.

"With any luck, in two or three days," Laurence said.

A couple of them joked about that. It can take between seven and ten days for letters to go from a soldier in the field in Vietnam to the States, and one man had wanted to write his family and tell them there was going to be a TV show about his base.

"Anyhow, you can't be sure," said Laurence. "You never know what's going to get on."

Another asked him, "What kind of film are you using?"

"Sixteen-millimetre color," said Laurence.

The Marine thought for a moment. "If you're shooting color, you really ought to go down to Khe Sanh, because of the beautiful greens and browns," he said. "You know, they have six different shades of green down there."

After about a forty-minute drive, the convoy stopped at Cam Lo, which was once a village but is now just another Marine artillery battery. The road from Dong Ha to Cam Lo is reasonably safe these days (except at night), but the road from Cam Lo north to Con Thien hasn't been so successfully pacified as yet. There had been two ambushes within the last ten days—some Marines had been killed in the first one—so the convoy waited for two tanks and two ONTOS (an ONTOS is a track vehicle, a little smaller than a tank, mounting a cluster of six 106-mm. rifles, six 50-calibre spotting rifles, and one 30-calibre machine gun) to come up and join it. During the ride from Dong Ha, Laurence had noticed a seemingly introspective young Marine, sitting toward the front of the truck, who had something written on the back of his flak jacket, and while they were stopped he asked him about it. The Marine—Corporal Edward Broderick—said it was a poem he'd written a few months before. Laurence asked him if he would recite it on camera. The Corporal nodded. Kay clambered down from the cab of the truck, Dan adjusted his sound equipment, and Laurence held the mike.

"I don't know that I can remember it right off," the Corporal said, looking at Laurence's mike.

"Well, try it once on your own," said Laurence.

The Corporal took off his flak jacket, read the poem, then put the flak jacket back on again. "O.K.," he said.

Kay's camera started whirring. The Marine stared straight ahead and recited. "When youth was a soldier," he began, his voice low and flat, "and I fought across the sea,/We were young and cold hearts, of bloody savagery,/Born of indignation, children of our times,/We were orphans of creation, and dying in our prime." Everyone in the truck was very silent.

Kay was shooting back through Laurence and the Corporal to the other trucks in the convoy.

"What made you write that poem?" Laurence asked.

"Well, just the way things are," the Corporal said. He then went on to say some things about how it was better anyway to be in the front lines at Con Thien than back at some base camp like Danang.

Laurence asked him what his overriding feeling about the war was right now.

The Corporal thought for a moment. "Better to be fighting the Communists here than fighting them back in San Diego," he said.

Two tanks appeared, rumbling down the road from Cam Lo, and Laurence called to Kay that he was going to try to do an "open" (meaning an opening for the film piece) before the convoy got under way.

"We don't have much time," Kay said.

"I'll ad-lib it," Laurence said. He moved to the seat in the truck that was nearest the tailgate. Kay once again took up his station near the cab and started up his camera. Laurence, still holding the mike, stared at the floor for a moment. "The convoy for Con Thien goes once a day, and it does not stay long. It is the only source of supply for the Marine outpost on the Demilitarized Zone; it rides the only road that goes there," he began. "The convoy carries food, water, and ammunition, and returns the few men who have been lucky enough to get away for a few days. . . ."

When the convoy started up again, the Marines seemed to be in a changed mood. Some went back to reading comics, but the road was really too bumpy, and for the most part they just sat in silence and stared out at the muddy, reddish-brown dirt on either side of the road, the dry-looking scrub, the rolling, dark-green hills extending into the distance. Shortly, one by one, they started inserting ammunition clips in their M-16s and putting them on safe. Laurence nodded at Kay, and Kay's camera began whirring. Twenty minutes farther on, at a place called Charlie Two, near the entrance to a Marine battery, the convoy passed the burned hulk of a light tank, lying abandoned twenty feet off the road. One of the Marines took hold of Laurence's arm and started telling him about the ambush ten days before (he'd been one of its victims), pointing to where it had happened, describing how the tank had been hit, telling him in an intense, informative way what a serious fight it had been. The men had now stopped every other activity, and were only looking out on either side of the road with peering, impassive faces. The convoy bumped along. The sun grew hotter. For the first time, some of the men began to sweat a little.

Around noon, the trucks reached Con Thien—the end of the road. The road points directly toward the camp, then stops at the base of a slight hill. The convoy stopped, and there was a good deal of discussion among the drivers as to how far the trucks should go up toward the camp, because of the accuracy of the enemy artillery across the D.M.Z., and because of the mud, and because many of the trucks were carrying ammunition. "Hell, let's take 'em right up," the driver of Laurence's truck said, and the trucks roared up the hill.

Everybody quickly clambered out. Beyond the hill is a shallow valley, and in the valley sit the gun emplacements, just the barrels of the guns showing, the rest hidden behind sandbags, and everything in view—sandbags, terrain (there are no trees, no vegetation, just sandbags, guns, empty shell cases, and boxes of ammunition)—light brown, the color of dry dirt. Laurence and his crew walked down the hill, each man wearing a pack, and Kay and Dan carrying their equipment besides. Laurence asked someone which was the command bunker (since most of the men were either naked to the waist or wearing olive-colored T-shirts, it was hard to tell rank), and the man pointed to the largest bunker in the camp, built right into the side of the hill. The executive officer came out to greet them—a Marine major in his mid-thirties, who seemed a bit tense.

"Hi," said Laurence. "I'm Jack Laurence, of C.B.S. News.

We've come up to take pictures of you winning the war up here."

"How long are you planning to stay?" the major asked.

"Oh, just as long as we need to get some action," said Laurence. "A day, a week."

"You really want to spend the night up *here*?" the major said. "We haven't had any press around in about three weeks."

Laurence and his crew threw their packs off outside the bunker and followed the major in. Inside, it was very dark; a few men were sitting silent at tables, with candles for light. Four military-band field radios were squawking. There was a large map standing upright in the center of the bunker, about eight feet high and divided into three panels, like a screen.

"What about something to eat?" Kay whispered to Laurence. "I haven't had anything all morning."

The major walked over. "Come on," he said, "I'll give you a briefing."

Laurence and Kay and Dan stood in front of the big map, and the major pointed out the various places where the battalion's companies were now operating.

A soldier came hurrying in with a message for the major.

"Kilo Company is in contact with snipers," the major said, and showed them where Kilo Company was on the map.

The major finished the briefing at last, and Laurence, Kay, and Dan (whose Vietnamese face had been stared at suspiciously by some of the officers in the bunker) stumbled out into the sun, where the sergeant major came over and handed them each a can of C rations—in this case, something described on the label as "turkey loaf."

A man in a green T-shirt who had a bright-red mustache came over and introduced himself as Captain Jansen, and began to tell Laurence about how to take cover during an artillery barrage. "Above all, don't follow me when you see me running down the side of the hill," Jansen said. "I like to be off by myself when the shells come in. I have this feeling that the round that has your number on it shouldn't kill anyone else—and I certainly don't want to get someone else's round. Actually, the best thing for *you* to do is watch the other guys.

When they start running, hurry after them." Jansen went off to sit on the ground nearby and read *Stars & Stripes.*

Everything seemed relaxed. Laurence took out his pocket compass and fooled around with it. A soldier came up to him and said that Lieutenant Colonel Lee R. Bendel, the battery commander, was still tied up but would be available shortly. Laurence wandered off to take a look around, walking away from the command bunker up toward the top of the hill, and stepping over cast-off shell cases and the ruins of the Colonel's shower, which had been destroyed by an incoming round. At the top, he stood for a moment trying to figure out from his compass where true north was. From a bunker nearby, a voice was saying, "I swear I got the actual word. We're going in four days. Colonel's orders." Other voices chimed in from other bunkers. "Hey, we're getting out. We're getting out of here."

A corporal came up and asked Laurence to come down the hill a bit and see the new infrared radar beam—a large green machine, on the order of a searchlight, that was mounted on a jeep. The corporal explained in a proud manner how the infrared beam worked—you turn it on at night and wear infrared goggles, and then you can see the V.C. when they move across the ground in the dark. Suddenly, in midsentence, the corporal's head turned toward the north. He quickly got down on his knees and seemed to be looking at the ground. He glanced up at Laurence. "Hell, no sense staying out here," he said. "Let's get in a bunker." Laurence and the corporal started walking quickly, then ran. From somewhere, a voice yelled, "Incoming!" There was a large explosion quite far away. Laurence and the corporal tumbled into a bunker where there were about twelve other men. Everyone else seemed very casual.

"I'm Jack Laurence, from C.B.S. News," said Laurence.

"Have a beer," said one of the men.

Some of them were talking about the war, and Laurence took out a small tape recorder and turned it on. "What do you think of the enemy?" he asked.

A big Southern corporal leaned forward. "When we first came up here, we used to call the enemy Victor Charlie," he said. "But now we call him Charles. Mister Charles."

"Lord Charles," somebody else said, and laughed.

The men talked on—with Laurence recording their words—about their frustrating efforts to get at the enemy artillery. "Our shelling don't seem to have much effect, because those enemy guns keep hitting the camp every day," said one. "Often, we get about a hundred rounds a day."

"Why are you crazy enough to come up to Con Thien?" one man asked Laurence.

"You're here," said Laurence. "We might as well tell the people back home how well you're doing."

After about twenty minutes, in which there was no more shelling, the corporal in charge of the infrared radar machine told Laurence it was O.K. to leave. "I'll show you the observation post," he said. They walked toward it—the sun now very hot, everything hot and dry. A voice again yelled, "Incoming!," and Laurence and the corporal ran forward and tumbled into a small, open bunker, with a telescopelike object, a field radio, and two young soldiers all lying on the bottom. This turned out to be the observation post. There was another big explosion, also far away. The two soldiers didn't seem to be frightened, but they both had their heads flat to the ground. A voice came over the field radio. "Do you see where those rounds are coming from?" One of the soldiers raised his head sufficiently to reply to the radio. "No, sir. Don't see a thing," he said, and he grinned at Laurence. "Every time we get incoming, that lieutenant calls on the radio and asks us if we see where it's coming from, and every time we say, 'No, sir, we don't see a thing.' The fact is, those damned guns of theirs are firing from the back slopes in the D.M.Z., and they're too far away and too well camouflaged for us to do much about them."

After ten minutes or so, when the shelling again seemed to have stopped, Laurence got out of the observation post and ran back to the command bunker to look for Kay and Dan. Colonel Bendel was there. Kay was seated on the floor inside the bunker, reloading his camera, and when he had finished plugging it into the battery pack over his shoulder, Laurence and his crew went outside again, quickly following the Colonel, who had muttered something about wanting to get a "better vantage point" from which to see his two companies.

The better vantage point turned out to be on the rim of the same hill Laurence had been standing on earlier, only on the far side, in the direction of the road, away from the camp and out of sight of it. It was a lonely-seeming spot, which had obviously not been much used—at least, not by Americans. Near where they were standing, Laurence spotted five small foxholes dug into the side of the hill. The shelling now seemed to have stopped completely. The Colonel was standing on a small, jutting piece of ground, peering below him through binoculars. "You can see Kilo Company moving down there," the Colonel said. "Look—three fingers to the right of this tree." He pointed. "See them?"

Laurence, who wears glasses, peered below him and, about three-quarters of a mile away, saw a line of Marines walking in the open across a field. Just at that moment, there was a loud, sharp pop, pop, pop-pop-pop, pop, and a few seconds later a string of mortar rounds exploded in a line across the field, in the midst of the Marines. There was a moment of absolute silence.

"Are you sure those are *our* troops?" Laurence asked the Colonel incredulously. "Aren't *we* shelling *them*?"

Some of the Marines in the field could now be seen to run forward, and a few seconds later another barrage of shells exploded, this time making a much deeper sound. Laurence heard Kay's camera whirring, and turned back to him to ask, "How much of that can we get?"

"Just the smoke," Kay said. "The damned lens isn't long enough."

"Well, get a little of the smoke out there," Laurence said. "Perhaps it can be used."

"O.K.," said Kay. "But it's not going to be very clear."

Captain Jansen came up with a field radio on his back and stood beside the Colonel. The Colonel alternately listened to chatter coming out of the radio and peered down through his binoculars at the again silent field. Laurence dropped on one knee to get out of Kay's picture, and extended his mike toward the Colonel.

"Every time we move, we take heavy fire," a man's voice said over the radio.

"O.K., it looks like we've got the grid on the one that's

getting—that you're getting the incoming from," the Colonel replied. "Hold your present positions. I hope you're in holes there as best you can."

Two jets suddenly appeared above the Marines in the field—narrow, pointed F-4Cs, circling at about five thousand feet. Kay aimed his camera toward them. One of the jets went into a dive, came in very low—no more than a couple of hundred feet above the ground—passed over the field, and then climbed again.

"A dud," said Captain Jansen.

The second jet came in and made the same pass, and suddenly the far edge of the field exploded with a black-and-orange flash, and a bright sheet of fire rushed forward very fast.

"Maybe that will show up," said Kay. "But don't count on it."

The radio was now very active, with several excited voices talking back and forth. "We're in very heavy contact here," one man's voice was saying tensely.

The Colonel, speaking calmly, asked the man to tell him which way he was facing and where his platoons were.

"Tell him to make his strafing runs one hundred metres in another direction!" a second voice called.

"We're *still* in very heavy contact!" the first voice called.

The Colonel put down his binoculars and held the radio. "O.K., Bill," he said, speaking in a fatherly tone. "Just try to pull your people together and get them linked up to Mike Company. This is still your show."

There was silence for a moment. Then the voice came back: "I think we may have to have help. We might get overrun."

"All right, Bill," the Colonel said, still in a fatherly voice. "I'm going to try to bring Mike Company up to you. I'm positioning tanks to fire in your support. But I *have* to have your coördinates—your position."

Just then, somebody yelled, "Incoming!," and Laurence, who until that instant had been kneeling on the ground beside the Colonel trying to tape the dialogue, jumped into one of the foxholes, and so did Kay and Dan. Kay's camera was still whirring, although he was holding it to cover his face. A shell exploded somewhere on the other side of the hill. Laurence looked over the edge of the foxhole and saw the Colonel and his staff all flattened out on the ground, the radio chattering but none of the Marines talking—just olive-green backs on the ground.

"We've *got* to get some of this," Laurence said to Kay.

Kay raised his head from the foxhole and pointed his camera at the Colonel and his staff. At that moment, Captain Jansen turned his head and saw Kay, and then immediately the staff jumped to its feet as several shells burst with great thumping noises. The Captain organized the staff into separate foxholes. Laurence moved forward into the foxhole now occupied by the Colonel and Captain Jansen, and motioned to Kay to continue taking pictures. The artillery barrage was coming in steadily, with two or three very loud, ground-shaking explosions at a time. The staff were all crouched low in the foxholes, except for the Colonel, who was standing up, with one foot on the edge of the hole, and leaning forward. Laurence huddled low over his microphone and spoke in a soft voice: "You don't spend long in Con Thien before the action starts. Some time ago, two companies from the battalion defending this outpost ran into enemy contact, and it has become increasingly heavy. Colonel Bendel is watching the action less than a mile away and moving his troops into position."

"O.K., look," the Colonel was saying to an officer who had come up. "Do you see where that smoke is?"

"Yes, sir."

"That far, where the shells landed, is about three hundred metres," the Colonel was saying. "Right where that big tree is out there, three hundred to four hundred metres southeast."

The noise from the battlefield now became very intense as the air strikes continued: a loud roaring of jet engines, sounds of gunfire and machinegun fire, the constant explosions of the shells, and then some strange little buzzing sounds, which, Jansen explained to Laurence, were made by bullets going by very close. The Colonel, who was on the radio again, trying to get Mike Company to move around toward Kilo Company, also appeared a little mystified and irritated by the buzzing. "Don't worry about them," said Jansen. "They're almost spent."

In the middle of the shelling, a major appeared, running across the hill. "I've got to have those coördinates!" he yelled. "I can't fire if I don't have those coördinates!"

The Colonel repeated the request over the radio, and a voice came back apologetically: "I didn't have my map, but I have it now. I'm trying to figure where we are."

The major turned to go back, caught his foot on the wire running between Laurence's mike and Dan's sound box, and sent the mike spinning out of Laurence's hand and across the ground. "Goddam wire!" he said.

The Colonel turned. "Look, some of you people just move on back."

"You're all right where you are," Jansen said to Laurence.

Kay, in the meantime, had run back to the command bunker to get some more equipment, and was now crouched in his foxhole trying to change film inside his changing bag—a black cloth affair with two sleeves in which he had inserted his arms. It took about five minutes, and he finished just as a fresh barrage hit, apparently right inside the camp.

More and more bullets were now buzzing by. The Colonel continued to stand with one foot on the edge of the foxhole. Jansen was seated on the edge. Laurence got up beside Jansen, and, with Kay's camera on the three of them, again spoke softly into the mike. "That whistling sound you hear is incoming artillery fire," he said. "You may actually be able to see it landing."

Kay somehow overheard him and quickly panned his camera from right to left, and just at that point four artillery rounds burst, with great crashes, inside the camp. The Colonel looked around. "Let's make sure we spread out here," he said.

"That one landed about one hundred and fifty yards away," Laurence said into his microphone, and then glanced back and saw that Kay was furiously taking his camera case apart.

"Goddam camera won't work!" Kay yelled to Laurence. In a moment, he had it working again.

Two helicopters came into view and landed beside the camp, their engines roaring, the dust blowing up around them. Soldiers appeared from within the camp carrying men on stretchers—men who had been wounded by the artillery bombardment. Kay's camera was rolling on them; then, once again, he stopped and began to pull his camera apart. This time, it wouldn't start up again. Kay was cursing and muttering as he and Dan crouched in their foxhole, pieces of Arriflex littered around them.

"What is it?" Laurence called.

"It's the battery pack," said Dan. "It's out of power."

Kay and Dan continued to fiddle with the camera. More shells landed nearby. Captain Jansen remained seated on the edge of the foxhole. One shell landed very close by, shattering the ground, and sending off shock waves. Laurence, with nothing to do and suddenly edgy, tumbled back into the hole. "It's O.K.," Jansen said to him. "It's not close enough to hurt you, and the next shell won't be in on top."

Kay called to Laurence that the camera was really dead.

"Are you sure?" Laurence asked.

"I'm sure," said Kay.

"If you want to get out of here, you can go back with the convoy," Jansen said.

Laurence considered for a moment. "O.K.," he said. "I guess we will."

The three C.B.S. men got all their gear together, while the Colonel went on directing Mike Company up to a position on Kilo Company's flank. "Now, if you'll just get everyone linked up . . ." the Colonel was saying into the radio. Jansen formed Laurence, Kay, and Dan into a line, spaced about ten feet apart, and walked them down the side of the hill toward the road. The Colonel looked at them over his shoulder. "That's a real fine squad you got there, Jansen," he said. Jansen, seeming embarrassed, waved at him. Just as they neared the foot of the hill, another incoming round came in, and they all dived into a tiny three-foot-deep pit, sprawling on their backs on top of each other—except for Jansen, who sat on the edge, remarking, "I'll know when it's going to hit us." An incredibly loud explosion burst nearby, making the ground shake, and they all looked up, to see that a fire had started in the midst of a stack of wooden crates containing 105-mm. ammunition.

A sergeant appeared, running. It was the convoy sergeant, who had just brought the ammunition up. "If that stuff blows, we're dead," he said.

A lieutenant also appeared on the run. "Get back! Get back!" he yelled. "It's going to blow!"

A number of men rushed out of the nearby bunkers and ran away from the fire. No one had told Laurence what to do, and he stood transfixed beside Jansen, who continued to sit still, watching. A Marine with a small hand-held fire extinguisher appeared briefly, made some dancing motions toward the fire, and then sped off.

A captain appeared a little distance away, yelled, "Everybody in the hole!," and disappeared.

The fire continued to blaze.

"For Chrisake!" the convoy sergeant said. "*Somebody's* got to put it out!"

"Incoming!" a voice yelled, and this time Laurence and Jansen both dived into the tiny hole with the others. When they stuck their heads up again, the convoy sergeant was walking back across the ground toward them holding an empty five-gallon water can. "Fire's out," he said. He dropped the can on the ground. "If you're all coming with me," he said, "let's get the hell out of here." He pointed to a jeep about fifty yards away and started to run toward it.

Laurence, Dan, and Kay chased after him, their packs bouncing on their backs. The sergeant clambered into the jeep, which was a small one, and the others began to fall in after him.

A voice in the distance yelled, "Incoming!"

"Everybody in?" the sergeant called, starting to pull away as Laurence dived into the back, his legs sticking out behind the tailgate. A couple of shells landed nearby—great crunches. The sergeant had his foot all the way down on the accelerator and was tearing across the terrain—skidding, turning, with all four wheels sometimes leaving the ground as they hit a bump—muttering incessantly, "Don't worry. We're going to make it." A huge explosion hit just behind, shaking the jeep. "Goddammit, they're trying to get us," he said, and added excitedly, "But they're gonna have to catch us!" He pushed the accelerator to the floor again and, reaching down between the legs of the man beside him—it was Kay—picked up a sub-machine gun and handed it back to Laurence, saying, "Hey, kid, know how to use this?"

Laurence took the gun, looked at it in bewilderment, and passed it to one of the soldiers, who put it on the floor beside him. Two more loud explosions hit, off to one side of the jeep. The sergeant was driving at top speed, the jeep screeching around the curves of the hill. In a couple of minutes, he reached the rest of the convoy—a line of trucks parked at the edge of the road, with Marines standing beside them.

"Everybody onto the trucks!" the sergeant yelled. "Let's get the hell outa here!"

Laurence, Kay, and Dan climbed onto a truck with six or seven Marines, and in a second all the trucks were moving, with Marines hanging on to the backs and sides and being hauled inside by friends. The convoy hurtled south along the road to Cam Lo.

About halfway to Cam Lo, gunfire started from the right side of the road, its source invisible—sharp cracks and pings, a few at first, and then more and more. The Marines fired back as they sped by. One truck was hit and caught on fire. The rest of the convoy reached Cam Lo in forty minutes, and stopped. The sergeant came around the truck to see Laurence. His eyes were very bright, and his right hand was bleeding. "I've had enough today," he said. "I'm not going any farther." He glanced abstractedly at his hand. "Come on and stay with us tonight," he said. "I'll buy you boys a beer." It was about six o'clock.

Laurence went into one of the tents, took off his pack, sat down on a bed, and started to write in a small notebook. The sergeant brought him a can of beer, which Laurence placed on the floor beside him, and when he had finished writing he called to Dan, who was just outside the tent setting up his sound equipment, that he was now ready to do the "voice-over," meaning a tape of his voice to be used with various filmed sequences of action. Laurence thereupon took a pillow from one of the beds, put it in the center of the bed, put his microphone on the pillow, and sat down on the edge of the bed.

"Level," called Dan from outside the tent.

"The enemy is one hazard, nature another. . . ." Laurence said.

"O.K.," said Dan.

Laurence took a breath. "Convoy to Con Thien," he said into the microphone. "Narration. Cameraman, Kay. Sound man, Dan." He paused. "The enemy is one hazard, nature another," he began, glancing at the notebook, which was on the bed beside him. "Two days of rain have nearly washed out the soft dirt road. It will be impassable within a month, with the coming of the fall monsoon. The convoy arrives safely, unloads quickly, and turns around, because the camp is continually under artillery attack." He paused again for a moment. "Every few minutes, and sometimes every few seconds, the guns go off, their guns and our guns, whistling and pounding with the incessant, methodical efficiency of a carpenter hammering nails. In the battle outside the camp, at least twenty men are killed on both sides, perhaps a hundred wounded, as each recovers its casualties quickly and prepares for the night of shelling, and the following day of fighting."

The convoy spent Thursday night in Cam Lo, and the next day it went back to Dong Ha, running into a company of Marines along the way—in a field a few hundred feet off to the side of the road—who were being shelled by rockets. Kay's camera was working again (he had had it recharged with a generator in Cam Lo), and, crouching with Laurence and Dan in a hole by the side of the road, he photographed some of the action—tanks racing out of range, soldiers running—for the few minutes that the shelling lasted. The convoy reached Danang an hour or so later.

Laurence called Edward Fouhy, the C.B.S. bureau chief in Saigon, who asked him to ship the film down to him right away, in the hope of getting it home in time for the Saturday-evening news. Then Laurence ran back inside the C.B.S. hut in the Danang press center and quickly scribbled out a "voice-over close," and, with his mike on the bed, as at Cam Lo, and Dan outside the door with his equipment, recited it in a measured voice: "The next day, on the road to Con Thien, another American company is shelled in an open field a hundred yards ahead, again with amazing accuracy, this time with rockets.

One tank is hit, a tread knocked apart, and the rest of the tanks, vulnerable to rockets, pull back out of range. They carry away some of the casualties from the rocket attack—some of the young men the Corporal wrote his poem about." He paused, then added, "John Laurence, C.B.S. News, on the road to Con Thien."

After that, Laurence packed the cans of film and tape in a big yellow net bag and took them to the Danang airbase, where he put them aboard an Air Force flight to Saigon. A C.B.S. man in Saigon rushed them onto the Pan American flight to San Francisco, where they were put aboard a United Airlines flight to New York. The film didn't arrive in time for the Saturday news, so it was shown on Monday night, when it ran for four minutes and prompted a congratulatory telegram to Laurence, Kay, and Dan from Walter Cronkite.

The New Yorker, September 30, 1967

from *The Armies of the Night*

by Norman Mailer

5: *The Witches and the Fugs*

SINCE the parking lot was huge as five football fields, and just about empty, for they were the first arrivals, the terminus of the March was without drama. Nor was the Pentagon even altogether visible from the parking lot. Perhaps for that reason, a recollection returned to Mailer of that instant (alive as an open nerve) when they had seen it first, walking through the field, just after the March had left the road on the Virginia side of the Potomac; there, topping a rise, it appeared, huge in the near distance, not attractive. Somehow, Mailer had been anticipating it would look more impressive than its pictures, he was always expecting corporation land to surprise him with a bit of wit, an unexpected turn of architectual grace—it never did. The Pentagon rose like an anomaly of the sea from the soft Virginia fields (they were crossing a park), its pale yellow walls reminiscent of some plastic plug coming out of the hole made in flesh by an unmentionable operation. There, it sat, geometrical aura complete, isolated from anything in nature surrounding it. Eras ago had corporation land begun by putting billboards on the old post roads?—now they worked to clean them up—just as the populace had finally succeeded in depositing comfortable amounts of libido on highway signs, gasoline exhaust, and oil-stained Jersey macadam—now corporation land, here named Government, took over state preserves, straightened crooked narrow roads, put up government buildings, removed unwelcome signs till the young Pop eye of Art wept for unwelcome signs—where are our old friends?—and corporation land would succeed, if it hadn't yet, in making nature look like an outdoor hospital, and the streets of U.S. cities, grace of Urban Renewal, would be difficult to distinguish when drunk from pyramids of packaged foods in the aisles of a supermarket.

For years he had been writing about the nature of totalitarianism, its need to render populations apathetic, its instrument—the destruction of mood. Mood was forever being sliced, cut, stamped, ground, excised, or obliterated; mood was a scent which rose from the acts and calms of nature, and totalitarianism was a deodorant to nature. Yes, and by the logic of this metaphor, the Pentagon looked like the five-sided tip on the spout of a spray can to be used under the arm, yes, the Pentagon was spraying the deodorant of its presence all over the fields of Virginia.

The North Parking Lot was physically separated from the Pentagon by a wide four-lane highway. Corporate wisdom had been at work—they might have been rattling about in the vast and empty parking lot of a modern stadium when no game is being played. Being among the first hundred to arrive, they found themselves in a state of confusion. No enemy was visible, nor much organization. In the reaches of the parking lot where they had entered was some sort of crane, with what appeared to be a speaker's platform on the end of its arm, and that was apparently being gotten ready for more speeches. Lowell, Macdonald, and Mailer discussed whether to remain there. They were hardly in the mood for further addresses, but on the other hand, combat was getting nearer—one could tell by the slow contractions of the gut. It was not that they would lose their courage, so much as that it would begin to seep away; so the idea of listening to speeches was not intolerable. There would be at least company.

But a pleasant young woman accompanied by her child had come up to greet Lowell, and she now mentioned that the hippies were going to have a play at the other end of the parking lot and music seemed by far the better preparation for all battle, and music was indeed coming from that direction. So they set out, a modest group in the paved empty desert of the North Parking Area, and strolled toward the sounds of the band which were somehow medieval in sound, leaving behind the panorama of marchers slowly flowing in. On the way, they agreed again that they would be arrested early. That seemed the best way to satisfy present demands and still get back to New York in time for their dinners, parties, weekend parts. The desire to get back early is not dishonorable in Lowell and Macdonald; they had stayed on today, and indeed probably had come this far because Mailer had helped to urge them, but Mailer! with his apocalyptic visions at Lincoln Memorial and again on the March, his readiness to throw himself, breast against breast, in any charge on the foe, why now in such a rush? Did he not respect his visions?

Well the party that night looked to be the best coming up in some time; he simply hated to miss it. Besides, he had no position here; it was not his March on the Pentagon in conception or execution; he was hardly required to remain for days or even hours on the scene. His function was to be arrested—his name was expendable for the cause. He did not like the idea of milling about for hours while the fine line of earlier perception (and Vision!) got mucked in the general confusion. Besides, he was a novelist, and there is no procurer, gambler, adventurer or romantic lover more greedy for experience in great gouts—a part of the novelist wished to take the cumulative rising memories of the last three days and bring them whole, intact, in sum, as they stood now, to cast, nay—shades of Henry James—to *fling* on the gaming tables of life resumed in New York, and there amass a doubling and tripling again. He was in fact afraid that within the yawning mute concrete of the parking lot this day which had begun with such exultation would dissipate into leaderless armies wandering about, acting like clowns and fools before the face of the authority; or worse, raw massacres, something more than bones broken: actual disasters—that was also in the air. He did not know if he was secretly afraid too much would happen or too little, but one thing he knew he hated—that would be to wait, and wait again, and nerve up to the point of being arrested, and get diverted and wait again while the light of the vision went out of the day and out of his head until hungry and cold they would all shamble off shamefacedly to New York on a late plane, too late for everything all around. One could not do that to this day. Great days demanded as much respect as great nights—Victorian, no Edwardian, were Mailer's more courtly sentiments.

And in his defense, one decent motive. He had the conviction that his early arrest might excite others to further effort:

the early battles of a war wheel on the hinge of their first legends—perhaps his imagination, in lockstep to many a montage in many an old movie, saw the word going out from mouth to ear to mouth to ear, linking the troops—in fact cold assessment would say that was not an inaccurate expectation. Details later.

Yes, Mailer had an egotism of curious disproportions. With the possible exception of John F. Kennedy, there had not been a President of the United States nor even a candidate since the Second World War whom Mailer secretly considered more suitable than himself, and yet on the first day of a war which he thought might go on for twenty years, his real desire was to be back in New York for a party. Such men are either monumental fools or excruciatingly practical since it may be wise to go to every party you can if the war is to continue for two decades. Of course, the likelihood is that the government— old corporation land—knew very well how wise it was to forge an agreement in negotiation to stage (dump) the marchers on arrival in the North Area's parking—coming off the March and into the face of a line of troops at the Pentagon, Mailer along with a good many others would not have been diverted with thoughts of New York whereas the parking area was so large and so empty that any army would have felt small in its expanse.

Well, let us move on to hear the music. It was being played by the Fugs, or rather—to be scrupulously phenomenological—Mailer heard the music first, then noticed the musicians and their costumes, then recognized two of them as Ed Sanders and Tuli Kupferberg and knew it was the Fugs. Great joy! They were much better than the last time he had heard them in a grind-it-out theater on Macdougal Street. Now they were dressed in orange and yellow and rose colored capes and looked at once like Hindu gurus, French musketeers, and Southern cavalry captains, and the girls watching them, indeed sharing the platform with them were wearing love beads and leather bells—sandals, blossoms, and little steel-rimmed spectacles abounded, and the music, no rather the play, had begun, almost Shakespearean in its sinister anouncement of great pleasures to come. Now the Participant recognized that this was the beginning of the exorcism of the Pentagon, yes the

papers had made much of the permit requested by a hippie
leader named Abbie Hoffman to encircle the Pentagon with
twelve hundred men in order to form a ring of exorcism sufficiently powerful to raise the Pentagon three hundred feet.
In the air the Pentagon would then, went the presumption,
turn orange and vibrate until all evil emissions had fled this
levitation. At that point the war in Vietnam would end.

The General Services Administrator who ruled on the permit consented to let an attempt be made to raise the building
ten feet, but he could not go so far as to allow the encirclement. Of course, exorcism without encirclement was like cu-
linary art without a fire—no one could properly expect a meal.
Nonetheless the exorcism would proceed, and the Fugs were
to serve as a theatrical medium and would play their music
on the rear bed of the truck they had driven in here at the
end of the parking lot nearest to the Pentagon some hundreds
of yards from the speaker's stand where the rally was to take
place.

Now, while an Indian triangle was repeatedly struck, and a
cymbal was clanged, a mimeographed paper was passed
around to the Marchers watching. It had a legend which went
something like this:

October 21, 1967, Washington, D.C., U.S.A., Planet Earth
    We Freemen, of all colors of the spectrum, in the name of God,
Ra, Jehovah, Anubis, Osiris, Tlaloc, Quetzalcoatl, Thoth, Ptah,
Allah, Krishna, Chango, Chimeke, Chukwu, Olisa-Bulu-Uwa, Imales,
Orisasu, Odudua, Kali, Shiva-Shakra, Great Spirit, Dionysus, Yahweh,
Thor, Bacchus, Isis, Jesus Christ, Maitreya, Buddha, Rama do
exorcise and cast out the EVIL which has walled and captured the
pentacle of power and perverted its use to the need of the total machine and its child the hydrogen bomb and has suffered the people
of the planet earth, the American people and creatures of the mountains, woods, streams, and oceans grievous mental and physical
torture and the constant torment of the imminent threat of utter
destruction.
    We are demanding that the pentacle of power once again be used
to serve the interests of GOD manifest in the world as man. We are
embarking on a motion which is millennial in scope. Let this day,
October 21, 1967, mark the beginning of suprapolitics.
    By the act of reading this paper you are engaged in the Holy Ritual

of Exorcism. To further participate focus your thought on the casting out of evil through the grace of GOD which is all (ours). A billion stars in a billion galaxies of space and time is the form of your power, and limitless is your name.

Now while the Indian triangle and the cymbal sounded, while a trumpet offered a mournful subterranean wail, full of sobs, and mahogany shadows of sorrow, and all sour groans from hell's dungeon, while finger bells tinkled and drums beat, so did a solemn voice speak something approximate to this: "In the name of the amulets of touching, seeing, groping, hearing and loving, we call upon the powers of the cosmos to protect our ceremonies in the name of Zeus, in the name of Anubis, god of the dead, in the name of all those killed because they do not comprehend, in the name of the lives of the soldiers in Vietnam who were killed because of a bad karma, in the name of sea-born Aphrodite, in the name of Magna Mater, in the name of Dionysus, Zagreus, Jesus, Yahweh, the unnamable, the quintessent finality of the Zoroastrian fire, in the name of Hermes, in the name of the Beak of Sok, in the name of scarab, in the name, in the name, in the name of the Tyrone Power Pound Cake Society in the Sky, in the name of Rah, Osiris, Horus, Nepta, Isis, in the name of the flowing living universe, in the name of the mouth of the river, we call upon the spirit . . . to raise the Pentagon from its destiny and preserve it."

Now spoke another voice. "In the name, and all the names, it is you."

Now the voice intoned a new chant, leaving the echo of the harsh invocation of all giants and thunders in the beat of cymbals, triangles, drums, leather bells, the sour anguish of a trumpet reaching for evil scurried through the tents of a medieval carnival.

Then all the musicians suddenly cried out: "Out, demons, out—back to darkness, ye servants of Satan—out, demons, out! Out, demons, out!"

Voices from the back cried: "Out! . . . Out! . . . Out! . . . Out!" mournful as the wind of a cave. Now the music went up louder and louder, and voices chanting, "Out, demons, out! Out, demons, out! Out, demons, out!"

He detested community sing—an old violation of his child-hood had been the bouncing ball on the movie screen; he had wanted to watch a movie, not sing—but the invocation deliv-ered some message to his throat. "Out, demons, out," he whispered, "out, demons, out." And his foot—simple Amer-ican foot—was, of course, tapping. "Out, demons, out." Were any of the experts in the Pentagon now shuddering, or glory of partial unringed exorcism—even vibrating? Vibrating ex-perts? "Out, demons, out! Out, demons, out!" He could hear Ed Sanders' voice, Ed of the red-gold head and red-gold beard, editor and publisher of a poetry magazine called *Fuck You*, renaissance conductor, composer, instrumentalist and vo-calist of the Fugs, old protégé of Allen Ginsberg, what mighty protégés was Allen amassing. Sanders spoke: "For the first time in the history of the Pentagon there will be a grope-in within a hundred feet of this place, within two hundred feet. Seminal culmination in the spirit of peace and brotherhood, a real grope for peace. All of you who want to protect this rite of love may form a circle of protection around the lovers."

"Circle of protection," intoned another voice.

"These are the magic eyes of victory," Sanders went on. "Victory, victory for peace. Money made the Pentagon—melt it. Money made the Pentagon, melt it for love."

Now came other voices, "Burn the money, burn the money, burn it, burn it."

Sanders: "In the name of the generative power of Priapus, in the name of the totality, we call upon the demons of the Pentagon to rid themselves of the cancerous tumors of the war generals, all the secretaries and soldiers who don't know what they're doing, all the intrigue bureaucracy and hatred, all the spewing, coupled with prostate cancer in the deathbed. Every Pentagon general lying alone at night with a tortured psyche and an image of death in his brain, every general, every general lying alone, every general lying alone."

Wild cries followed, chants: "Out, demons, out! Out, de-mons, out! Out! out! out! Out, demons, out."

Sanders: "In the name of the most sacred of sacred names Xabrax Phresxner."

He was accompanied now by chants of, "hari, hari, hari,

hari, rama, rama, rama, rama, Krishna, hari Krishna, hari, hari, rama, Krishna."

"Out, demons, out."

They all chanted: "End the fire and war, and war, end the plague of death. End the fire and war, and war, end the plague of death." In the background was the sound of a long sustained Ommmm.

On which acidic journeys had the hippies met the witches and the devils and the cutting edge of all primitive awe, the savage's sense of explosion—the fuse of blasphemy, the cap of taboo now struck, the answering roar of the Gods—for what was explosion but connections made at the rate of 10 to the 10th exponent of the average rate of a dialogue and its habitual answer—had all the TNT and nuclear transcendencies of TNT exploded some devil's cauldron from the past?—was the past being consumed by the present? by nuclear blasts, and blasts into the collective living brain by way of all exploding acids, opiums, whiskies, speeds, and dopes?—the past was palpable to him, a tissue living in the tangible mansions of death, and death was disappearing, death was wasting of some incurable ill. When death disappeared, there would be no life.

Morbid thoughts for the edge of battle, thoughts out alone without wings of whiskey to bring them back, but Mailer had made his lonely odyssey into the land of the witches, it had taken him through three divorces and four wives to decide that some female phenomena could be explained by no hypothesis less thoroughgoing than the absolute existence of witches. A lonely journey, taken without help from his old drugs, no, rather a distillate of his most difficult experience, and he had arrived at it in great secrecy, for quondam Marxist, nonactive editor of a Socialist magazine, where and how could he explain or justify a striking force of witches—difficult enough to force a Socialist eye to focus on what was existential. Now, here, after several years of the blandest reports from the religious explorers of LSD, vague Tibetan lama goody-goodness auras of religiosity being the only publicly announced or even rumored fruit from all trips back from the buried Atlantis of LSD, now suddenly an entire generation of acid-heads seemed to have said goodbye to easy visions of heaven, no, now the witches were here, and rites of exorcism, and black terrors of the night—hippies being murdered. Yes, the hippies had gone from Tibet to Christ to the Middle Ages, now they were Revolutionary Alchemists. Well, thought Mailer, that was all right, he was a Left Conservative himself. "Out, demons, out! Out, demons, out!"

"You know I like this," he said to Lowell.

Lowell shook his head. He looked not untroubled. "It was all right for a while," he said, "but it's so damn repetitious."

And Macdonald had a harsh glee in his pale eye as if he were half furious but half diverted by the meaninglessness of the repetitions. Macdonald hated meaninglessness even more than the war in Vietnam; on the other hand, he lived for a new critical stimulation: here it might be.

But to Lowell it was probably not meaningless. No, probably Lowell reacted against everything which was hypnotic in that music. Even if much of his poetry could be seen as formal incantations, halfway houses on the road to hypnosis and the oceans of contemplation beyond,

> O to break loose, like the chinook
> salmon jumping and falling back,
> nosing up the impossible
> stone and bone-crushing waterfall—

yes, even if Lowell's remarkable sense of rhythm drew one deep into the poems, nonetheless hypnotic they resolutely were not, for the language was particular, with a wicked sense of names, details, and places.

>   . . . Remember playing
> Marian Anderson, Mozart's *Shepherd King,*
> *il re pastore*? Hammerheaded shark,
> the rainbow salmon of the world—your hand
> a rose . . . And at the Mittersill, you topped
> the ski-run . . .

Lowell's poetry gave one the sense of living in a well, the echoes were deep, and sound was finally lost in moss on stone; down there the light had the light of velvet, and the ripples were imperceptible. But one lay on one's back in this well, looking up at the sky, and stars were determinedly there at night, fixed points of reference; nothing in the poems ever permitted you to turn on your face and try to look down into the depths of the well, it was enough you were in the well—now, look up! The world dazzled with its detail.

Lowell, drawn to hypnosis, would resist it, resist particularly these abstract clackety sounds like wooden gears in a noise-maker, "Hari, hari, hari, hari, rama, rama, Krishna, hari, rama, Krishna," and the whoop of wild Indians in "out, demons, out!" Nothing was more dangerous to the poet than hypnosis, for the *style* of one's entrance to that plain of sleep where all ideas coalesced into one, was critical—enter by any indiscriminate route, "Om, Om, Om," and who knows what finely articulated bones of future prosody might be melted in those undifferentiated pots—no, Lowell's good poetry was a reconnaissance into the deep, and for that, pirate's patrols were the best—one went down with the idea one would come back with more, but one did not immerse oneself with open guru Ginsberg arms crying, "Baa, baa, slay this sheep or en-rich it, Great Deep," no, one tiptoed in and made a raid and ideally got out good. Besides, the Fugs and Hindu bells and exorcisms via LSD were all indeed Allen Ginsberg's patch; poets respected each others' squatter's rights like Grenadiers before the unrolled carpet of the King.

But of course Lowell's final distaste was for the attraction itself of these sounds (which were incidentally lifting Mailer into the happiest sense of comradeship). Without a drink in him, he was nonetheless cheering up again at the thought of combat, and deciding it would be delightful to whack a bar-ricade in the company of Ed Sanders with the red-gold beard who had brought grope-freak talk to the Village and always seemed to Mailer a little over-liberated, but now suitable, yes, the Novelist was working up all steam in the "Out, demons, out."

But now these meanderings were interrupted by a sight to the rear of them and a battle cry, except there was not really a cry at all, just the unheard sense of a cry in the silent rush, the intent silence of a group of near a few hundred men, some wearing motorcycle helmets or fencing jackets or football shoulder pads, who were walking very rapidly, in fact almost at an odd run, in a long wedge perhaps two hundred feet long, forty or fifty wide at the base, and at the front, at the point, in the vanguard two or three carried standards, two or three blue and gold flags of the N.L.F., yes the American branch of the Vietcong was rushing across the parking lot for a first assault on the unseen Pentagon at a point not fifty yards from where the Fugs were playing.

On came the rush, the men carrying the standard running at an odd angle, as if the weight of the flag and pole brought their bodies and arms out too far ahead of their legs, so that they gave the impression, like Groucho Marx, of having torsos too large and too humped over for their limbs, (or perhaps this image came from the protection and stuffing they wore) and behind them were men carrying other standards and posters, a sea of slogans, (which could later be used for weapons—sticks and shards of broken masonite) nearly all the men at that odd incline forward from the vertical as if keening at the wind, and Mailer knew where he had seen this before, this posture of men running in a charge, yes it had been in the photographs by Mathew Brady of Union soldiers on the attack across a field, and on they came now, rolled up in some collective wave of purpose, their individual bodies seeming so much larger than their limbs, because their bodies were part of a mass, and one became aware of their feet as something more fragile and separated from them. The attack came on, The Wedge ran forward, this was a bona fide attack, a prepared attack, yes, and it jammed forward into some narrow exit out of the parking lot, some neck of road and fence and embankment and small pines and the body of troops in this attack, flags in the lead, charged by, went out of sight, and the rear of The Wedge galloping behind, rushed into a jam of bodies on the embankment, heaved to, pushed them forward, heaved, succeeded, pushed again, and ground finally to a straining equilibrium, then a halt.

For a few minutes, nothing happened. It was impossible to see what was going on at the head of the column, and the Fugs continued to play, "Out, demons, out!" From all over the parking lot, people were now streaming toward them to see what the attack had developed, many more people had arrived while they were listening to the music, and a man who knew Lowell or Macdonald came up to Mailer and said with a smile, "They're looking for you to speak at the other end."

But the other end was hundreds of yards away, far away from this unresolved action at their elbow. "Yes," said the man with a grin, "they said, 'will the real Norman Mailer stand up?'" It was a reference to two photographs he had used on the jacket of *Why Are We In Vietnam?*

"I'll get over in a while," said Mailer. It was mildly fatiguing to one specialized portion of the brain to keep preparing these variations on an extempore speech he still had not made. In fact, he had about decided he really did not wish to speak. It seemed a suggestion absurd in the face of the action now building, exactly the sort of thing to expect of a literary man. But his vanity was tempted. In a day of so many speeches, they ought to hear one piece of unorthodoxy.

Still, he did not want to leave. That sense of thin air and exaltation burning in the lungs, that intimation of living at high altitude had come back. "Let's try to see what's going on with that attack," he suggested.

They now left the Fugs and walked to the rear of the column jammed at that unseen exit. The men above were obviously packed too tightly for any late arrival to work himself up high enough to comprehend what was happening. It seemed foolish somehow to stand at the rear and ask questions, and they walked a few feet away and debated whether to go to the far end of the parking lot and hear speeches. The day was hovering again on anticlimax.

Abruptly—no warning—the men at the base of the stairs, the very troops who had carried the N.L.F. flags, were running toward the rear in a panic. Mailer had then that superimposition of vision which makes descriptions of combat so contradictory when one compares eyewitness reports—he did not literally see any uniformed soldiers or marshals chasing this civilian army down the embankment, there was nothing but demonstrators flying down toward them now, panic on their faces, but Mailer's imagination so clearly conceived MPs chasing them with bayonets that for an instant he did literally see fixed bayonets and knew in some other part of himself he didn't, like two transparent images almost superimposed. Then he saw nothing but the look of terror on the faces coming toward him and he turned to run in order not to be run down by them, conceiving for one instant MPs squirting Mace in everybody's eyes. Then panic was on him too. He didn't want Mace. He sprinted a few steps, looked over his shoulder, stepped in a drainage trough where the parking lot concrete was hollowed, almost fell with a nasty wrench of his back and abruptly stopped running, sheepishly, recognizing that some large fund of fear he had not even felt for a minute these three days had nonetheless lived in him like an abscess quick to burst now at the first mean threat. He was furious, furious at himself for fleeing and this shame was not balmed by the quick sight he had over one shoulder of Dwight Macdonald standing calm and still, while tens of people scrambled around him in panic. Macdonald had the quiet look on his face of a man who had lived his life, and had learned what he learned, and was not going to run from anyone.

They reassembled. It was confusing. Nobody knew why the men on the stairs had suddenly begun to flee. An attack had been mounted, had been stopped, and a retreat had gone off in their faces, partly swept them up in the terror and now had dissipated itself. His worst perspectives were being fulfilled. The one sequence he did not wish to follow on this late afternoon was in full prospect now—they would wander unattached to any troop or effort, always on the fringe, always ignorant of the next move, always confused. Then it would be dark. He had a picture again of three notables, silly to themselves, walking about with a candle, looking to be copped.

"Listen," Mailer said, "let's get arrested now." Stating the desire created it, and put a ligature across the rent in his nerve.

"Look, Norman," said Lowell, "if we're going to, shall we get away from here? I don't see any good that's accomplished if we're all picked up right next to a Vietcong flag."

This was not to be contested. Mailer had never understood how demonstrating with an N.L.F. flag was going to spark a mass movement to end the war. He could not argue with Lowell. The remark was sensible, and yet he felt uneasy, as if one should never be too sensible in war. Still—it was difficult enough for people to take him seriously without standing next to *that* flag!

So they moved on, looking for a line to cross, or a border, or a fence at the extremity of the parking lot, and came upon one in no time at all. To their left, perhaps fifty yards from where the attack had jammed, was a grassy field with United States MPs stationed in it. To their front was a low rope, not a foot off the ground. Protestors from the parking lot were standing behind this rope, two or three deep. Lowell, Mailer, and Macdonald worked into position until they had nothing in front of them but the rope, and the MPs.

6: A Confrontation by the River

It was not much of a situation to study. The MPs stood in two widely spaced ranks. The first rank was ten yards behind the rope, and each MP in that row was close to twenty feet from the next man. The second rank, similarly spaced, was ten yards behind the first rank and perhaps thirty yards behind them a cluster appeared, every fifty yards or so, of two or three U.S. Marshals in white helmets and dark blue suits. They were out there waiting. Two moods confronted one another, two separate senses of a private silence.

It was not unlike being a boy about to jump from one garage roof to an adjoining garage roof. The one thing not to do was wait. Mailer looked at Macdonald and Lowell. "Let's go," he said. Not looking again at them, not pausing to gather or dissipate resolve, he made a point of stepping neatly and decisively over the low rope. Then he headed across the grass to the nearest MP he saw.

It was as if the air had changed, or light had altered; he felt immediately much more alive—yes, bathed in air—and yet disembodied from himself, as if indeed he were watching himself in a film where this action was taking place. He could feel the eyes of the people behind the rope watching him, could feel the intensity of their existence as spectators. And as he walked forward, he and the MP looked at one another with the naked stricken lucidity which comes when absolute strangers are for the moment absolutely locked together.

The MP lifted his club to his chest as if to bar all passage. To Mailer's great surprise—he had secretly expected the enemy to be calm and strong, why should they not? they had every power, all the guns—to his great surprise, the MP was trembling. He was a young Negro, part white, who looked to have come from some small town where perhaps there were not many other Negroes; he had at any rate no Harlem smoke, no devil swish, no black, no black power for him, just a simple boy in an Army suit with a look of horror in his eye, "Why, why did it have to happen to me?" was the message of the petrified marbles in his face.

"Go back," he said hoarsely to Mailer.

"If you don't arrest me, I'm going to the Pentagon."

"No. Go back."

The thought of a return—"since they won't arrest me, what can I do?"—over these same ten yards was not at all suitable.

As the MP spoke, the raised club quivered. He did not know if it quivered from the desire of the MP to strike him, or secret military wonder was he now possessed of a moral force which implanted terror in the arms of young soldiers? Some unfamiliar current, now gyroscopic, now a sluggish whirlpool, was evolving from that quiver of the club, and the MP seemed to turn slowly away from his position confronting the rope, and the novelist turned with him, each still facing the other until the axis of their shoulders was now perpendicular to the rope, and still they kept turning in this psychic field, not touching, the club quivering, and then Mailer was behind the MP, he was free of him, and he wheeled around and kept going in a half run to the next line of MPs and then on the push of a sudden instinct, sprinted suddenly around the nearest MP in the second line, much as if he were a back cutting around the nearest man in the secondary to break free—that was actually his precise thought—and had a passing perception of how simple it was to get past these MPs. They looked petrified. Stricken faces as he went by. They did not know what to do. It was his dark pinstripe suit, his vest, the maroon and blue regimental tie, the part in his hair, the barrel chest, the early paunch—he must have looked like a banker himself, a banker gone ape! And then he saw the Pentagon to his right across the field, not a hundred yards away, and a little to his left, the marshals, and he ran on a jog toward them, and came up, and they glared at him and shouted, "Go back."

He had a quick impression of hard-faced men with gray eyes burning some transparent fuel for flame, and said, "I won't go back. If you don't arrest me, I'm going on to the Pentagon," and knew he meant it, some absolute certainty had come to him, and then two of them leaped on him at once in the cold clammy murderous fury of all cops at the existential moment of making their bust—all cops who secretly expect to be struck at that instant for their sins—and a surprising force came to his voice, and he roared, to his own distant pleasure in new achievement and new authority—"Take your hands off me, can't you see? I'm not resisting arrest," and one then let go of him, and the other stopped trying to pry his arm into a lock, and contented himself with a hard hand under his armpit, and they set off walking across the field at a rabid intent quick rate, walking parallel to the wall of the Pentagon, fully visible on his right at last, and he was arrested, he had succeeded in that, and without a club on his head, the mountain air in his lungs as thin and fierce as smoke, yes, the livid air of tension on this livid side promised a few events of more interest than the routine wait to be free, yes he was more than a visitor, he was in the land of the enemy now, he would get to see their face.

from *The Armies of the Night*, 1968

Hill 875

by Peter Arnett

HILL 875, Vietnam AP—Hour after hour of battle gave the living and the dead the same gray pallor on Hill 875. At times the only way to tell them apart was to watch when the enemy mortars crashed in on the exhausted American paratroopers.

The living rushed unashamedly to the tiny bunkers dug into the red clay.

The wounded squirmed toward the shelter of trees blasted to the ground.

The dead—propped up in bunkers or face down in the dust—didn't move.

Since Sunday the most brutal fighting of the Vietnam war has ebbed and flowed across this remote hill in the western sector of the Dak To battleground. The 2nd Battalion of the 173rd Airborne Brigade went up 875 first. It nearly died.

Of the 16 officers who led the men across the ridgeline Sunday, eight were killed and the other eight wounded. Eleven of the 13 medics died.

The battalion took its first casualties at midday Sunday as it crested Hill 875, one of the hundreds of knolls that dot the ridges in the Dak To fighting region near the Cambodian-Laotian border.

All weekend as the paratroopers moved along the jungle hills enemy base camps were uncovered. The biggest was on 875 and D Company lost several men in the first encounter with the bunkers.

A Company moved back down the hill to cut a landing zone and was chopped to pieces by a North Vietnamese flanking attack.

The remnants fled back to the crest of the hill while a paratrooper propped his gun on the trail and kept firing at the advancing enemy, ignoring orders to retreat with the others.

"You can keep gunning them down, but sooner or later

when there is enough of them they'll get to you," said Pfc. James Kelly of Fort Myers, Fla., who saw the machine gunner go down after killing about 17 North Vietnamese.

D Company, hearing the roar of battle below it, returned to the crest of the hill and established a 50-yard perimeter "because we figure we were surrounded by a regiment," one officer said.

As the battalion was regrouping late in the afternoon for another crack at the bunker system, one of the American planes striking at the nearby enemy dropped a 500-pound bomb too soon. About 30 of the paratroopers were killed.

"A foul play of war," said one survivor bitterly.

From then until a reinforcing battalion arrived the following night, the paratroopers on the hill dug in desperately. Only one medic was able to work on the many wounded, and the enemy kept driving off the rescue helicopters.

The relief battalion made it into the tiny perimeter on 875 Monday night. In the moonlight bodies of the dead lay spread-eagled across the ground. The wounded wimpered.

The survivors, hungry and thirsty, rushed up eagerly to get food and water, only to learn that the relief battalion had brought enough supplies for one day only and had already consumed them.

Monday night was sleepless but uneventful. On Tuesday the North Vietnamese struck with renewed fury.

From positions just 100 yards away, they pounded the American perimeter with 82mm mortars. The first rounds slapped in at daybreak, killing three paratroopers in a foxhole and wounding 17 others on the line.

For the rest of the day, the Communists methodically worked over the hill, pumping rounds in five or six at a time, giving new wounds to those who lay bleeding in the open and tearing through bunkers. The plop of the rounds as they left the enemy tubes gave the paratroopers a second or two to dash for cover.

The foxholes got deeper as the day wore on. Foxhole after foxhole took hits. A dog handler and his German shepherd died together. Men joking with you and offering cigarettes writhed on the ground wounded and pleading for water minutes later. There was no water for anyone.

Crouched in one bunker, Pfc. Angel Flores, 20, of New York City said: "If we were dead like those out there we wouldn't have to worry about this stuff coming in."

He fingered a plastic rosary around his neck and kissed it reverently as the rounds blasted on the ground outside.

"Does that do you any good?" a buddy asked him.

"Well, I'm still alive," Flores replied.

"Don't you know that the chaplain who gave you that was killed on Sunday?" said his buddy.

The day's pounding steadily reduced the platoon commanded by 1st Lt. Bryan Macdonough, 25, of Fort Lee, Va. He had started out Sunday with 27 men. He had nine left by noon Tuesday.

"If the Viets keep this up, there'll be none left by evening," he said.

The enemy positions seemed impervious to constant American air strikes. Napalm fireballs exploded on the bunkers 30 yards away. The earth shook with heavy bombs.

"We've tried 750 pounders, napalm and everything else, but air can't do it. It's going to take manpower to get those positions," Macdonough said.

By late afternoon a new landing zone was cut below the hill. The enemy mortars searched for it but the helicopters came in anyway. A line of wounded trudged down the hill and by evening 140 of them had been evacuated.

The arrival of the helicopters with food, water and ammunition seemed to put new life into the paratroopers. They talked eagerly of a final assault on the enemy bunkers.

As darkness fell flame throwers were brought up. The first stubborn bunker yielded, and the paratroopers were at last started on their way to gain the ridgeline which they had set out to take three days earlier.

AP wire copy, November 22, 1967

The Truest Sport:
Jousting with Sam and Charlie

by Tom Wolfe

DOWN a perfectly green tunnel, as cool and quiet as you can possibly imagine—no, it's not a tunnel, it's more like a hall of mirrors—but they're not mirrors, those aren't reflections, they're openings, one after another, on and on—just a minute! it's very familiar!—out of this cool green memory comes a steward, a tiny man, in uniform, a white jacket, perfectly starched and folded and creased like an envelope over his crisp little bones. Who doesn't know him! Here comes Bye Borty-bibe—

"Bye borty-bibe!"

He's saying it!

Dowd wakes up and it's 5:45 on the button, as always, and he looks across the stateroom at the steward. The steward is a little Filipino in a white jacket who hesitates, so as to make sure Dowd actually wakes up at bye borty-bibe, as he always pronounces it, and then he disappears down the passageway.

There is something eccentric in the way the day begins. It's terribly genteel!—having a little servant in a white jacket come by and respectfully summon you into consciousness so you can go hang your hide out for human skeet and sweat horribly. More servants will come in after Dowd leaves and make up his bed and clean up the stateroom and dust off the TV and the safe and clean off the desk and take out the laundry. *Only your laundryman knows for sure!* That was the usual joke, but there were some men who came aboard for the first time, and after a couple of hops north they would actually wonder whether it could get so bad—whether a man could get so frightened that he would literally lose control—*only your laundryman knows for sure!*—and whether later, in the bowels of the ship, in the laundry room, there might actually be some little laundry humper, some sweatback, some bye-bye steward of the soul, who would, in fact, *know*.

In the first moments, when you wake up, it's as if you're furiously scanning, painting all the stray trash on the screen, although usually that begins to fade as soon as you're on your feet. In a moment Dowd would be out in the good green passageway. The passageway is a very cool and immaculate green, not luxurious, you understand—in fact, every twenty feet there is a hatchway with a knee-knocker you have to step over, and as you look on and on through these hatchways, one after the other, it's like a hall of mirrors—but it is green and generally pleasing to the nervous system. Actually . . . that is not all there is to it. It is also good because, if the truth be known, being on this good green passageway means that you are traveling first-class, sleeping in a stateroom, with only one roommate, and you have the aforesaid servants standing by. It is not even a subject that one thinks about in so many words. And yet the ship is constructed in such an obvious fashion, in layers, that one can't help but know that down below . . . they are living in quite another way, in compartments, with thirty to forty souls to a compartment, and they wake up to a loudspeaker and make up their own bunks and run along to a loudspeaker through gray-and-beige tunnels and eat in a gray-and-beige galley off trays with scullion gullies stamped into them, instead of in a wardroom.

A wardroom!—also genteel in its way. Like the rest of them, Dowd is usually doing well if he gets up in time to make it to breakfast with his guy-in-back, Garth Flint, in the smaller wardroom, where they eat cafeteria-style. More than once he hasn't even managed that and has departed with nothing in his gullet but a couple of cups of coffee, notwithstanding all the lectures about the evil consequences this has for your blood-sugar level. But when they come back, Dowd and Flint and the others can enjoy the offerings of a proper wardroom, the formal one. They can take off the reeking zoom-bags, get dressed, sit down at a table with a white tablecloth on it, write out their orders on club slips, after the fashion of a men's club in New York or London, and more little Filipino stewards in white jackets will pick up the orders and serve dinner on china plates. The china has a certain dignity: it's white with a band of blue about the rim and a blue crest in the center. The silverware—now, that's rather nice! It's ornamental and heavy, it has curlicues and a noble gravity, the sort of silverware one used to see in the dining room of the good hotel near the railroad station. So they have dinner on a field of white and silver, while little stewards in white jackets move about the edges. The bulkheads (as the walls are known here) are paneled with walnut rectangles framed with more walnut; not actual wood, which is forbidden because it is inflammable, but similar enough to fool the eye. Off to the side are clusters of lounge chairs upholstered in leather and some acey-deucey tables. Silver and heavy glass wink out of a manly backdrop, rich as burled wood and Manila cigars; for here in the ward-rooms of the *Coral Sea* the Navy has done everything that interior decoration and white mess jackets can do to live up to the idea of Officers & Gentlemen, within the natural limits of going to war on the high seas.

The notion often crosses Dowd's mind: *It's like jousting.*

Every day they touch the napkins to their mouths, depart this gently stewarded place, and go forth, observing a checklist of written and unwritten rules of good form, to test their mettle, to go forth to battle, to hang their hides out over the skeet shooters of Hanoi-Haiphong . . . thence to return, after no more than two hours . . . to this linenfold club and its crisp starched white servitors.

One thing it is not good to think about is the fact that it would be even thus on the day when, finally, as has already happened to 799 other American aviators, radar-intercept officers, and helicopter crewmen, your hide is blown out of the sky. That day, too, would begin within this same gentlemanly envelope.

Fliers with premonitions are not healthy people. They are known as accidents waiting to happen. Now, John Dowd and Garth Flint are not given to premonitions, which is fortunate and a good sign; except that it won't make a great deal of difference today, because this is that day.

To get up on the flight deck of the *Coral Sea*, Dowd and Flint usually went out through a hatch onto a catwalk. The

catwalk hung out over the side of the ship just below the level
of the deck. At about midships they climbed a few feet up
a ladder and they would be on the deck itself. A simple,
if slightly old-fashioned, procedure, and by now second
nature—

—but what a marvelous low-volt amusement was available
if you were on the *Coral Sea* and you saw another mortal,
some visitor, some summer reservist, whoever, make his first
excursion out onto that deck. He takes a step out onto the
catwalk, and right away the burglar alarm sounds in his central
nervous system. Listen, Skipper!—the integrity of the circuit
has been violated somewhere! He looks out over the railing
of the catwalk, and it might as well be the railing of the goddamned Golden Gate Bridge. It's a sixty-foot drop to the sea
below, which is water—but what conceivable difference does
that make? From this height the water looks like steel where
it picks up reflections of the hull of the carrier, except that it
ripples and breaks up into queasy facets—and in fact the horizon itself is pitching up and down . . . The whole freaking
Golden Gate Bridge is pitching up and down . . . the big
wallowing monster can't hold still . . . Christ, let's get up on
the deck, away from the edge—but it's only when he reaches
the deck itself and stands with both feet planted flat that the
full red alert takes over.

This flight deck—in the movie or the training film the flight
deck is a grand piece of gray geometry, perilous, to be sure,
but an amazing abstract shape dominating the middle of the
ocean as we look down upon it on the screen—and yet, once
the newcomer's two feet are on it—ge*ome*try—my God, man,
this is a . . . skillet! It *heaves*, it moves up and down underneath his feet, it pitches up, it pitches down, as the ship moves
into the wind and, therefore, into the waves, and the wind
keeps sweeping across, sixty feet up in the air out in the open
sea, and there are no railings whatsoever—and no way whatsoever to cry out to another living soul for a helping hand,
because on top of everything else the newcomer realizes that
his sense of hearing has been *amputated entirely* and his voice
is useless. This is a *skillet!*—a frying pan!—a short-order
grill!—not gray but black, smeared with skid marks from one
end to the other and glistening with pools of hydraulic fluid

and the occasional jet-fuel slick, all of it still hot, sticky, greasy, runny, virulent from God knows what traumas—still ablaze!—consumed in detonations, explosions, flames, combustion, roars, shrieks, whines, blasts, cyclones, dust storms, horrible shudders, fracturing impacts, all of it taking place out on the very edge of control, if in fact it can be contained at all, which seems extremely doubtful, because the whole scorched skillet is still *heaving* up and down the horizon and little men in screaming red and yellow and purple and green shirts with black Mickey Mouse helmets over their ears are skittering about on the surface as if for their very lives (you've said it now!), clustering about twin-engine F-4 fighter planes like little bees about the queen, rolling them up a stripe toward the catapult slot, which runs through the deck like the slot in the back of a piggy bank, hooking their bellies on to the shuttle that comes up through the slot and then running for cover as the two jet engines go into their shriek and a huge deflection plate rises up behind the plane because it is about to go into its explosion and quite enough gets blown—quite enough!—quite enough gets blown off this heaving grill as it is, and then they explode—both engines explode into full afterburn, 37,000 pounds of force, and a very storm of flame, heat, crazed winds, and a billion blown steely particles—a very storm engulfs the deck, followed by an unbelievable shudder—*kaboom!*—that pounds through the skillet and destroys whatever may be left of the neophyte's vestibular system, and the howling monster is flung up the deck like something out of a red-mad slingshot, and the F-4 is launched, dropping off the lip of the deck tail down with black smoke pouring out of both engines in its furious struggle to gain altitude—and already *another* plane is ready on the *second* catapult and the screams and explosions have started again and the little screaming-yellow men with their Mouseketeer ears are running once more—

—and yet this flaming bazooka assembly line will, in the newcomer's memory, seem orderly, sublimely well controlled, compared to the procedure he will witness as the F-4's, F-8's, A-4's, A-6's return to the ship for what in the engineering stoicisms of the military is known as recovery and arrest. To say that an F-4 is coming back onto this heaving barbecue from out of the sky at a speed of 135 knots . . . that may be the truth on paper, but it doesn't begin to get across the idea of what a man sees from the deck itself, because it perhaps creates the notion that the plane is *gliding* in. On the deck one knows different! As the aircraft comes closer and the carrier heaves on into the waves and the plane's speed does *not* diminish—one experiences a neural alarm he has never in his wildest fears imagined before: This is not an *air*plane coming toward me, it's a brick, and it is not *gliding*, it's *falling*, a fifty-thousand-pound brick, headed not for a stripe on the deck, but for *me*—and with a horrible *smash!* it hits the skillet, and with a blur of momentum as big as a freight train's it hurtles toward the far end of the deck—another blinding storm!—another roar as the pilot pushes the throttle up to full military power and another smear of rubber screams out over the skillet—and this is normal!—quite okay!—a wire stretched across the deck has grabbed the hook on the end of the plane as it hit the deck tail down, and the smash was the rest of the twenty-five-ton brute slamming onto the deck, as if tripped up, so that it is now straining against the wire at full throttle, in case it hadn't held and the plane had "boltered" off the end of the deck and had to struggle up into the air again. And already the Mickey Mouse helmets are running toward their fiery monster . . .

The obvious dangers of the flight deck were the setting, the backdrop, the mental decor, the emotional scenery against which all that happened on the carrier was played out, and the aviator was he who lived in the very eye of the firestorm. This grill was *his* scenery. Its terrors rose out of his great moments: the launch and recovery. For that reason some crewmen liked to check out the demeanor of the aviators during these events, just as they might have in the heyday of the chivalric code.

When John Dowd and Garth Flint came out on deck in their green flight suits, carrying their helmets and their knee-boards, they were an unmistakable pair. Dowd was the tallest pilot on the ship, almost six feet five. Six years ago he was captain of the Yale basketball team. He was so tall, he had to slump his way through the physicals in order to get into flight training, where six four was the upper limit. He looked like a basketball player. His face, his Adam's apple, his shoulders, his elbows—he was a tower of sharp angles. Flint was Dowd's radar-intercept officer. He was five eight and rather solidly built. He was not small, but next to Dowd he looked like a little jockey.

Today they were to go out on a two-ship formation, with Dowd's roommate, Dick Brent, flying a second F-4B. Dowd's would be the lead ship; Brent's the wing. The usual monsoon overcast was down within about five hundred feet of the deck. It was another day inside the gray pearl: the ship, a tight circle of the waters of the Gulf of Tonkin around it, a dome of clouds, fog, mist, which was God's great gift to the North Vietnamese.

They climb aboard and Dowd eases the power on to taxi the ship toward the catapult, while the aircraft directors nurse it onto the slot. The catapult officer is out there on the deck with his Mousketeer ear baffles on and his yellow jersey flapping in the wind. Assuming the preliminary stages have been completed correctly, the catapult officer is supposed to hold up five fingers to show the pilot that all looks good for launch. If the gauges look okay, the pilot then shows that he is ready for his little slide-for-life . . . by saluting. At this point three things are supposed to happen in a very rapid sequence: the catapult officer drops to one knee (to avoid having his head removed by the wing) and throws his hand forward like a cheerleader doing the "locomotive"; the pilot cuts on full afterburn; and a seaman on a catwalk across the deck presses a black rubber button and throws both hands up in the air. This somewhat hopeless-looking gesture says: "It's done! We've fired the catapult! You're on your way! There's no stopping it!"

To Dowd this is another eccentric note. This man who fires the slingshot—or who seems to—actually he's signaling the steam-catapult crew below deck—this man, who appears to flick you into the sky or the sea with his finger, according to how things work out, is some little swabbo making seventy-eight dollars a month or whatever it is. Somehow this fact puts just that much more edge on the demeanor of the pilot's salute, because what that salute says is: "I hereby commit my hide to your miserable care, sir, to you and your sailor with

the button and your motherless catapult. I'm a human can-
nonball, and it's your cannon."

So it is that today, just before he cuts on full afterburn and
sets off the full 37,000-pound explosion and consumes the
skillet in the firestorm and braces the stick so he won't lose
control in the bad lurch of the slingshot, just before the big
ride, in the key moment of knightly correctness, Dowd rolls
his salute off his helmet with a languid swivel of his wrist, like
Adolphe Menjou doffing his hat . . . a raffish gesture, you
might say, with a roll to it that borders on irony . . . but a
friendly note all the same . . . For this is a good day! They
are flying again! There is no bomb load—therefore less
weight, therefore an easy launch! . . . a good day—otherwise
he might have, or would have been entitled to, according to
the unwritten and unspoken rules (especially since he has
more than one hundred missions behind him)—he might have
ended that cool rolling salute by leaving his middle finger
sticking up in the air, in an accepted fashion that tells one and
all: "You're only giving me the grand goose. Why should I
salute? (Here's one for you.)"

But this is a good day!—and Dowd surrenders to the catapult without even an ironic protest, and he feels a tremendous compression, so great that the surface of his eyeballs
flattens and his vision blurs, and the F-4B shrieks, and he and
Flint hurtle down the stripe and off the bow of the ship, half
blind and riding a shrieking beast, into the gray pearl. It
couldn't have been a smoother launch; it was absolutely
nominal.

Dowd heads on through the pearl, through the overcast,
with Brent's plane about five hundred yards back. The ride to
the coast of North Vietnam will take them about twenty
minutes. Just how high the cloud cover will be up around
Haiphong is impossible to say, which means that the game of
high-low may be a trifle too interesting. The weather has been
so bad, nobody has been up there. Well . . . now somebody's
going up there. Already, without any doubt, the Russian
trawlers in the gulf have painted the two aircraft on their radar
screens. *Painted!* Such a nice word for it! The phosphorescent
images come sliding onto the screen, as if a brush were doing

it. And with those two delicate little strokes on a Russian radar screen somewhere out there in the muck, the game is on again.

American pilots in Vietnam often ran through their side of the action ahead of time as if it were a movie in the mind . . . trying to picture every landmark on the way to the Red River delta, every razorback green ridge, all that tropical hardscrabble down below, every jut in the coast, every wretched misty snake bend in the Red River, every bridge around Haiphong harbor, every change of course, the angle of every bomb run from the assigned altitude . . . But just try to imagine the enemy's side of it. Try to imagine your own aircraft (encasing your own hide) sliding onto their screens like a ghost stroke (observed by what Russian?) and the trawler signaling the coast and the cannon crews and SAM battalions cranking up in the delta and devising (saying what exactly?) their black trash for the day, which could be inexplicably varied.

One day flying over Haiphong would be "a walk in Haiphong Park," as Dowd would put it. The next day the place would erupt with the wildest storms of ground fire since the bombing of Berlin, Merseburg, and Magdeburg in the Second World War, absolute sheets of 37-millimeter, 57-millimeter, and 85-millimeter cannon fire, plus the SAM's. The antiaircraft cannons now had sights that computed the leads instantly and automatically, and they were more accurate than anything ever dreamed of in the Second World War or the Korean war. But it was the SAM's that were the great equalizer. It was SAM's that made aerial combat in Vietnam something different from what the aces of wars gone by—admirable innocent fellows! —had ever known.

Dowd used to say to himself: "The SAM's come up, and the boys go down." One way or the other! The SAM's, the Russian surface-to-air missiles, were aimed and guided by radar. They climbed at about Mach 3, which was likely to be at least three times as fast as your own ship was going when you heard the warning over your radio ("I have a valid launch!"). The SAM's were not fired at random—each had a radar lock on your aircraft or somebody else's. The only way to evade a SAM was to dive for the deck, i.e., the ground. The SAM's own G-forces were so great they couldn't make the loop and come back down. "The SAM's come up, and the boys go down." And the merriment has just begun. The dive brings you down so low, you are now down into the skeet range of that insidiously well-aimed flak! This, as they say, put you between a rock and a hard place. Sometimes the North Vietnamese also sent up the Mig-21's. But they were canny about it. The Migs went up mainly to harass the bombers, the F-105's, A-4's, and A-6's, to force them to jettison their bomb loads (in order to gain speed to evade the Migs) before they reached the target. But occasionally the F-4's got a chance to tangle with them. What a luxury! How sporting! How nice to have a mere Mig to deal with instead of the accursed SAM's! Of course, you just might have both to contend with at the same time. The North Vietnamese were so SAM-crazy, once in a while they'd fire them up in the middle of a hassle and hit their own planes.

Dowd saw his first SAM last year when he was on a flak-suppression run. Other aviators had always told him they looked like "flying telephone poles," but the only thing he saw at first was a shower of sparks, like the sparks from a Roman candle. That was the rocket tail. And then he could make out the shaft—all of this happening in an instant—and it was, in fact, like a pale-gray telephone pole, moving sideways through the sky as if skidding on its tail, which meant the ship it was after had already dived for the deck and the SAM was trying to overcome its own momentum and make the loop. You were always reassured with the statement, "If you can see it"—meaning a SAM—"you can evade it"—but there were some pilots who were so egotistical they believed that the one they saw was the one that had their name on it. A fatal delusion in many cases!—for the SAM's came up in fans of six or eight, fired from different sites and different angles. "The SAM's come up, and the boys go down"—and Dowd and his whole formation hit the deck and got out of there. Not long after that, Dowd and Flint were hit by ground fire for the first time—it was to happen four more times—in the same sort of situation. They had just come down out of the dive when they took hits in the port ramp and intake duct. Fortunately it was 14.5-millimeter fire, instead of one of the big cannons, and they made it on back to the ship.

High-low! In what?—ten minutes?—Dowd will have to start playing the same game again this morning. Soon he will have to decide whether to go above the overcast or right on the deck. Above the overcast they will be safe from the gunners, who need visual sightings in order to use their automatic lead mechanisms. But right above the overcast is where SAM rules like a snake. More aviators have been wiped out by SAM's popping out of the clouds they're sitting on than any other way. Rather than contend with that automated blind beast, some pilots prefer to come in low over the terrain in the eternal attempt to get in "under the radar." But what is it really, a strategic defense or a psychological defense?

Such was the nature of the game that Dowd and every other pilot here had to play. Many of the pilots who flew over Vietnam had been trained by instructors who had flown in the Korean war. What tigers those old Korea jocks were! What glorious memories they had! What visions those aces could fill your skull with! What a tangy taste they gave to the idea of aerial combat over Southeast Asia! The Korean war brought on the first air-to-air combat between jet fighters, but it turned out to be dogfighting of the conventional sort nonetheless, American F-86's versus Soviet-built Mig-15's mainly —and it was a picnic . . . a field day . . . a duck shoot . . . American pilots, flying F-86's in all but a few dozen cases, shot down 839 Korean and Chinese Mig-15's. Only fifty-six F-86's were lost. Quite a carnival it was. Morale among American ground troops in Korea slid like the mud, but the pilots were in Fighter Jock Heaven. The Air Force was producing aces—fighter pilots who had shot down five planes or more—as fast as the Communists could get the Migs up in the air. By the time the war stopped, there were thirty-eight Air Force aces, and between them they had accounted for a total of 299.5 kills. High spirits these lads had. They chronicled their adventures with a good creamy romanticism such as nobody in flying had dared treat himself to since the days of Lufbery, Frank Luke, and Von Richthofen in the First World War. Why hold back! Jousting is jousting, and a knight's a knight. Colonel Harrison R. Thyng, who shot down five Migs in Korea (and eight German and Japanese planes in the Second World War), glowed like Excalibur when he described his Fourth Fighter-Interceptor Wing: "Like olden knights the F-86 pilots ride up over North Korea to the Yalu River, the sun glinting off silver aircraft, contrails streaming behind, as they challenge the numerically superior enemy to come on up and fight." Lances and plumes! Come on up and fight! Now there was a man having a wonderful time!

In Vietnam, however, the jousting was of a kind the good colonel and his knights never dreamed of. The fighter plane that the Air Force and the Navy were now using instead of the F-86—namely, the F-4—was competing with the new generation of Migs and was winning by a ratio of two to one, according to the air-to-air combat scoreboards, regular league standings, that were kept in various military publications. That was nothing like the fifteen-to-one ratio in Korea, of course—but more than that, it was not even the main event any longer. Not even the heroic word "ace" carried the old wallop. The studs-of-all-the-studs in Vietnam were not the pilots in air-to-air combat but the men who operated in that evil space between the rock and the hard place, between the SAM's and the automatic cannon fire.

In the past three years—1965, 1966, and the year just ending for John Dowd, 1967—the losses had been more brutal than the Air Force or the Navy had ever admitted. Jack Broughton, an Air Force colonel and commander of a wing of F-105's flying over Hanoi-Haiphong from out of Thailand, described the losses as "astronomical and unacceptable," and they were increasing sharply each year. What made the North Vietnamese game of high-low—SAM's and ground fire—so effective was a set of restrictions such as no combat pilots had ever had to contend with before.

Flying out over Hanoi and Haiphong was like playing on some small and sharply defined court. These two cities were by far the major targets in North Vietnam, and so there was very little element of surprise along the lines of switching targets. They could only be approached down a ridge of mountains ("Thud Ridge") from the west, out of Thailand, which would be the Air Force attacking with F-105 fighter-bombers, or across a wide-open delta (perfect for radar defenses) from the east, which would be the Navy attacking from carriers in the gulf. The North Vietnamese and the Russians packed so much artillery in around these two cities that pilots would come back saying, "It was like trying to fly through a rainstorm without hitting a drop."

God knows how many planes and pilots were lost just trying to knock out the North Vietnamese ground fire. The Air Force had Wild Weasel or Iron Hand units made up of pilots in F-105's who offered themselves as living SAM bait. They would deliberately try to provoke launches by the SAM battalions so that other ships could get a radar lock on the SAM sites and hit them with cluster-bomb strikes. This became the ultimate game of radar chess. If the SAM battalions beamed up at the Wild Weasels and committed too early, they stood to get obliterated, which would also allow the main strike force to get through to its target. On the other hand, if they refused to go for the bait, recognizing it for what it was, and shut down their beams—that might give the strike force just enough time to slip through unchallenged. So they'd keep shutting on and off, as in some lethal game of "one finger, two fingers." Their risk was nothing, however, compared to that of the Wild Weasel pilots, who were the first in and the last out, who hung around in the evil space far too long and stood to get snuffed any way the game went.

Navy pilots, Dowd among them, were sent out day after day for "flak suppression." The North Vietnamese could move their flak sites around overnight, so that the only way to find them was by leading with your head, as it were, flying over the target area until you saw them fire the cannons. This you could detect by the rather pretty peach-pink sparkles, which were the muzzle explosions. The cannons made no sound at all (way up here) and seemed tiny and merely decorative . . . with their little delicate peach-pink sparkles amid the bitter green of the scrabble. Dowd and his comrades could not unload on these flak sites just anywhere they found them, however. As if to make the game a little more hazardous, the Pentagon had declared certain areas bomb-free zones. A pilot could hit only "military targets," which meant he couldn't hit villages, hospitals, churches, or Haiphong harbor if there was a "third-party" ship there. So, naturally, being no fools, the North Vietnamese loaded the villages up with flak sites, loaded the churches up with munitions, put SAM sites behind the hospitals, and "welded a third-party ship to the dock" in Haiphong harbor, as Garth Flint put it. There always seemed to be some neutral flag in port there, with one of North Vietnam's best customers being our friends the British. One day one of Dowd's *Coral Sea* comrades came in for a run on a railroad freight depot, pickled his bombs too soon, went long, and hit a church—whereupon the bitter-green landscape rocked with secondary and tertiary explosions and a succession of fireballs. The place had gone up like an arsenal, which of course it was. Every now and then Dowd would be involved in a strike aimed at "cutting off" Haiphong harbor. This was not to be done, however, by mining the harbor or blowing the docking facilities out of the water or in any other obvious and easy manner. No, this had to be accomplished by surgically severing the bridges that connected the port with the mainland. This required bomb runs through the eye of a needle, and even if the bridges were knocked out, the North Vietnamese simply moved everything across by barge until the bridges were back.

If you were a pilot being flung out every day between the rock and the hard place, these complicated proscriptions took on an eerie diffidence, finally. They were like an unaccountable display of delicate manners. In fact, it was the Johnson Administration's attempt to fight a "humane" war and look good in the eyes of the world. There was something out to-lunch about it, however. The eyes of the world did not flutter for a second. Stories of American atrocities were believed by whoever wanted to believe them, no matter what actually occurred, and the lacy patterns that American bombing missions had to follow across Hanoi-Haiphong never impressed a soul, except for the pilots and radar-intercept officers who knew what a difficult and dangerous game it was.

If the United States was seriously trying to win the battle of world opinion—well, then, here you had a real bush-league operation. The North Vietnamese were the uncontested aces, once you got into this arena. One of the most galling things a pilot had to endure in Vietnam was seeing the North Vietnamese pull propaganda coup after propaganda coup, often with the help, unwitting or otherwise, of Americans. There was not merely a sense of humiliation about it. The North Vietnamese talent in this direction often had direct strategic results.

For example, the missions over N—— D——. Now, here was one time, in Dowd's estimation, when they had gotten the go-ahead to do the job right. N—— D—— was an important transportation center in the Iron Triangle area. For two days they softened the place up, working on the flak sites and SAM sites in the most methodical way. On the third day they massed the bomb strike itself. They tore the place apart. They ripped open its gullet. They put it out of the transport business. It had been a model operation. But the North Vietnamese now are blessed with a weapon that no military device known to America could ever get a lock on. As if by magic . . . in Hanoi . . . appears . . . Harrison Salisbury! Harrison Salisbury—writing in *The New York Times* about the atrocious American bombing of the hardscrabble folk of North Vietnam in the Iron Triangle! If you had real sporting blood in you, you had to hand it to the North Vietnamese. They were champions at this sort of thing. It was beautiful to watch. To Americans who knew the air war in the north firsthand, it seemed as if the North Vietnamese were playing Mr. Harrison Salisbury of *The New York Times* like an ocarina, as if they were blowing smoke up his pipe and the finger work was just right and the song was coming forth better than they could have played it themselves.

Before you knew it, massive operations like the one at N—— D—— were no longer being carried out. It was back to threading needles. And yet it couldn't simply be blamed on Salisbury. No series of articles by anyone, no matter what the publication, could have had such an immediate strategic effect if there weren't some sort of strange collapse of will power taking place back in the States. One night, after a couple of hops, Dowd sank back into an easy chair in the wardroom of the *Coral Sea* and picked up a copy of some newspaper that was lying around. There on the first page was William Sloane Coffin, the Yale University chaplain, leading a student antiwar protest. Not only that, there was Kingman Brewster, the president of Yale, standing by, offering tacit support . . . or at least not demurring in any way. It gave Dowd a very strange feeling. Out in the Gulf of Tonkin, on a carrier, one was not engulfed in news from stateside. A report like this came like a remote slice of something—but a slice of something how big? Coffin, who had been at Yale when Dowd was there—Coffin was one thing. But the president of Yale? There was Kingman Brewster with his square-cut face—but looked at another way, it was a strong face gone flaccid, plump as a piece of chicken Kiev. Six years before, when Dowd was a senior at Yale and had his picture taken on the Yale Fence as captain of the basketball team . . . any such Yale scene as was now in this newspaper would have been impossible to contemplate.

The collapse of morale, or weakening of resolve, or whatever it should be called—this was all taking place in the States at the very moment when the losses were beginning to mount in both the Navy and the Air Force. Aviators were getting shot down by the hundreds. Sometimes, at night, after dinner, after the little stewards in white had cleared away the last of the silver from off the white line, after playing a few rounds of acey-deucey in the lounge or just sinking into the leather billows of the easy chairs, after a movie in the wardroom, after a couple of unauthorized but unofficially tolerated whiskeys in somebody's stateroom—after the usual, in short, when he was back in his own quarters, Dowd would take out his mimeographed flight schedule for the day just completed and turn it over to the blank side and use it to keep a journal. In 1966 and 1967 more and more of these entries would make terse note of the toll of friends: "We lost Paul Schultz & Sully—presumably captured immediately on landing in parachute. Direct hit from SAM coming out of clouds—site near Kien An." Or: "Bill C. got it over Ha Tinh today—body seen bloody on ground."

Or they were about how John Dowd hadn't gotten his: "The Lord giveth and the Lord taketh away. I think today was a *give* day. 8 SAM's or so fired from multiple sites and it looked like a few had my no. on them. However they missed their mark & so this entry is made . . . Doc H. presented those who participated in the 'A' strike with a little vial of J. W. Dant cough medicine."

In light of all that, it may be of interest to note one fact concerning the mission to Haiphong and points north that Dowd has just headed off on: he did not merely volunteer for it—he thought it up!

For four days, which is to say, ever since Christmas Day, the coastal ports of Haiphong, Cam Pha, and Hon Gay have been socked in with bad weather. Dowd suggested and volunteered for a weather-reconnaissance hop to find out how bad it actually was, to see if the soup was moving at all, to see if the harbors were by any chance clear of third-party ships and therefore eligible for bombing, and so on. If anyone had asked, Dowd would have merely said that anything was better than sitting around the ship for days on end, doing makework.

But *any*thing—even playing high-low with SAM over the North?

The answer to that question perhaps leads to the answer to a broader one: How was it that despite their own fearsome losses in 1965, 1966 and 1967, despite hobbling restrictions and dubious strategies set by the Pentagon, despite the spectacle of the antiwar movement building back home—how was it that, in the face of all this, American fliers in Vietnam persisted in virtuoso performances and amazing displays of *esprit* throughout the war? Somehow it got down to something that is encoded in the phrase "a great hop."

The last time Dowd and Garth Flint were out was four days ago, Christmas Day, during the American Christmas cease-fire; and what a little tourist excursion that was. They flew a photo run over Route 1A in North Vietnam, came in under the cloud cover, right down on top of the "Drive-In," as it was called, fifty feet from the ground, with Garth taking pictures, and the Charlies were down there using Christmas Day and the cease-fire for all it was worth. The traffic jam at the Phun Cat ferry, going south to the Ho Chi Minh Trail, was so enormous that they couldn't have budged even if they thought Dowd was going to open up on them. They craned their heads back and stared up at him. He was down so low, it was as if he could have chucked them under their chins. Several old geezers, in the inevitable pantaloons, looked up without even taking their hands off the drafts of the wagons they were pulling. It was as if they were harnessed to them. The wagons were so full of artillery shells, it was hard to see how one man, particularly so spindly a creature, could possibly pull one, but there they were in the middle of the general jam-up, in with the trucks, bicycles, motorcycles, old cars, rigs of every sort, anything that would roll.

Now, that was a good hop—and Dowd so recorded it in his journal—an interesting hop, a nice slice of the war, something to talk about, but merely a photo hop . . . and not *a great hop*. There was such a thing as a great hop, and it was quite something else.

Sometimes, at night, when Dowd would write on the back of his flight schedule, he'd make such entries as:

"Great hop! Went to Nam Dinh and hosed down the flak sites around that city. Migs joined in the caper, but no one got a tally. Think I lucked out in a last-minute bomb run & racked up a flak site pretty well."

The atmosphere of the great hop had something about it that was *warlike* only in the sense that it was, literally, a part of combat. A word that comes closer is *sporting*. Throughout his tour of duty on the *Coral Sea*, no matter how bearish the missions became, Dowd seemed to maintain an almost athletic regard for form. Even on days he spent diving from SAM's and running the flak gauntlets, even on days when he was hit by flak, he would wind up his journal entries with a note about how well (or how poorly) he drove his F-4 back down onto the carrier, and often with a playful tone: "2nd pass was a beauty but only received an OK—which was an unfortunate misjudgment on the part of the LSO [landing signal officer]." Or: "Went to Haiphong Barracks. 3 SAM's launched—one appeared to be directed at yours truly—however with skill & cunning we managed to avoid it, although it cost us our first bombing run, which was in question due to lack of a target—no flak to suppress. After whifferdilling around we rolled in on a preplanned secondary target. What deleterious havoc this bombing caused the enemy is questionable. However the overall mission was quite successful . . . RTB good approach except for last ¼ mile. Received *cut*-1 for my efforts."

A great hop! *With skill & cunning we managed to avoid*

. . . death, to call it by its right name. But pilots never mentioned death in the abstract. In fact, the word itself was taboo in conversation. So were the words "bravery" and "fear" and their synonyms. Which is to say, pilots never mentioned the three questions that were uppermost in the minds of all of them: Will I live or die? Will I be brave, whatever happens? Will I show my fear? By now, 1967, with more than a hundred combat missions behind him, Dowd existed in a mental atmosphere that was very nearly mystical. Pilots who had survived that many games of high-low over North Vietnam were like the preacher in *Moby Dick* who ascends to the pulpit on a rope ladder and then pulls the ladder up behind him.

Friends, near ones and dear ones, the loved ones back home, often wondered just what was on the minds of the fliers as the casualties began to increase at a fearsome rate in 1966 and 1967. Does a flier lie on his back in bed at night with his eyes wide open, staring holes through the ceiling and the flight deck and into outer space, thinking of the little ones, Jeffrey and Jennifer, or of his wife, Sandy, and of the soft lost look she has when she first wakes in the morning or of Mom and Dad and Christmas and of little things like how he used to click the toggles on his rubber boots into place before he went out into the snow when he was eight? No, my dear ones back home—I'm afraid not! The lads did not lie in their staterooms on the *Coral Sea* thinking of these things—not even on Christmas Eve, a few days ago!

Well . . . what was on their minds?

(Hmmmm . . . How to put it into words . . . Should it be called the "inner room"?)

Dowd, for one, had entered the Navy in 1961 without the slightest thought of flying or of going to war. The Navy had no such designs for him, either. Quite the contrary. All they asked was that he keep playing basketball! At Yale, Dowd had been an aggressive player, the sort who was matched up against other college stars, such as Dave De Busschere of the University of Detroit (later of the New York Knicks). At the end of his last season, 1961, Dowd was drafted by the Cleveland entry in the new American Basketball Association. He had his naval R.O.T.C. obligation to serve out, however, and the Navy sent him to Hawaii to play ball for the fleet. This he did; his team won the All-Navy championship in 1962. There was nothing to stop him from playing basketball for the rest of his service stint . . . just putting the ball in the hoop for Uncle Sam in heavy-lidded Hawaii.

Now that he was in the military, however, Dowd, like many service athletes, began to get a funny feeling. It had to do with the intangible thing that made sports so alluring when you were in school or college, the intangible summed up in the phrase "where the action is." At Yale, as at other colleges, playing sports was *where the action was*—or where the applause, the stardom, and the honor were, to be more exact. But now that he was in the Navy, something about sports, something he had never thought about, became obvious. Namely, all team sports were play-acting versions of military combat.

It is no mere coincidence that the college sport where there is the greatest risk of injury—football—is also the most prestigious. But the very risk of injury in football is itself but a mild play-acting version of the real thing: the risk of death in military action. So a service athlete was like a dilettante. He was play-acting inside the arena of the real thing. The real thing was always available, any time one had the stomach for it, even in peacetime. There were plenty of ways to hang your side out over the edge in the service, even without going to war. Quite unconsciously, the service athlete always felt mocked by that unspoken challenge. And in the Navy there was no question but that *the* action-of-all-actions was flying fighter planes off carriers.

In his last year at Yale, Dowd had married a girl named Wendy Harter from his home town, Rockville Centre, Long Island. About a year and a half later they had a son, John Jr. And then, out in Hawaii, on those hot liquid evenings when the boy couldn't go to sleep, they would drive him out to Hickam Field to watch the airplanes. Both commercial liners and military fighters came into Hickam. By and by Dowd was taking his wife and his son out there even when the boy was practically asleep in his tracks. One night they were out at Hickam, and Wendy surprised Dowd by reading his mind out loud for him.

"If you like them so much," she said, "why don't you fly them?"

So he started training . . . with a vague feeling of *pour le sport*. This was 1963, when the possibility of an American war in Vietnam was not even talked about.

A man may go into military flight training believing that he is entering some sort of technical school where he is simply going to acquire a certain set of skills. Instead, he finds himself enclosed in the walls of a fraternity. That was the first big surprise for every student. Flying was not a craft but a fraternity. Not only that, the activities of this particular brotherhood began to consume all of a man's waking hours.

But why? And why was it so obsessive? Ahhhhh—*we don't talk about that!* Nevertheless, the explanation was: flying required not merely talent but one of the grandest gambles of manhood. Flying, particularly in the military, involved an abnormal risk of death at every stage. Being a military flight instructor was a more hazardous occupation than deep-sea diving. For that matter, simply taking off in a single-engine jet fighter, such as an F-102, or any other of the military's marvelous bricks with fins on them, presented a man, on a perfectly sunny day, with more ways to get himself killed than his wife and children could possibly imagine. Within the fraternity of men who did this sort of thing day in and day out—within the flying fraternity, that is—mankind appeared to be sheerly divided into those who have it and those who don't—although just what *it* was . . . was never explained. Moreover, the very subject was taboo. *It* somehow seemed to be the transcendent solution to the binary problem of Death/ Glory, but since not even the *terminology* could be uttered, speculating on the answer became doubly taboo.

For Dowd, like every other military pilot, the flying fraternity turned out to be the sort that had outer and inner chambers. No sooner did the novitiate demonstrate his capabilities in the outermost chamber and gain entrance to the next . . . than he discovered that he was once again a novitiate insofar as entry through the *next* door was concerned . . . and on and on the series goes. Moreover, in carrier training the tests confronted the candidate, the eternal novitiate, in more rapid succession than in any other form of flying.

He first had to learn to fly a propeller-driven airplane. Perhaps a quarter of an entering class might be eliminated, washed out, at this stage. Then came jet training and formation flight. As many as 50 percent of those left might wash out at these stages. But in naval flying, on top of everything else, there was the inevitable matter of . . . the heaving greasy skillet. That slab of metal was always waiting out in the middle of the ocean. The trainees first practiced touching down on the shape of a flight deck painted on an airfield. They'd touch down and then gun right off. This was safe enough—the shape didn't move, at least—but it could do terrible things to, let us say, the gyroscope of the soul. *That shape—it's so damned small!* And more novitiates washed out. Then came the day, without warning, when they were sent out over the ocean for the first of many days of reckoning with the skillet. The first day was always a clear day with little wind and a calm sea. The carrier was so steady it seemed to be resting on pilings—but what a bear that day was!

When Dowd was in training, aviators learned to land on the flight deck with the aid of a device that bore the horrible, appropriate name of the "meatball." This was a big mirror set up on the deck with a searchlight shining into it at a 3-degree angle—the angle of the flight deck—so that it reflected at the same angle. The aviator was to guide himself onto the deck by keeping the great burst of light, the meatball, visible in the center of the mirror. And many, many good souls washed out as they dropped like a brick toward the deck and tried to deal with that blazing meatball. Those who survived that test perhaps thought for a brief moment that at last they were regulars in Gideon's Army. But then came night landings. The sky was black, and the sea was black, and now that hellish meatball bobbed like a single sagging star in outer space. Many good men "bingoed" and washed out at this juncture. The novitiate was given three chances to land on the deck. If he didn't come in on his first or second approach and flew by instead, then he had to make it on his third, or the word "bingo!" would sound over his earphones—and over the entire flight deck, as he well knew—meaning that he would have to fly back to shore and land on a nice, safe immovable airfield . . . where everyone likewise knew he was a poor sad Bingo coming in from the carrier. It didn't take many bingos to add up to a washout.

One night, when Dowd had just started night training, the sea and the wind seemed to be higher, the clouds seemed lower, the night blacker than he thought possible. From up in the air the meatball seemed to bob and dart around in a crazy fashion, like a BB under glass in one of those roll-'em-in-the-hole games you hold in the palm of your hand. He made two passes and leveled off a good two hundred feet above the ship each time. On the third time around . . . it suddenly seemed of supreme, decisive, eternal importance that the word "bingo" not sound over *his* earphones. He fought the meatball all the way down in a succession of jerks, shudders, lurches, and whifferdills, then drove his plane onto the deck through sheer will, practically like a nail. The fourth and last deck wire caught him, and he kept the throttle pushed forward into the "full military power" position, figuring he was on the verge of boltering off the end and would have to regain altitude instantaneously. He had his head down and his hand thrust forward, with his engine roaring—for how long?—God knows—before it dawned on him that he was actually down safe and could get out. The whole flight deck was waiting for him to shut off his damned engine. As he climbed down from the aircraft, he heard the skipper's voice boom out over the speaker system:

"How do you like flying now, Lieutenant?"

He noted with some satisfaction, however, that they then closed down the deck because of the weather. And was he *now* in the fraternity at last? . . . Hardly. He was just *beginning*. Everything he had learned to do so far became merely the routine. He was now expected to perform such incredible stunts day in and day out, under conditions of fleet operations and combat.

Being a carrier pilot was like being a paratrooper in that it took a while to learn how many different ways you could be killed in the course of an ordinary operation. A fellow F-4 jock, a friend, an experienced aviator, comes in one night low on fuel, not sure he has enough for a second pass, touches down long, bolters, tries to regain altitude, can't, careens off the far end of the deck, fifty thousand pounds of metal and tubes, and sinks without a trace. It all happens in a matter of seconds, *just like that*. Another friend, with even more experience, a combat veteran, *gets his* without moving a muscle. He's in his F-4, in the flight line, waiting for his turn on the catapult, when the ship up ahead somehow turns at the wrong angle, throttles up without a deflection shield behind it, and the whole fifteen tons of thrust hits his F-4, and the man and his guy-in-back and the ship are blown off the deck like a candy wrapper and are gone forever—in an instant, a snap of the fingers, *just like that*.

Yet once an aviator was in combat, all that, too, became simply the given, the hazards of everyday life on the job, a mere backdrop. From now on one found new doors, new tests, coming up with a mad rapidity. Your first day in combat . . . your first bombing run . . . first strafing run . . . the first time you're shot at . . . the first time you see a SAM . . . which also means the first time you dive for the deck straight into the maw of the flak cannons . . . the first time your ship gets dinged by flak . . . and the first time you *see someone else* in your own formation blown out of the sky over the North—and in many ways what an aviator saw with his own eyes was more terrible than the sudden unseen things happening to himself.

For Dowd and Garth Flint this came one day during a bombing run near the Iron Triangle. They were closing in on the target, barreling through the eternal cloud cover, unable to see even the ships in their own wing, when all at once a great livid ghost came drifting straight across their path, from left to right. It was an F-4. It had taken a direct hit, and smoke was pouring out of the cockpit. The smoke enveloped the fuselage in the most ghostly fashion. The pilot had cobbed it to starboard in a furious effort to reach the water, the gulf, to try to bail out where Navy rescue planes could reach them. In the blink of an eye the ghastly cartridge disappeared, swallowed up by the clouds. They would never make it. Dowd and Flint plowed on to the target, following their wing command, even though the gunners below obviously had dead range on the formation. To have done anything else would have been unthinkable.

Unthinkable, to be sure. By late 1967 thinkable/unthinkable played on a very narrow band. The options had been cut back sharply. Both Navy and Air Force fliers were *getting theirs* at a rate that was "astronomical and unacceptable," by ordinary logic, as Jack Broughton had said. But fliers with a hundred missions over the North were people who by now had pulled the rope ladder up into the pulpit. Somehow they had removed their ties with the ordinary earth. They no longer lived on it. Home and hearth, loved ones and dear ones—it wasn't that they had consciously lost their love or dear regard for such folks and such things . . . it was just that the dear folks back home were . . . so far away, back there through such an incalculable number of chambers and doors. The fliers over the North now lived in, or near, the fraternity's innermost room. Or, at the very least, they now knew *who it was*, finally, who had access to that room. It was not merely he who could be called "brave." No, it was he who was able to put his hide on the line in combat and then had the moxie, the reflexes, the experience, the coolness to pull it back in the last yawning moment—and then was able to go out again *the next day*, and the next day, and every next day, and do it all over again, even if the series proved infinite. It was the *daily routine* of risking one's hide while operating a hurtling piece of machinery that separated military flying from all other forms of soldiering and sailoring known to history.

Even *without going into combat* career Navy fighter pilots stood one chance in four of dying in an accident before their twenty years were up, and one chance in two of having to punch out, eject by parachute, at some point. In combat, especially in Vietnam, God knew what the figures were. The Pentagon was not saying. No, the Pentagon itself seemed bent on raising the ante to ridiculous heights, imposing restrictions that every aviator knew to be absurd. And "the nation"? "our country"? "the folks back home"? They seemed to have lost heart for the battle. But even that realization seemed . . . so far away, back through so many doors. Finally, there was only the business of the fraternity and the inner room.

All of the foregoing was out-of-bounds in conversation. Nevertheless, there it was. The closest aviators came to talking about it was when they used the term "professionalism." Many extraordinary things were done in the name of profes-

sionalism. And when everything else went wrong, this professionalism existed like an envelope, in the sense that each
airplane was said to have a certain "performance envelope."
Inside, inside that space, the aviators remained one another's
relentless judges right up to the end, when not a hell of a lot
of people outside seemed to care any longer. They were like
casebook proof of something an English doctor, Lord Moran,
had written forty years before. Moran had been a doctor treating soldiers in the trenches during the First World War, and
he wrote one of the few analytical studies ever addressed specifically to the subject of bravery: *The Anatomy of Courage.*
In the wars of the future, he said, aerial combat, not soldiering, would have "first call on adventurous youth." But the
bravery of these adventurers, he said, would have a curiously
detached quality. For the pilot, "love of the sport—success at
the game—rather than sense of duty makes him go on."

The unspoken things! *Bye borty-bibe* . . . every morning
when he woke up and rolled out of bed in his stateroom, the
components of the game of high-low lit up in every aviator's
brain, and he would all too literally calculate the state of his
soul that morning by the composition of his bowel movement, with diarrhea being the worst sign of all. Well, not quite
the worst; for occasionally one would hear some poor soul in
another cubicle of the head . . . vomiting. One would be
curious . . . but in another way one would just as soon not
know who it was. (After all, he might be in my wing.) Since
none of this could be spoken, demeanor was everything. (*Only
your laundryman knows for sure!*) It *was* like jousting! One
did return to the carrier like a knight! . . . or as near to
knightly status as was likely to be possible in an age of mimeographed flight assignments and mandatory debriefings.

The most beautiful possible moments came when you
brought your aircraft back to the deck from battle half shot
up. Just a few weeks ago Dowd and Garth Flint came back
with an 85-millimeter shell hole shot clear through a rear stabilizer wing. It looked as if you could put your arm through
it, and it was no more than a yard from the fuselage. Dowd
and Flint had scarcely opened the cockpit before the Mouse-
keteers, the deckhands, were gaping at the damage. Dowd

climbed down to the deck, took off his helmet, and started walking away. Then, as if he'd just remembered something, he turned about and said to the onlookers: "Check that stabilizer, will you? Think maybe we caught a little flak."

How gloriously bored! The unspoken, unspeakable things! All the gagged taboos!

No doubt that was what made American airmen, while on leave, the most notorious bar patrons in the Philippines, Japan, and Thailand during the Vietnam years. In keeping with a tradition as old as the First World War, drink and drunkenness gave pilots their only license to *let it out*. Not to talk about the unspoken things—not to break the taboo—but to set free all the strangled roars, screams, bawls, sighs, and raving yahoos. Emotion displayed while drunk didn't count. Everybody knew that. One night Dowd was drinking at a bar at Cubi Point with an A-4 pilot named Starbird. It was getting to that hour of the night when you're so drunk you can't hear any more. Your skull itself is roaring and your screams and songs get beaten back by the gale. The bartender announces that the bar is now closed. He slides a brass pole under the handles on the tops of the big beer coolers behind the bar and locks them shut. Starbird reaches across the bar and grabs the brass pole and emits a roar of sheer gorilla fury and pulls it up out of its mooring, until it's looped in the middle like a piece of spaghetti, and announces: "The bar just reopened."

After a long season of such affronts by many roaring souls, Navy bars and officers' clubs in Subic Bay began ruling themselves off limits to pilots returning from tours in the North (Yankee Station). Then came a gesture from on high that Dowd would never forget. Admiral Red Hyland himself sent out a directive to all clubs and pubs within the purview of the Fleet, saying: It has come to my attention that the cocktail lounge conduct of aviators returning from Yankee Station has occasioned some negative responses. This is to inform all hands that the combat conduct of these men has been exemplary, despite the most trying conditions, and now hear this: THEY WILL BE ACCORDED THE FULL PRIVILEGES OF OFFICERS AND GENTLEMEN! (For you I bend the brass! The bars just reopened!)

At last!—someone had come close to saying it! to putting
it into words! to giving a tiny corner of the world some actual
inkling that they just might have . . . the ineffable . . . *it!*

That memo, like all memos, soon vanished down the memory
hole. Yet it meant more to Dowd than any medal he ever got.

High or low? The weather doesn't get any better as they
pull closer to Haiphong, and Dowd decides to play it low. It
looks like the kind of overcast the SAM's like best, high and
solid. Dowd, with Brent off his wing, comes into Haiphong
at about two hundred feet at close to Mach 1. Suddenly they
break out of the mist and they're over the harbor. They bank
for one turn around it, which immediately cuts their speed
down to about 450 knots. It's peaceful, just another inexplicable stroll in Haiphong Park. The overcast is down to four
hundred feet, meaning it's hopeless so far as a bombing strike
is concerned. Besides, the inevitable third-party ships are
welded in . . .

The weather is so bad, it's as if the enemy has decided to
take a holiday from the war, knowing no bombers will be
coming in. There's no sense loitering, however, and Dowd
heads out for a look at Cam Pha and Hon Gay, two ports
north of Haiphong. High or low . . . Dowd stays down low.
There's nothing below but a smattering of islands.

All at once Dowd sees a streak of orange shoot up over the
nose on the port side. Garth Flint, in the back seat, sees another streak come up under the nose on the starboard . . .
They both know at once: tracer bullets . . . *They go to school
with the tracer bullets* . . . The tracers show the gunners
whether or not they're near the mark . . . and without any
doubt they're near the mark. Then they hear a sound like
twack . . . It sounds like nothing more than a good-size rock
hitting an automobile . . . the shot hit the bottom of the nose
section . . . Dowd immediately cobs it, gives it full power in
a furious bid to get up into the cloud cover and out over the
gulf. Every warning light on the panel is lit up red, but he
still has control of the plane. Smoke starts pouring into the
cockpit. The heat is so intense he can barely touch sections of
the panel. It's so hot he can hardly hold the controls. The fire
seems to be in the hydraulics system of the wheel well. He

tries to vent the cockpit, but the vent doesn't work. Then he blows the canopy off to try to clear the smoke, but the smoke pours out so heavily he still can't see. Everything metal is becoming fiercely hot. He wonders if the ejection mechanism will still work. He can hardly hold the stick.

For Garth Flint, in back, with the canopy gone, it's as if a hurricane has hit, a hurricane plus smoke. Maps are blowing all over the place, and smoke is pouring back. It's chaos. They're going about 350 knots, and the rush of air is so furious Flint can no longer hear anything on the radio, not even from Dowd. He wonders: Can we possibly get back onto the carrier if the smoke is this bad and Dowd can't hear radio communications? Oddly, all his worries center on this one problem. An explosion right in front of him! In the roiling smoke, where Dowd used to be, there's a metal pole sticking up in the air. It's made of sections, like a telescope. It's something Flint's never seen before . . . the fully sprung underpinning of an F-4 ejection system, sticking up in the air as they hurtle over the Gulf of Tonkin. This spastic pole sticking up in the front seat is now his only companion in this stricken ship going 350 knots. Dowd has punched out!

Flint stares at the pole for perhaps two or three seconds, then pulls the ring under his seat. He's blasted out of the ship, with such force that he can't see.

Meanwhile, Dowd's furious ride is jerked to a halt by his parachute opening. He assumes Garth is floating down ahead of him. In fact, Dowd had yelled over the radio for Garth to eject and assumed he was on his way, not knowing Garth couldn't hear a word he said. Considering the way he had cobbed the engine and turned the plane to starboard and out over the gulf, Dowd expects to see water as he comes down through the clouds. Instead, little islands—and the live possibility of capture—are rising up toward him.

Reprieve! The wind carries him about a quarter mile from shore. Just the way the survival training told you, he prepares to shuck his parachute before he hits the water, at the same time keeping his life raft uninflated so the people onshore can't spot him so easily. He hits the water . . . it's surprisingly cold . . . he inflates the flotation device he's wearing—but feels himself being dragged under. The water, which looked

so calm from above, is running five- to seven-foot swells. It
pitches up and down in front of him and beneath him, and
he's being dragged under. He can't comprehend it—the parachute, which he thought he had so skillfully abandoned at
the textbook-proper second, has somehow wrapped around
his right leg in the slosh of the swells and he's going under.
He pulls out the knife that they're issued for just such a situation. But the nylon cords are wet and the damned knife
won't cut them. He's going under. For the first time since
the flak hit, the jaws of the Halusian Gulp have opened. *I'm
going to die.* At first it's an incredible notion. Then it's in-
furiating. To die by drowning out in this squalid pond after a
ten-cent shoot-down on a weather-recce mission—it's humiliating! Another fly-boy disappears into the Cosmic Yawn! He's
swept by a wave of the purest self-pity. It's actually about to
happen—*his death*—the erasure of John Dowd from human
existence—in a few seconds—*just like that!* The ineffable talent, the mystical power—*it!*—that let him hang his hide out
over the Jaws and always pull it back—he *doesn't* have it, after
all!—he is no more special than the hundreds of other pilots
who have already been swallowed up over the North! It's pathetic. It's a miserable and colossal affront. His whole life does
not roll before his eyes—only the miserable pity of the here
and now. He does not think of home and hearth. He does
not think of Mom at the shuttling sewing machine late at
night or the poignancy of seeing one's own child daydream-
ing. No, there is only the here and now and the sum total of
this total affront to all that comprises John Dowd—being
dragged down in a fish pond by a parachute, holding in his
hand a knife that the Navy issued for a task that it won't
perform—it's utterly piteous and pathetic! . . . *Jesus! How I
pity myself now!* . . . And that makes him furious. He gives
the parachute a ferocious yank. Whuh?—in that very explosion
of the final anger he discovers something: the damned thing
is caught—not around his leg but on his knee-board! . . .
The board is attached to his flight suit so he can jot down
figures, keep charts handy, whatever . . . one last breath! Now
he's completely underwater . . . He can't see . . . He grabs
the knee-board and rips it off his flight suit . . . a miracle!
. . . he's free! . . . The parachute is gone . . . the death

anchor . . . He bobs back to the surface . . . Christ! . . . the
hell with the colossal affront of fate . . . There's only *now!*
. . . Never mind! . . . He inflates the raft, as it says in the
manual . . . He's on the side of manual now! . . . Oh yes!
. . . Navy-issue! . . . Why not! . . . He climbs on the raft
. . . He's not drowning any more, he's on his belly on a raft
swooping up and down with the swells of the gulf . . . Never
mind the past! . . . He scans the water and the nearby island
. . . Not miserable Fate, but islanders with guns . . . That's
what he's looking for . . . Is that one of them? . . . But on
the water . . . there's Garth! . . . Flint is on a raft about two
hundred yards away, bobbing in and out of Dowd's line of
vision . . . It's all shaping up . . . Never mind Fate! The hell
with colossal affronts! He's pulled it back after all—out of the
Jaws . . .

Meanwhile, Dick Brent, in the other F-4B, has seen Dowd
and Flint eject. After about fifteen minutes of diving and fishing down through the clouds, Brent spots them on the water
below and radios the position. Brent sees a few people on the
shore of an island, looking out toward the two men, but the
islanders don't seem to be making any attempt to go out by
boat to retrieve Garth and Dowd, which also means capture
them. (In fact, the islanders had long since learned to leave
well enough alone. American pilots in the water were often
followed by screaming rescue aircraft that blew every boat out
of the tub.)

After about another thirty minutes Spads are coming in low
over the water. To Garth Flint it appears as if the Spad pilots
don't see him, only Dowd. Over his emergency radio Flint
says: "If you see two pilots, rock your wings." One of the
Spads rocks its wings. The Spads call in a helicopter known
as a Big Mother. The helicopter, too, heads straight for Dowd.
A morose thought crosses Flint's mind: "He's a lieutenant,
I'm only a lieutenant (j.g.)—so they're picking him up first."

Then it dawns on him that they're going after Dowd because he's in closer to shore and therefore more vulnerable to
gunfire or capture. Hell, it's going to be okay.

Back on the *Coral Sea* Dowd and Flint were debriefed in
the ready room. They drank coffee and tried to warm up. The

china had a certain dignity. It was white with bands of blue about the rims and blue crests here and there. The silverware—now, that was rather nice. It was ornamental and heavy. The questions came, one after the other, and they went through everything that happened. Yet during this debriefing the two men were waiting for *something else*. Surely, they would mention *something else*. But they didn't. It was a debriefing much like *every* debriefing. Just the facts! No quarter given! No slack in the line! Then the commander of their squadron said, with a note of accusation: "Why were you flying so low?"

Now, that was really too much! Why . . . you *bastard!* But they said nothing except the usual. What they wanted to say . . . well, how could they have put it into words? How, within the inner room, does one say: "My God, man, we've just been into the Jaws!—about as far into the goddamned Jaws as you can go and still come back again!—and you want to know why we flew so low! We've just been *there!* at the lost end of the equation! where it drops off the end of the known world! Ask us about . . . *the last things*, you bastard, and we will enlighten you!" There were no words in the chivalric code for such thoughts, however.

But all at once the skipper of the *Coral Sea*, the maximum leader, a former combat pilot himself, appeared—and he smiled! And that smile was like an emission of radio waves.

"We're glad to have you back, men."

That was all he said. But he smiled again! Such ethereal waves! Invisible but comprehensible, they said, "I know. I've been there myself." Just that!—not a sound!—and yet a doxology for all the unspoken things. How full my heart, O Lord!

Flint took one day off before going out on his next mission, on New Year's Eve. Dowd had suffered a back injury in the ejection from the F-4B, and so it was another two days before he climbed back into the metal slingshot, got slung off the skillet, and went flying over North Vietnam again.

from *Mauve Gloves & Madmen,*
Clutter & Vine, 1976

U.S. Aide in Embassy Villa Kills Guerrilla with Pistol

by Charles Mohr

SAIGON, South Vietnam, Wednesday, Jan. 31—The Vietcong terrorist attack on the United States Embassy ended this morning with a gun battle between an embassy official and a guerrilla on a staircase.

Col. George Jacobson, retired, who holds the title of United States Mission Coordinator, had been trapped in his white stucco villa in a corner of the spacious embassy grounds throughout the fierce fighting, which raged in the compound from about 3 A.M. until 9 A.M. today.

Using a .45-caliber automatic pistol that had been tossed to his second-story window by an American military policeman, Colonel Jacobson turned and killed a wounded Vietcong rifleman stumbling up the stairs to get away from tear gas fumes filling the ground floor.

"I was very lucky," said Colonel Jacobson. "He got in the first shots and shot three times but missed. I didn't do much because the military police and Marine guards had already crippled him and he couldn't shoot straight."

At least five American military policemen and two United States Marine guards were killed in a wild night that saw the Vietcong terror squad overrun and then hold a section of the embassy grounds against initial attempts by rescue forces to fight their way in.

Bodies of Vietcong littered the grass and graveled terrace around the modernistic eight-story chancery building.

An initial count by military policemen said that there were 17 bodies of Vietcong after the fight ended.

In one of the strangest scenes of the Vietnam war, helmeted American troops ran crouching across broad Thong Nhut Boulevard to assault the gate of their own embassy at dawn today.

557

Seven American helicopters landed on the roof to discharge a platoon of American paratroops who raced down the stairways to come to the aid of Marine guards fighting to keep the enemy out of the main chancery building.

Meanwhile, the rattle of gunfire and explosions could be heard from the area of the nearby Independence Palace and numerous other parts of Saigon as the guerrilla commando units fought scattered actions late into the morning.

The pierced concrete grille that shades the windows of the chancery building was broken in three places with jagged holes left by Soviet-designed B-40 antitank rockets fired by the guerrillas in their initial assault.

A 3.5-inch bazooka rocket had also torn a hole in the high reinforced concrete wall of the grounds.

Some guerrillas apparently crawled through this hole during the attack. Others shot their way through the gates guarded by United States Army Military Policemen. At the side gate of the grounds two young American soldiers lay dead, one of them shot in the face by a machine gun.

Many details of the embassy battle were unclear for the time being even though newsmen ran crouching with military policemen when the grounds were retaken.

It appeared, however, that the Vietcong commando unit shot its way into the grounds at about 3 A.M. Some of them were killed by the small contingent of United States Marine guards in the building.

Instead of giving up the attack and trying to flee, the guerrillas set up defensive positions on the grounds. Some of the attackers were said to have held the lower floors of the building itself for several hours.

When an American helicopter tried to land on the building's roof before dawn it was driven away by fierce automatic weapons fire from the guerrillas.

Besides the guerrillas inside the compound, American military policemen converging on the chancery building had to deal with snipers firing from nearby roofs and other locations.

Two military policemen getting out of a jeep across the street from the main embassy gate went down in a hail of bullets about 8 A.M.

"Get those men and get that sniper," shouted a Military

Police captain wearing a protective flak jacket emblazoned with the legend "In God We Trust."

While the Marine guard contingent held out in the main building, an American Military Police captain and a young private first class, Paul Healy, 20 years old, of Holbrook, Mass., led the way in a rescue assault into the grounds at first light.

Throwing grenades and firing their automatic M-16 rifles, they killed the guerrillas who tried to keep them out.

"One VC threw a grenade at me," said Private Healy. "It hit the wall and fell down about two feet from me. I dived for cover and didn't get hurt. I killed that man with a grenade and later got three more with another grenade."

His grim face was twitching with emotion as he told his story and a major gently put his arm around the youth's shoulders.

Private Healy, other Military Police and Marine guards fought their way across the flowered lawns to try to rescue Colonel Jacobson, the only embassy official who lives on the grounds.

"I saw raw courage tonight on the part of the Marine guards and military policemen," said Colonel Jacobson, his sleepy eyes drawn and haggard and his maroon sport shirt rumpled with sweat.

"I saw them advance straight into the direction of enemy fire and silence that fire. If you want to get more brave than that, I would rather not be around."

The first-floor foyer of the chancery building was a smoldering shambles. The reception desk with its elaborate push-button console telephone was wrecked.

Some of the bodies on the grounds—thought to be South Vietnamese—might prove to be those of embassy employees rather than Vietcong, since witnesses could see United States identification cards on two of the bodies.

An unexploded, live grenade and several Soviet-made rockets littered the grounds, presenting a demolitions hazard.

One Vietnamese was riddled by American machine-gun fire near the embassy this morning when he failed to stop his ancient black sedan after an American command to halt.

The New York Times, January 31, 1968

from *Tet!*

by Don Oberdorfer

The Plan

IN SEPTEMBER of 1967 an important meeting was held in a pagoda at Tay Ho hamlet, four miles east of the city. The man in charge was Hoang Van Vien, known as "Ba," secretary of the Hue City Committee of the Communist Party. Ba explained to his coworkers that the revolution against the Americans and their Saigon puppets was developing very fast, that conditions were ripe for the General Offensive and General Uprising and that preparations must be undertaken immediately to prepare for the liberation of Hue.

Comrade Son Lam, thirty-five years old and a native of the Hue area, was assigned the task of organizing the uprising for the Right Bank, the section of the city south of the Perfume River. He had joined the anti-French Resistance while attending high school in Hue in 1948, became a member of a Viet Minh secret intelligence cell in 1950, was ejected from the intelligence service in 1952 when his well-to-do parents were denounced as "oppressors of the people," regrouped to North Vietnam after the country was divided in 1954 and infiltrated south in 1962 as the head of a nine-man group of Hue-area natives working for the Party. Despite the fact that his older sister was married to a government policeman, Lam lived safely in his native hamlet just east of the city.

After receiving his instructions, Lam selected as aides the men who could work best within the city and sent them to prepare the way. One night in mid-October, he walked to Hue accompanied by a squad of bodyguards and took up residence in a rented house at the edge of town. He was an ideal organizer: he knew the city and the people, he understood them and they understood him. He began making the rounds of old friends and acquaintances and, with the aid of letters of introduction, called on Hue citizens whose relatives were working for the Party.

Within a week or two he had organized five cells of residents in the Right Bank district—two cells of small-business men and three cells of youths, including the framework of a "Young People's Democratic Group" to be unveiled at the proper moment. He went back to the countryside, where his recruits joined him in small groups for a week's instruction on the aims and organizing principles of the Party. Lam did not tell them when the General Uprising would erupt; he himself had been led to believe that N day would be sometime in March.

On January 26 the leadership committee of the Party completed an eight-page plan for the offensive and uprising in the Right Bank district, specifying general missions as well as targets, the jobs of particular leaders, headquarters locations and policy guidelines. The plan suggests that the leadership did not expect to be able to hold Hue for very long, for it emphasized destruction of "the enemy" over establishment and consolidation of the new order. As set forth in the Party plan, the general missions were:

1. Destroy and disorganize the enemy's restrictive administrative machinery from the province and district levels to city wards, streets and wharves. To pursue until the end spies, reactionaries, and reactionaries who exploit Catholics in and outside the country. To prevent them from escaping and to punish scoundrels, hoodlums, and robbers who kill the people and disturb peace and honor.

2. Motivate the people to take up arms, to pursue the enemy and to seize power and establish a revolutionary government.

3. Make every effort to establish strength in the military, political and economic fields in order to conserve the government. Our immediate mission is to pay particular attention to armed and security forces.

4. Make positive efforts to develop [our forces] in the city wards, streets and wharves in order to expand the guerrilla war.

5. Encircle the reactionaries who exploit Catholics and isolate them. Pay special attention to the Phu Cam area, Thien Huu and Binh Linh schools and at the same time try to gain the support of the Buddhist sects of Tu Dam and Bao Quoc pagodas.

6. Promptly motivate the people to participate in combat, transportation and supply activities and to serve the wounded soldiers, etc.

7. Maintain order and security in the city and stabilize the people's living conditions.

The plan divided the Right Bank into four tactical areas, each with its own priority targets and special missions, its own organization and assigned leaders. The forces were given an activity schedule for their first three days of occupation and specific instructions for handling prisoners in different categories. Important prisoners of war were to be closely guarded and evacuated from the city at the first opportunity; they were to be killed on the spot only if evacuation were impossible. "Cruel tyrants and reactionary elements" were to be imprisoned separately and moved outside the city for "punishment," a euphemism for execution. As for foreign civilians such as teachers, newsmen and artists, the attack force was instructed to "gain the sympathy" of the French residents but to arrest Americans, Germans and Filipinos.

Viet Cong agents had prepared a profusion of reports on the defenses and defenders of the city, the deployment and habits of military and police patrols at night, the identity and activities of political opponents, government officials and foreigners and even the schedule of doctors on duty at the Central Hospital. Working from this mass of information, Viet Cong intelligence prepared two documents for security forces moving into the city. One was a target list for each area of the city of United States and "puppet" civil and military installations. The other list, more detailed and important, included 196 targets in the city to be given priority attention, arranged by street location. For example, these were the items for Duy Tan Street on the Right Bank:

The Garrison Town Office is located on Duy Tan Street at the corner and adjacent to Truong Dinh Street.

U.S. personnel live at No. 4 Duy Tan Street.

Thua Thien [Province] Sector Headquarters is located at Phan Sao Nam Camp, No. 3 Duy Tan Street.

Pham Tra Dang, native of Quang Nam, teacher at the high school, long-standing Vietnamese Nationalist Party member, an extremely anti-revolutionary element, lives at No. 34 Duy Tan Street.

U.S. personnel live at Thuan Hoa Hotel, No. 5 Duy Tan Street.

A house used by U.S. personnel is at No. 21 Duy Tan Street.

No. 52 Duy Tan Street is the house of the concubine of Captain

Pham Lien, Phu Thu District Chief. He was formerly Duc Hoa District Chief and was active against us. He usually sleeps at his concubine's house at night.

No. 71 Duy Tan Street is the home of Nguyen Giang, father of Nguyen Vi Hoc. Hoc is chief of the Psywar office of the Province Rural Development Group. Hoc is also a member of the Dai Viet Party. He usually comes and stays at his father's house.

No. 59 Duy Tan Street is the home of Nam, a member of the National Police Service, Nam Hoa District.

Comrade Son Lam, who moved back to the city from the countryside in early January, was awakened by a messenger in the night at 2 A.M. on January 30, the first day of Tet. His presence was required immediately outside of town. At a meeting in a family chapel north of the city he was informed for the first time that the General Offensive and General Uprising would coincide with the Lunar New Year. The troops were moving, the hour of attack was close at hand. In order to maintain security, no one was permitted to leave the meeting.

The main force units began arriving shortly after dark. Lam was assigned as liaison officer between the troop units which would occupy the Right Bank and the political organization he had built. The provisional battalion, composed half of North Vietnamese regulars and half of South Vietnamese Liberation Army forces, began its march a little after 10 P.M., crossing rice fields, highways and streams and arriving at the jumping-off point after midnight. There in darkness and in silence the soldiers waited at the edge of a rice paddy only a few blocks from the headquarters of the American advisers. Son Lam was excited and anxious, but he was not fearful. He had waited twenty years for this day. His ears were eager for the "signal from above," the mortar and rocket barrage which was to be the call to battle.

United States and South Vietnamese government intelligence, charged with keeping up with threats to the city, was confused, uncoordinated and ineffective. The government police, headed by a former sports announcer who kept a bottle of Johnnie Walker Black Label on his desk, did not customarily exchange intelligence—if indeed it had any—with the 1st

South Vietnamese Division. The small CIA station in the city, which advised the police, rarely exchanged information with the U.S. military advisory team which worked with the provincial troops. The forces within the city rarely received any intelligence of value from the U.S. air, logistical and ground installation at Phu Bai, just eight miles southeast of the city along Route 1.

On January 22 the U.S. Command in Saigon informed the Pentagon in Washington of good evidence in hand that the enemy would attempt a multibattalion attack on Hue. Whatever the good evidence was, it did not reach the people most immediately endangered. Both United States and Vietnamese government forces in Hue were unprepared for a major attack.

About January 28 a U.S. military adviser in Huong Thuy district just east of the city reported signs that three North Vietnamese/Viet Cong battalions had recently left their mountain base camp and were now located in his lowland district. The officer was known at U.S. advisory headquarters in Hue as a habitual worrier and, in the absence of corroborating information, his report was discounted. The following night many of the American and Vietnamese military intelligence officials celebrated New Year's Eve at a party in the back room of the best Chinese restaurant in the city. There was plenty of food and drink, and not a whisper of impending disaster.

On January 30, New Year's morning, Brigadier General Ngo Quang Truong, commander of the 1st South Vietnamese Division, attended the flag-raising ceremony near the Emperor's Gate of the Citadel to mark the coming Year of the Monkey. Shortly after the ceremony he received reports of the attacks on Da Nang, Nha Trang and other cities during the night just past. Many of Truong's men were on Tet holiday, but he placed his remaining forces on alert and called his division staff officers to their posts at division headquarters for the night. This precautionary action preserved the command structure of the division and saved the lives of many staff officers whose residences were in unprotected areas of the city.

At this point, strong evidence of Communist troop movements converging on Hue was in U.S. hands at nearby Phu Bai, but neither Truong nor the U.S. advisory team in Hue was aware of it. The evidence consisted of telltale signals from radio transmissions, picked up by the U.S. radio intercept field station at Phu Bai on January 30. Under Army procedures of the time, this information was not forwarded directly to Hue but was sent back to Da Nang regional headquarters for posting and analysis before being relayed from there to Hue via teletype. The usual bureaucratic delays at headquarters were compounded by the attack on Da Nang itself. By the time the radio intercept reports arrived in Hue, the "signal from above" had already been fired, the Communist units had attacked from all sides and nearly the entire city had been taken over.

Marked Men

The first travail was of those who had been named as targets on the Viet Cong intelligence lists: Vietnamese officials, military officers, political figures and functionaries and Americans and foreigners other than the French. Most of them tried to hide and some of them managed to flee, but many were caught in their homes. They were marched down the nearly empty streets, their arms bound behind their backs, to prisoner collection points in the city.

Lieutenant Colonel Pham Van Khoa, the province chief, fled from his house and made his way in the darkness to Central Hospital six blocks away. There he hid for a week in an attic while a Viet Cong unit conducted the business of a command post on the floor below. Khoa, who had risen to high authority from a lowly position as a personal retainer of the Diem family, was badly shaken by the experience. He was relieved of his post a few weeks later and ultimately assigned to a less important military job in Da Nang.

The senior American adviser in Hue, Philip W. Manhard, radioed the U.S. Command in Saigon on the first morning that his house was surrounded and that he and two assistants were going into a hiding place within the residence. Manhard, a veteran Foreign Service officer, was captured and taken away. As this is written, he has not been heard from since.

Stephen H. Miller, a twenty-eight-year-old Foreign Service officer assigned to Hue as a United States Information Agency representative, had dinner the night before with James R.

Bullington, a Foreign Service classmate who had previously served in Hue and was engaged to marry a Hue girl. The girl's uncle, the son of an old mandarin, had heard rumors that the night would be very dangerous, but the two young Americans had heard such talk before and they were unconcerned. They stayed up late drinking and singing college songs before Miller went home to his house on Phan Dinh Phung Street.

All hell broke loose during the night and in the morning a neighbor boy reported to Miller that many, many Viet Cong were about, including more than thirty at the very next corner. Miller was invited by Vietnamese friends to flee with them to the big Catholic cathedral nearby, but he decided to remain in his house. When his friends returned, the house was occupied by a platoon of Viet Cong who said they had discovered the Foreign Service officer and another American hiding in a closet. Miller's body was found a few days later in a field behind a Catholic seminary which had been used as a prisoner collection point. His arms had been tied and he had been shot to death.

Bullington was luckier. Since he was not regularly assigned to Hue at the time, he was staying in the guesthouse of a friend, who hid him, in turn, with Vietnamese neighbors who had no connection with the government or the Americans. For eight days he watched North Vietnamese troops in khaki patrol the neighborhood and once saw men in black pajamas rumbling down the street in a captured American tank. On the ninth day the North Vietnamese fled and U.S. Marines liberated the house where he was hidden.

Courtney Niles, an NBC International official serving under contract as a radio-television technical adviser, was staying with a U.S. Army communications crew in a house in the Right Bank area. For two days nothing happened. On the third day a Viet Cong team marched up to the house and pounded on the front door. One of the Americans opened fire, a Viet Cong soldier fell dead and the rest of the team withdrew. The Americans gathered their weapons and steeled themselves for a last stand—but again, nothing happened. The invaders were all over the area, walking back and forth through the streets with leafy camouflage hanging from their shoulder packs, carrying mortar tubes and projectiles, machine guns and other weapons, but they simply ignored the Americans in the marked house.

Two or three nights later the attack on the house came, beginning with dynamite charges which blew out a wall without warning. Niles and several others fled. The NBC official was hit in the legs but made it nearly to the church where he had decided to seek refuge. A friend saw him fall in the street. His body was found after the area was cleared. Some of the other Americans in the house surrendered; they were bound and marched off to the Ashau Valley and have never been heard from since.

Father Elizalde, a Spanish Jesuit who lived two blocks from the U.S. advisory compound, was awakened by the barrage in the night and then by a message from the invading troops— delivered by his cook—to open all the doors or suffer the consequences. The troops swarmed in, setting up machine gun posts and mortar pits. The Spaniard and his superior, a Belgian, retreated to the little villa behind their garden while the war erupted around them.

During a pause in the fighting on the third day, a Viet Cong patrol shot off the lock on their door and a political officer summoned them, in broken English, to come outside with their hands in the air. The leader wore khaki shorts and shirt with a green and red arm band and a Ho Chi Minh medal, and he carried a clipboard full of papers describing inhabitants of the area. Copies of identity card pictures were pasted on many of the sheets. He handed the Jesuits a pamphlet printed in English containing the Communist version of American activities all over the world and of the cries of people that "Americans go home."

The priests protested that they were not Americans and that the school had nothing to do with politics or the war, but their arms were bound and they were marched across a field and through a nearby seminary, crowded with North Vietnamese soldiers, to the residence of the senior American adviser. Manhard was nowhere to be seen but five other Americans were crowded into temporary confinement in the shower stall, their arms bound behind them. The priests were searched and then interrogated. The Spaniard said he was from "south of France" and the Belgian from "north of France" and both repeated the humanitarian and non-political nature of their mission. They were vouched for by Vietnamese university students of their acquaintance who seemed to be working with the invading troops. After a while the senior Viet Cong commander on the scene wrote out a safe-conduct pass and let them go. The Americans were later marched away, except for one badly wounded civilian who was left behind.

Dr. Horst Gunther Krainick, a German pediatrician and professor of internal medicine, had come from the University of Freiburg in December of 1960 to help establish a medical school at Hue University. With the assistance of the German and Vietnamese governments, teams of German doctors—mostly from Freiburg—had labored under increasing difficulties to bring first-class medical education to a region and nation woefully short of physicians. Dr. Krainick and his wife, Elisabeth, were torn between their love of Hue and the memories of the happy early years and the growing hostility and bureaucratic difficulties at the university. They were planning to return to Germany as soon as the school year ended and the small class of senior medical students had graduated.

During the Buddhist uprising of 1966, the Germans had been left alone and as non-combatants and medical workers they felt certain they would be left alone at Tet. They placed their German identification on their door in the university faculty apartments and watched the Viet Cong from the windows. They had no way to know that the Viet Cong order was to pick up Germans and that they were listed—though not by name—in Item 65 of the Right Bank target list.

On Sunday morning, the fifth day of the occupation, a well-armed squad wearing red arm bands, neat uniforms and boots arrived in a jeep and a cream-colored Volkswagen bus and began searching the building. The Krainicks stayed put and the Viet Cong went away. Three hours later they returned and entered the Krainicks' apartment. Elisabeth Krainick screamed and when she and her husband were led away she was heard to shout in English, "Keep your hands off my husband." The couple and the two other German doctors in residence, Dr. Raimund Discher and Dr. Alois Altekoester, were taken away in the Volkswagen bus. The four bodies were found later in a shallow grave in a potato field a half mile away, all victims of executioner's bullets. Vietnamese nuns who knew them gently washed the bodies and wrapped them in black cloth and then white cloth in traditional fashion for the long trip home to Germany.

Father Urbain and Father Guy, two French Benedictine priests at the Thien An Mission in the tall pines on a bluff south of the city, had been able to coexist with the local Viet Cong who dominated the area. When the fighting began, several thousand local peasants flocked to the monastery seeking refuge, and they were followed by Communist troops. Father Urbain's body was found in a common grave with ten other victims near the monumental tomb of the Emperor Dong Khanh (1883–89), who was installed on the throne by the French and whose reign was marked by a bloody Vietnamese attack on the French at Hue. Father Urbain had been bound hand and foot and buried alive. Father Guy's body was found nearby. His cassock had been removed and he had been allowed to kneel before being shot in the back of the head.

Three fourths of Hue's Roman Catholics lived in the Phu Cam area of the Right Bank, and the Right Bank plan contained special instructions to "destroy the power and influence of reactionary ring leaders" there. On the fifth day troops came in force to Phu Cam Cathedral and ordered out about four hundred men and boys, some by name and others apparently because they were of military age or prosperous appearance. When the group was assembled, the Viet Cong leader told everyone not to fear, they were merely being taken a half mile away to Tu Dam Pagoda, headquarters of their Buddhist adversaries, for political reorientation. They marched away to Tu Dam and two days later troops returned to the cathedral to ask the women to prepare packages of food and clothing for their loved ones. After this was done, the group disappeared, marching south, and was not heard of for a long time.

Nineteen months later three Viet Cong defectors led the U.S. 101st Airborne Brigade through the royal tombs area, across a river and through some of the most rugged country of central Vietnam to a creek bed deep in double-canopy jungle ten miles from Hue. There spread out for nearly a hundred yards in the ravine were the skulls, skeletons and shards of bone of the men of Phu Cam, washed clean and white by the running brook. The skulls showed they had been shot or brained with blunt instruments. Hue authorities later released a list of 428 victims. About 100 were South Vietnamese servicemen, including two officers; about 100 were students; the rest were civil servants, village and hamlet officials, government workers and ordinary citizens.

Of all instances of Catholic leaders singled out for slaughter, none was more poignant than that of Father Buu Dong, the radiant and popular parish priest of a village east of the city. The area was inhabited by many Viet Cong, and Father Dong worked hard to stay on good terms with both sides in the war. In 1967 he invited Viet Cong and government soldiers to sit down together for Christmas dinner and, according to local legend, he carried it off. He kept a picture of Ho Chi Minh in his room and told his parishioners that he prayed for Ho because "he is our friend too." At the same time, he accepted sewing machines for the people from the American AID program.

On the first day Viet Cong troops led Father Dong to a nearby pagoda for questioning but released him after a passionate appeal by the elders of the parish. Five days later the troops returned. They searched the rectory, seized his binoculars, camera, typewriter and his picture of Ho Chi Minh and led Father Dong and two seminarians away.

The remains of his body were found twenty-two months later in a shallow grave in the coastal sand flats along with the remnants of three hundred other victims. In the priest's eyeglass case were three letters. One was to his aged parents, another to his brothers, sisters and cousins. The third, to his parishioners, said:

My dearly beloved children,

This is my last chance to write to you my children and remind you of the lesson of St. Peter on the boat in the storm (three illegible words) the faith.

My words of greeting at this beginning of Spring are a hope that my works in the faith among you will make you remember (two illegible words) as my life is about to end by the will of God.

Love one another and forgive my wrongs, thanking God with me.

Ask God to forgive all my sins and remember to love and pray for me that I will live in belief and patience during difficulties to bring about the peace of Christ and serve the spirit of God and the interests of everyone in Mother Mary.

Please pray that I will be serene and clear-headed and brave in every adversity of the spirit and of the body and will send my life to God through the hands of the Blessed Mother.

With a promise to meet again in Heaven,

I hope for grace for all of you, my children.

From the position of his body and the lack of visible wounds, it is believed that Buu Dong was buried alive and left to die.

from *Tet!*, 1971

A Third of Mytho Destroyed in Delta Fighting

by Lee Lescaze

MYTHO, South Vietnam, Feb. 5—A third of Mytho is destroyed. Perhaps 50 per cent of this prosperous Mekong Delta city's people have lost their homes.

No one is sure how many civilians have been killed. About 200 are known dead, some killed by allied bombing, others by the Vietcong or after being caught in a crossfire. More than 1000 wounded have been treated in the provincial hospital.

Rue Pasteur on the west side of the city is a dusty line between piles of broken brick and a few standing walls. Twenty-one bent and burned out buses stand where they were parked last Tuesday night, before three Vietcong battalions, operating from a command post in the bus station, opened the battle for Mytho at 3 A.M., Wednesday.

The Vietcong began infiltrating Mytho on Jan. 29, according to American officials trying to reconstruct the battle. They arrived in small groups by bus, motor scooter, sampan and foot. People now say they noticed numbers of men entering the city with heavy parcels and without the wives or children of family groups traveling for the Tet holidays.

Police officials said many of these men went straight to a barbershop and came out minutes later without their parcels. The barber was not questioned because no one wanted to embarrass him, one account has it.

In the first hours Vietcong patrols were in almost every part of the city. U.S. civilians, none of whom was injured during the battle, watched from windows and rooftops.

Those that fired, such as deputy senior province adviser Peter Brownback of Arlington, Va., were quickly pinned down by Vietcong automatic weapons.

"I've seen a lot of scrawny, little Vietcong prisoners and

corpses," one American said, "but that night the Vietcong outside my window looked 7 feet tall."

The 32d Vietnamese Rangers blunted part of the Vietcong offensive at their headquarters on the edge of town. Although the Rangers had fired off a lot of ammunition the night before to celebrate Tet and had about 300 of their 550 men away on holiday leave, they made a brave and successful stand.

Rangers dropped hand grenades from the second floor of their headquarters at Vietcong who had penetrated three lines of barbed wire surrounding the building. After clouding the courtyard with smoke grenades, the Rangers counterattacked and routed the enemy. Of the 360 Vietcong bodies reported in Mytho, 102 were killed in this clash.

The 1st Battalion of the Vietnamese 11th Regiment, which was guarding the 7th Division headquarters and Mytho, was also down to less than 200 men when the Vietcong attacked. The Tet holiday appears to have worked both ways, however. A number of Vietnamese armored personnel carriers, which usually patrol Highway 4 around the city, were in Mytho the morning of the attack.

The armored units and the infantry battalion kept the Vietcong away from division headquarters, the provincial headquarters for Dinhtuong Province and other key buildings. By the afternoon of the 31st, about 12 hours after the fighting started, the Vietcong occupied the north and west sections of the city, but were no longer active in other areas.

Brig. Gen. Nguyen Viet Thanh, commander of the 7th Division, considered calling for air strikes and infantry battalions from the U.S. 9th Infantry Division camp three miles west. For the moment, he decided the battle of Mytho was going to be a Vietnamese show.

The next day, however, Gen. Thanh changed his mind and jets and helicopter gunships began to blast the city. Two battalions of U.S. infantry from Dongtam arrived 24 hours later.

Most Americans here believe the bombing was necessary to save other sections of the city and the lives of the thousands of people who had left their homes to camp in the streets and park on the southeast corner of the city.

The area bombed was one of the poorer sections of Mytho—and one of the most crowded. Bombs and artillery shells touched off numerous secondary explosions as they hit Vietcong ammunition storage areas and parts of the area are blackened by fire.

As for the casualties, all Vietnamese doctors and nurses were away for Tet and many have been unable to get back to Mytho. U.S. and Filipino medical teams handled most of the emergency patients but couldn't get at many needed medical supplies that had been locked up.

Mytho still smells of death. Most of the bodies—Vietcong and friendly—have been removed from the streets, but some remain. In the wreckage of their homes, people are looking for things to save.

There is little emotion and less noise: For a crowded area in Vietnam it is almost impossibly quiet.

In recent months Mytho knew that the Vietcong were coming closer to the city but it has been years since Mytho was attacked by Vietcong troops.

The city has grown rapidly to about 80,000 people because of the war in the countryside and because of its prosperity. It is the first important city south of Saigon and supplies much of the capital's food from its rice and vegetable fields.

Vegetable farming was pushed by American advisers and it was a great success here. Now Highway 4, which must carry the produce to Saigon, is closed—cut in 48 places in Dinhtuong Province both north and west of Mytho with main bridges out and one bridge on the outskirts of this city still in Vietcong hands today. No vegetables can be shipped and many will rot.

Before the coordinated Vietcong attacks against 31 of Vietnam's 44 province capitals plus Saigon and other major cities last week, the road from Saigon to Mytho was one of the most secure in Vietnam. No one knows how long it will be closed.

The Vietcong have been driven out of Mytho but they are staying close to the city. Mortar rounds landed last night and there was a small probe against the power stations.

Initially, Vietnamese officials have responded quickly to the problems of reconstruction. Seven committees have been established and the 5000 to 7000 homeless are being taken care of in schools and churches. The majority of the estimated

40,000 whose homes were destroyed have been taken in by family and friends.

"The attack made the official community realize this isn't a play war," one official said. It is too early to tell what the people of Mytho are thinking, most observers agree. Their respect for the power of the Vietcong has been increased, it is generally acknowledged, but, they are also angry that the attack came during the Tet holiday.

One result of their anger has been a new willingness to give information to the South Vietnamese army and the Americans. "They're going out of their way to tell us things now they never would have volunteered before," an American said.

The Washington Post, February 6, 1968

Life in the V Ring

by John T. Wheeler

KHE SANH, Vietnam (AP)—The first shell burst caught the Marines outside the bunkers filling sandbags. More exploding rockets sent showers of hot fragments zinging. The Americans dove for cover.

"Corpsman! Corpsman!"

The shout came from off to the right.

"We've got wounded here!"

"Corpsman! Corpsman!" The shouts now came from the distance. You could see the men dragging a bleeding buddy toward cover.

Inside the bunkers the Marines hugged their legs and bowed their heads, unconsciously trying to make themselves as small as possible. The tempo of the shelling increased and the small opening to the bunker seemed in their minds to grow to the size of a barn door. The 5,000 sandbags around and over the bunker seemed wafer thin.

Although it could increase their chances of survival only minutely, men shifted their positions to get closer to the ground.

Some measured the angle to the doorway and tried to wiggle a bit more behind those next to them.

There were no prayers uttered aloud. Two men growled a stream of profanity at the North Vietnamese gunners who might snuff out their lives at any moment.

Near misses rocked the bunker and sent dirt cascading down everyone's neck.

Outside the random explosions sent thousands of pounds of shrapnel tearing into sandbags and battering already damaged messhalls and tent areas long ago destroyed and abandoned for a life of fear and filth underground.

This is the life in the V Ring, a sharpshooter's term for the inner part of the bull's eye. At Khe Sanh the V Ring for the

North Vietnamese gunners neatly covers the bunkers of Bravo Company, 3rd Reconnaissance Battalion. In three weeks, more than half the company had been killed or wounded. It was recon's bad luck to live in an area bordered by an ammunition dump, a flightline loading area, and the 26th Marine Regiment's command post.

Shrapnel and shell holes cover the area. The incoming rounds could hardly be noticed once the barrage stopped, such is the desolation.

And then the shells did stop. Silent men turned their faces from one to the other. Several men scrambled out of the bunker to see if more dead or wounded men from their unit were outside. Medics scurried through the area, crouching low.

Inside one bunker a Marine returned to his paperback book, a tale of Wild West adventure. Another man whose hand had stopped in the midst of strumming a guitar resumed playing. Two men in a card game began flipping the soggy pasteboards again.

The shelling wasn't worth discussing. It was too commonplace and none from Bravo Company had been hit this time. Like jungle rot, snipers and rats, artillery fire was something to be hated and accepted at the same time.

But the shellfire had taken its toll. Minutes before the barrage opened, Army Spec. 4 William Hankinson had drifted off from the other members of his communications team assigned to this Marine base.

When the first shell hit, he dived into a Marine bunker. After the explosions stopped, he talked with the Marines awhile before starting back to his bunker.

A white-faced Leatherneck joined the group.

"You look kind of sick," a Marine buddy said. "What happened?"

"The whole Army bunker got wiped out," he replied. "Jesus, what a mess."

Hankinson started to run toward the smashed bunker where his friends' shattered bodies lay. Marines caught and blocked him. Then with a tenderness not at all out of place for hardened fighting men, they began to console the Army specialist, a man most had never spoken to before that day.

One dud mortar round was half-buried in the runway of

the airstrip. Planes carrying priority supplies had to be waved off until the round could be removed.

Two demolition experts raced from shelter with fire axes and chopped it out of the aluminum sheet runway. Neither would give his name. Both had told their families they were safely out of the war zone.

"An awful lot of Marines are big liars on that point," one said.

The men of No. 2 gun, Charlie Battery, didn't think of cover when the shelling began. After what they had been through when the main ammunition dump 200 yards away exploded during an earlier barrage, "This is coasting," one gunner said.

And alone of the Marines at Khe Sanh, the artillery could fire back at the enemy. No 2 gun, commanded by Cpl. Anthony Albo, kept pouring out 105mm rounds even though a shell splinter had started a fire in the gun's ready ammo bunker.

At Charlie Med, the main casualty clearing station, wounded were coming in. Some were on stretchers, some hobbled by themselves, some were hauled in across the shoulder of a comrade.

One prayed, a few cried, some were unconscious. Many showed shock on their faces.

In between shellings, Lance Cpl. Richard Noyes, 19, of Cincinnati, Ohio, roughhoused on the dirt floor of his bunker with a friend. Noyes lives with five buddies in the center of the V Ring. The war was pushed far into the background for a moment as ripples of laughter broke from the tangled, wrestling forms.

Then the first shell of a new barrage hit.

Both men recoiled as if a scorpion had been dropped between them. Even though they were underground in a bunker, everyone put on helmets. Across the front of his "brain pot," Noyes long ago had written in ink, "God walks with me."

A blank stare in the eyes of some is not uncommon at Khe Sanh where the Communists have fired up to 1,500 rounds of rockets, artillery and mortar shells in a single day.

It is called the 1,000-yard stare. It can be the sign of the beginning of combat fatigue.

For Noyes and thousands of others at this surrounded combat base, the anguish is bottled up within tolerable limits.

Noyes had had luck, lots of it. A rocket once drove through the bunker's sandbags and exploded, killing 4 and wounding 14 of the 20 men inside. Noyes was slightly wounded.

It was Noyes' second Purple Heart. One more and he automatically would be sent out of Vietnam under Marine regulations. Noyes doesn't want the third medal.

Despite heavy casualties, the survivors of the recon company are frightened but uncowed. When the call for stretcher bearers comes, the young Marines unhesitatingly begin wriggling through the opening in their bunker to help.

At night the men in Noyes' bunker sit and talk, sing, play cards, almost anything to keep from being alone with their thoughts. During a night when more than 1,000 rounds hit Khe Sanh, Noyes turned to a buddy and said:

"Man, it'll be really decent to go home and never hear words like incoming shells, mortars, rifles, and all that stuff. And the first guy who asks me how it feels to kill, I'll . . ." A pause. Then: "You know, my brother wants me to go duck hunting when I get home. Man, I don't want to even see a slingshot when I get out of here."

Lt. C. J. Slack of Carlsbad, Calif., said: "When I get back to California, I'm going to open a bar especially for the survivors of Khe Sanh. And any time it gets two deep at that bar, I'll know someone is lying."

Noyes smokes heavily and his hands never seem to be entirely still. Looking at the side of a cigarette pack, Noyes said with a wry smile, "Caution, Khe Sanh may be hazardous to your health. Oh, man, yeah."

Still later, he called out, "Okay, we're going to sing now. Anyone who can't sing has to hum. Because I said so. Okay, let's hear it."

Lance Cpl. Richard Morris, 24, of North Hollywood, Calif., began playing a guitar. Two favorites that night were "Five Hundred Miles" and "Where Have All the Flowers Gone?"

A hard emphasis accompanied the verse that went: "Where

have all the soldiers gone? To the graveyard every one. When will they ever learn? When will they ever learn?"

Finally the two small naked light bulbs were turned out and the Marines struggled toward sleep.

AP wire copy, February 12, 1968

AFTERMATH OF TET: FEBRUARY 1968

"We Are Mired in Stalemate . . ."

by Walter Cronkite

TONIGHT, back in more familiar surroundings in New York, we'd like to sum up our findings in Vietnam, an analysis that must be speculative, personal, subjective. Who won and who lost in the great Tet offensive against the cities? I'm not sure. The Vietcong did not win by a knockout, but neither did we. The referees of history may make it a draw. Another standoff may be coming in the big battles expected south of the Demilitarized Zone. Khesanh could well fall, with a terrible loss in American lives, prestige and morale, and this is a tragedy of our stubbornness there; but the bastion no longer is a key to the rest of the northern regions, and it is doubtful that the American forces can be defeated across the breadth of the DMZ with any substantial loss of ground. Another standoff. On the political front, past performance gives no confidence that the Vietnamese government can cope with its problems, now compounded by the attack on the cities. It may not fall, it may hold on, but it probably won't show the dynamic qualities demanded of this young nation. Another standoff.

We have been too often disappointed by the optimism of the American leaders, both in Vietnam and Washington, to have faith any longer in the silver linings they find in the darkest clouds. They may be right, that Hanoi's winter-spring offensive has been forced by the Communist realization that they could not win the longer war of attrition, and that the Communists hope that any success in the offensive will improve their position for eventual negotiations. It would improve their position, and it would also require our realization, that we should have had all along, that any negotiations must be that—negotiations, not the dictation of peace terms. For it seems now more certain than ever that the bloody experience of Vietnam is to end in a stalemate. This summer's almost certain standoff will either end in real give-and-take negotiations or terrible escalation; and for every means we have to escalate, the enemy can match us, and that applies to invasion of the North, the use of nuclear weapons, or the mere commitment of one hundred, or two hundred, or three hundred thousand more American troops to the battle. And with each escalation, the world comes closer to the brink of cosmic disaster.

To say that we are closer to victory today is to believe, in the face of the evidence, the optimists who have been wrong in the past. To suggest we are on the edge of defeat is to yield to unreasonable pessimism. To say that we are mired in stalemate seems the only realistic, yet unsatisfactory, conclusion. On the off chance that military and political analysts are right, in the next few months we must test the enemy's intentions, in case this is indeed his last big gasp before negotiations. But it is increasingly clear to this reporter that the only rational way out then will be to negotiate, not as victors, but as an honorable people who lived up to their pledge to defend democracy, and did the best they could.

This is Walter Cronkite. Good night.

from Who, What, When, Why (CBS report), February 27, 1968

"An Ending of His Own"

by Don Oberdorfer

THERE NOW occurred in Washington, on March 25 and 26, a remarkable event, perhaps unique in American history, which demonstrated in unmistakable fashion the bankruptcy of the war policy on the home front. At the invitation of the President, another gathering of "Wise Old Men" was convened to hear briefings on the war and express their views. These were former Cabinet secretaries, ambassadors and generals, some of whom had helped design the nation's policies toward Vietnam and nearly all of whom were conservative and cautious men with personal ties to their successors in the high posts of the government. The November meeting of Wise Old Men, attended by roughly the same group with only a few changes, had ended in a nearly unanimous endorsement of the government's policy. This time, by a margin of two to one, the senior outside advisers told the President they no longer believed in the war as it was being waged. Several of them expressed the view that the American people would not long support it. It would have to be changed.

At the White House meeting earlier in March, Clark Clifford had suggested to the President that the senior advisers from November, plus additional men as appropriate, be reconvened to take a new look at the Vietnam problem. Clifford had an idea that Johnson would be surprised at the shift in opinion. The President, perhaps influenced by the strong support he received in November, welcomed the suggestion for a new meeting and suggested to several callers—among them Arthur Goldberg, who came to discuss his bombing halt plan—that they should try their ideas on the senior advisers.

The Wise Old Men assembled at the office of the Secretary of State at 7:30 P.M. on Monday, March 25. The outside advisers present were Dean Acheson, George Ball, Omar Bradley, McGeorge Bundy, Arthur Dean, Douglas Dillon, Abe Fortas,

Robert Murphy, Matthew Ridgway and Cyrus Vance. Henry
Cabot Lodge and General Maxwell Taylor, both former Am-
bassadors to Vietnam, held positions in the State Department
and White House, respectively, but were also considered
senior advisers. Those present as senior officials of the gov-
ernment were Dean Rusk, Clark Clifford, Richard Helms,
Walt Rostow, Nicholas Katzenbach, Paul Nitze, Averell
Harriman, Arthur Goldberg, William Bundy and General
John McConnell of the Air Force, representing the Joint
Chiefs.

The meeting was secret, but Lyndon Johnson, who was in
the State Department building that evening to address a Conference on Farm Policy and Rural Life, almost gave it away.
"Secretary Rusk is having a meeting with some wise men in
the next room," said the President in his opening remarks,
but none of the White House reporters got the reference. The
November meeting had not been publicized, and few members of the press had ever heard of the "Wise Old Men." After
his speech to the farmers, Johnson slipped away to the room
where the senior advisers and government officials were dining, and shook hands all around.

In a meeting after dinner and another the following morning at the State Department, they discussed the problems in
Vietnam and the choices facing the United States. Three mid-
dle-rank government officials briefed the assembled group:
Deputy Assistant Secretary of State Philip Habib on the political situation in Vietnam; Major General William DePuy on
the military situation; and George Carver of the Central Intelligence Agency on pacification and the state of the enemy.
The briefers presented factual, carefully balanced accounts
with little indication of their personal views. Even so, some of
the senior advisers were struck with the change in tone and
substance from the highly optimistic briefings of November.
Douglas Dillon, the New York investment banker who had
served President Eisenhower as Undersecretary of State and
President Kennedy as Secretary of the Treasury, got the strong
impression from the November briefings that the war would
be pretty well cleaned up in a year. Now he asked how long
it would take to expel the North Vietnamese and pacify the

country. "Maybe five years, maybe ten years," was the answer. Dillon was stunned, and instantly came to the opinion that the American people would never stand for such a thing.

Clark Clifford described the choices open to the United States as he saw them: (1) expansion of the war—a major increase in ground troops, national mobilization, extension of ground action in Laos, Cambodia and perhaps the southern part of North Vietnam, stepped-up bombing in the North; (2) muddle along—perhaps a few thousand more troops for Vietnam but no change in national strategy; and (3) a "reduced strategy"—reduction in the bombing, abandonment of isolated positions such as Khe Sanh, and the use of American troops as a shield around populated areas while the Vietnamese government and its troops were given time to assume the burden of the war.

Former Secretary of State Acheson, the senior man present in terms of prior governmental responsibility, said he had changed his views since November. He had reached the conclusion that it was not possible to achieve the nation's objectives in Vietnam by military means. Therefore, he opposed the dispatch of more American troops and noted there were always more troops in North Vietnam as well. Arthur Goldberg made his plea for total cessation of the bombing of North Vietnam. Averell Harriman spoke earnestly about the dangers of military escalation. Acheson's turnabout appeared to have considerable impact on the group, as did the change in Clifford's views since he had been one of the outsider advisers at the November meeting.

At midday Tuesday most of the senior advisers, accompanied by a few of the senior government officials, went to the White House to submit their views. They were joined in the family dining room by the President, Vice-President Humphrey, General Wheeler (who had just returned from Clark Field) and General Creighton Abrams, who flew back with Wheeler. After lunch, Abrams briefed the group on the progress of the South Vietnamese Army. Then the President dismissed Rusk, Clifford and most of the other government officials, and adjourned to the Cabinet Room to hear the views of the senior advisers. Those present were Johnson,

Humphrey, Wheeler, Taylor and Lodge, and nine outsiders: Acheson, Ball, Bradley, McGeorge Bundy, Dillon, Fortas, Murphy, Ridgway and Vance.

McGeorge Bundy, president of The Ford Foundation and former White House foreign policy assistant to Presidents Kennedy and Johnson, summarized the views of the advisers. The predominant view was that of Dean Acheson—that American objectives could not be achieved within the limits of time and resources available, and therefore the policies would have to be changed. Bradley, Fortas and Murphy, it was noted, dissented from the general view.

The President was quite visibly taken aback. He went around the table, calling on each man to state his opinion.

The bombing of North Vietnam had been undertaken in February 1965 at the specific recommendation of McGeorge Bundy, who helped sell it to Johnson then as a low-cost way to stave off defeat in South Vietnam and raise the potential price of insurgencies around the world. Later Bundy saw the bombing of the North essentially as a negotiating chip at some future bargaining table, and twice in the fall of 1967 he let the President know that he did not favor giving it up. Now he reversed himself, on the grounds that the bombing was more damaging to support for the war at home than it was militarily beneficial abroad. He recommended that the bombing should be stopped completely, not partially, and opposed sending additional American troops to Vietnam.

Henry Cabot Lodge, twice U.S. Ambassador to South Vietnam and the Republican political cover on Vietnam for both Kennedy and Johnson, read a statement he had written in longhand the night before. Lodge urged urgent consideration to a shift from "search and destroy" and "war of attrition," which he said pointed to an unobtainable goal of military victory, to a new strategy of using American military power as a shield behind which South Vietnam would be organized. "Less stress on search and destroy would mean fewer casualties, less destruction, fewer refugees, less ill will and more public support at home," Lodge said. More stress on the organization of Vietnamese society would "put the egg in the cake before putting on the frosting." He conceded that his strategy would take a long time, and concluded that "U.S.

forces therefore should be in numbers sufficient only to enable us to keep faith with our troops in exposed positions such as Khe Sanh, and not to continue the past emphasis on search and destroy."

Douglas Dillon, another prominent Republican, said the United States should send no additional troops, it should stop the bombing completely and try to move toward a negotiated settlement. The President asked Dillon how he came to change his mind about the war. The financier said the briefing of the night before had an impact on his views, that it was quite clear to him the United States did not have five or ten years to conclude this war. Johnson seemed surprised, and said he wanted to hear the briefings.

Dean Acheson, sitting on the President's right at the Cabinet table, went over his position in detail. As summarized by one of the participants later that day, Acheson declared that the "belligerency" in Vietnam could not be brought to the point where the South Vietnamese government could handle it by the use of any permissible means within the time allowed this or any other President by the American people. "This fact, together with our broader interests in Southeast Asia, Europe and in connection with the dollar crisis, requires a decision now to disengage within a limited time," Acheson said. No actions should be taken inconsistent with this goal, and there should be some evidence of a new policy by mid-summer, he urged. The fundamental problem in South Vietnam, in his view, was the missing element of popular support, which the United States could not supply. And the fundamental problem in the United States was lack of popular American support for the war. Acheson did not think the public would permit the government to continue its efforts in Vietnam for more than a year or so, and probably the time available would be shorter in the absence of a clear turn toward peace by midsummer. "One thing seems sure—the old slogan that success is just around the corner won't work."

George Ball, the former Undersecretary of State who had been the most articulate "devil's advocate" against the war within high Administration councils, recommended an immediate cessation of all bombing of North Vietnam. At one point Ball began to speak of the political problems in the

United States, but the President cut him off. "That's the last thing that would affect me," he said.

General Matthew Ridgway, the field commander of U.S. troops in Korea after the dismissal of MacArthur and later Army Chief of Staff, recommended that the Vietnamese government be given arms and equipment and two years' time to prepare its armed forces to take over the fighting. The Vietnamese would be told that after two years the United States would begin withdrawing its troops. Ridgway did not know if this would work, but it would be worth trying; he himself had opposed the Vietnam intervention from the very start.

Cyrus Vance had been Deputy Secretary of Defense during the period of the Vietnam build-up, and a solid defender of the policy until a severe back ailment forced him to retire to private life in mid-1967. Had Vance remained in government, he would probably have become Secretary of Defense in early 1968, and he might well have continued to support the military effort—for it was his return to private life which shattered his earlier views. Back in New York in the law firm he had left a decade previously, Vance was stunned by the depth of feeling against the war on the part of nearly everyone he met: his law partners, their wives, the junior associates, the people at dinner parties, the clients of his law firm. For the first time, Vance understood how insulated he had been in government, hearing the briefings and reading the reports, making speeches calling for patience and never understanding that the people were not behind the war.

As a young lawyer, Vance had come to Washington in 1957 to be special counsel to Senator Lyndon Johnson's Preparedness Investigating Subcommittee, and he had always been considered Lyndon Johnson's man. When there was trouble in the Panama Canal zone in 1964, the new President sent Vance as his personal emissary; when the Dominican crisis erupted, he did the same; when the Detroit ghettos burst into flames, when Greece and Turkey were locked in dangerous conflict over Cyprus, when South Korea was in crisis after the Blue House raid, Johnson's answer was the same—send Cy Vance. Now Vance sat in the Cabinet Room and told the President that the war was dividing the country and it was time to change the policy. The government must find a way to move to negotiations, he said.

Justice Fortas, Johnson's old friend and still a solid supporter of the war, objected that this was not a favorable time for negotiations. Moreover, Fortas thought there had been too much emphasis among the senior advisers on the words "search and destroy." That did not mean big offensives, but was merely a synonym for fighting the enemy, he said.

General Wheeler agreed on both points. He had told Westmoreland at Clark Field that "search and destroy" was in bad repute—he had better find another term. (The U.S. Command subsequently banned the term from its lexicon and began referring to its offensive mobile operations as "combat sweeps," "reconnaissance in force," "spoiling attacks" or simply "raids.")

An objection was raised to Acheson's assertion that existing United States policy was bent on a military solution in Vietnam. "What in the name of God have we got 500,000 troops out there for—chasing girls? You know damned well this is what we're trying to do—to force the enemy to sue for peace," the blunt-spoken Acheson declared. "It won't happen —at least not in any time the American people will permit."

Retired General Omar Bradley, the World War II commander and former Chairman of the Joint Chiefs, had been to Vietnam on a semiofficial inspection tour in 1967 and returned publicly backing the policy. He continued his support of the basic policy now, but indicated it might be necessary to lower the sights of the nation's objectives.

Former Ambassador Robert Murphy continued to back the war in strong terms.

The President looked increasingly glum as one man after another spoke. His grandson, nine-month-old Lyn Nugent, had been brought in during the meeting, and the chief executive held the baby on his lap while the Wise Men gave their judgments on the war. "As I understand it, with the exception of Murphy, Bradley, Taylor, Fortas and General Wheeler, all of you favor disengagement in Vietnam," the President summed up. Lodge spoke up that he did not favor disengagement, but wanted to use American power in different fashion. Bundy quarreled with the word. (He decided later the word he preferred was "deescalation.") The others were silent. Johnson thanked them all and said goodbye.

The following day the President summoned the men who had briefed the senior advisers and ordered them to repeat their briefings. DePuy and Carver did so (Habib was out of town) and Johnson asked questions. Finally he decided that the briefings could not have been the cause of the disaffection.

Dean Rusk, Clark Clifford, Walt Rostow, William Bundy and speech writer Harry McPherson met on March 28 at the State Department to "polish the speech" which the President was to deliver three days later. McPherson's original drafts had undergone many changes since the last speech-writing meeting six days previously, but it was still a "more of the same" address. At this stage, it reflected the decision to send only a small number of additional troops to the war but said nothing about a halt or reduction in the bombing.

On March 23 the State Department had submitted twenty pages of proposed speech language, including a section announcing a bombing halt at the 20th parallel of North Vietnam, but the President would not allow this or any other suggestion of a bombing limitation to be circulated. Always secretive about his decisions, he was doubly so about this initiative. A leak would complicate his negotiations with the Saigon government and the Joint Chiefs of Staff and rob the proposal of the surprise and drama that he loved. He was holding even more closely to his chest another, more explosive secret—his own resolve to announce at the end of the Vietnam speech that he would not be a candidate for reelection.

The night before the March 28 "polishing" session Clifford read the latest draft of the Vietnam speech, and he thought it a disaster. The President was going to the country to speak of the war in the same old terms the country was rejecting, to ask again for sacrifice, perseverance, patience and fortitude. Over lunch in Secretary Rusk's office at the State Department, Clifford told his colleagues that the country would not buy it. This was a speech for more war, and the President needed a speech about peace. Clifford marshaled the conclusions he had reached in the months since Wheeler's return—the problems and difficulties of the war, the futility of more of the same, the state of mind of the American public, the loss of confidence by private leaders. A democratic nation could not carry forward a war without broad support among the public. "Boys, it's not there," Clifford said emphatically. He argued that the President should reduce the bombing in a move toward peace, and give a peace speech.

Rusk did not argue. At the end ·of the meeting, it was agreed that McPherson would draft a whole new speech for the President. McPherson had come to hate the war and its effect on the President and the country. He left for the White House in high spirits.

After a nod from Rusk, William Bundy drafted a cable to Saigon instructing Bunker to clear the 20th parallel bombing halt with President Thieu. It was to be made clear that if Hanoi did not respond, the bombing limitation would be temporary. At 6:30 P.M. Rusk went to the White House for a private discussion with the President, and a little later there was a telephone call to the State Department. The cable was on its way, in code, by 8 P.M.

The Joint Chiefs considered the 20th parallel bombing halt in formal deliberations, and approved the plan after considerable debate with certain specific provisos. The United States would resume bombing throughout North Vietnam if the Hanoi regime failed to respond to the peace initiative by the time the weather cleared in a month or two, and it would resume the bombing if the Communists made a big military push in the South. The Joint Chiefs did not expect the limited cessation of bombing to be permanent, but there were serious misgivings. Some of the military men feared that once the bombing of the northern part of North Vietnam was stopped, it would be politically impossible to resume it.

On Sunday, March 31, the leaders of Lyndon Johnson's campaign for reelection met in Marvin Watson's office in the west wing of the White House to discuss the bleak prospects in the April 2 Wisconsin primary and plan strategy for the tough campaign ahead. Watson, Lawrence O'Brien and James Rowe were joined for the first time by Terry Sanford, who had agreed to be the campaign manager in a telephone conversation with the President at the beginning of that very week. Johnson greeted Sanford briefly, but did not participate in the strategy session. The political pros were told that the President would announce a limited bombing halt in the speech that night. Nothing was said about his political decision.

In the family quarters of the White House, the President was working with Horace Busby, a trusted former aide and sometime speech writer, on the surprise peroration announcing that he would not run again. Except for the final ending, the full speech had been discussed and approved line by line by the President and his advisers in a long session the previous day. When they came to the end of the prepared text, Johnson had told the group he might have an ending of his own.

Never having had sons of his own, Lyndon Johnson felt an almost paternal affection for several of the young men on the White House staff, among them Harry McPherson. McPherson was a fellow Texan and had been working for Johnson off and on since he came to Washington as a Senate aide in 1956. McPherson was working in his office in the west wing of the White House late in the afternoon when the President telephoned.

"Do you think it is a good speech?" the President asked his aide. McPherson thought it was.

"Do you think it will help?" McPherson thought it would, particularly at home.

"Do you think Hanoi will talk?" The aide was much less certain—the chances seemed to him to be less than 50-50.

"I'm going to have a little ending of my own to add to yours," the President told his aide and friend. McPherson had heard that it was in the works, and he caught a hint the day before of what Johnson might do.

"Do you know what I'm going to say?" Johnson asked. There was a pause. Yes, he thought so.

"What do you think?"

"I'm very sorry," said McPherson softly.

"Okay," responded the President with a Texas lilt in his voice—"so long, pardner."

McPherson put away the papers on his desk and left the

White House. He went to a neighbor's house and proceeded to drink most of a fifth of bourbon.

Richard Nixon had scheduled a nationwide radio address for 6:30 P.M. on March 31 to begin to define his position on future strategy in the war. In the New Hampshire primary campaign, Nixon had "pledged" to end the war, but he gave no clue of how he would go about it. Political opponents and the press ridiculed him for implying he had a plan without explaining what it was, and there was a growing demand that he state a clear position. Nixon preferred to keep his views ambiguous for maximum political appeal and maneuverability, but in late March he reluctantly decided that the political cost of remaining silent was even higher than the cost of speaking up.

The radio address he had planned for March 31 was characteristically cautious, but it represented a significant departure from his original hawkish stand. "The answer to failure is not simply more of the same," he planned to say, making the point that Vietnam was basically a political war, which could be resolved only on a political basis. He planned to urge great diplomatic efforts to obtain a settlement, especially efforts to enlist the Soviet Union's support for an early end to the war, perhaps as part of a far-reaching agreement. He planned to say that a more effective military strategy might involve fewer American troops—not more troops. The working draft of the radio speech was a first step toward a Nixon commitment to liquidate the war, and implicit in it was the abandonment of the idea of military "victory."

The day before his address Nixon received word that Lyndon Johnson had requested television time for the same night. With relief mixed with curiosity, Nixon immediately canceled his own talk "in deference to the President." After he heard the speech, Nixon announced the first of a long series of self-imposed moratoriums on Vietnam comment, on the grounds that he should not "even inadvertently" say anything that might cause difficulty for U.S. negotiators. As his campaign for the presidency developed, he was never forced to state a clear position on the war.

*

Dean Rusk was aboard an Air Force jet flying over the Pacific to a previously scheduled meeting of the Vietnam War allies at Wellington, New Zealand, when he received a radiotelephone call from a White House aide. "There's going to be a final paragraph on the President's address," the aide said cryptically over the insecure radio channel. Rusk knew immediately what the message meant.

The President called Soviet Ambassador Dobrynin to the White House at 6 P.M. to explain the partial bombing cessation and give personal emphasis to the bid for peace. High-ranking American officials in Washington and around the world began similar briefings for other foreign leaders.

About 8 P.M. Clark Clifford and his wife, Marny, and Walt Rostow and his wife, Elspeth, arrived for drinks in the family quarters of the White House. After a few minutes the President called Clifford and Rostow into his bedroom and handed them a copy of his secret peroration. Clifford was very surprised, and asked Johnson if he had thought it through from every aspect. The President had; it was final. Rostow said little. Mrs. Rostow was on the verge of tears after her husband told her the news.

A few minutes before the scheduled air time of 9 P.M., the President, a few aides and guests walked over to the west wing. Johnson told Marvin Watson to begin calling members of the Cabinet and others who should know of his political decision, and then he stepped before the cameras in the Oval Office. Lady Bird looked radiant and happy, but Lynda and Luci, who cried when they heard the news, did not. Lynda had returned from California only that morning after seeing her husband off to combat duty in Vietnam. She desperately wanted the war to end, and felt her father was the man to do it. She was afraid she would never see her husband again.

The President sat down behind his desk. The still photographers came in and took their pictures. The producer checked the sound and lighting. The red light went on.

"Good evening, my fellow Americans:
"Tonight I want to speak to you of peace in Vietnam and Southeast Asia. No other question so preoccupies

our people. No other dream so absorbs the 250 million human beings who live in that part of the world. No other goal motivates American policy in Southeast Asia.

"For years, representatives of our Government and others have traveled the world—seeking to find a basis for peace talks. Since last September, they have carried the offer that I made public at San Antonio. . . . Hanoi denounced this offer, both privately and publicly. Even while the search for peace was going on, North Vietnam rushed their preparations for a savage assault on the people, the government and the allies of South Vietnam.

"Their attack—during the Tet holiday—failed to achieve its principal objectives. It did not collapse the elected government of South Vietnam or shatter its army—as the Communists had hoped. It did not produce a 'general uprising' among the people of the cities as they predicted. The Communists were unable to maintain control of any of the more than thirty cities that they attacked. And they took very heavy casualties.

"But they did compel the South Vietnamese and their allies to move certain forces from the countryside into the cities. They caused widespread disruption and suffering. Their attacks, and the battles that followed, made refugees of half a million human beings.

"The Communists may renew their attack any day. They are, it appears, trying to make 1968 the year of decision in South Vietnam—the year that brings, if not final victory or defeat, at least a turning point in the struggle.

"This much is clear: If they do mount another round of heavy attacks, they will not succeed in destroying the fighting power of South Vietnam and its allies. But tragically, this is also clear: Many men—on both sides of the struggle—will be lost. A nation that has already suffered twenty years of warfare will suffer once again. Armies on both sides will take new casualties. And the war will go on.

"There is no need for this to be so. There is no need to delay talks that could bring an end to this long and this bloody war.

"Tonight, I renew the offer I made last August—to

stop the bombardment of North Vietnam. We ask that talks begin promptly, that they be serious talks on the substance of peace. We assume that during those talks Hanoi will not take advantage of our restraint.

"We are prepared to move immediately toward peace through negotiations. So tonight, in the hope that this action will lead to early talks, I am taking the first step to de-escalate the conflict. We are reducing—substantially reducing—the present level of hostilities. And we are doing so unilaterally, and at once.

"Tonight, I have ordered our aircraft and our naval vessels to make no attacks on North Vietnam, except in the area north of the demilitarized zone where the continuing enemy buildup directly threatens allied forward positions and where the movements of their troops and supplies are closely related to that threat. . . ."

In Saigon, the hour of the President's address coincided with a scheduled meeting of the U.S. Mission Council. The high officials—including Ambassador Bunker, General Westmoreland, Robert Komer, Barry Zorthian, the CIA chief, and Colonel George Jacobson, the Mission coordinator—had gathered in the third-floor conference room of the Chancery building. Most of the physical damage done by the Viet Cong commando team had been repaired, temporary gun nests had been built and the Embassy compound was a bristling fortress.

Several of the officials had been briefed in detail on the President's address, and a text of his prepared remarks had been transmitted from Washington several hours earlier. The Saigon Embassy officials listened without enthusiasm—there was much feeling that this was a step in the wrong direction—as Lyndon Johnson's voice floated into the room via Armed Forces Radio. As the President reached the end of the text, one of the officials stood up to turn off the radio—but, unaccountably, the President continued talking:

"Finally, my fellow Americans, let me say this: Of those to whom much is given, much is asked. I cannot say, and no man could say, that no more will be asked of us. Yet, I believe that now, no less than when the decade began, this generation of Americans is willing to 'pay any price, bear any burden, meet any hardship, support any friend, oppose any foe to assure the survival and the success of liberty.' Since those words were spoken by John F. Kennedy, the people of America have kept that compact with mankind's noblest cause. And we shall continue to keep it.

"Yet, I believe that we must always be mindful of this one thing, whatever the trials and the tests ahead. The ultimate strength of our country and our cause will lie not in powerful weapons or infinite resources or boundless wealth, but will lie in the unity of our people. . . . What we won when all of our people united just must not now be lost in suspicion, distrust, selfishness and politics among any of our people.

"Believing this as I do, I have concluded that I should not permit the Presidency to become involved in the partisan divisions that are developing in this political year.

"With America's sons in the fields far away, with America's future under challenge right here at home, with our hopes and the world's hopes for peace in the balance every day, I do not believe that I should devote an hour or a day of my time to any personal partisan causes or to any duties other than the awesome duties of this office—the Presidency of your country.

"Accordingly, I shall not seek, and I will not accept, the nomination of my party for another term as your President. . . ."

When Lyndon Johnson had finally finished, there was a self-conscious silence in the Embassy conference room. The men sat there looking at one another, measuring each other's surprise and wondering about the future of the war the President had led and the future of those whose careers had been tied to his. Westmoreland remembered the half-forgotten conversation with Johnson in November, but no one else in the room had had the slightest warning. For the second time in eight weeks, the wheel of life was turning with a velocity and in a direction that no one had quite foreseen.

from *Tet!*, 1971

Hanoi—March 1968

by Mary McCarthy

"Attachez vos ceintures, s'il vous plaît." "Fasten your seat belts." The hostess, plump, blonde, French, brown-eyed, in a light-blue smock, passed through, checking. It was funny to find a hostess on a military plane. Like the plane itself, loaded with mail, canned goods, cases of beer, she was a sort of last beep from the "other" world behind the mountains in Vientiane. Born in Hanoi, she had been making the run from Saigon with the I.C.C.—Poles, Indians, Canadians, of the inspection team—six times a month, weather permitting, for thirteen years, practically since the Geneva Accords.

As the I.C.C. plane, an obsolete non-pressurized Convair, circled in the dark above Hanoi, waiting to get the OK to land, out the window, by stretching against our seat belts, we could see tiny headlights of cars moving on the highways below and then the city all lit up like a big glowworm. In Phnom Penh, at the North Vietnamese Delegation, where they issued our visas, they had prepared us for this surprise, but it remained a surprise nonetheless. I thought of the Atlantic coast during World War II and the blackout curtains we had had to buy on the Cape—a Coast Guard order designed to foil enemy submarines. When the Convair taxied to a stop, it instantly doused its lights, though, and the hostess held a flashlight for the boarding officials to examine our papers. But then the airport, brilliant white and blazing with electricity. "You really don't have a blackout!" I exclaimed to the delegation from the Vietnamese Peace Committee who had come to meet us, with bouquets of snapdragons, pink sweet peas, pale-pink roses, larkspur, and little African daisies. A Japanese author and a journalist from a Tokyo paper were receiving bouquets, too. The Vietnamese did not know the word "blackout," and I tried *couvre-feu*. They dismissed the term "curfew" with laughter. "Passive defense!" In fact, there was no curfew of any sort in Hanoi—except the bell that rang at eleven o'clock nightly, closing the hotel bar—though there was one in Saigon. It was only when the sirens blew that the lights of the city went out and the cars and trucks halted and waited for the All Clear.

On the way from Gia Lam Airport into the city, we had our first alert—a pre-alert, really, given by loud-speakers; the pre-alert usually means the planes are sixty kilometers away; it is not till they are within thirty kilometers of the center that the sirens scream. Suddenly, still deep in the countryside, the driver braked the car; he had heard the pre-alert on his radio. He turned off the engine. I sat in the back seat, holding my bouquet in my lap and feeling quite apprehensive. On March 17, two days before, the much-feared swing-wing F-111A's had appeared in Thailand; there had been pictures of them in the Bangkok papers. The driver got out of the car. "He is looking for the shelter," one of my companions explained. "He has found the shelter," they announced a few minutes later, and we all climbed out of the car. In the moonlight, we could see the remains of a brick house, with its roof torn off; up the lane, there had been a hamlet, but now there were only indistinct masses of debris and, somewhere in the dark, the shelter, which I never actually saw. It was enough to know that it was there.

Outside Hanoi, the driver's first job, I discovered, was to look for a shelter for the passengers whenever the alert or the pre-alert sounded. Every hamlet, sometimes every house, is equipped with a loud-speaker, and the alarm is rung out by the hamlet bell—the same bell that calls the peasants to work in the fields. When there is no hamlet nearby, a band of young soldiers, tramping along with a transistor radio, may warn you that the planes are coming. Once, in Hoa Binh Province, out in the west, I sat huddled in the car with the thin, large-eyed young woman interpreter while the driver conducted the search; he came back, and there was a quick conference in Vietnamese. "Here there is no shelter," she whispered, gravely touching my arm, as we listened to the bombs, fortunately some miles off. Though the shelter may be only a hole in the ground, the assurance that there is such a burrow handy gives a sort of animal comfort—possibly not unlike the ostrich's. Or maybe it is a grateful sense that somebody, an unknown friend, has thought about your safety; even if the uncovered earth shelter cannot protect you from a direct hit, the thought, as they say of small presents, is what counts.

In the city, there are individual cement cylinders, resembling manholes, every few feet, with round fitted covers of cement or of plaited reeds—good against fragmentation bombs. In a pinch, they will accommodate two small Vietnamese. But what happened, I wondered, if there were more people on a given street when the alarm sounded than there were shelters to hold them? As in a game of going to Jerusalem or musical chairs, who would be left outside? It is a schoolmen's problem, that of the outsider, which is posed in the scramble of extreme situations, and I was curious—anxious, even—about the socialist solution. But I never was able to observe for myself what did in fact occur: in my two and a half weeks in North Vietnam, it chanced that only once was I in the city streets during an alert and then only long enough to see the people scattering as our driver raced toward the hotel and its communal shelter. And I felt that it would be somehow impolite to express my curiosity in the form of a point-blank question; there are many questions one does not want to ask in Hanoi.

In any case, the target of the Hanoi government is one shelter per person within the city limits—I am not sure whether this ratio takes into account the communal shelters attached to institutions. During my stay, hundreds of brand-new cylinders were lying along the sidewalks, waiting for the pavement to be dug up and holes sunk to contain them, and every day trucks kept dumping more. Production and delivery were ahead of the picks and shovels. "Manufacturing shelters is one of our principal industries now," people remark, rather ruefully, watching the gray cylinders being put into place. What can be done with these grim manholes, war memorials, when and if peace comes? The only answer I could think of was to plant flowers in them.

Johnson's speech of March 31—and the subsequent eerie absence of alerts—did not cause even a momentary flagging in the shelter program. Yet, so far as I could tell, the shelters

were more a symbol of determination than places to scuttle
to when the planes approached. The city population had a
certain disdain for using them. "There are toads in them," a
pretty girl said, making a face. Like the white-gowned surgeon
I met, a Hero of Labor, who had calculated the statistical
probabilities of being killed by a bomb in the night and decided that he preferred to stay in bed, to be fresh for operating
the next morning, many people in Hanoi decline to leave their
beds or their offices when the peremptory siren shrills; it is a
matter of individual decision. Only foreign visitors are hustled
to safety by their guides and interpreters and told to put on
their steel helmets or their pellet-absorbent hats of woven
reeds or straw. A pellet in the brain is the thing most dreaded
by the Vietnamese—a dread that as a brain-worker I more
than shared; unfortunately the hat they gave me was too small
for my large Western head, and I had to trust to my helmet,
hurriedly strapping it on as I trotted down the hotel stairs to
the communal shelter and glad of the excuse of social duty to
do what private fear was urging.

Your guides are held responsible by the authorities if anything happens to you while you are in their care. This applies
particularly to guests invited by North Vietnamese organizations (which we were); accredited journalists are allowed more
rein. I was asked not to go out into the street alone, even for
a short walk, though the rule was relaxed when the bombing
of Hanoi stopped on April 1—Hanoi time. This of course
limited one's bodily freedom, but I accepted it, being a law-
abiding person. Our hosts of the Peace Committee told us
that they had been severely reprimanded because some frisky
young South Americans had eluded their control last summer
and roved unsupervised about the country; one got a pellet
in the brain and had to be sent by plane to Moscow to be
operated on; he lived. Whenever we traveled, one of the comrades of the Peace Committee made sure I had my helmet by
personally carrying it for me. I was never alone, except in bed
or writing in my room. In the provinces, when we stayed at
a guest house or came to inspect a village, each time I went
to the outlying toilet, the young woman interpreter went with
me as far as the door, bearing my helmet, some sheets of tan
toilet paper she had brought from Hanoi, and, at night, the

trusty flashlight. She waited outside till I was through and then softly led me back.

That first night, driving in from the airport, everything was novel. The driver had left the radio turned on in the car when he switched off the lights. We could hear it talking, as if to itself, as we paced up and down, and I had the foolish notion that the planes, wherever they were, might hear it, too. Other shadowy sedans and passengers were grouped by the roadside; there had been a great influx at the airport that night because for over three weeks, four times running, the I.C.C. flight had not been able to make it down the narrow air corridor from Vientiane to Hanoi. On the road we had passed several cars with diplomatic license plates, one, surely, containing the Indonesian ambassador, who had boarded the plane with his golf clubs; he used them to exercise on his lawn. Now abruptly all the headlights went on again; motors started. "They are going away. They are going away," the radio voice had said in Vietnamese; the pre-alert was over.

Activity resumed. A chattering stream of people, mostly young, was flowing along the highway from the city, walking or riding bicycles and motor bikes: boys in work clothes or uniforms, with camouflage leaves in their helmets, girls and women, some riding pillion, carrying baskets of salad greens and other provisions; now and then a wrinkled old peasant, in black, with balance-pole on shoulder or pushing a cart. A cow raised its head from a field. All that nocturnal movement and chatter gave an impression of revelry, as if a night ball game or a theater had just let out; probably a work shift had ended in the factories. Along the road's edge cases of supplies were stashed, covered with jute or tarpaulin. Jeeps and military trucks, some heavily camouflaged, were moving steadily in the opposite direction.

We were passing pretty rows of small, compact trees—perhaps pruned fruit trees; it was too dark to tell—a pre-alert to the fact that Hanoi is a shady, leafy city, like Minneapolis or Warsaw; like Minneapolis, too, it has lakes, treated as a municipal feature, with parks and promenades. The people are proud of the trees, particularly of the giant camphor, wreathed in a strange parasite with dangling coinlike leaves. Near the bombed brick house where we waited during the alert, there was a big bare blasted trunk, maybe an oak, which was putting out a few new leaves; my companions eagerly pointed them out, making sure I did not miss the symbol of resistance and rebirth. To the North Vietnamese, I soon became aware, everything is now a symbol, an ideogram, expressing the national resolve to overcome. All of Nature is with them, not just the "brother socialist countries." Nodding their heads in time with a vast patriotic orchestra, they are hearing tongues in trees, terrible sermons in stones and the twisted metal of downed aircraft. In Hung Yen Province, you eat a fresh-caught carp under a red-and-white-nylon canopy, like a billowing circus tent enclosing the whole room; it is the giant parachute of the pilotless reconnaissance plane they have shot down. Near Hanoi, in a village co-operative, raising model pigs and making handicrafts, they show you a small mute cluster bomb, olive drab, and, beside it, the mute rusty primitive soil-scratching implement the young peasant was using in the co-operative fields when pellets from the cluster bomb killed him. Visual education, they feel, for the people, and they are not afraid of hammering the lesson in. But it is Johnson, finally, they wish to give food for thought.

Growth statistics, offered everywhere, on bicycle ownership, irrigation, rice harvests, maternity clinics, literacy are the answer to "the war of destruction," which began February 7, 1965; a bombed oak putting out new leaves is a "reply" to the air pirates of the Air Force and the Seventh Fleet. All Communist countries are bent on furnishing growth statistics (it is their form of advertising), but with Hanoi this is something special, carrying a secondary meaning—defiance. On a big billboard in the city center, the number of U.S. planes shot down is revised forward almost daily in red paint—2,818, they claimed when I left, and the number keeps growing. In villages, the score is kept on a blackboard. Everything they build is dated, down to the family wells in a hamlet—a means of visibly recording progress, like penciling the heights of children, with the dates opposite, on a door. And each date has a clear significance in the story of resistance: 1965 or 1966, stamped on a well, proclaims that it was built *in spite of* the air pirates.

Hanoi, it is whispered, is going underground, digging shel-

ters, factories, offices, operating theaters, preparing for "the
worst," *i.e.*, for saturation bombing by the B-52's or even—
draw a deep breath—for atom bombs, although if you mention those to one of the leaders, he tersely answers that Johnson is not crazy. This feverish digging, while dictated no
doubt by a very practical mistrust of the Pentagon, seems to
have a secondary meaning, too—mythic, as though the city
were an allegorical character. Hanoi appears to be telling its
people that it is ready to go underground, harrow hell, to rise
again like the rice plants from the buried seed. To a Westerner,
this sounds fantastic, so much so that I hesitate to bring it up;
after all, you can tell me, Hanoi's leaders are Marxists, and
Marxists do not believe in resurrection stories.

Yet the Vietnamese folk beliefs are highly animistic; they
venerate (or did) the souls of their ancestors, resting in the
rice fields, and the souls of rocks and trees. Their classic relief
sculpture surprises you with delicate, naturalistic representa-
tions of plants, birds, animals, and flowers—much more typical of Vietnamese art than grotesque images of gods and the
Buddha. The love of Nature is strong in their literature, too,
and is found even in the "captured enemy documents" the
U.S. is fond of distributing for publication. This helps explain
their root-attachment to the fatherland, as every observer has
noticed, going deeper than politics, into some sphere of
immanence the foreigner is almost embarrassed to name—
"spiritual," "religious"? Much is made in the North of the
fatherland's sacred, indivisible unity, and, despite or because
of a history of partitions like Poland's, the sentiment of being
one country seems to be authentic and shared, incidentally,
by the South Vietnamese firebrands who would like to "march
on Hanoi." As a symbol of that unity, the North has planted
the coconut palm; the visitor may be slow to grasp the significance of this. "Coconut trees." "Yes, I see them." "Before, here in the North, we did not have the coconut tree. It
is a native of Saigon."

In Hanoi you find cabbages and tomato plants growing in
the ornamental garden of a museum, in parks, around an anti-
aircraft unit; the anti-aircraft battery has planted a large flower
garden as well and it has chickens running around the gun-
emplacements. Today the abundant use of camouflage—exu-

berant sprigs of plants, fronds, branches, leaves of coconut and banana on helmets, anti-aircraft, military vehicles, even tied to the backs of school children—cannot be meant entirely to fool the enemy overhead. For one thing, the foliage on the anti-aircraft artillery does not begin to conceal the guns' muzzles. This camouflage, snatched from Nature, must be partly a ritual decoration, a "palm" or "laurel" of prowess and connected with ancient notions of metamorphosis—pursued by a powerful enemy, you could "survive" in the verdant form of a tree. In Hanoi, the innocent protective mimicry of coconut leaves "disguising" military hardware always made me think of Palm Sunday in a Catholic country and the devout coming out of church with palm leaves or olive branches—a pre-Easter mood. In the country, a column of army trucks and half-tracks proceeding under its thatch of greenery made me feel that Birnam Wood was rolling on to Dunsinane: "Your leavy screens throw down,/And show like those you are."

The determination of Hanoi appears at first incredible—legendary and bizarre; also disturbing. We came eventually to the pontoon bridge, floating on bamboo, the replacement, for automobiles, of the Paul Doumer Bridge that still hangs, half bombed, like a groping tentacle, over the Red River. On the bridge, the traffic goes single file, and you wait for the oncoming cars to finish their turn before a policeman gives you the signal to advance. This waiting in line by the river's edge is scary—there has been a lot of bombing in the area, as you can see by looking around—and it is even scarier when you start across the frail, wavy bridge; traffic moves very slowly, with many halts, and if the bombers should come while you are there, suspended over the water, there would be no escape; useless to look for shelters on the insubstantial bridge, obviously, and you could not jump into the dark, quite swift river. You just have to put your mind on something else, make conversation; I always dreaded this crossing, the sense of being imprisoned in a metal box, a helpless, all-but-motionless target, and I had the impression that the Vietnamese did not care for it either; each time, there was a general easing of tension when the bridge was finally negotiated.

In the hotel, to my stupefaction, there was hot water, plenty of it. During nearly a month spent in South Vietnam the year before, I had had *one* hot bath—on the U.S.S. *Enterprise*. In my room at the Continental in Saigon, there was only cold water, and when I was once offered a bath in the room of a New York *Times* correspondent, the water ran dark red, too rusty to get into. In theory, they had hot water in the Marine Press Base at Da Nang, but in practice they didn't. Other luxuries I found at the Thong Nhat Hotel were sheets of toilet paper laid out on a box in a fan pattern (keys at the desk were laid out in a fan pattern, too), a thermos of hot water for making tea, a package of tea, a teapot, cups and saucers, candies, cigarettes, and a mosquito net draped over the bed and tucked in; in Saigon, I had been tortured by mosquitoes.

It was obvious that the foreigners at the Thong Nhat lived better than the general population, but this could be said, too, of the foreigners at the Continental, who moreover had to pay for what they got, whereas in Hanoi a guest of a Vietnamese organization was not allowed to pay for anything—I never had to change so much as a dollar bill into dongs. The knowledge of living much better than others (the meals were very good) and at the expense of an impecunious government whose food-production areas were being pounded every day by my government produced a certain amount of uneasiness, which, however, wore off. There was nothing to be done about it anyway, and I soon was able to verify that outside no families were sleeping in the streets, as they had been in Saigon, nobody was begging or in rags, and the people appeared healthy, though tired in some cases, particularly those who were old and had doubtless been hungry a good part of their lives.

On opening the window, I found that there was an extraordinary amount of traffic, extremely noisy traffic, though nobody in Hanoi owns a private car—only bicycles and motor bikes. The honking of horns and screeching of brakes went on all night. To someone who lives in a European city where it is against the law to honk your horn, the constant deafening noise seems very old-fashioned. My ears had forgotten those sounds, as they had forgotten the clanging of streetcars and the crowing of cocks at 4:00 A.M. Hanoi still has both cocks and streetcars, and you can hear the whistle of trains, as well as the more up-to-date noise of MIGs overhead and the almost continuous voice of the loud-speakers, invariably feminine and soothing, sugared, in tone. Unless you know Vietnamese, you cannot guess whether they are announcing an air raid or telling you the planes have left or simply giving a news broadcast or a political diatribe.

There is a good deal in North Vietnam that unexpectedly recalls the past. Waiting to cross the Red River recalled my first trip to Italy, just after World War II, when most of the bridges were down ("Bombed by the Liberators," in Italian, was scrawled all over the devastated cities and towns) and our bus crossed the Po or the Adda on a tremulous pontoon bridge; the loud-speaker outside the hotel window ("Attention, citizens, attention") recalled the loud-speakers in Florence during a spring election campaign (*"Attenzione, cittadini, attenzione"*). Jouncing along a highway deeply pitted by pellets from cluster bombs made me think of my childhood: bumpy trips in northern Minnesota; Grandma in a motoring hat and duster; and how each time we struck a pothole her immense white head, preceded by the hat, would bounce up and hit the car's canvas top. North Vietnam is still pioneer country, where streams have to be forded; the ethnic minorities, Meos, Muongs, and Thais, in the mountains of the wild west, though they do not wear feathers, recall American Indians. The old-fashioned school desks and the geometry lesson on the blackboard in an evacuated school, the kerosene lamps in the villages, the basins of water filled from a well to use to wash up before meals on an open porch, the one- or two-seater toilets with a cow ruminating outside brought back buried fragments of my personal history. I was aware of a psychic upheaval, a sort of identity crisis, as when a bomb lays bare the medieval foundations of a house thought to be modern.

The daytime alerts in the hotel reminded me very much of fire drill in school. During my stay there was no bombing near the hotel, though the siren sometimes sent us to the shelter as often as six times in twenty-four hours. After a while you estimate the distance of the explosions you hear—six kilometers, ten, fifteen—and you think you can tell the dull, resounding noise a bomb makes from the crackle of ack-ack. In the hotel, I began to have a feeling of security, like the veteran correspondents who usually did not bother to get up during night raids or who, if they were up already, wandered out into the street to watch the anti-aircraft activity. In the daytime, it became a slightly tiresome routine to walk, not run, to the shelter, where a delegation of Chinese in gray uniforms—who never spoke to anyone—were always the first arrivals, and wait for the All Clear. And as in the case of fire drill, I began to half wish for some *real* excitement, for the bombs to come a bit nearer and make a louder bang. It got to be a disappointment if the alert was a false alarm, *i.e.*, when you simply sat in the shelter and heard no action at all. The other foreigners must have felt the same way, for when the explosions were noisy and the guns replied, the conversation in the shelter became much livelier, and there were giggles.

An alert was also a social event; you saw new faces and welcomed back old friends—that is, people you had known a few days—reappearing from a trip to Haiphong or Nam Dinh. One day in the shelter I met the Danish ambassador to Peking, and another time a whole diplomatic dinner party, men in dark suits, large, freshly waved ladies from the bloc countries in low-cut silks and satins, an Indian lady in a truly beautiful blue sari, joined us drab "regulars" on the underground benches, having left their double rows of wine glasses and their napkins on the table of the hotel's private dining room, reserved for parties—this eruption, as of a flight of butterflies, was a momentary wonder in our somewhat mothy, closet-like existence.

The late-night alerts were different. Though I had concluded that there was no real danger of bombing in the immediate neighborhood of the hotel—unless Johnson escalated again, with B-52's or "nukes," in which case my personal survival was not of any interest; I would not care to survive—at night, when the shrilling of the siren waked me, I forgot and would jerk up from the pillow with my heart pounding, grope my way out of the mosquito netting, find the flashlight in the dark, slippers, dressing gown, et cetera, and stumble, still unnerved, down the stairs and out through the hotel garden, pointing my flashlight down, searching for the entrance to the shelter. Those late-March night raids made everybody angry. According to the Vietnamese, who were experts on such matters, they consisted of one or two planes only, whereas before they had come in large purposeful waves; their object now must be psychological—without any military pretext—to harass the population at random, deprive it of sleep, while at the same time lessening the risk to themselves of being shot down, for it is harder to hit a single plane in the sky than to pick off one or two out of a serried dozen or twenty.

No planes, so far as I know, were shot down over Hanoi during my stay, though one, they said, an Intruder, had been shot down the day of our arrival. The foreign correspondents agreed that the bombing was slowing down, at least in the region of Hanoi, and they wondered whether the Americans could be short of planes, on account of the number destroyed or damaged in the late-January Têt offensive. The date of manufacture stamped on a shot-down plane was always of great interest; if a plane manufactured in July was shot down in August, this suggested that stocks were low.

In fact, though we did not know this in Hanoi, the "return" of the bombing, in dollars terms, had been added up early in the year by the accountants in Washington. The April number of *Foreign Affairs* was revealing that it had cost the U.S. six billion dollars to destroy an estimated 340 million dollars' worth of facilities: clearly a low-yield investment. The cost in lives of U.S. pilots in comparison with estimated North Vietnamese losses seems not to have been computed—where, on the balance sheet, would the lone target, working in a rice field, of an anti-personnel bomb figure? Left out of the calculations also—surely an oversight?—was the cost to the North Vietnamese government of the shelter program, not to mention the cost of the loud-speakers and the personnel to man them.

Only once in the city while I was there did a bomber "sneak through" the warning system. It happened once in the country, but there it was less spectacular to hear the thud of bombs before, so to speak, listening to the overture of the sirens; in the country, as I said, there are no sirens anyway and surprises were to be expected. In Hanoi, it happened one evening at the Museum of War Crimes, when we were sitting down to little cups of tea at a long table following a tour of the exhibits. Suddenly, there was a long-drawn-out, shrill, banshee-like, shrieking noise, succeeded by a shattering explosion. At the same time, out the window, we could see a plane streak across the sky. The museum director, an officer in uniform, rushed us out into the garden; guiding me by the arm, he was propelling me toward the shelter. Big red stars looking like sky-rockets were bursting in the dark overhead. Then the siren must have blown, though I have no memory of hearing it. In the museum's shelter, we heard more bombs exploding. "The museum is near the bridge," the interpreter murmured, as if to excuse the fact that a raid had come so close. When the All Clear sounded, we went in and found the tea cold in our cups. Back at the hotel, during the next alert, one of the guests told us that there had been three bombs and a Shrike.

To return from a shelter to a disarrayed table where the tea has grown cold in the cups and resume a conversation at the precise point it had left off ("You were saying . . . ?") is a daily, sometimes an hourly, occurrence in the North—inevitably so, since tea is served visitors on every ceremonious occasion, and all occasions, however sickening or painful, are ceremonious. Hospitality requires that tea should be served at the beginning and end of any visit: tea, cigarettes, candies, and long slender little cakes that taste of bananas. The exceptions were the Journalists' Union and the War Crimes Commission, both of which served beer, and the prison where the captured pilots were held, which offered a choice of beer or a soft drink, plus bananas. I could never make out the reason behind these slight variations of an otherwise inflexible precept. It was easy to guess why beer was served to journalists (newsmen drink), while the Writers' and Artists' Union served tea, but why beer at the War Crimes *Commission* and tea at the War Crimes *Museum*? Maybe beer is more expensive, and Mr. Luu Quy Ky of the Journalists' Union and Colonel Ha Van Lau of the War Crimes Commission had bigger budgets than the others. In some instances, tea was followed by coffee.

Perhaps I should have asked, but the Vietnamese are sensitive, and to wonder aloud why beer was served instead of the customary tea might have been taken, I thought, as a criticism of the hospitality: "Why did they *not* serve tea?" In the same way, I was reluctant to ask why in some co-operatives, factories, and associations there were portraits of Marx, Engels, Lenin, Stalin, and Ho, while in others there was only Ho. Was it a matter of personal preference on the part of the administrator? That did not appear likely. Once, in a village co-operative I thought I saw Marx, Engels, Lenin, and Ho, and no Stalin—which made a joyful impression on me—but when I got up from my chair, I found that Stalin had been behind me all along, chuckling. The explanation may be that if the center you are visiting is a branch headquarters of the Lao Dong (Workers') Party, you get the whole pantheon; otherwise, only Ho. The absence of portraits of Mao and of the current Soviet leaders seemed self-explanatory ("Vietnam asserts its independence"), but it could not be remarked on, any more than you can remark to a host on the absence of certain persons who you might have thought would be invited to a party.

In the War Crimes Museum, that evening, among the exhibits they had showed us a Shrike, so that the sudden advent of the live missile had the air, to us, of a coincidence ("Speak of the devil . . ."), but of course, to the North Vietnamese, nearly all the exhibits in the museum "matched" what was befalling them regularly. The museum, unlike that at Auschwitz, is strictly contemporary. There were cluster bombs—guavas and pineapples—some of the delayed-action type, regarded as the most fiendish, ordinary placid TNT bombs of varying weights, ranging from babies of 200 to big daddies of 3,000 pounds, rockets, an assortment of missiles, crop-spraying powders (with the results in a bottle), tear gases, front and rear views of patients hit by a spray of pellets from the "mother" bomb, X rays of pellets in human skulls, photos of napalm and phosphorus victims (napalm has not been used in the vicinity of Hanoi and Haiphong, or, as the Vietnamese say, "not yet"), quite a collection of exhibits. And shuffling about among the displays was a small middle-aged Vietnamese woman in a bunched sweater, wide trousers, and sandals, who was staring, as if drawn by some morbid, fascinated curiosity, at the weapons and devices in the glass cases, at the big bombs arranged, like modern metal sculptures, on the floor; she bent to read the labels, sometimes furtively touched. They told us, lowering their voices, that she had been haunting the museum ever since she had lost her twenty-year-old son early in the year.

An American apologist might claim that she was an exhibit, too, a "plant" to invoke the sympathy of soft-headed pacifists and other bleeding hearts, but in fact the museum personnel seemed somewhat put out by her presence and by the occasional snuffling, sobbing noises she made, interrupting the scholarly presentation of the material. In short, they reacted like museum officials anywhere who were not lacking in heart but had their professional duties, which included discouraging nuts and people with "troubles" from intruding on official visits. It was true, she *was* causing our attention to stray. Then, as if guiltily conscious of being a disturbance, she would hastily quiet down and regain her composure, peering into the glass cases with an air of timid wonder, like a peasant viewing the tools of modern civilization and wondering what they were for. She seemed to be trying to put her lost son and these efficient implements together in some satisfactory manner, as though to make a connection and localize the source of her pain. Sometimes, appearing to find it for a moment, she actually smiled and nodded to herself.

She had gone, I guess, when the Shrike came. Perhaps one of the museum employees had persuaded her to go home finally or given her some tea in the kitchen. To tell the truth, when the Shrike came I forgot about her; I had got used to the fact that during an alert the ordinary Vietnamese—chambermaids, cooks, waiters, desk clerks, tea servers—vanished from sight, only to reappear when the alert was over. Either they proceeded to their own shelters, separate from those for foreign guests, or, like the chambermaids in the hotel who doubled as militia, they shouldered guns and went up to the roof, or they continued quietly with their jobs, like the cook I once glimpsed in the hotel sitting in his white apron and hat at the kitchen table when the All Clear blew. The siren was a Last Trump separating the sheep—us—from the nimble goats. At the National Liberation Front Delegation, the distinction was marked by a heavy dark-brown curtain dividing the communal shelter between personnel, on one side, and, on the other, the Chief of Mission, his immediate staff, and his guests. To an American, such a frank distinction appears *ipso facto* undemocratic.

At the museum, in a parting ceremony, they presented us with rings made from downed U.S. aircraft. Like a wedding ring, mine is engraved August 1, 1966—the day the plane was shot down—and has the initials H. Y., which must stand for Hung Yen Province. They also gave me a woman's comb of the same material. Such souvenirs seem to be popular in Hanoi, but though, as they watched, I murmured *"Merci beaucoup"* and hurriedly, like one rapidly swallowing medicine, tried the blunt ring on my finger, I instantly slid it off and dropped it into my handbag; luckily, I had the excuse that it was a man's ring: too big. Back in the hotel, I shut it up in a drawer out of sight, but it kept troubling my mind, making me toss at night, like an unsettled score. For some reason, the comb, scalloped in the Vietnamese style, did not bother me.

Perhaps, if I had had the courage, I might have declined to take the ring, handed it back to the Vietnamese as soon as I realized what it was. As my grandmother tried to teach me, one need never be afraid to say no. But from their point of view, it was a symbol of friendship, a medal pinned on my chest. They were proud to bestow it. What was it that, deeper than politeness, which was urging me to do so, made it impossible for me to keep it on my finger, even for a few minutes—just not to give offense? Maybe the premonition that if I once put it on, I could never take it off; I could not sport it for the rest of my stay and then get rid of it as soon as I left the country—that would be base. Yet equally repugnant to my nature, to my identity, whatever that is, to the souls of my ancestors, would be to be wedded for life or at least for the duration of this detestable war to a piece of aluminum wreckage from a shot-down U.S. war plane. Or was it just the fact that it did not "go" with my other jewelry?

Nor could I drop it in the wastebasket of my hotel room. The chambermaids would find it and return it to me: *"Votre bague, madame."* Or, worse, they would feel that, to me, their friendship band was rubbish. But if respect for the feelings of others forbade my junking it in a wastebasket of the Thong Nhat Hotel, then there was no sea anywhere deep enough for me to drop it into. I had to keep it. The comb, presenting no problem, a simple keepsake and rather pretty, remained openly on my bureau in the Thong Nhat with my other toilet articles. Yet I now slowly realize that I never passed it through my hair. Mysterious. I cannot explain the physical aversion, evidently subliminal, to being touched by this metal. Quite a few of the questions one does not, as an American liberal, want to put in Hanoi are addressed to oneself.

from Hanoi, 1968

The U.S. Negro in Vietnam

by Thomas A. Johnson

SAIGON, South Vietnam—The Army sergeant with the coal-black face muttered: "What in the hell am I doing here? Tell me that—what in the hell am I doing here?"

But there was a smile on his face.

At the moment, he and the men of his under-strength platoon—about half of them Negroes—were crouching on a jungle trail as artillery shells pounded the brush 100 yards away.

At the same time, some 50,000 other Negroes in Vietnam were unloading ships and commanding battalions, walking mountain ranges and flying warplanes, cowering in bunkers and relaxing in Saigon villas.

They were planning battles, moving supplies, baking bread, advising the South Vietnamese Army, practicing international law, patrolling Mekong Delta canals, repairing jets on carriers in the Tonkin Gulf, guarding the United States Embassy, drinking in sleazy bars and dining in the best French restaurants in Saigon, running press centers, digging latrines, driving trucks and serving on the staff of Gen. William C. Westmoreland, the American commander.

They were doing everything and they were everywhere. In this highly controversial and exhaustively documented war, the Negro, and particularly the Negro fighting man, has attained a sudden visibility—a visibility his forefathers never realized while fighting in past American wars.

Fourteen weeks of interviews with black and white Americans serving here reveal that Vietnam is like a speeded-up film of recent racial progress at home. But Vietnam also demonstrates that the United States has not yet come close to solving its volatile racial problem.

Why was the sergeant—a 34-year-old career soldier—in Vietnam?

He talked with good humor of the "good Regular Army" to a Negro correspondent, he shuddered with anger recalling that his home-town paper in the Deep South called his parents "Mr. and Mrs." only when referring to their hero son, and he pointed out that he had stayed in the Army because his home town offered only "colored" jobs in a clothing factory where whites did the same work for higher pay.

Most often, Negro and white civilians and career soldiers see Vietnam as a boon to their careers and as a source of greater income than at home. It was not unusual to hear civilians and career soldiers—Negro and white—express such views as, "Hell, Vietnam's the only war we've got."

For the Negro there is the additional inducement that Southeast Asia offers an environment almost free of discrimination.

One civilian remarked, "Bread and freedom, man, bread and freedom."

To the ordinary Negro fighting man, Vietnam means not only integration but also an integral role in American life—or at least this aspect of American life.

" 'The man' can't overlook talent when he wants the job done," said S. Sgt. James Frost, a 29-year-old Negro from Youngstown, Ohio.

In the job of battle, fighting prowess and dependability quickly erase color barriers. Staying alive becomes more important than keeping stateside racial patterns.

During the battle for Hue in February, a knot of white and Negro marines stood knee deep in the mean red mud beside their tank. They were grimy-faced, beard-stubbled and grease-spattered.

They peered across the Huong (Perfume) River, where, more than 300 yards away, unseen North Vietnamese gunners had just given up a mortar and artillery duel.

"They're through for now," said Sgt. Eddie Dailey, a Negro from York, Pa.

"It looks like it," said a white marine with field glasses.

It was 9 A.M., but from somewhere a bottle of liberated Black and White scotch was produced and passed around. "Integration whisky," someone commented.

"And that's just what's winning this Goddamn battle," the Negro sergeant said.

A white lance corporal agreed. "You're damn straight, bro," he said. The Negro shorthand for "soul brother" seemed to slip out naturally.

As the corporal, John Tice of Savannah, Ga., passed the bottle, a tattoo could be seen on his bare right arm. It showed a Confederate flag and the words "Johnny Rebel."

"That's just what's gonna win this Goddamn war," Sergeant Dailey spat. "Integration, Goddamn it."

With the integration of the armed forces in the late nineteen-forties and early fifties, the military quickly outdistanced civilian efforts at breaking down color barriers. This has continued to a point where young Negro men flock to military service for the status, careers and security that many cannot find in civilian life.

A junior infantry officer, who is white, commented:

"It's an awful indictment of America that many young Negroes must go into the military for fulfillment, for status—and that they prefer service overseas to their homeland."

The war in Vietnam is filled with ironies, and one of the biggest is that the ordinary Negro fighting man—and especially the teen-age front-line soldier—is not aware of the Negro's participation in previous American wars.

An 18-year-old Marine private at Dongha said proudly: "The brother is here, and he's raising hell. We're proving ourselves."

Officers in Saigon at the headquarters of the Military Assistance Command, Vietnam, say the heavily Negro 173d Airborne Brigade is the best performing unit in Vietnam.

This correspondent went in with the second helicopter wave when the Fourth Battalion of the 173d struck a Vietcong supply base in a thickly forested area of Phuyen Province.

Taking cover in tall grass, he found himself with a young Negro paratrooper, a private first class whose face had not yet sprouted a serious growth of beard.

"What you doin' here, bro?" the paratrooper asked. "You gonna do a story on the Fourth Battalion?"

Without waiting for an answer he kept talking.

"You tell them that the 173d is the best Goddamn outfit on this rock. We were the first brigade-size combat unit in Vietnam."

His squad was ordered forward, but he kept talking:

"Tell them we made the first combat jump in Vietnam on Operation Junction City, and that the Fourth Battalion is the best in the 173d. You tell them that—tell them we took Hill 875 at Dakto and that we are steadily kicking Charlie's rear."

Only then did the paratrooper stand up, and as he ran with his squad he called back:

"You tell them, you hear?"

Capt. Robert Fitzgerald, a Harlem-born intelligence officer on General Westmoreland's staff, commented:

"They feel they're the first Negroes to fight because their history books told only of white soldiers, and their movies showed that John Wayne and Errol Flynn won all American wars."

The 31-year-old officer went on: "The only uniform they've seen on Sidney Poitier was a chain-gang suit, and—oh, yes—that of an Army truckdriver once."

Talk of race often leaves white servicemen bored, embarrassed or annoyed. Many say the problem is overly stressed, and many Negro servicemen, especially the teen-aged, first-hitch foot soldiers, say the same thing.

But a Negro sailor stationed in Saigon noted:

"The question of race is always there for the Negro. He would either be blind or insane if it were not. But Vietnam is a buffer or isolation ward to the whole question of race as we know it."

If Vietnam is an isolation ward, then combat is a private room off the ward where the ordinary G.I. can bring to bear the special skill for which he has been trained—killing. And white or black, the G.I.—usually referred to here as a "grunt" or a "crunch"—is adept at his specialty. The élite units—the airborne, Marines, air cavalry and Special Forces—to which Negro youths flock are among the best of these specialists.

A paratroop officer commented:

"The crunch wants to fight, pure and simple. He's one hell of a fighter, and we couldn't win any war without him because he lives, eats and sleeps to fight. You don't fight wars with gentlemen—that is, you don't win wars with gentlemen."

The grunt is no gentleman.

His average age is 19, and he left high school without finishing. His skills are with the M-16 rifle, the M-60 machine gun, the M-79 grenade launcher, hand grenades and bayonets.

He brags and swears and swaggers, and he runs to a fight. He runs into battle when the first shot is fired, screaming or cursing, as if he does not believe he can be killed.

He can be, however, and he is.

He is killed and wrapped in a green paper blanket and put off to one side until a truck or a helicopter can take him to the rear.

Then he is remembered during quiet times by other young soldiers and marines who still rush into battle, screaming and cursing as if they cannot be killed.

And during those quiet times other things come out.

Like that night in a pitch-black front-line bunker, when it was comforting to hear one another's voices, and the correspondent learned how it was after the Fourth Battalion of the 173d took Hill 875 from a determined enemy force, a force that "had chewed up the Second Battalion."

"We hugged and kissed one another like Girl Scouts, and we cried," said a voice in the darkness.

An Army chaplain comments: "Their anxiousness to prove themselves as men makes them quickly absorb the lesson the military is anxious to teach."

That lesson, an infantry platoon sergeant said, "is to make every man feel that he's in the best army, the best division, the best brigade, the best battalion, the best company, the best platoon, the best squad—and that he's the best Goddamn man in that squad."

And the Negro youngster—from the high-school basketball team, the sharecropper's farm or the riot-ready slums—has consistently volunteered for the élite of the military fighting forces.

"You take a good look at an airborne rifle company and it'll look like there ain't no foreign [white] troops there," one Negro commented.

Dr. Kenneth B. Clark, the Negro psychologist, has noted

that a "status not readily available in civilian life" causes Negroes to join the military service at a rate two to three times greater than that for whites, and then to volunteer for élite units.

"There is no chance of asserting his manhood and demonstrating his sense of worth in civilian life," said Dr. Clark, who heads the Metropolitan Applied Research Center in New York.

Dr. Clark said the ferocity demonstrated by young front-line soldiers could be related to their youth and their eagerness to prove themselves. He noted that after the 1943 riots in Harlem he interviewed a youth who "got a terrific boost out of the destruction."

Dr. Clark added: "A few months later he was a soldier, in uniform and with a riding crop, and getting an even bigger kick out of potential destruction he could legally cause."

The Negro makes up 9.8 per cent of the military forces in Vietnam, but close to 20 per cent of the combat troops and more than 25 per cent of such élite Army units as the paratroops. Estimates of Negro participation in some airborne units have been as high as 45 per cent, and up to 60 per cent of some airborne rifle platoons.

A Negro private first class in the Fourth Battalion of the 173d Airborne Brigade said that when he joined the unit in the summer of 1967 "there were 20 brothers and 8 foreign troops" in his platoon.

About one in every four of the Army's front-line supervisors in the grades of sergeant first class and master sergeant is a Negro, a fact attesting to the higher Negro re-enlistment rate in the armed forces in general and the Army in particular.

The re-enlistment rate for first-term Army men in 1965 was 49.3 per cent for Negroes and 13.7 per cent for whites; in 1966 the figures were 66.5 and 20.0. Re-enlistment figures for 1967 have not been completed, a Pentagon spokesman said. Generally, the rate in the Army runs at least three times as high as for whites, and in the other services two times as high.

The present Negro death rate in Vietnam is 14.1 per cent of total American fatalities; for 1961 to 1967 it was 12.7 per cent. Late in 1965 and early in 1966 the Negro death rate soared to about 25 per cent, and the Pentagon ordered a cut-back in front-line participation by Negroes.

It is in the front lines that commonly shared adversity has always sprouted quickly into group loyalty and brotherhood. And whether between white and white, Negro and Negro, or Negro and white, Vietnam is no exception to the tradition of battlefield brotherhood.

"The stereotypes they had believed just sort of melt away," said Capt. Richard Traegerman, a 25-year-old West Pointer from Philadelphia. "Whites see Negroes are as intelligent and brave as anyone else, and Negroes see whites are just guys with the same strengths and weaknesses as anyone else."

A Negro soldier said he felt that the Negro underwent more of a change than the white.

"The Negro sees the white boy—really sees him—for the first time," he said. "He's just another dude without all those things to back him up and make him bigger than he is—things like a police department, big job or salary."

And a long-time front-line observer said:

"It's the most natural thing in the world to come out closer than brothers after a few days on the line. Up here it's a real pleasure to just be warm and dry or to feel a cool breeze; to have fresh water, a heat cube for C rations; to wash or take off your shoes or to be alive when others are dying. This will make any two people brothers."

For the most part, Negroes in Vietnam say that the closest thing to real integration that America has produced exists here.

"It's the kind of integration that could kill you, though," a Negro sailor remarked.

There are reports of racial discrimination, racial fights and instances of self-segregation, but most Negroes interviewed said these instances were greatly outweighed by racial coop-eration.

In effect, while participating in a war that pits yellow people against yellow people, America is demonstrating that its black and white people can get along.

So pervasive is this demonstration that some Negroes, in discussing the prejudice of lowland Vietnamese toward the mountain-dwelling and usually primitive montagnard tribes-men, convey the idea that discrimination against Negroes has ended at home as well as in Vietnam.

Oscar Roberts, an Army captain stationed at Pleiku as an adviser to the South Vietnamese Army, pointed up this atti-tude when he remarked: "The montagnards are treated the way we used to be treated back home."

But then he smiled and added: "The way we used to be and still are treated some places back home."

Other Negroes did not remember, or smile, or correct themselves.

Race is quite often a laughing matter among servicemen in Vietnam.

Sgt. Charles C. Hardy, a 21-year-old marine from Chicago, was on duty one night in Danang and gave his bed to a vis-iting white friend, but not without some specific admonitions.

"That sack has lots of soul," he said. "It's a soul-recharging station, so you'd better be careful. I don't want to see you wake up tomorrow morning thinking you can talk trash and trying to dance the boogaloo and the philly dog, you hear me?"

Some of the "brothers" in an airborne unit held a "soul session" to "cuss Chuck," the white man. When a late-arriv-ing brother inquired what a "couple of Chucks" were doing attending a soul session, it was explained that they were "hon-orary souls," and the Chuck-cussing continued.

And after watching a plea for brotherhood on a television set in a bunker in the Central Highlands, a youth of Mexican origin spoke up.

"All right," he said. "Which one of my Goddamn brothers is going to buy me a beer?"

He got the beer, but not before the whites and Negroes unleashed a barrage of anti-Mexican remarks that included: "Give me, give me, give me! A Goddamn spec 4 in the Reg-ular Army and he still thinks he's on relief! Give me, give me, give me!"

Even the highly potent taboo on interracial sex is much less a taboo in Vietnam than it was in the military in past years.

A white officer from North Carolina visited the luxurious Saigon apartment of a Negro officer from Illinois, carrying a dozen red roses for the Vietnamese Lunar New Year, Tet. Their friendship dated from the time they both commanded segregated airborne companies at Fort Bragg, N.C., in the late forties.

While discussing a double date with Vietnamese girls that the Negro was arranging, they reminisced about the "German broads" and Japanese women they had known.

Walls and lockers, from neat hotels in Saigon to red-earth bunkers in Khesanh, have both white and Negro pinups, regardless of the race of the serviceman.

Some bars tend to be predominantly white or predominantly Negro. This is especially true in the rear areas where the permanently assigned and normally noncombatant troops gather every day. In Saigon, for example, it is mostly whites who frequent the bars along Tu Do Street, while Negroes predominate in the Khanh Hoi area across the Saigon River along Trinh Minh The Street.

It is not uncommon, though, to find both races in both locations, and to see integrated teams making "skivvy runs"—forays in search of bar girls. And white and Negro servicemen talk to the same bar girls.

Still, there is much off-duty separation of the races, and most of it is voluntary separation by Negroes. There are several reasons, not the least of which was expressed by a high Negro civilian official:

"Wherever you have a lot of American whites with a lot of time for relaxing," he said, "then you can figure that the brother is in for a little difficulty."

A German in Vietnam asked a Negro civilian if he was aware of how some American whites talked about Negroes when they were alone. The Negro said he was.

"Do you know that they call you animals," the German said, "that they say you have tails and that they seem especially anxious that foreigners—myself and the Vietnamese—hear this?"

"I know," the Negro said.

"What's wrong with them?" the German asked.

"They're white Americans," he was told, "a strange breed of people."

A Negro field-grade officer said he relaxed only around

Negroes and put up an "aloof" and "even unfriendly" front around whites.

"You don't want to overextend yourself because you never know when whites are for real," he explained. He went on to suggest that the Negro officer must often be a "super Negro."

"I see white officers bringing Vietnamese girls into our quarters and getting away with it," he said, "and I wouldn't think of joining them. Whites prove every day how vulnerable the 'successful' Negro is in our society. If they can go to such great length and bend the rules to kick Adam Powell out of Congress and take Cassius Clay's title, they can certainly get to me. I don't intend to give them the chance."

Still, separation and aloofness are not rigid situations and attitudes.

A Negro specialist 4 in an infantry outfit said:

"I got some white friends who are 'for real' studs, and, hell, they could call me anything and do anything they want, because I know they are for real. I know some other Chucks who I'd most likely punch in the mouth if they said good morning to me, because I know they are some wrong studs."

A rear-echelon Negro private first class, sitting in a bar in Saigon's Khanh Hoi with a white friend with a Deep South accent, started to discuss why Negroes segregate themselves.

"White people are dull," he said. "They have no style and they don't know how to relax."

"What do you mean?" the white youth interrupted.

"Shut up," the Negro said. "I'm not talking about you, nigger. I'm talking about white people."

Another Negro, explaining why he frequented the Negro-owned "soul food" places in Saigon—such as the L & M and the C.M.G. Guest House, both of which have white and Negro clientele—said:

"Look, you've proven your point when you go out and work and soldier with Chuck all day. It's like you went to the Crusades and now you're back relaxing around the Round Table—ain't no need bringing the dragon home with you."

The term "soul session" is often used here to describe Negro efforts to "get away from 'the man,'" to luxuriate in blackness or to "get the black view." These sessions occur in front-line bunkers and in Saigon villas, and quite often they include some "for real" whites.

Negro V.I.P.'s who come to Vietnam find that despite full schedules a "brother" will get to them with a dinner invitation so the visitors can get "down to the nitty-gritty."

Senator Edward W. Brooke of Massachusetts, Whitney M. Young Jr. of the Urban League and the Rev. Ralph D. Abernathy of the Southern Christian Leadership Conference are among those who have got the benefit of the black view.

"Sometimes it doesn't do too much good, from what some of the black V.I.P.'s have said when they got back home," one soul-session advocate said later.

Self-segregation does not attract all Negroes, and there are some who shun any appearance of Negroes' getting together, no matter what the purpose.

There are Negro officers and civilians in Saigon hotels who prominently display record albums by Mantovani and Lawrence Welk and hide albums by such soul-sound purveyors as James Brown and Aretha Franklin.

"A lot of the brothers feel they can't be themselves and integrated," said Lieut. Col. Felix L. Goodwin, a Negro veteran of 27 years of Army service.

"This dates back to the time the Army was first integrated and we all felt we had to show whites we were not prejudiced," the colonel added. "Most of us feel comfortable enough now to be both black and integrated, and we think this is healthy."

While integration is fairly recent in the military, Negro participation in American wars is as old as the country's history.

Negroes were with Columbus, the Conquistadors and Henry Hudson. They fought the Indians in Nieuw Amsterdam and the English in the Revolutionary War. Three thousand fought in the War of 1812, and Commodore Oliver H. Perry described them as "insensible to danger."

In the Civil War, more than 200,000 black men wore Union uniforms, and the Confederacy began organizing Negro units toward the end of the war.

Negroes were at Little Big Horn with Custer. They helped to chase the Sioux into Canada, they captured Geronimo and they pursued Billy the Kid across the Southwest. Some runaway black slaves and their descendants fought on the side of the Indians.

Ten thousand Negroes fought in the Spanish-American War, and a group of Negro cavalrymen rescued Theodore Roosevelt's Rough Riders in the battle of El Caney.

A controversy over the fighting qualities of the Negro combat soldier began in World War I. The all-Negro 369th Infantry Regiment stayed under fire for 191 days without relief—longer than any other American unit—and was the first to fight its way to the Rhine.

But the 368th, also all Negro, was sent to the rear as a result of confusion and disorder after five days at the front in the Oise-Aisne offensive.

The controversy was renewed in World War II as a result of reports that the all-Negro 92d Infantry Division in Italy "melted" when it met German troops. After an investigation a Negro aide to the Secretary of War reported that some units—not all—had made "panicky and disorderly" retreats and had shown "a lack of will to fight."

But the report also pointed out that many of the men did not know how to use their weapons, and the Army learned during World War II that the efficiency of any unit fell off sharply when more than 10 per cent of its men had scored in the lowest grade of the general classification test. The 92d went into battle with 50 per cent of its men in the lowest grade and 90 per cent in the two lowest.

The controversy subsided during the Korean war as a growing number of units were integrated racially.

The Negro's ability and willingness have not been questioned in the war in Vietnam, and have in fact been consistently praised.

In a speech to fellow South Carolinians last year, General Westmoreland said: "The performance of the Negro serviceman has been particularly inspirational to me. They have served with distinction. He has been courageous on the battlefield, proficient, and a possessor of technical skills."

Courage—and often bravado—is the young combat soldier's long suit.

"When America invented the grunt, she legalized thuggery," one front-line observer said. "When I'm out with grunts and the Vietcong fires on us, I'm damn glad she invented them."

A young Negro marine in war-ravaged Hue typified the grunt's bravado, his eagerness to fight, his disbelief that he can be hurt or killed.

The marine sat on a naval landing craft on the Huong River, bound for the Citadel, once the seat of the Vietnamese imperial government and now, during the Tet fighting, South Vietnam's major killing ground.

"Put me in your paper," the marine told a correspondent.

"What can I say about you?" the newsman asked.

"You can say Lance Cpl. Raymond Howard, 18, better known as 'Trouble,' from Bay Manette, Ala., squad leader, Second Platoon, Delta Company, First Battalion, Fifth Marine Regiment, is going 'cross the river to kick him a few behinds."

The New York Times, April 29, 1968

from
The Siege of Chicago

by Norman Mailer

THEY WERE young men who were not going to Vietnam. So they would show every lover of war in Vietnam that the reason they did not go was not for lack of the courage to fight; no, they would carry the fight over every street in Old Town and the Loop where the opportunity presented itself. If they had been gassed and beaten, their leaders arrested on fake charges (Hayden, picked up while sitting under a tree in daylight in Lincoln Park, naturally protested; the resulting charge was "resisting arrest") they were going to demonstrate that they would not give up, that they were the stuff out of which the very best soldiers were made. Sunday, they had been driven out of the park, Monday as well, now Tuesday. The centers where they slept in bedrolls on the floor near Lincoln Park had been broken into by the police, informers and provocateurs were everywhere; tonight tear-gas trucks had been used. They were still not ready to give up. Indeed their militancy may have increased. They took care of the worst of their injured and headed for the Loop, picking up fellow demonstrators as they went. Perhaps the tear gas was a kind of catharsis for some of them, a letting of tears, a purging of old middle-class weakness. Some were turning from college boys to revolutionaries. It seemed as if the more they were beaten and tear-gassed, the more they rallied back. Now, with the facility for underground communication which seemed so instinctive a tool in their generation's equipment, they were on their way to Grant Park, en masse, a thousand of them, two thousand of them, there were conceivably as many as five thousand boys and girls massed in Grant Park at three in the morning, listening to speakers, cheering, chanting, calling across Michigan Avenue to the huge brooding facade of the Hilton, a block

wide, over twenty-five stories high, with huge wings and deep
courts (the better to multiply the number of windows with a
view of the street and a view of Grant Park). The lights were
on in hundreds of bedrooms in the Hilton, indeed people
were sleeping and dreaming all over the hotel with the sound
of young orators declaiming in the night below, voices rising
twenty, twenty-five stories high, the voices clear in the spell
of sound which hung over the Hilton. The Humphrey headquarters were here, and the McCarthy headquarters. Half the
Press was quartered here, and Marvin Watson as well. Postmaster General and Presidential troubleshooter, he had come
to bring some of Johnson's messages to Humphrey. His suite
had a view of the park. Indeed two-thirds of the principals at
the convention must have had a view early this morning, two
and three and four A.M. of this Tuesday night, no, this
Wednesday morning, of Grant Park filled across the street with
a revolutionary army of dissenters and demonstrators and college children and McCarthy workers and tourists ready to take
a crack on the head, all night they could hear the demonstrators chanting, "Join us, join us," and the college bellow of
utter contempt, "Dump the Hump! Dump the Hump!" all
the fury of the beatings and the tear-gassings, all the bitter
disappointments of that recently elapsed bright spring when
the only critical problem was who would make a better President, Kennedy or McCarthy (now all the dread of a future
with Humphrey or Nixon). There was also the sense that police had now entered their lives, become an element pervasive
as drugs and books and sex and music and family. So they
shouted up to the windows of the Hilton, to the delegates
and the campaign workers who were sleeping, or shuddering
by the side of their bed, or cheering by their open window;
they called up through the night on a stage as vast and towering as one of Wagner's visions and the screams of police cars
joined them, pulling up, gliding away, blue lights revolving,
lines of police hundreds long in their sky-blue shirts and
sky-blue crash helmets, penning the demonstrators back of
barriers across Michigan Avenue from the Hilton, and other
lines of police and police fences on the Hilton's side of the
street. The police had obviously been given orders not to attack the demonstrators here, not in front of the Hilton with

half the Democratic Party watching them, not now at three in the morning—would anyone ever discover for certain what was to change their mind in sixteen hours?

Now, a great cheer went up. The police were being relieved by the National Guard. The Guard was being brought in! It was like a certificate of merit for the demonstrators to see the police march off and new hundreds of Guardsmen in khaki uniforms, helmets, and rifles take up post in place, army trucks coughing and barking and filing back and forth on Michigan Avenue, and on the side streets now surrounding the Hilton, evil-looking jeeps with barbed-wire gratings in front of their bumpers drove forward in echelons, and parked behind the crowd. Portable barbed-wire fences were now riding on Jeeps.

Earlier in the week, it had been relatively simple to get into the Hilton. Mobs of McCarthy workers and excited adolescents had jammed the stairs and the main entrance room of the lobby chanting all day, singing campaign songs, mocking every Humphrey worker they could recognize, holding station for hours in the hope, or on the rumor, that McCarthy would be passing through, and the cheers had the good nature and concerted rhythmic steam of a football rally. That had been Saturday and Sunday and Monday, but the police finally had barricaded the kids out of the lobby, and now at night covered the entrances to the Hilton, and demanded press passes, and room keys, as warrants of entry. The Hilton heaved and staggered through a variety of attacks and breakdowns. Like an old fort, like the old fort of the old Democratic Party, about to fall forever beneath the ministrations of its high shaman, its excruciated warlock, derided by the young, held in contempt by its own soldiers—the very delegates who would be loyal to Humphrey in the nomination and loyal to nothing in their heart—this spiritual fort of the Democratic Party was now housed in the literal fort of the Hilton staggering in place, all boilers working, all motors vibrating, yet seeming to come apart from the pressures on the street outside, as if the old Hilton had become artifact of the party and the nation.

Nothing worked well in the hotel, and much didn't work at all. There was no laundry because of the bus strike, and the house phones usually did not function; the room phones were tapped so completely, and the devices so over-adjacent, that separate conversations lapped upon one another in the same earpiece, or went jolting by in all directions like three hand-balls at play at once in a four-wall handball court. Sometimes the phone was dead, sometimes it emitted hideous squawks, or squeals, or the harsh electronic displeasure of a steady well-pulsed static. Sometimes one got long distance by taking it through the operator, sometimes one got an outside line only by ringing the desk and demanding it, sometimes one could get the hotel operator only by dialing the outside line. All the while, a photograph of Mayor Daley the size of a postage stamp was pasted on the cradle of the phone. "Welcome to the 1968 National Democratic Convention," it said. Often, one could not even extract a whimper from the room phone. It had succumbed. Sometimes the phone stayed dead for hours. Success in a convention is reduced to success in com-munications, as the reporter was yet to learn; communications in the headquarters of the largest party in the nation most renowned for the technology of its communications was breaking apart under strikes, pressure, sabotage, security, se-curity over-check, overdevelopment and insufficient testing of advanced technical devices: at the base of the pyramid, sheer human inefficiencies before the combined onslaught of pres-sure and street war.

The elevators worked abominably. On certain floors the sig-nal did not seem to ring. One could wait a half hour for an elevator to stop on the way down. After a time everybody went up to the top in order to be able to go down. Yet one could not use the stairs, for Secret Servicemen were guarding them. It could, at worst, demand an hour to go to one's room and go down again. So it might have been better to live in a hotel across the Loop; but then there were traffic jams and police lines and demonstrators every night, demonstrators marching along with handkerchiefs to their noses.

This night with the demonstrators up and aroused in Grant Park, tear gas was blowing right into the hotel. The police had tried to gas the kids out of the park when they first arrived in numbers from Lincoln Park, but the wind blew the wrong way, blew the tears across the street into the air conditioning of the Hilton lobby, and delegates and Press and officials walked about with smarting eyes, burning throats, and the presentiment that they were going to catch a cold. The lobby stunk. Not from the tear gas, but from stink bombs, or some advanced variety of them, for the source of the odor was either mysterious, or unremovable, or had gotten into the very entrails of the air-conditioning since it got worse from day to day and drenched the coffee shop and the bars and the lobby with a stench not easily forgettable. Standing near someone, the odor of vomit always prevailed from the bombs—no, it was worse than vomit, rather like a truly atrocious body odor which spoke of the potential for sour vomit in every joint of a bad piece of psychic work. So personal relations were curious. One met attractive men or women, shook hands with them, chatted for a time, said good-bye. One's memory of the occasion was how awful it had smelled. Delegates, powerful political figures, old friends, and strangers all smelled awful.

So nothing worked well in the hotel, and everything stank, and crowds—those who could get in—milled about, and police guarded the entrance, and across the street as the reporter moved through the tight press of children sitting packed together on the grass, cheering the speakers, chanting "Join us! Join us!" and "Dump the Hump" the smell of the stink bombs was still present, but different now, equally evil and vomitous but from a faded odor of Mace. The nation divided was going to war with stinks; each side would inflict a stink upon the other. The years of sabotage were ahead—a fearful perspective: they would be giving engineering students tests in loyalty before they were done; the F.B.I. would come to question whoever took a mail order course in radio. It was possible that one was at the edge of that watershed year from which the country might never function well again, and service in American hotels would yet be reminiscent of service in Mexican motels. Whatever! the children were alive with revolutionary fire on this fine Tuesday night, this early Wednesday morning, and the National Guard policing them was wide-awake as well. Incidents occurred. Flare-ups. A small Negro soldier started pushing a demonstrator with his rifle, pushing him in sudden fury as at the wild kickoff of a wild street fight; the demonstrator—who looked to be a kindly divinity student—aghast at what he had set off; he had not comprehended the Negro wished no special conversation from him. And a National Guard officer came running up to pull the Negro back. (On the next night, there would be no Negroes in the line of National Guards.)

The kids were singing. There were two old standards which were sung all the time. An hour could not go by without both songs. So they sang "We Shall Overcome" and they sang "This Land Is Your Land," and a speaker cried up to the twenty-five stories of the Hilton, "We have the votes, you have the guns," a reference to the polls which had shown McCarthy to be more popular than Hubert Humphrey (yes, if only Rockefeller had run for the Democrats and McCarthy for the Republicans this would have been an ideal contest between a spender and a conservative) and then another speaker, referring to the projected march on the Amphitheatre next day, shouted, "We're going to march without a permit—the Russians demand a permit to have a meeting in Prague," and the crowd cheered this. They cheered with wild enthusiasm when one speaker, a delegate, had the inspiration to call out to the delegates and workers listening in the hundreds of rooms at the Hilton with a view of the park, "Turn on your lights, and blink them if you are with us. If you are with us, if you are sympathetic to us, blink your lights, blink your lights." And to the delight of the crowd, lights began to blink in the Hilton, ten, then twenty, perhaps so many as fifty lights were blinking at once, and a whole bank of lights on the fifteenth floor and the twenty-third floor went off and on at once, off and on at once. The McCarthy headquarters on the fifteenth and the twenty-third were blinking, and the crowd cheered. Now they had become an audience to watch the actors in the hotel. So two audiences regarded each other, like ships signalling across a gulf of water in the night, and delegates came down from the hotel; a mood of new beauty was in the air, there present through all the dirty bandaged kids, the sour vomit odor of the Mace, the sighing and whining of the army trucks moving in and out all the time, the adenoids, larynxes, wheezes and growls of the speakers, the blinking of lights in the Hilton, yes, there was the breath of this incredible crusade where fear was in every breath you took, and so breath was tender, it came into the lungs as a manifest of value, as a gift, and the children's faces were shining in the glow of the headlights of the National Guard trucks and the searchlights of the police in front of the Hilton across Michigan Avenue. And the Hilton, sinking in its foundations, twinkled like a birthday cake. Horrors were coming tomorrow. No, it is today. It is Wednesday already.

* * *

Meanwhile, a mass meeting was taking place about the bandshell in Grant Park, perhaps a quarter of a mile east of Michigan Avenue and the Conrad Hilton. The meeting was under the auspices of the Mobilization, and a crowd of ten or fifteen thousand appeared. The Mayor had granted a permit to assemble, but had refused to allow a march. Since the Mobilization had announced that it would attempt, no matter how, the march to the Amphitheatre that was the first purpose of their visit to Chicago, the police were out in force to surround the meeting.

An episode occurred during the speeches. Three demonstrators climbed a flag pole to cut down the American flag and put up a rebel flag. A squad of police charged to beat them up, but got into trouble themselves, for when they threw tear gas, the demonstrators lobbed the canisters back, and the police, choking on their own gas, had to fight their way clear through a barrage of rocks. Then came a much larger force of police charging the area, overturning benches, busting up members of the audience, then heading for Rennie Davis at the bullhorn. He was one of the coordinators of the Mobilization, his face was known, he had been fingered and fingered again by plainclothesmen. Now urging the crowd to sit down and be calm, he was attacked from behind by the police, his head laid open in a three-inch cut, and he was unconscious for a period. Furious at the attack, Tom Hayden, who had been in disguise these last two days to avoid any more arrests for himself, spoke to the crowd, said he was leaving to perform certain special tasks, and suggested that others break up into small groups and go out into the streets of the Loop "to do what they have to do." A few left with him; the majority remained. While it was a People's Army and therefore utterly unorganized by uniform or unity, it had a variety of special troops and regular troops; everything from a few qualified Kamikaze who were ready to charge police lines in a Japanese snake dance and dare on the consequence, some vicious beatings, to various kinds of small saboteurs, rock-throwers, gauntlet-runners—some of the speediest of the kids were adept at taunting cops while keeping barely out of range of their clubs—not altogether alien to running the bulls at Pamplona. Many of those who remained, however, were still nominally pacifists, protesters, Gandhians—they believed in non-violence, in the mystical interposition of their body to the attack, as if the violence of the enemy might be drained by the spiritual act of passive resistance over the years, over the thousands, tens of thousands, hundreds of thousands of beatings over the years. So Allen Ginsberg was speaking now to them.

The police looking through the plexiglass face shields they had flipped down from their helmets were then obliged to watch the poet with his bald head, soft eyes magnified by horn-rimmed eyeglasses, and massive dark beard, utter his words in a croaking speech. He had been gassed Monday night and Tuesday night, and had gone to the beach at dawn to read Hindu Tantras to some of the Yippies, the combination of the chants and the gassings had all but burned out his voice, his beautiful speaking voice, one of the most powerful and hypnotic instruments of the Western world was down to the scrapings of the throat now, raw as flesh after a curettage.

"The best strategy for you," said Ginsberg, "in cases of hysteria, overexcitement or fear, is still to chant 'OM' together. It helps to quell flutterings of butterflies in the belly. Join me now as I try to lead you."

The crowd chanted with Ginsberg. They were of a generation which would try every idea, every drug, every action—it was even possible a few of them had made out with freaky kicks on tear gas these last few days—so they would chant OM. There were Hindu fanatics in the crowd, children who loved India and scorned everything in the West; there were cynics who thought the best thing to be said for a country which allowed its excess population to die by the millions in famine-ridden fields was that it would not be ready soon to try to dominate the rest of the world. There were also militants who were ready to march. And the police there to prevent them, busy now in communication with other detachments of police, by way of radios whose aerials were attached to their helmets, thereby giving them the look of giant insects.

A confused hour began. Lincoln Park was irregular in shape with curving foot walks; but Grant Park was indeed not so much a park as a set of belts of greenery cut into files by major parallel avenues between Michigan Avenue and Lake Michigan half a mile away. Since there were also cross streets cutting the belts of green perpendicularly, a variety of bridges and pedestrian overpasses gave egress to the city. The park was in this sense an alternation of lawn with superhighways. So the police were able to pen the crowd. But not completely. There were too many bridges, too many choices, in effect, for the police to anticipate. To this confusion was added the fact that every confrontation of demonstrators with police, now buttressed by the National Guard, attracted hundreds of newsmen, and hence began a set of attempted negotiations between spokesmen for the demonstrators and troops. The demonstrators finally tried to force a bridge and get back to the city. Repelled by tear gas, they went to other bridges, still other bridges, finally found a bridge lightly guarded, broke through a passage and were loose in the city at six-thirty in the evening. They milled about in the Loop for a few minutes, only to encounter the mules and three wagons of the Poor People's Campaign. City officials, afraid of provoking the Negroes on the South Side, had given a permit to the Reverend Abernathy, and he was going to march the mules and wagons down Michigan Avenue and over to the convention. An impromptu march of the demonstrators formed behind the wagons immediately on encountering them and ranks of marchers, sixty, eighty, a hundred in line across the width of Michigan Avenue began to move forward in the gray early twilight of 7 P.M.; Michigan Avenue was now suddenly jammed with people in the march, perhaps so many as four or five thousand people, including onlookers on the sidewalk who jumped in. The streets of the Loop were also reeking with tear gas—the wind had blown some of the gas west over Michigan Avenue from the drops on the bridges, some gas still was penetrated into the clothing of the marchers. In broken ranks, half a march, half a happy mob, eyes red from gas, faces excited by the tension of the afternoon, and the excitement of the escape from Grant Park, now pushing down Michigan Avenue toward the Hilton Hotel with dreams of a march on to the Amphitheatre four miles beyond, and in the full pleasure of being led by the wagons of the Poor People's March, the demonstrators shouted to everyone on the sidewalk, "Join us, join us, join us," and the sidewalk kept disgorging more people ready to march.

But at Balbo Avenue, just before Michigan Avenue reached the Hilton, the marchers were halted by the police. It was a long halt. Perhaps thirty minutes. Time for people who had been walking on the sidewalk to join the march, proceed for a few steps, halt with the others, wait, get bored, and leave. It was time for someone in command of the hundreds of police in the neighborhood to communicate with his headquarters, explain the problem, time for the dilemma to be relayed, alternatives examined, and orders conceivably sent back to attack and disperse the crowd. If so, a trap was first set. The mules were allowed to cross Balbo Avenue, then were separated by a line of police from the marchers, who now, several thousand compressed in this one place, filled the intersection of Michigan Avenue and Balbo. There, dammed by police on three sides, and cut off from the wagons of the Poor People's March, there, right beneath the windows of the Hilton which looked down on Grant Park and Michigan Avenue, the stationary march was abruptly attacked. The police attacked with tear gas, with Mace, and with clubs, they attacked like a chain saw cutting into wood, the teeth of the saw the edge of their clubs, they attacked like a scythe through grass, lines of twenty and thirty policemen striking out in an arc, their clubs beating, demonstrators fleeing. Seen from overhead, from the nineteenth floor, it was like a wind blowing dust, or the edge of waves riding foam on the shore.

The police cut through the crowd one way, then cut through them another. They chased people into the park, ran them down, beat them up; they cut through the intersection at Michigan and Balbo like a razor cutting a channel through a head of hair, and then drove columns of new police into the channel who in turn pushed out, clubs flailing, on each side, to cut new channels, and new ones again. As demonstrators ran, they reformed in new groups only to be chased by the police again. The action went on for ten minutes, fifteen minutes, with the absolute ferocity of a tropical storm, and watching it from a window on the nineteenth floor, there was something of the detachment of studying a storm at evening through a glass, the light was a lovely gray-blue, the police had uniforms of sky-blue, even the ferocity had an abstract elemental play of forces of nature at battle with other forces, as if sheets of tropical rain were driving across the street in patterns, in curving patterns which curved upon each other again. Police cars rolled up, prisoners were beaten, shoved into wagons, driven away. The rain of police, maddened by the uncoiling of their own storm, pushed against their own barricades of tourists pressed on the street against the Hilton Hotel, then pressed them so hard—but here is a quotation from J. Anthony Lukas in *The New York Times*:

> Even elderly bystanders were caught in the police onslaught. At one point, the police turned on several dozen persons standing quietly behind police barriers in front of the Conrad Hilton Hotel watching the demonstrators across the street.
>
> For no reason that could be immediately determined, the blue-helmeted policemen charged the barriers, crushing the spectators against the windows of the Haymarket Inn, a restaurant in the hotel. Finally the window gave way, sending screaming middle aged women and children backward through the broken shards of glass.
>
> The police then ran into the restaurant and beat some of the victims who had fallen through the windows and arrested them.

Now another quote from Steve Lerner in *The Village Voice*:

> When the charge came, there was a stampede toward the sidelines. People piled into each other, humped over each other's bodies like coupling dogs. To fall down in the crush was just as terrifying as facing the police. Suddenly I realized my feet weren't touching the ground as the crowd pushed up onto the sidewalk. I was grabbing at the army jacket of the boy in front of me; the girl behind me had a stranglehold on my neck and was screaming incoherently in my ear.

Now, a longer quotation from Jack Newfield in *The Village Voice*. (The accounts in *The Voice* of September 5 were superior to any others encountered that week.)

At the southwest entrance to the Hilton, a skinny, long-haired kid of about seventeen skidded down on the sidewalk, and four overweight cops leaped on him, chopping strokes on his head. His hair flew from the force of the blows. A dozen small rivulets of blood began to cascade down the kid's temple and onto the sidewalk. He was not crying or screaming, but crawling in a stupor toward the gutter. When he saw a photographer take a picture, he made a V sign with his fingers.

A doctor in a white uniform and Red Cross arm band began to run toward the kid, but two other cops caught him from behind and knocked him down. One of them jammed his knee into the doctor's throat and began clubbing his rib cage. The doctor squirmed away, but the cops followed him, swinging hard, sometimes missing.

A few feet away a phalanx of police charged into a group of women, reporters, and young McCarthy activists standing idly against the window of the Hilton Hotel's Haymarket Inn. The terrified people began to go down under the unexpected police charge when the plate glass window shattered, and the people tumbled backward through the glass. The police then climbed through the broken window and began to beat people, some of whom had been drinking quietly in the hotel bar.

At the side entrance of the Hilton Hotel four cops were chasing one frightened kid of about seventeen. Suddenly, Fred Dutton, a former aide to Robert Kennedy, moved out from under the marquee and interposed his body between the kid and the police.

"He's my guest in this hotel," Dutton told the cops.

The police started to club the kid.

Dutton screamed for the first cop's name and badge number. The cop grabbed Dutton and began to arrest him, until a Washington *Post* reporter identified Dutton as a former RFK aide.

Demonstrators, reporters, McCarthy workers, doctors, all began to stagger into the Hilton lobby, blood streaming from face and head wounds. The lobby smelled from tear gas, and stink bombs dropped by the Yippies. A few people began to direct the wounded to a makeshift hospital on the fifteenth floor, the McCarthy staff headquarters.

Fred Dutton was screaming at the police, and at the journalists to report all the "sadism and brutality." Richard Goodwin, the ashen nub of a cigar sticking out of his fatigued face, mumbled, "This is just the beginning. There'll be four years of this."

The defiant kids began a slow, orderly retreat back up Michigan Avenue. They did not run. They did not panic. They did not fight back. As they fell back they helped pick up fallen comrades who were beaten or gassed. Suddenly, a plainclothesman dressed as a soldier moved out of the shadows and knocked one kid down with an overhand punch. The kid squatted on the pavement of Michigan Avenue, trying to cover his face, while the Chicago plainclothesman punched him with savage accuracy. Thud, thud, thud. Blotches of blood spread over the kid's face. Two photographers moved in. Several police formed a closed circle around the beating to prevent pictures. One of the policemen then squirted Chemical Mace at the photographers, who dispersed. The plainclothesman melted into the line of police.

Let us escape to the street. The reporter, watching in safety from the nineteenth floor, could understand now how Mussolini's son-in-law had once been able to find the bombs he dropped from his airplane beautiful as they burst, yes, children, and youths, and middle-aged men and women were being pounded and clubbed and gassed and beaten, hunted and driven, sent scattering in all directions by teams of policemen who had exploded out of their restraints like the bursting of a boil, and nonetheless he felt a sense of calm and beauty, void even of the desire to be down there, as if in years to come there would be beatings enough, some chosen, some from nowhere, but it was as if the war had finally begun, and this was therefore a great and solemn moment, as if indeed even the gods of history had come together from each side to choose the very front of the Hilton Hotel before the television cameras of the world and the eyes of the campaign workers and the delegates' wives, yes, there before the eyes of half the principals at the convention was this drama played, as if the military spine of a great liberal party had finally separated itself from the skin, as if, no metaphor large enough to suffice, the Democratic Party had here broken in two before the eyes of a nation like Melville's whale charging right out of the sea.

A great stillness rose up from the street through all the small noise of clubbing and cries, small sirens, sigh of loaded arrest vans as off they pulled, shouts of police as they wheeled in larger circles, the intersection clearing further, then further, a stillness rose through the steel and stone of the hotel, congregating in the shocked centers of every room where delegates and wives and Press and campaign workers innocent until now of the intimate working of social force, looked down now into the murderous paradigm of Vietnam there beneath them at this huge intersection of this great city. Look—a boy was running through the park, and a cop was chasing. There he caught him on the back of the neck with his club! There! The cop is returning to his own! And the boy stumbling to his feet is helped off the ground by a girl who has come running up.

Yes, it could only have happened in a meeting of the Gods, that history for once should take place not on some back street, or some inaccessible grand room, not in some laboratory indistinguishable from others, or in the sly undiscoverable hypocrisies of a committee of experts, but rather on the center of the stage, as if each side had said, "Here we will have our battle. Here we will win."

The demonstrators were afterward delighted to have been manhandled before the public eye, delighted to have pushed and prodded, antagonized and provoked the cops over these days with rocks and bottles and cries of "Pig" to the point where police had charged in a blind rage and made a stage at the one place in the city (besides the Amphitheatre) where audience, actors, and cameras could all convene, yes, the rebels thought they had had a great victory, and perhaps they did; but the reporter wondered, even as he saw it, if the police in that half hour of waiting had not had time to receive instructions from the power of the city, perhaps the power of the land, and the power had decided, "No, do not let them march another ten blocks and there disperse them on some quiet street, no, let it happen before all the land, let everybody see that their dissent will soon be equal to their own blood; let them realize that the power is implacable, and will beat and crush and imprison and yet kill before it will ever relinquish the power. So let them see before their own eyes what it will cost to continue to mock us, defy us, and resist. There are more millions behind us than behind them, more millions who wish to weed out, poison, gas, and obliterate every flower whose power they do not comprehend than heroes for their side who will view our brute determination and still be ready to resist. There are more cowards alive than the brave. Otherwise we would not be where we are," said the Prince of Greed.

Who knew. One could thank the city of Chicago where drama was still a property of the open stage. It was quiet now, there was nothing to stare down on but the mules, and the police guarding them. The mules had not moved through the entire fray. Isolated from the battle, they had stood there in harness waiting to be told to go on. Only once in a while did they turn their heads. Their role as actors in the Poor People's March was to wait and to serve. Finally they moved on. The night had come. It was dark. The intersection was now empty. Shoes, ladies' handbags, and pieces of clothing lay on the street outside the hotel.

from *Miami and the Siege of Chicago*, 1968

A Visit to Chicago: Blood, Sweat, & Tears

by Steve Lerner

CHICAGO—At half past midnight last Tuesday, the occupants of Lincoln Park were stormed by the Chicago police. It was not the first day, nor was it to be the last, that the Old City—the Lincoln Park area—had come under attack. During the previous two nights the Mayor's ordinance to clear the park by 11 p.m. had been vigorously enforced with nightsticks and tear gas.

Around midnight on Tuesday, some 400 clergy, concerned local citizens, and other respectable gentry joined the Yippies, members of Students for a Democratic Society, and the National Mobilization Committee to fight for the privilege of remaining in the park. Sporting armbands decorated with a black cross and chanting pacifist hymns, the men of God exhorted their radical congregation to lay down their bricks and join in a non-violent vigil.

Having foreseen that they could only wage a symbolic war with "little caesar Daley," several enterprising clergymen brought with them an enormous wooden cross which they erected in the midst of the demonstrators under a street lamp. Three of them assumed heroic poses around the cross, more reminiscent of the Marines raising the flag over Iwo Jima than any Christ-like tableau they may have had in mind.

During the half-hour interlude between the arrival of the clergy and the police attack, a fascinating debate over the relative merits of strict non-violence versus armed self-defense raged between the clergy and the militants. While the clergy was reminded that their members were "over 30, the opiate of the people, and totally irrelevant," the younger generation was warned that "by calling the police 'pigs' and fighting with them you become as bad as they are." Although the conflict was never resolved, everyone more or less decided to do his own thing. By then the demonstrators, some 800 strong,

643

began to feel the phalanx of police which encircled the park moving in; even the most militant forgot his quibbles with "the liberal-religious sell-out" and began to huddle together around the cross.

When the police announced that the demonstrators had five minutes to move out before the park was cleared, everyone went into his individual kind of panic. One boy sitting near me unwrapped a cheese sandwich and began to stuff it into his face without bothering to chew. A girl standing at the periphery of the circle who had been alone all evening walked up to a helmeted boy with a mustache and ground herself into him. People all over the park were shyly introducing themselves to each other as if they didn't want to die alone: "My name is Mike Stevenson from Detroit; what got you into this?" I heard someone asking behind me. Others became increasingly involved in the details of survival: rubbing Vaseline on their face to keep the Mace from burning their skin, buttoning their jackets, wetting their handkerchief and tying it over their nose and mouth. "If it's gas, remember, breathe through your mouth, don't run, don't pant, and for Christsake don't rub your eyes," someone thoughtfully announced over the speaker. A boy in the center of the circle got up, stepped over his seated friends, and made his way toward the woods. "Don't leave now," several voices called in a panic. The boy explained in embarrassed tones that he was just going to take a leak.

Sitting in a cluster near the main circle, Allen Ginsberg, Jean Genet, William Burroughs, and Terry Southern were taking in the scene. Ginsberg was in his element. As during all moments of tension during the week, he was chanting OM in a hoarse whisper, occasionally punctuating the ritual with a tinkle from his finger cymbals. Burroughs, wearing a felt hat, stared vacantly at the cross, his thin lips twitching in a half smile. Genet, small, stocky, bald-headed, with the mug of a saintly convict, rubbed his nose on the sleeve of his leather jacket. I asked him if he was afraid. "No. I know what this is," he replied. But doesn't knowing make you more afraid, I asked. He shook his head and started to speak when the sky fell on us.

It happened all in an instant. The night which had been

filled with darkness and whispers exploded in a fiery scream. Huge tear gas canisters came crashing through the branches, snapping them, and bursting in the center of the gathering. From where I lay, groveling in the grass, I could see ministers retreating with the cross, carrying it like a fallen comrade. Another volley shook me to my feet. Gas was everywhere. People were running, screaming, tearing, through the trees. Something hit the tree next to me, I was on the ground again, someone was pulling me to my feet, two boys were lifting a big branch off a girl who lay squirming hysterically. I couldn't see. Someone grabbed onto me and asked me to lead them out of the park. We walked along, hands out-stretched, bumping into people and trees, tears streaming from our eyes and mucus smeared across our face. I flashed First World War doughboys caught in no man's land during a mustard gas attack. I couldn't breathe. I felt sure I was going to die. I heard others choking around me. And then every-thing cleared.

Standing on the sidewalk at the edge of the park I looked back at a dozen little fires which lit up the woods, still fogged with gas. The police were advancing in a picket line, swatting at the stragglers and crumpled figures; huge trucks, usually used for cleaning the streets, swept toward us spraying more gas. Kids began ripping up the pavement and hurling snow-ball-size chunks at the truck windows. Then they flooded out into the streets, blocking traffic, fighting with plainclothesmen who awaited our exodus from the park, and bombarding hap-less patrol cars which sped through the crowds.

The ragged army split up into a series of mobs which roamed through the streets breaking windows, setting trash cans on fire, and demolishing at least a dozen patrol cars which happened to cruise down the wrong street at the wrong time. Smoke billowed from a house several blocks from me and the fire engines began arriving. A policeman ran from an angry brick-throwing mob, lost his cap, hesitated, and ran away without it. At the intersection of Clark and Division, four cop cars arrived simultaneously and policemen leapt out shooting in the air. From all four sides the demonstrators let them have it; most of the missiles were overthrown and hit their comrades or store windows on the other side of the street. Diving down into the subway, I found a large group of refugees who had escaped the same way. The tunnel looked like a busy bomb shelter; upstairs the shooting continued.

Everyone knew that Wednesday was going to be the big one. Rumors circulated among the police that a cop had been killed in Tuesday's "white riot." The demonstrators had their own beef: not only had they been gassed and beaten, not only had one of their leaders, Tom Hayden, been arrested twice on trumped-up charges of inciting to riot, disorderly conduct, resisting arrest, and letting the air out of the tires of a police vehicle, but the police had also broken into their community centers up near Lincoln Park.

Finally, the demonstrators were also set on marching to the Amphitheatre where what they called the Convention of Death was going through the motions of nominating Hubert. Crossing the bridge from the park in front of the Hilton to the bandshell in the middle of Grant Park, demonstrators filed into their seats listening to the prophetic words of Bob Dylan's "The Times They Are A-Changing." The police had already surrounded the park, the National Guard held all the bridges leading across the railroad tracks to Chicago's downtown Loop area, and helicopters filled the skies like hungry mosquitos.

The Mayor had been good enough to circulate an announcement telling the demonstrators that they were welcome to stay at the bandshell all day and enjoy themselves, but that no march on the convention would be tolerated. His instructions, however, were apparently too subtle for his henchmen who saw the demonstrator as the enemy and couldn't wrestle the idea of a truce into their image. Accordingly, when a demonstrator replaced the American flag with revolutionary red, the police became incensed at the unpatriotic slur and moved in to restore decency and the American way of life. (Jerry Rubin, accused of "soliciting to mob action" and out of jail on $25,000, says that one of the demonstrators who claims to have taken part in the lowering of the American flag was his personal bodyguard assigned to him by the Mobilization. The same young man later turned out to be an under cover agent who had been keeping Rubin under surveillance.)

In the police charge which was ostensibly aimed at lowering the red banner, the police went considerably out of their way to crack the skull of Rennie Davis, spokesman and leader of the Mobe, along with four or five others who had been sitting on their benches in the open-air auditorium listening to anti-war speeches by Vietnam veterans and the ever present Phil Ochs. Medics scrambled over broken benches (later used as ammunition against the police) in a display of greater enthusiasm than efficiency. Within minutes the program continued as if nothing extraordinary had occurred. "The merchants of death are trying to make themselves present in the delivery room of our movement," Carl Oglesby, once chairman of SDS, screamed over the microphones as the police withdrew to the periphery of the crowd. Hayden, furious at the indifference with which people learned that Davis was "stretched out," exhorted the People's Army to break up into small groups and invade the streets of the Loop, "to do what they have to do." Some of the hard heads followed him, but the vast majority of the demonstrators stayed with Ginsberg who was organizing a non-violent march to the Amphitheatre.

While Genet, Burroughs, and Southern chose to stay with the marchers, Norman Mailer provided brief comic relief when he made his excuses, saying that he would not march because he was writing a long piece about the convention and demonstration, and that he couldn't write it from jail. "But you all know what I'm full of if I don't show up on the next one," Mailer said with his characteristic hurumph for emphasis after the last word in the key sentence. Mailer ended by comparing the Chicago demonstrators favorably with those he had written about at the Pentagon march last October.

Once outside the bandshell and onto the sidewalk of a highway which runs through the park, the marchers were immediately halted by a line of Guardsmen who blocked the route. Seeing a confrontation emerging, hundreds of newsmen rushed to the front of the line to be in on the action. Instead they formed a protective barrier between the troops and the demonstrators, a pattern which was to be repeated frequently

during the next two days. After hours of frustrating negotiations which led nowhere, the demonstrators moved in a block
toward one of the bridges which lead back to the Hilton. It
too was barricaded with troops as were the next four bridges,
where tear gas was used to keep the demonstrators from trying to break through.

Most of us got across the fifth bridge and joined the
mule-drawn covered wagons of the Poor People's Campaign
which were headed for the Hilton. Michigan Avenue, for the
first time in anyone's memory, clearly belonged to the people.
There was a sense of victory and momentum as the mob of
some 8000 to 10,000 people converged on the Hilton. Everyone was still sneezing and spitting from the gas, but they felt
high at having outfoxed the police who had clearly meant to
isolate them in the park or split them up before they got to
the Hilton.

A police line across Michigan Avenue on the doorstep of
the hotel finally halted the march and people began to mill
around, undecided on the best strategy.

Finally the police solved the problem by taking the initiative. To put it neatly, they decided to clear the street. In the
process of allowing for the circulation of vehicular traffic they
sent some 300 demonstrators to the hospital with split skulls
and broken bones. When the charge came there was a stam-
pede toward the sidelines. People piled into each other,
humped over each other's bodies like coupling dogs. To fall
down in the crush was just as terrifying as facing the police.
Suddenly I realized my feet weren't touching the ground as
the crowd pushed up onto the sidewalk. I was grabbing at the
army jacket of the boy in front of me; the girl behind had a
strangle-hold on my neck and was screaming incoherently in
my ear.

Across the street, the other half of the crowd was being
squashed against the walls of the Hilton. The pressure was so
great that a plate glass window shattered. Terrified demonstrators were pulled through the window by a Life correspondent and a sympathetic waitress gave them instructions as to
where they could hide. Within minutes police piled into the
hotel to protect the clientele by beating the protestors senseless in the plush corridors of the Hilton.

Outside, demonstrators were being peeled off the wall one at a time, sprayed with Mace, beaten, and occasionally arrested. More forays by the police into the park across from the hotel sent people headlong into trees. During one of these maneuvers I watched a medic throw himself over the bloody head of a demonstrator—like a GI clutching a live grenade to his gut. When I saw him emerge from the fracas the medic's head was in a worse state than the patient's.

By 10 p.m. the National Guard had pinned one group in the park in front of the Hilton and pushed the other two groups north and south down Michigan Avenue. A paddy wagon was caught in one of the mobs and demonstrators started rocking it back and forth in an attempt to overturn it. A busload of police got to them before they succeeded.

Down the side streets groups of 50 to 100 demonstrators broke off from the main action to disrupt the town. They moved quickly, leaving a trail of overturned garbage and shattered glass in their wake. Chased by police, they would split up and reform with other groups. One contingent, calling itself the Flower Cong, was particularly well organized and effective. I was following them up State Street when I caught sight of a blonde girl, a member of the Resistance, whom I'd talked to earlier in the day. I caught up with her just as the street filled up with cops. We turned to run in opposite directions and I lost sight of her until it was all over. Having seen that the police had blocked both ends of the street, I took refuge in a drugstore with several others. When I came out she was trying to sit up in the street, blood soaking through her hair, running down her chin and neck, and collecting in her collar. A car stopped and offered to take her to the hospital, so I carried her over and laid her out in the back seat. The car owner wanted to put newspaper under her head so she wouldn't stain the seats.

My hotel was nearby so I decided to go up and get rid of my shirt which was covered with her blood. At the main entrance I was stopped by a security guard who wouldn't let me in. I showed him my key but he still refused. After two similar rebuttals I was finally allowed to sneak in the back entrance and up the service elevator. "We don't want you walking around the lobby like that," one of the hotel policemen advised me. Up in my room I turned on the tube just as Daley was being asked by an interviewer if there was any evidence of brutality. Outside my window I could hear screams. I opened the shades and leaned out as the police pinned a bunch of demonstrators against the wall of the hotel. From the window above me someone heaved a roll of toilet paper and screamed "Pigs." When the street cleared, four bodies were lying in the gutter. Daley's voice droned on about how he had received no indication of police brutality.

Later that evening the McCarthy delegates, having lost the football game, as one Flower Cong put it, joined the demonstrators in a dramatic candlelight procession. It was irrational but I hated them. I hated them for having come to the blood fest late. I hated them as I hated every necktie in the Hilton. I hated them not because they had tried to win the football game, but because their very presence among the real demonstrators co-opted and made respectable the blood and snot that speckled the streets of Chicago. The earlier crowd, the scruffy-hippie-commie-beatnik-agitators, were the ones who had exposed the military backbone of the liberal system. It took blood to prove to the prime time viewers that Civil Rights, the right to dissent, the right to assemble, the right to pass freely in the streets, the right to be tried before being clubbed, were all okay as long as you didn't actually try to use them.

The delegates were received with mixed feelings. Outwardly almost everyone welcomed them, even those who earlier had shouted "McCarthy is not enough." They represented a kind of vindication of the demonstration. In addition they lent respectability and a certain amount of protection to protestors who had been kicked around for five long days. But in spite of this there was a feeling among most of those who had been initiated by violence that the support of the delegates would only be tolerated as long as the movement in the streets remained the property of those who had grown and suffered with it.

Wednesday was the bloody catharsis, Thursday was farce. There is a certain credible nature about a policeman's nightstick which inspires a kind of defiant respect. But a tank is hard to take seriously. I know a lot of people who cracked up when they saw the tank sitting in the middle of the street, pawing at the pavement like a lost rhinoceros who has wandered out of the jungle into the city by mistake. Mortars, flame throwers, machine guns, and bazookas, who are they kidding?

Standing in line, waiting to be arrested in Thursday's march to Dick Gregory's house, I happened to end up next to a very stoned young couple groping at each other and taunting the troops with their sexual freedom. "Fuck don't fight," the young man pleaded with the troops as he fondled his woman. A black army medic finally responded with a smile, "Is it true that all you people run around without any clothes on up in Lincoln Park?" Then the jokes were over and they turned on the gas. Four times in all until they had pushed us back to the Hilton. Then another three times in front of the Hilton just in case the tv crews had missed anything.

The absurdity of the police and military over-reaction to the demonstrators had been driven home to me earlier in the day when I was stopped by five policemen under the tramway on Wabash Avenue. One of them grabbed me and looked at my press credentials, making some wise-assed remark about the hippie underground press from New York. His buddies laughed and I thought I was going to be let go. "Let's see your underarms, kid," my interrogator said. Earlier in the week I had heard some Yips complaining about a similar request, but I never had figured out why anyone wanted to check their pits. Taking my jacket off I held my hands over my head thinking that maybe this was the new slang for "reach for the sky." But that wasn't it. They wanted me to take off my shirt, and when I refused they ripped it under both arms and by God they checked my armpits. Satisfied, I guess, that I wasn't carrying either concealed weapons or drugs, they chased me away with a warning. After that nothing sounded too absurd.

Walking past a group of Guardsmen who were resting up for their next stint of duty, Abbie Hoffman, a Yip leader, was being razzed about his appearance. Finally, without a blink,

Hoffman walked up to one of them and said, "Hey listen, I'll lay a nickel bag that you guys could whip the cops any day of the week." A pensive look came across the trooper's face.

The Village Voice, September 5, 1968

from
The Selling of the President 1968

by Joe McGinniss

ONE DAY Harry Treleaven came into his office with two reels of movie film under his arm.

"Come on," he said. "I think you'd like to see this." We went into the big meeting room and he gave the film to a man in the projection booth.

The film was in black and white. There was a title: *A Face of War*. It had been made in Vietnam. It was the story of three months of fighting done by a single infantry platoon. There was no music or narration. Just the faces and sounds of jungle war.

Halfway through the first reel, Len Garment and Frank Shakespeare came in. They were there for a one o'clock meeting. They took seats and began to watch the film. Neither spoke. They watched the men crawling single file through the jungle, heard the sound the leaves made as they brushed the faces of the men and heard the sound of rain and bullets and mortar shells in the night. The reel ended. The meeting was due to begin. Harry Treleaven turned to the projection booth. "Play the second reel," he said. Ruth Jones came in for the meeting and watched the film for three minutes and left. "I can't sit through that," she said.

No one else spoke. There were only the men trying to kill and trying to avoid being killed in the jungle.

Twenty minutes later, with the film still running, Art Duram said, "Don't you think we'd better start?" No one moved or gave any sign of having heard.

"It's half past one already."

Harry Treleaven sat up in his chair and looked at his watch. "All right, that's enough," he said to the man in the projection booth.

The lights came on in the room. No one spoke for a moment. Each man was still staring at where the film had been.

"That's the most powerful thing I've ever seen," Len Garment said.

"What is it?" Frank Shakespeare said.

Harry Treleaven stood and stepped toward the projection booth. "It's called *A Face of War*," he said, "and it was made by the man I want to hire to do our spot commercials."

Originally, Treleaven had wanted David Douglas Duncan, the photographer, to make commercials. Duncan was a friend of Richard Nixon's but when Treleaven took him out to lunch he said no, he would be too busy. Then Duncan mentioned Eugene Jones.

Treleaven had wanted Duncan because he had decided to make still photography the basis of Richard Nixon's sixty-second television commercial campaign. He had learned a little about stills at J. Walter Thompson when he used them for some Pan American spots. Now he thought they were the perfect thing for Nixon because Nixon himself would not have to appear.

Treleaven could use Nixon's voice to accompany the stills but his face would not be on the screen. Instead there would be pictures, and hopefully, the pictures would prevent people from paying too much attention to the words.

The words would be the same ones Nixon always used— the words of the acceptance speech. But they would all seem fresh and lively because a series of still pictures would flash on the screen while Nixon spoke. If it were done right, it would permit Treleaven to create a Nixon image that was entirely independent of the words. Nixon would say his same old tiresome things but no one would have to listen. The words would become Muzak. Something pleasant and lulling in the background. The flashing pictures would be carefully selected to create the impression that somehow Nixon represented competence, respect for tradition, serenity, faith that the American people were better than people anywhere else, and that all these problems others shouted about meant nothing in a land blessed with the tallest buildings, strongest armies, biggest factories, cutest children, and rosiest sunsets in the world. Even better: through association with the pictures, Richard Nixon could *become* these very things.

Obviously, some technical skill would be required. David Douglas Duncan said Gene Jones was the man.

Treleaven met Jones and was impressed. "He's low-key," Treleaven said. "He doesn't come at you as a know-it-all."

Gene Jones, also in his middle forties, had been taking movies of wars half his life. He did it perhaps as well as any man ever has. Besides that, he had produced the Today show on NBC for eight years and had done a documentary series on famous people called *The World of* . . . Billy Graham, Sophia Loren, anyone who had been famous and was willing to be surrounded by Jones's cameras for a month.

Jones understood perfectly what Treleaven was after. A technique through which Richard Nixon would seem to be contemporary, imaginative, involved—without having to say anything of substance. Jones had never done commercial work before but for $110,000, from which he would pay salaries to a nine-man staff, he said he would do it for Nixon.

"A hundred and ten thousand dollars," Frank Shakespeare said after seeing *A Face of War*. "That's pretty steep."

"I wouldn't know," Treleaven said. "I have nothing to compare it to."

"It's pretty steep."

"He's pretty good."

"Yes, he is."

"What do you think?"

"Oh, I have no objection. That just hit me as a very high price."

"I'd like approval to pay it right now. I want to hire him immediately."

"Fine," Frank Shakespeare said. "You've got it."

A day or two later Jones came down to Treleaven's office to discuss details such as where he should set up a studio and what areas the first set of spots should cover.

"This will not be a commercial sell," Jones said. "It will not have the feel of something a—pardon the expression—an agency would turn out. I see it as sort of a miniature *Project 20*. And I can't see anyone turning it off a television set, quite frankly."

That same day Jones rented two floors of the building at 303 East Fifty-third Street, one flight up from a nightclub called Chuck's Composite. Within three days, he had his staff at work. Buying pictures, taking pictures, taking motion pictures of still pictures that Jones himself had cropped and arranged in a sequence.

"I'm pretty excited about this," Jones said. "I think we can give it an artistic dimension."

Harry Treleaven did not get excited about anything but he was at least intrigued by this. "It will be interesting to see how he translates his approach into political usefulness," Treleaven said.

"Yes," Frank Shakespeare said, "if he can."

Gene Jones would start work at five o'clock in the morning. Laying coffee and doughnuts on his desk, he would spread a hundred or so pictures on the floor, taken from boxes into which his staff already had filed them. The boxes had labels like VIETNAM . . . DEMOCRATIC CONVENTION . . . POVERTY: HARLEM, CITY SLUMS, GHETTOS . . . FACES; HAPPY AMERICAN PEOPLE AT WORK AND LEISURE . . .

He would select a category to fit the first line of whatever script he happened to be working with that day. The script would contain the words of Richard Nixon. Often they would be exactly the words he had used in the acceptance speech, but re-recorded in a hotel room somewhere so the tone would be better suited to commercial use.

Jones would select the most appropriate of the pictures and then arrange and rearrange, as in a game of solitaire. When he had the effect he thought he wanted he would work with a stopwatch and red pencil, marking each picture on the back to indicate what sort of angle and distance the movie camera should shoot from and how long it should linger on each still.

"The secret is in juxtaposition," Jones said. "The relationships, the arrangement. After twenty-five years, the other things—the framing and the panning, are easy."

Everyone was excited about the technique and the way it could be used to make people feel that Richard Nixon belonged in the White House. The only person who was not impressed was Nixon. He was in a hotel room in San Francisco one day, recording the words for one of the early commercials. The machine was turned on before Nixon realized it and the end of his conversation was picked up.

"I'm not sure I like this kind of a . . . of a format, incidentally," Nixon said. "Ah . . . I've seen these kinds of things and I don't think they're very . . . very effective. . . ."

Still, Nixon read the words he had been told to read:

"In recent years crime in this country has grown nine times as fast as the population. At the current rate, the crimes of violence in America will double by nineteen seventy-two. We cannot accept that kind of future. We owe it to the decent and law-abiding citizens of America to take the offensive against the criminal forces that threaten their peace and security and to rebuild respect for law across this country. I pledge to you that the wave of crime is not going to be the wave of the future in America."

There was nothing new in these words. Harry Treleaven had simply paraphrased and condensed the standard law and order message Nixon had been preaching since New Hampshire. But when the words were coupled with quickly flashing colored pictures of criminals, of policemen patrolling deserted streets, of bars on storefront windows, of disorder on a college campus, of peace demonstrators being led bleeding into a police van, then the words became something more than what they actually were. It was the whole being greater than the sum of its parts.

In the afternoons, Treleaven, Garment and Shakespeare would go to Gene Jones' studio to look at the films on a little machine called a movieola. If they were approved, Jones would take them to a sound studio down the street to blend in music, but they never were approved right away. There was not one film that Garment or Shakespeare did not order changed for a "political" reason. Anything that might offend Strom Thurmond, that might annoy the Wallace voter whom Nixon was trying so hard for; any ethnic nuance that Jones, in his preoccupation with artistic viewpoint, might have missed: these came out.

"Gene is good," Treleaven explained, "but he needs a lot

of political guidance. He doesn't always seem to be aware of the point we're trying to make."

Jones didn't like the changes. "I'm not an apprentice," he said. "I'm an experienced pro and never before in my career have I had anyone stand over my shoulder telling me to change this and change that. It might sound like bullshit, but when you pull out a shot or two it destroys the dynamism, the whole flow."

The first spot was called simply *Vietnam*. Gene Jones had been there for ninety days, under fire, watching men kill and die, and he had been wounded in the neck himself. Out of the experience had come *A Face of War*. And out of it now came E.S.J. [for Eugene S. Jones] #1, designed to help Richard Nixon become President. Created for no other purpose.

VIDEO	AUDIO
1. OPENING NETWORK DIS-CLAIMER: "A POLITICAL AN-NOUNCEMENT."	
2. FADEUP ON FAST PACED SCENES OF HELO ASSAULT IN VIETNAM.	SFX AND UNDER
3. WOUNDED AMERICANS AND VIETNAMESE,	R.N. Never has so much military, economic, and diplomatic power been used as ineffectively as in Vietnam.
4. MONTAGE OF FACIAL CU'S OF AMERICAN SERVICEMEN AND VIETNAMESE NATIVES WITH QUESTIONING, ANXIOUS, PERPLEXED ATTITUDE.	And if after all of this time and all of this sacrifice and all of this support there is still no end in sight, then I say the time has come for the American people to turn to new leadership—not tied to the policies and mistakes of the past.
5. PROUD FACES OF VIETNAMESE PEASANTS ENDING IN CU OF THE WORD "LOVE" SCRAWLED ON THE HELMET OF AMERICAN G.I. AND PULL BACK TO REVEAL HIS FACE.	I pledge to you: we will have an honorable end to the war in Vietnam.
	MUSIC UP AND OUT.

Harry Treleaven and Len Garment and Frank Shakespeare thought this commercial was splendid.

"Wow, that's powerful," Treleaven said.

Dead soldiers and empty words. The war was not bad because of insane suffering and death. The war was bad because it was *ineffective*.

So Richard Nixon, in his commercial, talked about new leadership for the war. New leadership like Ellsworth Bunker and Henry Cabot Lodge and U. Alexis Johnson.

Vietnam was shown across the country for the first time on September 18. Jack Gould did not like this one any more than he had liked Connie Francis.

"The advertising agency working in behalf of Richard Nixon unveiled another unattractive campaign spot announcement," he wrote. "Scenes of wounded GIs were the visual complement for Mr. Nixon's view that he is better equipped to handle the agony of the Vietnamese war. Rudimentary good taste in politics apparently is automatically ruled out when Madison Avenue gets into the act."

The fallen soldiers bothered other people in other ways. There was on the Nixon staff an "ethnic specialist" named Kevin Phillips, whose job it was to determine what specific appeals would work with specific nationalities and in specific parts of the country. He watched *Vietnam* and sent a quick and alarmed memo to Len Garment: "This has a decidedly dovish impact as a result of the visual content and it does not seem suitable for use in the South and Southwest."

His reasoning was quite simple. A picture of a wounded soldier was a reminder that the people who fight wars get hurt. This, he felt, might cause resentment among those Americans who got such a big kick out of cheering for wars from their Legion halls and barrooms half a world away. So bury the dead in silence, Kevin Phillips said, before you blow North Carolina.

Another problem arose in the Midwest: annoyance over the word "Love" written on the soldier's helmet.

"It reminds them of hippies," Harry Treleaven said. "We've gotten several calls already from congressmen complaining. They don't think it's the sort of thing soldiers should be writing on their helmets."

Len Garment ordered the picture taken out of the commercial. Gene Jones inserted another at the end; this time a
soldier whose helmet was plain.

This was the first big case of "political" guidance, and for
a full week the more sensitive members of the Gene Jones
staff mourned the loss of their picture.

"It was such a beautiful touch," one of them said. "And
we thought, what an interesting young man it must be who
would write 'Love' on his helmet even as he went into combat."

Then E.S.J. Productions received a letter from the mother
of the soldier. She told what a thrill it had been to see her
son's picture in one of Mr. Nixon's commercials, and she
asked if there were some way that she might obtain a copy of
the photograph.

The letter was signed: Mrs. William Love.

Almost all the commercials ran sixty seconds. But Jones did
one, called E.S.J. #3: *Look at America*, that went more than
four minutes.

VIDEO	AUDIO
2. FADEUP ON FAST, DRAMATIC RIOT IN CITY, FLAMING BUILDINGS.	ELECTRIC MUSIC UP FULL.
3. VIETNAM COMBAT.	ELECTRONIC MUSIC CONTINUES AND UNDER.
4. G.I. IN VIETNAM SLUMPS DEJECTEDLY.	R.N. America is in trouble today not because her people have failed, but because her leaders have failed. Let us look at America. Let us listen to America. We see Americans dying on distant battlefields abroad.
5. RIOTS & FIRES.	We see Americans hating each other; fighting each other; killing each other at home.

We see cities enveloped in smoke and flame.

6. FIRE ENGINES.

We hear sirens in the night.

7. PERPLEXED FACES OF AMER-
   ICANS.

As we see and hear these things, millions of Americans cry out in anguish.

Did we come all the way for this?

8. MONTAGE URBAN & RURAL
   DECAY—(hungry in Appalachia—poor in ghetto—ill-
   clothed on Indian reservations. Unemployment in cities and welfare in small
   towns).

MUSIC UP AND UNDER.

9. MONTAGE OF AMERICANS
   "CREATING AND CONTRIB-
   UTING" MOTIVATES INTO
   CU'S OF FACES.

R.N.
Let us listen now to another voice. It is the voice of the great majority of Americans—the non-shouters; the non-demonstrators.

They are not racists or sick; they are not guilty of the crime that plagues the land.

They are black and they are white—native born and foreign born—young and old.

They work in America's factories.

They run American business.

They serve in government.

They provide most of the soldiers who died to keep us free.

CONTINUING MONTAGE OF
"CREATIVE & CONTRIBUTING
FACES."

They give drive to the spirit of America.

They give lift to the American Dream.

They give steel to the back-bone of America.

They are good people, decent people; they work, they save, they pay their taxes, they care. Like Theodore Roosevelt, they know that this country will not be a good place for any of us to live in unless it is a good place for all of us to live in.

This, I say, is the real voice of America. And in this year 1968, this is the message it will broadcast to America and to the world.

10. STRENGTH AND CHARACTER OF AMERICANS—BUSY FACTORIES, FARMS, CROWDS & TRAFFIC, ETC.	Let's never forget that despite her faults, America is a great nation.
11. INTO MONTAGE OF SCENIC VALUES OF AMERICA FROM THE PACIFIC OCEAN TO DESERTS, TO SNOW-COVERED MOUNTAINS. BESIDE A STILL POND A MAN WAITS.	R.N. America is great because her people are great. With Winston Churchill, we say: "We have not journeyed all this way across the centuries, across the oceans, across the mountains, across the prairies, because we are made of sugar candy."
12. DOLLY TOWARD SUNRISE. HOLD. FADEOUT.	America is in trouble today not because her people have failed, but because her leaders have failed. What America needs are leaders to match the greatness of her people. MUSIC UP AND OUT.

"Run it through again, would you please, Gene?" Len Garment said. "There's something there that bothers me."

The film was rewound and played again.

"There, that's it," Garment said. "Yeah, that will have to be changed."

"What will have to be changed?" Jones said.

The film had been stopped just as Richard Nixon, reciting his litany to the "forgotten Americans," had said, "They provide most of the soldiers who died to keep us free." The picture that went with those words was a close-up of a young American soldier in Vietnam. A young Negro soldier.

Len Garment was shaking his head.

"We can't show a Negro just as RN's saying 'most of the soldiers who died to keep us free,' " he said. "That's been one of their big claims all along—that the draft is unfair to them—and this could be interpreted in a way that would make us appear to be taking their side."

"Hey, yes, good point, Len," Frank Shakespeare said. "That's a very good point."

Harry Treleaven was nodding.

Gene Jones said okay, he would put a white soldier there instead.

from *The Selling of the President 1968*, 1969

A Small Contribution

by Kevin Buckley

EARLY in the morning, while the mist still clung to their base camp at Loc Ninh, about 180 men of Alpha and Delta companies, First Battalion of the 28th Infantry, First Infantry Division, set off on what seemed likely to be nothing more than a grueling trudge in the mud. Their mission was to reconnoiter the scene of an earlier battle in the vast rubber forest west of the camp and to make sure that all North Vietnamese troops had left the area.

For the first few hours, the going was easy. The sun was not yet overhead, and the earth, dark in the shade of the rubber trees, was cool and soft. In the distance, we heard the rattle of gunfire, and soon the radio crackled with the news that another unit, patrolling south of Loc Ninh, had run into an ambush. But for us, the only disconcerting experience came when Delta Company, which was in the lead, spotted what appeared to be a partially concealed land mine and sent a man up to detonate it. The "mine" turned out to be an overturned rubber dish, a soup-bowl-shaped container that workers hang from the trees to collect the sticky, white latex.

By late morning we had reached the scene of the earlier fighting. There were big gouges in the rubber trees, and caved-in enemy bunkers were everywhere. But there seemed to be no sign of life and Delta Company passed through the battleground without incident. Then, as Alpha Company came up, the whole area erupted. North Vietnamese automatic-weapon fire came pouring out of the jungle and we all scrambled for cover. Curiously, one of the first things that caught my eye were tracer bullets—ricochets from enemy sniper fire—floating up into the trees like strange, glowing embers.

As the men of Alpha Company began to return the fire, Lt.

Edward J. Knoll, 21, the company commander, strode out into the open and started to pump round after round into the underbrush. Then, suddenly seized by doubt, he stopped. "Cease fire, cease fire," he shouted. "That might be Delta in there . . . Cease fire, damn you!"

There was a moment of stillness and then a fresh burst of enemy fire came blasting out of the jungle, trimming the leaves over our heads. "Screw it! Fire! They're gooks all right," yelled Knoll. "Gimme a blooper [grenade launcher] quick. We're gonna get some gooks."

The din resumed, louder and more intense than before. Up ahead, Delta Company was exploding smoke grenades to mark the edges of its position so that Alpha would not fire in that direction. With enemy fire chipping the bark off the trees around him, Sp/4 Washington Norfleet, a Negro from Baltimore, raced up to Knoll and handed him a blooper. "Move down! Cut them off!" screamed Knoll. Then he and Norfleet—who had taken over the lieutenant's sawed-off M-16—moved out ahead, pumping bullets and grenades into the jungle.

After a while, Knoll called a halt to the firing and shouted for a South Vietnamese interpreter who was along with us. Knoll wanted the interpreter to call on the enemy to *chieu hoi*—give themselves up. But the Vietnamese, who had "Make Love, Not War!" written on his helmet, was flat behind a tree, his head wrapped in his arms, and he refused to budge. "No chieu hoi. Just kill them," he called out. Then he raised himself slightly, spoke the words "chieu hoi" and flopped down again. At this point, possibly out of disgust, Knoll indulged in pure bravado by relieving himself against a tree in what seemed to me to be full view of the enemy troops.

Strangely enough, the Communists seemed to hold their fire until Knoll was through. Then they opened up again. "I don't think they want to chieu hoi," said Knoll reflectively—at which point someone shouted, "There they go." A handful of enemy soldiers were trying to make a run for it from the brush jungle to bunkers and interconnecting spider holes, and Alpha, moving after them, opened up with everything it had. "Good work, good work," I heard Knoll say over and over.

"I saw one little bastard," he said to one man. "He peeked out from behind that tree and started going and I got him with my blooper right in the head."

Finally, the shooting stopped again. What was left of the enemy unit had fled, and now, at Knoll's order, we moved forward to investigate. There were four enemy dead—all disfigured with gaping wounds. "OK, you mother, you tried to kill my buddies, didn't you," said one GI as he hefted the corpse of the first dead North Vietnamese we came to. "Look at that. He's got a hat made out of one of our poncho liners. The rotten little bastard. I'm gonna wear that hat now, blood and all."

Quickly, the men of Alpha Company stripped the dead enemy soldiers of their gear—star-buckled belts, knives and AK-47 assault rifles. Then they placed "Big Red One" shoulder patches on each dead face before leaving the battlefield for the trip back to camp. "We let those people know who's been through the area," Norfleet said as we moved out.

Newsweek, October 14, 1968

"We Lived for a Time Like Dogs"

by Zalin Grant

Frank Anton: Willie Watkins slowly took over as camp leader. He was the strongest. When there was work to be done he did it. From there it grew to his having the crucial say about what and when to cook. He then began to make other decisions too. It was never outward that he ran the place. He didn't say, "I'm the chief." But he was. I guess you would call Watkins a good-looking Negro. He was a little over six feet tall, lanky, with very dark skin and penetrating eyes. He kept his hair short and himself neat. He was wiry and hard as a rock, could carry two sixty-pound baskets of manioc easier than I could walk. And he seemed never to get sick.

At the beginning Kushner, Williams, and myself got together and discussed what we should do. The person who led the camp had to be physically strong. None of us was. We decided to try to use our influence as a group. We made no attempt to create a military organization. The VC warned us individually several times that if we did we would be punished. Moreover, we weren't sure of our legal rights in the matter. Kushner was a captain but a doctor and therefore a noncombatant. I was a warrant officer, a pilot with no command responsibility. Williams was a first sergeant but wounded.

Eventually Watkins let us know that since we couldn't work our decisions would be limited. Some of the others followed him, saying, "That's right. Anybody who tells me what to do has to work at least as hard as I do." Willie had the Negroes organized on some questions. He got them off to the side and spoke to them about what they should do. I don't know what they talked about, but it was bad for our morale. At times they took care of each other. At other times they were split.

No racial comments were made in camp, although a couple

of guys didn't like Negroes. Joe Zawtocki, for example, didn't talk about Willie being a Negro but being Watkins. "I hate that black sonofabitch," he would say. Strictland got along with the blacks okay because he could work. Harker did too but he didn't like Willie. Actually it came down to who could work and who couldn't.

The Vietnamese went to Willie when they wanted to know something about the camp or to organize an activity. Watkins got the information from them and told us. In this respect he had pushed out Russ Grissett, who served at first as our communications link with the VC because he'd been there longest and spoke a little Vietnamese. But the VC hated Russ and they liked Willie. They liked him mainly because he worked hard and never talked back. Willie, unlike most of us, always called Garwood Mr. Dao, as the VC ordered us to do. He hated Garwood, that was obvious, but he kept it to himself. He was very secretive.

Daly. Russ Grissett told us when we first got to camp, "In the jungle the lion is king. To survive you must live like an animal." Kushner and I tried to argue that it didn't have to be that way. But eventually it was exactly as Grissett said. We fought and carried on. We lived for a time like dogs. I even took part in it myself, yes.

Anton. Watkins could have whipped anybody in camp—that was the point. Everyone thought so. Davis, who was several inches shorter and also very strong, had a certain influence over Watkins. Frequently Davis disagreed with him but they never fought. Willie liked Davis. He would bargain and barter with him before it came to blows. Several people tried to fight Willie. Lewis was one. Watkins took care of him with a single lick.

Daly. That's true. Everybody was afraid of getting beat. Watkins once pounded the stew out of Joe Zawtocki. Kushner and Anton swore they would make Watkins pay for it if they ever got back to the States. They didn't say this in front of Watkins, though. I thought since we were a military group the leadership responsibility should have been Captain Kushner's. He always said the obligation was not his because he was a noncombatant. He said the one who should be in charge was Sergeant Williams. But Williams was wounded. Many people felt Kushner was using this as an excuse to avoid responsibility.

We all admired Captain Kushner. He helped us with his medical advice. But the man was lazy. The first time we argued was when I told him it was his turn to sweep the hootch floor. He refused. He said he hadn't gone to college for so many years to sweep floors. I said, "Wait a damn minute. I didn't go to school for twelve years to sweep either. But everyone has to take his turn." He also said that before he would carry manioc he wouldn't eat them. You couldn't believe he was so lazy. But he did change. Anton never did.

Harker. Dr. Kushner was an intellectual caught in a situation where physical strength was the chief virtue. He was, as his wife Valerie said in *Life* magazine, the type of guy who would tell her to mow the lawn because he didn't want to mess up his hands. I was famous for jumping on his back. I guess I was letting off steam. Davis was the serious type. He believed, like Watkins and Strictland, in working or else. He would get into hassles with Kushner but Kushner would sweet talk him out of it. It was true that Kushner and Anton were sick. But we were all sick. And sometimes you simply had to push yourself beyond your limitations.

Watkins. Kushner was a nice guy, easy to get along with, but he was soft, and I was especially suspicious of him. I felt he was strong enough to pick manioc. All of us felt that way. We thought it was mainly laziness. He said he couldn't go. We said, "If you don't bring back more than two or three that will be helping." He said walking was bad for his feet, that he could hardly make it. We said we felt the same way. Still, if we didn't pick them we would probably starve. Finally we told him, okay, no work, no eat.

Anton. I didn't like Watkins but I had respect for him. What he did was wrong. Yet he didn't do it with malice. He did it because he was strong and lacked judgment. He took over without really trying. He did a lot for people who were sick, so much that I would have to overlook the bad part. He helped people when they were down and did not say anything about it whether he thought they were faking or not. Willie hated Williams. Why we could never figure out. Yet he helped Williams. He carried him to the latrine when he was down. He was that type of guy; he could hate but still help you.

Everybody at first tried to work. That's my opinion. Right away people got sick. I myself was sicker than the others because I didn't eat rice in the beginning. Kushner and I went down fast. We remained weak after that. At first we went for firewood. We had to get it every day because we could never get enough, and there were no complaints. Then my load got smaller and smaller. If I carried a piece the other prisoners wanted to know why I couldn't carry ten pieces. If ten pieces, why not twenty? When I carried none I heard the snide comments, "Last time you carried some, why can't you do it now?" I didn't mind it so much when it was said to my face. But I knew they were talking behind my back. I couldn't pick manioc at all.

Kushner didn't think that being a doctor excused him from working. He was sicker than everybody realized. All they understood was that "I'm doing all the work and he's eating half the food." That's the way it was. Kushner confided to me he felt terrible about not being able to help more. He would get depressed and go off by himself. The VC jumped on him more than anybody else. Some of this, of course, was his own fault. He would argue with anybody about anything.

The Vietnamese saw what was happening to us. I don't know whether they planned it. But there were signs they encouraged our antagonisms. I remember Mr. Ho said that so and so doesn't work yet he eats as much as the others. He told Watkins and Davis they should have more because they did half the work.

Yet it was not the VC but a skin disease that pushed us into our darkest period and caused a near-fatal split between us. Daly came down with it first, which was unusual since the blacks were less susceptible than we were to disease. But he was lighter-skinned than the other four, a coffee-and-cream color, and though big, perhaps more fragile. It quickly spread, some catching it worse than others.

Harker. The disease was probably caused by a lack of vitamins and oil. It was unlike anything ever seen by Dr. Kushner. The epidermis cracked open with water-blister-type sores that

first ran clear serum and then pus. Scratching was almost sexual in its relief but only made the disease worse. The pus dried,
gluing our pajamas to our backsides. The pain was horrible.
Eighteen of us were jammed together on the bed. It was excruciatingly hot. But we had to sleep under our blankets to
ward off hordes of mosquitoes. Men cried out at night, "Kill
me! I want to die!" Guys began to schiz out in the daytime
by pulling blankets over their heads to shut out the world.
The disease was combined with our growing dysentery and
malaria. The hootch smelled like a septic tank. It was best not
to get up at night unless absolutely necessary. Probably you
would step in excrement while walking down the aisleway.

The skin disease broke out before Mr. Ho arrived. It
jumped from man to man. Ho saw the condition we were in.
It was he who ordered the VC to build us another hootch.
The VC had divided us several months earlier into two nine-
man squads. At the time it meant nothing. The squad leaders
were mostly responsible for giving the VC a head count in
the mornings and evenings. Now Watkins' squad was moved
to the new hootch. Our squad, headed by Strictland, who
replaced Grissett, stayed in the old hootch.

Ho possibly had ideas about Strictland, and maybe that was
why he was made a squad leader. All of us thought constantly
about being freed. But even though you wanted to go along
with the VC for this reason things sometimes got so ridiculous
that you questioned them before you could catch yourself.
"You don't understand," the VC would say. "You imperialists
have aggressed us."

"Oh, yeah, how could I ever forget?"

Strictland made few mistakes of this sort. He was quiet and
went along without arguing. He was rather short, boyish-
looking, with cool blue eyes and light freckles. He was strong
as a bull and a hard worker. He had been brought up on a
tobacco farm in North Carolina and was drafted after high
school. That's what the VC liked about him. Their idea of a
"progressive" was someone who killed himself working.

Strictland. I did anything they said. Other guys argued with
them. Some they'd have to hit in the head to make them get
out of bed. The VC might come to the hootch and say, "We
need five guys to carry grass to build us a house."

I'd say, "I'll go." Watkins and this guy Davis, we'd go do it. I didn't mind. I felt like I was just getting by. Surviving.

Anton. The VC separated the two nine-man squads into two hootches and it just so happened that most of the strong and healthy men were concentrated in one squad. Watkins, Davis, Denny, Joe Zawtocki. In fact myself and Long, who was captured when a special forces camp was overrun, were about the only ones in our squad who couldn't work. But almost everyone in the other squad was sick with the skin disease or other ailments. Harker and Strictland were the stronger members of the second squad. Harker had a terrible case of the skin disease. Strictland had serious kidney trouble, he was pissing blood.

Separating us into two hootches turned out to be like putting us into two different countries. We became enemies. At first there was a compromise about work. Watkins told the other hootch, "You send two guys on a manioc run and we'll send three or four." Then it got to the point where we'd send three and they'd send just one. Resentments built up. I irritated the other squad because I wasn't working, yet my squad was complaining about them. No one said much about Long because he was ill from the moment he arrived in camp.

The VC killed a pig on September 2 to celebrate North Viet Nam's Independence Day. Before going to eat with the Vietnamese, Grissett said, "Let's show them today how Americans act. No reaching and grabbing. Two people serve and no one eats till everyone has his food." Everyone agreed. The food was placed on the table. Grissett and someone else began politely serving the others.

Suddenly Grissett said, "Fuck this," and dumped half a plate of meat into his bowl, squatted on his haunches, and began to shovel it in. The meal deteriorated into the usual reach and grab.

That's where we were at this point. Our mental condition had begun to match our physical condition. We had no shoes, toothpaste, soap, or mosquito nets. All of us had bed sores from the hard bamboo. Rats ran rampant through the hootch at night. They were unbelievably brave. Sometimes they crawled up and sat on our arms. I guess they sensed we were one of them.

Davis. The split began one day in my hootch. Watkins, Denny, and Joe Zawtocki were talking about the guys in the other hootch being lazy. Everybody had the skin disease. We returned from manioc runs with our hands swollen and bleeding. Petty irritations became hard resentments and then anger. Some of my squad thought some of the other squad were goofing off. Some thought Dr. Kushner had too much education to work. Everybody was sick and feeling sorry for themselves, that's what it was. So we said why don't we split up and let each hootch worry about itself.

Harker. We hadn't had to work while Ho was there. The Vietnamese had done everything for us so we could attend class. The quality and quantity of our food was a little better during this time. The vacation ended and we had to face the reality of scrambling for ourselves again. The skin disease and the separation into two hootches opened the way for the breach.

The split started the day after the September 2 celebration. The other hootch said they had taken a vote at the end of August and had decided that my squad must henceforth gather its own firewood and manioc and do its own cooking.

We said, "You're crazy. Somebody will die."

They said, "This is the way it's going to be."

I was mad at Watkins. I later found that Denny had a big say in the matter too. It was like a slap in the face. I thought Watkins didn't understand the situation. A lot of men in my squad were deathly sick.

The decision to split apart was theirs. But we played the game like them. All of us played. Things became competitive and petty. Some of my squad were in the Vietnamese kitchen after the September 2 celebration and saw a pot of leftover pig fat. We brought it back to our hootch. Instead of going eighteen ways, it went nine.

Anton. We had one kitchen, a small shed with a mud-packed stove and an underground chimney to disperse the smoke. During the split we took turns using it. The other squad took an extra long time when they cooked. Whether on purpose or not I don't know. In retaliation the people cooking for us also took an extra long time. We ended up eating only two meals a day instead of three. And for about a week each group had only one meal; one group in the morning, the other in the afternoon, because they couldn't get into the kitchen till then.

Harker and Strictland did most of the work for the other squad. Harker had lost a lot of weight and like myself was very thin. He was of medium height, with a shock of brown wavy hair, a full mouth, and teeth that could have used braces when he was a kid. He was basically a loner. He and I simply ignored each other at first and seldom spoke. He was a hard worker, though, and good with his hands. Everybody respected him for this.

Davis. There was animosity. Some guys from one squad didn't talk to the other squad while the split was on; but I did.

McMillan. My foot hadn't completely healed. A lot of people said I was shamming. They thought I should have gotten up quicker. But I couldn't walk well, it was impossible to hump up and down the rocks. Kushner would go on a manioc run and couldn't bring back but two or three. He wasn't built for it, he just couldn't do it. Daly couldn't carry a heavy load either, would stumble and fall and tear up two manioc baskets before he got off one run. Fred could do nothing; he was swollen with edema. Even Grissett had fallen very sick.

Watkins did a lot of things to piss people off. It wasn't that he was sympathizing with the VC. But, goddamn, he was trying to cover his ass in the long run. He didn't do that much to be progressive. Kushner did everything to be done because he was an officer and the VC were always on his back—they forced him to do it. Watkins didn't do any more than Kushner. But the fact was Watkins was truthful about the things he did. He was honest. That was one reason why the Vietnamese liked him.

But he didn't understand our situation. Even before the split Watkins told Kushner, Daly, and myself that either we worked or he would cut off our chow. In fact he did cut us for one day. It surprised me as a black man that he would do that to another black man. I said, "This dude must be crazy." Any man in his right mind could have seen we weren't able to work. If he had a little sympathy he would have known.

Will didn't look at things that way. He was hard. One day

I walked into the kitchen to get some water when he was cooking. He told me to wait a few minutes till chow was ready. I tried to get the water anyway. He said, "If you get it I'm gonna knock your teeth down your throat."

Damn, man, I'm looking up at a big dude, almost twice as big as I am. Plus that he had once boxed in the Golden Gloves. I said, "Okay, man, if that's the way you want it."

Davis was in that squad with Watkins and Denny. Davis wanted to get along with everybody and he did; everybody liked him. But as I said to Kushner, "If a man tells Davis to jump off a mountain, he'll jump." I told Davis this to his face. I said, "If I'm in a situation where a man told me not to cook your rice and said he would beat me if I did, I wouldn't cook for you. But I would at least take some of my rice to you."

During the split, don't get me wrong, some guys were talking to each other. But I wasn't speaking to no damn body.

Davis. I didn't want any part of the camp leadership. I didn't want to be always hassling others about what they should do. We were all men. I was about as strong as Watkins. If it had come down to a fight it would have been a pretty good one. He never gave me any static. Maybe because we were both black and there was a mutual respect.

Harker. I got up before dawn early in September and went to take a leak. When I returned I saw Cannon lying on the floor near the firepit. He often sat up at night and slept in the daytime. He was in terrible pain and there was so little room on the bed that his movements disturbed the others. He was making a strange noise. I went to investigate. He said, "I'm trying to get back on the bed." But he wasn't moving. I realized he was in a sad state. He went into a coma later that day, and passed away after a few hours.

The VC made a bamboo coffin. We dug his grave. They came to the hootch and said, "Here are some white clothes to bury him in."

We said, "Take your clothing back. We don't want anything. You didn't give him anything when he was alive." They were insulted, and left.

They must have realized that we felt very strongly about it for us to talk back to them. Later they called us to a meeting.

The camp commander said, "Why do you think Cannon died?"

We said, "Because he did not have proper medical care or adequate food."

The VC said, "No, he died because of his wounds and because he didn't clean himself."

We argued with them. They became irritated. We backed off.

Anton. Williams had grown weaker after the political course. He had a bad case of edema. The fluid had swollen his testicles to three times their normal size, they were unreal, watery looking; his legs and stomach were swollen and the fluid had begun to press toward his heart. If Kushner had had the simple diuretics available in any pharmacy, he could have saved his life. It was especially hard on him watching men die whom he knew he could save if medicines were available. But nothing was available, or if it was the VC waited as usual until it was too late.

Williams lay fatally ill some days. Watkins carried him to the latrine, others washed him. The VC gave him a can of condensed milk. Kushner warned him not to drink it without diluting it because it was too sweet in concentrated form and would complicate his dysentery. By this time, however, Williams was practically incoherent. He drank it straight. One morning several weeks after Cannon died we awoke to hear Williams breathing strangely. In a couple of hours he was dead.

A few weeks after Williams it was Sherman's turn. He had never recovered from the time spent in stocks after the escape attempt. He had hung on the following months like a walking zombie, sitting outside when the sun was out, inside on the bed when it wasn't. We reminded him of his Marine Corps stories, trying to make him talk and take an interest in living. He couldn't remember them. Sometimes he laughed and smiled. But he wasn't there. And finally he died.

McMillan. Usually the two squads didn't talk to each other but that night in November we did. Joe Zawtocki was up by the kitchen when he called me. Me and Joe got along pretty good because Joe blew pot. All the guys who blew got along,

I associated with them. Anyway, Joe says to me, "Hey, Ike, want some pussy?"

I said, "Yeah, man."

He said, "You're gonna have to eat it."

I went to see what he wanted. He had the camp cat with him. Grissett, Harker, and Strictland had planned to kill the cat and eat him. Trouble was, nobody could catch him. I returned and told everyone we had the cat.

Somebody asked, "Who's gonna kill him?"

I said, "I'm not gonna kill him. I've done had enough of bad luck with cats."

They said, "What do you mean?"

I remember when I was small I used to aggravate cats—set them on fire, shoot them with my BB gun. I'd do this for devilment. My grandfather used to beat me. Ohhh, did he beat me! One time I caught this cat and poured kerosene on his back and lit him up. He looked like a shooting star. That night when I was asleep, that same cat jumped on my bed. I grabbed a window stick and started beating him. He didn't move. I got a Coke bottle and threw it at him. He still didn't move. I screamed for my grandmother. When she came the cat disappeared. I knew I had seen the cat, but now he was gone.

You can ask my wife. If a cat crosses me I'll turn around and go the other way. Any cat. That's me today. I respect cats. And it went through my head that I shouldn't bother this VC cat. But I said, "Hell, I can't have no worse luck than I'm having right now."

Davis. I didn't want them to kill it actually. I liked the cat and thought it was bad luck to kill one. I also knew the camp authorities would miss it. I told them to let me hold the cat. They said, "No, you'll turn him loose." And I would have too.

The cat was miaowing loudly. He knew something was up, all the guys were gathered round petting him. They tried first to drown him in a pot a boiling water. But he jumped out scratching and spitting and almost got away. Then Grissett said, "I'll kill him."

McMillan. Russ took the cat outside. Two or three minutes later we heard this *ka-loomph!* He returned. The cat's head was bashed in. Someone got a rusty razor blade and began to skin it. Kushner was detailed to hide the fur and entrails in the latrine. Strictland watched for the guards.

Some guys from Watkins' hootch were there and we said, "Hey, there are too many of us here. Somebody should go." They left.

We started jiving around, wondering how it would taste because it was all lovely pink meat.

"Jeez, look at those thighs!"

Strictland whistled a warning. We stashed the cat. A guard arrived. He asked us what we were doing.

"Boiling water," we said. "We're thirsty." It looked strange because we weren't supposed to have a fire at night. He told us to go to bed. Then he left.

We resumed our work. Ten minutes later a guard we called College Joe slipped in without Strictland seeing him. He walked up behind us, scaring us half to death. He saw the cat but didn't recognize it. He said, *"Tot lam,"* and laughed. He thought we had killed some sort of wild animal.

Then Qua the montagnard guard came in and began poking around.

He spotted the paws, which we hadn't been able to skin, and shouted, *"Meo! Meo!"* All of us ran from the kitchen and left the cat laying there. Went to our hootch and jumped on the bed.

The VC and Garwood arrived with lamps. They ordered us outside. Fred was the only one from our hootch who hadn't been in the kitchen, he was too sick. Before we left the hootch we agreed that no matter what happened we wouldn't admit anything. Outside, they called me and Harker to the front.

"Who killed the cat?" Mr. Hom asked.

"I don't know, Mr. Hom," I said.

He asked Harker.

Harker said, "I don't know, Mr. Hom."

He went down the line asking each person. Everybody stood firm.

Anton. We watched from our hootch. It was an eerie scene. The lamp light distorted the Viet Cong's features and made them appear even more sinister.

They said, "You have killed the camp's cat. The camp com-

mander loves his cat. All the guards love the cat." It was ridiculous. They had loved the camp dog too. Yet one day
several months earlier when meat was in short supply they had
beaten their lovable dog to death with sticks and eaten him.
They had had a pet parakeet they were going to teach to talk.
It too had disappeared into their pot. "The baby loved the
cat." The younger cook, Hannah, had a two-year-old boy
who ran around the camp bare-assed. "You must tell us who
killed the cat."

McMillan. We stood firm for half an hour. Then Russ said,
"I killed the cat. I heard a noise by the john and I threw a
rock and accidentally killed him." That wouldn't wash. The
VC jerked him out of line. They kicked and beat him. He fell
to the ground. They pounded him terribly.

Harker. Garwood came down the line and punched me in
the ribs. He said, "Somebody's gonna pay for letting Russ
take all the blame." The blow stunned me. Not because it was
thrown hard but because I was weak. I stumbled backward.
A guard removed Kushner's glasses and slapped him brutally.

McMillan. The VC tied us up. Daly and I were fastened to
a pole so tightly as to cut off our circulation. I started vomiting. The medic girl ran to see what was happening. The VC
untied me. Several hours later they untied everyone but Grissett. Several guys were made to bury the cat. Next morning
the supply director worked Grissett over with a cane. It was
his cat, brought to camp to keep the rats out of the rice supply. As the guards passed by they kicked Grissett and pinched
his ears. Around noon they untied him. The camp commander
called us to a meeting. He asked for our opinions about what
had happened the night before.

Kushner told him the guards were cruel savages. The camp
commander had this slinky look on his face. That's why we
called him Slime. He giggled like the Vietnamese do when
they're nervous and asked the others what they thought.
Everyone said the same thing. Then Slime apologized for the
beatings we'd received. He said if he had been there it
wouldn't have happened. It was true—he wasn't there. Ol'
Ratface, the North Vietnamese, was in charge. He didn't care
what happened. Slime was like that. When someone died he
came around and apologized. The ARVN POWs told us he

was dangerous, that he would execute you, and we believed he would. But at least Slime seemed to show a little sympathy. The rest didn't.

Anton. We could not understand why Grissett confessed to killing the cat. It wasn't necessary. He never recovered from the incident. Perhaps he'd been hurt more deeply than we realized when he lost his influence over us as Watkins assumed the role of camp commander. I know his failure to be released after Ho's indoctrination course hurt him. And then taking that terrible beating must have made him give up all hopes of being freed. He became quiet and meek. He quit talking about going home, stopped eating, and began to regress. He lay on his bed all day long in the fetal position with a blanket pulled over his head, sucking his thumb and whimpering like a baby.

Strictland. After we learned the camp routine we didn't want Grissett to tell us what to do. Someone like him needed to have authority. A lot of guys said that was what caused him to go downhill.

If Grissett decided not to work, he wouldn't even though he might be in better shape than others. Some mornings he said, "I'm sick." He'd tell so and so he could have his rice. If someone offered you rice, you grabbed for it. You always gave your rice to someone in your squad. You looked after them first; that was natural. Anyway, after the other guys went to work Grissett would get up and say, "Where's my rice?"

We said, "We thought you were sick and gave yours to someone."

He said, "I'm better now." He had a morning sickness called work disease. He was the type of guy to take his rice back.

Grissett would get hungry and say he was going on the next manioc run.

"Okay, I'm going too," I'd tell him. Manioc might not have done me any good but I was sure going to carry them so I could eat them.

Russ would get a basket of manioc. When he returned he wouldn't let anybody touch them. He would eat them himself. And when he finished he wanted somebody else's.

Then we said, "You didn't let us eat any of yours. Now you can't have any of ours."

At the last Grissett squatted in a corner of the bed with a blanket pulled over his head. The medic girl had four or five dull needles. She bulled them but it didn't do any good. When she gave a shot, half of it wouldn't go in. She gave me one and my shoulder got infected. I still have a hole in it. The VC brought doctors in when people started dying. Kushner told them what the prisoner needed to survive and after the guy was about dead they brought the medicine. When Grissett was unconscious they let Kushner give him I don't know how many shots. But it was too late.

Davis. Everybody pitched in when someone was really down. Personal differences were forgotten. Russ had dysentery very badly. We washed his clothes and brought food to his bed. He developed a case of bronchial pneumonia. We thought he was gone. Suddenly he popped out of it. One morning he awoke and began to move around, did some exercises and looked like his old self. He said he was going to be all right. Then several days later he sank back into it. We tried to make him eat, make him get up and move about. We were fighting against impossible odds. At a certain point in starvation a lack of vitamins brings a loss of appetite. A man will ultimately lie down and die staring at food piled in front of him.

Harker. Russ went harder than anyone. Kushner and I stayed up all night with him. He fought it so. He knew he was dying. He asked us to tell his sister that he loved her. He passed away about 3:30 in the morning the day before Thanksgiving. The medic girl came to the hootch. At first when we got to camp she had been cool toward us. But as people fell ill, as she saw she could do nothing to help because of her lack of knowledge and equipment, she became sympathetic; and we began to consider her our friend. We could see she was truly sad that Russ had died.

Several days after Thanksgiving it was Bill Port. You could tell by his bone structure that Port had once been a very big guy. He was from the First Cav. He was taking a squad from LZ Baldy to reinforce a unit getting hit. Just as they jumped from the choppers mortars started coming in. And then a ground attack. There was mass confusion. Port remembered seeing Viet Cong darting around the landing zone. He was hit by a mortar round. One of his ears was half blown off, his toes were completely ripped away, and his left arm had a deep wound that drained continually. He had powder burns on his face and severely limited vision in his left eye. At dusk he would be almost blind and someone had to lead him to the latrine. After he was first captured the VC took him to a field hospital. There they treated his wounds and fed him eggs and monkey meat regularly. He improved a little. But not enough to justify their transferring him to our camp. Why they did that we never knew. Through it all Port kept a good sense of humor. He was taken in his sleep.

McMillan. The split between the two squads lasted till people started dying like hell. Nobody brought it up to anyone's face. But the people in the other squad who wanted the split saw what was happening. They started thinking. They could see others were run-down and might die too. It didn't end all of a sudden. We gradually got back together in early December. The Vietnamese had something to do with ending it. They moved us five blacks into another hootch, making it three squads instead of two. They also told us we had to have two permanent cooks. After the split was over and we were back together I didn't say anything about it. But I was still mad. I intended to get even with some of those guys.

Harker. The VC half-stopped it in a way, and we did too. The split was so absurd and should never have happened; and didn't. No one spoke about it.

Daly. The Vietnamese separated us into three groups because they could see we weren't getting along. From the very first moment they reorganized us, people got together and things began to change. The VC tried to make us black fellows think they did this because we were sort of special. Mr. Ho had given us this idea one night in July when he called us to his hootch. He didn't say so directly. But he asked had we heard of the Black Panthers and when we said no, he told us all about them. That's all Ho talked about, black this and black that, how the Front sympathized with the blacks. He said, "You should be in the States to tell of your experiences. What would you do if we released you?"

We said, "Oh, good night! We would tell about the war and what's happening over here and everything!" We thought when they moved the blacks together in a third hootch that maybe they were preparing to release us.

During the split everything was filthy. It wasn't so much the fault of the Vietnamese as our own dirty sanitation. One group would cook and wouldn't wash the pans. The other squad would do the same thing. Overnight rats and bugs ate what was left in the pans and we got up and cooked out of them again. Nobody wanted to wash the rice before cooking it. If you didn't wash it sometimes almost half the ration was rat feces. Still, people cooked without washing it. The Vietnamese claimed that was why people were getting sick. So they said they wanted us to have only two cooks. And mama-san was assigned to teach us how to cook properly.

The POWs voted for whom they wanted as cooks. Harker and I were elected. Since I had prior cooking experience I became head cook. The assistant cook was responsible for preparing the fire and making sure enough wood was on hand. Harker didn't mind the work but he hated to get up at 3:00 A.M. After several weeks he quit. Lewis came on. He lasted till he had an argument with mama-san. Lewis didn't eat manioc. Sometimes when mama-san cooked she mixed them with the rice. She was doing this one day and Lewis said, "No, no, we no eat this way." She continued what she was doing. Lewis pulled off the pot top. Mama-san went hollering to the VC area. Mr. Hom came down and chewed Lewis out. The VC removed him as assistant cook. McMillan took over.

We had three large pots. One was for boiling water, another for cooking rice, and the third for manioc. First thing each morning we made drinking water. We had washed the rice and cut the manioc and covered it up the night before, so everything was prepared. The rice took about ten minutes to cook. Some guys wanted manioc and rice together, others wanted them separately. Some wanted a few, others forced themselves to eat a lot just to be full. Occasionally if we had extra cooking oil I cooked manioc patties or manioc soup. We ate with chop sticks we carved ourselves. Later we received American-made spoons.

Every day, three hundred sixty-five days a year, someone came to me and said, "What're we having for lunch?"

I started cussing. "What do you think we're having? Manioc and rice!"

There were times we cooked three times a day, times we cooked twice or once, and times we didn't cook at all. It was sort of an unwritten rule when it came your time to cook under the old rotation system that you screwed everybody else. But the truth is, when I became permanent cook I never took any extra. Guys kidded me about tasting the manioc soup too much. I guess everybody thought I looked surprisingly healthy. I never lost much weight like everybody else. I was five foot eleven and most of the time weighed about a hundred seventy. But that was the story of my life, it has always been like that.

Anton. I practically went into a state of shock when people started dying. Most of those who died had beriberi to some extent, and I had it too. Beriberi is primarily caused by a severe deficiency of vitamin B_1. The disease is inevitable when you have a steady diet of polished rice. It killed many American POWs in Asian camps during World War II and Korea. You get dysentery at the outset, then a swelling called edema, which is caused by a retention of body fluids. My legs ballooned up. My testicles looked like baseballs. I moved in slow motion. The edema retarded respiration. The VC gave me B_1 and iron shots. I received a hundred shots in two months. None I thought did any good.

McMillan. Anton was lazy long before he got to Viet Nam. He said after he graduated from warrant officer's school his father, an air force colonel, told him that was the first successful thing he had ever done. Anton was tall and so skinny that we called him Bones. He weighed about a hundred ten pounds. He had a thin mouth and bushy black eyebrows that moved up and down like dark thunderclouds when he grumbled, and he talked in a nasal tone. He thought we were down on him because we tried to make him get up and do. He lay under his blanket all day long. If we hadn't pushed him and made him get up, he would have died. All of us knew that.

Harker. We had a small celebration Christmas Eve. The VC gave us a banner with a star on it. We hung it behind the bed in Joe Zawtocki's hootch and found a little tree and decorated it with bits of paper. We listened to Radio Hanoi that afternoon. Several pilots held in Hanoi read beautiful warm messages about how they missed home and the children who were growing up without them. We allowed ourselves to linger over thoughts of our families. The VC returned to Watkins his New Testament, and he read the Christmas Scriptures. We said the Lord's Prayer and sang a few carols. Bob Garwood was there, he was a friend of Joe's, and he sang with us.

The camp commander made a brief speech. "You are allowed to enjoy Christmas because of the Front's lenient and humane policy. We are sorry you are not with your family. But Johnson prolongs the war. Maybe next year you will be back home." He didn't promise but he sounded almost certain that Nixon, who had been elected the month before, would end the war. We clutched at his optimism. Our spirits rose.

Anton. The Vietnamese gave us some candy. We divided it into equal shares. Garwood saw we had split it up. He reported us to the Vietnamese. The camp commander told us collect the candy, said we had to eat it community style.

"Put it in the middle of the bed and you can have it at midnight."

We said, "Midnight?"

They wanted us to stay up because captured U.S. pilots were to sing Christmas carols over Radio Hanoi at 12:00.

The pilots already had read messages saying they had ham, turkey, and cranberry sauce. We said, "If we could have but one bite of it!"

We tried to be happy but couldn't. People were showing tears. Anyway, when the camp commander said we couldn't split the candy we said, "It's our Christmas. If we can't divide it the way we want, you keep it. Or give it to Garwood."

Finally he gave in.

Harker. We received an extra can of rice for our Christmas meal and two chickens. On New Year's we had another celebration, with extra rice and several cans of U.S. Army B-ration ham. But if our spirits were rising, they suddenly fell the next day.

Anton. Fred was captured on his first mission. He had been in Viet Nam six days. He was on the tail end of the patrol and fell asleep from exhaustion during a ten-minute break. The others were gone when he awoke. He seemed to think they had left him on purpose because they didn't like him. He didn't smoke, didn't drink, didn't swear. He wasn't an average marine. He had been an excellent student and had won a scholarship to Notre Dame. He was having problems at home. He considered his father weak. His mother wore the pants in the family. Instead of going to Notre Dame, he joined the Marine Corps to prove he was a man.

Harker. You watch the changes in him. His legs swell with edema. You see his hair becoming frizzy, it stands up on his head. His eyes begin to bulge. Before he was a nice-looking guy. Now he looks foreign, strange. Kushner punched me one night. Five of us were in the hootch, McMillan had built a fire, and we had let Fred come over to sit by it. For being a good boy that day. It gets down to the ridiculous but you try to develop some sort of incentive for making them want to live. "Fred you can have your blanket if you wash yourself." Or "Fred you can sit by the fire if you don't crap in your pants today." He had that faraway look in his eyes. When he saw us watching he smiled gently. I wanted to cry.

Anton. He began to make a lot of noise at night, crying over and over, "Mama, oh, Mama . . . I want my Mama."

Once in the middle of the night someone, I don't remember who, yelled, "Die, motherfucker, die!"

No one was shocked. Several people laughed. It was that kind of situation, so pathetic, but the realism of the moment because nobody could get any sleep. Later people talked about it and said what a rotten thing to do.

Harker. You could confront him with it. "You're dying, Fred. You've got to try. You've got to get back. Your mom wants to see you, your dad does too. You mean so much to them."

He'd reply, "Yes, I want to. But I can't. I just can't."

"Why? You can. All you have to do is eat."

"Doesn't taste good."

"The food doesn't taste good to any of us. But you've got to eat to live. You ate it before."

"All I want is to be warm. Please let me sit by the fire."

Prison didn't change him as it did others, didn't make him harsh and nasty, foulmouthed like many of us became. He kept his manners through the hardest of times, always said thank you for the smallest gestures, and remained a devout Catholic when others had their faith shaken. When he died the day after New Year's all of us realized that some part of ourselves had died with him. He was nineteen.

from *Survivors*, 1975

Our Town: The War Comes Home to Beallsville, Ohio

by Jeffrey Blankfort

WASHINGTON (AP) *The Pentagon has rejected a plea to withdraw from Viet-Nam combat the servicemen from a little Ohio town that had five native sons killed in action. . . .*

[Congressman Clarence] Miller made the request in letters to Laird and President Nixon after residents of the town of 450 expressed fear their younger generation was being decimated.

I WENT to Beallsville a little more than a month after the town had buried its fifth son, Naval Corpsman Robert Lucas, in a plot of ground overlooking the high school where he and the four other boys had been schoolmates. Three of them now lie with him in the same graveyard and another is buried a few miles away.

Beallsville, on the fringes of Appalachia, is a sleepy southeastern Ohio town, made up of a general store, churches, a post office, farms, frame houses and a cemetery. Intersected by three state highways, it is located 12 miles up a winding road from the Ohio River. The road is State Highway 556, but in Beallsville it is known as Rural Route 3.

Viet-Nam has taken a toll from Beallsville that is 75 times the national average. ("They won't be getting many more of our boys," said Mayor Gramlich. "They drafted the last one of draft age this month.") The war has come home to Beallsville with unique severity, and America's confusions and contradictions about it are sharpened there: the acute consciousness of the waste, against the ingrained heartland patriotism; deep resentment over the lost sons, against the need to be proud of their sacrifice.

688

I talked to the parents about their sons and the war.

The Pittmans live in a two-story, many-gabled frame house on a farm six miles up the road from the Beallsville Corporation limits. With no one but themselves now, they use only the first floor. Mr. Pittman works at the Ormet Aluminum plant in Hannibal. In the fall they can peaches from their orchard.

Mrs. Maegene Pittman—whose son Jack was drafted at nineteen, was sent to the infantry and became the town's first casualty—expressed it this way: "They just took him and that was it. We never knew there was a Viet-Nam or anything until he had to go. And to think in eight months we had him back and buried."

Hurt and bitter at the loss of their only child, Mrs. Pittman and her husband, Earl, refused a military funeral. "Jack would have wanted it that way," she said. "He didn't understand the Viet-Nam thing any more than we do. We were bitter. We didn't want no part of a military funeral. I just think we have no business over there. If they were attacking our country, that's different."

Her husband saw things differently: "They're fighting over there with their hands tied behind them is the way I look at it. I always thought they ought to declare war and do it right if they're going to be over there."

"Why do you think we are there?" I asked.

He smiled. "Politics."

And you, Mrs. Pittman?

She looked over at her husband and then back at me. "It's a political war."

As I talked with the Pittmans, I sat beneath a case containing a photograph of their son and the trophies he had won at Beallsville High where he had been captain of the football and basketball teams. Before he was drafted, his mother said, he had taken "a little team of eighth graders under his wing to teach them basketball. He was a good Christian boy.

"Being our only son, we just gave everything we had to our country. We've got each other," said Mrs. Pittman, exchanging glances with her husband. "But when you get our age you look for your grandchildren, your family to multiply.

Now both of us is left with, we might as well say, no future. When you lose your only child, you don't have any future."

11

On the same road, back toward town, Kenneth and Betty Rucker live in a blue frame house on the edge of a small farm. Their son Richard was killed on Memorial Day last year. Also drafted at nineteen, he had served eight months in combat with the infantry.

Mr. Rucker works, when work is available, as an electrical lineman. A veteran of World War II, he was eager to talk about his son:

"He was very clean-cut. All his hobbies were clean. He didn't smoke, he didn't chew, he didn't drink, and he didn't specially want to go to the service much. But he was a boy that wouldn't object. Whatever he had to do, he did it and did it willingly."

What do you think about the war, Mr. Rucker? What would you do?

"There is not much you can do," he replied. "I do what they tell me, but I see this thing is out of hand and we shouldn't have been involved—which he didn't want to be. But he was that kind of boy. He wouldn't shirk no part of his American body for communism."

Betty Rucker, Richard's stepmother who raised him from the first grade, broke down in tears when she started to talk about him.

"There's just no sense to it. Just a slaughter. A lot of young kids going over there to get killed for no reason at all. We have no business over there.

"They hadn't even started their lives yet. They give them a few weeks training and they say, 'Well, you're ready, boy, go ahead.' What can you do? They don't know anything. Only kill or be killed. That's all Rich thought about, kill or be killed.

"They tell us we're over there to fight communism," she said. "If the South Vietnamese want to fight, let them fight their own battles."

Richard, in his last month of combat, had been showing signs of mental fatigue. "They checked him and said he was just a little nervous," said his father, "and then in three days he was killed."

Two days before he died, Richard wrote home:

"Well, we got into the shit again here. This is near suicide. Every day I say, you are going to make it Rich, you are going to make it."

"I gave my boy a full military funeral," said Kenneth Rucker, "but it was rough."

III

Duane Greenlee joined the Marines in January, 1966, at the age of eighteen. He was sent to Viet-Nam that July and served 44 days before he was killed.

Shortly after Duane's death, his parents separated. His father, Duane Sr., moved to Bellaire, Ohio, a few miles from Wheeling, while his mother, three brothers and four sisters relocated in Clarington, 12 miles from Beallsville.

I talked with Mrs. Greenlee over her morning cup of coffee.

"It don't seem like Duane's gone yet. It's really hard. It hits me at times and it's pretty hard to take. I know what all the other mothers feel like. I wanted to go to each one of their funerals but I just couldn't. I just stayed away and thought about it as though they were my own boys. It's hard to talk about it.

"I knew all the boys but Jack. The others had all been to my house with Duane at different times.

"I'm certainly proud of my boy. All his life he wanted to be a Marine. When he was home on furlough before he went over, we asked him if he was scared. He said he wasn't scared but he'd rather go there and fight for mom and dad and his brothers and sisters than have them come over here and fight.

"I have a son thirteen coming up and he can't wait to get in the Marines. He's going to. They're all real proud of their brother."

Do you know, or did Duane know, why he was over there?

"Duane really wanted to go and help out but he said he didn't know what he was going over there for. He wrote home in letters he didn't know what he was fighting for. He didn't see any sense in it and I don't see where we've gained anything at all by any of them being over there. I just wish it was all over.

"I believe if I had been President," she said, and dropped her voice, "I would have done like Hiroshima."

IV

"Our kid, he done most of the farming," Mr. Ernest Schnegg recalled. "I was doing construction work down at the Norton mine. Charles worked three days a week at Timken Roller Bearings in Cincinnati and when he was off he came home and took care of things."

Ernest and Esther Schnegg now live and work in Barnesville, 19 miles north of Beallsville. Their farm in Beallsville, on which they raised eight children, can no longer support them. Mr. Schnegg works seven days a week at a greenhouse and Mrs. Schnegg is a nurse's aide at Barnesville Hospital.

Charles, their oldest son, was drafted on December 5, 1966, and one day short of a year later was killed, serving with the infantry in Viet-Nam.

Their oldest daughter, Shirley, seventeen, and Roger, now their oldest son at sixteen, live on the farm and attend Beallsville High School.

Mr. Schnegg was tired. He had been working hard all day and his pants were rolled up and his feet were bare.

"I was counting on Charles to work on the farm. He was a farmer. Charles was all I had. The government took him and didn't give anything in return."

V

On March 7 of this year, the day before his son died in Viet-Nam, Robert Lucas Sr., age thirty-eight, had a heart attack. As a result he could not attend the funeral. Lucas lives with his wife and his remaining three sons and three daughters in a gaunt, gray two-story farmhouse eight miles outside of Beallsville.

Mr. Lucas came out to the back porch as I drove up, wearing the green work uniform that is a familiar sight in the area. I asked him how he felt. As far as the heart, all right, he guessed. He told me that his wife didn't want to talk to reporters so we sat down on the edge of the porch while his two dogs studied me curiously and we talked for a few minutes about his son and the war.

"Well, I hope to think he died for a purpose."

Do you have any feelings about what the purpose was?

"No."

You have a thirteen-year-old boy. Will he have to go, too?

"Well, I hope not, but if there ever comes a time when he has to defend his country, why I'm sure he'll do it."

Do you think the other boys from Beallsville should be moved from the combat zone?

"Well, the Defense Department, whatever you call it, can't do anything like that, can't favor one boy and put another in, they just can't do it. It's a business same as anything else."

What do you think we should do in Viet-Nam?

"Well, I know what I would do."

What?

"If I had my way, in a week's time it would be over. I'd draw the boys out of there and there wouldn't be no Viet-Nam to it."

YOU'VE HEARD OF APPALACHIA?

After the death of young Lucas, Keith Harper, the Beallsville undertaker, called Monroe County Treasurer Ray Starkey, and said, "Ray, you've got to do something." Starkey, a 50-year resident of the Beallsville area, called their congressman, Clarence Miller. Miller said he would "see if he could 'get the boys moved around a little bit so this won't happen again right away,'" recalls Starkey, "or maybe I said that to him. Doesn't make any difference who said what, that's what he undertook to do."

Congressman Miller contacted the Department of Defense and was turned down.

I asked Starkey about the standard of living in Beallsville.

"It's certainly not plush. You can see that. This is Appalachia. You've heard that term? That's exactly what it is.

"The economic level isn't good here at all. 'Course now

the mine has helped the area a bit in the past couple of years. Prior to that, no. Now the aluminum plant complex we've had since '56 has been a big help. If it hadn't been for that I couldn't envision, in the name of peace, what this place would be like. I heard one guy say we'd be making change in possum skins, if it weren't for the plant."

Starkey was referring to the Olin Mathieson Chemical plant in Hannibal, Ohio, 16 miles southeast along the Ohio River, and its adjacent subsidiary, Ormet, owned jointly with Revere Copper and Brass. Ormet has 2500 employees, approximately 90 from the Beallsville area. Olin Mathieson has about 50 employees from Beallsville.

The chemical plant fabricates aluminum sheeting, plating and coil and Ormet turns it into everything from Revere pots and pans to shells for Viet-Nam. The wage scale at both plants runs from $2.84 to $4.60 an hour.

The only other large-scale employment for the area comes from its coal mines operated by North American Coal Company and Ogilby-Norton.

Due to the presence of the mines and aluminum plants, Monroe County workers earn the highest weekly wage of any county in Ohio, an average of $127 a week—for those who get work. But there is also widespread unemployment and, according to Ralph Yoss, county welfare director, 40 per cent of the 4500 families in Monroe County have annual incomes below the official poverty level of $3000.

In the Beallsville area, which is defined by the limits of the Beallsville School District and includes approximately 1000 people, 87 families are receiving some form of federal or local assistance. Besides Beallsville, the school district includes the towns of Malaga, Jerusalem, Aladonia, Switzer, Ozark and Armstrong Mills, crossing over a short way into Belmont County. It is from this general area with its larger population that the five boys originate.

There are at least six more boys from Beallsville stationed in Viet-Nam and several more apparently on their way.

In the first group is Randy Gramlich, son of Beallsville Mayor Ben Gramlich. "I'm not a dove," the mayor told me. "I never said I was a hawk, either. Still, this war, I can't see where it's any different than the rest. It's just to preserve freedom in the world."

Mr. Gramlich owns one of the town's two cafes, Jacqueline's Place, which is run by his wife. In the back he maintains the "J.F.K. Recreation Center," a free pool hall for Beallsville teenagers. Since the restaurant cannot bring in enough business to support the family, the mayor works the night shift at Olin Mathieson.

A short distance down the street I heard a sharp note of dissent from Ferrell McClelland. Tall and lean, in his late fifties or early sixties, he has spent 30 years in the coal mines. His youngest son, Roger, enlisted in the Army and has been in Viet-Nam since December.

"We ain't got no damn business over there to start with," he snapped. "I can't see what good they're gonna do over there. The one tape we got from him [Roger] said 'we don't know what we're over here for'; said 'it wouldn't be so bad if we knew what we were fighting for.' "

Beallsville Postmaster Vern Jeffers is a World War I veteran and an active member of his American Legion post. He delivered mail in Beallsville for 40 years and has been postmaster for the past eight. He is gray and bespectacled, with the voice and manner of an old family doctor.

"I enlisted in World War I. I was the youngest enlistee from Monroe County. We had as a slogan then, 'the war to end all wars.' We attended the American Legion 50th anniversary banquet recently and one of the boys said to me, 'Well, you were an enlistee, would you do it again?' Yes, I told him, under the same circumstances I would, because I really thought it was going to end all war, but we see—we have seen all these years since—that the slogan was meaningless.

"So, under the present circumstances I don't think I would enlist. If I were drafted, I certainly would go without hesitation. I wouldn't enlist because I don't feel, and I think I represent practically everybody in the community, I don't think this is a war to defend America or to make America a better place to live in. I just don't see it that way.

"I don't think it justifies the lives of these boys, over and above the expense of the war. Doesn't justify it at all. There was not a boy that really wanted to go over there that was killed. I know. I've known every one personally, all these years, since they were born. Most of the boys were from small farms and they didn't want to go over there and fight.

"And when we have been told we are working with one of the most corrupt governments in the whole world, it makes it still harder for us to believe we should sacrifice the lives of our boys for that cause."

Referring to his fellow legionnaires, Jeffers told me, "Almost, not unanimously, but by far the greater majority of them, do not think there is any justification for the war.

"I don't mean we should draw them out now," he added. "Anyone knows that would be the wrong thing. But I do think they should take definite and positive steps to bring it to a close. What we need is diplomacy.

"Diplomats," he said almost confidentially, "we're short of."

Mrs. Jean Nelson, the first woman to serve on the Beallsville Council, is serving as secretary on a committee for building a flagpole monument and memorial park in honor of the five boys who have been killed. "I feel so bitter about the war in Viet-Nam," she told me, "because it seems such a useless war, that my feeling is, any guy who can get out of it for whatever reason, more power to him.

"I don't think, however, that there has been a single solitary person in this community that has ever thought of protesting. What should we hope to accomplish? It's not going to bring our boys back.

"So many street marches! This is the type of person I would like to see shipped to Viet-Nam. Then he could be doing some good for his country!"

This strong reaction to public protest seemed to be universal in Beallsville, and there is little likelihood of a draft resistance movement forming there at the present time.

The principal of Beallsville High School, Timothy Haught, described to me what happened when a reporter from the Wheeling News-Register interviewed the senior boys after the last two deaths.

"Some expressed the fact that the war seemed at a considerable distance. Some expressed the fact that they were not entirely aware of all the implications of the war. But generally speaking, in both classes, the boys reflected the view that if called upon, they would serve."

There are 24 boys in the current Beallsville senior class.

Ramparts, July 1969

Hamburger Hill: The Army's Rationale

by David Hoffman

PHUBAI, South Vietnam, May 22—The Army commanders who ordered, approved and led what Sen. Edward M. Kennedy described as a "senseless and irresponsible" charge up Hamburger Hill disputed the Senator today.

They did so indirectly, with tact and also with passion.

"That hill was in my area of operations, that was where the enemy was, that's where I attacked him," said Maj. Gen. Melvin Zais, commander of the 101st Airborne Division, whose battalions led the 11-day assault.

"If I find him [the enemy] on any other hill in the Ashau, I assure you I'll attack him," the 53-year-old general told newsmen here this afternoon.

Dong Apbia, the rugged hill in question, known militarily as Hill 937, looks down upon the Ashau Valley, a traditional Communist invasion route winding east from Laos toward the big coastal cities of Hue and Danang.

Three 101st Airborne battalions and one South Vietnamese battalion finally gained its 3000-foot summit Tuesday, after battling uphill through triple-canopy jungle and stands of dense bamboo. Hill 937 cost the Americans 50 killed and 410 wounded.

"How can we justify sending our boys against a hill a dozen times or more until soldiers themselves question the madness of the action?" Kennedy asked the Senate. It is "both senseless and irresponsible to continue to send our young men to their deaths to capture hills and positions that have no relation to ending this conflict," declared the Massachusetts Democrat.

Zais acknowledged that the hill itself "has no tactical significance." All that distinguished it from countless similar redoubts bracketing the crater-pocked Ashau Valley was that

Hill 937 had elements of two North Vietnamese regiments dug in on top of it, the general said.

Why, then, did the allies storm it? Was not clearing the hill a job tailor-made for B-52 bombers? Is it not possible for an American army to shun such casualty-producing assaults and to still wage effective war?

Zais answered with considerable emotion:

"You can't go into the Ashau and leave the hills alone because then you're on the bottom of the floor of the Ashau and the enemy is on the hill and he won't leave you alone. The enemy doesn't leave us alone anywhere."

The general continued without pausing:

"It's a myth that somebody perpetuated, that if we don't do anything nothing will happen to us. It is not true . . . if we just sit, they try to overrun us. They'd kill us. It's just a myth that we can pull back and be quiet and everything will settle down. If we pulled back and were quiet, they'd kill us in the night.

"They'd come in and crawl under the wire and they'd drop satchel charges on our bunkers and they'd mangle and maim and kill our men. The only way I can in good conscience lead my men and protect them is to insure that they're not caught in that kind of a situation."

The grey-haired general was somber and intent as he addressed an informal press conference at division headquarters here.

Zais has been nominated for a third star and his promotion must still be confirmed by the Senate. In that context, his outspoken plea here for battlefield freedom was considered courageous by fellow officers. If confirmed as a lieutenant general, he is scheduled to assume command of the U.S. 24th Corps early this summer.

Either an imaginative newspaper correspondent or a frustrated GI dubbed Hill 937 "Hamburger Hill." The operation that led to its seizure last Tuesday was conceived by the 24th Corps headquarters and was called Apache Snow. The Corps, in turn, reports to the 3d Marine Amphibious Force, the supreme U.S. military headquarters in South Vietnam's five northernmost provinces.

It is entirely possible that the U.S. commander in Vietnam,

Gen. Creighton Abrams, gave Apache Snow his personal ap-
proval, for it involved major elements of three divisions—the
U.S. 101st Airborne, the 1st South Vietnamese and U.S.
Marines.

According to Zais, the 101st's mission was to enter the
northern Ashau Valley and, in conjunction with the South
Vietnamese, "destroy enemy forces there. I've never received
orders to hold down casualties," Zais said. "If they wanted to
hold down casualties then I'd be told not to fight."

Asked about American casualties in this battle, Zais said, "I
didn't consider them high at all." In terms of the 10-to-1 kill
ratio the battle produced, he remarked that the fight consti-
tuted a "tremendous, gallant victory. We decimated a large
North Vietnamese unit and people are acting as if it were a
catastrophe."

Arrayed against Zais's division were elements of the 9th and
29th North Vietnamese Army independent regiments. The
last time the 101st and the 9th Regiment tangled was on
March 12, near Fire Support Base Veghel, about halfway between Hue and Hill 937.

"I ask you," said Zais, "was it better for me to fight the
9th Regiment on the western edge of the Ashau Valley or on
the western edge of Hue?"

Zais had obviously been briefed on Sen. Kennedy's speech
in the Senate Tuesday. Asked for his reaction, the general said,
"He's performing as a Senator to the best of his ability in
Washington . . . (but) I know for sure he wasn't here" during
the battle.

The battle for Hamburger Hill began on May 10, when a
battalion of the 101st's 3d Brigade was landed by helicopter
approximately half a mile northwest of the summit. Its companies fanned out to the south and west, reaching the Laotian
border little more than a mile away. They encountered no
resistance.

The next day, May 11, all companies wheeled eastward toward Hamburger Hill. According to Lt. Col. Weldon F.
Honeycutt, 38, the battalion commander, Bravo Company
surprised an enemy "trail-watching squad and hosed them
down" with automatic-weapons fire.

All of the enemy were killed; none was taken prisoner. The

best estimate that afternoon was that a North Vietnamese company or less occupied Hamburger Hill. One battalion would be more than a match for it, the allied commanders reasoned.

On May 12, Honeycutt's battalion, the 3d Battalion of the 187th Regiment, ran into heavy rocket-grenade and automatic-weapons fire from enemy soldiers in deep bunkers. The bunkers were superbly designed with interlocking fields of fire and almost no visible silhouettes, according to Col. Joseph B. Conmy Jr., commander of the 3d Brigade.

Honeycutt held back, calling artillery and air strikes on his prospective line of march to the summit. On May 13, he sent two companies against the northwest ridges of the hill. They, too, encountered fierce fire and were ordered to fall back. Throughout that night and the following morning, artillery and tactical fighter-bombers pummeled the summit ridgeline with high explosives and napalm.

On May 14, Honeycutt sent his full battalion against the enemy's position. But the commander of his lead company was wounded and the company's radio silenced. Again Honeycutt ordered a tactical retreat and called for air strikes and artillery.

In the meantime Honeycutt's battalion had been reinforced by three others, two from the 101st Airborne Division and one from the South Vietnamese 1st Division. These took up positions to the northeast, southeast and south of Hamburger Hill, virtually surrounding it.

On May 18, after 36 additional hours of artillery and air bombardment, two of the battalions attacked again. Honeycutt's moved southeast and the 1st Battalion of the 506th Regiment moved north. By 3 p.m., some of Honeycutt's platoons clawed their way to the summit, but a thunderstorm drenched the hill and visibility dropped to zero.

Soldiers carrying ammunition, mortars and water lost their footing in the mud, and Honeycutt ordered a fourth retreat.

Between 9 a.m. and 10 a.m. on May 20, every artillery piece within range of Hill 937 was firing at the ridgeline. The hill had turned a dirty brown as shells stripped the trees of leaves and peeled away underbrush.

At 10 a.m., all four battalions attacked, and by 3 p.m. the hill had fallen.

According to Conmy, the attackers killed 544 North Vietnamese soldiers and captured three more. During the 11-day battle, more than 21,500 artillery rounds landed on and around the hill. Air Force jets dropped more than 1000 tons of bombs and 117 tons of napalm, so there was no way of telling how many of the enemy actually died at the hands of the allied infantry.

Newsmen asked repeatedly why, prior to the last three assaults, the battalions were not pulled back to permit B-52 strikes. As pieced together from Zais, Conmy and Honeycutt, the answer comes in several parts:

First, the army thought until the final assault and the hill's capture that not more than a reinforced battalion of enemy troops was lodged on its summit. By the time the battlefield commanders realized that they faced even a battalion, their companies were set up in good assault position.

Second, to order the three-mile pullback required to bring in B-52s, in the opinion of Zais, would have demoralized men who had fought hard for the already occupied hillside. Such a retreat would have also made it easier for the enemy units to escape back to Laos.

Third, tactical commanders were receiving good artillery and air support. Fighter-bombers, they said, were dropping 1000-pound bombs on the hill with good accuracy. B-52s carry only 750-pound bombs or smaller. As Honeycutt put it later, "I got everything I asked for—the only thing I could have used that I did not get was an ice cream cone."

Zais, Conmy and Honeycutt denied requesting B-52 strikes on the hill.

Conmy was interviewed at Fire Base Berchtesgaden on the opposite side of the Ashau Valley, due east from Hill 937. Asked for his reaction to Kennedy's speech, Conmy said, "He's trying to do his job as a Senator, I'm trying to do mine as a brigade commander . . . I don't want to get into a discourse on that."

Conmy was ceremonial aide to President Johnson for 4½ years, during which he commanded the Old Guard at Ft.

Meyer. During the April, 1968, riots in Washington, D.C., Conmy led the first federal troops into the city.

Honeycutt's battalion, which did most of the fighting and took a majority of the casualties, was airlifted out of the Ashau Valley yesterday and has spent the time since swimming at Eagle Beach, south of Hue.

The Washington Post, May 23, 1969

Black Power in Viet Nam

by Wallace Terry

BEFORE the war went stale and before black aspirations soared at home, the black soldier was satisfied to fight on an equal basis with his white comrade-in-arms in Viet Nam as in no other war in American history. But now there is another war being fought in Viet Nam—between black and white Americans. "The immediate cause for racial problems here," explains Navy Lieut. Owen Heggs, the only black attorney in I Corps, "is black people themselves. White people haven't changed. What has changed is the black population."

When an American force stormed ashore south of Danang this summer, young blacks wore amulets around their necks symbolizing black pride, culture and self-defense. They raised their fists to their brothers as they moved side by side with white Marines against their common Communist enemy. "Ju Ju" and "Mau Mau" groups have organized to protect themselves against white prejudice and intimidation. In remote fire-support bases near the Cambodian border, blacks register their complaints as a group. Tanks fly black flags. At Danang, Black Power Leader Ron Karenga's followers have designed a flag: red for the blood shed by Negroes in Viet Nam and at home, black for the face of black culture, and green for youth and new ideas. Crossed spears and a shield at the center signify "violence if necessary," and a surrounding wreath "peace if possible" between blacks and whites.

White pinups have been replaced by black ones. One all-black hootch in Danang sports more than 500 such photographs. "I don't want any stringy-haired beast* broad on my wall. Black is beauty." In a Saigon "soul kitchen," blacks greet

---

*"Beast," a term that originated with the Black Panthers, is rapidly replacing "Chuck" as the black soldier's standard epithet for the white man.

each other over spareribs and chittlins with 57 varieties of Black Power handshakes that may end with giving the receiver "knowledge" by tapping him on the head or vowing to die for him by crossing the chest, Roman legion style.

Many of today's young black soldiers are yesterday's rioters, expecting increased racial conflict in Viet Nam and at home when they return. Elaborate training in guerrilla warfare has not been lost upon them, and many officers, black and white, believe that Viet Nam may prove a training ground for the black urban commando of the future. As in America, the pantheon of black heroes has changed. The N.A.A.C.P.'s Roy Wilkins is a "uniform tango"—military phonetics for U.T., or Uncle Tom—and Massachusetts Senator Edward Brooke is an "Oreo" cookie—black on the outside, white on the inside. "The N.A.A.C.P., Urban League and Martin Luther King were good for their time and context," says Marine Corporal Joseph Harris of Los Angeles, "but this is a new time." King and Robert Kennedy, once among the young black soldier's idols, have died violently. Says Wardell Sellers, a rifleman from New York: "They were trying to help the brothers—you can see what that got them." Now many blacks see the case of Edward Kennedy as a plot to remove one more hope. "Just like King and Bobby Kennedy," says Pfc. Carl Horsley, 19. "They gon' try to hang Teddy 'cause he was on the side of the brothers." To most black soldiers, Nixon doesn't even bear discussion. "If he were a brother," says Ronald Washington, a black sailor from Los Angeles, "he'd be the number one Uncle Tom."

In the jungle lies death for a cause that many black soldiers don't understand or dismiss as white man's folly. "Why should I come over here when some of the South Vietnamese live better than my people in 'the world'?" asks a black Marine. "We have enough problems fighting white people back home."

Black racism is strong, but so are provocations by white soldiers. Soon after Martin Luther King was killed, crosses were burned at Danang and Cam Ranh Bay. Confederate flags still fly from barracks and trucks, and are even worn as shoulder patches on the uniforms of helicopter pilots stationed at

Phu Loi. Black soldiers at Con Thien grimace when whites call a Negro sergeant "brown boy" and a mongrel puppy "soul man." Base club operators who accept country and western but not soul music from their entertainers have paid a toll. Clubs were wrecked in Chu Lai, Qui Nhon and a dozen other places in the past twelve months. Two white sailors were recently tried for inciting a riot at the Tun My Club.

Violence has reached such a peak in the Danang area that lights have been installed on the streets of Cap Tien Sha to curb roving bands of white and black sailors who were attacking each other at night. At Dong Tam in the Delta and Dien Hoa north of Saigon, bands of black soldiers still waylay whites. A white officer in Danang was critically injured when a black Marine rolled a grenade under his headquarters. At the officer's side was a black sergeant with a reputation for not tolerating Afro haircuts and Black Power salutes.

Unrest among the blacks often turns on real discrimination or the failure of the military to accept the trappings of black soldiers bent on "doing their thing." Promotions, awards and coveted rear-area assignments are too often slow in coming the black soldiers' way, however well they fight or however high their proportion of casualties. Some 13% of battle deaths are black, while Negroes make up 11.1% of the American population and 9.2% of the military.

For all that, the black soldier in the bush still helps his white comrade and wants his help as well. At Phuoc Vinh, a black 1st Cavalry trooper recently dragged a wounded white from a rocketed hootch when no other black or white dared to venture in. A black Navy medic who had been in Viet Nam only two weeks fell on a grenade near Danang to save a white Marine and lost his own life. When black Lieut. Archie Bigger was three times wounded capturing enemy artillery pieces, eleven whites held him aloft above the suffocating napalm smoke until a rescue chopper arrived. On Hamburger Hill, a white paratrooper tried vainly to breathe life into a fallen black medic.

Yet the violence at home and in "the Nam" leaves the black man with radically divided loyalties. Thus, says Lieut. Colonel Frank Peterson, the senior black officer in the Marine Corps, "the average black who has been here and goes back to the

States is bordering somewhere on the psychotic as a result of having grown up a black man in America—having been given this black pride and then going back to find that nothing has changed.''

Personal interviews conducted with 400 black enlisted men from Con Thien to the Delta provide a measure, though by no means a scientific sample, of the attitudes of black men in Viet Nam.

▶ 45% said they would use arms to gain their rights when they return to "the world." A few boasted that they are smuggling automatic weapons back to the States.

▶ 60% agreed that black people should not fight in Viet Nam because they have problems back home. Only 23% replied that blacks should fight in Viet Nam the same as whites.

▶ 64% believed that racial troubles in Viet Nam are getting worse. Only 6% thought that racial relations were improving. "Just like civilian life," one black Marine said, "the white doesn't want to see the black get ahead."

▶ 56% said that they use the Black Power salute. Only 1% condemned its use.

▶ 60% said they wear their hair Afro style. 17% wanted to, but said their commanders refused to let them. One Marine reported that he had been reduced in rank for refusing to get his hair cut closer.

▶ 55% preferred to eat their meals with blacks, 52% preferred to live in all-black barracks.

▶ 41% said they would join a riot when they returned to the U.S. However, a nearly equal number, 40%, said they would not.

▶ 28% said they believed that weapons would help the black cause back home, while 35% thought that they would be harmful to it. "What the beast has done for me which is going to screw him," said a black Marine, "is teach me how to use a weapon. The Marines taught me how to improve."

Combat inevitably sharpens both emotions and rhetoric. It is an incendiary combination to be young, black, armed, 10,000 miles from home and in persistent danger of death in "a white man's war." When the men return to "the world," their perspective may shift, and doubtless many black soldiers will become so busy with their own affairs that their militance will fade somewhat. Even in Viet Nam, 53% of the black men interviewed said that they would not join a militant group such as the Black Panthers when they return to the U.S. Says Major Wardell Smith: "A lot of what they say they will do, they just won't. They won't be so closely knit, and they will have girls, wives, families and jobs to worry over." Nevertheless, a significant number seems likely to continue to believe that the U.S. owes the black soldier a debt both for his service in Viet Nam and his suffering at home. These men are a new generation of black soldiers. Unlike the veterans of a year or two ago, they are immersed in black awareness and racial pride. It is only this fall and winter that they will be returning to civilian life in the cities. If they find that nothing has changed there, then they could constitute a formidable force in the streets of America, schooled and tempered in all the violent arts as no generation of blacks has ever been.

Time, September 19, 1969

Casualties of War

by Daniel Lang

LIKE their predecessors in all wars, American veterans of the Vietnamese campaign who are coming home to civilian life have their heads filled with memories that may last the rest of their days, for, no matter how far from the front a man may have spent his time as a soldier, he will remember it as a special time, when, fleetingly, his daily existence appeared to approach the heroic. Former Private First Class Sven Eriksson—as I shall call him, since to use his actual name might add to the danger he may be in—has also come back with his memories, but he has no idea what the future will do to them. Honorably discharged in April, 1968, this new war veteran, who is twenty-four and comes from a small farming community in northwestern Minnesota, isn't even sure that he would care to hold on to his recollections, if it were possible for him to control his memory. Naturally, Eriksson's experiences in Vietnam were varied, and many of them impressed themselves vividly on his mind. Just seeing an Asian country, for instance, was an adventure, Eriksson says, its landscape so different from the frozen plains of his corner of Minnesota; he had never before splashed through paddy fields, he told me, or stood blinking in the sudden sunlessness of lush, entangled jungle, or wandered uncertainly through imprisoning fields of towering elephant grass. An infantryman, Eriksson saw a fair amount of action, so, if he chose, he could reminisce about strong points he helped take and fire fights in which he was pinned down, and one ambush, in particular, in which half his unit was wounded. But, as Eriksson unhesitatingly acknowledges, the fact is that when he thinks of his tour of duty in Vietnam it is always a single image that comes to his mind. The image is that of a Vietnamese peasant girl, two or three years younger than he was, whom he met, so to speak, on November 18, 1966, in a remote hamlet in the Central Highlands, a few miles west of the South China Sea. Eriksson and four other enlisted men were then on a reconnaissance patrol in the vicinity of the girl's home. Eriksson considers himself hazy about the girl's looks. He does remember, though, that she had a prominent gold tooth, and that her eyes, which were dark brown, could be particularly expressive. He also remembers that she was wearing dusty earrings made of bluish glass; he noticed the trinkets because they gave off a dull glint one bright afternoon when he was assigned to stand guard over her. Like most rural women, she was dressed in loose-fitting black pajamas. They obscured her figure, Eriksson says, but he has the impression that she was slender and slight, and was perhaps five feet two or three inches tall. For as long as she lived, Eriksson did not know her name. He learned it, eventually, when the girl's sister identified her at court-martial proceedings—proceedings that Eriksson himself instigated and in which he served as the government's chief witness. The girl's name—her actual name—was Phan Thi Mao. Eriksson never exchanged a word with her; neither spoke the other's language. He knew Mao for slightly more than twenty-four hours. They were her last. The four soldiers with whom he was on patrol raped and killed her, abandoning her body in mountain brush. One of the soldiers stabbed her three times, and when defense counsel challenged Eriksson at the court-martial proceedings to describe the sound that the stabbings made, he testified, "Well, I've shot deer and I've gutted deer. It was just like when you stick a deer with a knife—sort of a thud—or something like this, sir."

Eriksson talked with me at his home in (I shall say) Minneapolis, where, since leaving the Army, he has been earning his living as a cabinetmaker at a local department store. He and his wife, Kirsten, have a neat, modest apartment of three rooms, its walls decorated with paintings by Mrs. Eriksson, a Sunday artist, who was present while we talked; she is twenty-three and is employed as a receptionist in an insurance office. The two have no children. They were married four years ago, shortly after Eriksson was drafted. They had known each other

since childhood, their fathers having been neighboring farmers, who both had difficulty making ends meet. This was true
of many farmers in the area, Mrs. Eriksson told me, adding
that most of its inhabitants were of Scandinavian background.
"It's a part of the country where we pride ourselves on not
being demonstrative," she said. A small, pretty blonde with
an alert, intelligent manner, she offered me coffee and cake
the instant I set foot in the apartment. She was pleased, she
told me, that I had asked to hear about the episode involving
Mao. She herself had thus far been the only person with
whom her husband had discussed it since returning from Vietnam, and even with her he had not gone into much detail.
"It'll do him good to talk to someone else," she said, her
tone lively and teasing. Sitting by himself on a sofa, Eriksson
smiled somewhat ruefully, a deep dimple forming in one
cheek. He is a short man of fair complexion, blond and
blue-eyed, and he is not voluble. In the hours we spent together, there were intervals that may have lasted as long as a
minute when he sat silent, a brooding expression on his face,
before resuming his account. At the start, he spoke laconically,
but gradually his natural reticence thawed out, and there were
times—generally after one of his silences—when he produced
such a burst of talk that it seemed to cost him an effort to
bring it to a halt.

At the very outset, Eriksson told me that the last thing he
wished to do was discuss Mao's murder in any legalistic vein.
It was certainly possible to do so, as I knew for myself from
having read the court record of the trials he had brought
about: seven bulky volumes in the offices of the Clerk of
Courts, U.S. Army Judiciary, in Falls Church, Virginia, which
included Eriksson's testimony against the members of the patrol; their convictions and appeals; interminable correspondence between judges and opposing counsel; and depositions
concerning the character of individual defendants. Having appeared as a witness before four tribunals in Vietnam, Eriksson
told me, he had had his fill of the judicial process—of the
dogged grillings by lawyers and the repeated strictures of
judges insisting on precise answers to questions that were often vague. As far as he was concerned, Eriksson said, it had
all seemed a morass of cleverness, but then, he conceded, he

may well have entered the military courtroom in the Central Highlands, where the four trials were held, with unwarranted expectations, for it had been his hope that the trials would help him unravel his reactions to Mao's fate. Unreasonably, he granted, he had come into court with the idea that he and the others on hand would wonder aloud, in a kind of corporate searching, how it was possible for the young girl to meet the end she did. He had imagined that he would be able to ask how it was that he alone of the patrol had come to act as he had. He had wanted to tell of the way the episode with Mao had affected him, and why it was that he had felt impelled to report the others—four young Americans like him, each dependent on the others for survival deep in enemy territory. He had wanted to unburden himself of his doubts about whether he had done all he might have done for Mao in her travail—doubts that gnaw at him to this day. With me, he said, he trusted he would be able to go into these matters freely, but he had early discovered that in a court of law they were of little interest.

Launching into his unlegalistic account, Eriksson told me that it seemed clear to him in retrospect that he should have been prepared for Mao's death. It had been preceded by any number of similar occurrences. In one form or another, he said, they took place almost daily, but he was slow, or reluctant, to perceive that they were as much a part of the war as shells and targets were. Eriksson now believes he should have foreseen that sooner or later one of these incidents was bound to strike him with special, climactic force. He had scarcely landed in Vietnam, in October, 1966, when he was made aware of these occurrences, each of them apparently impulsive and unrelated to military strategy. He told me that beatings were common—random, routine kicks and cuffings that he saw G.I.s administer to the Vietnamese. Occasionally, official orders were used for justifying gratuitous acts of violence. Thus, early in his tour of duty, Eriksson recalled, G.I.s in his unit were empowered to shoot any Vietnamese violating a 7 P.M. curfew, but in practice it was largely a matter of individual discretion whether a soldier chose to fire at a stray Vietnamese hurrying home a few minutes late to his hootch—the American term for the mud-and-bamboo huts in which most natives lived. Similarly, it was permissible to shoot at any Vietnamese seen running, but, as Eriksson put it, "the line between walking and running could be very thin." The day after the one on which his squad was ambushed and half its members were wounded, several enemy prisoners were taken, and, in retaliation, two were summarily killed, "to serve as an example." A corporal who was still enraged over the ambush tried to strangle another of the prisoners; he had knotted a poncho, nooselike, around the captive's neck and was tightening it when a merciful lieutenant commanded him to desist.

Needless to say, Eriksson continued, the kind of behavior he was describing was by no means limited to Americans. The enemy did the same thing, and much of the evidence for this came from the Vietnamese themselves. They constantly reported rapes and kidnappings by the Vietcong; in fact, the Vietcong committed these crimes so indiscriminately that the victims were sometimes their own sympathizers. On one occasion that he knew of, Eriksson said, American troops, attracted by the familiar odor of decomposing bodies, had found a pit piled high with Vietnamese men and women who had been machine-gunned by the V.C. But, as Eriksson pointed out, he could not give me many such first-hand accounts of V.C. depredations. Necessarily, he said, he was in a position to speak only of the behavior of American soldiers, since they were the people he fought and lived with.

Ending the first of his brooding silences, Eriksson said, "From one day to the next, you could see for yourself changes coming over guys on our side—decent fellows, who wouldn't dream of calling an Oriental a 'gook' or a 'slopehead' back home. But they were halfway around the world now, in a strange country, where they couldn't tell who was their friend and who wasn't. Day after day, out on patrol, we'd come to a narrow dirt path leading through some shabby village, and the elders would welcome us and the children come running with smiles on their faces, waiting for the candy we'd give them. But at the other end of the path, just as we were leaving the village behind, the enemy would open up on us, and there was bitterness among us that the villagers hadn't given us warning. All that many of us could think at such times was that we were fools to be ready to die for people who defecated in public, whose food was dirtier than anything in our garbage cans back home. Thinking like that—well, as I say, it could change some fellows. It could keep them from believing that life was so valuable—anyone's life, I mean, even their own. I'm not saying that every fellow who roughed up a civilian liked himself for it—not that he'd admit in so many words that he didn't. But you could tell. Out of the blue, without being asked, he'd start defending what he'd done maybe hours ago by saying that, after all, it was no worse than what Charlie was doing. I heard that argument over and over again, and I could never buy it. It was like claiming that just because a drunken driver hit your friend, you had a right to get in your car and aim it at some pedestrian. Of course, I was a foot soldier all this time. I was operating in a forward area and probably seeing the war at its ugliest. In daylight it was search-and-destroy missions, and at night it was setting ambushes for the enemy. I discovered it's not difficult to kill a human being—in combat it's as instinctive as ducking bullets. You never knew whose turn it was to die, and that isn't how it was in rear areas. The farther back you got, the closer you approached the way people lived in civilian life."

On November 16, 1966, the commanding officer of Eriksson's platoon, a Negro lieutenant, Harold Reilly (whose name, like every soldier's name in this account, has been changed), assigned him as one of five enlisted men who were to make up a reconnaissance patrol, its mission to comb a sector of the Central Highlands for signs of Vietcong activity. Testifying later in court, Lieutenant Reilly characterized the mission as "extremely dangerous," and said that to carry it out he had picked members of the best of the four squads in the platoon. Special care had been taken with the operation, he stated, since it had been conceived by the battalion command, a higher echelon than the company command, to which Reilly was ordinarily responsible. Explaining his choice of the patrol, Reilly testified, "These people, I felt, knew what they were doing, and a second reason was because the company commanding officer asked for good people." On the following afternoon, November 17th, the members of the newly formed patrol met in a corner of the platoon's headquarters area, near the village of My Tho, where, relaxed as they stood or sat on the ground, they listened to a briefing from their leader, who was seated on a low stool. He was Sergeant Tony Meserve, a slim, black-haired man of medium height who was twenty years old and came from a town in upstate New York, near the Canadian border. According to Eriksson, Meserve, who was assertive and confident, was both the patrol's youngest soldier and its most experienced one, being a volunteer of three years' standing who had fought in Vietnam for a year and had been decorated several times; he was due to go back to the United States in a month. The group's second-in-command was Ralph Clark, a corporal who came from a town near Philadelphia. He was twenty-two, a stringbean in physique, and blond, with eyes that were a pale, cold blue. Again according to Eriksson, Clark was given to quick movements and to seemingly abrupt decisions that reflected Meserve's thinking in an exaggerated form. The two other G.I.s in the combat team were a year younger than Eriksson, who was then twenty-two. They were cousins named Diaz—Rafael, known as Rafe, whose home was near Amarillo, Texas, and Manuel, who came from a town some distance north of Santa Fe, New Mexico. Eriksson remembers Rafe as a tall, swarthy, round-faced man with a disposition that was naturally sunny and amiable. As for Manuel, who was fair-skinned and stockier than his cousin, his manner was on the jumpy side. Like Clark, he was given to quick movements, but his behavior had nothing to do with embellishing Meserve's thinking. Manuel showed no initiative in that regard, Eriksson told me, his attitude toward authority being simple and automatic: he heeded it devoutly. In mild contrast, Rafe was capable of questioning authority, Eriksson said, but he generally wound up by going along with whoever seemed to be the leader—"just to keep from making trouble."

Returning to the patrol's briefing, Eriksson told me that Meserve was all business as he plunged into his talk. Echoing the instructions that a battalion officer had given him earlier, the Sergeant informed the four men of the duties that each was expected to carry out, of the chain of command in the field, and of radio-communication arrangements with the platoon command, and then, consulting the grid coördinates of a map he was holding, the Sergeant described a precise westerly route that the patrol was to follow. It was to take them, ultimately, to Hill 192—a height, in the Bong Son valley, that overlooked a ravine laced with a cave complex, which was suspected of serving as a Vietcong hideout. But caves weren't all that the five men would be looking for. Bunkers, trenches, trails that were not marked on maps, caches of enemy equipment—these, too, were to be reconnaissance objectives. Naturally, Meserve said, if the men could spot any Vietcong in the open, that would be all to the good, but the patrol's orders—and these had been spelled out in no uncertain terms by the battalion command—were to avoid any shooting matches with the enemy except in self-defense; as a so-called pony patrol, he said, they were out to collect "early-warning" information concerning enemy intentions.

The men were to be gone five days, the Sergeant revealed —a fairly long time for a reconnaissance mission—and on hearing this Eriksson experienced a sense of exhilaration, just as he had at the prospect of far shorter patrols in which he had taken part. He felt that way, he explained, because out in the field, in territory that could turn hostile at any moment, the men in the patrol would be very much on their own, and this would be so even if a high-ranking officer were in charge. "You could never tell how a man was going to behave under pressure," Eriksson said. "He might turn out to be dumb or brave or to have a wonderful stock of jokes. Sure, there were always advance plans to do this or that, but they didn't often stand up in the field. The only thing you could count on out there was that the unexpected would happen." Usually, Eriksson said, it took time for the unexpected to develop, but now—more than half a day before the patrol was to leave platoon headquarters—it happened with stunning abruptness. It happened when the Sergeant, having delivered his instructions, concluded the briefing by telling the assembled men that they were going to have a good time on the mission, because he was going to see to it that they found themselves a girl and took her along "for the morale of the squad." For five days, the Sergeant said, they would avail themselves of her body, finally disposing of it, to keep the girl from ever accusing

them of abduction and rape—both listed as capital crimes in
the Uniform Code of Military Justice. Rafe later testified at
his court-martial, "Meserve stated we would leave an hour
ahead of time so that we would have time to find a woman
to take with us on the mission. Meserve stated that we would
get the woman for the purpose of boom boom, or sexual
intercourse, and at the end of five days we would kill her."
And in Manuel's testimony one finds: "After we were briefed
by Meserve, he said that we would take a girl with us on
patrol, or that we would try to take a girl with us to have
some fun. . . . He said it would be good for the morale of
the squad."

The Sergeant had made his announcement with a straight
face, leaving his men to interpret it as they would. Clark at
once greeted it with enthusiasm. The two Diazes laughed,
either out of embarrassment, Eriksson conjectures, or because
they thought Meserve was joking, in view of his remark about
"the morale of the squad"—an old gag in the platoon.
Eriksson told me that he himself reacted silently but that after
Meserve and the men had broken up to go their separate ways
until morning he sought out his friend Corporal Curly
Rowan, a West Virginian, who had been in Vietnam, and with
the platoon, just as long as Meserve had. Rowan listened with
astonishment as Eriksson apprised him of the Sergeant's plan,
but when Eriksson asked his friend whether he thought
Meserve's statements should be reported to an officer before
the patrol left camp, Rowan immediately shook his head, replying, as the court record shows, "Meserve wouldn't dare
do such a fool thing." This incredulity notwithstanding, the
news of Meserve's briefing left Rowan unhappy. The two men
had arrived in Vietnam at the same time, and he had known
Meserve as a considerate, agreeable man. However, in the last
month or so, Rowan told Eriksson, the Sergeant, apparently
undergoing changes, had exhibited a mean streak toward the
Vietnamese; a couple of weeks before, Rowan said, Meserve
had shot at and wounded one of them, giving as his reason
afterward that he had "felt like it." "The way Curly talked
about him, Meserve sounded as though he had become a kind
of war casualty," Eriksson told me.

At four-thirty the following morning, Meserve diligently

checked his men's gear at the edge of camp, seeing to it that their chow, star clusters, rounds of ammunition, smoke and hand grenades, and other supplies were in order. Once this was done, the patrol filed out of the camp in the faintly humid darkness, the men still uncertain of their leader's intent. Twenty minutes later, they knew what it was. By then, moving unhurriedly in the gray dusk, Meserve's squad had dutifully followed him two thousand metres to the east, which, as Eriksson and the others realized, was a flagrant deviation from the westward route the Sergeant had described so precisely at the briefing. By then, too, the men were approaching the hamlet of Cat Tuong, in the district of Phu My, and Eriksson was cursing himself for having listened to Rowan. In disbelief and confusion, his heart palpitating, Eriksson saw that Meserve was losing no time in carrying out his plan, for, with Clark at his heels, the Sergeant had embarked on a systematic search of the hamlet's hootches. The pair had emerged empty-handed from five or six of the huts when Rafe, ever his amiable, accommodating self, pointed to a white hootch ahead and called out, "There's a pretty girl in there! She has a gold tooth!" Instantly, the Sergeant said, "That's the girl we'll find." Astounded by the enormity of his own suggestion, Rafe looked miserably at Manuel and Eriksson as Meserve and Clark, quickening their steps, made for the white hootch that contained the pretty girl with a gold tooth. While Eriksson, Manuel, and the now wretched Rafe hovered outside, Meserve and Clark entered the hut—Mao's home. They lingered in it longer than they had in the other hootches, but since Eriksson was standing outside the hut he is unable to describe what went on inside. However, Mao's sister, Phan Thi Loc, who was present, has done this at one of the trials. Translating the testimony of Loc, who was two years younger than Mao, an interpreter informed the court, "She said they come in, use flashlight and shone around the house and saw her mother's face and her sister's face and all of them wake up at the same time. It was six in morning and dark." The father was away in Phu My market, the interpreter went on. The mother wept and pleaded, and her daughters, clinging to one another, cowered against the wall. Loc was spared, but Mao was seized by the two soldiers, who bound her hands behind her back with a length of coconut rope. Reporting another of Loc's answers at the trial, the court interpreter stated, "She said her sister have gold tooth, right side in lower jaw."

When Meserve and Clark rejoined their comrades, Eriksson told me, they had the bound Mao well in tow. Clark was holding her elbow, and he pushed her forward when Meserve ordered the patrol to get moving. "Daylight was coming on fast, and he wanted the girl in the light as little as possible," Eriksson told me. "Helicopter crews might spot her." Before the patrol left the hamlet, a swarm of local children materialized, chattering agitatedly in a circle around Mao, and then out of the white hootch came Loc. The two sisters looked at each other. "Their eyes were terrified," Eriksson remembers. Departing from the hamlet with their prize, the soldiers moved west toward the main trail they should have been on. They had gone scarcely twenty metres when a cry of distress halted them. It came from Mao's mother, who was giving chase. Meserve testified at his court-martial, "The mother came out, like they always do, started crying, talking. We just tell them to *dee dee*"—meaning to go away. The mother, Eriksson told me, was waving a scarf and laboriously propelling herself forward. Panting, she finally reached the soldiers, indicating to them that the scarf was Mao's and that she would like her daughter to have it; the woman's cheeks were wet and her manner was imploring. It was an awkward moment, Eriksson said, and Clark terminated it. A smile spreading on his face, he took the scarf and stuffed it into Mao's mouth. In an affidavit that Manuel later signed, he stated, "Clark gagged the girl to keep her from yelling out. It was still dark in the area, and no civilians attempted to stop us." Leaving the mother behind, the patrol resumed its march, prodding Mao to match its stride. The hamlet was barely out of sight when Manuel, perhaps competing with Clark, untied Mao's hands, then slipped his pack from his shoulders and loaded it onto the girl's.

The five men and Mao kept up a steady pace. Meserve saw to that, for a brilliant sun had come up, its glare exposing the bizarre party as clearly as it did the landscape. "We were advancing through nice country," Eriksson told me. "We were on a plateau in the Highlands, and all around us were small mountain ranges, hazy and green. Below was a valley with a winding stream, and along its banks were paddy fields with neat little dikes around them. The country we were moving through was mostly all shades of green, but we also passed barren stretches and, here and there, places that had been browned by napalm. The land was very changeable. It would be open for a while, and then there'd be sections so thick with thorny vines tearing at our clothes that we couldn't see each other, even though we were spaced no farther apart than you and I are, right here in this room." Around eight o'clock, Meserve permitted his squad a half hour's break for chow. Mao was ungagged but was given no food; noticing that she was flushed and coughing slightly, Meserve handed her an aspirin. Only one piece of military action occurred that morning, and it could have been dispensed with. Gazing into the valley below, Rafe thought he spied a Vietnamese in a native type of straw hat standing in the stream. Deciding that he was looking at a V.C., Rafe let fly with a couple of rounds from his M-16 rifle. His target turned out to be the rump of a wallowing water buffalo, the animal raising itself from the shallow stream in clumsy panic and lumbering out of view. Rafe had flouted the order against unnecessary shooting, confirming Eriksson's observation that plans could mean little in the field and that out there any patrol was a unit only in theory. "We were each acting the way we had to," he told me. Meserve said nothing to Rafe; nor did he say anything to any of the others when, as the mission unfolded, they committed similar derelictions. Under cross-examination at his court-martial concerning this disregard of his commanding officer's instructions, the Sergeant stated, "Sir, most of the time everybody agrees with his C.O. Sometimes you have your disagreements, and sometimes you don't voice them, you keep them to yourself."

At ten-thirty, a short distance below the summit of Hill 192, Meserve found what he was looking for—a command post for the day. It was an abandoned hootch, eight feet square and eight feet high, with a window on the east side, a door on the west, and two slits facing north and south; there was a stream a few metres away, giving the patrol a ready source of water.

The hootch contained a table, a low bench built against a wall, and tattered remnants of a straw mat strewn in a dark corner, and the dirt floor was littered with scrap metal, rocks, and cans. The structure was in a state of extreme disrepair, and had a number of large holes in its mud walls. However, it was essentially intact, and Meserve quickly converted it into a weapons depot, dumping ammunition stocks, and also food supplies, on its dirt floor. In addition, the hootch served as a place to hide Mao. Ordering Eriksson and Rafe to clean up the hootch, and leaving Mao in their charge, the Sergeant went off with Clark and Manuel to have a careful look around. In the hootch, Eriksson recalled, Mao, now relieved of Manuel's pack, watched him and Rafe heave out junk for a while, and then, unasked, the girl lent the G.I.s a hand. "She had no idea the kind of place she was helping to prepare," Eriksson said.

Meserve and the others returned an hour later, toward noon, and had a hearty snack, eating it outdoors, near the entrance to the hut. Sprawled on the ground after the meal, Meserve, refreshed, glanced at his fellows and then, with a knowing smile, indicated the partly ruined structure. "It's time for some fun," he said. Clark appeared to be beside himself with anticipation, Eriksson told me, and Manuel and Rafe appeared less so. He himself, he imagines, must have looked glum. "It was the way I felt," he said. "It was impossible for me to have any part of what I knew was about to take place." He suspects that Meserve sensed this, for before anything else happened the Sergeant confronted him, demanding to know whether he would enter the hootch when his turn came. Eriksson shook his head. Incensed, the Sergeant uttered the first of a series of threats. Unless Eriksson went along with the others, Meserve warned, he would run the risk of being reported "a friendly casualty." Clark seconded this vociferously, and both Diazes concentrated puzzled stares on the difficult member of the patrol. Eriksson shook his head again. "I had had enough of watching beatings and stranglings with ponchos," he told me. Rebuffed a second time, Meserve lashed out with an attack on Eriksson's manliness, deriding him as "queer" and "chicken." The attack didn't bother him, Eriksson told me, but it appears from the court record that it did affect Rafe, who testified that he could not have withstood the epithets he heard Meserve heap on Eriksson; it was his fear of such derision, Rafe stated, that caused him to join those who entered the hootch he had helped make tidy. Manuel gave similar testimony. "I was afraid of being ridiculed, sir," he told the prosecutor. Asked why, he answered, "O.K., let's say you are on a patrol. These guys right here are going to start laughing you out. Pretty soon, you're going to be an outcast from the platoon. 'That guy, he's scared of doing this, he's scared of doing that.' Everybody is going to make fun of you. When you go out on a patrol, you ain't going to be as good as you want to be, because these guys ain't helping you do anything. It is going to be yourself. There is going to be four people on that patrol and an individual."

Once Meserve had delivered his estimate of Eriksson's virility, the ill-fated bacchanal got under way. Just before it did, Eriksson moved away from the entrance to the hootch, where he had been standing, and sat down alone on the grassy turf to one side of the structure; periodically, he raised his field glasses to gaze at distant points. Cross-examined at Meserve's trial as to why he had shifted his position, Eriksson testified, "Well, sir, these gentlemen seemed to me—oh, I should say kind of enthused about what was going on. The whole thing made me sick to my stomach. I figured somebody would have to be out there for security, because there were V.C. in the area."

The Sergeant was the first man to enter the hootch, and soon, Eriksson told me, a high, piercing moan of pain and despair came from the girl. It repeated itself in waves, broken only, Eriksson assumed, by Mao's need to summon fresh breath. After several minutes, the moan turned to a steady sobbing, and this did not cease until, after a half hour, Meserve reappeared in the open. He was shirtless; his face wore an expression of swaggering irresistibility. "She was real good—pretty clean," he said. Pointing to the hootch, he signalled to Rafe to be his successor, and Rafe, sparing himself ridicule, walked in. In court, Rafe said that he found Mao naked, lying on the table, her hands bound behind her back. "The girl looked so innocent, so calm," he testified. But Rafe stayed, and again the moan and the sobbing, slightly diminished, rose from the hootch. Outside, according to the court record, Clark was watching his comrade through a hole in the mud façade and letting out whoops of delight that mingled with Mao's cries. His manner became momentarily subdued when Meserve waved him in as the third man, but Clark was his jaunty self again when he returned. "I held a knife to her throat," he told the others. He displayed a hunting knife. It was ten inches long, and its handle was wrapped with tape that bore a pattern of tiny diamonds. The men were familiar with the knife; it had recently been given to Clark by a close friend in the platoon who had been wounded. As Manuel was going into the hootch, Mao's sounds could be heard, weak and conquered. The four soldiers' visitation lasted nearly an hour and a half, and two minutes after it was terminated the men, to conceal themselves from any Vietcong who might be in the vicinity, reëntered the hootch together. Eriksson was now with them, and he saw that Mao had retreated to a corner of the hut, frightened, watchful, her eyes glistening with tears, her presence made known chiefly by a cough that had grown more pronounced since morning. The girl was dressed and her hands had been freed. The men ate, again without feeding her, and reminisced about their communal feat, comparing Mao with other girls they had known, and talking about how long it had been since they had had a woman. After fifteen or twenty minutes, Meserve, as though he were finally bored with the topic, abruptly reminded the unit of its mission; he wanted the men to do some more reconnoitring that afternoon. This time, he said, it would be Clark who would stay behind to guard Mao and the weapons in the hootch.

The day continued eventful. Exploring the mountain further, often making their way through shoulder-high vegetation, Eriksson, Meserve, Manuel, and Rafe pushed on toward the summit. Though the men had to struggle for footing, Eriksson related, they made a point of keeping an eye on the stream that ran near the hootch; it had its source high up on the mountain, flowing down past a number of rice fields. After half an hour, their watch on the stream paid off, producing a more interesting sight than Rafe's water buffalo. Three Vietnamese were spotted walking along the edge of the water, and though they wore no uniforms, Meserve assumed they were

V.C., and he and his men, including Eriksson, opened fire on them. None of the four hit anything, and the Sergeant radioed the platoon command for artillery support, which was quickly granted; the coöperation, Eriksson recalled, pleased Meserve no end, since it implicitly conferred an importance on the skirmish. Deciding to close in on the three Vietnamese, Meserve dispatched Eriksson and Rafe to the hootch to pick up a supply of smoke grenades. Arriving on the run, the two explained their errand to Clark, who heard the news eagerly, then pulled rank on Eriksson and ordered him to take his place in guarding the hootch. As Clark and Rafe left, Eriksson told me, he realized that he was about to exchange one kind of excitement for another—the encounter with the three Vietnamese, that is, for the quieter, more complicated ordeal of being alone with Mao. He was uncertain how he would act with her, he said, even though, oddly, he felt he knew her well; her cries, he said, had thrown him into a turmoil he had never before experienced. As he listened to her, he said, it had even crossed his mind to shoot her assailants, but then, he observed to me, "I'd have had the bodies of four men to justify." Asked in court for his thoughts during the period he had sat on the grassy turf he testified, "Well, sir, I was wishing I wasn't in the situation I was in. I might say I was praying to God that if I ever got out of there alive I'd do everything I could to see that these men would pay for what they did."

Eriksson now lapsed into the longest of his silences with me, and when he spoke again, it was, for him, at great length. "When Mao saw me come into the hootch, she thought I was there to rape her," Eriksson said. "She began to weep, and backed away, cringing. She looked weary and ill, and she seemed to be getting more so by the minute. I had a feeling she had been injured in some way—not that I could tell. She had her black pajamas on. I gave her crackers and beef stew and water. It was her first food since she'd been taken away from her hamlet—it had been still dark then, and here it was the middle of the afternoon. She ate, standing, and it was whimper, then eat, whimper, then eat. She kept looking at me, as though she was trying to guess what my game could be. When she finished eating, she mumbled something in Vietnamese; maybe it was 'Thank you'—I wouldn't know.

And I told her, in English, 'I can't understand you.' I wanted to tell her other things. I wanted to say, 'I apologize to you for what's happened, but don't ever accept my apology or anyone else's for that. Please don't ask me to explain why they did it. I'll never know. You're hurt, I can see, but how are you? I mean, if I let you go, do you think you can make it home?' I wish Mao and I could have talked," Eriksson said, his voice tightening. "She might have helped me know what to do, instead of my having to figure it out alone—it was her life that was at stake. I stepped outside the hootch to be by myself awhile, and out there I could hear the muffled noise of artillery off in the distance. I had no idea where my unit was. I didn't know then that they were four hundred metres away, at the top of Hill 192, or that it would be a whole hour before they returned. It might have influenced my thinking if I'd had that information, but I'm not sure. As a disciplined soldier, I knew I wouldn't abandon the weapons in the hootch to the enemy, but, just the same, I was dizzy with thinking how to save Mao. I thought again of letting her go, but what would I tell Meserve when he got back? That this weak, coughing girl had overpowered me? Besides, she was in no condition to reach home or anywhere else. Then I thought of taking off together with her. We couldn't have gone very far, I realized, but it was going to be dark soon and we might find a hideout somewhere in the brush. After that, we'd have to stay out of sight until the third day of the patrol's mission—that was the day the patrol was supposed to rendezvous with another unit for fresh supplies. I knew the rendezvous spot, and if Mao and I could show up there at the right time, there was no question in my mind but that the fellows in the re-supply squad would help us both. But I couldn't think any of my brainstorms through. I knew I had cut myself off from the rest of my patrol, refusing to go into that hootch, and I had this idea that the fellows were watching the place from the brush, waiting for me to make just one false move with Mao. I had this picture that when we did, they'd fire at us, or, at least, Meserve would have me up on charges of desertion. The guys would back him up, of course. They'd say there had never been a girl with the patrol, and I'd be left looking crazy."

Shifting uneasily on the sofa, Eriksson went on, "When I stepped back into the hootch, I saw that Mao had made up her mind that I wasn't going to harm her. She had stopped whimpering, and there was even a little look of trust in her eyes. There shouldn't have been, because I had decided, outside, that there wasn't a thing in the world I could do for her. It was the hardest decision I've ever had to make, and it couldn't have been the best possible one, or Mao wouldn't be gone today."

In the time that elapsed before the patrol's return, Eriksson said, Mao's condition worsened noticeably. The men found her feverish and coughing, and Clark was all for rescheduling her death hour to that evening. Meserve, however, counselled patience. A good night's rest might do wonders for Mao's health, he pointed out, in which case he, for one, wouldn't mind revisiting her in the morning. Rafe subsequently testified that the Sergeant was in an expansive mood, cheerfully observing to his men that it wasn't every day he could rate artillery support and have himself a woman as well. The patrol and Mao shared the hootch that night, the girl spending it in a corner by herself. The soldiers set up a night watch, each man pulling guard duty outside in the moonlight, alert for any lurking enemy. Mao coughed throughout the night, and at one point, Eriksson recalls, Clark again urged that the girl be finished off forthwith. Eriksson said, "He told Meserve her coughing was going to give away our position, but I didn't think it was Charlie he had on his mind. I thought he wanted to destroy living evidence."

In the morning, everyone got up shortly after six, and it wasn't long before Mao's fate was sealed. "Events happened fast that day," Eriksson said. The first of them, he told me, was that Mao woke up less alluring than when she had gone to bed. Her fever and coughing had increased overnight, he said, and that didn't do her cause any good. Meserve, he noticed, paid scarcely any attention to her. The Sergeant seemed more attracted by the possibility of military action, to judge by the speed with which he had his charges break camp. His last order before they left was to send Eriksson, Rafe, and Manuel to fetch the day's supply of water from the stream.

When they returned, Eriksson told me, they discovered that Clark was no longer alone in advocating Mao's early demise. Meserve was now an ally, he and his second-in-command apparently having arrived at a meeting of minds while the others were filling the patrol's canteens. As Mao stood listening, mute and uncomprehending, Meserve said that she had to be got out of the way; if they ran into action, he pointed out, she would be a hindrance, and even if they didn't, helicopter crews scouting the area might want to know who she was. All that awaited decision, Meserve went on, was the moment and method of the girl's murder, but, whatever was settled on, the Sergeant's thought was to have Eriksson do the job; if Eriksson refused, Meserve said, he would be reported as K.I.A.—killed in action. Manuel later told agents of the Army's Criminal Investigation Division, "Meserve said to Eriksson that inasmuch as he did not do anything to the girl [the day before], Eriksson would have to kill the girl, but Eriksson said that he would not have anything to do with that." Meserve, however, didn't follow through on his threat. To Eriksson's astonishment and deep relief, the Sergeant abruptly shifted his attention to the Diazes, asking first Rafe and then Manuel to carry out the murder. "Both refused," Eriksson said. "They were very definite. It excited me." Impatiently, Clark volunteered his services, but Meserve wouldn't have that, insisting that they collaborate. Clark could knife the girl from the front, the Sergeant said, while he bayoneted her from behind; the body would then be tossed over a cliff from the summit of Hill 192, where the patrol had reconnoitred the previous day. Accordingly, at nine the group struck out for the cliff. The climb took longer than it had the day before, the men's pace slowed by the packs they bore. This morning, Manuel carried his own. Serving as radioman, he was in the vanguard with Meserve and Clark; Mao walked ten metres behind, wearily ascending the rugged terrain, with Rafe as her forward guard and Eriksson bringing up the rear. It took an hour to negotiate the climb, and the group had barely attained the ridge when Rafe, his eyes sweeping the vista below, saw five Vietnamese in peasant dress making their way along a mountain trail toward the paddy fields near the stream. The Vietnamese proved to be V.C., for the moment

they were aware that they had been seen they fired at the
patrol with small arms, then changed their direction and
passed temporarily out of sight. Meserve at once radioed the
platoon command, reaching Lieutenant Reilly, to whom he
suggested that the V.C. be ambushed. Agreeing, the Lieutenant said that he would order another squad, operating at the
base of the mountain, to coördinate its movements with those
of Meserve's patrol, and that he would also dispatch two other
squads to the area. In addition, Meserve learned that he was
again to be the recipient of artillery support; in a short while,
Reilly said, helicopter gunships—aircraft equipped with rocket
artillery and machine guns—would be in the area. "It was
going to be a big outlay, considering the few men we were up
against," Eriksson said. Ordinarily, he conjectured, the promise of such generous support would have cheered Meserve,
but Mao's presence seemed to confuse matters. Glancing at
the girl with distaste, the Sergeant ordered Eriksson and Rafe
to stay with her on the ridge, whereupon he, Clark, and
Manuel began a cautious descent of the mountain, their purpose to stalk the Vietcong. Thirty metres down, they came to
a curiously shaped rock formation composed of two jutting
ledges. Using the upper one as a vantage point, they spied the
small band of V.C. making slow progress toward the refuge
of the cave complex, which was three hundred metres away,
almost at the bottom of the ravine. But the Sergeant did nothing about the escaping V.C., for he was now powerfully distracted from the enemy; in the distance, still inaudible and
looking miniaturized, were four approaching gunships. Acting
fast, he sent Manuel backtracking to the summit to tell
Eriksson and Rafe to report to him with Mao. In ten minutes,
they were all together again; by then, too, the helicopters had
grown larger and their engines were faintly audible. Rafe later
testified, "There were helicopters flying around, and everyone
was getting jumpy about having the girl."

Before Meserve could devise any next step, Clark took hold
of Mao's arm. "Let's kill her and get it over with," he said,
according to the court record.

"All right, go ahead," Meserve said, and he instantly turned
his attention to the enemy, ordering Eriksson to the lower

ledge of rock while he and Manuel returned to the upper one, with Rafe to their rear.

Rafe was the man closest to Clark and Mao—only a few metres away—and because he was, his testimony concerning the events that now took place carried special weight with the court. He stated at the trial, "From where I was, I observed Clark grab the girl by the arm and take her into the bushes nearby . . . I saw that Clark had his hunting knife hidden in one of his hands." It was in the next seconds that deer-gutting sounds issued from the bushes. "I then heard the girl cry out, but not too loud," Rafe continued. "Clark came back to where we were. Meserve asked him if he had finished the girl." Clark had just replied yes when Mao, like a wounded apparition, was seen crawling rapidly downhill and then disappearing into the thick foliage. As Rafe recounted it, "Meserve saw her and said, 'There she goes.' Clark said, 'Why, that bitch, I stabbed her more than twice.' Meserve told us all to shoot her before she could get away. We were all told to look for the girl." All five men shot, but Eriksson aimed his weapon—a grenade launcher, which looks like a shotgun—down into the valley, away from the general direction of Mao. In addition, Rafe flatly said, "Eriksson could not see the girl," despite which, Rafe also testified, "Eriksson stated, 'Oh, no,' like he regretted that he had fired." Rafe himself let go with a burst from his M-16, which, inexplicably, caused his rifle to jam. However, he did call Clark's attention to a bush directly ahead. It was rustling. "I couldn't tell whether it was Charlie or the girl," Rafe testified. Clark, who was several metres in front of Rafe, yelled back to him that it was the girl. "I saw him raise his rifle," Rafe stated, adding that he then started toward Clark. Moving in on the bush, Clark blazed away with his M-16, and at once the rustling foliage grew still. "You want her gold tooth?" Clark called over his shoulder to Rafe, who was then, he testified, a foot away and was staring, aghast, at Mao. "When I got up to the girl, I saw that her head was partially blown away," he testified. "She was dead, I'm sure."

Immediately after the murder, Eriksson told me, the men appeared to assume a self-protective air of disbelief at what had taken place. Straggling uphill, he said, they gravitated toward their leader, who stood, unflustered, near the jutting rock formation, surveying the combat situation. It had built up sharply. The gunships were now unmistakably in the area, their motors sending up a storm of noise as the machines hovered low and their crews searched out the enemy. Now the V.C., flushed from their temporary hideout, continued to beat a desperate retreat, relying on sniper fire to fend off their attackers, who were converging on them from both sides of the stream. Small artillery spotter planes had arrived, heralding the imminent use of ground-artillery support. The court record attests that it was in the midst of this encircling racket that Meserve chose to initiate radio contact with Lieutenant Reilly, the burden of the Sergeant's message being that he wanted to report "one V.C., K.I.A." Under cross-examination at Meserve's court-martial, Reilly, appearing as a defense witness, testified, "Sergeant Meserve called me up and informed me in the middle of the fire fight that a girl was fleeing up the side of the mountain, and I informed him to get the girl. He called me back in a few minutes, or a couple of minutes, and informed me that he could not catch the girl, that he had had to shoot her. . . . I called him back and commended him on the job that he did and reported it, in turn, to the company headquarters."

Meserve fought well that day. With Mao out of the way, he was able to concentrate on the action at hand, managing his patrol, working in concert with the other squads, and helping to guide the diving gunships, whose presence he now welcomed. Among them, Eriksson said, these sizable elements, advancing toward the cave complex, succeeded in killing one V.C. and wounding another. Two escaped, and the fifth man made it to the caves, where he holed up for a last-ditch stand. The man was never captured, Eriksson said, despite the fact that he became the single target of the gunships' rockets and the infantry's bullets and grenades. Moreover, Eriksson told me, the enemy soldier inflicted casualties on the infantrymen deployed around the cave complex, which was some two hundred metres long and had numerous mouths. At the time the fifth V.C. entered the caves, he said, the patrol had long ago left the vicinity of the curiously shaped rock formation, and

had descended so deep into the valley that the men were practically able to touch the thick, rough outer walls of the caves.
Meserve, Clark, and Manuel, together with members of the
other squads, were shooting away at the solitary V.C., who
was behind an aperture that measured perhaps six inches wide
and a couple of inches high. As for himself, Eriksson told me,
Meserve had ordered him to a ledge from which he could
overlook the complex as he trained his grenade launcher on
two cave mouths in particular, either one of which, the Sergeant thought, could afford the entombed V.C. an exit. For
Rafe, the fighting had ended an hour earlier—well before the
patrol reached the cave complex. As the men had raced to
get there, clambering and sliding, Rafe had slipped and fallen
from a ledge, dislocating an elbow and a shoulder. Evacuated
by a medical helicopter, he was flown to a hospital at Qui
Nhon. There, corpsmen deposited him on a bed alongside
that of a battalion officer he knew and liked. At Rafe's
court-martial, it was disclosed that for several days the two
patients in the hospital ward seemingly talked about whatever
came into their heads but that Rafe never mentioned Mao.
Testifying in his own defense, Rafe stated, "I was afraid to tell
[the officer], because I might be the only one who brought
it up. I didn't know Eriksson brought it up. I wanted to find
out first what Meserve and Clark might do."

The fire fight in the ravine lasted several hours, the attackers
finally breaking off after dark. The holed-up V.C. (who escaped the following morning) wounded five Americans, and
Meserve displayed considerable courage in rescuing the most
seriously injured of them, a G.I. whose ammunition pouch,
girding his midriff, had exploded as the result of a hit. "The
poor guy's guts were out," Eriksson said. "It was as though
he had shot himself with two rounds of his own ammo." The
wounded man lay helpless, directly in front of the small opening from which the V.C. was shooting, and Meserve, braving
a fusillade of bullets, crept forward and pulled the man out of
the V.C.'s line of fire. For this action, Meserve was nominated
for a Bronze Star.

Eriksson had no occasion to fire his grenade launcher, and
that was just as well, he told me, since his mind was on Mao—
on the part of the war that, as he put it, "had got to me."

Perched on the mountainside, listening to the gunfire and the helicopters, he found his thoughts returning repeatedly to the fact that Rafe and Manuel had refused to kill the girl. Transitory though their show of character may have been, he said, it encouraged him in reaching a private resolve, for as he kept watch above the cave complex, Eriksson told me, he was suddenly seized with the overwhelming realization that unless he took it upon himself to speak out, the fact of Mao's death would remain a secret. "No one would ever know what had become of her!" he exclaimed. "Who else would tell but myself? All the others in the patrol had raped or killed her. I knew I wouldn't rest until something was done about Mao's murder. It was the least I could do—I had failed her in so many ways. The only thing that could stop me was if I became a friendly casualty."

Looking back, Eriksson thinks that the small band of V.C. may have rescued him from Meserve. The outmanned, outgunned enemy put up so strong a fight, he said, that the Sergeant, Clark, and Manuel ran out of ammunition, and the patrol had to interrupt its five-day mission long enough to go back for fresh supplies of bullets and grenades. This meant going to platoon headquarters—the home of four squads, and only a few minutes' walk from company headquarters, where there were officers who outranked Reilly, the platoon's lone lieutenant. Arriving at the platoon area, Eriksson told me, he felt as though he had reached the promised land; the anxiety in which he had lived the past two days yielded to what he described as an almost tangible sense of safety. Since the patrol would be going out again, Eriksson said, he knew he had to act fast, but that seemed no big deal. In the first place, he wanted to act fast, and, besides, he had no doubt that once he did act, there would be fast results. Once he was inside the camp perimeter, he assumed, it would be a simple matter to bring Meserve and the others to judgment. All he need do, he believed, was report that they had committed rape and murder, and the military authorities would investigate with the same alacrity that civilian authorities are expected to show in such situations. During his first hour back in camp, he recalls, no one could have persuaded him otherwise.

In any event, Eriksson went on, he lost little time in seeking out his friend Curly Rowan to tell him the story of Mao. He had barely begun it, however, when Clark, seeing the two in conversation, descended on them, demanding to know what they were talking about. "We made up something to get him to go away," Eriksson told me. "He had a wild manner—he couldn't stand still, and his eyes looked every which way. All of us in the patrol had long ago stopped pretending nothing horrible had happened. All of us had come back scared and upset, but Clark, I thought, showed it the most." Once Clark had left them, Eriksson continued with his story, feeling an immense relief when he had finished telling it. "At last, someone outside the patrol knew of Mao," he said. He had no illusion, though, that Rowan himself could do much about what he had just learned, but at that, Eriksson said, his friend did what he could, immediately relaying news of the murder to the sergeant of his own squad. In turn, the sergeant passed the news on to Lieutenant Reilly, who sent for Eriksson.

Arriving at the austere hootch that Reilly used as a command post, Eriksson told me, he imagined that the Lieutenant, if only conversationally, would express dismay over the murder. No such dismay was expressed. Instead, to Eriksson's astonishment, Reilly chose that moment to offer a reminiscence. Calmly and easily, he told Eriksson about an experience that he had undergone three years earlier, when he drove his wife, also a Negro, to an Alabama hospital to have their first child. She was in an advanced stage of labor, the Lieutenant related, but she had been refused admittance to the hospital, on racial grounds, and she had eventually had her baby on the floor of its reception room. Wild with rage, Reilly had tried to wreck the place, whereupon hospital orderlies summoned the police, and the new father was arrested and jailed. In his cell, Reilly went on, he had made plans to shoot various officials at the hospital, but when he was finally released he gave up the idea of vengeance. "By the time I got out of jail," he told Eriksson, "I was saying to myself, 'What's happened is the way things are, so why try to buck the system?' And take it from me, Eriksson, it's even more hopeless to try to buck it in the middle of a war—there's more of a system then than ever. Better relax about that Vietnamese girl,

Eriksson. The kind of thing that happened to her—what else can you expect in a combat zone?" His recollection out of the way, the Lieutenant informed Eriksson that the patrol, having replenished its ammunition stocks, would be leaving camp at any moment to resume its five-day mission. Eriksson wouldn't be going along, though; the Lieutenant had assigned another G.I. in his stead. Acknowledging the danger in which Eriksson had placed himself, the Lieutenant told him, "If I sent you out with that patrol, you'd never make it back."

As the court transcript shows, Reilly didn't let matters rest there. The atrocity that Eriksson had reported was too big for that. Reilly was aware that if it came to public knowledge it would tarnish the image of the officers commanding the platoon, the company, the battalion, perhaps even the regiment; the officers might be made to appear incapable of controlling the conduct of the men in their commands. Reilly's immediate superior, Captain Otto Vorst, as was later brought out in court, was out in the field at the time on "a tactical problem." He was not due back until November 22nd, the day Meserve's patrol was scheduled to conclude its mission. The Captain—a "lifer," or career Army man—had left instructions that he was to be sent urgent messages only, but shortly after Eriksson took leave of Reilly, the Lieutenant, confident that the murder merited his superior's attention, radioed word of it to Vorst. As it happened, the Captain heard about it from a second source as well—from Eriksson himself. Out on a search-and-destroy mission the morning after leaving Meserve's command, Eriksson told me, he encountered a small group of American military men reconnoitring the vicinity of the cave complex. Vorst was in the group, and Eriksson, detaching himself from his unit, went up to the Captain and told him about Mao. "Leave it to me. I'll handle everything," Vorst said. A moment later, the two groups went off in different directions.

On November 22nd, Meserve, Clark, and Manuel, weary from their five-day stint (Rafe was still hospitalized), had scarcely dropped into their foxholes back in the platoon area when they were ordered to appear at Captain Vorst's command post—a hootch somewhat larger than Reilly's but equally bare. They found the company commander, who had himself only just returned, waiting impatiently to confront them with Eriksson's report. In his affidavit for Army investigators, Manuel gave what is probably a comprehensive account of the confrontation that took place in the Captain's quarters. "This was about 1400 hours," Manuel stated. "Captain Vorst handed Meserve a piece of paper with three words printed on it—Kidnapping, Rape, Murder. We all looked at the paper, and he asked us what this was all about. At first, we all denied any knowledge about it. He first asked Sergeant Meserve, 'Do you know anything about this?' To which Meserve said, 'We don't know what you're talking about.' He then directed the same question to all of us, 'Do you people know what you've done up there?' Captain Vorst then asked me did I know what would or could happen to me. I said, 'Probably the firing squad, sir.' He then said something to the effect, 'I could send you all back to the States for courts-martial,' or he could court-martial us out here and still have a firing squad. Then the C.O. said something to the effect, 'You people acted like animals up there and do not deserve to live.' He said he would have never learned about this but one man had the balls to tell [the officers] about it. Then he proceeded to tell us that if anything happened to Eriksson, our souls would belong to him." Possibly to help them retain their souls, Vorst announced that he was breaking up the patrol. Rafe, hospitalized at Qui Nhon, was already accounted for; Clark was to take a relatively rear-area post, at battalion headquarters; Meserve was to be shifted to another platoon. Only Manuel would remain anywhere near Eriksson; he was being reassigned to a different squad in the same platoon.

Eriksson saw Vorst shortly after the three soldiers left the company command post. At the time, Eriksson told me, he had no idea that the Captain had chewed them out. If he had known this, he thinks, he might have realized then, as he did later, that the Captain was in a bind; that is, he was torn between the dictates of his conscience, which condemned the crime, and concern for his Army career, which, Eriksson later discovered, the battalion commander—who outranked Vorst, and who was also a "lifer"—was in the habit of admonishing the Captain to bear in mind. Initially, however, Eriksson discerned no signs of inner conflict in Vorst. As far as he could make out, the company C.O. held a clear, uncomplicated view of the crime, and that view was that its repercussions should be kept to a minimum. "That word 'handle'!" Eriksson said reminiscently. "Three times I saw the C.O. about Mao, and three times he used it—'I'll handle everything,' 'I'll handle everything,' 'I'll handle everything.' Maybe he did, but not in a way that had anything to do with anyone's making amends." At his meeting with Vorst the day of the Captain's return, he went on, he noticed that—like Reilly, who was present—the company commander failed to deplore the murder, and instead stressed its potentialities as a scandal. Reilly later testified in court, "Captain Vorst stated to Eriksson, 'I guess you realize how serious this incident is, and that it could cause an international issue.' Eriksson stated that's why he reported the incident—because he knew it was serious. Eriksson also stated that the entire taking of the girl, the rape, and killing of the girl were preplanned . . . that he [had] thought [at first] the men were just joking about really completing the acts." Throughout, Eriksson told me, he had the distinct impression that his position and Vorst's were at variance. Despite Vorst's generally negative tone, Eriksson said, he believed that the company commander would eventually take steps to bring Meserve and the others to justice. At one point, Eriksson recalled, the Captain warned him that if the incident did result in courts-martial, he might face rough going on the witness stand. When Eriksson replied that he was prepared to take his chances on that, Vorst asked whether Eriksson might not care to transfer out of the company—or, for that matter, out of the infantry altogether. Eriksson replied that he wouldn't mind a change—not that it would deter him from pressing charges. He wouldn't mind being a door gunner aboard a helicopter, he told Vorst, citing as his qualifications for such a post that he had been trained as a machine gunner and that he was fond of flying. Vorst filled out transfer forms, and Eriksson signed them. As he was leaving, he told me, the Captain called out reassuringly, "I'll handle everything!"

When Eriksson heard nothing from Vorst for four days, he sought an interview, which was granted. It was the final talk between the two men. They were alone this time, Eriksson told me, and when Eriksson inquired what progress there had been in the murder case, the Captain seemed not to hear but posed a series of questions. He was merely asking, Vorst said, but had Eriksson really thought through what he was doing in pushing his charges? Had he taken into account the amount of suffering that Americans had already undergone in behalf of the Vietnamese? Had he stopped to think of the consequences to himself of accusing four fellow-G.I.s—thereby adding to that suffering? Besides, what if the four were court-martialled and found guilty? Did Eriksson know that military judges and jurors were notoriously lenient in their sentencing? Unlike their civilian counterparts, Vorst said, the law officers (the term by which military judges were known) and members of the court (as jurors were known) had a sympathetic understanding of the pressures a combat man faced in risking his life daily; military jurists didn't expect foot soldiers to be on their best behavior in a war zone. Here, the C.O. went on, it was mild sentences that were the order of the day, and, what was more, they became even milder when they were up for review; safe and professionally idealistic back home, he said, the legal experts of military appellate bodies invariably looked with suspicion upon the administration of justice in war zones. Thus, Vorst concluded, coming to the last of his questions, if the men in the patrol were actually convicted, Eriksson could anticipate their being freed in short order, and when that happened Eriksson himself might not feel so free—for was it really inconceivable that one or more of the ex-convicts would seek revenge? And wasn't it just possible that the victim might not necessarily be Eriksson himself but, rather, his new bride? Eriksson stated in court, "Captain Vorst said that the men would get off with hardly any or no sentence at all, then myself and my family would really have something to worry about."

In the weeks immediately following Mao's death, Eriksson's home continued to be the platoon area, and his routine consisted of patrols—search-and-destroy by day, ambush by night. These were always demanding and hazardous, yet they could not distract him from the intense feeling of frustration that now beset him. After his last talk with Vorst, he told me, that

frustration was always with him—eating at him, keeping him
remote from his fellow-G.I.s, costing him sleep. Lying awake
nights, listening to Asian birdsong and the squealing of mon-
keys in the jungle nearby, he said, he found himself constantly
mulling over the phenomenon of military discipline—the
chain-of-command system. As in all armies, he believed, it per-
vaded every facet of military life, embracing officers and
enlisted men, volunteers and draftees, and, for that matter,
men with college degrees, like Vorst and Reilly, and men with
meagre educations, like Meserve and him. He was at his wit's
end for a way to circumvent the system, Eriksson told me,
because he was convinced that it was this system that lay at
the heart of his difficulties. He saw now how wrong he had
been in thinking that a report of rape and murder would
evoke instant action, as in civilian life. In the Army, he had
discovered, that kind of action depended entirely on the discretion of one's superior—unless it was possible to figure out
some way of bypassing him. It was maddening, Eriksson said,
to realize that military discipline threatened to make Mao its
victim again, just as it had on Hill 192, when all that certified
Meserve's orders was his rank as sergeant. "They scare that
discipline into you in basic training," Eriksson told me. "It's
obey the man over you, follow the chain of command, or into
the stockade you go." Something that added to his feeling of
frustration in those trying weeks was that he could not find
it within himself to single out Vorst as the arch-villain, from
whom all evil flowed. Eriksson said to me, "It only looked as
though he was the one out to do everything in, but the C.O.,
I knew, had someone over him, and *his* superior had a superior. That was the thing about the chain of command—you
couldn't tell who was to blame for what. It had nothing to
do with a man's being responsible for his own behavior. Just
as long as he stayed in line, just as long as he kept the set-up
going, he could do whatever he wanted."

Perhaps the most jarring of all the discoveries he made during this unhappy period, Eriksson told me, was that his fellow-
G.I.s took a dim view of his efforts in behalf of Mao. To be
sure, there were a few individuals, like Rowan, who shared his
outlook, but the great majority saw things the way their officers did. Time and again, at chow or during a break out in

the field, someone would tell him (as Vorst had told him) that it was pointless to throw good lives after bad by having Meserve and the others up on charges, since (as Reilly had said) violence was the language of war, and, naturally, it could not always be controlled. Continually, Eriksson recalls, he heard the familiar argument that the V.C. also kidnapped, raped, murdered. "Hey, Sven, how do you know that girl wasn't a V.C.?" an Oklahoma rifleman asked one night as he and Eriksson were settling down to sleep in their foxholes. Each day, Eriksson said, he felt as though he were at war with war, a troublemaker out to undermine some careful, desperate code of survival. When he first got back from Hill 192, he said, he had imagined that it might have been his peculiar misfortune to draw a patrol made up of psychopaths, but now each time a new G.I. rallied to the patrol's defense that idea seemed less tenable. "Listening to the fellows, I had the feeling there might be any number of Meserves and Clarks around me," he said. "It was like living in an overorganized jungle—full of names, ranks, and serial numbers but not much else."

Dispiriting though he found the atmosphere in the platoon area, Eriksson went on, there were traces of conscience there. It took him a while to realize this, he said, and, curiously, he became persuaded of its prevalence as a result of thinking about Vorst's negative "handling." As he went over it in his mind for the hundredth time, he began to suspect the existence of cracks in the Captain's seemingly certain, untroubled façade. If there weren't any, Eriksson asked himself, why hadn't the C.O. simply told him to bug off from the word go? Why had he bothered to discuss Mao with him three times? Nor could the concern that the C.O. had shown for Eriksson's safety be explained unless those cracks existed. Why else had Vorst seen fit to reshuffle the patrol, leaving only Manuel within shooting distance, so to speak? And then there was Vorst's invitation to Eriksson to transfer out of the company. It seemed like a deal, but why was it, Eriksson asked himself, that a captain should feel constrained to bargain with a lowly enlisted man? Why make all this effort to dismiss the death of an unknown peasant girl if it weren't that the C.O. recognized that there were forces of conscience that might have to be contended with? Thinking along these lines,

Eriksson said, he arrived at a kind of strategy in regard to Mao. "Whatever I could do about her depended on finding someone with both the rank and the conscience to help me," he told me. "Otherwise, I'd stay boxed in by the chain of command."

On the last day of November, Eriksson was in a patrol that was chasing two or three V.C. down a trail between two hedgerows when the patrol was suddenly fired upon from one side. "Hit it!" the patrol leader shouted, and his men hit the ground, the bullets from the still invisible attackers raising columns of dust all around the flattened G.I.s. In a matter of seconds, the shooting broke off, and another patrol, consisting of another squad in Reilly's platoon, emerged from behind the hedgerow. Eriksson's patrol leader delivered a tongue-lashing to his counterpart, who apologized. It had all been a mistake, he said—he and his men had been dozing when the sound of running feet aroused them, and instinctively they had assumed it was the enemy. He had stopped the shooting as soon as he heard an American voice yell "Hit it!" Still fuming as the two patrols stood facing each other awkwardly, Eriksson's sergeant declared that in all the time he had spent in Vietnam he had never before experienced any such "mistake." As Eriksson waited for his sergeant to cool off, he idly scanned the men in the other squad, his eyes stopping abruptly when they met the expressionless gaze of a familiar face. "It was Manuel," Eriksson told me. "We just looked at each other, without saying hello. Seeing him made me think at once of two questions I would have liked to ask him or his sergeant. Just who, I wanted to ask, was the man in Manuel's patrol who started the shooting? And who was the man who fired the last shot? I couldn't even guess at the answers—not without knowing what kind of jam Manuel thought he was in."

Whatever the answers, Captain Vorst saw to it that Eriksson left his command early the following morning, sending the enlisted man seventy miles away to Camp Radcliff, the 1st Cavalry (Airmobile) Division base, near the small city of An Khe. Eriksson was to remain there until his reassignment as a door gunner came through, Vorst having sent his transfer papers on for official approval by the helicopter command. In the meantime, Eriksson's orders placed him on temporary duty with a carpentry detail that was constructing additional housing for the base, whose population came to twenty thousand. Eriksson was delighted with this duty, since he had had a passion for carpentry all his life. However, he welcomed the shift to Radcliff for a more important reason. He was confident, he told me, that he stood a better chance of finding help there than in the confines of the platoon area. Far from where the daily, relentless fighting was going on, he pointed out, Radcliff was probably less disposed to take gratuitous violence in stride; besides, there were infinitely more people at the division base, and that gave him a better chance of finding the effective ally he needed. "From the minute I got to Radcliff, I was on the lookout for him, whoever he might turn out to be," Eriksson said.

His break came after just a week—by accident, which was the only way it could come. Late one afternoon, when he and about twenty other G.I.s putting up a barracks were about to knock off for the day, he saw a fellow-carpenter, Boyd Greenacre, detach himself from the crew to have a talk with a passing chaplain, a blond, long-nosed six-footer wearing a captain's bars; the two men, Eriksson could see, were on cordial terms. Eriksson had never laid eyes on the chaplain before. For that matter, he said, he knew almost nothing about Greenacre—only that he was a cowboy from Arizona, a wiry type, who put in a good day's work as a carpenter and didn't have much to say. Now, watching the chaplain depart, Eriksson decided that Greenacre was very much worth cultivating. Eriksson was determined to meet the Arizonan's friend, he told me, for he had a feeling that the long-nosed chaplain was the man who would help him bring Mao's case to light. Seeing him and Greenacre chatting together, Eriksson went on, had made him realize that the only chance he had of escaping the chain of command was through a chaplain. Actually, Eriksson told me, he had once asked Reilly for permission to discuss Mao's murder with a chaplain, but the Lieutenant had discouraged the idea. Perhaps, Eriksson said, he remembered that idea just then because of his recent stewing about Vorst and conscience. At any rate, he felt that he was on the right track, since chaplains were professionally concerned with conscience. "Conscience was one thing that crossed over from civilian life to war," he said. "It was as much a part of us as our legs and arms."

His spirits on the upswing, Eriksson set about trying to meet the chaplain. "It had to be him, and no other chaplain," he recalled, smiling. "And it had to be Boyd Greenacre who would introduce me. That was how my hunch went, and I didn't dare change it in any way." Eriksson moved cautiously. He didn't see how he could just walk up to Greenacre and state his business. Greenacre might react disapprovingly, as the fellows in the platoon had—or, for all Eriksson knew, Greenacre might turn out to be Meserve's best friend. As a result, Eriksson spent the next two days surreptitiously doing a kind of security check on Greenacre's character. "I needed more of an impression of Boyd than I had," Eriksson said. "What if he refused to arrange an introduction for me? I had to know whether he could at least be trusted to keep quiet about what I was up to." As indirectly and offhandedly as he could, Eriksson sounded out various members of the work detail about Greenacre—none of whom, he remarked, he knew any better than he knew the Arizonan. He remembers that he talked with one of them while they were both shaving, and that in shooting the breeze with another he led the conversation around to Greenacre when the man mentioned that Arizona was where he dreamed of spending his first postwar vacation. Before long, Eriksson told me, his sleuthing established that Greenacre was well thought of, and one evening, after the carpenters had finished eating, he invited Greenacre to take a walk with him. Even though the two were alone, Eriksson remained cautious, revealing nothing about Mao's murder. He did, however, speak of her abduction and rape, and that, it turned out, was quite enough to make Greenacre propose that he and Eriksson walk over to the chaplain's quarters immediately. On the way, Greenacre told Eriksson that the chaplain, Captain Gerald Kirk, came from Ogden, Utah; he was a Mormon, Eriksson learned, and so was Greenacre.

Mrs. Eriksson, who was once more plying her husband and me with coffee and cake, put in, "Sven and I are Lutherans. In our part of Minnesota, just about everyone is."

It was ten at night when Eriksson sat down to talk with

Kirk, and he found he was able to speak more freely than he had even to Curly Rowan. Eriksson remembers having a deep feeling of ease and calm, as though he were at long last ceasing to be a fugitive from injustice. Greenacre was present throughout the talk, at Eriksson's insistence. "Boyd had been a big help," he told me. "I hadn't let out anything to him about the murder, but as long as I was with Chaplain Kirk, I thought he was entitled to hear everything." The gesture impressed him, the chaplain has since told me. "With Greenacre there, it meant that Sven was waiving his right to my silence," he said. Impressed though he may have been, he heard Eriksson out with some skepticism, for before Kirk entered the Mormon priesthood he had spent ten years as a policeman on the Salt Lake City force. "I listened to Sven's story with a cop's ear," the chaplain said. "I wanted to be very sure that he himself hadn't taken part in the rape. Coming to me, the way he did, he might have been trying to save his neck by turning state's evidence, so to speak." Kirk therefore interrupted Eriksson frequently, challenging him to tie together details that at first seemed contradictory. Gradually, though, the cop's ear gave way to the chaplain's. "I decided I was hearing an individual who wished he could have saved that girl but hadn't been able to," Kirk told me. "I can assure you he wasn't being paranoid in thinking he might be shot in the back for seeing me. In war—at least, the war we were in—it was nothing unusual to hear shots that were unexplained, to find a body that might or might not have been shot in combat. Where we were, it was a time and place for thousands of men to play for keeps, and that certainly included Meserve and the others in the patrol, because if they wanted to eliminate Sven as a potential witness they had the M-16s to do it with."

Eriksson finished telling his story to the chaplain toward midnight, whereupon Kirk pressed him closely, as Vorst had done earlier, to determine whether he was certain in his mind that he was prepared to endure not just the cross-examinations but the risks attendant upon appearing as a government witness in open court. When Eriksson reaffirmed that he was, Kirk picked up his phone and called the Criminal Investigation Division office at Camp Radcliff. "I'd never known the Army had any such unit," Eriksson told me. In ten minutes, a pair of agents entered the chaplain's quarters, and Eriksson, as his affidavit shows, told them, in a signal example of understatement, "This [the rape and murder] has been bothering me since it happened, and I went to the chaplain tonight and told him what had happened." The agents interrogated him with a cool, neutral competence. "They weren't shocked, or anything like that," Eriksson recalls. "They were just doing their job." Once the pair had assessed the gravity of the crimes being charged, they moved swiftly. "The next thing I knew, I was in jail," Eriksson told me. "They locked me up in a steel box, in solitary. For protective custody, they said."

From that point on, Eriksson's life in the Army was radically changed. Released from jail in a few hours, he found himself no longer a lone, underground accuser but, instead, a cog in an elaborate law-enforcement machine, whose purpose was to gather evidence, question suspects, and generally determine whether "a case" existed. Once the investigation of Mao's murder had been set in motion, Eriksson was frequently consulted by a variety of experts, among them pathologists, C.I.D. agents, lawyers, and ballistics and firearms specialists. Even his routine duties as a G.I. now had to do with law enforcement, for he was reassigned to the 545th Military Police Company at Camp Radcliff, in which outfit he guarded high-ranking officers, pulled gate duty, made periodic "sweeps" of the base area for signs of infiltrating V.C., and, every day at 4 P.M., climbed into "the drunk wagon," which was an M.P. bus that collected G.I.s who had fallen on hard times in "Sin City," a section of bars and bordellos in An Khe, two miles away. "The C.I.D. wouldn't let me become a door gunner," Eriksson told me. "They put a hold on my transfer forms. They said that door-gunner duty was too dangerous—that if I was going to be any use as a witness I had to stay alive."

Eriksson recognized the abrupt transformation of his military life the morning after his meeting with Kirk. Almost before he was awake, M.P.s escorted him from his cell to the Provost Marshal's office, where he underwent a further interrogation. "Technically, I myself was a suspect," Eriksson told me. "The C.I.D. carefully explained that to me, informing me of my legal rights, one of which was to shut up." When the interrogation was over, he was asked to lead a search party to the spot on Hill 192 where he had claimed that Mao's body could be found. Accompanied by a squad of armed enlisted men, as a precaution against an enemy ambush, the search party set out early the following morning, December 9th, flying from An Khe to an airstrip near Captain Vorst's company headquarters. In charge of the group were a colonel, a major, and, after they reached the airstrip, Captain Vorst himself, who maintained silence toward Eriksson. Among its members were C.I.D. agents, photographers, a firearms expert, and a ballistics man. The group walked from the airstrip to Hill 192. It was a six-hour trek, over difficult terrain, and when the men finally stood just below the summit, several of them, who were unaccustomed to tramping so long, were near exhaustion. Eriksson himself stood scanning the landscape intently, looking for the curiously shaped rock formation where the stabbed girl had been shot. Eriksson had considered the jutting and twisted rock a highly unusual one, but now, refamiliarizing himself with his surroundings, he saw, to his surprise, that it had a practically identical twin close by. It had to be on one of the two rocks that the girl lay, Eriksson knew, and to spare the others in the party unnecessary exertion he screened out the nearer rock by himself, doggedly plunging through formidable brush to reach it. Mao wasn't there, and Eriksson, rejoining the waiting group, pointed to the other rock. "That's where she is," he said, with certainty. After the others fell in behind him, he walked silently to the second rock, seventy-five metres away. In due course, they came upon Mao, her remains a rigid crescent settled grotesquely in a half nest of soil and rocks and matted foliage. She had lain moldering there for three weeks and her body was badly decayed. As the others clustered around it, Eriksson withdrew to the fringes of the circle, made uncomfortable by everyone's purposeful curiosity. "It was another case of people doing their job," he told me. "They hadn't ever heard Mao's voice or seen her carrying Manuel's pack."

Going about their tasks with unrelieved efficiency, the men staked out an area thirty feet square in which to conduct their operations, soon gathering a harvest of clues, among them lead fragments of spent bullets, for the ballistics and firearms men, and parts of Mao's remains, for the pathologists. The corpse itself was placed in an Army "casualty bag"—a rubberized olive-drab shroud, originally designed for fallen soldiers. There was to be an autopsy at the United States Army mortuary in Saigon, by a Japanese anthropologist, Professor Tadao Furue, of Tokyo University, and Colonel Pierre A. Finck, commanding officer of the 9th Medical Laboratory. (Dr. Finck, a well-known Army pathologist, was one of the team of three physicians that performed the autopsy on the late President Kennedy.) Throughout, Eriksson recalls, dozens of pictures were taken, for possible use as trial exhibits, the flashes of the photographers' bulbs pale in the afternoon sun. Additional pictures were taken a week later, when Eriksson led a second pilgrimage to Hill 192. The search party was a smaller one this time, Eriksson said, its assignment to make certain that nothing of any conceivable courtroom value still lay hidden in the area around Mao's body; eventually, a C.I.D. agent, poking through leaves with a bayonet, found teeth, finger bones, and yet more bullet fragments, all of which he deposited in a plastic bag.

The evidence gained as a result of the two field trips played an important part in the judicial proceedings, Eriksson told me. For example, the ballistics and firearms specialists, working together, were able to analyze the lead bullet fragments as having come from an M-16 rifle and to offer it as their judgment in court that Mao had been shot at close range—a judgment that afforded a presumably objective basis for incriminating Clark, at least, as one of her assassins. Professor Furue and Colonel Finck also appeared as witnesses, to offer information based on clinical studies they had made of Mao's skeletal parts in Saigon. The experts' findings established conclusively that Mao had been stabbed three times, in the rib cage and the neck, and that her skull presented a "crushed" appearance, "showing the shattering effects of two high-velocity-missile wounds." Classifying her "racial stock" as Mongoloid, Professor Furue placed Mao's age at between eighteen and twenty and her height at five feet four and a half inches—somewhat greater than Eriksson had estimated it to be in talking with me. A veteran of thirty-five thousand autopsies, Professor Furue told the court, "Compared with other female Mongoloids, Mao's remains were well developed, a well-balanced body build."

Meserve, Clark, and the two Diazes were taken into custody the day after the first search party made its visit to Hill 192. Arrested by military policemen at scattered points, the four soldiers passed through Vorst's area in the late afternoon and saw the Captain briefly. His farewell to them was succinct. Recalling it for investigators later on, Manuel stated, "He told us he had attempted to keep the incident quiet but that now he couldn't give us any further advice or help." The M.P.s took the enlisted men to the Provost Marshal's office at An Khe, where they were given an initial interrogation before being remanded to the stockade at Long Binh. It didn't take many further interrogations to convince the law-enforcement officers that they had "a case," for Rafe and Manuel readily signed affidavits whose substance supported Eriksson's account of "the incident on Hill 192"—the name by which Mao's murder became known among the military. (Asked by a C.I.D. man, "Who raped or had sexual intercourse with the girl?," Manuel replied, "Sergeant Meserve, Clark, R. Diaz, and myself. Eriksson did not have sexual intercourse or harm her in any way.") Meserve and Clark denied any wrongdoing, and the leader of the misbegotten patrol insisted that his motives had been misconstrued. He had only been fooling, he testified, when he talked of having "fun" on the reconnaissance mission. As he recalled his briefing, he had told the men, "It'd be nice if we could pick up five women for the five days up there and have an orgy," and then, he said, "everybody had made comments and laughed." As for going to Mao's hamlet, the Sergeant said that he had led the patrol there to look for V.C., and that he had captured the girl because she had behaved suspiciously inside her hootch. When Meserve ended his testimony, the prosecutor inquired how many times and to whom he had "told the story you just told on the witness stand."

"Numerous times, sir," the Sergeant replied. "Mostly to my lawyer."

*

The four courts-martial took place in the winter of 1967, within a period of about ten days in the middle of March. The trials were held in a courthouse at Camp Radcliff, a frame structure measuring thirty feet by thirty and roofed with tin. The weather had turned hot and dry, Eriksson remembers, and the interior of the courtroom throbbed with the whirr of electric fans. Outside, a diesel generator, the base camp's source of electricity, made a constant racket, causing the law officers frequently to request witnesses to raise their voices. The participants in the cases, including lawyers, witnesses, law officers, and members of the court, lived in tents near the courthouse, and often at night the vicious thump of artillery shells, enemy-bound, from the edges of the division base disturbed the quiet of the legal encampment.

Throughout each trial, Eriksson said, the exponents of military law strove diligently to apply judicial rules largely borrowed from civilian law, as though they were seeking to re-create a semblance of civilian life. Eriksson found it impressive that these procedures should be so punctiliously observed within easy artillery range of the enemy—which, he added, was not to say that he was unaware of various shortcomings. Uninitiated though he was in the ways of jurisprudence, Eriksson said, he found it odd that defense lawyers could freely engage him in conversation during court recesses, questioning him on subjects that he was later asked about under oath when the court session was resumed. And, in fact, Eriksson told me, a C.I.D. man attending the sessions assured him that this was highly improper. "But then I don't know how much the C.I.D. fellows knew about law," Eriksson said. "One of them, I know, goofed on his interrogation of Manuel—he forgot to read off one of Manuel's rights before he started asking questions." In addition, Eriksson told me, he would have appreciated it if the prosecutor—whom he looked upon as his lawyer—had tutored him slightly in how to conduct himself in court; despite his status as the Army's chief witness, Eriksson said, he took the stand practically cold. However, he acknowledged that the prosecutor did warn him, as Vorst and Kirk had previously, of the possible consequences to him and his wife of his testifying for the government. "He said for me to think that over again very carefully," Eriksson recalled. "He sounded genuinely concerned." Something else the prosecutor did was to advise him to see a psychiatrist before the trials started. The prosecutor, it appeared, counted it a safe bet that the defense attorneys would attempt to portray Eriksson as some kind of repressed nut for having failed to join in the festivities on Hill 192. To counter any such strategy, the prosecutor wanted to have on hand a statement attesting to his chief witness's mental stability. Thus, a couple of weeks before the first court-martial opened, Eriksson found himself sitting in a cubbyhole office at Camp Radcliff face to face with a stocky medical captain with an extremely close crew cut who wanted to know whether the young infantryman loved his mother and whether he heard from his wife. Recalling the interview, Eriksson said, "I'd answer a question, then he'd wait and I'd have to wait along with him, then he'd ask another question, real fast, and in I'd come with my next answer. His questions didn't take long—maybe twenty minutes—and when they were over he wrote down on a piece of paper, 'Has no speech defects, steady manner.'" Offering an evaluation of his own, Eriksson added, "He seemed like a nice guy. When he stopped asking me questions, he started talking about Meserve and the others, sort of thinking aloud what it was that came over fellows in wartime. He sounded as though the war would have to come to an end before his work could make much sense."

For Eriksson, the trials were totally unlike anything he had anticipated. He had thought of them uneasily, imagining that the act of testifying might force him to relive the macabre episode on Hill 192. No such thing happened. From his point of view, as he had indicated at the beginning of our talk, the legal consideration of the crime was a field day of fencing and distortion, of quibbling and traps. No matter how close the questioning, and no matter how detailed the testimony he gave, or heard, it all seemed related to Mao's murder in only a surface sense. "The lawyers were playing a game," he said. "To listen to them, and to the testimony that the guys in the patrol gave, Mao was probably living happily in her hamlet." As early as the opening day of Rafe's trial, which was the first one held, he realized that it was idle to consider whether the G.I.s' punishment would, or could, fit the crime. Through-

out, he told me, the single belief that sustained him was that
in serving as the defendants' principal accuser he was carrying
out the resolve he had made as he trained his grenade launcher
on the cave complex; namely, to let the world know of Mao's
fate.

Enacting the role of chief government witness was not an
edifying experience, Eriksson went on. Just as the prosecutor
had foreseen, the defense attorneys did try to make Eriksson
look odd, but that was among the milder of their insinuations.
By the time he concluded his last appearance on the stand, he
had been accused of lying, of cowardice, and even of Mao's
murder. One of the defense lawyers hammered away at the
point that Eriksson had killed the girl when, in obeying the
Sergeant's command to shoot her, he fired his grenade
launcher. But the assertion was a hard one to prove, for Rafe
was on hand to testify that Eriksson was so situated in that
feverish moment that Mao wasn't even in his line of vision.
Besides, as the defense could not dispute, the jacket containing the explosive charge of a grenade launcher is made not of
lead but of copper, and the search parties' experts had found
only the lead of numerous bullets from an M-16 rifle littering
the immediate vicinity of Mao's body.

In all four trials, the court records show, defense lawyers
made a studied effort to depict Eriksson as less than lion-
hearted, presumably on the theory that proving him to be
craven would automatically exonerate their clients. "Are you
afraid of Sergeant Meserve?" Eriksson was asked at one point,
and he replied, "That's affirmative, sir. . . . I am not afraid
of him if he has no weapons." Eriksson answered, "That is
negative, sir," when a defense counsel, taking up the pre-Hill
192 patrol in which half of Eriksson's squad had been
wounded, inquired, "Isn't it true, Eriksson, that you allowed
the squad to walk into the ambush area without warning, because you were hiding in the bushes?"

Undeterred by Eriksson's denial, the lawyer persevered with
his line of questioning.

Q: How did you react to this particular ambush, Eriksson?
Did you fire your weapon?

A: I was in the rear of the column, and didn't have a chance.

Q: Were you afraid?

A: No, sir.

Q: You were not afraid?

A: No, sir.

Q: Isn't it true you were so afraid you could hardly move?

A: No, sir.

Q: You think your fear was apparent to anyone else?

A: No, sir.

Another defense attorney repeatedly taxed Eriksson with having "fabricated" his charges against Meserve and the others in order to escape further assignments to hazardous infantry missions. When Eriksson was able to state that he had put in for door gunner aboard helicopters, which could hardly be considered safe duty, the lawyer persisted in reminding him that "you testified you wanted to get out of the platoon."

Eriksson agreed. "I wanted to get out of the platoon," he stated. "I wanted to get out of the whole company, because I could not see staying in a company that would do anything such as here. I realize that we are over here fighting a war, but to go out and kill an innocent person has nothing to do with the war."

Accused of shrewdness in seeking to evade infantry duty, Eriksson found himself also accused of a lack of shrewdness in failing to let Mao escape when he was alone with her in the hootch. He was asked, "Couldn't you have thought up a story [for Meserve] to the effect that you heard some noises or heard some V.C. and went out to check, and she got away from you, right out of the hootch?"

"No, sir," Eriksson replied.

"You traded the girl's life for your well-being," he was told.

At times, Eriksson displayed a certain poise on the stand. Asked whether Meserve might not have been searching the hootches of Mao's hamlet for the strictly military purpose of finding "strange faces," he answered, "I wouldn't say this, sir. They were all strange faces." Asked whether Mao's continued presence on Hill 192 might not ultimately have "endangered the lives of the members of the patrol," Eriksson said, "Sir, this girl wasn't supposed to be on this patrol."

Before Eriksson was through, even his possession of a sense of humor became an issue. This arose when a defense witness, a sergeant in the platoon, said that Eriksson had none. "He didn't laugh and joke as much as the other guys did; he was much quieter," the sergeant said.

Cross-examining, the prosecutor asked, "When you say he didn't have a sense of humor, you mean he wasn't a jokester, running around making or seeing the funny side of everything?"

A: Yes, sir.

Q: Did he endeavor to actively join in with the free-time activity of the rest of the people, or did he have to be coaxed . . . or did he just refuse at all times?

A: Oh, no, sir, it was not that he was disliked in any way. It was just that he was less than average as far as being one of the guys, should we say? He was just more serious-minded.

Mao's sister, Phan Thi Loc, appeared as a prosecution witness, her very presence irrefutable evidence that Mao was not in fact living happily in her hamlet. Through an interpreter, Loc related that after the patrol finished with their hamlet, she and her mother had searched desperately for Mao. Accompanied by troops of the South Vietnamese government, the two women had eventually come to the hootch on Hill 192, where they had found Mao's brassiere, flecked with blood; the troops had burned down the hootch. Loc's mother was now missing. The Vietcong, Loc said, had abducted her, accusing her of having led South Vietnamese forces to a V.C. munitions cache on Hill 192. Loc and her father had moved from their native hamlet; they now lived in a village several miles from there.

Though Eriksson testified at greater length than anyone else, most of the witnesses who appeared in the close, noisy courtroom spoke in support of the defendants, extolling their gallantry, their sense of duty, and their other soldierly virtues. With few exceptions, these witnesses had fought alongside the defendants, and it was a powerful camaraderie they shared, forged, as it was, in combat, where they had all saved each other's lives more than once. Recurrently, the court records show, witnesses found it deplorable that the defendants should have to fight for their survival in a prisoner's dock when they might be far better employed doing that on the battlefield; in their every utterance these witnesses reflected the view that losing soldiers of Meserve's calibre could result only in gaining a stronger enemy.

Perhaps because Meserve had been the leader of the four accused, he came in for particularly heavy praise. In a sample encomium, Lieutenant Reilly declared that the Sergeant's "character and reputation are the best I have seen, and [he is] one of the best combat soldiers I have known." Reilly also called him "a fine soldier," and went on to say, "He never failed to accomplish the mission. I give him 'max' rating as a soldier." In other connections, it was brought out that the Sergeant had not waited to be drafted, that he was currently in line for the Bronze Star, and that in the course of his overseas duty he had been awarded five medals, of varying importance, and had a conduct rating of Excellent. It was adduced that even before Meserve left for Vietnam he was regarded as an exemplary soldier, since he had been selected to march in President Johnson's inaugural parade—an honor limited to two hundred men with unblemished records. Inevitably, though, the defense witnesses were unable to confine their remarks to Meserve's service record, for—almost tactlessly, it seemed—the prosecutor would inject the topic of Mao's murder, the implications of which had less to do with the conquest of an enemy than with the requirements of an ordered civilian life. Given this confusion of values, the legalistic consideration of Mao's death sometimes bordered on the incongruous. Thus, defense lawyers raised no objections when the prosecutor asked the defendants and the defense witnesses whether a soldier who was condemned for having committed civilian homicide, such as the killing of Mao, should be kept on as a member of the armed forces—that is, should be permitted to go on committing military homicide. Needless to say, the question was not examined philosophically in the Camp Radcliff courthouse; instead, it was employed narrowly as a government gambit for stumping a witness. If he said no, he would appear to be disowning the defendants, his comrades-in-arms; if he said yes, he would in effect be telling the jury that he regarded the war as a public-works project for criminals. The trial records make it clear that the question left the witnesses uncomfortable, for their responses were reluctant and tortured. Of those who were asked the question, only Captain Vorst, "lifer" though he was, stated that if Meserve was guilty of rape and murder, then he did not care to have the Sergeant in his command.

Vorst's executive officer, by contrast, could not countenance the thought of Meserve's being cashiered. Here is the interchange between the executive officer and the prosecutor:

Q: Do you feel there is a place in the United States Army for murderers?

A: Sir, Sergeant Meserve, he joined the unit in approximately February of last year, and he served under me when I was a rifle-platoon leader, and the reason he is a sergeant today is because we put the duties of squad leader upon him—

Q: I didn't ask you for a long elaboration. I simply asked, do you think a murderer should be retained in the United States Army? Yes or no?

A: Well, no, sir, until they've—not until they serve their sentence. Then, of course, after rehabilitation—I think there's a difference, sir. . . .

Q: You would suggest some minor form of punishment, in other words?

A: Well, in general, sir, [but] in this specific case—

Q: For a murder. I'm talking about a murder. I'm not talking about any specific case.

A: Well, yes, sir, I think if someone has been found guilty of murder, they should be punished, but, knowing Meserve as an individual, I would accept him back in the unit, yes, sir.

As for the defendants themselves, only Rafe showed contrition, the most striking manifestation of which was his decision to testify against Clark. The decision was not easily arrived at, for two days before Clark's trial was to begin, and when Rafe had already been convicted, Clark approached Rafe in the stockade at Long Binh, where both were jailed, and, appealing to Rafe's conscience, told him that if he gave unfriendly testimony against his comrades, "he would have it on his mind the rest of his life." Troubled by this, Rafe sought, and heeded, the counsel of a Catholic chaplain at Camp Radcliff in resolving the dilemma of choosing between his "moral obligation," as Rafe put it to the chaplain, and "loyalty to the patrol." Summoned to the stand by Clark's lawyer, the priest said he had advised Rafe that, as opposed to defending Clark's interest, he had "a greater obligation to his wife and his child and the young woman who, supposedly, I assume, was killed, and to justice and society." The priest also said he was asking a Franciscan brother in Texas to break the news of Rafe's conviction to his wife, "to help her absorb the initial shock."

By contrast, the general demeanor of the other defendants was that of incredulity at being tried; the impression they gave was that they thought only the sheerest, most improbable sort of accident could explain their being haled before a tribunal. Their testimony indicates that they were so inured to the epidemic, occupational violence of war that they found it hard to recognize their judicial plight as a type of retribution. In the case of Manuel (the father of a three-month-old girl), this attitude of mystification became so palpable that the prosecutor finally inquired, "Do you feel you are involved in any way in this rape and murder?" To which Manuel replied "No."

Q: You feel that the government has done you a grave injustice in bringing you here today for trial?

A: No, sir, I've got nothing against the government.

Q: Well, you feel you are not involved in any way?

A: Yes, sir, I feel that way.

Q: You shouldn't be on trial?

A: Well, yes, sir.

Q: As a matter of fact, you have complained [from the stockade] that your promotion is being held up?

A: I wrote my senator. I told him I was being wrongly brought to trial.

Manuel admitted to C.I.D. investigators before the trial started that he had committed rape, but when the subject came up in the courtroom, it appeared to be Manuel's judgment that he had taken part in a reasonable enterprise, and the justification that he gave for doing so was military discipline. Confirming Eriksson's ruminations on this subject, Manuel testified that at a special ten-day camp in Vietnam where G.I.s were trained intensively to cope with combat situations "it had been knocked into our heads, practically, to obey orders and . . . they said if you were fortunate enough to get in a group where you had an old-timer who had been

in Vietnam like six months longer than you had, if you followed what he said, you would live longer." Besides, Manuel
testified, if he had not gone into the hootch he would have
risked becoming an outcast. Asked by the prosecutor why he
thought Eriksson had stayed out of the hootch, Manuel answered, "Eriksson was different. He was brand-new. I'd been
there a month or three weeks longer."

When he went on to imply that Eriksson might be a
"chicken," the prosecutor asked, "How come he stood up to
Meserve? Do you consider yourself braver than Eriksson?"

A: I don't think I'm braver than Eriksson. I'm not going
to say that, sir.

Q: Why did you want other members of the squad to think
you were a rapist?

A: Better to go into the hootch, sir, and keep contentment
in the squad, and keep a better—well, how can I explain
it?—keep the thing running smooth. It makes for an easier
mission and no problems.

Q: You don't believe the military gives a choice between
rules, orders, and conscience?

A: The Army expects you to do it the Army way, and that's
follow orders.

In the end, the four juries sitting at Camp Radcliff found
the defendants guilty of one crime or another. All were dishonorably discharged, reduced in rank to private, and deprived of all pay, with the exception of Rafe, who was to go
on receiving pay but forfeit fifty dollars monthly for eight
years. All four soldiers were sentenced to hard labor at the
United States Army Disciplinary Barracks, Fort Leavenworth,
Kansas. There was little pattern to the verdicts, each of the
juries indulging in its own vagaries. Possibly because of his
coöperative attitude at the trials, Rafe was given the lightest
term—eight years, for the crimes of rape and unpremeditated
murder. Clark, convicted of rape and premeditated murder,
was to serve for life. Manuel received a sentence of fifteen
years, his punishment for rape. To Eriksson, Meserve's was
the most surprising of the verdicts, for the Sergeant was found
innocent of the charge of rape but guilty of unpremeditated
murder, for which he was sentenced to a term of ten years.
When Meserve had been convicted but not yet sentenced, he

was asked by the law officer, "Is there any particular thing that you would like to tell the court?" Standing before the bench, Meserve replied, "Well, sir, I've seen a lot of killing, which it is our duty to do, because it's kill or be killed. Sometimes you hate the enemy so bad. Well, during this Operation Thayer II, which started [last October], we ran into a hootch that was burned down. Some Vietnamese people were bringing children out of . . . the bunker in the hootch. They suffered from smoke inhalation. I had to give one small child mouth-to-mouth respiration and bring her back to life. That just shows you it isn't all combat over here." Meserve's lawyer, pleading for his client immediately after this, spoke of the pressures on "twenty-year-old sergeants . . . leading men on fifty, sixty, seventy patrols," and gave it as his opinion that "this incident did not occur as the normal incident." Making his chief point, Meserve's lawyer told the court, "There's one thing that stands out about this particular offense. . . . It did not occur in the United States. Indeed, there are some that would say it did not even occur in civilization, when you are out on combat operations."

Two weeks after the trials ended, one of the court interpreters, a Vietnamese schoolteacher, with whom Eriksson had made friends, brought word to him that Mao's sister was missing. Eriksson said to me, his voice urgent, as though he had just heard the news, "Charlie kidnapped her, just as he did Mao's mother. So now it's only the father who's left—or is he? Who says we don't get along with Charlie? Between us, we've taken care of that whole family."

Eriksson never did become a door gunner. Since the verdicts would automatically come under review and the government might again need him as a witness, he was kept on in the post of military policeman at the division base. Fortunately, he said, his assignments involved no murder or rape cases. Only minor infractions came his way, but even such a routine chore as driving the drunk wagon down to Sin City could make him conscious of the sense of justice in himself that had been so tumultuously aroused the preceding November. It was a consciousness he could have done without, he remarked, for its effect was to remind him of Mao, and, following the trials, he was in a mood to try to forget her. "I just wanted to feel quiet," he said. He had no impulse to talk about Mao—certainly not with his fellow-policemen. To do so, he believed, might only invite their censure, enforcers of the law though they were. As it turned out, they required no invitation to talk about her—particularly in the summer months, when the torrential monsoon rains drowned all possibility of outdoor routine. In that season, Eriksson told me, when the M.P.s yakked the hours away together in their quarters, one or another of his fellow-cops would periodically recall what Eriksson had chosen to do. Invariably, Eriksson said, he found himself reproved for the deed. "But they weren't as sure about it as the guys in the platoon had been," he said. "One M.P., I remember, told me he could have understood it if I'd gone to bat for a G.I. who was murdered, but how could I do it for a Vietnamese? But he was very tolerant about it. He said it was only human to make mistakes."

Eriksson's attempt to forget Mao proved futile, as he had really known it would. In addition to the occasional remarks he heard in the police barracks, a train of other developments served to remind him of the girl. In the late spring, for instance, he learned that a change of sentence might be in the making for Clark, whose lawyer, it appeared, had asked the jurors who convicted him to approve a petition urging clemency; all but two of them had agreed, and Eriksson was given to understand that this augured an almost certain reduction in sentence. Commenting on this, Eriksson told me, "I realized that nothing definite had happened yet, but I had the feeling it was the first sign that things were going to work out the way Captain Vorst had warned me they would—I mean, that the sentences would get shorter and shorter, maybe even disappear."

Late in July, Eriksson was handed a communication from the commanding officer of his division, the 1st Cavalry (Airmobile). It turned out to be a letter of commendation. Mrs. Eriksson fetched it for me from a bureau drawer, and I read:

1: You are to be commended for the important role you played in seeing that justice was done in the recent court-martial cases involving four soldiers charged with the rape and murder of a young Vietnamese woman. Your prompt reporting of this serious incident to your superiors and subsequent testimony in court were essential elements in the apprehension and trials of the men responsible for this brutal crime.

2: The great pressures you were subject to during those critical months are appreciated. Yours was not an easy task, but you did your duty as an American soldier. You should know that the courage and steadfastness you demonstrated make me proud to have you a member of this division.

> John J. Tolson
> Major General, U.S.A.
> Commanding

Eriksson's tour of duty in Vietnam came to an end on November 28, 1967, a year after the patrol paid its visit to Mao's hamlet. He thought of her as his plane, full of singing soldiers, took off from Cam Ranh Bay and he had his last look at the unhappy land below. "She was the big thing that had happened in the war for me," he told me. His plane was a commercial airliner, the Army having chartered it for a flight to Fort Lewis, Seattle, from which point the men, all of whom were going on leave, would be on their own. Eriksson was bound for Minnesota, for a month at home before his discharge in the spring, but when his plane put down at Seattle he found that he was ten dollars short for the final leg of his journey. Fortunately, he ran into a fellow-Minnesotan at the airport, an artilleryman with whom he had gone off to Asia thirteen months earlier; the artilleryman, also homeward bound, unhesitatingly lent Eriksson the ten dollars. When the two men were aloft and sitting side by side, the artilleryman suddenly glanced at Eriksson with fresh interest and said, "Say, weren't you the guy who turned in that patrol? That was a bum rap." Smiling, Eriksson remarked to me, "We were thirty thousand feet up by then, or he might have asked for his money back."

In Minnesota, Eriksson returned to the small apartment in Minneapolis where we were sitting, his wife having maintained it while he was gone. During his month's leave, he was always with her and with relatives and friends and, in a way, Eriksson said, with Mao. Mao seemed to figure constantly in his thoughts, he said, which were concerned mostly with how he would earn his livelihood after he left the Army, the following

April. The ideas that came to him, he said, had less to do with jobs than they had to do with life, and he attributed this to the incident on Hill 192. Sounding as though he felt he would be years mining its lessons, he told me, "I decided that whatever jobs I'd get, they weren't going to be as important to me as the way I lived. That had to have some purpose. If it didn't, then coming back from that patrol meant nothing."

Recalling her husband's arrival, Mrs. Eriksson said that when she went out to the airport to meet him, she could tell at once that there was a stronger kindness in him than when he had left. "The girl was very much with us when Sven came home that day, and maybe she always will be," Mrs. Eriksson said. "We'd had to support each other in a new way after she was killed. I made sure I wrote to him every day, and in each letter I put a packet of Kool-Aid, so that at least his water would be tasty. He was upset and frustrated—it was in all his letters. He had no one to talk to over there. Of course, I never bring up the girl now, because I know how much she's still on his mind, but Sven brings her up, and usually when I don't expect it." Eriksson and his wife spent Christmas of 1967 with members of their families in the small farm town up north that they both came from, and while they were there, an uncle of Eriksson's asked him about Mao. Eriksson was fond of his uncle, Mrs. Eriksson said, but, reluctantly, he answered, "I'm afraid I don't want to talk about her."

When Eriksson's leave was over, he finished out his two-year hitch at Fort Carson, Colorado, where many of the men were either completing their service, like him, or departing for war. Eriksson continued as an M.P., his duties generally less onerous than they had been in Vietnam, and his existence certainly more relaxed, since, as he observed to me, he was waking up every morning not only in his own country but in the presence of the Rockies. Besides, Eriksson said, none of the M.P.s at Fort Carson asked him about Mao—very likely, he assumed, because they didn't connect him with her. He made one particular friend at Fort Carson, a Marine captain who had seen eighteen months of combat in Vietnam and was also about to become a civilian. Perhaps as an earnest of his friendship, Eriksson told the Marine about Mao one afternoon, and the captain was shocked to hear what had happened to her. "His reaction interested me," Eriksson said. "There had been times when I'd thought that if I had been in Vietnam longer than just a month when the incident took place I might have felt differently about it—had the same attitude, that is, as most of the fellows. But here was this Marine, who had put in much more combat service than Meserve or Clark or anyone else I'd met, and he felt exactly as I did about the crime."

Eriksson now fell into one of his silences, and I imagined he was contemplating the mystery of human character. When he spoke, however, it was about his friendship with the Marine. He told me that their bond was religion and that the interest each of them took in it had been heightened by their experiences in the war. No doubt, Eriksson said, the close brushes that he and his friend had been through had something to do with this, but in his own case he had been deeply impressed while he was overseas by what he called an upside-down mentality, which he believed explained the general unconcern there about incidents like the one he had taken part in. He said, "We all figured we might be dead in the next minute, so what difference did it make what we did? But the longer I was over there, the more I became convinced that it was the other way around that counted—that *because* we might not be around much longer, we had to take extra care how we behaved. Anyway, that's what made me believe I was interested in religion. Another man might have called it something else, but the idea was simply that we had to answer for what we did. We had to answer to something, to someone—maybe just to ourselves."

Before Eriksson saw the last of Fort Carson, he again acted as a witness for the government. That occurred in February, 1968, when Manuel was granted a retrial on the ground that although his C.I.D. interrogators had apprised him of various rights he had, among them the right to remain silent and to have a lawyer, the interrogators had neglected to mention that he was entitled to have an "appointed" lawyer, meaning one whose services would be free of charge. In fact, it would have been difficult to find any other kind in Vietnam, since the Army was dispensing such benefits all over the place. And, in practice, neither Manuel nor any of the other defendants (nor

Eriksson, for that matter) paid a cent for legal services. However, a board of review in Washington, made up of three
senior officers, had noticed the C.I.D.'s oversight, and it had
resulted in a second chance for Manuel. ("He got a break.
Another board might have found differently," a colonel in the
Judge Advocate General's office told me.) As a result,
Eriksson left Colorado for Fort Leavenworth, where Manuel,
serving his time in the Disciplinary Barracks, was to be retried.
Eriksson told me that he felt weary at the mere prospect of
reappearing as a witness a year after the Radcliff trials. He felt
even wearier on arriving in Kansas, when he learned that there
was little point to his presence. Because of the C.I.D.'s slipup,
it appeared, practically all the pretrial information obtained by
the investigators could be successfully challenged in court by
the defense—which meant that Manuel's confession of guilt
would be inadmissible as evidence, and without that the government's case was as good as emasculated. Even the prosecutor predicted defeat, Eriksson told me, and during a short
break Eriksson heard the judge remark to the court reporter
that the trial was a waste of the taxpayers' money. Eriksson
himself helped Manuel's case by testifying briefly as a defense
witness, corroborating the fact that Manuel had refused to
obey Meserve's order to kill Mao. (Eriksson had done the
same for Rafe at his trial in Vietnam.) The *pro-forma* proceedings at Leavenworth took two days, at the conclusion of
which the jury came in with a verdict of acquittal. Grinning,
Manuel approached Eriksson, stuck out his hand, and said,
"No hard feelings." Before Eriksson could say anything,
Manuel turned and left the courtroom, a free man. "I
couldn't tell who was supposed to have the hard feelings—
Manuel or myself," Eriksson told me. "Flying back to Carson,
I thought to myself, So Manuel's out. That leaves three to
go."

In April, Eriksson received his honorable discharge from the
Army, and in April, too, he heard of further judicial developments. In Vietnam, the jurors' petition urging clemency for
Clark had been acted upon, with the result that the G.I.'s life
sentence had been commuted to a sentence of twenty years.
Now, six months later, Clark's case, forwarded from Vietnam,
had been gone over in the United States by a board of review,

which had reduced his term to eight years. At about the same time, other boards of review had dealt with Rafe's and Meserve's convictions. Rafe's sentence of eight years had been cut to four, and Meserve's ten years had been trimmed to eight. These varying decisions, it seemed, were attributable to a variety of factors, among them considerations of the defendants' character and background. Thus, it assumed pertinence that Meserve came from an impoverished home and that his father had deserted his mother, and the members of his board of review learned, further, through material furnished them by the commanding general at Fort Leavenworth, that the former sergeant had gone through the ninth grade, had no police record, was a lapsed Roman Catholic, had worked in a cannery in upstate New York, and had saved five thousand dollars while he was in the Army, and that he was confident that "even though war was a brutal business . . . he could control his aggressions in the future, like a professional prize-fighter." In Clark's case, the commanding general, who was responsible for deciding whether the evidence supported Clark's conviction and whether Clark's sentence should be lowered, was informed by a staff lawyer who had interviewed Clark that the soldier in the Disciplinary Barracks was "articulate and above average in intelligence," and that, if given a chance to reënter society, he hoped to earn a college degree in either English or philosophy. It was also noted that, like Meserve, Clark was the product of an impoverished and broken home.

"As if Sven had it so easy!" Mrs. Eriksson said to me when she heard of these findings. "As if his family had any money! He was all of seven when he was driving a tractor on the farm. He was ten when his father suddenly died. Or maybe it's our winters that make Sven so different from those other men—our Januaries, when it's fifty below and the snowdrifts are so high you can't get from the house to the barn without pulling on a rope."

Since returning to civilian life, a year and a half ago, Eriksson has been concerned primarily with what his wife calls "sorting things out." Once he had been separated from the service at Fort Carson, he came back to Minneapolis determined to find employment at something other than carpentry. Much as he loved it, he told me, it was what he had been working at before he was drafted, and, as is often true of new war veterans, he felt restless and in need of a change. The idea that came most easily to his mind was to continue in police work, in which he had been engaged since his days at Camp Radcliff, but on applying to the State Highway Patrol for a post as motorcycle cop he discovered that this was impracticable. "My height," Eriksson said. "I was an inch too short." Somewhat gratefully, he went back to his prewar, and well-paid, job of cabinetmaking at the small department store. For a number of months, though, he found it less than exhilarating to pick up where he had left off. Everything around him, he said, impressed him as pointless and arid—his fellow-workers, the monotony of clock punching, and even, at times, his beloved carpentry. His discontent abated when he managed to remind himself of the plan he had made during his leave to reach out beyond his jobs, whatever they might be. Acting on this, he enrolled in a non-credit course at the University of Minnesota designed to teach adults with an inadequate education how to study.

Speaking matter-of-factly, Mrs. Eriksson said, "Out in the boonies, where we come from, you get an A if you don't throw erasers."

His interest in religion still strong, Eriksson took part in church activities, he told me; he had recently supervised a group of high-school-age boys and girls making a two-week retreat on an island in a lake between Minnesota and Canada.

"Sven wasn't raised churchy," Mrs. Eriksson remarked. "His parents stayed home plenty of Sundays."

Eriksson expects that such steps as he has taken will be succeeded in time by others, though he has no idea at the moment what these may be. He hopes to open a small carpentry shop of his own in several years, but, ideally, he would like to be a farmer—a career that he doubts he will ever be able to afford. He has yet to come to terms with the incident on Hill 192, Eriksson told me. He still has a tendency to fight off its memory, he said, and he thinks the reason for this is that although the experience he had may have revealed certain strengths in himself, he is far more concerned with the limitations it exposed. The thought of them, he said, makes him feel discouraged at times about his future, which, he pointed out, could be a long one. "I'm still young," he said, and it took me a moment's effort to recall the fact of his youth, and the youth of Meserve and the rest of the patrol. Eriksson was confident, though, he told me, that the older he grew, the more accepting he would be of his memory. "Things will get sorted out," he said.

Rafe's case, I learned, had taken a fresh turn in recent weeks. Last winter, members of the Military Appeals Court —the military's highest appellate body—had decided that the admissions Rafe made in Vietnam were "tainted;" that is, like Manuel, he had made a confession without being fully informed of his rights. The judges had ordered that the incarcerated Rafe be given a new trial, which, like Manuel's, was held at Fort Leavenworth. Eriksson was not called upon to testify this time, and this was a vast relief, he told me, not only because he was eager to get on with his civilian life but because it looked to him as though Rafe's re-hearing would be a duplication of Manuel's second trial; that is, with Rafe's "tainted" admissions thrown out, the government's arguments would be undermined and a verdict of acquittal brought in. To Eriksson's surprise, the trial, which occurred in June, 1969, resulted in Rafe's second conviction, an inevitable finding, in view of the fact that Rafe pleaded guilty to the charge of unpremeditated murder. Rafe received a punishment of four years' imprisonment, plus a monthly forfeiture of fifty dollars in pay. It was the same sentence he had been serving, but now, having been transformed into a new verdict, it was subject to another review, the effects of which soon worked to Rafe's advantage, for in August, 1969, the commanding general at Fort Leavenworth shortened his term to twenty-two months. The G.I. already had more prison time than that to his credit, so the force of the general's ruling was to bring about Rafe's immediate release from confinement. He is now on duty as a soldier in the United States while awaiting further word on his case, which since September has been in the hands of a board of review. Inasmuch as the board may only affirm or reduce Rafe's sentence, any changes that it makes will necessarily fall under the heading of good news for him; for example, the board may decide that Rafe served too long a sentence by five or six months, in which event it will be incumbent upon the Army to restore back pay for that period; it is also within the board's power to reverse Rafe's dishonorable discharge.

Eriksson told me he has no qualms about Rafe's being at large, because Rafe's remorse over the criminal episode had been evident to everybody in the Radcliff courtroom. Eriksson conceded, however, that the prospect of Meserve's and Clark's freedom did disturb him. As far as he knew, he said, no legal developments were brewing in their behalf—not that it made much difference, he added, since he had learned just a few weeks earlier that Meserve and Clark stood to be declared eligible for parole before they had served even half their time at Fort Leavenworth. "They may be out in a few months," he said. "It will even be possible for them to join the Army again."

"Sven had to do what he did," Mrs. Eriksson said. "If he'd kept quiet, he would have been impossible to live with."

Regardless of when Meserve and Clark get out, Eriksson thinks, the atmosphere of civilian life may exert a moderating influence on their outlook. He has no idea to what extent that may operate, however; nor is he prepared, he said, to bank on anything so abstract. "Kirsten and I have talked about the day of their release," he told me, "and our realistic hope is that Meserve and Clark have been able to see for themselves what they've done."

"What else can we hope?" Mrs. Eriksson asked. "We would be fools to think those men couldn't do again what they did before."

He would never cease to condemn the members of the patrol personally for their crime, Eriksson said, but that didn't mean they were beyond pity. Other soldiers, he said, might just as easily have betrayed the weakness that the four men had betrayed on Hill 192, but it had fallen to Meserve and Clark and Rafe and Manuel in particular to act as they had. Speaking evenly, Eriksson said, "They were among the ones —among the few—who did what everyone around them wanted to do." Nor was he himself free of blame, he went on, without pausing—once again referring to the limitations within himself that he had glimpsed in Asia. He had yet to exonerate himself from the self-imposed charge of having failed to save Mao's life. He had no idea how long this feeling would continue, but for the present, he knew, he lived with the charge daily, often wondering how Mao might have fared in a time of peace. Six months ago, he said, he had taken a Minneapolis bus home from work and, being very tired, had dozed off. When he opened his eyes, a new passenger was sitting directly opposite him—a young Oriental woman. Still in the process of waking, and not yet thinking clearly, he said, he had transformed her into a peasant woman on her way to do a day's farming, such as he had seen many times in Vietnam; he had envisioned the passenger in a broad, peaked straw hat and black pajamas, carrying the traditional stick across her shoulders, with baskets at either end for holding crops. "Those baskets could get awfully heavy," Eriksson recalled. "Sometimes I didn't see what kept the stick from snapping. They were hard workers, those Vietnamese women, picking little bananas, shinnying up palm trees for coconuts. But on the bus the peasant woman across from me was going to work in paddy fields that were near Mao's hamlet, from which it was a nice walk downhill to a stream that flooded the rice fields. That's where the woman was going in the early morning, but it was peacetime and it wasn't necessary either for her or for the peasant women she was with to smell the bodies that were always rotting for miles around, no one knew where, when I was in the Central Highlands. The only thing these women had to do on their way to the stream was breathe pure mountain air."

The New Yorker, October 18, 1969

MAPS

CHRONOLOGY

BIOGRAPHICAL NOTES

NOTE ON THE TEXTS

NOTES

GLOSSARY

INDEX

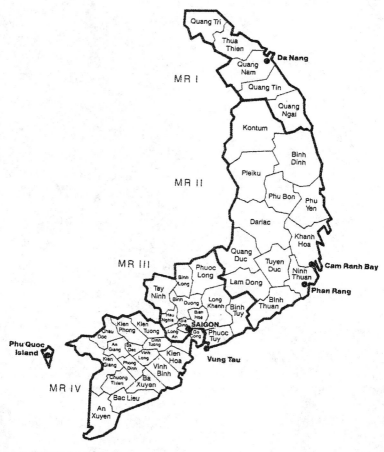

Quang Tri

Thua Thien

Da Nang

Quang Nam

MR I

Quang Tin

Quang Ngai

Kontum

Binh Dinh

Pleiku

Phu Bon

Phu Yen

Darlac

Khanh Hoa

MR II

Quang Duc

Tuyen Duc

Cam Ranh Bay

MR III

Phuoc Long

Lam Dong

Ninh Thuan

Phan Rang

Binh Long

Tay Ninh

Binh Duong

Long Khanh

Binh Tuy

Binh Thuan

Hau Nghia

Gia Dinh

Bien Hoa

Phu Quoc Island

Chau Doc

Kien Phong

Kien Tuong

Long An

SAIGON

Go Cong

Phuoc Tuy

An Giang

Sa Dec

Dinh Tuong

Kien Hoa

Vung Tau

Kien Giang

Phong Dinh

Vinh Long

Chuong Thien

Ba Xuyen

Vinh Binh

MR IV

Bac Lieu

An Xuyen

SOUTH VIETNAM
Provinces and Military Regions

Chronology, 1940–1995

1940   Defeat of France by Germany, May 10–June 22, increases vulnerability of French Indochina to Japanese expansionism. (Indochinese Union, formed in 1887, consists of five states: Cambodia, a French protectorate since 1863; Cochin China, a French colony since 1867; Annam and Tonkin, French protectorates since 1883; and Laos, a French protectorate since 1893.) Japanese forces attack French posts along the Chinese border in northern Tonkin, September 22–24; fighting ends after French governor-general agrees to allow Japanese to station troops and use airfields in Tonkin.

1941   Indochinese Communist Party holds conference in northern Tonkin in May under chairmanship of Nguyen Ai Quoc ("Nguyen the Patriot"), the party's founder, and establishes the Viet Nam Doc Lap Dong Minh (Vietnam Independence League) as a united front organization opposed to French and Japanese rule. Vichy French sign agreement on July 22 giving Japanese military control of Cochin China, including air and naval bases that can be used to attack Malaya, the Dutch East Indies, and the Philippines. Japan begins war against the United States and Great Britain on December 8 (December 7 in the U.S.).

1942–43   Vo Nguyen Giap, a Communist activist since the 1930s, begins recruiting and training Viet Minh guerrilla forces in mountains along the Chinese frontier. Nguyen Ai Quoc is arrested during visit to southern China in 1942 and is imprisoned by Chinese Nationalists until 1943. After his release he adopts Ho Chi Minh ("He Who Enlightens") as new political pseudonym and works in southern China with the Vietnam Revolutionary League, an anti-Japanese front controlled by the Chinese Nationalists. Free French movement led by Charles de Gaulle declares in December 1943 that Indochina will assume a new "political status within the French community" after the defeat of Japan.

1944   Ho Chi Minh returns to Vietnam in August and begins planning for a general uprising under Viet Minh leadership following the defeat of Japan. Giap leads small Viet Minh force in successful attacks on two French outposts on December 24.

1945   Japanese demands for rice and other crops cause severe famine in northern and central Vietnam (as many as two million Vietnamese die from hunger by 1946). Japanese overthrow French administration in Indochina on March 9 and install Bao Dai, heir to dynasty that ascended to the throne in 1802, as emperor of puppet Vietnamese state with authority over Annam and Tonkin. Viet Minh form army in April with Giap as its commander, and work with the Office of Strategic Services, American special operations organization, to collect intelligence and rescue downed Allied airmen in Indochina. Allies divide Indochina at the 16th parallel into Chinese Nationalist and British occupation zones for the purpose of disarming and repatriating Japanese troops following the surrender of Japan. Emperor Hirohito announces Japanese surrender on August 15. Ho Chi Minh issues call for general uprising on August 16. Viet Minh seize power in Hanoi on August 19 and control most of Tonkin by August 22. Bao Dai abdicates on August 23 and uprising spreads to Saigon on August 25. Provisional government of the Democratic Republic of Vietnam is formed with Ho as its president. Ho declares Vietnam independent at mass rally in Hanoi on September 2. Chinese Nationalist army enters northern Vietnam in early September. British, Indian, and French troops begin landing at Saigon on September 12. French seize key buildings in Saigon on September 23; fighting spreads throughout Cochin China as French, British, Indian, and rearmed Japanese troops attempt to suppress Viet Minh resistance. Indochinese Communist Party is officially dissolved in November as Ho, seeking to conciliate Chinese Nationalists, negotiates with other Vietnamese nationalist factions to form new coalition government in Hanoi (Communist Party apparatus continues to control Viet Minh).

1946   French military command declares Cochin China pacified in early February. Agreement signed by Ho and French emissary Jean Sainteny on March 6 provides for French recognition of Democratic Republic of Vietnam as a "free State" within the French Union, allows the French to station 25,000 troops in northern Vietnam for five years, and calls for a plebiscite to determine the status of Cochin China. Nationalist Chinese troops begin withdrawing from Vietnam after signing of Sino-French agreement on March 14 (withdrawal is completed in October; last British forces leave Vietnam in April). Ho holds further talks on status of Vietnam in France, June–September, that leave major issues unresolved. Viet Minh suppress rival nationalist parties in the north. Ho returns to Vietnam on October 20. Clashes between Viet Minh and French in Haiphong lead to bombardment of the city by the French navy on November 23 in which as many as 6,000 Vietnamese civilians are killed. Viet Minh begin offensive against French in Tonkin on December 19.

1947–48   French gain control of major towns in Annam and Tonkin by spring of 1947 as main Viet Minh forces and leadership retreat into the Viet Bac, mountainous region north of Hanoi. Major French offensive in the Viet Bac using paratroops and armored columns inflicts heavy casualties but fails to destroy the Viet Minh, October–November 1947. Guerrilla warfare continues throughout Vietnam as French concentrate on holding the Red River and Mekong deltas, major rice-growing regions in Tonkin and Cochin China. Using captured French and Japanese weapons, Viet Minh build army made up of local village militia, regional guerrilla units, and main-force infantry battalions; by the end of 1948 Viet Minh regain control of the Viet Bac and establish base areas along the central coast and in remote regions of southern Vietnam.

1949   Bao Dai signs agreement with French on March 8 consolidating Cochin China, Annam, and Tonkin into the State of Vietnam, an "associated state" within the French Union; under its terms, Bao Dai will serve as chief of state, with the French retaining control of Vietnamese foreign policy, finances, and defense. Agreements making Laos and Cambodia associated states are signed in July and November. French Expeditionary Corps in Indochina now numbers 150,000, and is composed of troops from France, Algeria, Morocco, Tunisia, Senegal, units of the Foreign Legion, and Indochinese recruits (for political reasons, French government does not send conscripts to serve in Indochina). Communist Chinese troops begin arriving along northern Vietnamese border on December 15 following defeat of Nationalists in the Chinese civil war.

1950   Ho Chi Minh declares Democratic Republic of Vietnam to be the sole Vietnamese government on January 14. After China and the Soviet Union extend diplomatic recognition to the Democratic Republic of Vietnam, the United States recognizes the Associated States of Vietnam, Laos, and Cambodia on February 7. Viet Minh use bases in southern China to organize, train, and equip regular infantry divisions and receive new weapons, including machine guns, mortars, and recoilless rifles, from the Chinese. President Truman approves sending $15 million in military assistance to French forces in Indochina on March 10. Aid is rapidly increased after Korean War begins on June 25 (U.S. will send $2 billion in military aid to Indochina by 1954). Viet Minh regulars overrun French outpost at Dong Khe, September 16–18, opening major offensive along northeastern Vietnamese-Chinese border. French abandon Lang Son, October 18, and retreat from northeastern border region after losing 6,000 men killed or captured in border battles. During autumn French build line of fortifications around Red River delta as Giap plans general offensive designed to capture Hanoi. French sign agreement with Bao Dai regime on December 8 establishing Vietnamese National Army.

1951   Viet Minh lose more than 10,000 men killed in three major attacks on Red River delta, January–June, before abandoning general offensive (French inflict many casualties with air-dropped napalm during Red River battles). Vietnamese Communist Party is overtly reestablished in February as the Lao Dong (Workers') Party. French drop paratroops on Hoa Binh, 40 miles west of Hanoi, on November 14, beginning campaign intended to draw Viet Minh into open battle against superior French firepower.

1952   Both sides suffer heavy losses in fighting around Hoa Binh before French withdraw on February 24. French give Vietnamese National Army increasing role in counter-guerrilla operations in southern and central Vietnam as French Expeditionary Corps is concentrated in northern Vietnam for operations against Viet Minh regulars. Viet Minh begin successful offensive on October 11 in highlands northwest of Hanoi but fail to overrun fortified airfield at Na San, November 23–December 1. Major French incursion into the Viet Bac, October 29–December 1, fails to significantly disrupt Viet Minh logistics.

1953   Viet Minh begin receiving trucks, anti-aircraft artillery, and heavy mortars from the Soviet Union. Armistice is signed in Korean War on July 27. French command decides to reoccupy abandoned airstrip at Dien Bien Phu, village in valley near the Laotian border over 180 miles west of Hanoi, and use it as a base to block Viet Minh operations into Laos. Dien Bien Phu operation begins with successful French parachute assault on November 20. Giap orders major reinforcements to Dien Bien Phu and begins planning siege of French base. French command reinforces Dien Bien Phu in hopes of inflicting major defeat on Viet Minh.

1954   Viet Minh surround Dien Bien Phu garrison of 10,000 men with force of 40,000 regulars and achieve three-to-one superiority over French in howitzers and heavy mortars. Intense bombardment of Dien Bien Phu begins on March 13; by March 17 Viet Minh capture three of the eight strongpoints held by the French forces. Eisenhower administration considers, and then rejects, proposals for the U.S. to launch airstrikes in support of the French garrison. Viet Minh overrun Dien Bien Phu on May 7 and capture 6,500 prisoners; more than 2,000 French troops and 8,000 Viet Minh are killed during the battle.

International conference on Indochina opens in Geneva on May 8, attended by delegations from France, Great Britain, the U.S., the Soviet Union, Communist China, the Democratic Republic of Vietnam, the State of Vietnam, Laos, and Cambodia. Ngo Dinh Diem becomes premier of the State of Vietnam on July 7. Cease-fire agreement is signed in Geneva July 21 between representatives of Viet Minh army and the French Expeditionary Corps; it provides for the exchange of prisoners and the "regrouping" of the opposing armies within 300 days north and south of a "provisional military demarcation line" near the 17th parallel. Separate cease-fire agreements are signed for Laos and Cambodia that call for the withdrawal of Viet Minh forces from both countries. The "Final Declaration" of the conference, which calls for holding internationally supervised general elections throughout Vietnam in July 1956, is not signed by any of the delegations, and the U.S. and the State of Vietnam refuse to "associate" themselves with it. Cease-fire goes into effect throughout Indochina by August 11. French Expeditionary Corps loses 75,000 men killed, including 21,000 from metropolitan France, during the Indochina War, while the Viet Minh lose at least 200,000 dead.

French withdraw from Hanoi in October as Lao Dong Party takes control of North Vietnam. Over 900,000 refugees, most of them Roman Catholic, move south from North Vietnam by May 1955, and between 50,000 and 90,000 Viet Minh move north, while about 10,000 Viet Minh remain in South Vietnam with instructions to engage in "political struggle" toward reunification. Authority of Diem is challenged within South Vietnam by the Cao Dai and Hoa Hao, politically powerful religious sects, and the Binh Xuyen, criminal organization that controls much of Saigon.

1955   Troops loyal to Diem drive Binh Xuyen from Saigon in intense fighting, April 28–30, and begin successful campaign against military forces of the Cao Dai and Hoa Hao. Diem declares on July 6 that South Vietnam is not bound by the Geneva agreements to hold national elections in 1956. Land reform campaign conducted by the Lao Dong Party in North Vietnam results in widespread denunciations, arrests, and executions. Diem ousts Bao Dai as head of state and on October 26 proclaims himself the first president of the Republic of Vietnam. U.S. establishes Military Assistance and Advisory Group Vietnam on November 1 to train and equip South Vietnamese army (new group succeeds MAAG-Indochina, which was established in 1950 to convey aid to the French).

1956   Diem regime begins repressive campaign aimed at Viet Minh in South Vietnam that results in the death or imprisonment of thousands of suspected Viet Minh supporters by the end of the 1950s. Last French troops leave South Vietnam on April 28. Land reform campaign in North Vietnam ends in November after resulting in 10,000–15,000 deaths.

1957–58   Former Viet Minh in South Vietnam begin forming small armed units and assassinating government officials, sometimes working with remnants of the Binh Xuyen, Cao Dai, and Hoa Hao military forces. (Communist-led insurgents in South Vietnam will become known as Viet Cong, from Viet Nam Cong San, "Vietnamese Communists," a term applied to them by the Diem regime.)

1959   Lao Dong Party leadership decides to use "armed struggle" as well as "political struggle" to overthrow Saigon government and reunify Vietnam. In May North Vietnamese organize secret transportation group to infiltrate cadre who "regrouped" north in 1954 back into South Vietnam along the Truong Son Strategic Route ("Ho Chi Minh Trail"), a network of paths running through the mountains of southeastern Laos. North Vietnamese also organize transportation groups for infiltration of men and supplies into South Vietnam by sea, and for sending supplies to Laos after fighting breaks out in July between the Communist Pathet Lao movement and the Royal Lao army. Viet Cong assassinations and ambushes increase (Communist forces assassinate more than 30,000 people in South Vietnam between 1957 and 1972).

1960   Military coup in Laos on August 9 leads to increased outside involvement in the Laotian civil war, with the U.S. supplying and training rightist forces and the Soviet Union airlifting military equipment to the Pathet Lao and its neutralist allies. Formation of National Liberation Front, an alliance of opponents of Diem regime, is announced in Hanoi on December 20 (insurgency in South Vietnam remains under control of the Lao Dong Party). U.S. military personnel serving in South Vietnam total 900 by the end of the year.

1961   U.S. Central Intelligence Agency begins arming Hmong (Meo) tribesmen to fight Pathet Lao in Laotian mountains and sending teams of South Vietnamese into North Vietnam on sabotage missions. Cease-fire is declared in Laotian civil war on May 11 and international conference on Laos convenes in Geneva on May 16. In response to requests by Diem for more American assistance in fighting the Viet

Cong, President John F. Kennedy decides in November
to increase the number of U.S. military personnel in South
Vietnam and expand their role in counter-guerrilla operations. In December U.S. helicopter units begin carrying
South Vietnamese troops on operations and American pilots begin flying combat missions in attack aircraft with
Vietnamese aircrew onboard (flights are officially described as training missions). American military personnel
in South Vietnam total 3,200 by the end of the year.

1962   General Paul D. Harkins becomes first commander of U.S.
Military Assistance Command Vietnam (MACV), new
headquarters established in Saigon on February 8 to control buildup of U.S. advisers and support personnel. U.S.
special forces begin organizing paramilitary units among
Montagnards in Central Highlands. With U.S. assistance,
Diem regime launches strategic hamlet program designed
to protect rural population from Viet Cong coercion.
American helicopters and armored personnel carriers increase mobility of government troops in counter-guerrilla
operations and allow the South Vietnamese to make offensive sweeps into Viet Cong base areas. Geneva conference on Laos ends on July 23 with signing of accords
under which the U.S. and North Vietnam agree to observe the neutrality of Laos and refrain from using Laotian
territory for military purposes. North Vietnam fails to
withdraw its troops from Laos by October 7 deadline and
continues to use Ho Chi Minh Trail to infiltrate men into
the South. U.S. curtails overt military aid to Laotian government in compliance with Geneva agreement, but continues covert support of the Royal Lao army and the
Hmong. Viet Cong begin forming battalion-sized main-
force units in South Vietnam. American military personnel
in South Vietnam total 11,300 by the end of the year.

1963   Viet Cong main-force troops repulse attack by numerically
superior South Vietnamese force equipped with helicopters, armored personnel carriers, and heavy artillery at Ap
Bac on January 2 before withdrawing from the battlefield;
engagement is hailed as major victory by Viet Cong propagandists and increases doubts among some American
advisers and journalists about fighting ability of South
Vietnamese army. Organized Buddhist opposition to

Diem regime increases after South Vietnamese troops kill nine persons during Buddhist celebration in Hue on May 8. Buddhist monk commits suicide by self-immolation in Saigon on June 11, the first of seven protest suicides by Buddhists in 1963. Paramilitary forces commanded by Ngo Dinh Nhu, Diem's brother and chief adviser, raid Buddhist temples in several major cities on August 21 as Diem imposes martial law. Kennedy administration loses confidence in ability of Diem to prevent Communist takeover in South Vietnam and secretly informs generals plotting to overthrow Diem that the U.S. would not oppose a coup. Group of military commanders led by General Duong Van Minh overthrow Diem on November 1, and Diem and Nhu are murdered on November 2 by officers participating in coup. Kennedy is assassinated on November 22 and Vice-President Lyndon B. Johnson becomes president. Lao Dong Party leadership decides in December to intensify military operations in South Vietnam by supplying new Chinese and Soviet weapons to the Viet Cong and by sending North Vietnamese cadre to the South. Strategic hamlet program declines. American military personnel in South Vietnam total 16,300 by the end of the year.

1964   General Nguyen Khanh overthrows ruling military committee in bloodless Saigon coup on January 30 (until February 1965 Khanh will remain central figure in period of continued South Vietnamese political turmoil). In February 1964 President Johnson authorizes raids against the North Vietnamese coast by South Vietnamese naval commando units operating under U.S. control. North Vietnamese undertake major expansion of Ho Chi Minh Trail network, building roads capable of bearing heavy truck traffic and extending trail into northeastern Cambodia (eventually a force of 50,000 North Vietnamese soldiers will guard and maintain the roads, supply depots, and anti-aircraft defenses of the trail). American pilots working for the CIA begin flying fighter-bomber missions over Laos in late May as Laotian fighting intensifies, and two U.S. navy jets flying reconnaissance missions over Laos are shot down in early June. General William Westmoreland succeeds Harkins as commander of MACV on June 20. Fighting in South Vietnam intensifies in July as Viet Cong increase attacks against government outposts.

U.S. destroyer *Maddox* is attacked by North Vietnamese torpedo boats in the Gulf of Tonkin on August 2 while on an electronic intelligence-gathering mission. On the night of August 4 the *Maddox* and another destroyer, *C. Turner Joy*, report a second attack by North Vietnamese torpedo boats (evidence indicates that reports of August 4 attack were probably the result of false radar contacts caused by tropical weather conditions). Johnson responds to reports of second attack by ordering first U.S. airstrikes against North Vietnam, and on August 5 navy aircraft attack five military targets. Administration submits Tonkin Gulf Resolution to Congress; it authorizes the president to "take all necessary measures to repel any armed attack against the forces of the United States and to prevent further aggression" in Southeast Asia. Resolution is passed by the House of Representatives, 416–0, and the Senate, 88–2, on August 7.

Rioting breaks out in Saigon and other cities, August 21–29, in response to unsuccessful attempt by Khanh to assume the presidency. Viet Cong kill five Americans in mortar attack on Bien Hoa airbase, November 1; U.S. does not respond with airstrikes against North Vietnam. Johnson is elected president on November 3. U.S. air force and navy aircraft begin bombing northern Laos on November 14 (raids will be publicly described as "armed reconnaissance"). North Vietnamese infantry regiments begin moving into South Vietnam. American military personnel in South Vietnam total 23,300 by the end of the year; more than 260 Americans have died in combat since the conflict began.

1965   South Vietnamese army loses 200 men killed in Viet Cong ambush near village of Binh Gia, 40 miles from Saigon, in early January. Viet Cong kill eight Americans in attack on U.S. bases at Pleiku on February 7. Johnson orders retaliatory airstrikes against North Vietnam, February 7–8. Viet Cong blow up barracks at Qui Nhon on February 10, killing 23 Americans; U.S. aircraft bomb North Vietnam on February 11. American aircraft begin intensive bombing of Viet Cong targets in South Vietnam on February 19 (raids are no longer required to be flown with South Vietnamese personnel onboard). General Khanh is removed from power on February 21 by military coup that leaves Phan Huy Quat, a civilian, serving as premier of South Vietnam.

U.S. begins sustained bombing of North Vietnam on March 2, using navy aircraft based on carriers in the South China Sea and air force planes based in Thailand and South Vietnam. First American ground combat units are deployed to South Vietnam on March 8 as marines land at Danang to protect its airbase against Viet Cong attack. U.S. begins sustained bombing of Ho Chi Minh Trail in Laos on April 3. Johnson authorizes marines to conduct offensive ground operations around Danang base on April 6. U.S. and South Vietnam begin naval interdiction operations off Vietnamese coast (patrols will significantly reduce maritime flow of supplies to Communist forces in South Vietnam). First national demonstration against U.S. intervention in Vietnam, held in Washington, D.C., on April 17, draws 20,000 protestors. American paratroopers begin guarding Bien Hoa airbase on May 5 as first U.S. army ground combat units are deployed to South Vietnam. North Vietnamese plan major offensive in Central Highlands with objective of capturing Pleiku and Qui Nhon and inflicting decisive defeat on South Vietnamese. Viet Cong defeat South Vietnamese forces in heavy fighting in Quang Ngai and Phouc Long provinces in late May and early June, inflicting over 1,200 casualties. Westmoreland warns his superiors that the South Vietnamese army is on the brink of collapse. Military government takes power in Saigon on June 19 with Air Vice-Marshal Nguyen Cao Ky serving as premier and General Nguyen Van Thieu as chief of state.

Johnson decides in late July to send up to 200,000 U.S. troops to South Vietnam to avert defeat of Saigon government, but does not order mobilization of the reserves or the national guard, forcing a major increase in monthly draft calls. Johnson also limits U.S. ground operations to South Vietnam, and will consistently reject proposals to invade North Vietnam or launch ground attacks against Communist supply routes and bases in Laos and Cambodia. U.S. aircraft continue bombing North Vietnam, concentrating on transportation targets in attempt to interdict flow of supplies into South Vietnam. Effectiveness of bombing campaign is limited by the increasing strength and complexity of North Vietnamese air defenses, which are equipped with Soviet-made anti-aircraft artillery, surface-to-air missiles, jet fighters, and radar control systems, and by changing series of restrictions on targets and tactics imposed by Johnson administration in effort to avoid Soviet or Chinese intervention in the war.

Marines conduct first major American ground operation, attacking Viet Cong regiment massed near Chu Lai airbase, August 18–24; 45 marines and more than 600 Viet Cong are killed in the fighting. About 100,000 demonstrators protest American intervention in marchs and rallies held in cities and on campuses throughout the U.S., October 15–16. U.S. special forces begin secret cross-border reconnaissance missions into southern Laos (missions continue until early 1971, and are also carried out in eastern Cambodia, 1967–70). North Vietnamese begin Central Highlands offensive with attack on Plei Me special forces camp in Pleiku province on October 19. Westmoreland sends American "airmobile" troops heavily equipped with helicopters to Pleiku in late October, beginning first major battle between American and North Vietnamese forces. Heaviest fighting occurs in two separate engagements in the Ia Drang Valley, November 14–18, in which 234 Americans and more than 1,000 North Vietnamese are killed. Campaign ends when North Vietnamese retreat into Cambodia and Americans return to base camp at An Khe in late November; U.S. victory increases confidence of American commanders that superior mobility and firepower of U.S. troops will give them decisive advantage in battles with North Vietnamese and main-force Viet Cong units. Johnson decides to extend Christmas bombing halt begun on December 24 in hopes of starting negotiations with the North Vietnamese. Over 184,000 American military personnel are in South Vietnam by the end of the year, and more than 1,300 Americans are killed in combat during 1965.

1966   Buildup of U.S. forces continues, with American combat troops deployed both to defend bases, installations, and roads, and to begin conducting offensive operations aimed at finding and destroying North Vietnamese and main-force Viet Cong units (U.S. commanders do not have sufficient combat troops to hold permanently large amounts of territory, and the majority of South Vietnamese forces are deployed to defend towns and cities). During the year most major U.S. army combat operations are conducted in the region between Saigon and the Cambodian border, especially Binh Long, Tay Ninh, and Hau Nghia provinces; in Kontum and Pleiku provinces in the Central Highlands; and in the northern coastal plains in Binh Dinh province. Most ground operations by U.S. marines are initially directed at securing populated areas around major bases at Phu Bai, Danang, and Chu Lai. U.S. resumes bombing of North Vietnam on January 31.

Ky government dismisses General Nguyen Chanh Thi, South Vietnamese commander in I Corps, on March 10, leading to rebellion against Saigon regime in northern cities of South Vietnam. Forces loyal to Ky retake Danang, May 15–24, and Hue, June 15–23.

U.S. aircraft bomb targets close to Hanoi and Haiphong for the first time on June 29, beginning campaign directed at petroleum and oil storage sites (Johnson continues to forbid bombing of Haiphong harbor or central Hanoi). Campaign against oil targets continues until September 4 and succeeds in destroying most major storage sites, but fails to create significant fuel shortage because of widespread dispersion of oil storage undertaken by North Vietnamese since 1965; focus of bombing shifts back to transportation targets.

North Vietnamese army begins moving in strength across the Demilitarized Zone (DMZ) into northern Quang Tri province in early July. Marines deploy along southern boundary of the DMZ, where they fight North Vietnamese in series of infantry engagements and begin constructing series of fortified combat bases and outposts. U.S. incursion into War Zone C, major Viet Cong base area in Tay Ninh province, results in heavy fighting, November 3–15, in which 155 Americans and as many as 1,000 Viet Cong are killed. Determined Viet Cong resistance leads American commanders to plan further attacks on Communist base areas in hopes of forcing the Viet Cong and North Vietnamese into battle. (American efforts to wage successful war of attrition are made difficult by ability of Viet Cong and North Vietnamese to evade many offensive sweeps; to fight many engagements at close range and from dug-in positions, thereby reducing the effectiveness of American airstrikes and artillery fire; and to withdraw successfully their surviving forces from the battlefield after most engagements.) More than 385,000 American military personnel are in South Vietnam by the end of the year, and more than 5,000 Americans are killed in combat during 1966.

1967   American ground combat units begin operations in the Mekong delta. U.S. forces launch major operation in War Zone C on February 22; over 280 Americans and at least 2,000 Viet Cong and North Vietnamese are killed by April 1. Disruption caused by offensive contributes to increasing use of base areas inside Cambodia by Communist forces, who purchase large amounts of Cambodian rice and receive arms shipped through port of Kompong Som (Sihanoukville) with the collusion of the Cambodian government and army. American troops continue operations against North Vietnamese and Viet Cong units in the Central Highlands and in Binh Dinh, Quang Ngai, Quang Tin, and Quang Ngai provinces. North Vietnamese begin shelling U.S. outposts along the DMZ with long-range Soviet artillery.

Senator Robert F. Kennedy gives speech on March 2 calling for a halt in the bombing of North Vietnam and the opening of peace negotiations. U.S. aircraft begin bombing major North Vietnamese industrial sites and electric power plants in early March. Campaign continues until May, when priority is again given to interdiction targets. Johnson administration internally debates continued bombing of the North as Robert S. McNamara, the secretary of defense since 1961, loses confidence in American policy. Anti-war march in New York City on April 15 draws at least 125,000 people; speakers at rally include Dr. Martin Luther King Jr. and pediatrician Dr. Benjamin Spock.

U.S. marines attack North Vietnamese troops entrenched in hills near Khe Sanh combat base, April 24–May 11; 155 Americans and 900 North Vietnamese are killed before North Vietnamese withdraw into Laos (heavy fighting continues in northern Quang Tri province during the spring and summer).

Civil Operations and Revolutionary Development Support (CORDS) program is established in May to consolidate pacification efforts of the U.S. military, CIA, Agency for International Development, and the State Department.

Lao Dong Party leadership decides during summer to stage "General Offensive–General Uprising" in South Vietnam. North Vietnamese begin planning widespread attacks on towns and cities using Viet Cong forces with goal of inflicting major defeat on the South Vietnamese army and causing a widespread revolutionary uprising among the urban population.

Nguyen Van Thieu is elected president and Nguyen Cao Ky vice-president of South Vietnam on September 3, winning 35 per cent of the vote out of field of 11 electoral slates.

Giap initiates series of major battles along borders of South Vietnam as first phase of General Offensive–General Uprising with objective of drawing U.S. combat forces away from major South Vietnamese cities. North Vietnamese begin heavy shelling of Con Thien, marine outpost along the DMZ, on September 11; siege lasts until October 31 as U.S. forces respond with prolonged bombardment involving coordinated use of heavy artillery, naval gunfire, fighter-bombers, and B-52 heavy bombers.

March on Pentagon on October 22 draws 50,000 people.

Viet Cong lose 900 killed in unsuccessful attack on Loc Ninh in northern Binh Long province, October 29–November 3. U.S. and North Vietnamese fight series of engagements in Central Highlands near Dak To, November 3–December 1; almost 300 Americans and at least 1,000 North Vietnamese are killed before North Vietnamese units withdraw into Cambodia.

Johnson administration seeks to counter growing public and Congressional opposition to the war by stressing "progress" being made in Vietnam. In speech given in Washington on November 21, Westmoreland states that American forces have reached "an important point where the end begins to come into view" and that "the enemy's hopes are bankrupt." Resignation of McNamara, effective February 29, 1968, is announced by Johnson on November 29. Senator Eugene McCarthy announces on November 30 that he will oppose Johnson in 1968 Democratic presidential primaries and calls for a negotiated settlement in Vietnam. Over 485,000 American military personnel are in South Vietnam by the end of the year, and more than 9,300 Americans are killed in combat during 1967.

1968   North Vietnamese mass large number of troops around Khe Sanh combat base and its garrison of 6,000 U.S. marines. Westmoreland and Lieutenant General Frederick C.

Weyand, American field commander in III Corps, decide on January 10 to move significant number of American combat troops away from the Cambodian border and closer to Saigon to guard against possible attacks in the capital region. North Vietnamese bombard Khe Sanh with heavy rocket and mortar fire on January 21, beginning 77-day siege. U.S. forces respond with sustained bombing and shelling of North Vietnamese positions in surrounding area, using intelligence from aerial reconnaissance and from signals sent by hundreds of seismic and acoustic sensors (U.S. also uses recently developed sensors to target airstrikes against the Ho Chi Minh Trail in Laos).

North Vietnamese and Viet Cong open second phase of General Offensive–General Uprising with ground attacks on over 100 cities and towns throughout South Vietnam during the Tet holiday truce, when many South Vietnamese soldiers are home on leave. Communist forces attack Danang and six other cities in I and II Corps in early hours of January 30. U.S. and South Vietnamese commanders cancel remainder of Tet truce, but are still surprised by intensity and extent of main wave of Tet attacks, which begin in early hours of January 31. Viet Cong and North Vietnamese troops capture much of Hue; during their occupation, Viet Cong murder at least 2,800 residents. In the Saigon area Viet Cong attack several key installations, including the presidential palace, the government radio station, the U.S. embassy, the South Vietnamese Joint General Staff headquarters, Bien Hoa air base, the U.S. army base at Long Binh, and Tan Son Nhut airbase, the site of MACV headquarters, where heavy fighting takes place between a large Viet Cong force and American base security troops, South Vietnamese paratroopers, and U.S. armored cavalry. Viet Cong in Saigon region fail to capture or hold any of their major objectives, and fail throughout the country to start popular uprisings or to cause South Vietnamese units to defect.

Lang Vei special forces camp, five miles from Khe Sanh, is overrun on February 7 as North Vietnamese use tanks in South Vietnam for the first time. By mid-February South Vietnamese and U.S. forces have retaken all of the cities attacked during Tet except for Saigon, where fighting continues in Cholon section, and Hue, where U.S. and South Vietnamese troops engage in house-to-house combat until city is recaptured on February 25. More than

1,700 Americans are killed in action during the Tet offensive, while South Vietnamese lose about twice as many men (20,000 South Vietnamese soldiers are killed in combat during 1968); Communist forces lose as many as 40,000 killed, most of them Viet Cong, including many veteran cadre.

Johnson asks Clark Clifford, who succeeds McNamara as secretary of defense on March 1, to conduct reassessment of U.S. policy in Vietnam after administration receives proposal from the military to send as many as 206,000 more troops to Vietnam by the end of 1968. Clifford becomes strong advocate for a major change in policy, arguing that a military victory in Vietnam is unachievable and that the U.S. must limit its commitment to South Vietnam. Johnson authorizes sending 13,500 more troops to Vietnam. McCarthy wins 42 per cent of the vote in the New Hampshire Democratic primary on March 12. Robert Kennedy announces on March 16 that he will seek the Democratic presidential nomination.

American infantry company murders between 200 and 500 unarmed South Vietnamese villagers at My Lai, hamlet in Quang Ngai province, on March 16. (U.S. army begins investigation of the atrocity in the spring of 1969, and the first press reports of the massacre appear in November 1969.)

North Vietnamese begin withdrawing some of their troops from the Khe Sanh area after suffering heavy casualties from sustained U.S. bombing and shelling. Johnson meets on March 26 with group of senior advisers, most of whom recommend reducing American involvement in Vietnam. In speech delivered on March 31, Johnson announces a partial halt in the bombing of North Vietnam in effort to start negotiations and declares that he will not seek reelection.

American forces begin major operation to relieve Khe Sanh on April 1. Bombing of North Vietnam is halted above the 20th parallel. North Vietnamese government announces on April 3 its willingness to meet with U.S. representatives. Assassination of Martin Luther King Jr. on April 4 is followed by widespread rioting in American cities and increase in racial tension among U.S. forces in Vietnam. Siege of Khe Sanh ends on April 8, though heavy fighting continues in region around base through June. U.S. begins major program to expand South Vietnamese armed forces and to provide them with modern equipment. North Vietnamese attack near Dong Ha begins series of engagements along eastern end of DMZ. Viet Cong launch two waves of attacks in Saigon area, May 5–13 and May 25–June 4, resulting in renewed fighting in Cholon and near Tan Son Nhut airbase in which South Vietnamese troops play a major role. Fighting is also intense in Quang Nam province, and over 100 towns and military bases in South Vietnam are hit by mortar and rocket attacks during May "mini-Tet" offensive. U.S. and North Vietnamese negotiators meet in Paris on May 13, but talks soon deadlock over North Vietnamese demand for an end to all U.S. bombing of the North. American combat deaths in May total more than 2,000, the highest loss of any month of the war.

Robert Kennedy is assassinated on June 5. General Creighton Abrams succeeds Westmoreland as commander of MACV on July 3. Marines abandon Khe Sanh base on July 5 in shift toward using more mobile tactics in defense of northern Quang Tri. North Vietnamese stage last wave of 1967–68 General Offensive in late August, launching unsuccessful ground attacks on city of Tay Ninh and the Duc Lap special forces camp in Quang Duc province. Heavy casualties suffered by Viet Cong during General Offensive, and its failure to bring a rapid end to the war, cause permanent decline in Viet Cong strength and force Communist commanders to send North Vietnamese replacements to serve with Viet Cong main-force units.

Police and protestors repeatedly clash in Chicago streets as Democratic National Convention meets, August 26–29, and nominates Vice-President Hubert H. Humphrey for president. U.S. and South Vietnamese troops continue combat operations designed to protect urban areas against further ground attack or rocket bombardment. Johnson announces complete halt in bombing of North Vietnam on October 31 as part of agreement to begin negotiations involving the U.S., North and South Vietnam, and the National Liberation Front. (Over 900 U.S. aircraft, most of them modern jets, are shot down over North Vietnam, 1965–68.) Republican candidate Richard M. Nixon wins presidential election on November 5. Negotiations in Paris deadlock over procedural issues. Over 536,000 American military personnel are in South Vietnam by the end of the year, and more than 14,500 Americans are killed in combat during 1968.

1969   First session of four-party peace talks is held in Paris on January 18. Nixon is inaugurated as president on January 20. U.S. marines conduct operation along Laotian border in western Quang Tri province, January 22–March 18, with aim of disrupting North Vietnamese supply system. (Capture of arms and food caches and protection of populated rural areas increasingly become major objectives of American operations during 1969 as less emphasis is placed on engaging large North Vietnamese and Viet Cong units in ground combat.) U.S. bombing of Ho Chi Minh Trail in Laos is increased as consequence of bombing halt over North Vietnam.

North Vietnamese and Viet Cong begin new offensive across South Vietnam on February 23; in effort to avoid high casualties suffered during 1967–68 General Offensive, Communist ground attacks on U.S. installations are increasingly carried out by small "sapper" units armed with explosive charges and trained in night infiltration tactics. More than 1,100 Americans are killed in action in first three weeks of the offensive, and heavy fighting continues for months in region between Saigon and the Cambodian border and in northern coastal plains. Nixon orders first in series of B-52 raids on Communist base areas in eastern Cambodia on March 18 (bombing is not disclosed to Congress or the American public). American troop strength in South Vietnam reaches peak level of 543,000 men in April; "Free World" forces in South Vietnam also include 50,000 troops from South Korea, 11,500 from Thailand, and more than 8,000 from Australia.

National Liberation Front delegation in Paris calls on May 8 for an unconditional U.S. withdrawal from Vietnam and the creation of a coalition government in Saigon; Nixon responds on May 14 by proposing the phased mutual withdrawal of American and North Vietnamese troops from South Vietnam. American troops conducting sweep through the A Shau Valley, a major North Vietnamese stronghold along the Laotian border 25 miles southwest of Hue, capture Hill 937 ("Hamburger Hill") on May 20 after ten-day battle in which at least 56 Americans and more than 500 North Vietnamese are killed. Engagement causes controversy in press and Congress over American tactics in Vietnam.

Nixon announces on June 8 that 25,000 American troops will be withdrawn from Vietnam as South Vietnamese armed forces assume greater role in the war (further withdrawals involving another 85,000 men will be announced on September 16 and December 15). National Liberation Front forms Provisional Revolutionary Government for South Vietnam on June 10. Nixon administration instructs Abrams in August to "hold down" U.S. casualties. Ho Chi Minh dies on September 2 after several years of poor health. Small group of senior officials, including Lao Dong Party general secretary Le Duan, premier Pham Van Dong, defense minister Vo Nguyen Giap, and party ideologist Truong Chinh, assume collective leadership of North Vietnam. Hmong forces drive North Vietnamese troops from the Plain of Jars in September as ground fighting in northern Laos intensifies.

Series of anti-war demonstrations held across the U.S. on October 15 draw large crowds, and 250,000 protestors attend rally in Washington on November 15. First draft lottery is held on December 1 as Selective Service moves to reduce number of draft deferments. U.S. forces in Vietnam suffer increasingly from declining morale, insubordination, racial tension, and drug use; breakdown in discipline is generally more severe among support troops in rear areas than in combat units. Control of Viet Cong "shadow government" over rural areas is reduced as aid administered through CORDS program increases size and effectiveness of village-based South Vietnamese paramilitary forces, and as U.S. and South Vietnamese forces achieve increasing success in capturing or killing Viet Cong political cadre. American military personnel serving in South Vietnam total 475,000 at the end of the year; more than 9,400 Americans are killed in action in 1969.

1970   U.S. air force uses B-52 bombers over northern Laos for the first time on February 17 as North Vietnamese overrun Hmong postions on the Plain of Jars. National security adviser Henry Kissinger holds first in series of secret negotiating sessions in Paris with Le Duc Tho, a senior member of the Lao Dong Party leadership, on February 21.

Prince Norodom Sihanouk is ousted as chief of state of Cambodia on March 18 in coup led by General Lon Nol,

who also demands that all North Vietnamese and Viet
Cong troops leave the country. South Vietnamese troops
begin series of raids into Communist base areas in Cambodia on March 27. North Vietnamese begin attacking
Cambodian army outposts in the border region on March
29. Hundreds of ethnic Vietnamese are murdered in Cambodia in April as Lon Nol regime incites anti-Vietnamese
hatred. U.S. continues airstrikes against Communist forces
in Cambodia and begins covertly sending weapons to the
Cambodian army. Nixon announces on April 20 that an
additional 150,000 U.S. troops will be withdrawn from
Vietnam by the spring of 1971. After intense debate within
the administration, Nixon approves "incursion" into
North Vietnamese base areas inside Cambodia on April 26
and announces operation on April 30. American troops
cross border on May 1. Four students are shot to death by
National Guardsmen during demonstration at Kent State
University in Ohio on May 4. As widespread protests continue across the U.S., Nixon announces on May 8 that all
American troops will be withdrawn from Cambodia by
June 30. U.S. and South Vietnamese forces capture large
amounts of weapons, ammunition, and rice as North Vietnamese and Viet Cong troops retreat into Cambodia (U.S.
troops are restricted from going further than 35 kilometers
across the border). Demonstration by construction workers in support of Nixon draws 100,000 people in New
York City on May 20. South Vietnamese troops continue
ground operations in Cambodia after June 30 with American air support. By the end of July North Vietnamese and
Viet Cong occupy most of eastern Cambodia and begin
organizing Cambodian insurgents to fight the Lon Nol
regime.

U.S. participation in ground combat in South Vietnam
decreases as most remaining American combat units prepare to withdraw and South Vietnamese army assumes responsibility for defending border areas against North Vietnamese incursions. Land reform program instituted by
Thieu increases support for government in rural areas.
North Vietnamese work to reestablish supply system in
Cambodia.

U.S. special forces raid camp at Son Tay in North Vietnam on November 21 in attempt to rescue 70 American
prisoners of war, but discover that camp has been abandoned. Congress passes amendment to defense appropri-

ations bill on December 22 forbidding deployment of U.S. troops or advisers in Laos and Cambodia. By the end of the year more than 334,000 U.S. military personnel remain in South Vietnam; more than 4,200 Americans are killed in action in 1970.

1971   South Vietnamese troops cross border into southern Laos west of Khe Sanh on February 8 in offensive designed to destroy North Vietnamese supplies and disrupt Ho Chi Minh Trail. U.S. provides extensive air support for operation, but recently passed legislation prevents U.S. advisers from accompanying South Vietnamese units on the ground. Advance is slowed by lack of coordination among South Vietnamese commanders. North Vietnamese begin series of counterattacks on February 18, using tanks, heavy artillery, and mass infantry assaults, and subjecting American supply helicopters to intense anti-aircraft fire. South Vietnamese enter town of Tchepone on March 6, then begin retreating from Laos on March 9. Operation ends on April 6 after South Vietnamese lose at least 1,700 men killed, many of them from elite airborne, marine, and ranger units. Encouraged by results of Laotian battle, North Vietnamese continue planning for major conventional offensive in South Vietnam.

The New York Times publishes on June 13 the first in series of excerpts from secret Defense Department study of U.S. involvement in Vietnam, prepared in 1967–68 on instructions from McNamara. Nixon administration obtains court order stopping publication of the "Pentagon Papers," but Supreme Court lifts injunction in 6–3 decision on June 30. (Attempt by Nixon administration to discredit Daniel Ellsberg, a former government official who gave the study to the press, results in illegal break-in in September 1971 conducted by operatives later involved in 1972 Watergate burglary.)

Thieu is relected president of South Vietnam on October 3, receiving 94 per cent of the vote after major opposition candidates withdraw from the race. Fighting in northern Laos continues as CIA hires increasing number of Thai soldiers to replace Hmong casualties. Cambodian army suffers series of defeats in engagements with North Vietnamese and Viet Cong troops, October–December. Nixon announces on November 12 that U.S. troops in Vietnam have ended offensive ground operations. More than 156,000 American military personnel remain in South Vietnam by the end of the year, and more than 1,300 Americans are killed in action in 1971.

1972   North Vietnamese launch massive invasion of South Vietnam ("Easter Offensive") on March 30, using hundreds of tanks, truck-drawn heavy artillery pieces, and surface-to-air missiles in cross-border attacks into Quang Tri, Binh Long, and Kontum provinces. Quang Tri offensive begins on March 30 and drives South Vietnamese from their bases along the DMZ by April 2. Binh Long offensive begins with capture of Loc Ninh, April 4–6. U.S. resumes bombing North Vietnam below the 20th parallel on April 6. North Vietnamese move south from Loc Ninh and surround An Loc on April 7. South Vietnamese hold defensive line along Cam Lo and Cau Viet rivers and halt offensive in Quang Tri on April 9. Offensive in Kontum province begins on April 12 with attacks on South Vietnamese bases at Tan Canh and Dak To. South Vietnamese repulse attack on An Loc on April 13 with intense U.S. air support. Nixon orders air attacks on Hanoi and Haiphong on April 16.

North Vietnamese resume offensive in Quang Tri on April 23 and overrun Tan Canh and Dak To on April 24. South Vietnamese troops abandon Quang Tri City on May 1 and retreat south of the My Canh river toward Hue on May 2. Major General Ngo Quang Truong assumes command of I Corps and organizes successful defense of Hue with heavy American air and naval gunfire support.

Nixon announces mining of North Vietnamese ports on May 8 while offering to withdraw all U.S. forces from Vietnam within four months after the signing of a cease-fire and the release of American prisoners. U.S. expands bombing of North Vietnam on May 10, attacking targets in the Hanoi-Haiphong area as well as rail lines and roads leading to the Chinese border; ability of American aircraft to destroy bridges and military targets in populated areas is greatly increased by use of new laser-guided bombs. (New air campaign operates under fewer political restrictions than the bombing carried out between 1965 and 1968.)

South Vietnamese repulse attacks on An Loc, May 11–14, and city of Kontum, May 14–30; air support controlled by American advisers includes helicopters firing new wire-guided anti-tank missiles and close-in B-52 strikes.

"Easter Offensive" ends in June after North Vietnamese lose as many as 100,000 men killed, wounded, or captured; on all three fronts, North Vietnamese operations suffer from poor coordination among artillery, tanks, and infantry, and from supply difficulties that prevent the quick exploitation of initial successes. General Frederick Weygand succeeds Abrams as commander of MACV. South Vietnamese begin counteroffensive north of Hue on June 28. Siege of An Loc is broken on July 11 as heavy fighting continues in Quang Tri province. South Vietnamese recapture Quang Tri City on September 15; counteroffensive in I Corps ends with North Vietnamese still holding much of the territory captured by them during the spring.

In meeting with Kissinger on October 8 Le Duc Tho drops previous North Vietnamese demand that a coalition government be formed in South Vietnam as part of any peace agreement; by October 12 negotiators have agreed on general terms of an agreement. Thieu strongly objects to proposed terms in series of meetings with Kissinger, October 18–23. Nixon halts bombing of North Vietnam above the 20th parallel on October 23. North Vietnamese make terms of tentative agreement public on October 26 and call for its signing by October 31. Kissinger holds press conference on October 26 during which he says "peace is at hand" while stating that many details in agreement remain to be worked out. Nixon wins reelection as president on November 7. Negotiations in Paris between Kissinger and Le Duc Tho over final agreement break down on December 13. Nixon orders renewed bombing of Hanoi and Haiphong. Bombing begins on December 18 with first B-52 raids of the war against Hanoi and continues, with 36-hour pause at Christmas, until December 29 as B-52s and other aircraft attack railroad yards, power plants, airfields, and military storage areas. U.S. loses 26 aircraft, including 15 B-52s, in raids, while more than 1,300 persons are killed in Hanoi during December bombing. Nixon halts bombing above 20th parallel on December 29 after North Vietnamese announce willingness to resume negotiations.

1973   Negotiations resume in Paris on January 8. Nixon halts all bombing of North Vietnam on January 15. Final agreement is initialed by Kissinger and Le Duc Tho on January 23 and formally signed in Paris by representatives of the

U.S., North Vietnam, South Vietnam, and the Provisional Revolutionary Government on January 27. Agreement calls for a cease-fire in place, the withdrawal of foreign troops from Vietnam, the release of prisoners of war, the establishment of a Council of National Reconciliation in South Vietnam, and the holding of elections under international supervision; under its terms, the North Vietnamese are not to reinforce their troops in South Vietnam or to seek reunification by other than peaceful means. Fighting continues after cease-fire goes into effect on January 28 as both sides attempt to seize control of disputed areas. (At the time of the cease-fire, Saigon government controls most of the population and the territory of South Vietnam, although the North Vietnamese occupy significant border areas in the northern provinces, in the Central Highlands, and along the Cambodian border north of Saigon.) Withdrawal of remaining 23,400 American troops in South Vietnam begins. Military draft is ended in the United States.

Cease-fire goes into effect in Laos on February 22 following the formation of a new coalition government. War in Cambodia between Lon Nol government and Communist insurgents (Khmer Rouge) continues. Thieu declares that he will not surrender any territory to the Communists, form a coalition government, negotiate with the Communists, or permit Communist political agitation. North Vietnamese continue to send reinforcements and new equipment into South Vietnam. General Van Tien Dung, who replaced Giap as commander of the North Vietnamese army after the failure of the 1972 spring offensive, orders major expansion of Communist supply system within South Vietnam.

Last U.S. troops are withdrawn from South Vietnam on March 29. North Vietnamese complete release of 566 military and 25 civilian American prisoners on April 1. Heavy U.S. bombing continues in Cambodia as Khmer Rouge advance on Phnom Penh. Congress passes legislation on June 30 prohibiting funding of combat operations in Cambodia, Laos, and North and South Vietnam after August 15. Khmer Rouge advance on Phnom Penh is halted in early August. Bombing of Cambodia ends on August 15 (American military aid to Lon Nol government continues; by the end of 1973 the Khmer Rouge control most of Cambodia but are unable to overrun government enclaves

around the major cities). Fighting in South Vietnam increases as Lao Dong Party leadership decides that Thieu
government can be overthrown only by "revolutionary
violence."

1974   North Vietnamese launch series of local attacks in South
Vietnam designed to protect new supply routes and to
position their troops for general offensive planned for
1976. Inflation and cuts by Congress in American aid program cause increasing shortages of fuel, ammunition, and
spare parts among South Vietnamese forces. Nixon resigns
as president on August 9 to avoid impeachment and Vice-
President Gerald Ford becomes president. North Vietnamese continue construction of new roads, fuel pipelines,
and radio and telephone networks within South Vietnam.
Dung reorganizes North Vietnamese army to increase coordination among infantry, artillery, and tank forces.
Widespread fighting continues in South Vietnam (more
than 50,000 South Vietnamese soldiers are killed in action
in 1973 and 1974). North Vietnamese begin offensive in
Phouc Long province on December 13.

1975   Khmer Rouge launch new offensive in Cambodia on January 1.
North Vietnamese complete capture of Phouc Long
province on January 6. Lack of American military response
encourages Lao Dong Party leadership, who approve plans
for a major offensive in the Central Highlands in 1975.
Offensive begins on March 4 as North Vietnamese troops
block roads around Ban Me Thuot in Darlac province.
North Vietnamese assault Ban Me Thuot on March 10 and
capture town on March 11. Thieu decides to withdraw
troops from much of I and II Corps and on March 14
orders South Vietnamese forces to evacuate Kontum and
Pleiku, move to the coast, and then recapture Ban Me
Thuot. Evacuation of Central Highlands begins on March
16; retreating columns come under intense North Vietnamese attack (of the 60,000 troops who leave the Highlands, only 20,000 reach the coast at Tuy Hoa on March
27). Redeployment of elite airborne troops from Quang
Tri to Saigon region weakens South Vietnamese forces in
I Corps. North Vietnamese overrun Quang Tri province
on March 19. Refugee flight and concern of soldiers for
safety of their families undermine morale of South Viet-

namese troops in northern provinces. Hue is abandoned on March 25 as soldiers and refugees flee toward Danang in hope of being evacuated by sea or air. North Vietnamese capture Danang on March 30 and Nha Trang on April 1.

Khmer Rouge close Mekong River to supply convoys and begin intense rocket bombardment of Phnom Penh and its airport.

Dung redeploys North Vietnamese army in preparation for "Ho Chi Minh campaign" aimed at capture of Saigon. North Vietnamese attack on Xuan Loc on April 9 is repulsed by determined South Vietnamese resistance.

Khmer Rouge capture Phnom Penh on April 17 and forcibly evacuate its population into countryside as war in Cambodia ends.

Thieu resigns on April 21 and goes into exile. North Vietnamese capture Xuan Loc on April 22 and complete encirclement of Saigon on April 27. Duong Van Minh, leader of 1963 coup against Diem, becomes president of South Vietnam on April 28. U.S. evacuates several thousand Americans and South Vietnamese by helicopter from Saigon, April 29–30. North Vietnamese army enters Saigon on morning of April 30 as Minh orders South Vietnamese forces to surrender.

Pathet Lao troops enter Vientiane on August 23, and People's Democratic Republic of Laos is proclaimed on December 2. Communists establish "reeducation" camps in South Vietnam, where more than 200,000 persons are eventually sent to perform forced labor and undergo ideological indoctrination under harsh conditions.

1976   Socialist Republic of Vietnam is proclaimed in Hanoi on July 2 as North and South Vietnam are formally united.

1977   President Jimmy Carter pardons Vietnam-era draft resisters and evaders. Fighting begins along Vietnamese-Cambodian border in late April after Khmer Rouge stage major raid into Vietnam. Pathet Lao and Vietnamese troops attack Hmong villages inside Laos (over 300,000 people flee Laos after 1975). Refugees continue to leave Vietnam by boat (over 900,000 Vietnamese, many of them ethnic Chinese, become refugees between 1975 and 1988, in addition to the 140,000 who fled the country during the Communist victory in 1975).

1978   Vietnamese-Chinese relations worsen as Vietnam forms
            closer ties with the Soviet Union. Vietnamese army in-
            vades Cambodia on December 25.

1979   Vietnamese capture Phnom Penh on January 7 and install
            new regime. Khmer Rouge retreat into western Cambodia
            and begin guerrilla warfare against Vietnamese, using Chi-
            nese weapons supplied through Thailand. Chinese invade
            border region of northern Vietnam on February 17; fight-
            ing causes heavy casualties on both sides before Chinese
            withdraw on March 16. U.S. refuses to recognize new
            Cambodian government and tightens economic embargo
            imposed on Vietnam in 1975.

1982   Vietnam Veterans Memorial is dedicated in Washington,
            D.C., on November 13.

1986   Le Duan dies. Nguyen Van Linh becomes general secre-
            tary of the Communist Party and begins extensive pro-
            gram of economic reform.

1989   Vietnamese troops withdraw from Cambodia.

1994   President Bill Clinton lifts embargo on trade with Vietnam
            in response to increased Vietnamese cooperation in re-
            solving cases of American servicemen missing in action.

1995   United States establishes full diplomatic relations with
            Vietnam on July 11.

More than 58,000 American military personnel died in
Indochina between 1959 and 1975; of these deaths, more
than 47,000 were the result of hostile action. Battle deaths
by service were approximately 31,000 in the army, 13,000
in the marines, 1,700 in the air force, and 1,600 in the
navy.

South Korea lost 4,400 men killed in action in Vietnam.
Australia and New Zealand lost almost 500 dead. Thai
losses in Vietnam and Laos are not known. The number
of persons killed in the fighting in Laos is not known,
although it is estimated that 30,000 Hmong died during
the war. Cambodia lost at least 180,000 dead between

1970 and 1975, and at least one million Cambodians were executed, starved, or worked to death under the Khmer Rouge between 1975 and 1978; the number of Cambodians and Vietnamese killed in Cambodia since 1979 is not known. South Vietnam lost at least 220,000 military dead and at least 300,000 civilian dead during the war, and tens of thousands of Vietnamese refugees died at sea after 1975. It is estimated that at least 50,000 civilians were killed by American bombing in North Vietnam. In 1995 the Vietnamese government stated that 1,100,000 North Vietnamese and Viet Cong soldiers died between 1954 and 1975.

Biographical Notes

JOSEPH ALSOP (October 11, 1910–August 28, 1989) Born in Avon, Connecticut; graduated Harvard in 1932. After five years on staff of New York *Herald Tribune* (1932–37), began column "The Capital Parade" with Robert Kintner for North American Newspaper Alliance. Co-authored two books with Kintner, *Men Around the President* (1939), and *American White Paper: The Story of American Diplomacy and the Second World War* (1940). Joined U.S. Navy in 1940; later served with American Volunteer Group in China (held prisoner by Japanese in Hong Kong, 1942), and with 14th Air Force. In 1946 joined brother Stewart Alsop to write syndicated column "Matter of Fact"; was sole author from 1958 to 1974. Winner of Overseas Press Club Award, 1951. Other books include *The 168 Days* (1938, with Turner Catledge), *We Accuse! The Story of the Miscarriage of American Justice in the Case of J. Robert Oppenheimer* (with Stewart Alsop, 1954), *The Reporter's Trade* (with Stewart Alsop, 1958), *From the Silent Earth: A Report on the Greek Bronze Age* (1964), *The Rare Art Traditions* (1982), and *FDR: A Centenary Romance* (1982). Died in Washington, D.C.

MICHAEL J. ARLEN (December 9, 1930–) Born in London; educated at Harvard University. Worked as reporter for *Life* for four years beginning in 1952; contributor and television critic for *The New Yorker* from 1957 to 1982. His books include *The Living-Room War* (1969), *Exiles* (1970), *An American Verdict* (1973), *Passage to Ararat* (1975, winner of National Book Award), *The View from Highway 1: Essays on Television* (1976), *Thirty Seconds* (1980), *The Camera Age: Essays on Television* (1981), and *Say Goodbye to Sam* (1984).

PETER ARNETT (November 13, 1934–) Born in Riverton, New Zealand. Began career in 1951 as reporter for New Zealand newpapers *Southland Times* and *The Standard*. Moved to Sydney, Australia, in 1956, working briefly for *Sydney Sun* and *TV Preview*. After travel in Southeast Asia, took job in 1958 as reporter for *Bangkok World*; joined Associated Press in 1959 as stringer. Started paper *Vientiane World* in 1960. In 1961, hired as Associated Press Jakarta correspondent; expelled for anti-government stories. From 1962 until fall of Saigon in 1975, served as AP Vietnam correspondent, winning Pulitzer Prize in 1966. After war, continued to work for AP in New York; naturalized as U.S. citizen in 1979. Joined Cable News Network in 1981 as global correspondent, reporting from El Salvador, Iran, Lebanon, the Soviet Union, and Panama. Covered 1991 Gulf War from Baghdad. Memoir *Live from the Battlefield: From Vietnam to Baghdad, 35 Years in the World's War Zones* published in 1994.

RUSSELL BAKER (August 14, 1925–) Born in Loudoun County, Virginia. Graduated from Johns Hopkins University in 1947. After college, worked for seven years for the *Baltimore Sun*. In 1954 joined Washington bureau of *The New York Times*; from 1962 onwards has written "Observer" column for *The New York Times*. Winner of 1979 Pulitzer Prize for commentary. Books include *City on the Potomac* (1958), *American in Washington* (1961), *No Cause for Panic* (1964), *All Things Considered* (1965), *Our Next President* (1968), *Poor Russell's Almanac* (1972), *The Upside Down Man* (1977), *So This Is Depravity* (1980), *Growing Up* (1982), *The Rescue of Miss Yaskell and Other Pipe Dreams* (1983), *The Good Times* (1989), *There's a Country in My Cellar* (1990).

HOMER BIGART (October 25, 1907–April 16, 1991) Born in Hawley, Pennsylvania. Educated at Carnegie Institute of Technology and New York University School of Journalism. While at NYU worked for New York *Herald Tribune* as copyboy; hired as a reporter in 1933. Traveled to Europe as war correspondent in 1942, moving to Pacific theater two years later. Went to Vietnam for *Tribune* in 1945, 1950, and 1953; won Pulitzer Prize in 1951 for coverage of Korean War. Left *Tribune* for *The New York Times* in 1955. Reported from the Middle East, and, in 1962, from Vietnam. Retired in 1972; died in Portsmouth, New Hampshire. Writings collected posthumously in *Forward Positions: The War Correspondence of Homer Bigart* (1992).

JEFFREY A. BLANKFORT (June 4, 1934–) Born in New York City; educated University of California at Los Angeles, graduating in 1957. Worked at *Los Angeles Examiner* while at UCLA. Began career as freelance photojournalist in mid-1960s, focusing on anti-Vietnam war protests in the U.S. and abroad, and domestic political movements; his photographs have appeared in *Newsweek, Esquire, Harper's, The Saturday Evening Post, Rolling Stone, Interview,* and *Ramparts,* among other publications. From 1988 to 1995, he edited *The Middle East Labor Bulletin*; currently teaching history at Richmond (California) High School.

MALCOLM W. BROWNE (April 17, 1931–) Born Malcolm Wilde Browne in New York City; attended Swarthmore College and New York University, graduating in 1952. After college worked for four years as a chemist and technical writer. Drafted in 1956; began journalism career as reporter for *Pacific Stars and Stripes* in Korea. On return to U.S., hired as newsman and copy editor for Middletown (New York) *Daily Record*; moved to Baltimore bureau of Associated Press two years later, in 1960. Worked in Vietnam as chief AP Indochina correspondent (1961–65) and Saigon correspondent for the American Broadcasting Corporation (1965–66). Shared 1964 Pulitzer Prize for coverage of fall of Diem regime. After two years as a freelance correspondent and writer, joined staff of *The New York Times* in 1968, serving as correspondent in Buenos Aires, South Asia (1971–73), and Eastern Europe (1973–77). Since 1977 has been *Times* science correspondent and writer; edited *Discover* for three years beginning in 1981. His books include *The New Face of War* (1965) and memoir *Muddy Boots and Red Socks* (1993).

KEVIN BUCKLEY (December 31, 1940–   )   Born in New York City. Graduated in 1962 from Yale University, where he was managing editor of *Yale Daily News* and campus correspondent for New York *Herald Tribune*. Joined staff of *Newsweek* as religion writer in 1963; for next eleven years worked for *Newsweek* in Chicago, Boston, London, Saigon (bureau reporter 1968–69, bureau chief 1970–72), and Hong Kong. Later served as editor at *New Times* (1978), *Look* (1979), *Lear's* (1986–87), *Geo*, and *Playboy* (1991–   ); has taught at Hampshire College, Boston University, and Columbia School of Journalism. Author of *Panama: The Whole Story* (1991).

WALTER CRONKITE (November 4, 1916–   )   Born Walter Leland Cronkite Jr. in St. Joseph, Missouri. While attending University of Texas at Austin, worked as campus correspondent for Houston *Post*, state capitol reporter for Scripps-Howard, and sports announcer for KCMO, a radio station in Kansas City. Joined staff of United Press International in 1937, covering World War II, and then served as Moscow correspondent (1946–48). Became a correspondent for Columbia Broadcasting System in 1950; from 1962 until 1981, served as anchor of *CBS Evening News*. Writer, editor, and narrator of television specials for CBS; author of *Eye on the World* (1971), *The Challenges of Change* (1971), and *A Reporter's Life* (1996).

BEVERLY DEEPE (June 1, 1935–   )   Born Beverly Ann Deepe in Hebron, Nebraska. Studied journalism and political science at University of Nebraska (B.A. 1957), journalism at Columbia University (M.S. 1958), and library and information science at the University of Hawaii (M.L.I.S. 1991). Beginning in 1962, worked as stringer for *Newsweek* and other publications in Saigon; later Vietnam correspondent for New York *Herald Tribune* (1964–66) and *Christian Science Monitor* (1967–69), and reporter for Capitol Hill News Service (1974–75). Married Charles J. Keever in 1969, taking his name. Joined faculty of University of Hawaii at Manoa in 1979, becoming associate professor in 1987. Co-editor of *U.S. News Coverage of Racial Minorities, A Sourcebook: 1934–1996* (1997).

BERNARD B. FALL (November 11, 1926–February 21, 1967)   Born in Vienna, Austria. Served in French Underground and Fourth Moroccan Mountain Division during World War II; after the war worked as war crimes investigator and tracing officer for Nuremberg War Crimes Trials (1946–50), and as district manager for *Stars and Stripes* in Nuremberg (1950–51). Educated at universities of Paris and Munich (1948–50), the University of Maryland overseas program (1951), and at Syracuse University, from which he received his doctorate in 1955. Taught in American universities beginning in 1954, as Asian studies instructor at Cornell, assistant professor at American University, and professor of international relations at Howard (1956–67). Received George Polk Award in 1966. Author of *The Viet-Minh Regime* (1954), *Street Without Joy: Indochina at War, 1946–54* (1961), *Two Viet-Nams: A Political and Military History*

(1963), *Viet-Nam Witness, 1953–66* (1966), *Hell in a Very Small Place* (1967), and editor of *Ho Chi Minh on Revolution: Selected Writings, 1920–1966* (1967). Killed by a booby-trap explosion on Highway 1, between Hue and Quang Tri, while covering operation by the U.S. Marines. Uncollected writings published posthumously as *Last Reflections on a War* (1967).

FRANCES FITZGERALD (October 21, 1940–   ) Born in New York City; educated at Radcliffe, graduating in 1962. Worked as freelance writer for *Herald Tribune Sunday Magazine, The Village Voice, Vogue, Atlantic,* and other magazines; writer for *The New Yorker* and other periodicals (1971–   ). Correspondent in Vietnam in 1966, 1971, 1973, and 1975; worked also in the Middle East, Central America, the Caribbean, and the U.S. Received Pulitzer Prize for contemporary affairs writing in 1973 and Overseas Press Club Award, 1972. Author of *Fire in the Lake: The Vietnamese and Americans in Vietnam* (1972, winner of National Book Award, Bancroft Prize), *America Revised* (1979), and *Cities on a Hill* (1986).

JOHN FLYNN (July 12, 1932–   ) Born in Portland, Oregon. From 1956 to 1957, served as analyst with U.S. Army Counterintelligence Corps in West Germany. Later began career in journalism, working as editor for *Westchester News-Advertiser* in Los Angeles, reporter and photographer for Torrance, California, *Daily Breeze,* correspondent for Associated Press in Los Angeles, and, beginning in 1963, correspondent for *Life,* serving as magazine's first permanent staffer in Vietnam. Joined CBS News in 1965, serving as reporter and field producer in New York, Saigon, and Los Angeles. From 1969 until his retirement in 1997, associated with KNBC-TV in Burbank, California, as assignment editor, writer, and producer.

MARTHA GELLHORN (November 1908–February 15, 1998) Born in St. Louis, Missouri; educated at Bryn Mawr. Worked in New York for *The New Republic* and in Albany as a reporter for *Times Union.* Traveled in Europe and around the U.S. in early 1930s; worked as field investigator for Federal Emergency Relief Administration. Reported on Spanish Civil War for *Collier's;* also covered Soviet-Finnish War and, beginning in 1943, war in Europe. After war, collaborated with Virginia Cowles on comedy about war correspondents, *Love Goes to Press* (1946); reported on Indonesian anticolonial rebellion and Nuremberg War Crimes Trials. In 1947 launched attack on House Un-American Activities Committee. Settled in England. Reported on Eastern Europe and the Middle East; traveled to Vietnam as correspondent for *The Guardian* in 1966, and to Israel in 1967 during Six-Day War; reported on El Salvador and Nicaragua during 1980s. Author of novels including *What Mad Pursuit* (1934), *A Stricken Field* (1940), *Liana* (1944), *The Wine of Astonishment* (1948; republished as *Point of No Return*), *His Own Man* (1961), and *The Lowest Trees Have Tops* (1967); story collections *The Trouble I've Seen* (1936), *The Heart of Another* (1941), *The Honeyed Peace* (1953), *Two by Two* (1958), *Pretty Tales for Tired People* (1965), and *The Weather in Africa* (1981); memoir *Travels with*

Myself and Another (1978); and *The Face of War* (1959), collected war reporting. Died in London.

HENRY F. GRAFF (August 11, 1921–) Born Henry Franklin Graff in New York City. Educated at the College of the City of New York (B.S.S. 1941) and Columbia University, from which he received a Ph.D. in history in 1949. Served in U.S. Army as Japanese linguist and cryptanalyst (1942–46). Taught history at Columbia (1946–91), becoming full professor in 1961. Author of *Bluejackets with Perry in Japan* (1952), *The Modern Researcher* (with Jacques Barzun, 1957), *The Tuesday Cabinet: Deliberation and Decision on Peace and War under Lyndon B. Johnson* (1970), *The Presidents: A Reference History* (1984), and several American history textbooks.

ZALIN GRANT (April 17, 1941–) Born Zalin B. Grant in Cheraw, South Carolina. Graduated from Clemson University in 1963; during college, worked as stringer for Associated Press. After two years of service in Saigon and Danang as U.S. Army intelligence officer and Vietnamese linguist, joined staff of *Time* magazine; reported on Vietnam from 1965 to 1967, and later from Washington and New York. Became Southeast Asia correspondent for *The New Republic* in 1968. Beginning in 1971, has been a freelance writer, living in Spain and France; has served as editorial director of Pythia Press since 1995. His books include *Survivors* (1975), *Over the Beach* (1986), *Facing the Phoenix* (1992), and *Flying Smart* (1995).

MEG GREENFIELD (December 27, 1930–) Born in Seattle, Washington; educated at Smith College (B.A. 1952) and, with a Fulbright scholarship, at Newnham College, Cambridge (1952–53). Joined staff of *The Reporter* in 1957, serving as Washington editor 1965–68; later worked for *The Washington Post* as editorial writer and editorial page editor (1968–). Began contributing columns to *Newsweek* in 1974. Received Pulitzer Prize for editorial writing in 1978.

DAVID HALBERSTAM (April 10, 1934–) Born in New York City; educated at Harvard University (B.A. 1955). After college took reporting job in West Point, Mississippi, with *West Point Daily Times Leader* (1955–56); later worked for Nashville *Tennessean* (1956–60), and as staff writer for *The New York Times* (1960–67), in Vietnam from 1962 to 1963. Shared Pulitzer Prize for reporting from Saigon and George Polk Award for foreign reporting, 1964. Left *Times* in 1967 to become contributing editor for *Harper's*. His books include *The Noblest Roman* (novel, 1961), *The Making of a Quagmire* (1965), *One Very Hot Day* (novel, 1968), *The Unfinished Odyssey of Robert Kennedy* (1969), *Ho* (1971), *The Best and the Brightest* (1972; winner of Overseas Press Club Award), *The Powers That Be* (1979), *The Breaks of the Game* (1981), *The Amateurs* (1985), *The Reckoning* (1987), *Summer of '49* (1989), *The Next Century* (1992), *The Fifties* (1993), *October 1964* (1994), and *The Children* (1998).

FRANK HARVEY (February 15, 1913–December 15, 1993)   Born Frank Laird Harvey in Pittsburgh, Pennsylvania. Attended Cornell University; graduated from Columbia University in 1937. After college, worked as copywriter for Bethlehem Steel; joined U.S. Navy in 1943, serving for three years. Worked for *Argosy* from 1950 to 1954 as contributing editor; later a freelance writer (1954–93). His books include *Jet* (1954), *Air Force* (1955), *The Lion Pit* (1961), *Strike Command* (1962), *Nightmare County* (1964), *Hudasky's Raiders* (1966), and *Air War—Vietnam* (1967). Died in Hackettstown, New Jersey.

RICHARD HARWOOD (March 29, 1925–   )   Born in Chilton, Wisconsin. Served with the U.S. Marine Corps for four years, beginning in 1942; graduated from Vanderbilt University in 1950. Reported for Nashville *Tennessean* while in college and for two years afterwards. Moved to Louisville *Courier-Journal and Times* in 1952, remaining for 13 years, four as Washington correspondent. Joined *The Washington Post* in 1966 as national correspondent and editor; later worked as assistant and deputy managing editor, ombudsman, and editorial columnist (1992–   ). Won 1967 George Polk Award for national reporting and 1972 award for criticism. Author of *Lyndon: A Biography of Lyndon Baines Johnson* (1968).

MARGUERITE HIGGINS (September 3, 1920–January 3, 1966)   Born in Hong Kong; grew up in Oakland, California. Educated at University of California and Columbia School of Journalism. Joined staff of New York *Herald Tribune* in 1942, working as war correspondent in England, France, and Germany (1944–45), as Berlin bureau chief (1944–50), Tokyo bureau chief (1950–51), and Washington correspondent. Won Pulitzer Prize in 1951 for coverage of battle of Inchon in Korea. In 1954 covered French defeat in Vietnam. Left *Tribune* in 1963 to write for New York *Newsday*. Traveled ten times to Vietnam between 1953 and 1965. Books include *War in Korea* (1951), *News Is a Singular Thing* (1954, memoir), *Red Plush and Black Bread* (1956), *Jessie Benton Fremont* (1962), *Tales of the Foreign Service* (1963, with Peter Lisagor), *Saigon Summary* (1964), and *Our Vietnam Nightmare* (1965). Died in Washington, D.C., of leishmaniasis, a tropical disease she contracted in Vietnam.

DAVID HOFFMAN (1932–February 15, 1985)   Born David Herbert Hoffman in Coral Gables, Florida; educated at University of Florida and Boston University, from which he received a master's degree in political science. After an early career as pilot for the Air Force and for Trans World Airlines, began writing for *Aviation Week and Space Technology*, and later became aviation editor for New York *Herald Tribune*. Joined *The Washington Post* in 1967; investigated My Lai massacre in 1969 as Saigon bureau chief. Left the *Post* in 1971, working briefly for *Miami Herald*, then returned to Washington as freelance writer. Died in Arlington, Virginia.

THOMAS A. JOHNSON (October 11, 1928–   )   Born in St. Augustine, Florida. Moved to New York City as a child; in 1954, graduated from Long Island

University with a degree in English and journalism. Worked as social worker, Department of Welfare investigator, public relations man, and freelance writer before joining staff of *Newsday* in 1963. Joined *The New York Times* in 1966; served as national and local reporter, metropolitan desk assignment editor, and as foreign correspondent in Africa, Europe, the Caribbean, and Vietnam (December 1967–March 1968). Taught at New York University from 1969–72 as adjunct professor of journalism. Retired from *Times* in 1981 to become president of Thomas A. Johnson Associates, a Manhattan public relations firm.

WARD S. JUST (September 5, 1935–) Born Ward Swift Just in Michigan City, Indiana; educated at Trinity College, Hartford, Connecticut. Began career as reporter for Waukegan (Illinois) *News-Sun* (1957–59); later worked for *Newsweek* (1959–65) and *The Washington Post* (1965–70), in Vietnam from December 1965 to June 1967. His nonfiction works include *To What End: Report from Vietnam* (1968), and *Military Men* (1970); his fiction *A Soldier of the Revolution* (1970), *The Congressman Who Loved Flaubert, and Other Washington Stories* (1973), *Stringer* (1974), *Nicholson at Large* (1975), *A Family Trust* (1978), *Honor, Power, Riches, Fame, and the Love of Women* (1979), *In the City of Fear* (1982), *The American Blues* (1984), *The American Ambassador* (1987), *Jack Gance* (1989), *Twenty-One: Selected Stories* (1990), *The Translator* (1991), *Ambition and Love* (1994), and *Echo House* (1997).

STANLEY KARNOW (February 4, 1925–) Born in New York City. Served with U.S. Army Air Forces for three years beginning in 1943; later educated at Harvard, the Sorbonne, and the Ecole des Sciences Politiques. Began career in Paris as correspondent for *Time* (1950–57); worked subsequently as Time-Life bureau chief in North Africa (1958–59) and Hong Kong (1959–62), special correspondent for *London Observer* (1961–65) and *Time* (1962–63), and foreign correspondent for *The Saturday Evening Post* (1963–65). Joined staff of *The Washington Post* in 1965 as Far East correspondent, covering Vietnam, Southeast Asia, and China; was diplomatic correspondent for the *Post* in 1971 and 1972. Worked as NBC News correspondent from 1973 to 1975; later became associate editor of *The New Republic* (1973–75), King Features columnist (1975–88), and *Newsweek* columnist (1977–81). Was chief correspondent for PBS series *Vietnam: A Television History* (1983) and *The U.S. and the Philippines: In Our Image* (1989). Books include *Southeast Asia* (1963), *Mao and China: From Revolution to Revolution* (1972), *Vietnam: A History* (1983), *In Our Image: America's Empire in the Philippines* (1989, winner of the 1990 Pulitzer Prize for history), and *Paris in the Fifties* (1997).

DANIEL LANG (May 30, 1915–November 17, 1981) Born in New York City; educated at University of Wisconsin, graduating in 1936. After two years as reporter for *New York Post* (1939–41), joined staff of *The New Yorker*. Reported from North Africa, Italy, and France during World War II; later became a regular *New Yorker* contributor and freelance writer. Winner of 1977 George Polk Award for magazine reporting. Author of *Early Tales of the Atomic Age*

(1948), *The Man in the Thick Lead Suit* (1954), *From Hiroshima to the Moon* (1959), *A Summer's Duckling* (children's book, 1963), *An Enquiry into Enoughness: Of Bombs and Men and Staying Alive* (1965), *Casualties of War* (1969), *Patriotism without Flags* (1975), and *A Backward Look: Germans Remember* (1979). Died in New York City.

STEVE LERNER (February 9, 1946–   ) Born Stephen Daedalus Lerner in New York City. Graduated Harvard University in 1968; at Harvard, reported on antiwar events for *Harvard Crimson* and as stringer for *The New York Times*. After college hired as staff writer for *The Village Voice* (1968–69). Traveled overland through Asia for two years; upon return worked in tool factories, a pottery, an orchard, and in construction (1971–75). Since 1976 has served as research director for Commonweal (nonprofit health and environmental organization); editor and publisher of *Common Knowledge* (1977–82). Books include *The CYA Report: Conditions of Life at the California Youth Authority* (1982), *Bodily Harm: The Pattern of Fear and Violence at the California Youth Authority* (1986), *Reforming the CYA* (1988), *The Good News about Juvenile Justice* (1990), *Beyond the Earth Summit* (1992), and *Eco-Pioneers* (1997).

LEE LESCAZE (December 8, 1938–July 26, 1996) Born Lee Adrien Lescaze in New York City. Studied English and Chinese at Harvard University, graduating in 1960. Began working at *The Washington Post* in 1963 as copyboy; later served as local reporter, assistant foreign editor, Saigon correspondent (1967–68), Hong Kong correspondent (1970–73), foreign editor (1973–75), national editor (1975–77), New York correspondent (1977–80), presidential campaign and White House correspondent (1980–81), and managing editor for Style section (1981–82). Joined *The Wall Street Journal* in 1983, serving as foreign editor and weekend editor. Died in New York City.

MARY MCCARTHY (June 21, 1912–October 25, 1989) Born in Seattle, Washington. Graduated Vassar College in 1933, then worked in various jobs in New York City: as book reviewer for *The Nation* and *The New Republic* (1933–36), editor at Covici Friede (1936–37), ghostwriter for H.V. Kaltenborn (1937), editor of *Partisan Review* (1937–38), and drama critic (1937–62). Taught literature at Bard College, Sarah Lawrence, and University of London. Her works of fiction include *The Company She Keeps* (1942), *The Oasis* (1949), *The Groves of Academe* (1952), *A Charmed Life* (1955), *The Group* (1963), *Birds of America* (1965), *Cannibals and Missionaries* (1979), *The Hounds of Summer and Other Stories* (1981); her nonfiction: *Cast a Cold Eye* (1950), *Sights and Spectacles, 1937–1956* (1956), *Venice Observed* (1956), *Memories of a Catholic Girlhood* (1957), *The Stones of Florence* (1959), *On the Contrary* (1961), *Mary McCarthy's Theatre Chronicles* (1963), *Vietnam* (1967), *Hanoi* (1968), *The Writing on the Wall and Other Literary Essays* (1970), *Medina* (1972), *The Mask of State: Watergate Portraits* (1974), *The Seventeenth Degree* (1974), *Ideas and the Novel* (1980), *Occasional Prose* (1985), and *How I Grew* (1987). Died in New York City.

JOE McGINNISS (December 9, 1942–   )   Born in New York City; graduated from Holy Cross in 1964. After college worked as reporter for *Port Chester Daily Item* (1964), *Worcester Telegram* (1965), *Philadelphia Bulletin* (1966), and *Philadelphia Inquirer* (1967–68). Since 1968, has been a freelance writer and a lecturer in writing at Bennington College. Among his books are *The Selling of the President, 1968* (1969), *The Dream Team* (1972), *Heroes* (1976), *Going to Extremes* (1980), *Alaskan Episodes* (1980), *Fatal Vision* (1983), *Blind Faith* (1988), *Cruel Doubt* (1991), and *The Last Brother* (1993).

NORMAN MAILER (January 31, 1923–   )   Born in Long Branch, New Jersey; educated at Harvard University (B.S. 1943) and the Sorbonne (1947–48). Served in U.S. Army from 1944 to 1946 as field artillery observer and infantry rifleman in Philippines and Japan; novel *The Naked and the Dead* (1948) based on wartime experiences. Subsequent novels include *Barbary Shore* (1951), *The Deer Park* (1955), *An American Dream* (1965), *Why Are We in Vietnam?* (1967), *A Transit to Narcissus* (1944, first published 1978), *The Executioner's Song* (1979, winner of Pulitzer Prize for fiction), *Ancient Evenings* (1983), *Tough Guys Don't Dance* (1984), *Harlot's Ghost* (1991), and *The Gospel According to the Son* (1997); nonfiction books include *The Armies of the Night* (1968, winner of National Book Award and Pulitzer Prize for general nonfiction), *Miami and the Siege of Chicago* (1969), *Of a Fire on the Moon* (1970), *The Prisoner of Sex* (1971) *King of the Hill: On the Fight of the Century* (1971), *St. George and the Godfather* (1972), *Marilyn: A Biography* (1973), *The Fight* (1975), and *Oswald's Tale: An American Mystery* (1995). Among collections of his works are *The White Negro: Superficial Reflections on the Hipster* (1957), *Advertisements for Myself* (1959), *Cannibals and Christians* (1966), *The Short Fiction of Norman Mailer* (1967), and *Pieces and Pontifications* (1982). Candidate for New York City Democratic mayoral nomination in 1969.

CHARLES MOHR (June 18, 1929–June 16, 1989)   Born Loup City, Nebraska. Educated at University of Nebraska, graduating in 1951; worked for a year while an undergraduate as reporter for *Lincoln Star*. After college became reporter for United Press International in Chicago; three years later joined staff of *Time*, resigning in 1963 over magazine's rewriting of his critical reports from Vietnam. Hired by the *The New York Times*, he became chief Southeast Asia correspondent in 1966; reported from Vietnam until 1970. Spent five years in 1970s reporting from Africa; also covered Carter presidential campaign, and the 1967 and 1973 wars in Middle East. Shared 1986 Pulitzer Prize for reporting on "Star Wars" missile defense system. Died in Bethesda, Maryland.

DON MOSER (October 19, 1932–   )   Born Donald Bruce Moser in Cleveland, Ohio. Served in U.S. Army, 1953–55. Graduated from Ohio University in 1957; also attended Stanford and the University of Sydney. Worked for *Life* as reporter and assistant editor (1961–64), West Coast bureau chief (1964–65), Far East bureau chief (1966–69), and assistant managing editor (1970–72). After five years as a freelance writer (1972–77) became editor of *Smithsonian*

(1977–). Author of *The Peninsula: A Story of the Olympic Country in Words and Photographs* (1962), *The Pied Piper of Tucson* (1968, with Jerry Cohen), *The Snake River Country* (1974), *Central American Jungles* (1975), *A Heart to the Hawks* (1975), and *China-Burma-India Theater* (1977).

DON OBERDORFER (May 28, 1931–) Born Donald Oberdorfer Jr. in Atlanta, Georgia. Graduated from Princeton University in 1952, after which he served for two years in U.S. Army in Korea. Began career in journalism as staff writer for *Charlotte Observer* (1955–61) and *The Saturday Evening Post* (1961–65). Reported from Vietnam beginning in 1965, first as staff writer for Knight and later for *The Washington Post*. Remained with *Post* until 1993, when he became journalist-in-residence at the Nitze School of Advanced International Studies, Johns Hopkins University. His books include *Tet!* (1971), *The Turn: From the Cold War to a New Era* (1991), *Princeton University: The First 250 Years* (1995), and *The Two Koreas: A Contemporary History* (1997).

McCANDLISH PHILLIPS (December 4, 1927–) Born John McCandlish Phillips in Mount Vernon, New York. After graduation from high school, worked briefly as editor of *Boston Sport-Light* and for a weekly paper in Brookline, Massachusetts. Upon discharge from U.S. Army in 1952, joined *The New York Times* as editorial trainee; promoted to reporter in 1955. Left *Times* in 1973, continuing to accept spot assignments until 1980. Currently an elder and co-administrator of New Testament Missionary Fellowship, which he co-founded in 1964; also serves as general manager of Thomas E. Lowe, Ltd., a religious publishing house. Author of *The Bible, the Supernatural, and the Jews* (1970), *The Spirit World* (1972), *City Notebook: A Reporter's Portrait of a Vanishing New York* (1974).

JONATHAN RANDAL (February 14, 1933–) Born Jonathan C. Randal in Buffalo, New York. Graduated Harvard University in 1955, served for two years in U.S. Army, then worked in Paris for a year for United Press and Agence France-Presse. Subsequently served as UPI correspondent in London (1958) and Geneva (1959–60), correspondent for *The Paris Herald* (1960–61), *Time* correspondent in Africa and the Middle East (1962–66), *The New York Times* correspondent in Vietnam (1966–67) and Eastern Europe (1967–69), and *The Washington Post* Paris correspondent (1969–75), with a long tour in Vietnam in 1972. Since 1975, has been *Washington Post* roving correspondent, principally in Middle East, Africa, and Balkans. Books include *Going All the Way: Christian Warlords, Israeli Adventurers and the War in Lebanon* (1983) and *After Such Knowledge, What Forgiveness: My Encounters with Kurdistan* (1997).

ROGER RAPOPORT (May 7, 1946–) Born Roger Dale Rapoport in Detroit, Michigan; educated at the University of Michigan, graduating in 1968. Since college, has worked as a freelance journalist. His books include *Is the Library Burning?* (with L.J. Kirshbaum, 1969), *The Great American Bomb Machine* (1971), *The Super-doctors* (1975), *The California Catalogue* (with

Margot Lind, 1977), *The Big Player* (with Ken Uston, 1977), *California Dreaming* (1982), *22 Days in California* (1988), *22 Days in Asia* (with B. Willes, 1989), *22 Days around the World* (1990), *Into the Sunlight: Life after the Iron Curtain* (1991), *Great Cities of Eastern Europe* (1992), *The Wolf* (1994), and *The Rattler* (1994).

HARRISON E. SALISBURY (November 14, 1908–July 5, 1992) Born Harrison Evans Salisbury in Minneapolis, Minnesota; graduated from University of Minnesota in 1930. Began career in journalism in 1928 as reporter for *Minneapolis Journal*. After college joined United Press International, working as reporter, London manager, Moscow manager, and foreign editor. From 1949 to 1954 served as *The New York Times* Moscow correspondent; received Pulitzer Prize in 1955 for articles on Soviet Union. Later based in New York as reporter (1955–61), national editor (1962–64), assistant managing editor (1964–70), and op-ed page editor (1971–75). In addition to two novels, *The Northern Palmyra Affair* (1962) and *The Gates of Hell* (1975), and a book of photographs, *Children of Russia* (1967), he is the author of: *Russia on the Way* (1946), *American in Russia* (1955), *The Shook-up Generation* (1958), *To Moscow—and Beyond: A Reporter's Narrative* (1960), *Moscow Journal: The End of Stalin* (1961), *A New Russia?* (1962), *The Key to Moscow* (1963), *Russia* (1965), *Orbit of China* (1967), *Behind the Lines—Hanoi, December 23, 1966–January 7, 1967* (1967), *The Coming War between Russia and China* (1969), *The 900 Days: The Siege of Leningrad* (1969), *The Many Americans Shall Be One* (1971), *To Peking—and Beyond: A Report on the New Asia* (1973), *Travels around America* (1976), *Black Night, White Snow: Russia's Revolutions, 1905–1917* (1978), *The Unknown War* (1978), *Russia in Revolution: 1900–1930* (1978), *Without Fear or Favor: The New York Times and Its Times* (1980), *China: 100 Years of Revolution* (1983), *A Journey for Our Times: A Memoir* (1983), *The Long March: The Untold Story* (1985), *A Time of Change: A Reporter's Tale of Our Time* (1988), *The Great Black Dragon Fire: A Chinese Inferno* (1989), *Tiananmen Diary: Thirteen Days in June* (1989), *The New Emperors: China in the Era of Mao and Deng* (1992), and the posthumous *Heroes of My Time* (1993).

JONATHAN SCHELL (August 21, 1943–) Born in New York City. Graduated from Harvard University in 1965. Worked as writer for *The New Yorker* from 1967 to 1987, and as columnist for *Newsday* from 1990 to 1996. His books include: *The Village of Ben Suc* (1967), *The Military Half: An Account of the Destruction of Quang Ngai and Quang Tin* (1968), *The Time of Illusion* (1976), *The Fate of the Earth* (1982), *The Abolition* (1984), *History in Sherman Park* (1987), *Observing the Nixon Years* (1989), *Writing in Time* (1997), and *The Gift of Time* (1998).

NEIL SHEEHAN (October 27, 1936–) Born Cornelius Mahoney Sheehan in Holyoke, Massachusetts; graduated from Harvard University in 1958. Served as Saigon bureau chief for the Associated Press from 1962 to 1964. Joined *The New York Times* in 1964, working as reporter in New York, foreign correspondent in Indonesia (1965) and Vietnam (1965–66), Pentagon correspondent (1966–68), White House correspondent (1968–69) and special investigative reporter based in Washington (1969–72). Instrumental in 1971 publication of the Pentagon Papers. Has published books including *The Arnheiter Affair* (1972), *A Bright Shining Lie: John Paul Vann and America in Vietnam* (1988, National Book Award and Pulitzer Prize for nonfiction), and *After the War Was Over: Hanoi and Saigon* (1992).

SUSAN SHEEHAN (August 24, 1937–) Born Susan M. Margulies in Vienna, Austria; naturalized as U.S. citizen in 1946. Educated at Wellesley College, receiving degree in 1958. Began career after college as editorial researcher for *Esquire-Coronet*; later freelance writer in New York (1960–61), and staff writer for *The New Yorker* (1961–). Married Neil Sheehan in 1965. Her books include *Ten Vietnamese* (1967), *A Welfare Mother* (1976), *A Prison and a Prisoner* (1978), *Is There No Place on Earth for Me?* (1982, Pulitzer Prize for general nonfiction), *Kate Quinton's Days* (1984), *A Missing Plane* (1986), and *Life For Me Ain't Been No Crystal Stair* (1993). Since 1997, has been contributing writer for *Architectural Digest*.

JACK P. SMITH (April 25, 1945–) Born in Paris, grew up in London; moved to Washington, D.C., at age 12. Enlisted in the U.S. Army in 1964. Served in Vietnam from 1965 to 1966 with 1st Cavalry Division; wounded at Landing Zone Albany in the Ia Drang Valley, November 17, 1965. Left Army late in 1967 to study history at Carnegie-Mellon (B.A. 1971) and Oxford (B.A. 1974). Worked while at Carnegie-Mellon as news producer for WIIC-TV in Pittsburgh. Joined ABC in 1974, reporting from Paris from 1976 to 1980, and from Washington beginning in 1980; was principal correspondent for *This Week with David Brinkley* for nine years, beginning in 1985; currently contributor to ABC *World News Tonight* and *Nightline*.

WALLACE TERRY (April 21, 1938–) Born in Indianapolis, Indiana; graduated from Brown University in 1959, where he was reporter and editor-in-chief of *Brown Daily Herald*. Worked as civil rights reporter for *The Washington Post* from 1960 to 1963, then joined staff of *Time* as Washington correspondent. Went to Vietnam for *Time* in 1967 as deputy bureau chief; covered Tet offensive and Ashau Valley campaigns. Returned to U.S. in 1969, reporting again from Washington. Began academic career in 1974, teaching for eight years at Howard University, and also at the University of District of Columbia, Grinnell, Yale, Middle Tennessee State, Brown, the College of William and Mary, and the University of North Carolina. Has served as commentator and producer for CBS Radio, National Public Radio, and Mutual Radio Network, and as contributing editor of *Parade Magazine*. Author of *Bloods: An Oral History of the Vietnam War by Black Soldiers* (1984).

WILLIAM TUOHY (October 1, 1926–) Born in Chicago, Illinois. Served with U.S. Navy in China and the Philippines during World War II; educated at Northwestern University (B.S. 1951). Worked as copyboy, reporter, and night city editor for *San Francisco Chronicle* (1952–58), then as associate editor, national political correspondent, and foreign correspondent for *Newsweek* (1959–66). In 1966 joined *Los Angeles Times* as Vietnam correspondent and Saigon bureau chief; winner of Pulitzer Prize for Vietnam reporting and Overseas Press Club Award, 1969. Subsequently served as *L.A. Times* Middle East correspondent in Beirut (1968–72), and bureau chief in Rome (1972–77), London (1977–85), Bonn (1985–90), and London (1990–95). Published *Dangerous Company*, a memoir, in 1987.

JOHN T. WHEELER (August 19, 1930–   )   Born John Tipton Wheeler in El Paso, Texas; graduated from University of Missouri School of Journalism in 1952. After college, served for five years in Strategic Air Command of U.S. Air Force as navigator-bombardier; later joined staff of *Santa Cruz Sentinel* as city hall reporter, and the Associated Press, working in New York and San Francisco. Reported for AP in Vietnam from 1965 to 1969, returning occasionally to Kuala Lumpur and New York; also spent a year in Cambodia, returning to the U.S. in 1971. Went into public relations in early 1970s, working for Booz, Allen & Hamilton and DuPont; retired to become full-time amateur triathlete.

TOM WOLFE (March 2, 1931–   )   Born Thomas Kennerly Wolfe Jr. in Richmond, Virginia; educated at Washington and Lee University and Yale, receiving a Ph.D. in American Studies in 1957. Began career in journalism as reporter for Springfield, Massachusetts, *Union* (1956–59); subsequently reporter and Latin American correspondent for *The Washington Post* (1959–62), city reporter for New York *Herald Tribune* (1962–66), contributing editor for *New York* (1968–76) and *Esquire* magazines (1977–   ), and contributing artist for *Harper's* (1978–81). Books include *The Kandy-Kolored Tangerine-Flake Streamline Baby* (1965), *The Electric Kool-Aid Acid Test* (1968), *The Pump House Gang* (1968), *Radical Chic & Mau-Mauing the Flak Catchers* (1970), *The Painted Word* (1975), *Mauve Gloves & Madmen, Clutter & Vine* (1976), *The Right Stuff* (1979), *In Our Time* (1980), *From Bauhaus to Our House* (1981), *The Purple Decades: A Reader* (1982), and *The Bonfire of the Vanities* (1987).

Note on the Texts

This volume collects newspaper and magazine articles, excerpts from books, and the transcript of a television broadcast, written between 1959 and 1976 and dealing with events connected with the Vietnam War in the period between July 1959 and October 1969. Excerpts from books are taken from first editions; in some cases, the excerpts include material that had earlier appeared in magazines in different form.

The following is a list of the sources of the texts included in this volume, listed alphabetically by author (or, for anonymous items, by title of periodical). For untitled pieces and untitled book excerpts, a title is supplied and is enclosed in quotation marks.

Afro-American. No Room in the Cemetery: *Afro-American* (Baltimore), June 4, 1966. Reprinted by permission of Afro-American Newspapers Archives and Research Center.

Joseph Alsop. In the Gia Long Palace: New York *Herald Tribune*, September 20, 1963. Copyright © 1963, New York Herald Tribune, Inc. All rights reserved. Reprinted by permission.

Michael J. Arlen. A Day in the Life: *The New Yorker*, September 30, 1967. Copyright © 1967 by Michael J. Arlen. Reprinted by permission of Donadio & Ashworth, Inc.

Peter Arnett. Hill 875: Associated Press wire copy, November 22, 1967. Reprinted by permission of Associated Press.

Russell Baker. Befuddled in Asia: *The New York Times*, March 2, 1965. Copyright © 1965 by The New York Times Company. Reprinted by permission.

Homer Bigart. A "Very Real War" in Vietnam—and the Deep U.S. Commitment: *The New York Times*, February 25, 1962; Vietnam Victory Remote Despite U.S. Aid to Diem: *The New York Times*, July 25, 1962. Copyright © 1962 by The New York Times Company. Reprinted by permission.

Jeffrey Blankfort. Our Town: The War Comes to Beallsville, Ohio: *Ramparts*, July 1969. Reprinted by permission of Jeffrey Blankfort.

Malcolm W. Browne. Paddy War: Malcolm Browne, *The New Face of War* (New York: Bobbs-Merrill, 1965), pp. 1–8; "The Enemy Had Left a Display for Us": *New Face of War*, pp. 87–101; "He Was Sitting in the Center of a Column of Flame": *New Face of War*, pp. 175–81. Reprinted with permission of Simon & Schuster. Copyright © 1965, 1968 by Malcolm W. Browne.

Kevin Buckley. A Small Contribution: *Newsweek*, October 14, 1968. Copyright © 1968, Newsweek, Inc. All rights reserved. Reprinted by permission.

Walter Cronkite. "We Are Mired in Stalemate . . .": "Who, What, When, Where, Why" (CBS broadcast, February 27, 1968), The New York Times and CBS News, *The War in Vietnam: A Multimedia Chronicle from CBS News & The New York Times* (Macmillan Digital USA CD-ROM, 1995). © 1968 CBS Inc. All rights reserved.

Beverly Deepe. Christmas Eve Bomb in Saigon: New York *Herald Tribune*, December 25, 1964. Copyright © 1964, New York Herald Tribune, Inc. All rights reserved. Reprinted by permission.

Bernard B. Fall. Master of the Red Jab: *The Saturday Evening Post*, November 24, 1962. Reprinted with permission from *The Saturday Evening Post*. Vietnam Blitz: A Report on the Impersonal War: *The New Republic*, October 9, 1965; "Unrepentant, Unyielding": An Interview with Viet Cong Prisoners: *The New Republic*, February 4, 1967. Reprinted with permission. Copyright © 1965, 1967, Dorothy Fall.

Frances FitzGerald. "The Long Fear": *Vogue*, January 1967. (Title originally appeared in quotation marks.) Courtesy of *Vogue*. Copyright © 1967 (renewed 1995) by Condé Nast Publications, Inc.

John Flynn. Marines Get Flowers for a Tough Mission: *Life*, March 19, 1965. Copyright © Time, Inc. Reprinted by permission.

Martha Gellhorn. "Suffer the Little Children . . .": *Ladies' Home Journal*, January 1967. (Title originally appeared in quotation marks.) Copyright © 1967, Meredith Corporation. All rights reserved. Used with the permission of *Ladies' Home Journal*.

Henry F. Graff. Teach-In on Vietnam By . . . the President, the Secretary of State, the Secretary of Defense and the Under Secretary of State: *The New York Times Magazine*, March 20, 1966. Copyright © 1966 by The New York Times Company. Reprinted by permission.

Zalin Grant. "We Lived for a Time Like Dogs": Zalin Grant, *Survivors* (New York: W. W. Norton, 1975), pp. 155–76. Copyright © 1975 by Claude Renee Boutillon. Reprinted by permission of W. W. Norton & Company, Inc.

Meg Greenfield. After the Washington Teach-In: *The Reporter*, June 3, 1965. Reprinted by permission of Meg Greenfield.

David Halberstam. "An Endless, Relentless War": David Halberstam, *The Making of a Quagmire*. (New York: Random House, 1965), pp. 117–24; "They Can Win a War if Someone Shows Them How": *Quagmire*, pp. 163–78. Copyright © by David Halberstam.

Frank Harvey. "Only You Can Prevent Forests": Frank Harvey, *Air-War— Vietnam*. (New York: Bantam Books, 1967), pp. 39–43. Copyright © 1967 by Frank Harvey. Used by permission of Bantam Books, a division of Bantam Doubleday Dell Publishing Group, Inc.

Richard Harwood. The War Just Doesn't Add Up: *The Washington Post*, September 3, 1967.

Marguerite Higgins. The Diem Government, Pro and Con: New York *Herald Tribune*, September 1, 1963. Copyright © 1963, New York Herald Tribune, Inc. All rights reserved. Reprinted by permission.

David Hoffman. Hamburger Hill: The Army's Rationale: *The Washington Post*, May 23, 1969. Copyright © 1969, The Washington Post. Reprinted with permission.

Thomas A. Johnson. The U.S. Negro in Vietnam: *The New York Times*, April 29, 1968. Copyright © 1968 by The New York Times Company. Reprinted by permission.

Ward S. Just. Saigon and Other Syndromes: Ward S. Just, *To What End: Report from Vietnam*. (Boston: Houghton Mifflin, 1968), pp. 1–32; Reconnaissance: *To What End*, pp. 166–191. Copyright © by Ward Just. Reprinted by permission.

Stanley Karnow. Diem Defeats His Own Best Troops: *The Reporter*, January 19, 1961. Reprinted by permission of Stanley Karnow; The Fall of the House of Ngo Dinh: *The Saturday Evening Post*, December 21, 1963. Reprinted by permission from *The Saturday Evening Post*.

Daniel Lang. Casualties of War: *The New Yorker*, October 18, 1969. Copyright © 1969 by Daniel Lang. Copyright renewed 1997 by Margaret Lang, Frances A. Labaree, Cecily G. Lang, and Helen Lang.

Steve Lerner. A Visit to Chicago: Blood, Sweat, & Tears: *The Village Voice*, September 5, 1968. Reprinted by permission of Steve Lerner.

Lee Lescaze. A Third of Mytho Destroyed in Delta Battle: *The Washington Post*, February 6, 1968. Copyright © 1968, The Washington Post. Reprinted with permission.

Mary McCarthy. Hanoi—March 1968: Mary McCarthy, *Hanoi* (New York: Harcourt, Brace & World, 1968), pp. 1–24. Copyright © 1968 by Mary McCarthy, renewed 1996 by James West. Reprinted by permission of Harcourt Brace & Company.

Joe McGinniss. From *The Selling of the President 1968*: Joe McGinniss, *The Selling of the President 1968* (Trident Press, 1969), pp. 83–95. Copyright © 1969 by Joe McGinniss.

Norman Mailer. From *The Armies of the Night*: Norman Mailer, *The Armies of the Night* (New York: New American Library, 1968), pp. 116–31. Copyright © 1968 by Norman Mailer. Used by permission of Dutton Signet, a division of Penguin Putnam Inc.; from *The Siege of Chicago*: Mailer, *Miami and the Siege of Chicago* (New York: World Publishing, 1968), pp. 153–59, 165–74. Copyright © 1968 by Norman Mailer. Reprinted with the permission of The Wylie Agency, Inc.

Charles Mohr. U.S. Aide in Embassy Villa Kills Guerrilla with Pistol: *The New York Times*, January 31, 1968. Copyright © 1968 by The New York Times Company. Reprinted by permission.

Don Moser. Eight Dedicated Men Marked for Death: *Life*, September 3, 1965; The Vietcong Cadre of Terror: *Life*, January 12, 1968. Copyright © Time, Inc. Reprinted by permission.

Don Oberdorfer. From *Tet!*: Don Oberdorfer, *Tet!* (Garden City, New York: Doubleday and Company, 1971), pp. 205–16; "An Ending of His Own": *Tet!*, pp. 308–23. Copyright © 1971 by Don Oberdorfer. Used by permission of Doubleday, a division of Bantam Doubleday Dell Publishing Group, Inc.

McCandlish Phillips. Two Hilltops in a Marine's Life: *The New York Times*, March 6, 1966. Copyright © 1966 by The New York Times Company. Reprinted by permission.

Jonathan Randal. U.S. Marines Seize 3d Hill in Vietnam after 12-Day Push: *The New York Times*, May 6, 1967. Copyright © 1967 by The New York Times Company. Reprinted by permission.

Roger Rapoport. Protest, Learning, Heckling Spark Viet Rally: *The Michigan Daily*, March 26, 1965. Copyright Roger Rapoport.

Harrison E. Salisbury. U.S. Raids Batter 2 Towns; Supply Route Is Little Hurt: *The New York Times*. December 27, 1966. Copyright © 1966 by The New York Times Company. Reprinted by permission.

Jonathan Schell. From *The Military Half: An Account of the Destruction in Quang Ngai and Quang Tin:* Schell, *The Military Half: An Account of the Destruction in Quang Ngai and Quang Tin* (New York: Alfred A. Knopf, 1968), pp. 3–16, 35–52, 70–109, 117–25, 130–42, 150–65, 178–98. Copyright © 1968 by Jonathan Schell.

Neil Sheehan. Vietnamese Ignored U.S. Battle Order: *The Washington Post*, January 7, 1963; Not a Dove, But No Longer a Hawk: *The New York Times Magazine*, October 9, 1966. Copyright © 1966 by The New York Times Company. Reprinted by permission.

Susan Sheehan. A Viet Cong: *Ten Vietnamese* (New York: Alfred A. Knopf. 1967), pp. 149–66. Copyright © 1967 by Susan Sheehan. Reprinted by permission.

Jack P. Smith. Death in the Ia Drang Valley: *The Saturday Evening Post*, January 28, 1967. Reprinted with permission from *The Saturday Evening Post*.

Wallace Terry. Black Power in Viet Nam: *Time*, September 19, 1969. Copyright © Time, Inc. Reprinted by permission.

Time. Death at Intermission Time: *Time*, July 20, 1959. Copyright © Time, Inc. Reprinted by permission.

William Tuohy. A Big "Dirty Little War": *The New York Times Magazine*, November 28, 1965. Copyright © 1965 by The New York Times Company. Reprinted by permission.

U.S. News & World Report. "We Are Losing, Morale Is Bad . . . If They'd Give Us Good Planes . . .": *U.S. News & World Report*, May 4, 1964. (Title originally appeared in quotation marks.) Copyright © 1964 by U.S. News & World Report.

John T. Wheeler. Life in the V Ring: Associated Press wire copy, February 12, 1968. Reprinted by permission of Associated Press.

Tom Wolfe. From *The Electric Kool-Aid Acid Test*: Wolfe, The Electric Kool-Aid Acid Test (New York: Farrar, Straus and Giroux, 1968), pp. 216–26. Copyright © 1968 and copyright renewed © 1996 by Tom Wolfe; The Truest Sport: Jousting with Sam and Charlie: Wolfe, *Mauve Gloves & Madmen, Clutter & Vine* (New York: Farrar, Straus and Giroux, 1976), pp. 26-65. Copyright © 1976 by Tom Wolfe.

The map on page 771 in this volume is taken from Arnold R. Isaacs, *Without Honor: Defeat in Vietnam and Cambodia* (Baltimore: Johns Hopkins University Press, 1983), p. 22. Copyright © 1983 by The Johns Hopkins University Press. Reprinted by permission. The maps on pages 772 and 773 of this volume are taken from Clarence R. Wyatt, *Paper Soldiers: The American Press and the*

Vietnam War (New York: W.W. Norton, 1993), pp. 10–11. Copyright © 1993 by W.W. Norton & Company. Reprinted by permission.

Great care has been taken to trace all owners of copyrighted material included in this book; if any have been inadvertently omitted or overlooked, acknowledgment will gladly be made in future printings.

This volume presents the texts listed here without change except for the correction of typographical errors, but it does not attempt to reproduce features of their typographic design. The following is a list of typographical errors, cited by page and line number: 22.21, of into; 28.39, trying eliminate; 30.12, 19,000; 67.18, Donald; 68.10, resuce; 69.4, ad; 88.28, are in; 91.4, SIAGON; 127.33, FAD; 135.34, Vienamese; 144.19, croned; 176.23, 352th; 200.23, Hunt; 255.20, "Concentrate; 259.33, dispite; 260.5 out-of-the way; 260.25, pauper's; 266.35, Christ; 274.26, .105 . . . .155; 283.28, shotgun" roar; 300.5, seminarans; 310.23, foresaken; 326.21, Fleeet; 327.3, averages,; 344.19, batallions; 405.12, was go; 442.29, altogether,; 496.35, Bender; 523.31, at time; 568.32, Volkswagon; 576.7, tcover; 576.19, wafe; 577.19–20, commoplace; 578.25, sheelings; 578.35, witten; 584.2, Taylor both; 586.5, While; 586.16, lost-cost; 586.23, then; 596.20, chief and; 604.23, root—; 629.24, critcal; 636.20, troops the; 643.12, Yippies members; 650.24, oay; 698.35, reboubts; 699.13, prepetuated; 702.30, Zias.

Notes

In the notes below, the reference numbers denote page and line of this volume (the line count includes headings). No note is made for material included in standard desk-reference books such as Webster's *Collegiate, Biographical,* and *Geographical* dictionaries. Biblical references are keyed to the King James Version. Quotations from Shakespeare are keyed to *The Riverside Shakespeare,* ed. G. Blakemore Evans (Boston: Houghton, Mifflin, 1974). Footnotes and bracketed editorial notes within the text were in the originals. For historical background see Chronology in this volume. For weapons and military terms not identified in the notes, see Glossary in this volume. For further historical background and references to other studies, see Stanley Karnow, *Vietnam: A History* (revised edition; New York: Viking Penguin, 1991); Harry G. Summers Jr., *Vietnam War Almanac* (New York: Facts on File Publications, 1985); and *Encyclopedia of the Vietnam War,* ed. Stanley I. Kutler (New York: Macmillan Reference USA, 1996). For further background on Vietnam war journalism, see Clarence R. Wyatt, *Paper Soldiers: The American Press and the Vietnam War* (New York: W. W. Norton, 1993). For more detailed maps, see Harry G. Summers Jr., *Historical Atlas of the Vietnam War* (Boston: Houghton Mifflin, 1995).

1.3   *Death at Intermission Time*]   This story, which appeared in *Time* on July 20, 1959, was based on a dispatch filed from South Vietnam by Stanley Karnow.

1.16–17   1957 . . . Americans.]   Bombs were set off in Saigon on October 22, 1957, at buildings used by the Military Assistance Advisory Group and the United States Information Service, wounding 13 Americans.

1.35–36   Ovnand . . . Buis]   Ovnand and Buis were the first American servicemen to be killed in the Republic of Vietnam.

13.1   Elbridge Durbrow]   U.S. ambassador to South Vietnam, 1957–61.

16.33–34   Malaya . . . emergency]   A state of emergency was declared in Malaya, then a British colony, in June 1948 after a Communist revolt. The state of emergency was ended in July 1960, three years after Malaya became independent.

18.27–30   Thao . . . Diem]   Thao played a major role in the coups against Diem in November 1963, against Duong Van Minh in January 1964, and against Nguyen Khanh in February 1965. He was murdered in the summer of

1965 by South Vietnamese police officers allied with Nguyen Cao Ky. The Communists transferred his remains to a "patriots' cemetery" after their victory in 1975, and it is now believed that Thao served as a clandestine Communist agent after his apparent defection in 1954.

30.29   Frederick E. Nolting] U.S. ambassador to South Vietnam, 1961–63.

47.31   a copy . . . Spock] *Baby and Child Care* by Dr. Benjamin Spock, first published in 1946.

49.4–6   neutralist forces . . . civil war] See Chronology, 1960–62.

54.28–29   a book of mine] *Street Without Joy* (1961).

63.12   Robert McNamara] Secretary of Defense from January 1961 until February 1968.

68.6   Wednesday's battle] January 2, 1963.

68.14   American military man] Identified by Neil Sheehan in his book *A Bright Shining Lie: John Paul Vann and America in Vietnam* (1988) as Lieutenant Colonel John Paul Vann.

70.9   One U.S. adviser] Identified in *A Bright Shining Lie* as Vann.

86.7   top American diplomat] Identified by Marguerite Higgins in her book *Our Vietnam Nightmare* (1965) as John Richardson, the Central Intelligence Agency station chief in Saigon.

87.13   last Sunday] August 25, 1963.

94.2   *The Fall . . . Ngo Dinh*] Stanley Karnow used material from this article in writing "The End of Diem," chapter 8 in his book *Vietnam: A History* (1983, revised 1991), which includes information regarding American involvement in the overthrow of Diem unavailable to him in 1963.

104.38   tank-corps major] Identified by Karnow in *Vietnam: A History* as Duong Huu Nghia. Karnow also writes in *Vietnam* that General Minh gave the order to kill Diem and Nhu to his bodyguard, Captain Nguyen Van Nhung, and that Nhung and Nghia both shot the Ngo brothers inside the armored vehicle.

106.12   Poulo Condore] In Vietnamese, Con Son; an island 150 miles south of Saigon, used as a political prison by the French, the South Vietnamese government, and by the Communists after their victory in 1975.

108.6   battle of Ap Bac] See pp. 68–70 in this volume.

110.1   Cao and Dam] Colonel Huynh Van Cao, commander of the South Vietnamese 7th Division, 1959–62, and Colonel Bui Dinh Dam, commander of the 7th Division, 1962–63.

112.1   PIO's] Public Information Officers.

122.30–31   Vann . . . Vietnam] In *A Bright Shining Lie* Neil Sheehan writes that Vann was already planning to retire from the army in 1963 before he went to Vietnam in 1962, believing that his investigation by the army on statutory rape charges in 1959 would prevent him from ever being promoted to brigadier general.

124.5   *Capt. "Jerry" Shank*] In a short profile that appeared with this article in *U.S. News & World Report*, the magazine's editors wrote that Edwin Gerald Shank Jr. was born on June 21, 1936, in Winamac, Indiana, and graduated from Notre Dame in 1959 with a B.S. degree in architecture. Shank joined the Air Force ROTC while in college, was called into active service in August 1959, and was assigned to duty in South Vietnam on October 15, 1963.

131.6   multi] Multi-engined aircraft.

131.32   Hurlburt] Hurlburt Field, near Fort Walton Beach, Florida.

135.40   sinking . . . Card] The *Card*, an escort carrier used to transport helicopters and aircraft to South Vietnam, was sunk at its dock in Saigon by an explosive charge. The ship was later raised.

138.10–11   Rusk . . . Bundy] Rusk was Secretary of State during the Kennedy and Johnson administrations, 1961–69. Bundy served as the presidential national security adviser, 1961–66.

138.17   Panmunjom] Site of the Korean War armistice negotiations, 1951–53.

140.9   subsequent crises.] See Chronology, 1965.

143.9–10   another Munich] During a conference held in Munich on September 29–30, 1938, British prime minister Neville Chamberlain, French premier Éduoard Daladier, and Adolf Hitler agreed that Czechoslovakia would cede the Sudetenland to Germany.

143.26–27   I. F. Stone's rebuttal . . . paper"] The State Department issued a 64-page illustrated booklet, *Aggression From the North: The Record of North Viet-Nam's Campaign To Conquer South Viet-Nam*, on February 17, 1965. Journalist I. F. Stone extensively criticized the document in the March 8, 1965, number of his publication *I. F. Stone's Weekly*.

145.10–11   national teach-in . . . Washington] The event was held on May 15–16, 1965.

147.20   Dominican action] The United States sent 20,000 troops to the Dominican Republic after a coup and counter-coup split the ruling military junta in late April 1965. On May 6, 1965, the Organization of American States voted to establish an inter-American peace-keeping force in the Dominican Republic; U.S. troops became part of this force, which remained until after elections were held in 1966.

148.15   Carmine De Sapio] Leader of the New York City Democratic Party, 1949–61.

149.3   mote-and-beam]   Cf. Matthew 7:3–5, Luke 6:41–42.

155.29–30   top of these pages]   The photographs are reproduced on pp. 156–57 of this volume.

158.3–4   coups . . . overthows]   See Chronology, 1964–65.

175.16–17   Dr. Strangelove missions]   Several scenes in the film *Dr. Strangelove; or, How I Learned to Stop Worrying and Love the Bomb* (1963) take place onboard a B-52 bomber.

177.14   Chulai operation]   See Chronology, August 1965.

177.31   battle near Ankhé]   Fought on September 18–19, 1965, between 224 paratroopers of the 101st Airborne Division and a force of about 600 Viet Cong main-force troops. More than 200 Viet Cong and 13 Americans were killed in the engagement.

178.4   Task Force Alfa]   Task Force Alpha, a corps-level headquarters established at Nha Trang in August 1965 to control American military operations in the Central Highlands. It was renamed I Field Force Vietnam in March 1966.

178.14   Siegfried Line]   Fortifications along the western German frontier in World War II, made with steel-reinforced concrete.

180.27   bombed . . . Embassy]   A car bomb exploded outside the U.S. embassy in Saigon on March 30, 1965, killing 22 people; the bombing resulted in the construction of a new embassy building, which was attacked by the Viet Cong during the 1968 Tet Offensive.

181.39–40   executes VC . . . servicemen.]   Three alleged members of the Viet Cong political cadre were shot by South Vietnamese authorities in Danang on September 23, 1965. A Communist radio broadcast on September 26 announced that two U.S. soldiers captured in 1963 had been executed in reprisal.

182.26–27   newsreel . . . lighters,]   On August 3, 1965, a CBS television news team headed by correspondent Morley Safer filmed U.S. marines using cigarette lighters to burn huts in the village of Cam Ne after receiving sniper fire from the village. The footage was broadcast on CBS on August 5.

183.10   torture in Algeria]   During the Algerian War of Independence, 1954–62.

184.28   Hoa-Binh and Cao-Bang]   For Hoa Binh, see Chronology, November 1951–February 1952. The French garrison retreating from the northeastern border outpost of Cao Bang was annihilated in October 1950.

185.23   redoubt of "Zone D"]   A major Viet Cong base area north of Bien Hoa.

185.32–33   in 1951 . . . Tassigny]   Lattre de Tassigny commanded the successful defense of the Red River Delta; see Chronology, January–June 1951.

186.4   Huks] A Communist-led guerrilla movement that staged an unsuccessful insurgency against the Philippine government, 1949–55.

187.27–29   two . . . terrorists] See note 181.39–40.

190.17–18   General Westmoreland] Commander of the Military Assistance Command Vietnam from June 1964 until June 1968.

194.34   village of Cam Ne] See note 182.26–27.

196.16   'Catch 22'] Novel by Joseph Heller (1961).

198.8   rally in Berkeley] Held on October 15, 1965.

198.19   Free Speech . . . Savio] Mario Savio was the leader of the Free Speech Movement, formed in the autumn of 1964 to oppose restrictions on political activity on the Berkeley campus of the University of California.

199.13   Birchers] Members of the John Birch Society, an extreme right-wing political group.

201.29   the Tonton Macoute] Haitian secret police.

207.1–2   Martin . . . Selma] Civil rights demonstrators attempting to march from Selma, Alabama, to the state capitol in Montgomery were severely beaten by state troopers after crossing the Edmund Pettus Bridge on March 7, 1965. Martin Luther King Jr. led a second march across the bridge on March 9, but then had the marchers stop and return to Selma in order to avoid further violence. After federal district judge Frank Johnson Jr. issued an order restraining further state interference, King led a march from Selma to Montgomery, March 21–25, 1965, that was protected by federal troops.

208.5–6   1ST BATTALION . . . four days] The 1st Battalion, 7th Cavalry, made a helicopter assault into Landing Zone X-Ray in the Ia Drang Valley on the morning of November 14, 1965.

208.33   Charlie Company] Charlie Company, 2nd Battalion, 7th Cavalry, reached Landing Zone X-Ray on November 16, 1965.

210.8   Richards] This name, as well as the others used in this article, is a pseudonym.

211.34–37   The XO . . . crawl away] The body of the executive officer of Charlie Company was recovered by American troops on November 18, 1965.

222.16–17   about 150 . . . killed] 155 American soldiers were killed in the fighting at Landing Zone Albany.

223.18   1956 elections] See Chronology, 1954–55.

233.35   revolutionary war council] The ruling military committee in South Vietnam.

236.4–5   Tarrytown] Tarrytown, New York.

236.27 letters . . . Marks] Marks' letters were later collected in *The Letters of Pfc. Richard E. Marks, USMC* (1967).

239.12–13 Two companies . . . battalion] Marines from the 3rd Reconnaissance Battalion skirmished with the Viet Cong on April 22, 1965; one marine was wounded.

239.36 "Sam Durell" books] Series of paperback original novels by Edward S. Aarons, beginning with *Assignment to Disaster* (1955); 20 titles were published through 1964.

242.11–12 Honolulu . . . Johnson] At their conference in Honolulu, held February 6–9, 1966, Johnson promised Premier Ky that the U.S. would increase economic aid to South Vietnam.

242.24–25 George W. Ball] Undersecretary of State, 1961–66.

243.6–7 peace offensive . . . January] Johnson halted the bombing of North Vietnam between December 24, 1965, and January 30, 1966.

245.21–22 T.S. Eliot . . . a bang."] Cf. "The Hollow Men" (1925).

248.36 Khrushchev threaten . . . Berlin] At their summit meeting in Vienna in June 1961.

249.2 time . . . missile crisis] October 1962.

249.29 test-ban treaty] The treaty, which was signed by the United States, the Soviet Union, and Great Britain, prohibited the testing of nuclear weapons in space, underwater, or in the atmosphere, but permitted continued underground testing. It went into effect on October 10, 1963.

250.3 Senator Morse] Senator Wayne Morse of Oregon, one of two senators who voted against the Tonkin Gulf Resolution in August 1964.

250.30 bombing pause . . . May] Johnson suspended the bombing of North Vietnam from May 13 to May 17, 1965.

251.2 the Four Points] Set forth by North Vietnamese premier Pham Van Dong on April 8, 1965, the points called for an end to the bombing of North Vietnam and a complete U.S. withdrawal from South Vietnam, an end to U.S. military aid to South Vietnam, the acceptance of the political program of the National Liberation Front, and the peaceful reunification of Vietnam.

252.8–9 Vietcong . . . last year] The U.S. command claimed that 34,585 Viet Cong and North Vietnamese soldiers were killed in 1965.

252.33–34 Senator Fulbright] J. William Fulbright, a Democrat from Arkansas, was chairman of the Foreign Relations Committee.

253.16–37 'The Steaming . . . H.F.G.] This passage appeared as a sidebar in the original magazine article.

254.37   SEATO treaty]   The Southeast Asia Treaty Organization was created under the terms of a treaty signed on September 8, 1954, by representatives of Australia, New Zealand, Pakistan, the Philippines, Thailand, France,
Great Britain, and the United States. Members pledged to "act to meet the
common danger" in the event of "aggression by means of armed attack"
against territory covered by the treaty; under the terms of a separate protocol,
Laos, Cambodia, and southern Vietnam were included in the treaty area.
SEATO was dissolved in 1977.

255.35   enclave idea]   Proposed strategy that would restrict the mission of
U.S. ground forces in South Vietnam to defending populated coastal areas.

256.19–20   Churchill . . . streets]   In a speech to the House of Commons
on June 4, 1940.

256.30   Alamo . . . Houston]   The Alamo was captured by the Mexicans
on March 6, 1836; Texas forces under Sam Houston won a decisive victory at
the Battle of San Jacinto on April 21, 1836.

259.29   Civil Rights Act]   The 1964 Civil Rights Act.

263.38   101st Airborne Brigade]   101st Airborne Division.

266.35   Chris Verlumis]   Chris C. Vurlumis.

269.1   A. J. Liebling]   Writer for *The New Yorker* whose war reporting
was collected in *The Road Back to Paris* (1944) and *Mollie & Other War Pieces*
(1964).

280.8–9   Carpenter . . . overrun]   The napalm bombing on June 8, 1966,
temporarily halted the North Vietnamese attack, giving the American unit
time to establish a secure perimeter. One American soldier was killed by the
airstrike and another 11 were burned. Carpenter was awarded the Distinguished Service Cross for his actions during the engagement.

280.11–12   1,200 . . . 250 of their own]   The U.S. command announced
that 48 Americans and 531 North Vietnamese were killed during Operation
Hawthorne.

281.9   2-4D]   Chemical component used in a number of defoliants, including Agent Orange. The human health problems linked to exposure to
Agent Orange are believed to be caused by dioxin, a manufacturing contam-
inent present in another chemical component, 2,4,5-T.

282.2   Ky's Coup Squadron]   Ky had threatened to bomb rebel troops
during coup attempts in September 1964 and February 1965.

284.7   six-by]   A truck using six-by-six wheel drive.

314.26–27   Third Marine Amphibious Force]   Corps-level headquarters in
Danang that controlled marine operations in the northern provinces of South
Vietnam.

317.25–26   slim Northerner]   Ky was originally from North Vietnam.

326.14–16   Namdinh . . . military objective]   The Department of Defense responded to this story by stating that Nam Dinh contained a major railroad yard, a petroleum and oil storage depot, and a thermal power generating plant. Salisbury was also criticized by U.S. government officials for not acknowledging that some of the information in his story was taken from *Report on U.S. War Crimes in Nam-Dinh City*, a pamphlet published in North Vietnam in October 1966.

327.6–7   target . . . dike]   Irrigation dikes were not designated as targets during the American bombing of North Vietnam.

333.11   gas]   Nonlethal CS tear gas.

336.2–3   enterprising . . . lighters]   See note 182.26–27 in this volume.

337.33   American . . . suicide]   Norman Morrison, a 32-year-old Quaker who burned himself to death outside of the Pentagon on November 2, 1965.

338.25–26   *Et . . . chemin*]   And if it had to be done over / I would follow the same path.

339.31   "Indonesia?"]   In September 1965 the Indonesian army defeated a Communist coup attempt; by December 1965 at least 200,000 suspected Communists had been killed during the ensuing repression of the Indonesian Communist party.

342.35–36   Lord Russell]   In 1966 the British philosopher Bertrand Russell had organized an International War Crimes Tribunal. The tribunal held a public meeting in Stockholm in May 1967 and issued a report condemning the U.S. for committing crimes against humanity in Vietnam.

349.10–20   Baby, baby . . . symphony]   Cf. "I Hear a Symphony" by Brian Holland, Lamont Dozier, and Eddie Holland (1965).

353.20–21   1965 . . . Embassy]   See note 180.27.

354.40   *Kim Van Kieu*]   *The Tale of Kieu*, by Nguyen Du (1765–1820).

355.7   Cham]   Civilization in central Vietnam conquered by the Vietnamese in the 15th century during their southward expansion.

355.20   Snopeses]   Fictional family in works by William Faulkner, including *The Hamlet* (1940), *The Town* (1957), and *The Mansion* (1959).

361.8   McChristian? . . . Ellsberg?]   Major General Joseph McChristian was chief of intelligence for MACV, 1965–67. John Paul Vann returned to Vietnam as a civilian in March 1965 and became a pacification adviser in Hau Nghia Province; he later served as the senior American pacification official in III Corps (1966–69) and IV Corps (1969–71). In May 1971 he became the senior American adviser in II Corps, with authority over both military and civil operations, and served until his death in a helicopter accident on

June 9, 1972. Daniel Ellsberg served with the U.S. embassy as a pacification adviser, 1965–67. In 1971 he was indicted for espionage for having given the Pentagon Papers to the press; the charges against him were dismissed in 1973 on grounds of government misconduct.

363.23   *101st Airborne Brigade*]   101st Airborne Division.

365.13   Charlie Byrd]   American jazz guitarist.

365.25   *Guardian*]   A British newspaper.

366.27   Matthews]   Herbert Matthews, who reported on the Spanish Civil War for *The New York Times.*

369.4–5   SEATO agreements]   See note 254.37.

369.22   mortaring . . . Pleiku]   See Chronology, February 1965.

391.29   *corvée*]   Forced labor

397.8   * * *]   These asterisks, and the asterisks on pages 409, 440, 446, 455, and 467 of this volume, indicate the end of one extract from *The Military Half* and the beginning of another.

417.10   COSVN]   Central Office for South Vietnam.

417.29   Allen Dulles' book about intelligence]   *The Craft of Intelligence* (1963). Dulles served as director of the CIA from 1953 until 1961.

459.33   'The Swinger.']   American film comedy starring Ann-Margret and Tony Franciosa, released in 1966.

481.19–20   Presidential . . . September 3rd,]   The South Vietnamese presidential election, see Chronology, 1967.

486.17–18   pacification . . . Komer]   Komer headed the Civil Operations and Revolutionary Development Support program from its founding in May 1967 until November 1968, when he was succeeded by William Colby.

486.35–36   company . . . virtually annihilated]   Out of a total strength of 137 men, the unit lost 76 men killed and 23 wounded in the engagement fought on June 22, 1967.

491.23   106-mm. rifles]   Recoilless rifles.

506.6–7   terminus of the March]   The march, held on October 21, 1967, began at the Lincoln Memorial.

509.31   Macdougal Street]   A street in the Greenwich Village section of New York City.

514.20–23   O to . . . waterfall—]   From "Waking Early Sunday Morning," the first part of "Near the Ocean" (1967), by Robert Lowell.

514.28–33   Remember playing . . . ski-run] From "1958" (1967) by Robert Lowell.

522.14   Sunday] November 19, 1967.

523.2–3   machine gunner go down] Private First Class Carlos Lozada was posthumously awarded the Medal of Honor.

524.8–9   the chaplain . . . killed] Major Charles Joseph Watters, a Roman Catholic priest, was killed by the bomb that fell within the American lines on November 19. For several hours before his death Watters moved about the battlefield under fire, carrying, aiding, and comforting wounded men. He was posthumously awarded the Medal of Honor.

524.31   gain the ridgeline] The 173rd Airborne Brigade captured the crest on the morning of November 23, 1967, after losing 158 men killed and 402 wounded in the fighting on Hill 875.

532.9   Adolphe Menjou] American film actor.

536.24–27   Jack Broughton . . . unacceptable] In his book *Thud Ridge* (1969).

539.4   N—— D——] Nam Dinh.

539.7   Iron Triangle area] The Hanoi–Haiphong–Thanh Hoa region of North Vietnam.

539.15–16   Harrison Salisbury! . . . *Times*] See pp. 325–30 and note 326.14–16 in this volume.

555.27   Spads] See A-1 in Glossary.

557.23–24   five American . . . guards] Four U.S. army military policemen and one marine guard were killed defending the embassy.

558.29–30   attackers . . . several hours] American commanders subsequently announced that the Viet Cong did not enter the chancery building.

559.31–32   bodies . . . embassy employees] Four South Vietnamese embassy employees were killed during the attack; one of them is believed to have been a Viet Cong agent.

560.12–13   General . . . Uprising] See Chronology, 1967–68.

565.31–36   Manhard . . . heard from since] Manhard was released in Hanoi on March 16, 1973.

568.22   Buddhist . . . 1966] See Chronology, March–June 1966.

569.37   101st Airborne Brigade] 101st Airborne Division.

581.4   TONIGHT . . . New York] These concluding observations were preceded in the half-hour broadcast by reports filmed in Vietnam by Cronkite and other CBS correspondents.

583.14   November meeting] Held in November 1967.

583.22   Clark Clifford] Secretary of Defense from March 1, 1968, until the
end of the Johnson administration in January 1969.

583.29–30   Arthur Goldberg] U.S. Ambassador to the United Nations
since 1965.

583.34   George Ball] Undersecretary of State, 1961–66.

583.35   Bundy . . . Dillon] Bundy served as the White House national
security adviser, 1961–66. Dean served as a negotiator in Korea in 1953 and at
the Geneva disarmament talks, 1961–62. Dillon was Secretary of the Treasury,
1961–65.

584.1   Vance] Vance served as Secretary of the Army, 1962–63, and as
Deputy Secretary of Defense, 1964–67.

584.6–9   Helms . . . McConnell] Helms was director of the CIA,
1966–73. Rostow served as national security adviser to Johnson, 1966–69. Katzenbach was Undersecretary of State, 1966–69. Nitze served as Deputy
Secretary of Defense, 1967–69. Harriman had been serving since 1965 as an
ambassador-at-large with responsibility for Southeast Asia. For Goldberg,
see note 583.29–30. William Bundy was Assistant Secretary of State for Far
Eastern Affairs, 1964–69. McConnell was Chief of Staff of the U.S. Air Force,
1964–68.

585.33   General Wheeler] Earle Wheeler, Chairman of the Joint Chiefs of
Staff, 1964–70.

585.34   Abrams] General Abrams served as deputy commander of MACV,
1967–68, before succeeding General Westmoreland in the summer of 1968.

587.22   dollar crisis] In March 1968 the dollar came under severe speculative pressure in the international currency markets.

588.37   Blue House raid] North Korean commandos infiltrated across the
Korean Demilitarized Zone on the night of January 21, 1968, in an attempt
to kill Park Chung Hee, the president of South Korea. They were intercepted
by South Korean security forces one mile from the Blue House, the official
presidential residence in Seoul.

594.32   afraid . . . husband again] Charles Robb, a captain in the marines, returned from Vietnam. He was elected to the U.S. Senate from Virginia
in 1986 and reelected in 1992.

595.7   offer . . . San Antonio] In a speech delivered in San Antonio,
Texas, on September 29, 1967, Johnson offered to halt the bombing of North
Vietnam if the North Vietnamese would agree to enter into substantive peace
negotiations and not take military advantage of the cessation.

597.3–4   spoken . . . Kennedy] In his inaugural address, January 20, 1961.

597.34–35 Westmoreland . . . November] In November 1967 Johnson told Westmoreland that he might not seek reelection.

598.12 I.C.C.] International Control Commission, established under the Geneva Accords of 1954.

605.16–17 "Your leavy . . . are."] *Macbeth*, V, vi, 1–2.

618.6 Operation Junction City] The parachute assault was made in War Zone C on February 22, 1967.

618.19–20 Poitier . . . truckdriver] In the films *The Defiant Ones* (1958) and *Red Ball Express* (1952).

624.12 Clay's title] Muhammad Ali (Cassius Clay) was stripped of his world heavyweight boxing title in 1967 after he refused on religious grounds to be drafted into the armed forces.

628.15 Sunday] August 25, 1968.

633.17 Russians . . . Prague] The Soviet Union invaded Czechoslovakia on August 20, 1968.

634.6 * * *] These asterisks indicate the end of one extract from *The Siege of Chicago* and the beginning of another.

634.7 Meanwhile] While the convention delegates were debating the platform plank on Vietnam.

643.4 last Tuesday] August 27, 1968.

647.9 Phil Ochs] American folk singer.

649.22 the Resistance] Political group organized in 1967 to promote resistance to the draft.

651.9 Dick Gregory's] Gregory, a comedian, had been active in the civil rights movement since the early 1960s.

653.6 Harry Treleaven] Creative director of advertising for the Nixon campaign.

653.16–17 Garment . . . Shakespeare] Directors of media and advertising for the Nixon campaign.

653.24 Ruth Jones] Buyer of radio and television time for the Nixon campaign.

653.29–30 Art Duram] President of the advertising agency hired by the Nixon campaign.

654.27 acceptance speech] Delivered at the Republican National Convention in Miami Beach on August 8, 1968.

659.9 U. Alexis Johnson] A foreign service officer who served as the deputy ambassador to South Vietnam, 1964–65.

659.11–12 Gould . . . Francis] Gould, a writer for *The New York Times*, had previously criticized a commercial in which the singer Connie Francis endorsed Nixon.

662.22 Churchill, we say:] In a speech to the Canadian parliament, December 30, 1941.

664.2 *A Small Contribution*] This article appeared in *Newsweek* with a headnote that described it as a "report on a small contribution to Communist casualty figures."

665.18 sawed-off M-16] A version of the M-16 rifle manufactured with a shortened barrel and a telescoping stock, known as the CAR-15 or Colt Commando.

667.3 *"We Lived . . . Dogs"*] This excerpt from the book *Survivors* describes events that took place in a Viet Cong prison camp in western Quang Nam province.

667.5 *Anton . . . Watkins*] Anton, an army helicopter pilot, was captured on January 5, 1968. Watkins, an army infantryman, was captured on January 9, 1968.

667.16 Kushner, Williams] Captain Floyd William Kushner, an army doctor, was captured after his helicopter crashed in November 1967. Richard Williams, an army sergeant, was captured on January 8, 1968, after receiving a severe wound to his right hand.

668.1 Zawtocki] A marine captured during the 1968 Tet Offensive.

668.3–4 Strictland . . . Harker] Jim Strictland and David Harker, army riflemen captured on January 8, 1968, along with Sergeant Williams.

668.10 Russ Grissett] Member of a marine reconnaissance unit, captured early in 1966.

668.15 Garwood Mr. Dao] Robert Garwood, a marine private, was captured near Danang on September 28, 1965, and defected to the Viet Cong during 1967. Garwood chose to remain in North Vietnam after the signing of the 1973 cease-fire agreement, but returned to the United States in 1979. He was found guilty of collaboration by a court-martial in 1981 and dishonorably discharged from the marines. In 1968 the Viet Cong gave Garwood the name Huynh Chien Dao, "Brave Liberation Fighter."

668.18 *Daly*] James Daly, an army rifleman captured with Watkins on January 9, 1968.

668.25 Davis] Tom Davis, an army mortarman captured on March 12, 1968.

670.27 Mr. Ho] Viet Cong political cadre who came to the camp in the summer of 1968 to indoctrinate the prisoners.

672.6   Denny] Dennis Hammond, a marine captured during the 1968 Tet Offensive.

674.15   *McMillan*] Ike McMillan, an army mortarman captured along with Davis on March 12, 1968.

675.24   Cannon] Francis Cannon, an army rifleman captured on January 8, 1968, along with Strictland, Harker, and Williams.

676.28–30   Sherman's . . . escape attempt] Robert Sherman, a marine captured in 1967 who was confined to wooden stocks for almost two months after a failed escape attempt in the spring of 1968.

681.37–682.2   Port . . . ground attack] Port was posthumously awarded the Medal of Honor for his actions on January 12, 1968.

688.10–11   *Miller . . . Laird*] Miller, a Republican, served in Congress from 1967 until 1993. Melvin Laird was Secretary of Defense during the first Nixon administration, 1969–73.

700.19   Fire . . . Veghel] Named after a village in Holland captured by the 101st Airborne Division in September 1944.

700.25   Tuesday] May 20, 1969.

702.32   Fire Base Berchtesgaden] Named after the site of Hitler's Bavarian mountain villa, captured by the 101st Airborne Division in May 1945.

702.39   Old Guard] U.S. army ceremonial unit.

705.21–22   case . . . Kennedy] Senator Edward M. Kennedy was the driver in an automobile accident on Chappaquiddick Island, Massachusetts, on the night of July 18–19, 1969, in which Mary Jo Kopechne, his passenger, died. Kennedy pleaded guilty on July 25, 1969, to leaving the scene of an accident and received a suspended sentence. A judicial inquest in 1970 found probable cause that negligence by Kennedy contributed to the accident, but no further charges were brought against him.

718.2   star clusters] Signal flares.

Glossary of Military Terms

Notes on U.S. military organization appear at the end of the Glossary.

A-1]   Single piston-engined fighter-bomber used by both the navy and the air force. The "Skyraider" had a maximum speed of 325 mph, was armed with four rapid-firing 20 mm. cannon, and could carry up to 8,000 pounds of bombs or air-to-ground rockets. It was manufactured in both single-seat (A-1H) and two-seat (A-1E) models, and was sometimes called a "Spad," after the World War I French biplane.

A-3]   Twin-engined jet aircraft, used by the U.S. navy for electronic jamming and aerial refueling missions over North Vietnam.

A-4]   Single-seat, carrier-based jet fighter-bomber. The "Skyhawk" had a maximum speed of 670 mph, was armed with two rapid-firing 20 mm. cannon, and could carry up to 8,200 pounds of bombs.

A-6]   Carrier-based jet attack aircraft. The "Intruder" had a crew of two, a cruising speed of 480 mph, and could carry up to 15,000 pounds of bombs. It was equipped with an electronic navigation and bombing system and was often used to attack targets at night or in bad weather.

AC-47]   Gunship version of the C-47 transport aircraft, known as "Spooky" and "Puff." It had a crew of seven, a cruising speed of 150 mph, and was armed with three six-barreled machine guns firing bullets 7.62 mm. in diameter; each "minigun" could fire up to 6,000 rounds per minute (the aircraft carried 24,000 rounds of ammunition, as well as dozens of parachute flares for illuminating targets at night).

AD-6]   Alternate designation for the A-1 Skyraider.

Air America]   Charter airline covertly owned by the Central Intelligence Agency that operated in Southeast Asia from 1959 until 1976. It was especially active in providing logistical support to American-backed forces in Laos.

AK-47]   Soviet rifle, also manufactured in Communist China, that fired a 7.62 mm. bullet and was capable of both semiautomatic and full automatic fire. It was fed from a 30-round magazine, had an effective range of 330 yards, and weighed 10.5 pounds when loaded. The AK-47 was increasingly used by Viet Cong main-force units after 1965 and was the standard-issue rifle of the North Vietnamese army; it proved to be a highly reliable weapon under combat conditions.

AR-15 Armalite]   Name used in the early 1960s for the rifle later designated as the M-16.

ARVN]   Army of the Republic of Vietnam; the South Vietnamese army.

B-26]   Twin piston-engined medium bomber. The "Invader" had a crew of three, a cruising speed of 284 mph, was armed with six .50 caliber machine guns, and could carry up to 6,000 pounds of bombs. (Until 1948, this aircraft was designated as the A-26.)

B-40]   Soviet rocket-propelled grenade, also manufactured in Communist China. The grenade had a diameter of 82 mm. and an effective range of 150 yards; it was fired from a shoulder-carried tube launcher, and contained a shaped charge that could penetrate armor plate.

B-52]   Eight-engined jet heavy bomber. The B-52 had a crew of six, a cruising speed of 520 mph, and was armed with four .50 caliber machine guns mounted in the tail; the B-52F, used in Southeast Asia in 1965–66, could carry up to 38,000 pounds of bombs, while the B-52D, used in 1966–73, could carry a bombload of up to 60,000 pounds. B-52 crews usually bombed from an altitude of 30,000 feet after using electronic equipment to locate their targets.

B-57]   Twin-engined jet bomber. The B-57 had a crew of two, a cruising speed of 476 mph, was armed with four rapid-firing 20 mm. cannon, and could carry up to 6,000 pounds of bombs.

BAR]   Browning automatic rifle, used by American infantry during World War II as a light machine gun. It fired a .30 caliber bullet, was fed from a 20-round magazine, had an effective range of over 600 yards, and weighed 19 pounds.

Bullpup]   Air-to-ground guided missile that could be visually tracked and directed by radio toward the target by the pilot after it was fired. It carried a 250-pound warhead.

C-47]   Twin piston-engined American transport aircraft, the military version of the DC-3 passenger plane.

C-123]   Twin piston-engined transport aircraft designed for use on short runways.

C-rations]   American canned field rations that could be eaten hot or cold.

Carbine]   A short rifle. The American M-1 carbine, first used in World War II, was a semiautomatic weapon with a 15- or 30-round magazine; it fired a .30 caliber bullet, had an effective range of 300 yards, and weighed six pounds. Another model, the M-2, was capable of both semiautomatic and full automatic fire.

Chinook]   Twin-rotor transport helicopter that could carry 33 troops or up to 16,000 pounds of cargo.

F-4]   Jet fighter and fighter-bomber used by both the navy (F-4B) and the air force (F-4C, F-4D). The "Phantom" had a crew of two, a maximum speed of 816 mph at sea level, and could carry up to 16,000 pounds of bombs. When used as an escort fighter it could carry up to four heat-seeking and four radar-guided air-to-air missiles; in 1967 air force F-4s also began carrying a rapid-firing 20 mm. cannon mounted in an external pod.

F-105]   Single-seat air force jet fighter-bomber. The "Thud" had a maximum speed of 839 mph at sea level, was armed with a rapid-firing 20 mm. cannon, and usually carried 6,000 pounds of bombs on missions against North Vietnam. A two-seat version was used as a "Wild Weasel" aircraft to locate and attack surface-to-air missile sites.

F-111A]   Air force jet bomber that saw limited operational service in 1968. The F-111A had a crew of two, a cruising speed of 665 mph, and could carry up to 20,000 pounds of bombs.

FAC]   Forward Air Controller. FACs directed airstrikes either from the ground or from a light airplane flying over the battlefield.

4.2-inch mortar]   U.S. mortar that fired a 24-pound shell 4.2 inches in diameter, with a maximum range of over 2.5 miles (4,500 yards).

Howitzer]   An artillery gun capable of having its barrel elevated past 45°.

Huey]   Popular name for the UH-1 Iroquois, the most widely used helicopter of the Vietnam War. The Huey could carry 8–12 troops or 3,000 pounds of supplies into assault landing zones and was also used for medical evacuation missions; gunship versions carried a variety of weapons, including multi-barreled 7.62 mm. "miniguns," multi-tubed launchers for firing 2.75-inch diameter rockets, and 40 mm. automatic grenade launchers.

Intruder]   See A-6.

JUSPAO]   Joint United States Public Affairs Office.

L-19]   See O-1.

M-1 rifle]   Standard U.S. infantry rifle of World War II that was widely used by South Vietnamese forces until the late 1960s. A semiautomatic weapon, it fired a .30 caliber bullet, held eight rounds in its magazine, had an effective range of 550 yards, and weighed over nine pounds.

M-16]   American rifle firing a 5.56 mm. bullet and capable of both semiautomatic and full automatic fire. It was fed by a 20-round magazine, had an effective range of 430 yards, and weighed seven pounds. The M-16 frequently jammed under combat conditions in 1965–67, but modifications to its design, the widespread issue of cleaning kits, and improved training significantly reduced problems with the weapon after 1968.

M-60]   American light machine gun issued to the weapons squad of infantry platoons and usually operated by a two-man team, although it could be fired by one man. It fired a 7.62 mm. bullet, was fed by a metal belt, weighed 23 pounds, and had an effective range of 1,100 yards when used with its bipod mount. The M-60 was also used by door gunners on Huey helicopters and was often mounted on M-113 armored personnel carriers.

M-79]   Single-shot grenade launcher that fired a projectile 40 mm. in diameter. It weighed six and a half pounds and had a maximum range of 400 yards.

M-113]   Armored personnel carrier capable of transporting 11 troops. It weighed 12 tons, had a maximum speed of 40 mph, and was often armed with three machine guns. Although its armor gave protection against bullets and shell fragments, the M-113 proved vulnerable to rocket-propelled grenades and large land mines.

MACV]   Military Assistance Command Vietnam; the headquarters that commanded American forces in South Vietnam, 1962–73.

MATS]   Military Air Transport Service.

MiG]   Soviet single-seat jet fighter used for air defense by the North Vietnamese. The MiG-17 had a maximum speed of 661 mph at sea level and was armed with one 37 mm. and two 23 mm. rapid-firing cannon, while the MiG-21 had a maximum speed of 684 mph at sea level and was armed with one 30 mm. cannon and two heat-seeking air-to-air missiles; both aircraft were highly maneuverable in aerial combat.

O-1]   Single piston-engined observation plane. The O-1 had two seats, a maximum speed of 118 mph, and carried four rockets for marking targets with smoke.

O-2]   Twin piston-engined observation plane, with its engines in a tractor-pusher tandem arrangement. The O-2 had two seats, a maximum speed of 199 mph, and carried four rockets for marking targets with smoke.

105]   American howitzer that fired a 33-pound shell 105 mm. in diameter, with a maximum range of almost seven miles (12,200 yards).

155]   American howitzer that fired a 95-pound shell 155 mm. in diameter, with a maximum range of over nine miles (16,000 yards).

175]   American artillery gun that fired a 175-pound shell 175 mm. in diameter, with a range of over 20 miles (35,600 yards).

Phantom]   See F-4.

Popular Forces]   South Vietnamese village-based militia.

SAM]   Surface-to-air missile. The Soviet SA-2 used by the North Vietnamese was a two-stage missile with a range of 25 miles and a 288 pound warhead; it could accelerate to a maximum speed of Mach 3 and was guided by a radio beam linked to a tracking radar.

Skycrane]   Transport helicopter capable of carrying over 20,000 pounds of cargo in an underslung load.

Skyraider]   See A-1.

Shrike]   Air-to-ground missile with a 145-pound warhead and a range of 10 miles, designed to home in on enemy radar sites.

T-28]   Single piston-engined fighter-bomber. The T-28 had a crew of two, a maximum speed of 346 mph, was armed with two .50 caliber machine guns, and could carry 1,800 pounds of bombs.

TAC]   Tactical Air Command.

Thompson submachine gun]   American submachine gun used in World War II. It fired a .45 caliber bullet, had a 20-round magazine, an effective range of 100 yards, and weighed 12 pounds.

U.S. ARMY AND MARINE ORGANIZATION

Platoon]   Unit of about 40 men at full strength, commanded by a second lieutenant.

Company]   Unit made up of three rifle platoons and one weapons platoon, and other troops, usually commanded by a captain. The equivalent unit in the air and armored cavalry is a troop.

Battalion]   Unit usually made up of four rifle companies, one support company, and a headquarters company, usually commanded by a lieutenant colonel. The equivalent unit in the cavalry is a squadron.

Regiment]   In the marines and the armored cavalry, a formation made up of three battalions or squadrons plus supporting troops, commanded by a colonel. During the Vietnam War army infantry battalions were identified by the names of their historic regimental affiliations, but were operationally organized into brigades.

Brigade]   Formation made up of between two and four battalions plus supporting troops, commanded by either a colonel or a brigadier general.

Division]   Formation made up of three brigades (in the marines, three regiments) plus supporting troops. American divisions in Vietnam had between 15,000 and 22,000 men and were commanded by a major general. By 1969 the U.S. had seven army and two marine divisions in Vietnam, along with four separate brigades and an armored cavalry regiment.

Index

A Shau Valley, South Vietnam, 567, 698–703
Abernathy, Rev. Ralph D., 625, 636
Abrams, Gen. Creighton, 585, 700
Acheson, Dean, 583, 585–87, 589
Adda River (Italy), 607
Aden, 184
Adinolfi, 1st Lt. Jack, 345–46
Agency for International Development (AID), U.S., 43, 60, 64, 295, 322, 348, 356, 570
Agricultural Adjustment Act, 257
Air America, 319
Aladonia, Ohio, 694
Algeria, 183–84
Algerian rifle battalions, 343
Alleg, Henri, 183
Alsop, Joseph, *91–93*, 178
Altekoester, Alois, 568
American Code of the Fighting Man, 181
American Friends Service Committee, 149
American Legion, 695
Amphitheatre (Chicago), 633–34, 637, 641, 646–47
An Diem, South Vietnam, 394
An Giang Province, South Vietnam, 319, 322–23
An Khe, South Vietnam, 177, 740, 744–45, 747
An Quang Pagoda (Saigon), 81
An Xuyen, South Vietnam, 33–36, 319, 323–24
Anatomy of Courage, The (Moran), 550
Anderson, Marian, 514
Andersonville National Cemetery (Georgia), 259
Angola, 184
Anton, Frank, 667–69, 672–73, 676, 678, 680, 684–86
Ap Bac, South Vietnam, 68–69, 108, 111, 113, 486
Appalachia, 175, 688, 693

Apple, R.W., Jr., 484
Arlen, Michael J., *490–505*
Arlington National Cemetery, 241
Arlington, Virginia, 572
Armed Forces Radio Network, 135, 362–63, 596
Armstrong Mills, Ohio, 694
Army of the Republic of Vietnam (ARVN), 7, 36, 60, 64, 68, 73, 76, 86–87, 118, 120, 155, 168, 177, 183–84, 232–33, 332, 343, 350, 357–60, 368, 386, 389, 391–92, 395, 408–409, 420, 454, 456, 462, 464–66, 472, 478–79, 483, 575, 585, 615, 622
Arnett, Peter, 484, *522–24*
Arnoni, M.S., 202
At Ease (Eisenhower), 434
Auschwitz, 611

Bac Lieu, South Vietnam, 73, 77–78
Bach Duc Hach, 172
Bach Thanh, 172
Baez, Joan, 200
Baker, Col. Basil Lee, 117
Baker, Russell, *138–39*
Balbo Avenue (Chicago), 637
Baldwin, Hanson, 246
Ball, George W., 242–45, 247, 583, 586–87
Baltimore, Maryland, 665
Bangkok, 419, 442, 599
Bao An. *See* Civil Guard, South Vietnamese.
Bao Dai, Emperor, 67, 299–301, 390
Bao Quoc Pagoda (Hue), 561
Barnesville, Ohio, 692
Baton Rouge, Louisiana, 2
Bay Be, 376–78
Bay Coc Street (Saigon), 383, 384
Bay Manette, Alabama, 627
Bay of Pigs, Cuba, 248
Beallsville, Ohio, 688–97
Beatles, the, 200, 205
Beckett, Samuel, 348
Beethoven, Ludwig van, 365

841

Bellaire, Ohio, 691
Belmont County, Ohio, 694
Ben Cat, South Vietnam, 331
Ben Suc, South Vietnam, 331–35, 342
Ben Tre, South Vietnam, 59
Bendel, Col. Lee R., 495–500
Bergmann, Prithjof, 144
Berkeley, California, 199, 207
Berlin, Germany, 54, 248, 250, 252, 533
Bien Hoa, South Vietnam, 1, 129, 131, 135, 177, 232, 235
Big Sur, California, 200
Bigart, Homer, *26–32, 58–67*
Bigger, Lt. Archie, 706
Binh Dinh Province, South Vietnam, 389–90
Binh Duong Province, South Vietnam, 374, 378
Binh Hung, South Vietnam, 35–36
Binh Linh school (Hue), 561
Binh Long Province, South Vietnam, 137
Binh Son district, South Vietnam, 393–94, 396, 410
Binh Thuan, South Vietnam, 223–24, 226–27, 229
Binh Thuy, South Vietnam, 284
Black Lady mountain (South Vietnam), 230
Black Panthers, 682, 708
Black River. *See* Dao River.
Blairsburg, Iowa, 1
Blankfort, Jeffrey, *688–97*
Blue House raid (South Korea), 588
Bogart, Humphrey, 355
Bollardière, Brig. Gen. de la, 183
Bones. *See* Anton, Frank.
Bong Son, South Vietnam, 177, 716
Boone, Pat, 46
Boston, Capt. Howard, 1
Boswell, Lt. Corky, 415
Boulding, Kenneth, 142, 148
Boupacha, Djamila, 183
Bradley, Gen. Omar, 583, 586, 589
Brady, Col. Larry, 117
Brady, Matthew, 516
Brandeis University, 146
Brazil, 5
Brent, Dick, 531–32, 552, 555
Brewster, Kingman, 539–40
Briarcliff College, 149

Bridges, Mr. —, (teacher), 239
Brink, Brig. Gen. F.G., 136
Brinks B.O.Q. (officers' billet, Saigon), 136, 366–67
British advisory mission, 86
Broderick, Cpl. Edward, 491–92
Brooke, Edward W., 625, 705
Broughton, Jack, 536, 549
Brown, James, 625
Brownback, Peter, 572
Browne, Malcolm W., *18–25, 33–46, 79–85*
Bryant, Sgt. Pellum, 270, 275–76
Buckley, Kevin, *664–66*
Buckley, Thomas, 484
Budapest, Hungary, 340
Buddhist Association (South Vietnam), 88
Bui Chu Province, North Vietnam, 299–300
Bui Van Cach, 165–67
Buis, Maj. Dale, 1
Bullington, James R., 565–66
Bundy, McGeorge, 138, 145–47, 151, 583–84, 586, 590–91
Bunker, Ellsworth, 591, 596, 659
Burgin, Maj. Bill, 77
Burma, 51
Burroughs, William, 644, 647
Busby, Horace, 592
Butler, Maj. James, 77
Buu Dong, 570–71
Byrd, Charlie, 365

C.M.G. Guest House (Saigon), 624
Ca Mau, South Vietnam, 33–39, 367
Ca Mau Peninsula, South Vietnam, 33, 71–78, 263, 355
Cam Au, South Vietnam, 323–24
Cam Lo, South Vietnam, 490–92, 503–4
Cam Ne, South Vietnam, 182, 194
Cam Pha, North Vietnam, 541, 552
Cam Ranh Bay, 705, 759
Cambodia, 3, 16, 47, 51, 185, 316, 585
Cambodian consulate (Saigon), 82
Cambodian Mobile Battalion, 343
Camp Radcliff, South Vietnam, 740–41, 743–44, 748–49, 753, 756, 762, 764, 766
Camp Zama, Japan, 222

Can Lao Nhan Vi. *See* Revolutionary Labor Party, South Vietnam.

Can Tho, South Vietnam, 284, 317, 487

Canada, 625, 764

Cannon (POW), 675–76

Canton, Ohio, 399

Cao Bang, North Vietnam, 184

Cao Dai (religious sect, South Vietnam), 67

Cap St. Jacques, South Vietnam, 98, 355

Cap Tien Sha, South Vietnam, 706

Capitol billet (Saigon), 380

Caravelle Hotel (Saigon), 136, 361–65

Caraway, Hattie, 258

Card (U.S. aircraft ferry), 135

Carlsbad, California, 579

Carlton Hotel (London), 54

Carpenter, William S., 280

Carrillo, Juan, 206

Carver, George, 584, 590

Cassady, Neal, 200–1

Cat Tuong, South Vietnam, 718

Catch 22 (Heller), 196, 273

Central Hospital (Hue), 562, 565

Central Intelligence Agency (CIA), 66, 93, 97, 99, 486, 564, 584, 596; Combined Studies Group of, 35

Central Office of South Vietnam (COSVN), 417

Cercle Sportif (club, Saigon), 103, 355

Charade (film), 239

Chau Doc, South Vietnam, 320

Chicago, Illinois, 137, 353, 622, 628, 634, 640–41, 643, 646–47, 650

Chico, California, 415

Chieu Hoi, 230–35, 363, 456–58

China, 6, 8, 16, 33, 35, 50, 57, 162, 244–46, 248, 250–51, 255–56, 258, 268, 365, 403, 417

Cholon (district of Saigon), South Vietnam, 94, 103–4, 355, 378

Chop Vum (mountain, South Vietnam), 443–44, 446–47, 465

Chu Lai, South Vietnam, 177, 240, 338, 402, 413, 423, 429, 432, 436, 438, 442, 446, 450, 452, 467, 706

Chuck's Composite (nightclub, New York), 656

Churchill, Winston, 256, 369, 662

Cincinnati, Ohio, 692

Citadel (Hue), 627

Civic Action cadres, South Vietnamese, 416

Civil Guard, South Vietnamese, 25, 34–37, 40, 58, 120

Civil Rights Act (1964), 259

Civil War (U.S.), 365, 625

Civilian Irregular Defense Forces, South Vietnamese, 430

Clarington, Ohio, 691

Clark Field, Philippines, 585, 589

Clark Street, Chicago, 645

Clark, Kenneth B., 619–20

Clay, Cassius (Muhammad Ali), 624

Clay, Col. Frank B., 65

Cleveland, Ohio, 543

Clifford, Clark, 583–85, 590–91, 594

Clifford, Marny, 594

Cloy, Dick, 284

Coffin, William Sloane, 539–40

Collins, Gen. J. Lawton, 30, 66

Columbia Broadcasting System (CBS), 336, 490, 493, 495, 501, 504–5

Columbia University, 151

Columbus, Christopher, 625

Combat Youth, South Vietnamese, 35, 416

Command and General Staff College, U.S., 49

Committee for the Liberation of North Vietnam, 302

Committee of Responsibility for Treatment in the U.S. of War-Burned Vietnamese Children, 296

Commoner, Barry, 151

Con Thien, South Vietnam, 490–93, 496, 499, 504–505, 705, 707

Confederate States of America, 625

Confucius (K'ung Ch'iu), 355

Cong Ly, 355

Cong Ly Street, Saigon, 351–52

Congo, 52, 138–39

Congress, U.S., 624

Conmy, Col. Joseph B. Jr., 701–3

Constituent Assembly (South Vietnam), 321

Continental Palace Hotel (Saigon), 136, 355, 362, 606

Copperas Cove, Texas, 1

Coral Sea, U.S.S., 527–28, 538–39, 542–43, 555–56
Cornell University, 145
Country Joe and the Fish, 207
Cronkite, Walter, 505, *581–82*
Cu Chi, South Vietnam, 379
Cuban missile crisis, 249–50
Cubi Point, South Vietnam, 551
Custer, Lt. Col. George A., 222, 625
Cyprus, 184, 588

Da Lat, South Vietnam, 355
Dai Viet Party (South Vietnam), 104, 563
Dailey, Sgt. Eddie, 616–17
Dak To, South Vietnam, 263, 266, 280, 522, 618
Daley, Richard, 631, 634, 643, 646, 650
Daly, James, 668, 670, 674, 679
Dam Doi, South Vietnam, 33–35, 38–39, 41–43, 46
Dam Doi district, South Vietnam, 34, 36
Dam, Col. —, 114
Dan Ve. *See* Self-Defense Corps, South Vietnamese.
Danang, South Vietnam, 140, 155, 158, 181, 241, 283, 293, 311, 336, 419–20, 423, 434, 436, 478, 490, 492, 564–65, 606, 622, 698, 704–6
Dang Lao-Dong (Labor Party, North Vietnam), 52
Dang Sy, Maj., 80
Dang Van Quang, Gen., 317, 318
Dant, J.W., 540
Dao River, 327
Davis, Rennie, 634, 647
Davis, Tom, 668–70, 672–73, 675, 677, 681
De Sapio, Carmine, 148
Dean, Arthur, 583
Declaration of Independence, U.S., 277
Deepe, Beverly, *134–37*
Demilitarized Zone (DMZ), 262–63, 285, 387–88, 414, 488, 490, 492–93, 496, 581
Democratic Party (U.S.), 630, 633, 640, 698
Denny (POW), 672–73

Denver, Colorado, 122–23
Department of Defense, U.S., 64, 135, 693
Department of Justice, U.S., 259
Department of State, U.S., 30, 87, 122, 143, 146, 181, 187, 242, 296, 584, 590, 591
DePuy, Maj. Gen. William, 584, 590
Detroit News, 486
Detroit, Michigan, 349, 400, 588, 644
Deutscher, Isaac, 146–47
Diem. *See* Ngo Dinh Diem.
Dien Bien Phu, North Vietnam, 16, 182, 184–85, 300
Dien Hoa, South Vietnam, 706
Dillon, Douglas, 583–87
Dinh Tuong Province, South Vietnam, 194, 223, 319, 573–74
Dionne, Major Patrick H., 413–16
Discher, Dr. Raimund, 568
Division Street (Chicago), 645
Dobrynin, Anatoli F., 594
Do Cho, 168–70
Do Mau, Col., 96
Dominican Republic, 147, 340, 588
Dong Ap Bia, South Vietnam. *See* Hill 937.
Dong Ha, South Vietnam, 490–91, 504, 617
Dong Khanh, Emperor, 569
Dong Tam, South Vietnam, 573, 706
Dowd, John, 525–27, 530–48, 550–56
Dr. Strangelove (film), 175
Dresser, Maj. Ralph, 281–86
Drought, Spec. 4 Roger W., 400–1
Duc Hoa district, South Vietnam, 563
Duc Pho, South Vietnam, 391, 395, 397, 400–1, 404–5, 414–15, 423, 425, 435, 437, 468
Duc Pho district, South Vietnam, 406
Duc Tan, South Vietnam, 444, 446
Dulles, Allen W., 66, 417
Dulles, John Foster, 27, 66
Duncan, David Douglas, 654–55
Duong Pasteur (Saigon), 350
Duong Van Minh, Gen., 16, 18, 26, 33, 47–48, 51, 53–55, 57, 94, 96
Duram, Art, 653
Durand, M. — (IRC representative), 182
Dutton, Fred, 639

Duy Tan Street (Hue), 562–63
Dylan, Bob, 200, 646

E.S.J. Productions (advertising
    agency), 658, 660
Eagle Beach (South Vietnam), 703
Eastchester, New York, 236
803rd Regiment, Viet Minh, 182
Eighteenth Regiment, North
    Vietnamese, 344
Eighth Armored Squadron, South
    Vietnamese, 487
Eighth Infantry Regiment, South
    Vietnamese, 332
Eisenhower, Dwight D., 30, 66, 255,
    368, 434, 584
El Caney, battle of, 626
Eleventh Regiment (First Battalion),
    South Vietnamese, 573
Eliot, T. S., 245
Elizalde, Father, 567
Ellsberg, Daniel, 361
Eltige, Gen. Leroy, 400
Emerson, Lt. Col. Henry, 265
Engels, Friedrich, 611
Enterprise, U.S.S. 606
Escapade (magazine), 424

Faas, Horst, 484
Face of War, A (documentary), 653–55,
    658
Fairchild-Hiller (aircraft
    manufacturer), 281
Fall, Bernard B., *47–57, 175–86, 331–43*
Falls Church, Virginia, 711
Faust (Goethe), 355
Federal Bureau of Investigation (FBI),
    632
Fifth Armored Squadron, South
    Vietnamese, 487
Fifth Division, South Vietnamese, 332
Fifth Marine Regiment (Delta
    Company, First Battalion), U.S., 627
Finck, Col. Pierre A., 746
Fire Support Base Berchtesgaden, 702
Fire Support Base Veghel, 700
First Battalion, 506th Infantry, U.S.
    101st Airborne Division, 701
First Battalion, Seventh Cavalry, U.S.
    First Cavalry Division (Airmobile),
    208

First Battalion, 327th Infantry, U.S.
    101st Airborne Division, 263
First Battalion, 28th Infantry
    (Companies Alpha and Delta), U.S.
    First Infantry Division, 664, 666
First Brigade, U.S. 101st Airborne
    Division, 263, 387, 389, 397, 413, 418,
    423, 430, 438, 441, 443, 446, 461;
    Civil Affairs Office, 461–62, 467,
    483
First Cavalry Division (Airmobile),
    U.S., 208, 254, 314, 681, 706, 740,
    758
First Division, South Vietnamese,
    700–1
First Infantry Division, U.S., 332, 336,
    370, 664, 666
Fishel, Wesley, 146, 149
Fitzgerald, Capt. Robert, 618
FitzGerald, Frances, *316–24*
545th Military Police Company, U.S.,
    744
Flint, Garth, 526–27, 530–32, 534, 538,
    541, 548, 550, 552–53, 555–56
Florence, Italy, 607
Flores, Pfc. Angel, 524
Flower Street (Saigon), 373
Flynn, Errol, 618
Flynn, John, *140–41*
Ford Foundation, 586
Foreign Affairs, 609
Foreign Office (Hanoi), 49
Fort Benning, Georgia, 191, 213
Fort Bragg, North Carolina, 623
Fort Carson, Colorado 760–61, 763
Fort Leavenworth, Kansas, 49, 756,
    762–63, 765–66
Fort Lee, Virginia, 524
Fort Lewis, Washington, 759
Fort Meyer, Virginia, 702
Fort Myers, Florida, 523
Fort, Charles, 200
Fortas, Abe, 583, 586, 589
Foster Parents Plan, 294
Fouhy, Edward, 504
Fourth Battalion, 503rd Infantry
    (Airborne), U.S. 173rd Airborne
    Brigade, 617–20
Fourth Marine Regiment, U.S., 240
Fourth Military Region, Viet Cong,
    332

France, 5–6, 183–85, 295, 299–301, 338, 568
Francis, Connie, 659
Franklin, Aretha, 625
Free Speech Movement, 198
French and Indian Wars, 175
French Communist Party, 54
French-Indochina War, 18, 66, 72, 78, 177, 182, 300
French Socialist Party, 54
Frost, S. Sgt. James, 616
Fuck You (magazine), 512
Fugs, the, 506, 509–10, 512, 515–17
Fulbright, J. William, 252, 254, 258
Furue, Tadao, 746–47

Gamson, Albert, 143–44
Garcia, Pfc. Richard, 267–70, 273
Garment, Leonard, 653–54, 657, 659–60, 662–63
Garrison Town Office (Hue), 562
Garwood, Robert, 668, 678–79, 685
Gellhorn, Martha, *287–97,* 365–67
Genet, Jean, 644, 647
Geneva Accords, 4, 147, 181, 300, 598
Geneva Convention, 181, 183, 335, 341
Germany, 234, 342, 357–58, 402, 568–69
Geronimo, 625
Gia Lam Airport (Hanoi), 599
Gia Long Palace (Saigon), 91, 92, 117
Giap. *See* Vo Nguyen Giap, Gen.
Ginsberg, Allen, 200, 512, 515, 635, 644, 647
Goldberg, Arthur, 583–85
Goldwater, Barry, 256
Gonzales, S. Sgt. Pablo, 400–1
Good, Capt. Kenneth N., 68–69
Goodman, W.T., 260
Goodwin, Lt. Col. Felix L., 625
Goodwin, Richard, 639
Gould, Jack, 659
Graff, Henry F., *242–58*
Graham, Billy, 655
Gramlich, Ben, 688, 694–95
Gramlich, Randy, 694
Grant Park (Chicago), 628–29, 631, 634, 636–37, 646
Grant, Zalin, *667–87*
Gray, Rev. Fred, 260
Great Britain, 6, 295

Greece, 250, 339, 341, 365, 588
Greenacre, Boyd, 741–43
Greenfield, Meg, *145–52*
Greenlee, Duane, Jr., 691
Greenlee, Duane, Sr., 691
Greenlee, Mrs. Duane, 691
Greenville, New York, 345
Gregory, Dick, 651
Grey, Terry, 268, 272, 279
Griffith, Brig. Gen. Samuel B., 196
Grissett, Russ, 668, 671–72, 674, 677, 679–81
Gromyko, Andrei A., 250
Gruber, — (clerk), 222
Gruening, Ernest, 347
Guadalcanal, 175
Guam, 349
Guernica (Picasso), 366
Guerrilla and Counter-Guerrilla Warfare: Liberation and Suppression in the Present Period (Pomeroy), 186
Guevara, Che, 193
Guillaume Tell (restaurant, Saigon), 355
Gurdjieff, Georgei Ivanovitch, 202
Guy, Father, 569

Ha Dong Province, North Vietnam, 379
Ha Tinh, North Vietnam, 540
Ha Van Lau, Col., 610
Habib, Philip, 584, 590
Hackley School, 236–41
Hackworth, Maj. David, 263–65, 274–75
Hague, The, 181
Hai Duong, North Vietnam, 50
Haiphong, North Vietnam, 357, 369, 527, 532–33, 536–38, 541–42, 552, 608, 611
Halberstam, David, *71–78, 108–23*
Hamburger Hill. *See* Hill 937.
Hamlett, Gen. Barksdale, 120
Hang Thao. *See* Silk Street.
Hankinson, Spec. 4 William, 577
Hannibal, Ohio, 689, 694
Hanoi, 47–56, 325, 327–28, 330, 357, 369, 527, 536, 538–39, 598–614,
Hanoi University, 390
Hardy, Sgt. Charles C., 622
Harker, David, 668–86

Harkins, Gen. Paul Donal, 67, 101, 113–21
Harlem (New York), 54, 520, 618, 620
Harper, Keith, 693
Harriman, Averell, 584–85
Harris, Joseph, 705
Harter, Wendy, 544
Harvard University, 10, 106, 146
Harvey, Frank, *281–86*
Harwood, Ralph, 117
Harwood, Richard, *484–89*
Haught, Timothy, 696
Hayden, Tom, 628, 634, 646–47
Haymarket Inn (Chicago), 638–39
Healy, Pfc. Paul, 559
Heggs, Lt. Owen, 704
Hell's Angels, 199–201
Heller, Joseph, 273
Hellet, Maj. Jack, 2
Helms, Richard, 584
Hemingway, Ernest, 348, 366
Hickam Field (Hawaii), 544
Hickerson, Lt. Col. Elzie, 117
Higgins, Marguerite, *86–90*
Highway 1 (Vietnam), 155, 160, 163, 171–73, 327–30, 393–95, 405, 408–9, 415–16, 460, 541, 564
Highway 4 (Vietnam), 573–74
Higinbotham, Capt. Lewis, 264–80
Hill 69, 236
Hill 192, 716, 720, 725, 727, 738–39, 745–47, 749, 751–52, 760, 766
Hill 861, 345
Hill 875, 522, 618–19
Hill 881 North, 344–46
Hill 881 South, 345
Hill 937, 698–702, 706
Hilsman, Roger, 87
Hilton Hotel (Chicago), 628–31, 633–34, 637–40, 646, 648–51
Hiroshima, Japan, 195, 692
Hitler, Adolf, 238, 249, 369
Ho Chi Minh, 16, 47–48, 51, 53–55, 57, 148, 157, 162, 165, 252, 263, 301, 303, 313, 369, 390, 567, 570, 611
Ho Chi Minh Trail, 541
Ho, Mr. (VC political cadre), 670–71, 682
Hoa Binh Province, North Vietnam, 184, 599
Hoa Hao (religious sect), 67, 88, 319–21

Hoang Dinh Tho, Lt. Col., 420, 463, 465–66, 480
Hoang Van Vien, 560
Hoang, Brother, 374
Hoang, Maj., 37–38
Hobson, Ernest, 470
Hoffman, Abbie, 510, 651–52
Hoffman, David, *698–703*
Hofstra University, 151
Holbrook, Massachusetts, 559
Hom, Mr. (VC guard), 678, 683
Hon Gay, North Vietnam, 51, 541, 552
Honeycutt, Lt. Col. Weldon F., 700–3
Hong Kong, 298, 437
Honolulu, Hawaii, 238, 242, 305, 485
Horsley, Pfc. Carl, 705
Hotel Brink (Saigon), 135
Houston, Sam, 256
Howard University, 47
Howard, Lance Cpl. Raymond, 627
Howard, S. Sgt. James, 400
Huckleberry Finn (Twain), 355
Hudson River, 236
Hudson, Henry, 625
Hue, 4, 62, 80, 84, 154–55, 158, 162–63, 170, 173, 356–57, 383, 560–70, 616, 627, 698, 700, 703
Humphrey, Hubert H., 242, 247, 374, 585–86, 629, 633, 646
Hung Yen Province, North Vietnam, 603, 613
Huong River. *See* Perfume River.
Huong Thuy district, South Vietnam, 564
Hurlburt Field, Florida, 131–32
Hurt, Mississippi John, 200
Huyn Phu So (Hoa Hao prophet), 320
Huynh Van Kim, 223–35
Hyland, Adm. Red, 551

I Corps, 361, 419, 458, 466, 704
Ia Drang Valley, South Vietnam, 208, 222
Imperial Beach, California, 1
Independence Palace (Saigon), 374, 558
Indianapolis, Indiana, 277
Indonesia, 339

Ink Spots, the, 363
Institut de Recherches du Caoutchouc du Vietnam, 331
Interior Ministry, South Vietnamese, 38
International Control Commission (ICC), 48, 598, 602
International Red Cross (IRC), 10, 181–82, 290, 479, 639; Amputee Center (Saigon), 289
Inter-University Committee for a Public Hearing on Vietnam, 145
Iron Triangle, North Vietnam, 539, 548
Iron Triangle, South Vietnam, 331–33, 336, 343
Italy, 295, 607, 626
Iwo Jima, 207, 643

J.F.K. Recreation Center (Beallsville, Ohio), 695
Jacobs, Paul, 202–3
Jacobson, Col. George, 557, 559, 596
James, Henry, 508
Janesville, Wisconsin, 400
Jansen, Capt.—, 494–95, 497–502
Japan, 50, 63, 222, 238, 356, 402, 454, 551
Javits, Jacob K., 240
Jeffers, Vern, 695–96
Jerusalem, Ohio, 694
Johnson, Lyndon B., 63, 133, 138–39, 143, 149, 165, 242, 244, 249, 251, 253–55, 257–58, 312–13, 322, 327, 368, 369, 484, 486, 538, 583–97, 600, 603–4, 608, 629, 685, 702, 753
Johnson, Thomas A., *615–27*
Johnson, U. Alexis, 659
Joint Chiefs of Staff, U.S., 120–22, 312, 410, 485, 589–91
Joint U.S. Public Affairs Office (JUSPAO), 348, 357, 380
Jones, Eugene S., 198, 653–58, 660, 662–63
Jones, Ruth, 653
Jorden, William J., 145–46, 151
Journalists' Union (Hanoi), 610
JUSPAO. *See* Joint U.S. Public Affairs Office.
Just, Ward S., *262–80, 348–70,* 484

Kahin, George, 145, 149
Karch, Brig. Gen. Frederick, 140–41

Karenga, Ron, 704
Karnow, Stanley, *3–17, 94–107*
Katzenbach, Nicholas, 584
Kaufman, Arnold, 142
Kay, Keith, 490–505
Keene, New Hampshire, 136
Kelly, Pfc. James, 523
Kelman, Herbert, 148
Kennedy, Edward M., 698, 700, 702, 705
Kennedy, John F., 26–27, 61, 67, 86, 97, 115–16, 248, 250, 254, 368, 509, 584, 586, 597, 629, 746
Kennedy, Robert F., 639, 705
Kesey, Dale, 201
Kesey, Ken, 198–206
Khanh Hoi, South Vietnam, 623–24
Khartoum, Sudan, 184
Khe Sanh, South Vietnam, 344–45, 491, 576, 578–79, 581, 585, 587, 623
Khrushchev, Nikita, 54, 248–50
Kien An, North Vietnam, 540
Kien Giang, South Vietnam, 319
Kien Hoa Province, South Vietnam, 18
Kien Phong Province, South Vietnam, 120
Kim Van Kieu (Tale of Kieu, Nguyen Du), 354
King Chapel (Hackley School), 241
King, Martin Luther, Jr., 206–7, 705
Kinton, Spec. 4 Donald R., 399
Kirk, Roland, 200
Knoll, Lt. Edward J., 664–65
Komer, Robert, 486, 596
Kontum Province, South Vietnam, 262, 266, 268, 270, 273, 280, 355, 369, 403, 486
Korean War, 32, 109, 124, 127, 213, 246–47, 250, 252, 314, 342, 329, 370, 420, 453, 463, 533, 535, 626, 684
Krainick, Dr. Horst Gunther, 568
Krainick, Elisabeth, 568
Kramer, Mrs. Stephen, 237
Kraselsky, Lt. Robert L., 260
Krassner, Paul, 202–3, 205·
Kreole, Mississippi, 399
Kruger, Paul, 184
Krulak, Maj. Gen. Victor, 121
Kupferberg, Tuli, 509
Kushner, Capt. Floyd Harold, 667–70, 673–76, 678–79, 681, 686

Kushner, Valerie, 669
Ky Son American billet (Saigon), 379
Ky. *See* Nguyen Cao Ky.

Ladd, Lt. Col. Fred, 118, 120
Lai Khe, South Vietnam, 331, 343, 361
Laird, Melvin R., 688
Lam Son Square (Saigon), 362, 366
Lam Thao, North Vietnam, 50
L'Amiral (restaurant, Saigon), 355
Landing Zone Albany, 209
Landing Zone Baldy, 681
Lang, Daniel, *709–67*
Lang Son, North Vietnam, 48
Lansdale, Brig. Gen. Edward G., 66
Lao Dong (Workers') Party, 611
Laos, 7, 16, 27, 47, 49, 56, 185, 250,
    262, 267, 303, 312, 341, 345, 522, 585,
    698, 702
Lao-tse, 355
Laurence, John, 490–505
Le Nang, 140, 155, 158–60
Le Van Duyet Street (Saigon), 82,
    350
Legari, Vito, 399
Lenin, Vladimir Ilich Ulyanov, 147,
    611
L'Entente (newspaper), 52
Lerner, Max, 146
Lerner, Steve, 638, *643–52*
Lescaze, Lee, 486, *572–75*
Lewis, Robert, 668, 683
Li Tinh, South Vietnam, 458
Liebling, A.J., 269
Life, 141, 174–75, 236, 385, 391, 490,
    576, 584, 648, 669
Life of Agricola (Tacitus), 175
Lincoln Memorial (Washington), 508
Lincoln Park (Chicago), 628, 631, 636,
    643, 646, 651
Lippmann, Walter, 246
Loc Dien, South Vietnam, 153–73
Loc Ninh, South Vietnam, 664
Lodge, Henry Cabot, 87, 97, 101–2,
    116, 254, 257, 341, 353–54, 361, 584,
    586, 589, 659
London, England, 54, 146, 348, 352,
    361, 526
Long An Province, South Vietnam,
    120, 384, 486
Long Binh, South Vietnam, 747, 754

Long Island, New York, 399, 544
Long, Huey, 258
Long, Russell, 258
Long, Stephen, 672
Look at America (campaign
    commercial), 660
Loop, the (Chicago), 628, 631, 634,
    636, 647
Loren, Sophia, 655
Los Angeles, California, 64, 356, 705
Love, Mrs. William, 660
Lowell, Robert, 507–8, 514–16, 518–19
Luang Prabang, Laos, 354
Lucas, Robert, Jr., 688, 693
Lucas, Robert, Sr., 692
Lufbery, Raoul, 535
Lukas, J. Anthony, 638
Luke, Frank, 535
Luu Quy Ky, 610
Ly Tra, South Vietnam, 458, 462
Lynch, Lt. Col. Robert O., 465–66
Lynd, Staughton, 148

MacArthur, Gen. Douglas, 588
Macdonald, Dwight, 507–8, 514, 516,
    518–19
Macdonough, Lt. Bryan, 524
MACV. *See* Military Assistance
    Command Vietnam.
Madagascar, 184
Madrid, Spain, 352
Mafeking, South Africa, 184
Magdeburg, Germany, 533
Maginot Line, 285
Mailer, Norman, *506–21, 628–42,*
    647
Malaga, Ohio, 694
Malaya, 16, 32, 190, 339
Manchester Guardian, 365
Manhard, Philip W., 565, 567
Manh Dong, South Vietnam, 239
Manila, Philippines, 527
Mann, Richard, 145, 151
Mantovani (orchestra leader), 625
Mao Tse-tung, 6, 165, 177, 193, 196,
    410, 611
March on Washington (October
    1967), 506–9, 590
Marie Curie lycée (Saigon), 350
Marine Corps, South Vietnamese, 34,
    39–41, 44–45, 73, 96, 100, 456

Marine Corps, U.S., 140–41, 194, 236–38, 240, 311, 344–46, 392, 396, 433, 436, 438, 445, 470, 479, 488, 490–93, 497, 499, 503–504, 566, 576–80, 618–19, 676, 691, 700, 704, 707

Marks, Pfc. Richard E., 236–41

Marks, Robert B., 237

Marshall Plan, 148

Marx, Karl, 516, 611

Mata Hari, 377

Matthews, Herbert, 366

McCarthy, Eugene, 629–30, 633, 639, 650

McCarthy, Mary, *598–614*

McChristian, Maj. Gen. Joseph, 361

McClelland, Ferrell, 695

McClelland, Roger, 695

McConnell, Gen. John, 584

McGinniss, Joe, *653–63*

McGowan, John, 485

McMillan, Isaiah (Ike) 674, 676–77, 679, 682–84, 686

McNamara, Robert, 63, 121, 133, 139, 149, 242, 245–48, 251–52, 361, 485, 488

McPherson, Harry, 590–93

Mekong River Delta, 8, 18, 20, 23, 25, 27–28, 47–48, 60, 77, 109, 111–12, 117–20, 123–24, 131, 178, 188, 257, 265, 270, 283–85, 287–88, 294, 316–19, 322–24, 348, 352, 355–56, 487, 572, 615, 706–7

Melman, Seymour, 148–49

Merry Pranksters, 198–206

Merseburg, Germany, 533

Metro-Goldwyn-Mayer, 279

Metropole Hotel (Hanoi), 48

Metropole (enlisted men's billet, Saigon), 374, 376

Metropolitan Applied Research Center (New York), 620

Mexico, 238

Michigan Avenue (Chicago), 628–30, 634, 636–37, 639–40, 648–49

Michigan Daily, The, 142

Michigan State University, 146, 149

Military Assistance Advisory Group (MAAG), 1, 58

Military Assistance Command Vietnam (MACV), 67, 114–15, 117–19, 121, 307, 350, 354, 361, 367, 370, 387

Miller, Clarence, 688, 693

Miller, Glenn, 49

Miller, Stephen H., 565–66

Millet, Stanley, 149

Minh (shopkeeper), 383

Ministry of Information, South Vietnam, 460

Minneapolis, Minnesota, 602, 759, 763, 767

Mo Duc district, South Vietnam, 395–97, 404

Moby Dick (Melville), 543

Mohr, Charles, *557–59*

Monroe County, Ohio, 693–95

Monroe, Marilyn, 277

Montgomery, Alabama, 259

Morgenthau, Hans, 145, 148

Morris, Lance Cpl. Richard, 579

Morrison, Norman, 337

Morse, Wayne, 145, 250, 347

Moser, Don, *153–74, 371–85*

Moyers, Bill, 253

Munich Conference, 143

Murphy, Robert, 584, 586, 589

Museum of War Crimes (Hanoi), 609

Mussolini, Benito, 203–4, 640

Muste, A.J., 148

My Canh (restaurant, Saigon), 373–74, 379

My Tho, South Vietnam, 71, 100, 113, 287–89, 572–75, 715

Nagel, Ernest, 151

Nam Dinh, North Vietnam, 325–27, 542, 608

Nam Ha Province, North Vietnam, 327

Nam Hoa district, South Vietnam, 563

National Assembly (South Vietnam), 60–61, 353, 355

National Association for the Advancement of Colored People (NAACP), 705

National Broadcasting Corporation (NBC), 335–36, 362, 365, 566–67, 655

National Economic Council (South Vietnam), 62

National Guard, U.S., 206–7, 630, 632–34, 636, 646, 649

National Liberation Front, 153, 158, 171–72, 176, 226, 229, 231, 248, 251,

316, 318, 332, 336–39, 341–42, 385, 389–92, 394, 410, 412, 417–18, 469–70, 516–18, 612, 682, 685

National Mobilization Committee, 634, 643, 646–47

National Police Service (South Vietnam), 173, 374, 377, 563

National Security Council (U.S.), 62

Nelson, Jean, 696

Netherlands, 285, 295

New Life Hamlet Program (South Vietnam), 391

New York *Journal-American,* 122

New York Times, The, 32, 67, 77, 122, 241, 246, 248, 258, 347, 484, 487, 539, 606, 638

New York Times Magazine, The, 357, 410

New Zealand, 358

Newfield, Jack, 638

Newsweek, 175, 184

Newton Church of Christ (Montgomery, Alabama), 259

Nghia Hanh, South Vietnam, 395

Ngo Dinh Can, 4, 7, 61

Ngo Dinh Diem, 3–19, 24, 26–27, 29–30, 32, 34, 39, 44, 47, 55–56, 58, 60–63, 66–67, 79–80, 86–92, 94–107, 109, 113–15, 117, 120, 157–58, 165, 173, 192, 223, 302, 340, 350, 355, 369, 390, 463, 471, 488, 565

Ngo Dinh Nhu, 5, 7, 10, 13, 15, 29, 59–62, 89–92, 94–106, 114, 158

Ngo Dinh Nhu, Madam, 5, 61, 89, 92, 95, 128

Ngo Quan, 165

Ngo Quang Truong, Brig. Gen., 564

Ngo Truy, 153–54, 159–60, 166–67, 169–71, 173–74

Nguyen Ba, 162–63

Nguyen Cao Ky, Gen., 165, 257, 282, 300–1, 305, 317–18, 322, 487

Nguyen Che, 166

Nguyen Chuong, 98, 153, 167–68, 174

Nguyen Da, 171–72

Nguyen Dong, 156–59, 164, 167, 169–70, 172, 174

Nguyen Giang, 563

Nguyen Huu Co, Lt. Gen., 300

Nguyen Lac Hoa, 35–36, 45

Nguyen Lach, 167, 170, 173

Nguyen Thuan, 171–72

Nguyen Tien Canh, 327

Nguyen Truong, 161–62

Nguyen Van Sam, 371–73, 375, 378–80, 383–84

Nguyen Van Thieu, 591

Nguyen Vi Hoc, 563

Nguyen Viet Thanh, Brig. Gen., 573

Nha Trang, South Vietnam, 84, 351, 363, 564

Nhat Linh, 390

Nhu. *See* Ngo Dinh Nhu.

Nhu, Madam. *See* Ngo Dinh Nhu, Madam.

Nieuw Amsterdam, 625

Niles, Courtney, 566–67

Nimitz, Adm. Chester W., 242

1984 (Orwell), 52

Ninety-fifth Regiment, North Vietnamese, 344

Ninety-second Infantry Division, U.S. (WWII), 626

Ninth Armored Squadron, South Vietnamese, 487

Ninth Infantry Division, U.S., 486, 573

Ninth Medical Laboratory, U.S., 746

Ninth Regiment, North Vietnamese, 700

Nitze, Paul, 584

Nixon, Richard M., 593, 629, 654–60, 663, 685, 688, 705

Nolting, Frederick E., Jr, 63

Norfleet, Sp. 4 Washington, 665–66

North Atlantic Treaty Organization (NATO), 246

North Hollywood, California, 579

North Korea, 56, 453, 536

North Vietnamese Army (NVA), 51, 53, 181, 209–10, 212–13, 216, 220–21, 268, 309, 312, 389, 414, 486, 563

Noyes, Lance Cpl. Richard, 578–79

O'Brien, Lawrence, 591

Oakland, California, 203, 206, 266; Army Terminal, 199

Oberdorfer, Don, *560–71, 583–97*

Ochs, Phil, 647

Office of Strategic Services (OSS), 54

Ogden, Utah, 742

Oglesby, Carl, 142, 647

Ohio River, 688, 694
Oise-Aisne offensive (WW I), 626
Okinawa, 141, 239
Ol' Ratface (VC commander), 679
Old Town (Chicago), 628
101st Airborne Division, U.S., 177, 263, 280, 363, 387, 389, 397–98, 400, 413, 415, 418, 423, 430, 438, 441, 443, 446, 456, 461, 469, 482, 569, 698, 700–1
196th Light Infantry Brigade, U.S., 332, 387, 389, 394, 443, 469, 471, 481
173rd Airborne Brigade, U.S., 331–32, 522, 617–20
Ong Lanh marketplace (Saigon), 371
Open Arms program. *See* Chieu Hoi.
Operation Apache Snow, 699–700
Operation Benton, 397, 418, 423, 441, 443, 446, 456, 461–69, 482
Operation Cedar Falls, 334
Operation Hawthorne, 263, 280
Operation Hood River, 397, 413, 418, 423, 441, 446, 453
Operation Junction City, 618
Operation Lam Son Two, 360
Operation Malheur I, 397, 399, 423
Operation Malheur II, 397, 413, 415, 423
Operation Mastiff, 360
Operation Ranch Hand, 281–86
Operation Thayer II, 757
Orlovsky, Peter, 200
Orwell, George, 52, 348
Ovnand, Master Sgt. Chester, 1
Oxford Committee for Famine Relief (OXFAM), 296
Ozark, Ohio, 694

Palestine, 184
Palo Alto, California, 200–1
Pan Tho Airfield (South Vietnam), 128
Panama Canal Zone, 588
Panmunjom, Korea, 138
Paris, France, 5, 50, 183, 353, 362
Patton, Gen. George, 114
Paul Doumer Bridge (Hanoi), 605
Pearl Harbor, attack on, 138
Pearson, Brig. Gen. William, 264–65
Peking, 184, 244–45, 250, 340, 608
Peking Review, 340

Pentagon, the, 108–9, 120–22, 183, 245, 354–55, 488, 506–21, 537, 541, 549, 564, 604, 620–21, 647, 688
People's Army of Vietnam. *See* North Vietnamese Army (NVA).
People's Revolutionary Party, 339, 342, 417, 560
People's War, People's Army (Giap), 53
Perfume River, 80, 560, 616
Perry, Commodore Oliver Hazard, 625
Perry, Mert, 78
Peterson, Lt. Col. Frank, 706
Phai Tay, South Vietnam, 444–45
Pham Lien, Capt., 563
Pham Minh Cong, 399
Pham Ngoc Thao, Lt. Col., 96
Pham Quant Tan, Capt., 381–85
Pham Tan Dan, 490
Pham Tra Dang, 562
Pham Van Dong, 54–56, 302
Pham Van Khoa, Lt. Col., 565
Phan Dinh Phung Street (Saigon), 81–82, 566
Phan Rang, South Vietnam, 349
Phan Sao Nam Camp (Hue), 562
Phan Thi Loc, 718–19, 752
Phan Thi Mao, 710–12, 718–53, 757–62, 767
Phan Thiet, South Vietnam, 84
Philadelphia, Pennsylvania, 621, 715
Philippines, 339, 358, 551
Phillips, J. McCandlish, *236–41*
Phillips, Kevin, 659
Phillips, Rufus, 117
Phnom Penh, Cambodia, 6, 354, 598
Phu Bai, South Vietnam, 565, 698
Phu Cam area (Hue), 561, 569–70
Phu Cuong, South Vietnam, 333
Phu Loi, South Vietnam, 706
Phu My district, South Vietnam, 718
Phu Tho, South Vietnam, 355
Phu Thu district, South Vietnam, 563
Phu Ly, North Vietnam, 327
Phu Yen Province, South Vietnam, 617
Phun Cat, North Vietnam, 541
Phuoc Tho, South Vietnam, 394–95
Phuoc Tien, South Vietnam, 443, 466
Phuoc Vinh, South Vietnam, 27, 706
Pia Ouac, North Vietnam, 50
Piaf, Edith, 365

Pinter, Harold, 348, 356
Pisor, Robert, 486
Pittman, Earl, 689
Pittman, Jack, 689, 691
Pittman, Mrs. Maegene, 689
Plain of Reeds, South Vietnam, 69, 120
Playboy, 324, 353, 434, 460
Pleiku Province, South Vietnam, 222, 262–63, 338, 349, 363, 369, 622
Po River (Italy), 607
Poitier, Sidney, 618
Poland, 604
Pomeroy, William J., 186
Pompeii, 352
Poor People's Campaign, 636–37, 642, 648
Popular Forces, South Vietnamese, 159, 161, 166, 316, 415–16
Port, Bill, 681–82
Porter, Col. Daniel Boone, 118–20
Porter, William, 257
Potomac River, 506
Powell, Adam Clayton, 624
Prague, Czechoslovakia, 633
Pravda (newspaper), 340
Presidential Palace (Saigon), 59
Pruett, Maj. Jack G., 136

Qua (VC guard), 678
Quang Nam, South Vietnam, 361, 390, 562
Quang Ngai Province, South Vietnam, 308, 349, 358, 360, 386–93, 395, 397, 402, 405–6, 409–10, 412–16, 441–42, 445, 458, 464, 468–69, 476, 479, 483
Quang Ngai City, South Vietnam, 395, 409, 425
Quang Tin, South Vietnam, 386, 389–90, 392, 397, 413, 418, 420, 441, 443, 458, 463–65, 480, 483
Quang Tri Province, South Vietnam, 188, 488
Quantico, Virginia, 39, 41
Quarnstrom, Lee, 200
Question, The (Alleg), 183
Qui Nhon Province, South Vietnam, 291, 351, 706, 731, 735

Radio Hanoi, 685
Randal, Jonathan, *344–47*

Rapoport, Anatol, 149–50
Rapoport, Roger, *142–44*
Reader's Digest, 434
Realist, The (magazine), 202
Red River, 48, 50, 328, 533, 605, 607
Republican Party, U.S., 143, 633
Republican Youth Corps, South Vietnamese, 35
Reserve Officers' Training Corps (ROTC), 543
Resistance, the (antidraft organization), 649
Reston, James, 248
Revolutionary Development Program, 322, 413
Revolutionary Labor Party, South Vietnam, 5
Revolutionary War (U.S.), 625
Rhine River, 626
Richardson, John, 97
Richthofen, Manfred von, 535
Ridgway, Gen. Matthew, 584, 586, 588
Riverdale, New York, 241
RMK-BRJ (construction cartel), 354
Roberts, Oscar, 622
Roche, John P., 146
Rockefeller, Nelson, 633
Rockville Centre, New York, 544
Rocky Mountains, 760
Rome, Italy, 352–53, 362
Roosevelt, Franklin D., 257–58
Roosevelt, Theodore, 626
Ross, S/Sgt. James A., 399
Rostow, Elspeth, 594
Rostow, Walt, 584, 590, 594
Rough Riders (Spanish-American War), 626
Route 9, 490
Route 1. *See* Highway 1.
Rowan, Cpl. Curly, 717–18, 733, 738, 743
Rowe, James, 591
Rubin, Jerry, 646–47
Rucker, Betty, 690
Rucker, Kenneth, 690–91
Rucker, Richard, 690–91
Rusk, Dean, 138–39, 147, 181, 242, 246, 248–52, 488, 584–85, 590–91, 594; "Rusk Doctrine," 248
Russell, Bertrand, 342, 347

Saigon River, 331–32, 623
Salisbury, Harrison E., *325–30*, 539
Salt Lake City, Utah, 743
San Antonio, Texas, 286, 400, 595
San Diego, California, 492
San Francisco, California, 199, 505, 657
Sanders, Ed, 509, 512, 515
Sanders, Sol, 484
Sanford, Terry, 591–92
Santa Fe, New Mexico, 715
Savannah, Georgia, 617
Savio, Mario, 198
Scheer, Bob, 207
Schell, Jonathan, *386–483*
Schlesinger, Arthur M., Jr., 146–47
Schnegg, Charles, 692
Schnegg, Ernest, 692
Schnegg, Esther, 692
Schnegg, Roger, 692
Schnegg, Shirley, 692
Schultz, Paul, 540
Schulz, Charles, 435
Schweitzer, Maj. Robert, 137
Screaming Eagle, 398, 400, 415
Sea Swallows (South Vietnamese), 35–36, 45
Seattle, Washington, 759
Seburn, Roy, 201
Second Battalion, 503rd Infantry (Airborne), U.S. 173rd Airborne Brigade, 522
Second Moroccan Spahi Regiment, 343
Second Squadron, 17th Cavalry (Troop A), U.S. 101st Airborne Division, 400
Self-Defense Corps, South Vietnamese, 34, 58, 120
Sellers, Wardell, 705
Selma, Alabama, 207
Senate (U.S.), 181, 254, 255, 258, 592, 698, 699, 700; Committee on Foreign Relations, 248, 252
Seventeenth Parallel, 4, 300, 302, 329
Seventh Cavalry Regiment, U.S., 222
Seventh Division, South Vietnamese, 1, 65, 68, 70, 100, 115, 118, 573
Seventh Fleet, U.S., 307–8, 326, 603
Shakespeare, Frank, 653–56, 659, 663
Shakespeare, William, 239

Shank, Capt. Jerry, 124–33
Shank, Connie, 126
Sheehan, Neil, 68–70, 114, 116, *298–315*
Sheehan, Susan, *223–35*
Sheraton Park Hotel (Washington, D.C.), 145, 150
Sherman (POW), 676
Siam, Gulf of, 33
Siegfried Line, 178
Silk Street (Nam Dinh, North Vietnam), 326
Singapore, 54, 307
Sir! (magazine), 424
Slack, Lt. C.J., 579
Slavich, Maj. Ivan, 77
Slime (camp commander), 679–80
Smith, Bromley, 151
Smith, Jack P., *208–22*
Smith, Col. Jim, 114
Smith, Rick, 122
Smith, Maj. Wardell, 708
Soc Trang, South Vietnam, 127–28, 130
Son Lam, 560–63
Son Tinh district, South Vietnam, 394, 426
Son Tra, South Vietnam, 470, 472, 479–81
Song Chang (river), 443
Song of Roland, 355
Song Tien (river), 443–44
Song Tra Bong (river), 393–94, 473
Song Tra Kau (river), 395
Song Tra Khuc (river), 394–95, 413, 418, 429, 445
Song Tram (river), 443–44
Song Ve (river), 395–96, 408
South China Sea, 33, 262, 387, 389, 433, 710
South Korea, 9, 11, 15, 313, 588; South Korean marines, 389, 392, 394
Southeast Asian Treaty Organization (SEATO), 369
Southern Christian Leadership Conference, 625
Southern, Terry, 644, 647
Soviet Union, 185, 234, 243, 245–46, 249–50, 252, 417, 593
Spain, 358, 365–67
Spanish Civil War, 365
Spanish-American War, 626

Special Action Unit 69, Viet Cong, 373, 378, 382–83

Special Branch, South Vietnamese National Police, 377–78

Special Forces, Republic of Vietnam, 97

Special Forces, U.S. Army, 35, 61, 65, 97–98, 100, 102, 132, 263, 280, 284, 304, 366, 394, 430, 618

Spock, Dr. Benjamin, 47

St. Francis Xavier Church (Cholon, South Vietnam), 94

Stalin, Joseph, 147, 611

Stammel, Jared, 142

Starkey, Ray, 693, 694

Stars and Stripes (newspaper), 424, 495

State Planning Board (North Vietnam), 50–51

State Street (Chicago), 649

Stevenson, Mike, 644

Stilwell, Gen. Richard, 117

Stone, I.F., 143

Strategic Hamlet Program (South Vietnam), 391

Strictland, Jim, 668–74, 677–78, 680

Students for a Democratic Society (SDS), 643, 647

Su Lo Dong, South Vietnam, 165, 172–73

Subic Bay, Philippines, 551

Sukarno, 139

Sully (pilot), 540

Sun Tzu, 193

Supremes, the, 349

Sweezy, Paul, 148

Swinger, The (film), 459

Switzer, Ohio, 694

Switzerland, 5

Sydney, Australia 419

Tacitus, 175

Taiwan, 247, 255

Tam Ky, South Vietnam, 458, 463

Tan Son Nhut Airbase, South Vietnam, 187, 281, 298, 332, 348, 354, 355, 357, 362, 378

Tarrytown, New York, 236, 238

Task Force Alfa, U.S. Army, 178

Task Force Oregon, U.S. Army, 358, 387–89, 392, 413, 416, 424, 433, 436, 439, 441, 445, 456, 461, 463–67, 482

Task Force Oregon News Sheet, 424, 436–37

Tassigny, Marshal de Lattre de, 185

Tattered Dress, The (film), 1

Tay Ho, South Vietnam, 560

Tay Ninh, South Vietnam, 6, 227–230, 232, 338

Taylor, Gen. Maxwell, 61–62, 108, 114–15, 121, 175, 191, 342, 410, 584, 586, 589

Tennessee Valley, 257

Tenth Armored Squadron, South Vietnamese, 487

Terre des Hommes (Swiss war relief organization), 295–96

Terry, Wallace, *704–8*

Tet Offensive, 560–75, 581, 595, 597, 627

Thailand, 7, 51, 54, 358, 536, 551, 599

Thai-Nguyen steel complex (North Vietnam), 50

Thanh Phuoc, South Vietnam, 445, 447, 466

Thich Duc Nghiep, 79, 81

Thich Quang Duc, 83–85

Thich Tri Quang, 80–81

Thien An Mission (South Vietnam), 569

Thien Huu School (Hue), 561

Thieu. *See* Nguyen Van Thieu.

Third Battalion, Fourth Tunisian Rifles, 343

Third Battalion, 187th Infantry, U.S. 101st Airborne Division, 701

Third Brigade, U.S. Fourth Infantry Division, 387, 395, 397, 389, 404, 408, 438

Third Brigade, U.S. 101st Airborne Division, 700–1

Third Division, North Vietnamese, 414

Third Marine Amphibious Force, U.S., 314, 388, 396, 699

Third Marine Division, U.S., 178

Third Marine Regiment (Company E, Second Battalion), U.S., 344

Third Reconnaissance Battalion (Bravo Company), U.S. Marines, 577

Thirty-second Ranger Battalion, South Vietnamese, 573

Thirty Years War, 334

Thompson, J. Walter (advertising agency), 654
Thong Nhut Boulevard (Saigon), 557
Thong-Nhat (Unity) Hotel (Hanoi), 48, 606, 613–14
Thrash, Demp, 259–61
369th Infantry Regiment, U.S. (WWI), 626
338th Division, North Vietnamese, 337
325th Division, North Vietnamese, 176, 344
Thua Thien, South Vietnam, 562
Thuan Hoa Hotel (Hue), 562
Thurmond, Strom, 657
Thyng, Col. Harrison R., 535
Tibet, 514
Tice, John, 617
Tiger Force (reconnaissance unit, 1st Brigade, 101st Airborne Division), 264–66, 269, 280
Time, 78, 116
Timmes, Maj. Gen. Charles, 58
Tokyo, Japan, 419, 598
Tokyo University, 746
Tolson, Maj. Gen. John J., 759
Ton That Cao, 163–65
Tonkin, Gulf of, 531, 540, 553, 615
Traegerman, Capt. Richard, 621
Tran Thi Doan, 325, 326
Tran Van Kha, Capt., 36–37, 43–45
Tran Van Tan, 336
Treleaven, Harry, 653–57, 659, 663
Truoi Bridge, South Vietnam, 160, 163, 169
Truoi Mountain, South Vietnam, 153, 155, 163–64, 169, 171
Truoi River, 154–55, 158, 174
Truong Dinh Street (Hue), 562
Tshombe, Moise-Kapenda, 139
Tu Dam Pagoda (Hue), 80, 561, 569
Tu Do Street (Saigon), 350–51, 355, 362–65, 623
Tu Nghia, South Vietnam, 395
Tuan, — (demolitions expert), 376–78
Tugwell, Rex, 257
Tung, Capt. —, 168
Tuohy, William, *187–97*
Turkey, 588
Tuy Hoa, South Vietnam, 400

Tuyet Diem, South Vietnam, 396, 469–71, 473, 476–77, 479–81
Twentieth Tactical Air Support Squadron, U.S., 436
Twenty-eighth Infantry Regiment, U.S., 333, 664
Twenty-fifth Infantry Division, U.S., 332
Twenty-first Recon Company, South Vietnamese, 72
Twenty-first Division, South Vietnamese, 77, 118
Twenty-fourth Corps, U.S., 699
Twenty-ninth Regiment, North Vietnamese, 700
Twenty-sixth Marine Regiment, U.S., 577
226th Regiment, North Vietnamese, 269

U Minh Battalion, Viet Cong, 33
U.S. News & World Report, 122, 133, 484
Ukraine, 54
Ung Van Khiem, 18
Union of Soviet Socialist Republics (USSR). See Soviet Union.
United Jewish Appeal, 143
United Press International (UPI), 363
United States Information Agency (USIA), 565
United States Information Service (USIS), 92, 136
United States Strategic Bombing Survey (USSBS), 244
University of California at Berkeley, 198–201, 206
University of Chicago, 145
University of Detroit, 543
University of Freiburg, 568
University of Michigan, 145–46
University of Minnesota, 764
University of Notre Dame, 686
University of Pittsburgh, 240
Urbain, Father —, 569
Ut, Col. — (province chief), 38

Van Dien, North Vietnam, 330
Vance, Cyrus, 584, 586, 588

Vann, Lt. Col. John Paul, 70, 108–23, 361
Vassar College, 364
Vurlumis, Chris, 266–68, 272, 275–77
Vi Thanh, South Vietnam, 8
Victoria (officers' billet, Saigon), 376
Vienna, Austria, 250, 251, 348
Vientiane, Laos, 354, 602
Viet Tri, North Vietnam 50
Vietminh, 12, 18, 26, 72, 96, 157, 160–61, 165, 182, 223–24, 299–300, 323, 339, 378, 390–91, 414, 560
Vietnam (campaign commercial), 658–59
Vietnam Air Force (VNAF), 124, 420
Vietnam Day Committee, 198, 202, 205–206
Vietnam Railway (South Vietnam), 155
Vietnam-Polish Friendship senior high school (North Vietnam), 330
Village Voice, The, 638
Vinh Long, Prof., 336–39
Vo Nguyen Giap, Gen., 53, 193, 262–63
Vo Quang Anh, 51
Vo Van Diem, 163–64
Voice of America, 87

Wabash Avenue (Chicago), 651
Waikiki Beach, Hawaii, 238, 369
Waldorf-Astoria world peace conference, 148
Walker, George, 202–3
Wallace, George, 657
Walton, Frank, 64
War Crimes Commission (Hanoi), 610
War Crimes Museum (Hanoi), 610–11
War of 1812, 625
War Zone C, South Vietnam, 334
Warsaw, Poland, 602
Washburn, Pfc. Sam, 277–78
Washington Post, The, 70, 246, 484, 486–87
Washington, Booker T., 207
Washington, George, 242
Washington, Ronald, 705
Waskow, Arthur, 144, 148, 151
Watkins, Willie, 667–76, 678, 680, 685

Watson, Marvin, 591, 594, 629
Wayne, John, 139, 618
Weimar Republic (Germany), 54
Welk, Lawrence, 625
Wellington, New Zealand, 594
West Islip, New York, 399
West Point (New York), 68, 108, 114
Westmoreland, Gen. William C., 189–90, 193, 246, 253–54, 256–57, 262–63, 309, 335, 344–45, 374, 485–86, 589, 596–97, 615, 618, 626
Wetumpka, Alabama, 259–60
Wheeler, Gen. Earle, 121–22, 312, 485, 488, 585–86, 589–90
Wheeler, John T., *576–80*
Wheeling News-Register, 696
White House, the, 146, 151, 361, 484, 487–88, 583–86, 591–94, 656
Whiting, Peter, 236–41
Why Are We In Vietnam? (Mailer), 517
Wild Weasel missions, 537
Wilkins, Roy, 705
Williams, Jimmy, 260
Williams, Mrs. John, 259, 260
Williams, Sgt. —, 667, 669–70, 676
Wills, Pfc. Frank, 272
Wolfe, Tom, *198–207, 525–50*
Woodside, California, 201
World War I, 201, 419, 435, 535, 550–51, 626, 645, 695
World War II, 48, 94, 109, 114, 124–25, 157, 165, 182, 195, 202, 213, 269, 290, 313–14, 365, 390, 415, 453, 509, 533, 536, 589, 598, 607, 626, 684, 690
Wright, Mary, 149
Writers' and Artists' Union (Hanoi), 610

Xa Loi Pagoda (Saigon), 84–85
Xuan Mai, North Vietnam, 337
Xuan (South Vietnamese POW), 415

Yale University, 149, 530, 539–40, 543–44
Yalu River, 536
Yippies, 635, 639, 643
York, Pennsylvania, 616
Yorty, Sam, 356
Yoss, Ralph, 694

Young People's Democratic Group
    (Hue), 561
Young Pioneers (North Vietnam), 52
Young, Whitney M. Jr., 625
Youngstown, Ohio, 616

Zais, Maj. Gen. Melvin, 698–702
Zawtocki, Joe, 668, 672–73, 676–77,
    685
Zonker (Prankster), 201, 203, 205
Zorthian, Barry, 596

Library of Congress Cataloging-in-Publication Data

Reporting Vietnam
    p. cm. — (The Library of America ; 104–105)
  Includes indexes.
  Contents: pt. 1. American journalism 1959–1969 — pt. 2. American
journalism 1969–1975.
  ISBN 1–883011–58–2 (alk. paper : v. 1). — ISBN 1–883011–59–0
(alk. paper : v. 2)
  1. Journalism—United States—History—20th century.
2. Vietnamese Conflict, 1961–1975—Press coverage—United States.
I. Title: Reporting Vietnam.   II. Series.
PN4867.R45   1998
070.4′499597043—dc21   98–12267
                                                       CIP

THE LIBRARY OF AMERICA SERIES

1. Herman Melville, *Typee, Omoo, Mardi* (1982)
2. Nathaniel Hawthorne, *Tales and Sketches* (1982)
3. Walt Whitman, *Poetry and Prose* (1982)
4. Harriet Beecher Stowe, *Three Novels* (1982)
5. Mark Twain, *Mississippi Writings* (1982)
6. Jack London, *Novels and Stories* (1982)
7. Jack London, *Novels and Social Writings* (1982)
8. William Dean Howells, *Novels 1875–1886* (1982)
9. Herman Melville, *Redburn, White-Jacket, Moby-Dick* (1983)
10. Nathaniel Hawthorne, *Collected Novels* (1983)
11. Francis Parkman, *France and England in North America* vol. I, (1983)
12. Francis Parkman, *France and England in North America* vol. II, (1983)
13. Henry James, *Novels 1871–1880* (1983)
14. Henry Adams, *Novels, Mont Saint Michel, The Education* (1983)
15. Ralph Waldo Emerson, *Essays and Lectures* (1983)
16. Washington Irving, *History, Tales and Sketches* (1983)
17. Thomas Jefferson, *Writings* (1984)
18. Stephen Crane, *Prose and Poetry* (1984)
19. Edgar Allan Poe, *Poetry and Tales* (1984)
20. Edgar Allan Poe, *Essays and Reviews* (1984)
21. Mark Twain, *The Innocents Abroad, Roughing It* (1984)
22. Henry James, *Essays, American & English Writers* (1984)
23. Henry James, *European Writers & The Prefaces* (1984)
24. Herman Melville, *Pierre, Israel Potter, The Confidence-Man, Tales & Billy Budd* (1985)
25. William Faulkner, *Novels 1930–1935* (1985)
26. James Fenimore Cooper, *The Leatherstocking Tales* vol. I, (1985)
27. James Fenimore Cooper, *The Leatherstocking Tales* vol. II, (1985)
28. Henry David Thoreau, *A Week, Walden, The Maine Woods, Cape Cod* (1985)
29. Henry James, *Novels 1881–1886* (1985)
30. Edith Wharton, *Novels* (1986)
31. Henry Adams, *History of the United States during the Administrations of Jefferson* (1986)
32. Henry Adams, *History of the United States during the Administrations of Madison* (1986)
33. Frank Norris, *Novels and Essays* (1986)
34. W. E. B. Du Bois, *Writings* (1986)
35. Willa Cather, *Early Novels and Stories* (1987)
36. Theodore Dreiser, *Sister Carrie, Jennie Gerhardt, Twelve Men* (1987)
37. Benjamin Franklin, *Writings* (1987)
38. William James, *Writings 1902–1910* (1987)
39. Flannery O'Connor, *Collected Works* (1988)
40. Eugene O'Neill, *Complete Plays 1913–1920* (1988)
41. Eugene O'Neill, *Complete Plays 1920–1931* (1988)
42. Eugene O'Neill, *Complete Plays 1932–1943* (1988)
43. Henry James, *Novels 1886–1890* (1989)
44. William Dean Howells, *Novels 1886–1888* (1989)
45. Abraham Lincoln, *Speeches and Writings 1832–1858* (1989)
46. Abraham Lincoln, *Speeches and Writings 1859–1865* (1989)
47. Edith Wharton, *Novellas and Other Writings* (1990)
48. William Faulkner, *Novels 1936–1940* (1990)
49. Willa Cather, *Later Novels* (1990)
50. Ulysses S. Grant, *Personal Memoirs and Selected Letters* (1990)
51. William Tecumseh Sherman, *Memoirs* (1990)
52. Washington Irving, *Bracebridge Hall, Tales of a Traveller, The Alhambra* (1991)
53. Francis Parkman, *The Oregon Trail, The Conspiracy of Pontiac* (1991)
54. James Fenimore Cooper, *Sea Tales: The Pilot, The Red Rover* (1991)

55. Richard Wright, *Early Works* (1991)
56. Richard Wright, *Later Works* (1991)
57. Willa Cather, *Stories, Poems, and Other Writings* (1992)
58. William James, *Writings 1878–1899* (1992)
59. Sinclair Lewis, *Main Street & Babbitt* (1992)
60. Mark Twain, *Collected Tales, Sketches, Speeches, & Essays 1852–1890* (1992)
61. Mark Twain, *Collected Tales, Sketches, Speeches, & Essays 1891–1910* (1992)
62. *The Debate on the Constitution: Part One* (1993)
63. *The Debate on the Constitution: Part Two* (1993)
64. Henry James, *Collected Travel Writings: Great Britain & America* (1993)
65. Henry James, *Collected Travel Writings: The Continent* (1993)
66. *American Poetry: The Nineteenth Century,* Vol. 1 (1993)
67. *American Poetry: The Nineteenth Century,* Vol. 2 (1993)
68. Frederick Douglass, *Autobiographies,* (1994)
69. Sarah Orne Jewett, *Novels and Stories* (1994)
70. Ralph Waldo Emerson, *Collected Poems and Translations* (1994)
71. Mark Twain, *Historical Romances* (1994)
72. John Steinbeck, *Novels and Stories 1932–1937* (1994)
73. William Faulkner, *Novels 1942–1954* (1994)
74. Zora Neale Hurston, *Novels and Stories* (1995)
75. Zora Neale Hurston, *Folklore, Memoirs, and Other Writings* (1995)
76. Thomas Paine, *Collected Writings* (1995)
77. *Reporting World War II: American Journalism 1938–1944* (1995)
78. *Reporting World War II: American Journalism 1944–1946* (1995)
79. Raymond Chandler, *Stories and Early Novels* (1995)
80. Raymond Chandler, *Later Novels and Other Writings* (1995)
81. Robert Frost, *Collected Poems, Prose, & Plays* (1995)
82. Henry James, *Complete Stories 1892–1898* (1996)
83. Henry James, *Complete Stories 1898–1910* (1996)
84. William Bartram, *Travels and Other Writings* (1996)
85. John Dos Passos, *U.S.A.* (1996)
86. John Steinbeck, *The Grapes of Wrath and Other Writings 1936–1941* (1996)
87. Vladimir Nabokov, *Novels and Memoirs 1941–1951* (1996)
88. Vladimir Nabokov, *Novels 1955–1962* (1996)
89. Vladimir Nabokov, *Novels 1969–1974* (1996)
90. James Thurber, *Writings and Drawings* (1996)
91. George Washington, *Writings* (1997)
92. John Muir, *Nature Writings* (1997)
93. Nathanael West, *Novels and Other Writings* (1997)
94. *Crime Novels: American Noir of the 1930s and 40s* (1997)
95. *Crime Novels: American Noir of the 1950s* (1997)
96. Wallace Stevens, *Collected Poetry and Prose* (1997)
97. James Baldwin, *Early Novels and Stories* (1998)
98. James Baldwin, *Collected Essays* (1998)
99. Gertrude Stein, *Writings, 1903–1932* (1998)
100. Gertrude Stein, *Writings, 1932–1946* (1998)
101. Eudora Welty, *Complete Novels* (1998)
102. Eudora Welty, *Stories, Essays, & Memoir* (1998)
103. Charles Brockden Brown, *Three Gothic Novels* (1998)
104. *Reporting Vietnam: American Journalism 1959–1969* (1998)
105. *Reporting Vietnam: American Journalism 1969–1975* (1998)

This book is set in 10 point Linotron Galliard,
a face designed for photocomposition by Matthew Carter
and based on the sixteenth-century face Granjon. The paper is
acid-free Ecusta Nyalite and meets the requirements for permanence
of the American National Standards Institute. The binding
material is Brillianta, a woven rayon cloth made by
Van Heek-Scholco Textielfabrieken, Holland.
The composition is by The Clarinda
Company. Printing and binding by
R.R.Donnelley & Sons Company.
Designed by Bruce Campbell.